Lecture Notes in Computer Science 14657

The series Lecture Notes in Computer Science (LNCS), including its subseries Lecture Notes in Artificial Intelligence (LNAI) and Lecture Notes in Bioinformatics (LNBI), has established itself as a medium for the publication of new developments in computer science and information technology research, teaching, and education.

LNCS enjoys close cooperation with the computer science R & D community, the series counts many renowned academics among its volume editors and paper authors, and collaborates with prestigious societies. Its mission is to serve this international community by providing an invaluable service, mainly focused on the publication of conference and workshop proceedings and postproceedings. LNCS commenced publication in 1973.

Marc Joye · Gregor Leander
Editors

Advances in Cryptology – EUROCRYPT 2024

43rd Annual International Conference on the Theory
and Applications of Cryptographic Techniques
Zurich, Switzerland, May 26–30, 2024
Proceedings, Part VII

Springer

Editors
Marc Joye ⓘ
Zama
Paris, France

Gregor Leander ⓘ
Ruhr University Bochum
Bochum, Germany

ISSN 0302-9743   ISSN 1611-3349 (electronic)
Lecture Notes in Computer Science
ISBN 978-3-031-58753-5   ISBN 978-3-031-58754-2 (eBook)
https://doi.org/10.1007/978-3-031-58754-2

This Springer imprint is published by the registered company Springer Nature Switzerland AG
The registered company address is: Gewerbestrasse 11, 6330 Cham, Switzerland

Paper in this product is recyclable.

Preface

EUROCRYPT 2024 is the 43rd Annual International Conference on the Theory and Applications of Cryptographic Techniques. It was held in Zurich, Switzerland, during May 26–30, 2024. EUROCRYPT is an annual conference organized by the International Association for Cryptologic Research (IACR).

EUROCRYPT 2024 received 501 submissions, out of which 469 formally went to the review process. Every submission was assigned in a double blind way to three program committee members and, in some cases, one or two extra reviewers were added. The IACR version of the HotCRP software was used for the whole review process. In total, 1436 reviews were produced and 5200+ comments were made during the whole process. After a first round, 290 papers were pre-selected by the program committee to enter the second round. These remaining papers were offered a rebuttal to answer questions and requests for clarification from the reviewers. After several weeks of subsequent discussions, the committee ultimately selected 105 papers for acceptance.

The program committee was made up of 110 top cryptography researchers, all expert in their respective fields. For some papers, external sub-referees were appointed by the committee members. We warmly thank all the committee members and their sub-referees for the hard work in the peer review and their active participation in the discussions. We greatly benefited from the help of the area chairs: Shweta Agrawal for "Public Key Primitives with Advanced Functionalities", Serge Fehr for "Theoretical Foundations", Pierre-Alain Fouque for "Secure and Efficient Implementation, Cryptographic Engineering, and Real-World Cryptography", María Naya-Plasencia for "Symmetric Cryptology", Claudio Orlandi for "Multi-Party Computation and Zero-Knowledge", and Daniel Wichs for "Classic Public Key Cryptography". They each led the discussions and the paper selection in their respective area. The previous program chairs for IACR flagship conferences were also very helpful; in particular, we are grateful to Carmit Hazay and Martijn Stam for sharing their experience with EUROCRYPT 2023.

The IACR aims to support open and reproducible research within the field of cryptography. For the first time for a flagship conference, authors of accepted papers were invited to submit artifacts associated with their papers, such as software or datasets, for review, in a collaborative process between authors and the artifact review committee. We thank Martin Albrecht for having accepted to chair the artifact committee.

Three papers were awarded this year. The Best Paper Awards went to Pierrick Dartois, Antonin Leroux, Damien Robert and Benjamin Wesolowski for their paper "SQIsignHD: New Dimensions in Cryptography" and to Itai Dinur for his paper "Tight Indistinguishability Bounds for the XOR of Independent Random Permutations by Fourier Analysis". The Early-Career Best Paper Award was given to Maria Corte-Real Santos, Jonathan Komada Eriksen, Michael Meyer, and Krijn Reijnders for their paper "AprèsSQI: Extra Fast Verification for SQIsign Using Extension-Field Signing".

In addition to the contributed papers, EUROCRYPT 2024 featured two invited talks: "Cryptography in the Wild" by Kenny Paterson and "An Attack Became a Tool: Isogeny-based Cryptography 2.0" by Wouter Castryck. The conference also included a panel discussion on the future of publications; the panel was moderated by Anne Canteaut. The traditional rump session featuring short and entertaining presentations was held on Wednesday 29th.

Several people were key to the success of the conference. Our two general chairs, Julia Hesse and Thyla van der Merwe, did a fantastic job with the overall organization of EUROCRYPT 2024. Kevin McCurley ensured everything went smoothly with the review software and in the collection of the final papers. The conference relied on sponsors to help ensure student participation and reduce costs. We gratefully acknowledge the financial support of (in alphabetical order): Apple, AWS, CASA, City of Zürich, Concordium, Cosmian, Ethereum Foundation, Fair Math, Google, Huawei, IBM, Input/Output, NTT Research, SandboxAQ, Swiss National Science Foundation, Starkware, TII, Zama, and ZISC.

May 2024

Marc Joye
Gregor Leander

Organization

General Co-chairs

Thyla van der Merwe   Google, Switzerland
Julia Hesse   IBM Research Zurich, Switzerland

Program Co-chairs

Marc Joye   Zama, France
Gregor Leander   Ruhr-University Bochum, Germany

Area Chairs

Shweta Agrawal   IIT Madras, India
Serge Fehr   CWI Amsterdam and Leiden University, The Netherlands
Pierre-Alain Fouque   Université de Rennes, CNRS and Inria, France
María Naya-Plasencia   Inria, France
Claudio Orlandi   Aarhus University, Denmark
Daniel Wichs   Northeastern University and NTT Research, USA

Program Committee

Martin R. Albrecht   King's College London and SandboxAQ, UK
Diego F. Aranha   Aarhus University, Denmark
Nuttapong Attrapadung   AIST, Japan
Christof Beierle   RUB, Germany
Sonia Belaïd   CryptoExperts, France
Tim Beyne   KU Leuven, Belgium
Olivier Blazy   Ecole Polytechnique, France
Jeremiah Blocki   Purdue University, USA
Alexandra Boldyreva   Georgia Tech University, USA
Xavier Bonnetain   Inria, France
Jonathan Bootle   IBM Research Europe – Zurich, Switzerland
Christina Boura   University of Versailles, France

Stanislaw Jarecki	UC Irvine, USA
Jérémy Jean	ANSSI, France
Bhavana Kanukurthi	Indian Institute of Science, India
Shuichi Katsumata	PQShield LTD, UK, and AIST, Japan
Ilan Komargodski	Hebrew University of Jerusalem and NTT Research, Israel
Yashvanth Kondi	Aarhus University, Denmark
Venkata Koppula	IIT Delhi, India
Fabien Laguillaumie	Université de Montpellier, LIRMM, France
Wei-Kai Lin	University of Virginia, USA
Jiahui Liu	The University of Texas at Austin, USA
Chen-Da Liu-Zhang	HSLU and Web3 Foundation, Switzerland
Mark Manulis	Universität der Bundeswehr, Munich, Germany
Bart Mennink	Radboud University, The Netherlands
Pratyay Mukherjee	Supra Research, USA
Ruben Niederhagen	Academia Sinica, Taiwan, and University of Southern Denmark, Denmark
Svetla Nikova	KU Leuven, Belgium, and University of Bergen, Norway
Ryo Nishimaki	NTT Social Informatics Laboratories, Japan
Anca Nitulescu	Protocol Labs, France
Ariel Nof	Bar Ilan University, Israel
Kaisa Nyberg	Aalto University, Finland
Jiaxin Pan	University of Kassel, Germany and NTNU, Norway
Omer Paneth	Tel Aviv University, Israel
Arpita Patra	Indian Institute of Science, India
Duong Hieu Phan	Telecom Paris, France
Raphael C.-W. Phan	Monash University, Malaysia
Stjepan Picek	Radboud University, The Netherlands
Thomas Pornin	NCC Group, Canada
Manoj Prabhakaran	IIT Bombay, India
Carla Ràfols	Universitat Pompeu Fabra, Spain
Divya Ravi	Aarhus University, Denmark
Doreen Riepel	UC San Diego, USA
Matthieu Rivain	CryptoExperts, France
Mélissa Rossi	ANSSI, France
Adeline Roux-Langlois	CNRS, GREYC, France
Andy Rupp	University of Luxembourg, Luxembourg, and KASTEL SRL, Germany
Alessandra Scafuro	NC State University, USA
Peter Scholl	Aarhus University, Denmark

André Schrottenloher	Inria, Université de Rennes, IRISA, France
Peter Schwabe	MPI-SP, Germany, and Radboud University, The Netherlands
Yannick Seurin	Ledger, France
Mark Simkin	Ethereum Foundation, Denmark
Pratik Soni	University of Utah, USA
Akshayaram Srinivasan	University of Toronto, Canada
Damien Stehlé	CryptoLab, France
Siwei Sun	Chinese Academy of Sciences, China
Berk Sunar	Worcester Polytechnic Institute, USA
Yosuke Todo	NTT Social Informatics Laboratories, Japan
Junichi Tomida	NTT Social Informatics Laboratories, Japan
Serge Vaudenay	EPFL, Switzerland
Frederik Vercauteren	KU Leuven, Belgium
Ivan Visconti	University of Salerno, Italy
David Wu	UT Austin, USA
Mark Zhandry	NTT Research, USA

External Reviewers

Marius A. Aardal
Aysajan Abdin
Ittai Abraham
Damiano Abram
Hamza Abusalah
Anasuya Acharya
Léo Ackermann
Amit Agarwal
Ahmet Agirtas
Prabhanjan Ananth
Yoshinoro Aono
Ananya Appan
Nicolas Aragon
Arasu Arun
Gennaro Avitabile
Renas Bacho
Youngjin Bae
David Balbas
Marshall Ball
Fabio Banfi
Zhenzhen Bao
Manuel Barbosa

Augustin Bariant
Cruz Barnum
Khashayar Barooti
James Bartusek
Balthazar Bauer
Amit Behera
Shalev Ben-David
Shany Ben-David
Omri Ben-Eliezer
Loris Bergerat
Ward Beullens
Varsha Bhat
Ritam Bhaumik
Kaartik Bhushan
Alexander Bienstock
Alexander Block
Erica Blum
Jan Bobolz
Nicolas Bon
Charlotte Bonte
Carl Bootland
Joppe Bos

Katharina Boudgoust
Alexandre Bouez
Clemence Bouvier
Cyril Bouvier
Pedro Branco
Nicholas Brandt
Lennart Braun
Alessio Caminata
Matteo Campanelli
Sébastien Canard
Kevin Carrier
Ignacio Cascudo
Gaëtan Cassiers
Guilhem Castagnos
Wouter Castryck
Pierre-Louis Cayrel
André Chailloux
Debasmita Chakraborty
Hubert Chan
Anirudh Chandramouli
Rahul Chatterjee
Rohit Chatterjee
Mingjie Chen
Yanlin Chen
Yilei Chen
Yu Long Chen
Jesús-Javier Chi-Domínguez
Ilaria Chillotti
Hyeongmin Choe
Wonseok Choi
Wutichai Chongchitmate
Arka Ra Choudhuri
Hao Chung
Kai-Min Chung
Michele Ciampi
Sebastian Clermont
Benoît Cogliati
Daniel Collins
Brice Colombier
Sandro Coretti
Alain Couvreur
Daniele Cozzo
Wei Dai
Quang Dao
Debajyoti Das

Sourav Das
Pratish Datta
Emma Dauterman
Gareth T. Davies
Leo de Castro
Thomas De Cnudde
Paola de Perthuis
Giovanni Deligios
Cyprien Delpech de Saint Guilhem
Rafael del Pino
Amit Deo
Julien Devevey
Siemen Dhooghe
Zijing Di
Emanuele Di Giandomenico
Christoph Dobraunig
Rafael Dowsley
Leo Ducas
Jesko Dujmovic
Betül Durak
Avijit Dutta
Christoph Egger
Martin Ekera
Felix Engelmann
Simon Erfurth
Reo Eriguchi
Jonathan Komada Eriksen
Hülya Evkan
Thibauld Feneuil
Giacomo Fenzi
Rex Fernando
Valerie Fetzer
Rune Fiedler
Ben Fisch
Matthias Fitzi
Nils Fleischhacker
Pouyan Forghani
Boris Fouotsa
Cody Freitag
Sapir Freizeit
Daniele Friolo
Paul Frixons
Margot Funk
Phillip Gajland
Daniel Gardham

Rachit Garg
Francois Garillot
Gayathri Garimella
John Gaspoz
Robin Geelen
Paul Gerhart
Diana Ghinea
Satrajit Ghosh
Ashrujit Ghoshol
Emanuele Giunta
Kristian Gjøsteen
Aarushi Goel
Evangelos Gkoumas
Eli Goldin
Rishab Goyal
Adam Groce
Ziyi Guan
Zichen Gui
Antonio Guimaraes
Felix Günther
Kanav Gupta
Nirupam Gupta
Kamil Doruk Gur
Hosein Hadipour
Mohammad Hajiabadi
Ghaith Hammouri
Guillaume Hanrot
Keisuke Hara
Patrick Harasser
Dominik Hartmann
Keitaro Hashimoto
Rachelle Heim
Nadia Heninger
Alexandra Henzinger
Julius Hermelink
Julia Hesse
Hans Heum
Shuichi Hirahara
Taiga Hiroka
Marc Houben
James Hsin-Yu Chiang
Kai Hu
Yungcong Hu
Tao Huang
Zhenyu Huang

Loïs Huguenin-Dumittan
James Hulett
Atsunori Ichikawa
Akiko Inoue
Tetsu Iwata
Joseph Jaeger
Jonas Janneck
Dirmanto Jap
Samuel Jaques
Ruta Jawale
Corentin Jeudy
Ashwin Jha
Dan Jones
Philipp Jovanovic
Bernhard Jungk
Fatih Kaleoglu
Chethan Kamath
Jiayi Kang
Minsik Kang
Julia Kastner
Hannah Keller
Qiao Kexin
Mustafa Khairallah
Dmitry Khovratovich
Ryo Kikuchi
Jiseung Kim
Elena Kirshanova
Fuyuki Kitagawa
Michael Klooß
Christian Knabenhans
Lisa Kohl
Sebastian Kolby
Dimitris Kolonelos
Chelsea Komlo
Anders Konring
Nishat Koti
Mukul Kulkarni
Protik Kumar Paul
Simran Kumari
Norman Lahr
Russell W. F. Lai
Baptiste Lambin
Oleksandra Lapiha
Eysa Lee
Joohee Lee

Jooyoung Lee
Seunghoon Lee
Ryan Lehmkuhl
Tancrède Lepoint
Matthieu Lequesne
Andrea Lesavourey
Baiyu Li
Shun Li
Xingjian Li
Zengpeng Li
Xiao Liang
Chuanwei Lin
Fuchun Lin
Yao-Ting Lin
Fukang Liu
Peiyuan Liu
Qipeng Liu
Patrick Longa
Julian Loss
Paul Lou
George Lu
Steve Lu
Zhenghao Lu
Reinhard Lüftenegger
Vadim Lyubashevsky
Fermi Ma
Varun Madathil
Christian Majenz
Giulio Malavolta
Mary Maller
Nathan Manohar
Mario Marhuenda Beltrán
Ange Martinelli
Elisaweta Masserova
Takahiro Matsuda
Christian Matt
Noam Mazor
Pierrick Méaux
Jeremias Mechler
Jonas Meers
Willi Meier
Kelsey Melissaris
Nikolas Melissaris
Michael Meyer
Pierre Meyer

Charles Meyer-Hilfiger
Peihan Miao
Chohong Min
Brice Minaud
Kazuhiko Minematsu
Tomoyuki Morimae
Hiraku Morita
Mahnush Movahedi
Anne Mueller
Michael Naehrig
Marcel Nageler
Vineet Nair
Yusuke Naito
Varun Narayanan
Hugo Nartz
Shafik Nassar
Patrick Neumann
Lucien K. L. Ng
Ruth Ng
Dinh Duy Nguyen
Jérôme Nguyen
Khoa Nguyen
Ky Nguyen
Ngoc Khanh Nguyen
Phong Nguyen
Phuong Hoa Nguyen
Thi Thu Quyen Nguyen
Viet-Sang Nguyen
Georgio Nicolas
Guilhem Niot
Julian Nowakowski
Koji Nuida
Sabine Oechsner
Kazuma Ohara
Olya Ohrimenko
Jean-Baptiste Orfila
Astrid Ottenhues
Rasmus Pagh
Arghya Pal
Tapas Pal
Mahak Pancholi
Omkant Pandey
Lorenz Panny
Jai Hyun Park
Nikitas Paslis

Srivatsan Sridhar
Lukas Stennes
Gilad Stern
Marc Stöttinger
Bing Sun
Ling Sun
Ajith Suresh
Elias Suvanto
Jakub Szefer
Akira Takahashi
Abdullah Talayhan
Abdul Rahman Taleb
Suprita Talnikar
Tianxin Tang
Samuel Tap
Stefano Tessaro
Jean-Pierre Tillich
Ivan Tjuawinata
Patrick Towa
Kazunari Tozawa
Bénédikt Tran
Daniel Tschudi
Yiannis Tselekounis
Ida Tucker
Nirvan Tyagi
LaKyah Tyner
Rei Ueno
Gilles Van Assche
Wessel Van Woerden
Nikhil Vanjani
Marloes Venema
Michiel Verbauwhede
Javier Verbel
· Tanner Verber
Damien Vergnaud
Fernando Virdia
Damian Vizár
Benedikt Wagner
Roman Walch
Julian Wälde

Alexandre Wallet
Chenghong Wang
Mingyuan Wang
Qingju Wang
Xunhua Wang
Yuyu Wang
Alice Wanner
Fiona Weber
Christian Weinert
Weiqiangg Wen
Chenkai Weng
Ivy K. Y. Woo
Lichao Wu
Keita Xagawa
Aayush Yadav
Anshu Yadav
Saikumar Yadugiri
Shota Yamada
Takashi Yamakawa
Hailun Yan
Yibin Yang
Kevin Yeo
Eylon Yogev
Yang Yu
Chen Yuan
Mohammad Zaheri
Gabriel Zaid
Riccardo Zanotto
Arantxa Zapico
Maryam Zarezadeh
Greg Zaverucha
Marcin Zawada
Runzhi Zeng
Tina Zhang
Yinuo Zhang
Yupeng Zhang
Yuxi Zheng
Mingxun Zhou
Chenzhi Zhu

Contents – Part VII

Classic Public Key Cryptography (II/II)

Practical Attack on All Parameters of the DME Signature Scheme   3
   Pierre Briaud, Maxime Bros, Ray Perlner, and Daniel Smith-Tone

Signatures with Memory-Tight Security in the Quantum Random Oracle
Model 30
   Keita Xagawa

Key Exchange with Tight (Full) Forward Secrecy via Key Confirmation 59
   Jiaxin Pan, Doreen Riepel, and Runzhi Zeng

SLAP: Succinct Lattice-Based Polynomial Commitments from Standard
Assumptions 90
   *Martin R. Albrecht, Giacomo Fenzi, Oleksandra Lapiha,
   and Ngoc Khanh Nguyen*

Universal Composable Password Authenticated Key Exchange
for the Post-Quantum World 120
   You Lyu, Shengli Liu, and Shuai Han

Asymptotics and Improvements of Sieving for Codes 151
   Léo Ducas, Andre Esser, Simona Etinski, and Elena Kirshanova

Isogeny Problems with Level Structure 181
   Luca De Feo, Tako Boris Fouotsa, and Lorenz Panny

Key Recovery Attack on the Partial Vandermonde Knapsack Problem 205
   Dipayan Das and Antoine Joux

Cryptanalysis of Rank-2 Module-LIP in Totally Real Number Fields 226
   *Guilhem Mureau, Alice Pellet-Mary, Georgii Pliatsok,
   and Alexandre Wallet*

Provable Dual Attacks on Learning with Errors 256
   Amaury Pouly and Yixin Shen

Reduction from Sparse LPN to LPN, Dual Attack 3.0 286
   *Kévin Carrier, Thomas Debris-Alazard, Charles Meyer-Hilfiger,
   and Jean-Pierre Tillich*

Plover: Masking-Friendly Hash-and-Sign Lattice Signatures 316
Muhammed F. Esgin, Thomas Espitau, Guilhem Niot, Thomas Prest,
Amin Sakzad, and Ron Steinfeld

Updatable Public-Key Encryption, Revisited 346
Joël Alwen, Georg Fuchsbauer, and Marta Mularczyk

Author Index 377

Classic Public Key Cryptography (II/II)

Practical Attack on All Parameters
of the DME Signature Scheme

Pierre Briaud[1,2](✉)(iD), Maxime Bros[3], Ray Perlner[3],
and Daniel Smith-Tone[3,4](iD)

[1] Sorbonne Université, UPMC Univ Paris 06, Paris, France
[2] Inria, Team COSMIQ, Paris, France
`pierre.briaud@inria.fr`
[3] National Institute of Standards and Technology (NIST), Gaithersburg, MD, USA
{`maxime.bros,daniel.smith`}`@nist.gov`
[4] University of Louisville, Louisville, KY, USA

Abstract. DME is a multivariate scheme submitted to the call for additional signatures recently launched by NIST. Its performance is one of the best among all the candidates. The public key is constructed from the alternation of very structured linear and non-linear components that constitute the private key, the latter being defined over an extension field. We exploit these structures by proposing an algebraic attack which is practical on all DME parameters.

Keywords: Public Key Cryptography · Multivariate Cryptography · NIST Candidates · Algebraic Cryptanalysis

1 Introduction

After selecting a first collection of post-quantum algorithms to standardize, see [2], the National Institute of Standards and Technology (NIST) announced an expansion to their post-quantum cryptography standardization project and released a call for additional signature schemes [9][1].

One of the candidates is DME. Originally specified in [12], the basic idea is to use multiple rounds of the so-called "exponential maps" defined over a finite extension of $\mathbb{F}_q$ composed with affine maps. These two types of functions can be defined in terms of matrices whose structure is publicly known but whose entries are secret, for all rounds. The construction can also be used for encryption and it lead to a NIST submission in the KEM category already in 2017. This initial version employed two layers of exponential maps, hence the name "Double Matrix Exponentiation". Unfortunately, it was quickly observed in [4] that one can apply some generic attacks on the composition of functions [6,7]. Another attack of a different nature was given by the DME designers in [3]. In response to

---

[1] This work was partially supported by a grant from the Simons Foundation (712530, DCST).

M. Joye and G. Leander (Eds.): EUROCRYPT 2024, LNCS 14657, pp. 3–29, 2024.
https://doi.org/10.1007/978-3-031-58754-2_1

these threats, the authors increased the number of rounds of exponentiation in their new NIST submission [11] to $r = 3$ and they changed some specific design choices in order to avoid [3].

DME can be seen as a multivariate scheme for which signing boils down to inverting the public system over $\mathbb{F}_q$ in n variables obtained by composition of the different rounds. The hope is that its polynomials are complicated enough so that previous structural cryptanalysis does not apply. Interestingly enough, the analysis of Gröbner basis techniques in the DME submission is limited to lower bounding the solving degree of the public system by the degree of the field equations, i.e., q (see [11, Sect. 8.2]). While having equations of large enough degree might be necessary to counteract some attacks, a too high density for these polynomials would also lead to an unmanageable public key size. Thus, there are notable restrictions imposed on both the linear and the exponential maps to obtain a more compact key.

The NIST submission adopts a unique field extension $\mathbb{F}_{q^2}$ as well as the value $n = 8$ for all security levels. The observation on the Gröbner basis complexity explains that the main difference lies in the choice of q, namely $q = 2^{32}$, $q = 2^{48}$ and $q = 2^{64}$ for security levels I, III and V respectively. DME appears to be the fastest candidate for both signing and verification. The public key and signature sizes are also very attractive. This is quite understandable for the signature as it is a vector of length only 8 over $\mathbb{F}_q$ for all security levels. For the common "signature size + public key size" metric, DME ties with MAYO [5] (1481 and 1489 bytes respectively for level I) and it outperforms the rest of the multivariate candidates à la UOV. Due to this surprisingly competitive performance and its rather unusual design, it seems crucial to analyze the DME scheme.

Contribution. This paper presents an efficient attack on the version of DME submitted to the NIST competition [9]. At a very high level, we show that the added constraints which lead to a compact public key also induce a weakness for this construction.

More precisely, we are able to recover, at a very low cost, a candidate last round that can be completed into an equivalent key. The core idea of our attack is to view the scheme entirely over $\mathbb{F}_{q^2}$, the very same extension field over which the exponential maps are defined. This description allows us to exploit the specific structure of the linear and exponential layers coming from the added constraints, even though these maps remain private.

Our approach to invert one DME round is as follows. First, we observe that we can easily determine the monomial content of the polynomials that form the state before applying this round. The task of fully recovering them is then reduced to the one of finding their coefficients. By exploiting the design of the scheme, we achieve this by inverting multivariate equations whose variables are precisely these coefficients. While polynomial system solving is usually the bottleneck when attacking multivariate schemes, our situation is different. The shape of the exponential maps makes that our hardest system is a bilinear system in a small number of variables that is solved in degree only 2. Once we have recovered these polynomials, the full recovery of the "equivalent" last round is rather straightforward.

From this point, we can iterate our attack on the previous rounds or even use the known techniques applicable for $r = 2$ since all DME instantiations consider $r = 3$. In fact, as we essentially exploit a specific structure preserved throughout the rounds, our method suggests that DME might not be simply repaired by increasing (again) the value of r. Nonetheless, as is common in multivariate cryptography, there may still exist different ways to patch the scheme. In any case, we believe that such modifications should be analyzed with care as well as their effect on the performance of DME.

Outline. In Sect. 3, we briefly present the DME version submitted to NIST and in particular the added constraints to obtain compact keys. In Sect. 4, we introduce the description over the extension field $\mathbb{F}_{q^2}$ that we adopt and we derive from it some non-trivial and crucial properties. This material is used in Sect. 5 where we describe the steps to recover an equivalent last round.

2 Notation

Matrices will be written in **bold**. For a positive integer k, let $n = 2k$ denote the DME vector length. We have $k = 4$ for all security levels.

Finite Fields. For a positive integer e, let $q = 2^e$. Let $\mathbb{F}_q$ be a finite field with q elements and let $\mathbb{F}_{q^2}$ be a degree 2 extension of $\mathbb{F}_q$. One may construct this extension as $\mathbb{F}_{q^2} = \mathbb{F}_q[Y]/(g(Y))$, where g is a degree 2 irreducible polynomial over $\mathbb{F}_q$. From now on, we fix an element $U \in \mathbb{F}_{q^2} \setminus \mathbb{F}_q$ (a root of g, for example). In the following, we will often write $A \in \mathbb{F}_{q^2}$ in the form $A = a_1 + a_2 U$, where $a_1, a_2 \in \mathbb{F}_q$. Finally, we denote by $\phi : \mathbb{F}_q^n \to \mathbb{F}_{q^2}^k$ the isomorphism

$$\phi(x_1, \ldots, x_n) = (x_1 + x_2 U, \ldots, x_{n-1} + x_n U).$$

Polynomial Rings. We will consider the following two quotients

$$\mathcal{R} = \mathbb{F}_q[x_1, \ldots, x_n]/\langle x_1^q - x_1, \ldots, x_n^q - x_n \rangle,$$

$$\mathcal{S} = \mathbb{F}_{q^2}[X_1, \ldots, X_k]/\langle X_1^{q^2} - X_1, \ldots, X_k^{q^2} - X_k \rangle.$$

Powers of Two. Let $a \in \mathbb{Z}_{2e}$. In what follows, we will write $x^{[a]}$ (resp. $P^{[a]}$) instead of x^{2^a} (resp. P^{2^a}) when a scalar $x \in \mathbb{F}_{q^2}$ (resp. a polynomial $P \in \mathcal{S}$) is raised to the power 2^a.

3   Concise Description of DME

The main specificity of DME resides in the so-called "exponential" maps defined over $\mathbb{F}_{q^2}$. Any such map refers to a function $E_{\mathbf{A}} : \mathbb{F}_{q^2}^k \to \mathbb{F}_{q^2}^k$ defined from a matrix $\mathbf{A} = (a_{ij}) \in \mathrm{GL}_k(\mathbb{Z}_{q^2-1})$ by

$$E_{\mathbf{A}}(X_1, \ldots, X_k) = (X_1^{a_{11}} \cdots X_k^{a_{1k}}, \ldots, X_1^{a_{k1}} \cdots X_k^{a_{kk}}).$$

It works similarly to left multiplication by the matrix $\mathbf{A}$, except with the multiplication of coordinates replaced by exponentiation and with addition replaced by multiplication. We can naturally extend this definition to a map $F_{\mathbf{A}} : \mathbb{F}_q^n \to \mathbb{F}_q^n$ such that

$$F_{\mathbf{A}}(x_1, \ldots, x_n) = \phi^{-1} \circ E_{\mathbf{A}} \circ \phi(x_1, \ldots, x_n).$$

The similarity to matrix multiplication triggers some nice algebraic properties. For example, if $\mathbf{AB} = \mathbf{C}$, then $F_{\mathbf{A}} \circ F_{\mathbf{B}} = F_{\mathbf{C}}$. In particular, we have that the composition $F_{\mathbf{A}^{-1}} \circ F_{\mathbf{A}}$ is the identity of $\mathbb{F}_q^n$. This means that the inverse of an exponential map is another easy to compute exponential map, i.e. $F_{\mathbf{A}}^{-1} = F_{\mathbf{A}^{-1}}$.

A DME round corresponds the application of an exponential map followed by a linear layer $L : \mathbb{F}_q^n \to \mathbb{F}_q^n$ and an addition of constants $C : \mathbb{F}_q^n \to \mathbb{F}_q^n$. For instance, a DME public key $P : \mathbb{F}_q^n \to \mathbb{F}_q^n$ utilizing r rounds of exponentiation can be expressed as

$$P(x_1, \ldots, x_n) = C_r \circ L_r \circ F_{\mathbf{A}_r} \circ C_{r-1} \circ L_{r-1} \circ \cdots \circ C_1 \circ L_1 \circ F_{\mathbf{A}_1} \circ C_0 \circ L_0,$$

where we apply a prior affine component $C_0 \circ L_0$ before the first exponential map. This construction may look quite similar to the one of substitution-permutation networks (SPNs) from symmetric cryptography but the situation is in fact reversed. Indeed, the exponential components $F_{\mathbf{A}_i}$ apply to the whole state of size n while we will see that the linear maps act *locally*.

A public key of the above form can be seen as a set of n multivariate polynomials in the ring $\mathcal{R}$. However, such polynomials may be dense and of high degree even after a single round of exponentiation for a generic matrix in $\mathrm{GL}_k(\mathbb{Z}_{q^2-1})$ and a generic affine map, which would lead to an unmanageable key sizes. Thus, restrictions are imposed on both the linear and the exponential maps to obtain a more compact key. Roughly speaking, the idea is to guarantee some collisions among monomials present and to keep having exponents with low Hamming weight binary decomposition (see Definition 4 below). These modifications are quite simple. First, as mentioned above, the linear maps have a local nature. More precisely, each linear map is chosen as the direct sum of linear maps on $\mathbb{F}_q^2$. In other words, such a map can be expressed as a block diagonal matrix with blocks of dimension 2×2. Second, the entries of the matrices defining the exponential maps are restricted to powers of 2 with exponents less than $2e$ (we may view them as belonging to $\mathbb{Z}_{2e}$) and the number of nonzero entries in each row is limited to 1 or 2. Specifically, the submitted DME implementations utilize the following three exponential maps

$$\mathbf{A}_1 = \begin{bmatrix} 2^{a_0} & 0 & 0 & 0 \\ 2^{a_1} & 2^{a_2} & 0 & 0 \\ 0 & 0 & 2^{a_3} & 0 \\ 0 & 0 & 2^{a_4} & 2^{a_5} \end{bmatrix},$$

$$\mathbf{A}_2 = \begin{bmatrix} 2^{b_0} & 0 & 0 & 2^{b_1} \\ 0 & 2^{b_2} & 0 & 0 \\ 0 & 2^{b_3} & 2^{b_4} & 0 \\ 0 & 0 & 0 & 2^{b_5} \end{bmatrix}, \tag{1}$$

$$\mathbf{A}_3 = \begin{bmatrix} 2^{c_0} & 2^{c_1} & 0 & 0 \\ 0 & 2^{c_2} & 0 & 2^{c_3} \\ 0 & 2^{c_4} & 0 & 2^{c_5} \\ 0 & 0 & 2^{c_6} & 2^{c_7} \end{bmatrix},$$

with

$$c_1 = a_0 + b_0 + c_0 - a_1 - b_2 \pmod{2e}$$
$$c_7 = a_3 + b_4 + c_6 - a_4 - b_5 \pmod{2e} \tag{2}$$
$$c_4 = c_2 + c_5 - c_3 + d \pmod{2e},$$

and where the constants e and $d \in \mathbb{Z}_{2e}$ differ with the three security levels. For example, for NIST security level I, we have that $e = 32$ and $d = 57$.

Signing is accomplished by inverting each of the affine shifts C_i, linear maps L_i and exponential maps $F_{\mathbf{A}_i}$ in sequence. Since the inversion of the exponential maps requires the structure of the exponential maps defined over $\mathbb{F}_{q^2}$ (e.g., $E_{\mathbf{A}_i}$), we may naturally view DME as a multi-round big-field cryptosystem, see Fig. 1. Verification is performed by simply evaluating the public key at the signature. We may note here that the component maps $F_{\mathbf{A}_i}$ are not surjective; hence, it is not possible to use the public key without a construction to prevent signature failure. Still, since these maps are bijections of the image of the unit groups of $\mathbb{F}_{q^2}^k$ under ϕ^{-1} (see for instance [12, Theorem 1.2]), failure of inversion is a reasonably low probability event. The simple use of a salt mitigates the problem efficiently, allowing for isochronous signature generation. The specific choice of an analogue of the PSS00 construction of [1] is specified in [11].

4 Structure of DME over $\mathbb{F}_{q^2}$

As described in the previous section, we may view DME as a multi-round big field scheme. There are two important aspects of this identification. First, the maps over the extension field are still multivariate; thus, the scheme is similar in spirit to the so-called "intermediate field schemes" such as HMFEv-, see [14]. The second important aspect is the multi-round nature. This characteristic is obviously recurrent in symmetric cryptography but it is also present in some very old and rather well-known multivariate constructions such as the double

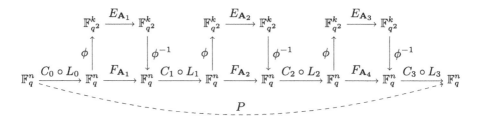

Fig. 1. A 3-round DME signature scheme.

round quadratic cipher, see [13]. We should note that both of these styles of multivariate cryptosystems were broken, see [10,15,17].

Let us expand the structure of DME over this extension field $\mathbb{F}_{q^2}$. Recall that each linear map L_i is the direct sum of maps on $\mathbb{F}_q^2$. We can thus write it as

$$L_i(x_1,\ldots,x_n) = (L_{i1}(x_1,x_2),\ldots,L_{ik}(x_{n-1},x_n)),$$

where L_{ij} is a linear map on $\mathbb{F}_q^2$ for $j \in \{1..k\}$. Note further that any $\mathbb{F}_q$-linear map L on $\mathbb{F}_q^2$ is isomorphic to an $\mathbb{F}_q$-linear polynomial $L_{\mathbb{F}_2} : \mathbb{F}_{q^2} \to \mathbb{F}_{q^2}$ by $L(x_1,x_2) = \phi^{-1}(L_{\mathbb{F}_2}(\phi(x_1,x_2)))$. In this way, we can easily construct an $\mathbb{F}_q$-linear map $\widehat{L}_i : \mathbb{F}_{q^2}^k \to \mathbb{F}_{q^2}^k$ equivalent to L_i. Similarly, each affine shift C_i consists of adding coordinate-wise constants $d_i \in \mathbb{F}_q$. Let us denote by $\widehat{C}_i$ the equivalent affine shift over $\mathbb{F}_{q^2}$ by adding the vector of constants $(D_{i1},\ldots,D_{ik}) = \phi(d_1,\ldots,d_n)$. With these two observations, we may complete our commutative diagram for the public key P to consider a calculation path $\widehat{P}$ entirely over the extension field $\mathbb{F}_{q^2}$, see Fig. 2. Given a formal input $(X_1,\ldots,X_k) \in \mathbb{F}_{q^2}^k$, we may implicitly view all big field polynomials as elements of the quotient ring $\mathcal{S} = \mathbb{F}_{q^2}[X_1,\ldots,X_k]/\langle X_1^{q^2} - X_1,\ldots,X_k^{q^2} - X_k\rangle$.

The rest of this section is dedicated to some crucial observations illustrating why the extension field is the correct arena in which to study the structure of DME. These properties are related to certain invariants of the composition of the exponential maps with the linear maps and affine shifts—the same invariants

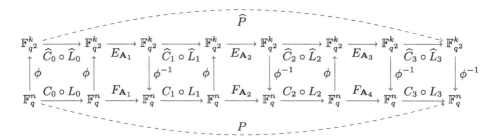

Fig. 2. The 3-round DME considering an equivalent "public" and private key over $\mathbb{F}_{q^2}$.

that guarantee efficiency and small key sizes. To establish a consistent language for discussing the structures, we define the DME round function over $\mathbb{F}_{q^2}$.

Definition 1 (Round function over $\mathbb{F}_{q^2}$). *Given an exponential map $E_{\mathbf{A}_i}$, an $\mathbb{F}_q$-linear map $\widehat{L}_i$ and an affine shift map $\widehat{C}_i$, the composition $R_i = \widehat{C}_i \circ \widehat{L}_i \circ E_{\mathbf{A}_i}$ is called the i-th DME round function over $\mathbb{F}_{q^2}$.*

With this notation we have $\widehat{P} = R_3 \circ R_2 \circ R_1 \circ \widehat{C}_0 \circ \widehat{L}_0$.

4.1 Stability by q-Powering

The first observation of importance is that the initial map $\widehat{C}_0 \circ \widehat{L}_0$ establishes a symmetry that is invariant under the application of DME round functions. Let us recall that each coordinate of $\widehat{L}_0$ is an $\mathbb{F}_q$-linear polynomial in $\mathbb{F}_{q^2}$. It is a classical result that such a polynomial is of the form $X \mapsto A_1 X + A_2 X^q$ for some A_1, $A_2 \in \mathbb{F}_{q^2}$. We thus obtain

$$\widehat{C}_0 \circ \widehat{L}_0(X_1, \ldots, X_k) = (A_{0,1}X_1 + A_{0,2}X_1^q + D_1, \ldots, A_{0,2k-1}X_k + A_{0,2k}X_k^q + D_k).$$

In each of the k coordinates, we notice that the relevant variable, i.e., X_i for the i-th one, occurs with the power 1 and q only. In order to generalize this property to more rounds, we introduce the following definition. Recall that $\mathcal{S} = \mathbb{F}_{q^2}[X_1, \ldots, X_k]/\langle X_1^{q^2} - X_1, \ldots, X_k^{q^2} - X_k \rangle$.

Definition 2 (q-symmetric orbit). *For a monomial $X_1^\alpha X_2^\beta \cdots X_k^\gamma \in \mathcal{S}$, the q-symmetric orbit is defined to be the set*

$$\{X_1^\alpha X_2^\beta \cdots X_k^\gamma, X_1^{q\alpha} X_2^\beta \cdots X_k^\gamma, X_1^\alpha X_2^{q\beta} \cdots X_k^\gamma,$$
$$X_1^{q\alpha} X_2^{q\beta} \cdots X_k^\gamma, \ldots, X_1^{q\alpha} X_2^{q\beta} \cdots X_k^{q\gamma}\}.$$

In other words, each of its elements is obtained by q-powering one or several variables present in the monomial.

Remark 1 *For the term "orbit" to make sense it might be more natural to authorize an arbitrary number of q-powerings. The above definition would not change as we have $X_i^{\alpha q^2} = X_i^\alpha \in \mathcal{S}$ for any $i \in \{1..k\}$ and any $\alpha \in \mathbb{N}$.*

Definition 3 (q-symmetric polynomial). *A polynomial $p \in \mathcal{S}$ is said to be q-symmetric if its set of monomials is a disjoint union of q-symmetric orbits.*

One may verify some simple properties of q-symmetric polynomials. We summarize the ones we require in the following. Their proofs are easy and the only subtlety lies in coefficient cancellations, see Appendix A.

Lemma 1. *The following statements on q-symmetric polynomials hold with high probability (easily estimated assuming a bound on the number of monomials),*

1. Let $D \in \mathbb{F}_{q^2} \subseteq \mathcal{S}$. Then D is q-symmetric (with probability 1).

2. Let p_1, $p_2 \in \mathcal{S}$ two q-symmetric polynomials. Then $p_1 + p_2$ is q-symmetric.
3. Let p_1, $p_2 \in \mathcal{S}$ two q-symmetric polynomials. Then $p_1 p_2$ is q-symmetric.
4. Let $p \in \mathcal{S}$ be a q-symmetric polynomial and let $r \in \mathbb{N}$. Then p^r is q-symmetric.
5. Let $p \in \mathcal{S}$ be q-symmetric and let $L : \mathbb{F}_{q^2} \to \mathbb{F}_{q^2}$ be an $\mathbb{F}_q$-linear map. Then the composition $L(p) \in \mathcal{S}$ is q-symmetric. Moreover, the monomial content of $L(p)$ is identical to that of p.

From these results, we see that all of the linear and affine layers preserve q-symmetry. This property is in fact critical in maintaining control on the growth of the number of monomials in the key as the number of rounds increases. Furthermore, since each coordinate of the exponential map $E_{\mathbf{A}_i}$ simply raises q-symmetric polynomials to powers and multiplies them together, Lemma 1 shows that the exponential maps preserve q-symmetry as well. Thus, we obtain

Corollary 1. *Given a k-tuple of q-symmetric polynomials as input, the DME round function over $\mathbb{F}_{q^2}$ produces another k-tuple of q-symmetric polynomials with high probability.*

4.2 Multi-hamming Weight

To analyze the specific structure of the polynomials produced by each round function, we will also use the following definition. As we work over $\mathcal{S}$, each variable exponent can be seen as an element in $\mathbb{Z}_{q^2-1}$. In the following, we may implicitly consider the unique representative in $\{0..q^2 - 2\}$.

Definition 4 (Multi-Hamming weight). *A monomial $X_1^\alpha X_2^\beta \cdots X_k^\gamma \in \mathcal{S}$ has multi-Hamming weight $(a, b, \ldots, c)$ if the binary representations of $\alpha, \beta, \ldots, \gamma$ are of Hamming weight $a, b, \ldots, c$, respectively.*

Clearly, raising a polynomial to a power of the form 2^s does not change the multi-Hamming weights of its monomials. More generally, since q is a power of two, we also observe that the multi-Hamming weight remains constant within one q-symmetric orbit. Note however that an arbitrary q-symmetric polynomial may contain distinct orbits having the same multi-Hamming weight.

We will restrict our notation to consider the parameters of DME provided in the submission package [11]. For the case of NIST security level I defined in [9], recall that we had $e = 32$ (thus, $q = 2^{32}$), $k = 4$ and 3 rounds. From the definition of DME, we see that the coordinates in the multi-Hamming weight can only grow by product between different components over $\mathbb{F}_{q^2}$. Due to the shape of the exponential maps $\mathbf{A}_i$, we also see that such a product involves at most 2 components. Finally, since there are only 3 rounds, we need to consider at most 3 such products. For these reasons the coordinates will remain small (we compute them explicitly in the next section). Since they will never be as large as 10, there will be no ambiguity in abbreviating $(a, b, \ldots, c)$ via concatenation: $ab \ldots c$. For example, we will denote the multi-Hamming weights of the input vector (X_1, X_2, X_3, X_4) as $(1000, 0100, 0010, 0001)$ instead of the much heavier

$$((1,0,0,0), (0,1,0,0), (0,0,1,0), (0,0,0,1)).$$

4.3 Monomial Content over $\mathbb{F}_{q^2}$

Using these notions, we can now describe more precisely the DME structure after each round. In our presentation, we will assume that no cancellation between coefficients occurs. We note that such an event should hold with very low probability under the choice of the linear and non-linear DME components.

Affine Layer $\widehat{C}_0 \circ \widehat{L}_0$. As observed above, the application of the first linear layer $\widehat{L}_0$ produces polynomials of the form $AX + BX^q$. The relevant weight vector remains $(1000, 0100, 0010, 0001)$ but this time we have created q-symmetric polynomials. Each of these equations contains one orbit with two monomials. Applying $\widehat{C}_0$ would then add the orbit $\{1\}$ but this first affine shift is in fact omitted in [11].

   In the subsequent rounds, we may focus on the exponential maps. This is because each affine map can be seen as acting coordinate-wise over $\mathbb{F}_{q^2}$ and because the monomial content of a q-symmetric polynomial does not change after applying an $\mathbb{F}_q$-linear map (statement 5 in Lemma 1). For $j \in \{1..3\}$, we will denote the j-th round output by $(G_1^{(j)}, G_2^{(j)}, G_3^{(j)}, G_4^{(j)})$.

Round Function R_1. The monomial content of the state $(G_1^{(1)}, G_2^{(1)}, G_3^{(1)}, G_4^{(1)})$ obtained at the end of R_1 is presented in Table 1. For each polynomial, we give the variables involved, the q-symmetric orbits (in the form "associated multi-Hamming weights: cardinality") and the total number of monomials.

Table 1. Variables, q-symmetric orbits and monomial counts for the output coordinates of R_1.

	Variables	Orbits	#Monomials
$G_1^{(1)}$	X_1	1000:2, 0000:1	3
$G_2^{(1)}$	X_1, X_2	1100:4, 0000:1	5
$G_3^{(1)}$	X_3	0010:2, 0000:1	3
$G_4^{(1)}$	X_3, X_4	0011:4, 0000:1	5

   This table can be easily obtained from the structure of $\mathbf{A}_1$ in Eq. (1). Raising a polynomial to a power of two does not change the multi-Hamming weights of its monomials and it does not affect the number of orbits. Then, each output is the product of at most two such 2-powered polynomials. In this first step we multiply polynomials with no variables in common: in this case, the multi-Hamming weight of a product is equal the sum of their multi-Hamming weights. Finally, as we apply $\widehat{C}_1$, we need to add the constant monomial.

Round Function R_2. We may continue in the same fashion to reveal the structure over $\mathbb{F}_{q^2}$ of the output of the round function R_2, see Table 2. The numbers of (complete) orbits and monomials present are still derived assuming no cancellation. We note that, once again, the polynomials being multiplied share no variables in common; thus, the multi-Hamming weight of the product of two monomials is equal to the sum of their multi-Hamming weights in all cases. We also note that given the monomial count from Table 1, the numbers of monomials in the output coordinates of the exponential layer correspond to products of numbers of monomials in the factors due to the fact that all of those monomials are distinct. In particular, the number of monomials in the output coordinates of R_2 will be these products unless there is cancellation of the coefficients due to the application of the linear layer, $\widehat{L}_2$, which is a low probability event.

Table 2. Variables, q-symmetric orbits and monomial counts for the output coordinates of R_2.

	Variables	Orbits	#Monomials
$G_1^{(2)}$	X_1, X_3, X_4	1011:8, 0011:4, 1000:2, 0000:1	15
$G_2^{(2)}$	X_1, X_2	1100:4, 0000:1	5
$G_3^{(2)}$	X_1, X_2, X_3	1110:8, 1100:4, 0010:2, 0000:1	15
$G_4^{(2)}$	X_3, X_4	0011:4, 0000:1	5

Round Function R_3. Deriving the q-symmetric orbits and the monomial support of the output coordinates of R_3 is more intricate.

The third round is the first in which products of monomials containing the same variables occur. Note that the product of a pair of orbits from R_2 no longer necessarily yields a unique q-symmetric orbit in R_3. Indeed, consider two orbits Ω and Ω' where a variable X appears with Hamming weight 1 and let us take representatives for these orbits with exponents 2^u and 2^v respectively. In other words, there exist monomials μ_Ω and $\mu_{\Omega'}$ not involving X such that $X^{[u]}\mu_\Omega \in \Omega$ and $X^{[v]}\mu_{\Omega'} \in \Omega'$. By doing the product we get monomials falling into two distinct orbits, namely $X^{[u]}X^{[v]}\mu_\Omega\mu_{\Omega'}$, $X^{[u+e]}X^{[v+e]}\mu_\Omega\mu_{\Omega'}$ on one side and $X^{[u+e]}X^{[v]}\mu_\Omega\mu_{\Omega'}$, $X^{[u]}X^{[v+e]}\mu_\Omega\mu_{\Omega'}$ on the other side.

Such a behaviour already occurs in the case when there are no imposed relations on the exponents in the exponential maps, see Table 3. For example, the product between the orbit of multi-Hamming weight 1011 in $G_1^{(2)}$ and the one of multi-Hamming weight 1000 in $G_2^{(2)}$ gives two orbits 2111(a) and 2111(b) of the same multi-Hamming weight and same cardinality 16 in $G_1^{(3)}$. The same phenomenon happens for the monomials of multi-Hamming weight 2100. Overall, a counting based on the multi-Hamming weights of all orbits would give 75 monomials for $G_1^{(3)}$ and $G_4^{(3)}$.

However, with the extra constraints of Eq. (2) imposed in the specification of DME, these polynomials actually contain only 65 monomials, see Lemma 2. More complete information on the monomial content is given in Table 4 below.

Table 3. Variables, q-symmetric orbits and monomial counts for the output coordinates when the matrices $\mathbf{A}_i \in \mathrm{GL}_k(\mathbb{Z}_{q^2-1})$ are chosen without the constraints of Eq. (2).

	Orbits	#Monomials
$G_1^{(3)}$	2111(a):16, 2111(b):16, 1111:16, 2100(a):4, 2100(b):4,	75
	1011:8, 1100:4, 0011:4, 1000:2, 0000:1	
$G_2^{(3)}$	1111:16, 1100:4, 0011:4, 0000:1	25
$G_3^{(3)}$	1111:16, 1100:4, 0011:4, 0000:1	25
$G_4^{(3)}$	1121(a):16, 1121(b):16, 1111:16, 0021(a):4, 0021(b):4,	75
	1110:8, 1100:4, 0011:4, 0010:2, 0000:1	

Table 4. DME case.

	Orbits	#Monomials
$G_1^{(3)}$	<u>2111:8</u>, <u>2100:2</u>, 1111:16, 1111(fall):16, 1011:8,	65
	1100:4, 1100(fall):4, 0011:4, 1000:2, 0000:1	
$G_2^{(3)}$	1111:16, 1100:4, 0011:4, 0000:1	25
$G_3^{(3)}$	1111:16, 1100:4, 0011:4, 0000:1	25
$G_4^{(3)}$	<u>1121:8</u>, <u>0021:2</u>, 1111:16, 1111(fall):16, 1110:8,	65
	1100:4, 0011:4, <u>0011(fall):4</u>, 0010:2, 0000:1	

Lemma 2. *Under the 3 constraints on the exponential maps given in Eq. (2), the number of monomials in $G_1^{(3)}$ and $G_4^{(3)}$ is generically equal to 65.*

Proof. Let us consider $G_1^{(3)}$. The case of $G_4^{(3)}$ is similar by replacing the first condition of Eq. (2) by the second one. First, notice from the definition of $\mathbf{A}_3$ given in Eq. (1) that the first output coordinate of $E_{\mathbf{A}_3}$ is

$$\left(G_1^{(2)}\right)^{[c_0]} \left(G_2^{(2)}\right)^{[c_1]}. \tag{3}$$

Thus, by Lemma 1, $G_1^{(3)}$ has the monomial structure of a product of polynomials with q-symmetric orbits and multi-Hamming weights as given in the first two rows of Table 2 since it is an affine function of this output. Moreover, without the 3 constraints of Eq. (2), its monomials would all be distinct and the total number would merely be the product of the number of monomials in $G_1^{(2)}$ and $G_2^{(2)}$ which is $15 \cdot 5 = 75$.

We now show that the constraints of Eq. (2) eliminate a total of 10 monomials. Most of the q-symmetric orbits of $G_1^{(2)}$ and $G_2^{(2)}$ involve disjoint variable sets and thus produce q-symmetric orbits of the expected multi-Hamming weight and number of monomials. The exceptions are products of the q-symmetric orbits of multi-Hamming weight 1011 with 1100 and 1000 with 1100, each of which giving a nontrivial interaction on the variable X_1.

Considering the sequence of operations that gives monomials of multi-Hamming weight 1011 and 1100 in $G_1^{(2)}$, there exists a representative for both of these orbits that contains the factor $X_1^{[a_0+b_0]}$. Similarly, we may trace the calculation of the q-symmetric orbit 1100 in $G_2^{(2)}$ and find that a representative includes a factor $X_1^{[a_1+b_2]}$. By definition of $\mathbf{A}_3$, we observe that the product of Eq. (3) has monomials including factors of the form

$$X_1^{[a_0+b_0+c_0]} X_1^{[a_1+b_2+c_1]},$$
$$X_1^{[a_0+b_0+c_0+e]} X_1^{[a_1+b_2+c_1]},$$
$$X_1^{[a_0+b_0+c_0]} X_1^{[a_1+b_2+c_1+e]},$$
$$X_1^{[a_0+b_0+c_0+e]} X_1^{[a_1+b_2+c_1+e]},$$

exactly as was considered above in the discussion on the number of orbits. Considering the first restriction from Eq. (2), we see that $a_0 + b_0 + c_0 = a_1 + b_2 + c_1 \pmod{2e}$ and thus $2^{a_0+b_0+c_0}$ and $2^{a_1+b_2+c_1}$ are equal in $\mathbb{Z}_{q^2-1}$. Therefore, the above monomial set simplifies in the form

$$\underbrace{X_1^{[a_0+b_0+c_0+1]}, \; X_1^{[a_0+b_0+c_0+e+1]}}_{\text{Hamming weight 1}} \quad \text{and} \quad \underbrace{X_1^{[a_0+b_0+c_0]} X_1^{[a_0+b_0+c_0+e]}}_{\text{Hamming weight 2}}.$$

Thus, we see that for actual parameters, the product of orbits involving X_1 does not split into two orbits of multi-Hamming weight 2111 (resp. 2100) as in the general case, but bifurcates into an orbit of multi-Hamming weight 2111 (resp. 2100), including factors of $X_1^{[a_0+b_0+c_0]} X_1^{[a_0+b_0+c_0+e]}$, and another orbit of multi-Hamming weight 1111 (resp. 1100), including factors of $X_1^{[a_0+b_0+c_0+1]}$ or $X_1^{[a_0+b_0+c_0+e+1]}$. These orbits are the ones which are underlined in Table 4.

To determine their sizes, we note that

$$\left(X_1^{[a_0+b_0+c_0]} X_1^{[a_0+b_0+c_0+e]}\right)^q = X_1^{[a_0+b_0+c_0+e]} X_1^{[a_0+b_0+c_0]},$$

and so they are determined by the powers of the remaining variables. For the 2111 orbit there are then 8 monomials (instead of 16) and for the 2100 orbit there are 2 monomials (instead of 4). Thus, there is a reduction of 10 monomials from the general case.

Finally, for the q-symmetric orbits that experience a multi-Hamming weight fall, the number of monomials is actually the same as in the generic case in which there is no such fall. In particular, $\left(X_1^{[a_0+b_0+c_0+1]}\right)^q = X_1^{[a_0+b_0+c_0+e+1]}$, so there are two possible powers of X_1 in such monomials. Thus, the atypical second instance of a multi-Hamming weight 1111 (resp. 1100) orbit contains the same 16 (resp. 4) monomials as the corresponding multi-Hamming weight 2111 (resp. 2100) orbit in the general case. $\square$

5   Algebraic Attack on DME

In this section, we describe our attack by recovering an *equivalent key* (recall that two secret keys are equivalent if they correspond to the same public key). More precisely, we will explain how to recover an *equivalent last round function*, i.e., whose knowledge allows to complete the attack in the same way as on a 2-round version of DME. Since all rounds have the same structure and since there are only 3 rounds, we argue that this latter step is not more costly (also, recall that 2-round DME has already been shown to be weak, see [4]).

More details on this completion will be given in Subsect. 5.5. Prior to that, Subsect. 5.1 presents tools that are used throughout this section and Subsects. 5.2, 5.3 and 5.4 are dedicated to the recovery of such an equivalent last round function. For the sake of clarity, our description will be limited to the level I parameter set with $e = 32$ (the values $k = 4$, $n = 8$ are common to all levels).

5.1   Using the Big Field Representation

In order to apply the results of Sect. 4, we start by deriving a public key $\widehat{P}$ whose 4 components lie in the ring

$$\mathcal{S} = \mathbb{F}_{q^2}[X_1, \ldots, X_4]/\langle X_1^{q^2} - X_1, \ldots, X_4^{q^2} - X_4 \rangle.$$

Recall that the initial public key P is an 8-tuple of polynomials in the quotient ring $\mathcal{R} = \mathbb{F}_q[x_1, \ldots, x_8]/\langle x_1^q - x_1, \ldots, x_8^q - x_8 \rangle$. To make the transformation, let ι be the inclusion $\iota : \mathcal{R} \to \mathbb{F}_{q^2}[x_1, \ldots, x_8]/\langle x_1^q - x_1, \ldots, x_8^q - x_8 \rangle$ and let $\psi : \mathcal{S} \to \mathbb{F}_{q^2}[x_1, \ldots, x_8]/\langle x_1^q - x_1, \ldots, x_8^q - x_8 \rangle$ be the unique ring morphism satisfying $\psi(X_i) = x_{2(i-1)+1} + U x_{2i}$ for $i \in \{1..4\}$ and $\psi(\lambda) = \lambda$ for $\lambda \in \mathbb{F}_{q^2}$. The latter has inverse

$$\psi^{-1} : \mathbb{F}_{q^2}[x_1, \ldots, x_8]/\langle x_1^q - x_1, \ldots, x_8^q - x_8 \rangle \to \quad \mathcal{S}$$
$$f \qquad\qquad \mapsto f(\xi_1, .., \xi_8),$$

where $\forall i \in \{1..8\}, \xi_{2(i-1)+1} = \frac{U X_i^q - U^q X_i}{U - U^q}$, and $\xi_{2i} = \frac{X_i^q - X_i}{U^q - U}$. Concretely, our approach starts by building the set of polynomials $\widehat{P} = (\widehat{P}_1, \ldots, \widehat{P}_4)$ defined by

$$\forall i \in \{1..4\}, \ \widehat{P}_i = \psi^{-1}\left(\iota(P_{2(i-1)+1}) + U\iota(P_{2i})\right).$$

Note that the above morphisms are used implicitly in the key generation of DME. In particular, constructing $\widehat{P}$ from P is extremely efficient.

From there, we may consider a calculation path entirely over $\mathbb{F}_{q^2}$. As observed in Sect. 4, the linear maps from the big field representation act *coordinate-wise*. This allows to exploit the following result, stating that such maps "nearly commute" coordinate-wise with power maps of exponent a power of two (the result is presented for general parameters).

Lemma 3 ("Nearly-commuting" trick). *Let $q = 2^e$, let $\widehat{L} : \mathbb{F}_{q^2}^k \to \mathbb{F}_{q^2}^k$ be a coordinate-wise $\mathbb{F}_q$-linear map and let $p = (p_1, \ldots, p_k) : \mathbb{F}_{q^2}^k \to \mathbb{F}_{q^2}^k$ be a map* *such that p_i raises the i-th input to a power of the form 2^{u_i}, $u_i \in \mathbb{Z}_{2e}$. Then there exists another coordinate-wise $\mathbb{F}_q$-linear map $\widehat{M} : \mathbb{F}_{q^2}^k \to \mathbb{F}_{q^2}^k$ such that*

$$p \circ \widehat{L} = \widehat{M} \circ p.$$

Proof. We only need to examine one single index i. To avoid confusion with the notation used for the linear layers, we may write the linear map at this coordinate as $\mathcal{L}_i(X) = AX + BX^q$ (in place of $\widehat{L}_i$). Then we observe that

$$p_i(\mathcal{L}_i(X)) = A^{[u_i]}X^{[u_i]} + B^{[u_i]}X^{[u_i+e]} = \mathcal{M}_i(p_i(X)),$$

where $\mathcal{M}_i(X) = A^{[u_i]}X + B^{[u_i]}X^q$.   □

Lemma 3 is instrumental to better grasp the set of possible equivalent keys. For example, assume that a secret key contains the composition of two round functions $R := \widehat{C} \circ \widehat{L} \circ E_A$ and $R' := \widehat{C'} \circ \widehat{L'} \circ E_{A'}$, where the matrices A and A' are of the same shape as in Eq. (1). The exponential map E_A may be written in a non-unique way as the composition of a power-of-two map p as in Lemma 3 followed by another exponential map $E_{A''}$. We then have

$$R \circ R' = \widehat{C} \circ \widehat{L} \circ E_A \circ \widehat{C'} \circ \widehat{L'} \circ E_{A'}$$
$$= \widehat{C} \circ \widehat{L} \circ E_{A''} \circ p \circ \widehat{C'} \circ \widehat{L'} \circ E_{A'}.$$

By linearity, we can write $p \circ \widehat{C'}$ as $\widehat{D'} \circ p$ where $\widehat{D'}$ is still an affine shift and eventually apply Lemma 3 to the composition $p \circ \widehat{L'}$. Namely, there exists a coordinate-wise $\mathbb{F}_q$-linear map $\widehat{M'}$ such that $p \circ \widehat{L'} = \widehat{M'} \circ p$. This gives

$$R \circ R' = \widehat{C} \circ \widehat{L} \circ E_{A''} \circ \widehat{D'} \circ \widehat{M'} \circ \underbrace{p \circ E_{A'}}_{:=E_{A'''}} := R'' \circ R''',$$

which is another composition of two round functions. Our attack will not require the full classification of equivalent keys but we already note that we can obtain other compositions by starting from a different factorization of E_A.

We will now see that Lemma 3 also plays a crucial role in the recovery of the equivalent last round. We will focus our attention on the 4 secret polynomials that constitute the input of the equivalent last round. These polynomials are entirely private but the analysis of Sect. 4.3 will allow to very efficiently identify the monomials present, see Subsect. 5.2. The associated coefficients, still unknown, will then be found in Subsect. 5.3 by solving polynomial systems. The recovery can be completed easily once these coefficients are known. Thus, polynomial system solving should represent the most costly part of the attack. We provide a complexity analysis of this step in Sect. 5.4.

5.2   Finding the Monomial Content of the Last Round Input

First, let us recall the relation with the public polynomials from $\widehat{P}$. We have

$$\widehat{P} = \widehat{C}_3 \circ \widehat{L}_3 \circ E_{A_3} \circ G,$$

where G is the input of the *genuine* last round R_3 and where

$$\mathbf{A}_3 = \begin{bmatrix} 2^{c_0} & 2^{c_1} & 0 & 0 \\ 0 & 2^{c_2} & 0 & 2^{c_3} \\ 0 & 2^{c_4} & 0 & 2^{c_5} \\ 0 & 0 & 2^{c_6} & 2^{c_7} \end{bmatrix}.$$

If we were to invert the last linear layer, we would obtain

$$\widehat{L}_3^{-1} \circ \widehat{C}_3^{-1} \circ \left(\widehat{P}_1, \widehat{P}_2, \widehat{P}_3, \widehat{P}_4\right) = \left(G_1^{[c_0]} G_2^{[c_1]}, G_2^{[c_2]} G_4^{[c_3]}, G_2^{[c_4]} G_4^{[c_5]}, G_3^{[c_6]} G_4^{[c_7]}\right)$$

$$= E_B \circ \left(G_1^{\alpha} G_2^{\beta}, G_2^{\beta} G_4^{[c_5]}, G_2^{[c_4]} G_4^{[c_5]}, G_3^{\gamma} G_4^{[c_5]}\right), \tag{4}$$

where $\alpha = [c_0 - (c_1 + c_3 - c_2 - c_5)]$, $\beta = [c_2 - c_3 + c_5]$, $\gamma = [c_5 + c_6 - c_7]$ and

$$B = \begin{bmatrix} 2^{c_1+c_3-c_2-c_5} & 0 & 0 & 0 \\ 0 & 2^{c_3-c_5} & 0 & 0 \\ 0 & 0 & 2^0 & 0 \\ 0 & 0 & 0 & 2^{c_7-c_5} \end{bmatrix}. \tag{5}$$

The goal here is to have a right-hand-side $\left(G_1^{\alpha} G_2^{\beta}, G_2^{\beta} G_4^{[c_5]}, G_2^{[c_4]} G_4^{[c_5]}, G_3^{\gamma} G_4^{[c_5]}\right)$ such that each of the 4 coordinates shares a factor in common with another. We will use this property later on in this subsection.

To recover the map E_B, we will use two facts. First, the maps $\widehat{L}_3$ and $\widehat{C}_3$ do not alter the monomial content of q-symmetric polynomials; thus, the monomial content of $\left(G_1^{[c_0]} G_2^{[c_1]}, G_2^{[c_2]} G_4^{[c_3]}, G_2^{[c_4]} G_4^{[c_5]}, G_3^{[c_6]} G_4^{[c_7]}\right)$ is public. Second, the discussion of Sect. 4.3 shows that the q-symmetric orbits in G are known. For instance, the following Table 5 is just Table 2 with the shorthand notation $(G_1, G_2, G_3, G_4) = (G_1^{(2)}, G_2^{(2)}, G_3^{(2)}, G_4^{(2)})$.

Table 5. Known q-symmetric orbits in G.

	Variables	Orbits	#Monomials
G_1	X_1, X_3, X_4	1011:8, 0011:4, 1000:2, 0000:1	15
G_2	X_1, X_2	1100:4, 0000:1	5
G_3	X_1, X_2, X_3	1110:8, 1100:4, 0010:2, 0000:1	15
G_4	X_3, X_4	0011:4, 0000:1	5

In the following, let QSymOrbit be a trivial procedure that computes the q-symmetric orbit of a monomial. For a given monomial μ and a set of indices $S \subset \{1..4\}$, we will also call *truncation of μ on S* the highest degree monomial ν in the variables X_s, $s \in S$ such that $\nu | \mu$. Applied to a polynomial p and such a set S, the procedure MONOMIALCONTENT will return the set of truncations of the monomials of p on S. For example,

$$\text{MONOMIALCONTENT}(X_1X_2X_3X_4 + X_1X_4, \{3,4\}) = \{X_3X_4, X_4\}.$$

We now explain how to recover the difference $c_3 - c_5$ from the public components $\widehat{P}_2$ and $\widehat{P}_3$, by using the peculiar property that G_2 and G_4 have disjoint variable supports; namely, their supports are $\{X_1, X_2\}$ and $\{X_3, X_4\}$, respectively. This difference is the power of two at which we have to raise $\widehat{P}_2$ so that the monomials in the result truncated on the variables $\{X_3, X_4\}$ match the truncation of those of $\widehat{P}_3$ on the same variables (they will correspond to the common factor $G_4^{[c_5]}$). More precisely, we apply the following Algorithm 1, on input $\widehat{P}_3$, $\widehat{P}_2$ and $\{3,4\}$.

Algorithm 1. RETRIEVEDIFFERENCE(H_1, H_2, S)

Input: H_1 and H_2 are polynomials and $S \subset \{1..4\}$ is a subset of indices.
Output: Difference Δ
1: $\Delta \leftarrow 0$
2: **for** $\mu \in$ MONOMIALCONTENT(H_1, S) **do**
3:      **for** r in $\{0..e-1\}$ **do**
4:          **if** QSYMORBIT$(\mu^{[r]}) \subseteq$ MONOMIALCONTENT(H_2, S) **then**
5:              $\Delta \leftarrow r$
6:          **end if**
7:      **end for**
8: **end for**
9: **return** Δ

The difference we are looking for belongs to $\mathbb{Z}_{2^e}$ and the algorithm will output this difference modulo e. The two possibilities for this difference will both yield equivalent keys (this can be seen from the discussion after Lemma 5). With the same ambiguity, we may recover the other exponents modulo e in an analogous way by

$$c_1 + c_3 - c_2 - c_5 = \text{RETRIEVEDIFFERENCE}(\widehat{P}_2^{[c_5 - c_3]}, \widehat{P}_1, \{2\}),$$

$$c_7 - c_5 = \text{RETRIEVEDIFFERENCE}(\widehat{P}_3, \widehat{P}_4, \{4\}).$$

Once the matrix $\boldsymbol{B}$ is recovered, we use Lemma 3 on Eq. (4) to verify the existence of a coordinate-wise $\mathbb{F}_q$-linear map $\widehat{M}$ and affine shift $\widehat{D}$ such that

$$E_{\boldsymbol{B}^{-1}} \circ \widehat{P} = \widehat{D} \circ \widehat{M} \circ \left(G_1^\alpha G_2^\beta, G_2^\beta G_4^{[c_5]}, G_2^{[c_4]} G_4^{[c_5]}, G_3^\gamma G_4^{[c_5]}\right),$$

where the left-hand side is now entirely known and where the monomial content of G_1^α, G_2^β, G_3^γ and $G_4^{[c_5]}$ is also known. This follows from the fact that the variable supports of G_2 and G_4 are disjoint and that each of the four coordinates shares a factor in common with another. The remainder of the recovery of an equivalent round 3 will consist in recovering the associated coefficients in G_1^α, G_2^β, G_3^γ and $G_4^{[c_5]}$ and then the ones of the maps $\widehat{D}$ and $\widehat{M}$, sequentially.

5.3   Finding the Unknown Coefficients

We start from the equation

$$\widehat{M}^{-1} \circ \widehat{D}^{-1} \circ E_{\boldsymbol{B}-1} \circ \widehat{P} = \left(G_1^\alpha G_2^\beta, G_2^\beta G_4^{[c_5]}, G_2^{[c_4]} G_4^{[c_5]}, G_3^\gamma G_4^{[c_5]} \right), \qquad (6)$$

that corresponds to 4 polynomial equalities. Our approach consists in viewing the unknown coefficients of all polynomials G_1^α, G_2^β, G_3^γ, $G_4^{[c_5]}$ and those of the 4 polynomials in $\widehat{M}^{-1}$ as formal variables in a multivariate polynomial ring and then in deriving equations in these coefficients. The equations will be solved using standard algebraic techniques.

Bilinear Modeling. Our first modeling is obtained from the second and third coordinates of $E_{\boldsymbol{B}-1} \circ \widehat{P}$. Specifically, we know that

$$\begin{aligned} \widehat{M}_2^{-1} \left(\widehat{P}_2^{[c_5-c_3]} - D_2 \right) &= G_2^\beta G_4^{[c_5]} \\ \widehat{M}_3^{-1} \left(\widehat{P}_3 - D_3 \right) &= G_2^{[c_4]} G_4^{[c_5]}. \end{aligned} \qquad (7)$$

Using Table 5, the number of formal variables we need to introduce is 5 for each of the polynomials $G_4^{[c_5]}$, $G_2^{[c_4]}$ and G_2^β (we arrange these variables as vectors $\boldsymbol{x}$, $\boldsymbol{y}$ and $\boldsymbol{z}$ respectively, all of length 5). Since these maps are linear, we also introduce 2 variables s_1, s_2 for $\widehat{M}_2^{-1}$ and 2 variables t_1, t_2 for $\widehat{M}_3^{-1}$, namely

$$\begin{aligned} \widehat{M}_2^{-1}(X) &= s_1 X + s_2 X^q, \\ \widehat{M}_3^{-1}(X) &= t_1 X + t_2 X^q. \end{aligned}$$

We consider the equations obtained by matching coefficients in front of the same monomial in the two polynomial equalities from (7). In both of them, the number of monomials present is 25 by using Table 4. Thus, we can obtain a total of $25 + 25 = 50$ equations. However, we cannot use the 2 equations corresponding to the constant terms since we do not include the secret coefficients D_2 and D_3 in our variables. Finally, we can divide the two equations in (7) by s_1 and t_1, respectively, to further reduce the number of variables.

Modeling 1. *We obtain in this way an affine bilinear system in* $\mathbb{F}_{q^2}[\boldsymbol{x}, \boldsymbol{y}, \boldsymbol{z}, s, t]$ *with* $s = s_2/s_1$ *and* $t = t_2/t_1$ *that contains 48 polynomials.*

- *the first equation in (7) gives a bilinear system in* $\mathbb{F}_{q^2}[\boldsymbol{x}, \boldsymbol{z}, s]$ *containing polynomials of the form*

$$x_i z_j + \ell_{i,j}(s),$$

  where $\ell_{i,j}(s)$ *linear affine in* s, *for any* $(i,j) \in \{1..5\}^2 \setminus \{(5,5)\}$;
- *the second equation in (7) gives a bilinear system in* $\mathbb{F}_{q^2}[\boldsymbol{x}, \boldsymbol{y}, t]$ *containing polynomials of the form*

$$x_i y_j + m_{i,j}(t),$$

  where $m_{i,j}(t)$ *linear affine in* t, *for any* $(i,j) \in \{1..5\}^2 \setminus \{(5,5)\}$.

Remark 2. *Anecdotally, Modeling 1 can be seen as a subset of* 48 *out of* 50 *equations which model two rank one MinRank problems in* $\mathbb{F}_{q^2}^{5 \times 5}$ *with matrices* $(\mathbf{M}_1, \mathbf{M}_2)$ *and* $(\mathbf{N}_1, \mathbf{N}_2)$ *respectively correlated in that we look for solutions* $\boldsymbol{x}^{\mathsf{T}} \boldsymbol{y} = \mathbf{M}_1 + s\mathbf{M}_2$ *and* $\boldsymbol{x}^{\mathsf{T}} \boldsymbol{z} = \mathbf{N}_1 + t\mathbf{N}_2$ *for the same* $\boldsymbol{x}$. *We simply do not consider the two equations coming from entry* $(5, 5)$.

In Lemma 4, we study the variety of Modeling 1 intersected with the coordinate ring of $\mathbb{F}_{q^2}^{17}$. This is also the variety (over the algebraic closure) of the ideal J generated by Modeling 1 together with the field equations from $\mathbb{F}_{q^2}$. For practical purposes, we do not, in practice, add equations of such a high degree into the system, since a Gröbner basis over an algebraic closure of $\mathbb{F}_{q^2}$ can be computed so easily on Modeling 1 alone.

Lemma 4. *Let J be the ideal generated by Modeling 1 along with the field equations from $\mathbb{F}_{q^2}$. The variety $V(J)$ has 1 degree of freedom over $\mathbb{F}_{q^2}$. Moreover, by fixing one variable different from s and t, we get a variety of size at least 2.*

Proof. If $(\boldsymbol{x}, \boldsymbol{z}, \boldsymbol{y}, s, t)$ is a solution in $V(J)$ then $(\lambda \boldsymbol{x}, \lambda^{-1} \boldsymbol{z}, \lambda^{-1} \boldsymbol{y}, s, t)$ is another solution for any non-zero $\lambda \in \mathbb{F}_{q^2}^*$. There is an additional symmetry coming from q-powering. Indeed, let us consider a solution $(\boldsymbol{x}, \boldsymbol{z}, \boldsymbol{y}, s, t)$ with a prescribed coordinate in $\boldsymbol{x}$, $\boldsymbol{y}$ or $\boldsymbol{z}$ (so that it is a solution to Modeling 1 specialized with this constraint). To simplify the notation, let us write S_i for the known polynomial $(E_{\mathbf{B}_1} \circ \widehat{P})_i$, $i \in \{2, 3\}$. Let also $(\overline{G}_4, \overline{G}_{2,1}, \overline{G}_{2,2})$ be the triple of polynomials corresponding to $(\boldsymbol{x}, \boldsymbol{z}, \boldsymbol{y})$. By q-powering the equalities

$$S_2^q + s^q S_2 = \overline{G}_{2,1} \overline{G}_4,$$
$$S_3^q + t^q S_3 = \overline{G}_{2,2} \overline{G}_4$$

we get

$$S_2 + s S_2^q = (\overline{G}_{2,1})^q (\overline{G}_4)^q,$$
$$S_3 + t S_3^q = (\overline{G}_{2,2})^q (\overline{G}_4)^q.$$

By dividing the first equality by s and the second one by t to adhere to the restriction in our modeling that the linear maps have a coefficient of 1 in front of X, we finally obtain

$$(1/s)S_2 + S_2^q = (\overline{G}_{2,1}^q / s)(\overline{G}_4)^q,$$
$$(1/t)S_3 + S_3^q = (\overline{G}_{2,2}^q / t)(\overline{G}_4)^q.$$

This yields the new solution $(\boldsymbol{x}^q, (\boldsymbol{z}^q / s), (\boldsymbol{y}^q / t), 1/s, 1/t)$ to Modeling 1. Note that, in general, the coordinate prescribed in the former solution $(\boldsymbol{x}, \boldsymbol{z}, \boldsymbol{y}, s, t)$ will here have a different value. However, by $\mathbb{F}_{q^2}$-linearity, exactly one of the other solutions $(\lambda \boldsymbol{x}^q, \lambda^{-1}(\boldsymbol{z}^q / s), \lambda^{-1}(\boldsymbol{y}^q / t), 1/s, 1/t)$ will have the right value at this coordinate. □

Due to Lemma 4, we have the freedom to specialize one of the variables other than s and t in Modeling 1 and retain a consistent system. Any choice of such a variable produces linear equations. However, choosing to fix a variable x_i for some $i \neq 5$ generates the greatest number of linear equations. In the following, we suppose that we fix the value of variable x_1.

The solution to the specialized system will provide candidates for the maps $\widehat{M}_2^{-1}, \widehat{M}_3^{-1}, G_2^{\beta}, G_2^{[c_4]}$ and $G_4^{[c_5]}$. There are, however, two complications. First, it is necessary to enforce the restriction that $\beta = [c_4 - d]$, i.e., $G_2^{\beta}/G_2^{[c_4-d]} = 1$, by computing this quotient $\tau \in \mathbb{F}_{q^2}$ and replacing G_2^{β} with τG_2^{β}. Second, the proof of Lemma 4 shows that, in particular, the candidate for $G_4^{[c_5]}$ might instead correspond to $\lambda G_4^{[c_5]}$ or $\lambda G_4^{[c_5+e]}$ for some $\lambda \in \mathbb{F}_{q^2}$. Since both multiplication by λ or τ and exponentiation by q are $\mathbb{F}_q$-linear, this is a not an issue as these operations can both be absorbed into the linear layer of the previous round (using the reasoning sketched right after Lemma 3). Thus, we may assume that we have the correct candidates. From these candidates, we can also recover the affine shift constants D_2 and D_3. Indeed, these solutions reveal all the quantities in Eq. (7) other than D_2 and D_3. In particular, these equations are readily solved for the correct values of the affine shift. In the following, we denote by $(\overline{G}_4, \overline{G}_{2,1}, \overline{G}_{2,2})$ the solutions found for $(G_4^{[c_5]}, G_2^{\beta}, G_2^{[c_4]})$.

Remaining Coefficients by Solving Linear Systems. The coefficients that we still have to recover of those of $\widehat{M}_i^{-1}$, $\widehat{D}_i$ for $i \in \{1, 4\}$ and those of the polynomials G_1^{α}, G_3^{γ}. To do so, we come back to Eq. (6) and we plug the solutions previously found into coordinates 1 and 4:

$$\widehat{M}_1^{-1} \left(\widehat{P}_1^{[c_2+c_5-c_1-c_3]} - D_1 \right) = G_1^{\alpha} \overline{G}_{2,1}$$
$$\widehat{M}_4^{-1} \left(\widehat{P}_1^{[c_5-c_7]} - D_4 \right) = G_3^{\gamma} \overline{G}_4. \tag{8}$$

By introducing formal variables for $\widehat{M}_1^{-1}$ and G_1^{α} in the first equation and for $\widehat{M}_4^{-1}$ and G_3^{γ} in the second equation, the reasoning used to obtain Modeling 1 yields two linear systems. These two systems contain $64 = 65 - 1$ equations (by using Table 4 and dropping the constant term) in $17 = 2 + 15$ variables (by using Table 2 or Table 5). These systems are much easier to solve than Modeling 1. From their solutions we can readily recover G_1^{α}, G_3^{γ} and $\widehat{M}_i^{-1}$ for $i \in \{1, 4\}$. Finally, we can retrieve D_1 and D_4 by coming back to Eq. (8) since all the other values are now known.

To unify notation, in the following let $\widetilde{L}_3$ be the recovered value for $\widehat{M}$ and let $\widetilde{C}_3$ be the recovered value for $\widehat{D}$. These values will be used in Subsect. 5.5 to derive an equivalent last round function (it remains to precise the exponential component). Prior to that, Subsect. 5.4 examines the complexity of recovering $\widetilde{L}_3$ and $\widetilde{C}_3$. Our discussion so far shows that we can restrict ourselves to the solving of Modeling 1.

5.4   Complexity of Solving Specialized Modeling 1

Recall that the equations in Modeling 1 are of the form $x_i z_j + \ell_{i,j}(s) = 0$ or $x_i y_j + m_{i,j}(t) = 0$ for $(i,j) \neq (5,5)$, were $\ell_{i,j}$, $m_{i,j}$ are univariate polynomials of degree 1. Recall also that we decided to set a constraint $x_1 = a$ in order to obtain a variety of expected size 2.

The Gröbner basis computation of the specialized system proceeds very simply. Setting $x_1 = a$ yields linear relations of the form $z_j + a^{-1}\ell_{1,j}(s) = 0$ and $y_j + a^{-1}m_{1,j}(t) = 0$. Thus, by substitution into the other equations that remain of degree 2, the entire system implicitly reduces to an overdetermined bilinear system of $38 = 48 - 10$ equations in the 6 variables s, t and x_i for $i \neq 1$ in which each relation contains a single quadratic monomial of the form $x_i s$ or $x_i t$. As outlined in detail in Appendix B, such a system is solved in degree 2. As suggested in Lemma 4, we find that the Gröbner basis consists of a single univariate quadratic equation and an otherwise linear system of equations producing precisely two solutions.

In fact, even a generic system consisting of 38 quadratic (not necessarily bilinear) equations and 10 linear equations in 16 variables[2] is solved at degree 2 (using standard arguments, e.g., Hilbert series). We may therefore provide a rather gross overestimate of the complexity of solving the system of Modeling 1 over $\mathbb{F}_{q^2}$ with the formula

$$\text{Complexity}_{\text{Modeling 1}} = \mathcal{O}\left(\binom{16+2}{2}^{\omega} \right),$$

in which ω is the linear algebra constant, typically assumed to be $\omega = 2.81$ for Strassen's Algorithm [16]. Finally, by using the standard formula

$$\# \text{ gates per } \mathbb{F}_q\text{-multiplication} = 2\left(\log_2 q\right)^2 + \log_2 q,$$

we obtain the following results on the NIST parameter sets (Table 6):

Table 6. Conservative estimate for the cost of solving specialized Modeling 1.

Level	Value of q	Gate Count
I	2^{32}	2^{31}
III	2^{48}	2^{32}
V	2^{64}	2^{33}

---

[2] For simplicity, our implementation does not use $17 - 1 = 16$ variables. Instead, it adds an equation of the form $x_1 - a$, resulting in a system of 49 equations in 17 variables.

5.5   Completing an Equivalent Round Function

We finally explain that we can efficiently recover an equivalent key from the maps $\widetilde{L}_3$ and $\widetilde{C}_3$ that have just been retrieved. Lemma 5 below shows that we can actually construct one which is identical to the genuine key in its first round.

Lemma 5. *Let $\widetilde{L}_3$ (resp. $\widetilde{C}_3$) denote the retrieved linear map (resp. affine shift), let $\boldsymbol{B}$ be the diagonal matrix of Eq. (5) and let*

$$\boldsymbol{C} = \begin{bmatrix} 1 & 1 & 0 & 0 \\ 0 & 1 & 0 & 1 \\ 0 & 2^{57} & 0 & 1 \\ 0 & 0 & 1 & 1 \end{bmatrix}.$$

Then the round function $\widetilde{R}_3$ given by the composition of $\widetilde{C}_3$, $\widetilde{L}_3$ and $E_{\boldsymbol{B}^{-1}\boldsymbol{C}}$ is an equivalent round function, in the sense that there exists a round function R_2' satisfying

$$\widehat{P} = \widetilde{R}_3 \circ R_2' \circ R_1 \circ \widehat{C}_0 \circ \widehat{L}_0.$$

Proof. Let $(\widetilde{G}_1, \widetilde{G}_2, \widetilde{G}_3, \widetilde{G}_4)$ be the components recovered in Subsect. 5.4. By the last equation in this subsection, they satisfy $\widehat{P} = \widetilde{C}_3 \circ \widetilde{L}_3 \circ E_{\boldsymbol{B}^{-1}\boldsymbol{C}}(\widetilde{G}_1, \widetilde{G}_2, \widetilde{G}_3, \widetilde{G}_4)$. We then obtain

$$\widehat{P} = \widetilde{C}_3 \circ \widetilde{L}_3 \circ E_{\boldsymbol{B}^{-1}\boldsymbol{C}}(G_1^\alpha, G_2^\beta, G_3^\gamma, G_4^{[c_5]}) = \widetilde{R}_3(G_1^\alpha, G_2^\beta, G_3^\gamma, G_4^{[c_5]})$$
$$= E_{\boldsymbol{A}_3}(G_1, G_2, G_3, G_4),$$

where the top equality is by definition of the $\widetilde{G}_i$'s and where the bottom one follows from the definition of $\boldsymbol{B}$ in Eq. (5) and from the condition on the exponents given by Eq. (2). By definition of (G_1, G_2, G_3, G_4) we also have

$$(G_1, G_2, G_3, G_4) = R_2 \circ R_1 \circ \widehat{C}_0 \circ \widehat{L}_0(X_1, \dots, X_4).$$

Thus, it remains to find a round function R_2' such that

$$R_2' \circ R_1 \circ \widehat{C}_0 \circ \widehat{L}_0 = E_{\boldsymbol{T}} \circ R_2 \circ R_1 \circ \widehat{C}_0 \circ \widehat{L}_0,$$

where $\boldsymbol{T}$ is the diagonal matrix with diagonal entries α, β, γ, and $[c_5]$. By Lemma 3, there exists a linear map $L_2' : \mathbb{F}_{q^2}^4 \to \mathbb{F}_{q^2}^4$ such that $E_{\boldsymbol{T}} \circ \widetilde{L}_2 = L_2' \circ E_{\boldsymbol{T}}$. If we denote by C_2' the affine shift derived from $\widehat{C}_2$ by raising the constants to the powers α, β, γ and $[c_5]$, then the round function

$$R_2' = C_2' \circ L_2' \circ E_{\boldsymbol{T}\boldsymbol{A}_2}$$

satisfies the criterion.   □

  Lemma 5 guarantees that we can view $(\widetilde{G}_1, \widetilde{G}_2, \widetilde{G}_3, \widetilde{G}_4)$ as the public key of a 2-round DME scheme. From there, we can apply the attack of Beullens [4] or iterate our procedure. In the latter case, the modelings derived to recover equivalent functions $\widetilde{R}_2$ and $\widetilde{R}_1$ will involve different components than the ones we described for $\widetilde{R}_3$. However, the shape of the exponent matrices $\boldsymbol{T}\boldsymbol{A}_2$ and $\boldsymbol{A}_1$ ensure that these systems will not be harder to solve than the bilinear system of above.

6   Experimental Results

A Magma implementation of the attack on the Level I parameters is available at https://github.com/ppbriaud/DMEattack. For this parameter set, the attack takes between roughly 500 ms and 1 s. Perhaps surprisingly, the main cost in practice corresponds to the application of Algorithm 1 and not to polynomial system solving. The reason is probably a poor implementation of this part.

The code can be easily adapted to the other security levels by changing the values of d and e, with no computational overhead other than the increased cost of the field arithmetic.

A   Proof of Lemma 1

Any scalar $D \in \mathbb{F}_{q^2}$ can clearly be viewed as a q-symmetric polynomial with monomial support reduced to the unique orbit $\{1\}$ if $D \neq 0$ and empty monomial support if $D = 0$. This proves Statement 1.

Statement 2 is similarly trivial. The monomial support of the sum $p_1 + p_2$ is perfectly controlled except if there is a cancellation when adding two coefficients for the same monomial. Assuming that the monomial support of both p_1 and p_2 are fixed and that their coefficients are randomly sampled, such a cancellation occurs with a probability bounded by the minimum of the numbers of monomials in the polynomials divided by $q^2 - 1$, which is assumed to be small.

The monomial support of a polynomial product is also perfectly understood with very high probability (which has nothing to do with q-symmetry). If we let M_i be monomial support of p_i for $\{1, 2\}$, the monomial support M of $p_1 p_2$ is included in the set $M_{\max}$ containing the distinct elements of the list

$$[\mu_1 \mu_2 : \mu_1 \in M_1, \ \mu_2 \in M_2].$$

This inclusion is strict precisely when there exists $\mu \in M_{\max}$ with cancellation

$$\sum_{\substack{\mu_1 \in M_1 \\ \mu_2 \in M_2 \\ \mu_1 \mu_2 = \mu}} \mathrm{coef}(\mu_1, p_1) \mathrm{coef}(\mu_2, p_2) = 0.$$

Just as in the previous case, this event is of very low probability. If now p_1 and p_2 are q-symmetric with $M = M_{\max}$, let us consider an arbitrary element $\mu = \mu_1 \mu_2 \in M_{\max}$ which is thus a monomial appearing in $p_1 p_2$. Any monomial $\widetilde{\mu}$ obtained by q-powering variables in μ can clearly be written as $\widetilde{\mu_1} \widetilde{\mu_2}$, where $\widetilde{\mu_i}$ belongs[3] to the q-symmetric orbit of μ_i for $\{1, 2\}$. By q-symmetry of p_1 (resp. p_2) we have $\widetilde{\mu_1} \in M_1$ (resp. $\widetilde{\mu_2} \in M_2$), hence $\widetilde{\mu} \in M_{\max}$ and this monomial necessarily appears in $p_1 p_2$. This shows Statement 3.

Statement 4 is obviously a particular case of Statement 3.

---

[3] Possibly $\widetilde{\mu_i} = \mu_i$.

Finally, Statement 5 is a consequence of the previous results along with the fact that every $\mathbb{F}_q$-linear map on $\mathbb{F}_{q^2}$ has a linearized polynomial form. Specifically, the reason that $L(p)$ has the same monomial content as p is because q-powering simply permutes the monomials of a q-symmetric polynomial and cannot create coefficient cancellations.

B   Gröbner Bases for Specialized Modeling 1

We detail the behaviour of the Gröbner basis algorithm on Modeling 1 when we fix one variable x_i for some $i \neq 5$ to a nonzero value $a \in \mathbb{F}_{q^2}^*$. This specialization may represent the most favorable case as we maximize the number of linear equations produced at the first step. Our description is made for a graded order $<$ such that $s < t < \boldsymbol{x}, \boldsymbol{y}, \boldsymbol{z}$ and our goal is mainly to describe the experimental steps reported in Fig. 3 below[4].

STEP 1. Former equations with leading terms divisible by x_i now become equations with leading terms z_j and y_k for $j, k \in \{1..5\}$. More precisely, we get $z_j - a^{-1}\ell_{i,j}(s) = 0$ for $j \in \{1..5\}$ and $y_k - a^{-1}m_{i,k}(t) = 0$ for $k \in \{1..5\}$. This should explain the 10 linear degree fall polynomials that are observed.

STEP 2. The second step is in degree 2. There, we use the degree fall polynomials found in STEP 1 to "remove" the $\boldsymbol{y}$ and $\boldsymbol{z}$ blocks in the initial modeling.

1. From the former equations with leading terms $x_5 z_j$ for $j \neq 5$, we now get 4 affine equations in $\mathbb{F}_{q^2}[x_5, s, 1]$ whose unique quadratic monomial is $x_5 s$. Similarly, we obtain 4 affine equations in $\mathbb{F}_{q^2}[x_5, t, 1]$ whose unique quadratic monomial is $x_5 t$ from the previous equations with leading terms $x_5 y_k$ for $k \neq 5$. In addition to this new leading term $x_5 s$ (resp. $x_5 t$) we thus expect 3 linear equations in $\mathbb{F}_{q^2}[x_5, s, 1]$ (resp. 3 linear equations in $\mathbb{F}_{q^2}[t, x_5, 1]$). By doing linear combinations between these degree 1 polynomials we may generate one degree 1 polynomial with leading term x_5 and one in $\mathbb{F}_{q^2}[s, t, 1]$ with leading term t. We cannot create a degree 1 equation with leading term s because we have > 1 solution (see Lemma 4).

2. From the former equations with leading terms $x_u z_j$ for $u \neq \{i, 5\}$, we now get 5 affine equations with leading monomial $x_u s$ and degree ≤ 1 part in x_u and s. Similarly, we obtain 5 affine equations with leading monomial $x_u t$ and degree ≤ 1 part in x_u and t from the previous equations with leading terms $x_u y_k$. This time we produce the leading terms $\{x_u s, x_u t\}$ as well as x_u for $u \neq \{i, 5\}$.

Overall, we create $2 + 3 \cdot 2 = 8$ new quadratic leading monomials and $2 + 3 \cdot 1 = 5$ new degree 1 leading monomials. This is in accordance with the behaviour observed in Magma.

---

[4] This figure was generated using the level I parameters but the behaviour would be analogous for the other levels since the only difference is the value of q.

```
*******
STEP 1
Basis length: 49, queue length: 310, step degree: 2, num pairs: 10
Basis total mons: 146, average length: 2.980
Number of S-polynomials: 10, different lcms: 10
Number of pair polynomials: 10, at 23 column(s), 0.000
Average length for reductees: 2.00 [10], reductors: 3.00 [10]
Symbolic reduction time: 0.000, column sort time: 0.000
10 + 10 = 20 rows / 23 columns out of 171 (13.450%)
Density: 10.87% / 13.854% (2.5/r), total: 50 (0.0MB)
Matrix construction time: 0.000
Matrix size: 20 by 23
Current max memory usage: 32.1MB (=max)
Before ech memory: 32.1MB (=max)
Row sort time: 0.000
    0.000 + 0.000 + 0.000 = 0.000 [10]
    Echelonization time: 0.000
After ech memory: 32.1MB (=max)
New rules time: 0.000
Num new polynomials: 10 (100.0%), min deg: 1 [10], av deg: 1.0
Degree counts: 1:10
Queue insertion time: 0.000
Number of linears: 10
New max step: 1, time: 0.000
Step 1 time: 0.000, [0.001], mat/total: 0.000/0.000, mem: 32.1MB (=max)


*******
STEP 2
Basis length: 59, queue length: 338, step degree: 2, num pairs: 38
Basis total mons: 176, average length: 2.983
Number of S-polynomials: 38, different lcms: 38
Number of pair polynomials: 38, at 53 column(s), 0.000
Average length for reductees: 3.00 [38], reductors: 3.00 [38]
Symbolic reduction time: 0.000, column sort time: 0.000
38 + 38 = 76 rows / 53 columns out of 171 (30.994%)
Density: 5.6604% / 9.7791% (3/r), total: 228 (0.0MB)
Matrix construction time: 0.000
Matrix size: 76 by 53
Current max memory usage: 32.1MB (=max)
Before ech memory: 32.1MB (=max)
Row sort time: 0.000
    0.000 + 0.000 + 0.000 = 0.000 [13]
    Echelonization time: 0.000
After ech memory: 32.1MB (=max)
New rules time: 0.000
Num new polynomials: 13 (34.2%), min deg: 1 [5], av deg: 1.6
Degree counts: 1:5 2:8
Queue insertion time: 0.000
Number of linears: 15
Step 2 time: 0.000, [0.001], mat/total: 0.000/0.000, mem: 32.1MB (=max)
```

Fig. 3. Trace of Magma's F4 algorithm [8] on Modeling 1 with one variable x_i, $i \neq 5$, fixed to a nonzero value (for security level I).

```
*******
STEP 3
Basis length: 72, queue length: 308, step degree: 2, num pairs: 8
Basis total mons: 215, average length: 2.986
Number of S-polynomials: 8, different lcms: 8
Number of pair polynomials: 8, at 15 column(s), 0.000
Average length for reductees: 3.00 [8], reductors: 3.00 [12]
Symbolic reduction time: 0.000, column sort time: 0.000
8 + 12 = 20 rows / 15 columns out of 171 (8.772%)
Density: 20% / 36.011% (3/r), total: 60 (0.0MB)
Matrix construction time: 0.000
Matrix size: 20 by 15
Current max memory usage: 32.1MB (=max)
Before ech memory: 32.1MB (=max)
Row sort time: 0.000
    0.000 + 0.000 + 0.000 = 0.000 [1]
    Echelonization time: 0.000
After ech memory: 32.1MB (=max)
New rules time: 0.000
Num new polynomials: 1 (12.5%), min deg: 2 [1], av deg: 2.0
Degree counts: 2:1
Queue insertion time: 0.000
Number of linears: 15
Step 3 time: 0.000, [0.001], mat/total: 0.000/0.000, mem: 32.1MB (=max)


*******
STEP 4
Basis length: 73, queue length: 300, step degree: 3, num pairs: 300
Basis total mons: 218, average length: 2.986
300 pairs eliminated
No pairs to reduce
Pair elimination time: 0.000

Do extern interreduction (length 25)
    INTERREDUCE 17 polynomial(s)
        Symbolic reduction time: 0.000
        Column sort time: 0.000
        17 + 0 = 17 rows / 19 columns
        Density: 15.48% / 35.791% (2.9412/r), total: 50 (0.0MB)
        Row sort time: 0.000
            0.000 + 0.000 = 0.000 [17]
            Echelonization time: 0.000
        Total reduction time: 0.000
    Reduction time: 0.000
Final extern interreduction time: 0.000

Final basis length: 17
Number of pairs: 56
Total pair setup time: 0.000
Max step: 2, time: 0.010
Max num entries matrix: 76 by 53
Max num rows matrix: 76 by 53
Approx mat cost: 8321.32, sym red cost: 338
Approx mat time: 0.000, sym red time: 0.000, total 0.000
Total symbolic reduction time: 0.000
Total column sort time: 0.000
Total row sort time: 0.000
Total matrix time: 0.010
Total new polys time: 0.000
Total queue update time: 0.000
Total Faugere F4 time: 0.010, real time: 0.004
```

Fig. 3. (*continued*)

STEP 3. We are left with the unique variable s if we simplify the system using the linear equations generated at STEP 2. The only degree 2 polynomial occurring at this step is univariate and it has leading monomial s^2.

References

1. IEEE standard specifications for public-key cryptography: IEEE Std 1363-2000, pp. 1–228 (2000). https://doi.org/10.1109/IEEESTD.2000.92292
2. Alagic, G., et al.: Status report on the third round of the NIST post-quantum cryptography standardization process. Technical report. NIST Interagency or Internal Report (IR) 8413, National Institute of Standards and Technology, Gaithersburg, MD, July 2022. https://doi.org/10.6028/NIST.IR.8413-upd1
3. Avendaño, M., Marco, M.: A structural attack to the DME-(3,2,q) cryptosystem. Finite Fields Appl. **71**, 101810 (2021). https://doi.org/10.1016/j.ffa.2021.101810, https://www.sciencedirect.com/science/article/pii/S1071579721000046
4. Beullens, W.: Round 1 official comments on DME. NIST CSRC (2017). https://csrc.nist.gov/CSRC/media/Projects/Post-Quantum-Cryptography/documents/round-1/official-comments/DME-official-comment.pdf
5. Beullens, W.: MAYO: practical post-quantum signatures from oil-and-vinegar maps. In: AlTawy, R., Hülsing, A. (eds.) Selected Areas in Cryptography: 28th International Conference, Virtual Event, 29 September–1 October 2021, Revised Selected Papers, pp. 355–376. Springer, Cham (2021). https://doi.org/10.1007/978-3-030-99277-4_17
6. Bouillaguet, C., Fouque, P., Véber, A.: Graph-theoretic algorithms for the "isomorphism of polynomials" problem. In: Johansson, T., Nguyen, P.Q. (eds.) Advances in Cryptology - EUROCRYPT 2013, 32nd Annual International Conference on the Theory and Applications of Cryptographic Techniques, Athens, Greece, 26–30 May 2013, Proceedings. LNCS, vol. 7881, pp. 211–227. Springer, Cham (2013). https://doi.org/10.1007/978-3-642-38348-9_13
7. Faugère, J., Perret, L.: An efficient algorithm for decomposing multivariate polynomials and its applications to cryptography. J. Symb. Comput. **44**(12), 1676–1689 (2009). https://doi.org/10.1016/j.jsc.2008.02.005
8. Faugére, J.C.: A new efficient algorithm for computing Gröbner bases (F4). J. Pure Appl. Algebra **139**(1), 61–88 (1999). https://doi.org/10.1016/S0022-4049(99)00005-5, https://www.sciencedirect.com/science/article/pii/S0022404999000055
9. Group, C.T.: Call for additional digital signature schemes for the post-quantum cryptography standardization process. NIST CSRC (2022). https://csrc.nist.gov/csrc/media/Projects/pqc-dig-sig/documents/call-for-proposals-dig-sig-sept-2022.pdf
10. Hashimoto, Y.: High-rank attack on HMFEv. JSIAM Lett. **10**, 21–24 (2018). https://doi.org/10.14495/jsiaml.10.21
11. Luengo, I., Avendaño, M.: DME: multivariate signature public key scheme. NIST CSRC (2023). https://csrc.nist.gov/Projects/pqc-dig-sig/round-1-additional-signatures
12. Luengo, I., Avendaño, M., Marco, M.: DME: a public key, signature and KEM system based on double exponentiation with matrix exponents. NIST CSRC (2017). https://csrc.nist.gov/Projects/post-quantum-cryptography/round-1-submissions

13. Patarin, J., Goubin, L.: Trapdoor one-way permutations and multivariate poly-
    nomials. In: Han, Y., Okamoto, T., Qing, S. (eds.) Information and Communi-
    cation Security, First International Conference, ICICS 1997, Beijing, China, 11–
    14 November 1997, Proceedings. LNCS, vol. 1334, pp. 356–368. Springer, Cham
    (1997). https://doi.org/10.1007/BFb0028491
14. Petzoldt, A., Chen, M., Ding, J., Yang, B.: HMFEv - an efficient multivariate
    signature scheme. In: Lange, T., Takagi, T. (eds.) Post-Quantum Cryptography
    - 8th International Workshop, PQCrypto 2017, Utrecht, The Netherlands, 26–28
    June 2017, Proceedings. LNCS, vol. 10346, pp. 205–223. Springer, Cham (2017).
    https://doi.org/10.1007/978-3-319-59879-6_12
15. Scemama, A.: A cryptanalysis of the double-round quadratic cryptosystem. In:
    Nam, K.H., Rhee, G. (eds.) Information Security and Cryptology - ICISC 2007,
    pp. 27–36. Springer, Heidelberg (2007). https://doi.org/10.1007/978-3-540-76788-
    6_3
16. Volker, S.: Gaussian elimination is not optimal. Numer. Math. **13**, 354–356 (1969)
17. Ye, D., Lam, K., Dai, Z.: Cryptanalysis of "2 r" schemes. In: Wiener, M.J. (ed.)
    Advances in Cryptology - CRYPTO 1999, 19th Annual International Cryptology
    Conference, Santa Barbara, California, USA, 15–19 August 1999, Proceedings.
    LNCS, vol. 1666, pp. 315–325. Springer, Cham (1999). https://doi.org/10.1007/3-
    540-48405-1_20

Signatures with Memory-Tight Security in the Quantum Random Oracle Model

Keita Xagawa[(✉)]

Technology Innovation Institute, Abu Dhabi, United Arab Emirates
keita.xagawa@tii.ae

Abstract. Memory tightness of reductions in cryptography, in addition to the standard tightness related to advantage and running time, is important when the underlying problem can be solved efficiently with large memory, as discussed in Auerbach, Cash, Fersch, and Kiltz (CRYPTO 2017). Diemert, Gellert, Jager, and Lyu (ASIACRYPT 2021) and Ghoshal, Ghosal, Jaeger, and Tessaro (EUROCRYPT 2022) gave memory-tight proofs for the multi-challenge security of digital signatures in the random oracle model.

This paper studies the memory-tight reductions for *post-quantum* signature schemes in the *quantum* random oracle model. Concretely, we show that signature schemes from lossy identification are multi-challenge secure in the quantum random oracle model via memory-tight reductions. Moreover, we show that the signature schemes from lossy identification achieve more enhanced securities considering *quantum* signing oracles proposed by Boneh and Zhandry (CRYPTO 2013) and Alagic, Majenz, Russel, and Song (EUROCRYPT 2020). We additionally show that signature schemes from preimage-sampleable functions achieve those securities via memory-tight reductions.

Keywords: memory-tight reductions · signature · provable security · post-quantum cryptography · quantum random oracle model (QROM) · plus-one unforgeability · blind unforgeability

1 Introduction

Memory-Tight Reductions: Provable security in cryptography consists of reductions and assumptions; we assume the hardness of a computational problem, design a cryptographic scheme, and then make a reduction algorithm $\mathcal{R}$ to solve the underlying problem by using an adversary $\mathcal{A}$ breaking the security of the scheme. The tightness of the reduction is measured by how close the resources of $\mathcal{R}$ and $\mathcal{A}$ are, where resources are success probability, running time, the number of queries, etc. The tightness of the security reduction is essential because it impacts the parameters of the cryptographic schemes and, thus, the scheme's efficiency. (See e.g., [11,19–21,35].)

Auerbach, Cash, Fersch, and Kiltz [7] explicitly put forth *memory tightness* of the reduction from the view of *memory usage*.[1] This concept is important when

---

[1] There are other studies considering memory-bounded adversary/reduction, e.g., Bernstein [12].

M. Joye and G. Leander (Eds.): EUROCRYPT 2024, LNCS 14657, pp. 30–58, 2024.
https://doi.org/10.1007/978-3-031-58754-2_2

the underlying computational problems are memory-sensitive; the problem can be solved efficiently with large memory. Examples of such problems are factoring, lattice problems, the learning-parity-with-noise (LPN) problem, and the multi-collision problem of the hash function.

After that, memory-tight reductions have gathered much attention and become an active area of cryptography: Auerbach et al. [7] gave several techniques to make security proofs memory-tight.[2] Using those techniques, they gave a memory-tight reduction for the standard security, the existential unforgeability under chosen-message attacks (EUF-CMA security), of RSA-FDH [11,41] in the random oracle model (ROM) [10]. Diemert, Gellert, Jager, and Lyu [24] studied memory-tight proofs of the *strong* existential unforgeability under chosen-message attacks in the *multi-challenge* setting (MsEUF-CMA security), where an adversary can submit multiple attempts of forgery and it wins if one of them is a 'new' forgery. They gave memory-tight reductions in the ROM for MsEUF-CMA security of RSA-PFDH [11], the BLS signature [15], and RFS-LID [1,27], where RFS denotes the Fiat-Shamir transform with random nonces and LID denotes a lossy identification. Ghoshal, Ghosal, Jaeger, and Tessaro [29] also gave a memory-tight proof of the MsEUF-CMA security of RSA-PFDH in the multi-challenge setting in the ROM. Bhattacharyya [13] and Jaeger and Kumar [33] gave memory-tight proofs for the security of key encapsulation mechanisms based on the variants of the Diffie-Hellman problem in the ROM. There are studies for symmetric-key cryptography, e.g., [25,29,30], and the lower bound of memory usage of black-box reductions [7,30,31,42].

Post-quantum Signatures and Quantum Random Oracle Model: Post-quantum signatures are an emerging area of cryptography as NIST had run the standardization of PQC and selected three post-quantum signatures (Falcon, Dilithium, and SPHINCS+) [3] and they started the standardization of additional signature schemes. The security of those post-quantum signatures is proven in the *quantum random oracle model (QROM)* [14], in which an adversary can make quantum queries to a random oracle. As far as we surveyed, the sEUF-CMA security proof for PSF-DFDH in Boneh et al. [14] is only one memory-tight proof for signature in the QROM, where PSF is preimage-sampleable functions [28] and DFDH is FDH derandomized by a pseudo-random function (PRF). The following natural question arises:

Can we construct memory-tight reductions for the MsEUF-CMA security of post-quantum PSF-based signatures in the QROM?

In addition, the memory-tight security proof of the MsEUF-CMA security of the signature scheme from LID in Diemert et al. [24] assumes that the underlying LID is perfectly correct and commitment-recoverable[3] and has statistical honest-

---

[2] Bernstein [12] proposed techniques (e.g., use PRF instead of lazy sampling) to reduce the memory of the adversary simulating the random oracles.

[3] The verification algorithm taking a transcript (w, c, z) computes commitment w' from challenge c and response z and accepts if and only if $w = w'$.

verifier zero-knowledge (HVZK) with a special simulator[4] and perfect unique response property[5]. Moreover, their proof is considered in the ROM. Thus, it is natural to ask the following question:

> Can we construct memory-tight reductions for the MsEUF-CMA security of post-quantum LID-based signatures in the QROM and eliminate the conditions on the underlying LID?

Quantum Signing Oracles: Furthermore, there are extended security models for signature schemes in the quantum setting by giving *quantum access* to the signing oracle. The first one is proposed by Boneh and Zhandry and dubbed EUF-qCMA security [16]. But, we call it plus-one unforgeability (PO security in short) following [5], because, in the security game, an adversary can access the signing oracle with q quantum queries and is required to output $q + 1$ distinct valid message/signature pairs. The other is proposed by Alagic, Majenz, Russell, and Song [5] and dubbed (strong) blind unforgeability (BU/sBU security in short). In the security game, an adversary can access the signing oracle with quantum queries, while some signatures are blinded if the corresponding messages are in a filter. The adversary is required to output a valid signature on a filtered message. Doosti, Delavar, Kashefi, and Arapinis [26] also gave parametrized security definitions using quantum signing oracles and showed that some of their definition are equivalent to the blind unforgeability.

Boneh and Zhandry [16] showed that the Lamport one-time signature and the Merkle signature are one-time PO-secure and PO-secure in the standard model, respectively. They further showed that some weakly-secure signature schemes under classical chosen message attacks can be converted into PO-secure signature schemes. They also directly showed that PSF-DFDH is PO-secure in the QROM. Chatterjee, Garg, Hajiabadi, Khurana, Liang, Malavolta, Pandey, and Shiehian [18] defined a PO-like security of ring signature and proposed a ring signature scheme satisfying their security notion. Chatterjee, Chung, Liang, and Malavolta [17] showed that PSF-DFDH is BU-secure in the QROM and their lattice-based signature is BU-secure in the standard model. They also extended a BU-like security of ring signature and proposed a ring signature satisfying their BU-like security. Majenz, Manfouo, and Ozols [39] showed that the Lamport one-time signature and the Winternitz one-time signature are BU-secure in the QROM by extending an argument in Alagic et al. [5]. Yuan, Tibouchi, and Abe [43] showed that a variant of SPHINCS+ is PO-secure in the QROM.

To the best of the authors' knowledge, there is no memory-tight proof for such enhanced securities for post-quantum signatures based on PSF and LID. Our third question is:

---

[4] Their deterministic simulator takes a challenge and a response chosen uniformly at random and outputs a commitment.

[5] For any (vk, w, c), where vk is honestly generated public key, there is at most one response z that makes the verifier accepting. See their proof of the third claim in [24, Appendix D, ePrint].

Can we construct memory-tight reductions for those extended securities (PO, BU, and sBU) of post-quantum signatures based on PSF and LID in the QROM?

1.1 Contributions

We affirmatively answer those three questions: The main contributions of this paper are four-fold. First, we give a *memory-tight* MsEUF-CMA security proof for LID-based signature schemes. We remove the constraints on the underlying LID scheme as much as possible, and we can employ lattice-based LID schemes with imperfect correctness, say, Dilitihium-QROM [22,34][6] and G+G [23]. Second, we extend the MsEUF-CMA security proof into (memory-tight) PO and sBU security proofs for LID-based signature schemes. Those are the first PO and sBU security proof of LID-based signature schemes. Third, we modify the existing sEUF-CMA, PO, and BU security proofs for PSF-based signature schemes into memory-tight MsEUF-CMA, PO, and sBU security proofs. Fourth, we pointed out a gap between BU security and PO security.

New Memory-Tight msEUF-CMA Security Proofs for LID-Based Signatures: We will give *memory-tight* MsEUF-CMA, PO, and sBU security proofs for LID-based signature schemes. Our starting point is the MsEUF-CMA security proof, and we extend it into PO and sBU security proofs.

The MsEUF-CMA *Security Proof for LID-Based Signatures:* We give a memory-tight MsEUF-CMA security proof for RFS-LID in the QROM, where LID can be *imperfectly* correct and not commitment-recoverable and can have *ordinal* statistical HVZK and *computational unique response* (CUR) property. As Diemert et al. [24], we first show the MsEUF-CMA1 security of FS-LID with memory-tight reduction, where CMA1 denotes chosen-message attacks in the *one-signature-per-message* setting [34] and FS denotes the Fiat-Shamir transform *with bounded aborts* [27,38]; we then obtain a memory-tight MsEUF-CMA security proof for RFS-LID by using a lemma in [24].

Our core contribution is a new memory-tight security proof of the MsEUF-CMA1 security of FS-LID. We carefully merge (and correct) the memory-tight MsEUF-CMA1 security proof in the ROM by Diemert et al. [24] and the memory-loose sEUF-CMA1 security proof in the QROM by Devevey, Fallahpour, Passelègue, and Stehlé [22], where the latter is a correction of the history-free programming proof in Abdalla, Fouque, Lyubashevsky, and Tibouchi [1] and Kiltz, Lyubashevsky, and Schaffner [34].

Let us briefly remind the Fiat-Shamir with aborts applied to the LID scheme. Let w, c, and z denote a commitment, a challenge, and a response of the underlying LID scheme, respectively. On a message m, the signer generates a commitment w and computes challenge $c = \mathsf{H}(m, w)$, where H is a random oracle,

---

[6] We need a statistical HVZK simulator in [22, Section 4] instead of a non-aborting HVZK simulator in [34].

and response z until $z \neq \perp$, and outputs a signature (w, z). The verifier verifies the transcript (w, c, z) via the LID's verification algorithm by computing $c = \mathsf{H}(m, w)$.

Our proof is summarized as follows: We first derandomize the signing oracle by using the random function. We next exclude the event that the signing oracle fails to produce a valid signature on the submitted message. This exclusion is required to invoke the CUR property of LID correctly. We then replace the winning condition that the adversary outputs a *new* pair of a message m^* and a valid signature (w^*, z^*) with the condition that the adversary's signature (w^*, z^*) on m^* is different from the signature $(\tilde{w}, \tilde{z})$ the signing oracle produces on m^* as Diemert et al. [24]. This modification allows us to remove the list containing a pair of messages queried by the adversary and signatures produced by the signing oracle and makes reductions memory-tight. In order to analyze the effect of this replacement, we will need to analyze the min-entropy of $\tilde{w}$ produced by the signing oracle carefully for imperfect-correct LID because the random oracle *leaks* the information of $\tilde{w}$. After those modifications, we follow the proof of Devevey et al. [22] to eliminate some events and simulate the signing oracle without the signing key. Before replacing the real verification key with the lossy one, we exclude the event that w^* in the adversary's signature is equivalent to $\tilde{w}$ in the signature produced by the signing oracle. This event cannot happen if LID has the CUR property. For the details, see Sect. 4. We then replace the verification key with a lossy one. In the final game, the adversary cannot win [1,34]. While merging the proofs carefully and removing the constraints are technical contributions, we have an additional technical byproduct discussed below.

Flaw in the Previous sEUF-CMA1 *Proofs in the QROM:* We found a flaw related to the CUR property in the previous sEUF-CMA1 proof in the QROM [22]. Roughly speaking, to reduce the sEUF-CMA1 security to the EUF-NMA security of the signature, we want the adversary to output a pair m^* and (w^*, z^*) such that *we do not program the random oracle at* (m^*, w^*). In order to do so, we exclude the event that $w^* = \tilde{w}$ where $\tilde{w}$ is a part of the signature $(\tilde{w}, \tilde{z})$ produced by the signing oracle on m^* and $(m^*, \tilde{w})$ is programmed.

Devevey et al. [22] and Barbosa et al. [8] pointed out that programming the random oracle only on succeeding signatures introduces a bias on the distribution of the signing oracle and the random oracle and the existing proofs do not care about the bias. To fix this error in the history-free programming approach [1,34], Devevey et al. [22] programmed the random oracle at $(m, \tilde{w}_i)$, where $\tilde{w}_i$ is the commitment for the i-th signer's attempt on the message m. Unfortunately, they ignored the fact that the adversary would output a message m^* and a signature (w^*, z^*) with $w^* = \tilde{w}$. To fix this problem, we exclude the event that $w^* = \tilde{w}_i$ for some i. We are interested especially in the case of $w^* = \tilde{w}$. To make a reduction to the CUR property, both the transcript $(\tilde{w}, \tilde{c}, \tilde{z})$ generated by the signing oracle and $(\tilde{w}, \tilde{c}, z^*)$ generated by the adversary's signature are valid. To ensure the validity of $(\tilde{w}, \tilde{c}, \tilde{z})$ generated by the signing oracle, we exclude the event that the signing oracle fails to output a valid signature. Thus, our security bound involves the term related to correctness.

Table 1. Summary of security proofs for LID-based signatures in the QROM. IND, CUR, and PRF in the column "Assumptions" denote the key indistinguishability of LID, the computational unique response of LID, and the pseudorandomness of PRF, respectively. The mark ✓ in the column "Adv." and "Time" indicates the multiplicative loss of advantage and time is $O(1)$, respectively. The marks ✓ and x in the column "Mem." indicate the additive loss of memory usage is $O(1) \cdot$ poly and $O(q) \cdot$ poly, respectively.

Proof	Scheme	Security	Assumptions	Adv.	Time	Mem.
KLS18+DFPS23 [22,34]	FS-LID	sEUF-CMA1	IND, CUR	✓	✓	x
KLS18+DFPS23 [22,34]	DFS-LID	sEUF-CMA	IND, CUR, PRF	✓	✓	x
Section 4	FS-LID	MsEUF-CMA1	IND, CUR	✓	✓	✓
Section 4	RFS-LID	MsEUF-CMA	IND, CUR	✓	✓	✓
Section 4	DFS-LID	MsEUF-CMA	IND, CUR, PRF	✓	✓	x
Section 4	DFS⁺-LID	MsEUF-CMA	IND, CUR	✓	✓	✓
Section 5	DFS-LID	PO	IND, CUR, PRF	✓	✓	x
Section 5	DFS⁺-LID	PO	IND, CUR	✓	✓	✓
(the full version)	DFS-LID	sBU	IND, CUR, PRF	✓	✓	✓

First (Memory-Tight) PO and sBU Security Proofs for LID-Based Signatures: We extend the security proof into the PO and sBU securities. We give a memory-loose PO security proof for DFS-LID and give a memory-tight PO security proof for DFS⁺-LID, where DFS and DFS⁺ denote the Fiat-Shamir transform derandomized by PRF and random oracle, respectively. We also give a memory-tight sBU security proof for DFS-LID. As far as we know, those are the first direct PO and sBU security proofs for the LID-based signature schemes in the QROM.

In order to consider memory tightness, we modify the PO security model with the forgery-checking oracle; the forgery-checking oracle maintains the list $\mathcal{Q}$ of the pairs of messages and valid signatures the adversary submits, and the adversary wins if the size of the list is larger than the number of quantum singing queries q_S, that is, $\#\mathcal{Q} > q_S$. In the PO security proof, we need to replace this winning condition A ($\#\mathcal{Q} > q_S$), which requires memory of $O(q_S)$ size, with the condition B that the adversary's signature (w^*, z^*) on m^* is different from $(\tilde{w}, \tilde{z})$ the signing oracle produced on the m^*. To treat this change, we first consider the difference between the winning condition A and the winning condition $A \wedge B$. Very roughly speaking, if the adversary makes the difference, it should guess $(q_S + 1)$ signatures on *distinct* messages. The min-entropy of $\tilde{w}$ allows us to upper-bound this guessing probability. After that, we relax the winning condition as B. This modification is the core of our PO security proof. For the details, see Sect. 5.

The sBU security proof is obtained by following the sEUF-CMA1 security proof, and we omit the details. For the details, see the full version (Table 1).

New Memory-Tight Security Proofs for PSF-Based Signatures: We extend the memory-tight sEUF-CMA security proof for PSF-DFDH in the QROM in Boneh et al. [14] into a memory-tight MsEUF-CMA1 security proof for PSF-FDH in the QROM. We then obtain a memory-tight MsEUF-CMA security proof for PSF-PFDH in the QROM by using the lemma in [24] as in the case of RFS-LID. Furthermore, we show a memory-loose PO security proof of PSF-DFDH and a memory-tight PO security proof of PSF-DFDH$^+$ in the QROM, where DFDH$^+$ denotes FDH derandomized by a random function. We also give a memory-tight sBU security proof of PSF-DFDH by modifying a memory-loose BU security proof of PSF-DFDH in the QROM by Chatterjee et al. [17]. See the full version for the details.

A Gap Between PO and BU Security: As a byproduct, we found that BU security does not imply PO security, which refutes the conjecture that BU security implies PO security of message authentication code (MAC) by Alagic et al. [5].[7] We exemplify this by constructing a BU-secure but PO-insecure MAC and signature scheme from a BU-secure MAC and signature scheme, respectively. We observe that PO-secure scheme should be sEUF-CMA-secure, but BU-secure scheme can be sEUF-CMA-insecure. Thus, making BU-secure MAC and signature scheme sEUF-CMA-insecure, the new scheme is PO-insecure. We think the conjecture should be that sBU security implies PO security. See the full version for the details.

Open Problems: We have managed the imperfect correctness of LID in the memory-tight security proofs of LID-based signature schemes by following the history-free approach [22,34] instead of the adaptive reprogramming approach [8, 22,32]. The history-free approach requires LID to have statistical honest-verifier zero-knowledge (HVZK). We leave it as an open problem to construct memory-tight security proofs treating *large* divergence HVZK and *computational* HVZK, which would require the adaptive reprogramming approach.

We currently can not give the memory-tight security proofs of the PSF-based signature scheme with *imperfectly correct* PSFs. Kosuge and Xagawa [37] gave memory-loose security proofs using the adaptive reprogramming technique [32]. We leave it as an open problem to give memory-tight security proof of signature schemes based on imperfectly-correct PSFs.

Jaeger and Kumar [33] gave memory-tight reductions for multi-challenge, multi-user CCA security of PKE/KEM. It is interesting to consider the multi-challenge, multi-user security of signature schemes with memory-tight reductions in the ROM and QROM.

1.2 Organization

Section 2 reviews basic notions and notations, quantum computations, and lossy identification. Section 3 reviews digital signatures, their security notions, and

---

[7] The conference version [5] claims that BU-secure MAC is also PO-secure, but, the newest version, '20230420:091107' [4] reported an error in their proof and removed the claim.

LID-based signature schemes. Section 4 and Sect. 5 show MsEUF-CMA and PO security of the LID-based signature schemes.

The full version contains the lemma on the Rényi divergence, the relation between PO security and BU security of MAC and signatures, the sBU-security proof of a LID-based signature scheme, and MsEUF-CMA, PO, and sBU security proofs of PSF-based signature schemes.

2 Preliminaries

The security parameter is denoted by $\kappa \in \mathbb{Z}^+$. We use the standard O-notations. For $n \in \mathbb{Z}^+$, we let $[n] := \{1, \ldots, n\}$. For a statement P, $[\![P]\!]$ denotes the truth value of P.

Let $\mathcal{X}$ and $\mathcal{Y}$ be two finite sets. $\mathsf{Func}(\mathcal{X}, \mathcal{Y})$ denotes a set of all functions whose domain is $\mathcal{X}$ and codomain is $\mathcal{Y}$. For a set of distributions over $\mathcal{Y}$ indexed by $x \in \mathcal{X}$, $D = \{D_x : x \in \mathcal{X}\}$, we define $\mathsf{Func}_{\mathcal{X},\mathcal{Y}}(D)$ as a distribution of f in $\mathsf{Func}(\mathcal{X}, \mathcal{Y})$ such that, for each $x \in \mathcal{X}$, $f(x)$ is independently drawn from a distribution D_x. When every D_x is the same as D' on every x, we simply write $\mathsf{Func}_{\mathcal{X},\mathcal{Y}}(D')$.

For two distributions D, D' over $\mathcal{Y}$, we say that D is ϵ-close to D' if the distance $|D - D'| := \sum_{y \in \mathcal{Y}} |D(y) - D'(y)|$ is at most ϵ.

For a distribution D, we often write "$x \leftarrow D$," which indicates that we take a sample x according to D. For a finite set $\mathcal{S}$, $U(\mathcal{S})$ denotes the uniform distribution over $\mathcal{S}$. We often write "$x \leftarrow \mathcal{S}$" instead of "$x \leftarrow U(\mathcal{S})$." If inp is a string, then "out $\leftarrow \mathsf{A}^O(\mathsf{inp})$" denotes the output of algorithm A running on input inp with an access to a set of oracles O. If A and oracles are deterministic, then out is a fixed value and we write "out $:= \mathsf{A}^O(\mathsf{inp})$." We also use the notation "out $:= \mathsf{A}(\mathsf{inp}; r)$" to make the randomness r of A explicit. For a probabilistic algorithm A, $\mathcal{R}_\mathsf{A}$ denotes the radnomness space of A.

For an algorithm or adversary A, $\mathsf{Time}(\mathsf{A})$ and $\mathsf{Mem}(\mathsf{A})$ denotes the time and memory complexity of the algorithm A, respectively. For a scheme S, $\mathsf{Time}(\mathsf{S})$ and $\mathsf{Mem}(\mathsf{S})$ denotes the maximum time and memory complexity of the algorithms in the scheme S, respectively.

For any function $f \colon \{0,1\}^n \to \{0,1\}^m$, a *quantum access* to f is modeled as oracle access to unitary $O_f \colon |x\rangle|y\rangle \mapsto |x\rangle|y \oplus f(x)\rangle$. By convention, we will use the notation $\mathsf{A}^{|f\rangle, g}$ to stress A's *quantum* and *classical* access to f and g.

2.1 Lemmas on Quantum Computations

Lemma 2.1 ([16, Lemma 2.5, ePrint]). *Let $\mathcal{X}$ and $\mathcal{Y}$ be two finite sets. Let $D = \{D_x\}$ and $D' = \{D'_x\}$ be two sets of efficiently sampleable distributions over $\mathcal{Y}$ indexed by $x \in \mathcal{X}$. let $\mathcal{A}$ be a quantum adversary making q (quantum) queries to an oracle $f \colon \mathcal{X} \to \mathcal{Y}$. If for each $x \in X$, $|D_x - D'_x| \le \epsilon$ holds, then $|\Pr[f \leftarrow \mathsf{Func}_{\mathcal{X},\mathcal{Y}}(D) : \mathcal{A}^{|f\rangle} = 1] - \Pr[f \leftarrow \mathsf{Func}_{\mathcal{X},\mathcal{Y}}(D') : \mathcal{A}^{|f\rangle} = 1]| \le \sqrt{(6q)^3 \epsilon}.$*[8]

---

[8] The value $6^3 = 27 \cdot 8$ is composed from 27 in [44, Corollary 7.5, ePrint] (denoted by C_0 in [16]) and 8 in [16, Lemma 2.5].

Lemma 2.2 ([16, **Lemma 2.6, ePrint**]). *Fix two finite sets $\mathcal{X}$ and $\mathcal{Y}$. Fix a set D of distributions D_x over $\mathcal{Y}$ indexed by $x \in \mathcal{X}$. Let α be the minimum over all $x \in \mathcal{X}$ of the min-entropy of the distribution D_x. Now, let $f : \mathcal{X} \to \mathcal{Y}$ be a function chosen according to $\mathsf{Func}_{\mathcal{X},\mathcal{Y}}(D)$. Then, any q-query quantum algorithm can only produce $(q + 1)$ input/output pairs of f with probability at most $(q + 1)/\lfloor 2^{\alpha} \rfloor$.*

2.2 Adversaries with Access to Random Functions

We adopt an adversary with access to random functions by following [29, Section 3]. The reductions in this paper are adversary $\mathcal{A}$ on the left side, consisting of a set of functions $\mathcal{F}$ and algorithm $\mathcal{A}_2$. We call such an adversary *an $\mathcal{F}$-oracle adversary.*

Adversary $\mathcal{A}^O(\mathsf{in})$	Adversary $\mathcal{A}_F^Q(\mathsf{in})$
1 : $f \leftarrow \mathcal{F}$	1 : $K \leftarrow \mathcal{K}$
2 : $\mathsf{out} \leftarrow \mathcal{A}_2^{O,|f\rangle}(\mathsf{in})$	2 : $\mathsf{out} \leftarrow \mathcal{A}_2^{O,|F_K\rangle}(\mathsf{in})$
3 : **return** out	3 : **return** out

Ghoshal et al. [29] defined the *reduced complexity* of $\mathcal{A}$ by $\mathsf{Time}^*(\mathcal{A}) := \mathsf{Time}(\mathcal{A}_2)$ and $\mathsf{Mem}^*(\mathcal{A}) := \mathsf{Mem}(\mathcal{A}_2)$. We employ $\mathcal{F}$-oracle adversaries as [29] for simplicity and clean notation. This approach is justified by pseudorandom adversary $\mathcal{A}_F$ on the right-hand side as long as the game $\mathcal{A}$ plays is efficient.

Lemma 2.3 ([29, **Lemma 2**], **quantum version**). *Let $\mathcal{A}$ be an $\mathcal{F}$-oracle adversary for a game G. Then, for any function family F with $F = \mathcal{F}$, there exists an adversary $\mathcal{A}_F$ such that*

$$|\Pr[\mathsf{G}(\mathcal{A})] - \Pr[\mathsf{G}(\mathcal{A}_F)]| \le \mathsf{Adv}_F^{\mathrm{pr}}(\mathcal{A}_F),$$
$$\mathsf{Time}(\mathcal{A}_F) = \mathsf{Time}^*(\mathcal{A}) + \mathsf{Time}(\mathsf{G}(\mathcal{A})),$$
$$\mathsf{Mem}(\mathcal{A}_F) = \mathsf{Mem}^*(\mathcal{A}) + \mathsf{Mem}(\mathsf{G}(\mathcal{A})),$$
$$\mathsf{Query}(\mathcal{A}_F) = q,$$

where q is an upper bound on the number of queries $\mathcal{A}_2$ makes to the oracle $|f\rangle$ or $|F_K\rangle$.

See [7] and [29, Lemma 2] for further discussions.

2.3 Lossy Identification

Abdalla et al. [1,2] defined lossy identification as a special case of a (cryptographic) identification scheme. A lossy identification scheme involves an additional *lossy* key-generation algorithm. The syntax follows:

Definition 2.1 (Lossy identification). *A lossy identification scheme* LID *consists of the following tuple of PPT algorithms* $(\mathsf{Gen}_{\mathsf{LID}}, \mathsf{LossyGen}_{\mathsf{LID}}, \mathsf{P}_1, \mathsf{P}_2, \mathsf{V})$

- $\mathsf{Gen_{LID}}(1^\kappa) \to (vk, sk)$: *a normal key-generation algorithm that, on input 1^κ, where κ is the security parameter, outputs a pair of keys (vk, sk). vk and sk are public verification and secret keys, respectively.*
- $\mathsf{LossyGen_{LID}}(1^\kappa) \to vk$: *a lossy key-generation algorithm that on input 1^κ outputs a lossy verification key vk.*
- $\mathsf{P_1}(sk) \to (w, s)$: *a first prover algorithm that takes as input signing key sk and outputs commitment w and state s.*
- $\mathsf{P_2}(sk, w, c, s) \to z$: *a second* deterministic *prover algorithm that takes as input signing key sk, commitment w, challenge c, and state s, and outputs response z.*
- $\mathsf{Vrfy}(vk, w, c, z) \to$ true/false: *a deterministic verification algorithm that takes as input verification key vk, commitment w, challenge c, and response z, and outputs its decision* true *or* false.

We assume that a verification key vk defines the challenge space $\mathcal{C}$ and the response space $\mathcal{Z}$.

Definition 2.2 (Completeness). *For non-negligible $\rho = \rho(\kappa)$, we call* LID *ρ-complete if*

$$\Pr\left[\begin{array}{l} (vk, sk) \leftarrow \mathsf{Gen_{LID}}(1^\kappa), (w, s) \leftarrow \mathsf{P_1}(sk), \\ c \leftarrow \mathcal{C}, z := \mathsf{P_2}(sk, w, c, s) \end{array} : \mathsf{V}(vk, w, c, z) = \mathsf{true} \right] \geq \rho(\kappa).$$

We call LID *perfectly complete if it is 1-complete.*

In order to analyze the completeness carefully, Devevey et al. [22] introduced another definition as follows:

Definition 2.3 (Correctness [22, Definition 2], adapted). *Let $\gamma, \beta > 0$. We call* LID *(γ, β)-correct if for every (vk, sk) generated by $\mathsf{Gen_{LID}}(1^\kappa)$, the following holds:*

- *The verifier accepts with probability at least γ if the response z is not $\bot$. That is,*

$$\Pr\left[\begin{array}{l} (w, s) \leftarrow \mathsf{P_1}(sk), \\ c \leftarrow \mathcal{C}, \\ z := \mathsf{P_2}(sk, w, c, s) \end{array} : \mathsf{V}(vk, w, c, z) = \mathsf{true} \;\middle|\; z \neq \bot \right] \geq \gamma.$$

- *The prover aborts with probability at most β. That is,*

$$\Pr\left[(w, s) \leftarrow \mathsf{P_1}(sk), c \leftarrow \mathcal{C}, z := \mathsf{P_2}(sk, w, c, s) : z = \bot \right] \leq \beta.$$

We note that if LID is $(1, \beta)$-correct, then it is $(1 - \beta)$-complete.

The security properties of a lossy identification scheme are defined as follows:

Definition 2.4 (Key indistinguishability [2, Definition 16]). *We say that* LID *is* key indistinguishable *if for any QPT adversary $\mathcal{A}$, its advantage $\mathsf{Adv}^{\text{ind-key}}_{\mathsf{LID},\mathcal{A}}(\kappa)$ is negligible in κ, where*

$$\mathsf{Adv}^{\text{ind-key}}_{\mathsf{LID},\mathcal{A}}(\kappa) := \left| \begin{array}{l} \Pr[(vk, sk) \leftarrow \mathsf{Gen_{LID}}(1^\kappa) : \mathcal{A}(vk) = 1] \\ - \Pr[vk \leftarrow \mathsf{LossyGen_{LID}}(1^\kappa) : \mathcal{A}(vk) = 1] \end{array} \right|.$$

Definition 2.5 (Lossiness [2, Definition 16], adapted). *We say that* LID *is* ϵ_ℓ-*lossy if for any unbounded adversary* $\mathcal{A}$, *its advantage* $\mathsf{Adv}^{\mathrm{imp}}_{\mathsf{LID},\mathcal{A}}(\kappa)$ *is at most* ϵ_ℓ, *where*

$$\mathsf{Adv}^{\mathrm{imp}}_{\mathsf{LID},\mathcal{A}}(\kappa) := \Pr\left[\begin{array}{l} vk \leftarrow \mathsf{LossyGen}_{\mathsf{LID}}(1^\kappa), \\ (w,s) \leftarrow \mathcal{A}(vk), \\ c \leftarrow \mathcal{C}, z \leftarrow \mathcal{A}(c,s) \end{array} : \mathsf{V}(vk,w,c,z) = \mathsf{true}\right].$$

Remark 2.1 (On Lossiness). In the original definition, adversary $\mathcal{A}$ can access the simulated transcript oracle to produce (w,s). However, since the simulated transcript oracle has no access to sk, we do need to consider this oracle.

Definition 2.6 (Statistical honest-verifier zero knowledge [22], adapted). *Let* (vk,sk) *be a key pair generated by* $\mathsf{Gen}_{\mathsf{LID}}(1^\kappa)$. *We call* LID ϵ_{zk}-*HVZK if there exists a PPT algorithm* Sim *that takes a public verification key* vk *and* c *as input and outputs* (w,z) *such that the distribution of* (w,c,z) *where* $c \leftarrow \mathcal{C}$ *and* $(w,z) \leftarrow \mathsf{Sim}(vk,c)$ *is* ϵ_{zk}-*close to the distribution of the real transcript between honest prover and verifier.*

Remark 2.2. In [2,34], "the distribution of the real transcript" is defined as follows: compute (w,c,z) by using the real prover and verifier; if $z = \perp$, then return $(\perp, \perp, \perp)$; otherwise return (w,c,z). Devevey et al. [22] pointed out that this definition is one of the causes of the error in the simulation. They defined "the distribution of the real transcript" as follows: compute (w,c,z) by using the real prover and verifier and output (w,c,z) as it is.

Definition 2.7 (Commitment recoverability [34, Definition 2.4]). *We say that* LID *is* commitment-recoverable *if for any* (vk,sk) *generated by* $\mathsf{Gen}_{\mathsf{LID}}(1^\kappa)$, $c \in \mathcal{C}$, *and* $z \in \mathcal{Z}$, *there exists a unique* w *such that* $\mathsf{V}(vk,w,c,z) =$ true. *In addition, we require that this unique* w *can be computed by a deterministic commitment-recovery algorithm* Rec, *that is,* $w = \mathsf{Rec}(vk,c,z)$.

Definition 2.8 (Computational unique response [34, Definition 2.7]). *We also say that* LID *has the* computational unique response (CUR) *property if for any QPT adversary* $\mathcal{A}$, *its advantage defined below is negligible in* κ:

$$\mathsf{Adv}^{\mathrm{cur}}_{\mathsf{LID},\mathcal{A}}(\kappa) := \Pr\left[\begin{array}{l} (vk,sk) \leftarrow \mathsf{Gen}_{\mathsf{LID}}(1^\kappa), \\ (w,c,z,z') \leftarrow \mathcal{A}(vk) \end{array} : \begin{array}{l} z \neq z' \\ \wedge \mathsf{V}(vk,w,c,z) = \mathsf{true} \\ \wedge \mathsf{V}(vk,w,c,z') = \mathsf{true} \end{array}\right].$$

Definition 2.9 (Min-entropy of commitment [34, Definition 2.6], modified). *We say that* LID *has* (α, ϵ_m)-*min-entropy if*

$$\Pr[(vk,sk) \leftarrow \mathsf{Gen}_{\mathsf{LID}}(1^\kappa) : H_\infty(w \mid (w,s) \leftarrow \mathsf{P}_1(sk)) \geq \alpha] \geq 1 - \epsilon_m.$$

In the original definition ([34, Definition 2.6]), ϵ_m is $2^{-\alpha}$. Devevey et al. [22, Definition 5] defined the min-entropy of commitment as $(\alpha, 0)$-min entropy in the above definition.

3   Digital Signature

The model for digital signature schemes is summarized as follows:

Definition 3.1. *A digital signature scheme* DS *consists of the following triple of PPT algorithms* (Gen, Sign, Vrfy):

- Gen$(1^\kappa) \to (vk, sk)$: *a key-generation algorithm that, on input* 1^κ, *where* κ *is the security parameter, outputs a pair of keys* (vk, sk). vk *and* sk *are called verification and signing keys, respectively.*
- Sign$(sk, \mu) \to \sigma$: *a signing algorithm that takes as input signing key* sk *and message* $\mu \in \mathcal{M}$ *and outputs signature* $\sigma \in \mathcal{S}$.
- Vrfy$(vk, \mu, \sigma) \to$ true/false: *a verification algorithm that takes as input verification key* vk, *message* $\mu \in \mathcal{M}$, *and signature* σ *and outputs its decision* true *or* false.

Definition 3.2 (Completeness). *We say that* DS *is* ρ-*complete if for any message* $\mu \in \mathcal{M}$, *we have*

$$\Pr[(vk, sk) \leftarrow \mathsf{Gen}(1^\kappa), \sigma \leftarrow \mathsf{Sign}(sk, \mu) : \mathsf{Vrfy}(vk, \mu, \sigma) = \mathsf{true}] \geq \rho.$$

Security Notions: We review the standard security notions of digital signature schemes. The standard security notion, existential unforgeability against chosen-message attack (EUF-CMA), is captured by the game $\mathsf{Expt}_{\mathsf{DS},\mathcal{A}}^{\mathrm{euf\text{-}cma}}(1^\kappa)$ in Fig. 1. The multi-challenge version allows an adversary to call FORGE freely [7]. We also consider a strong version, in which the adversary wins if its forgery (m^*, σ^*) is not equal to the pairs returned by SIGN. For signing oracles, we have two variants, one-signature-per-message/many-signature-per-message versions, which are denoted by CMA1 and CMA, respectively. We note that for deterministic signature schemes, CMA1 security implies CMA security. The formal definition follows:

Definition 3.3 (Security notions for digital signature schemes). *Let* DS $=$ (Gen, Sign, Vrfy) *be a digital signature scheme. For any* $\mathcal{A}$, *goal* $\in$ {euf, seuf, meuf, mseuf}, *and* atk $\in$ {cma, cma1}, *we define its* goal-atk *advantage against* DS *as follows:*

$$\mathsf{Adv}_{\mathsf{DS},\mathcal{A}}^{\mathrm{goal\text{-}atk}}(\kappa) := \Pr[\mathsf{Expt}_{\mathsf{DS},\mathcal{A}}^{\mathrm{goal\text{-}atk}}(1^\kappa) = 1],$$

where $\mathsf{Expt}_{\mathsf{DS},\mathcal{A}}^{\mathrm{goal\text{-}atk}}(1^\kappa)$ *is an experiment described in Fig. 1. For* GOAL $\in$ {EUF, sEUF, mEUF, msEUF} *and* ATK $\in$ {CMA, CMA1}, *we say that* DS *is* GOAL-ATK-*secure if* $\mathsf{Adv}_{\mathsf{DS},\mathcal{A}}^{\mathrm{goal\text{-}atk}}(\kappa)$ *is negligible for any QPT adversary* $\mathcal{A}$.

Security with Respect to Quantum Signing Oracles: Boneh and Zhandry [16] defined a new security notion of digital signature schemes with respect to a *quantum* signing oracle and dubbed it as EUF-qCMA security. We refer to this security notion as *plus-one security* (PO security) [5] because an adversary in

$\mathsf{Expt}^{\mathrm{goal}\text{-}\mathrm{atk}}_{\mathsf{DS},\mathcal{A}}(1^\kappa)$ for goal $\in \{\mathrm{euf}, \mathrm{seuf}\}$

$(vk, sk) \leftarrow \mathsf{Gen}(1^\kappa)$
$\mathcal{Q} := \emptyset;\ \mathrm{win} := \mathsf{false}$
$(m^*, \sigma^*) \leftarrow \mathcal{A}^{\mathrm{SIGN}}(vk)$
$\mathrm{FORGE}(m^*, \sigma^*)$
return win

$\mathrm{SIGN}(m)$ for atk $= \mathrm{cma}$

$\sigma \leftarrow \mathsf{Sign}(sk, m)$
$\mathcal{Q} := \mathcal{Q} \cup \{(m, \sigma)\}$
return σ

$\mathrm{FORGE}(m^*, \sigma^*)$ for goal $\in \{\mathrm{euf}, \mathrm{meuf}\}$

---

if $\mathsf{Vrfy}(vk, m^*, \sigma^*) = \mathsf{true}$ **then**
| **if** $\forall \sigma : (m^*, \sigma) \notin \mathcal{Q}$ **then**
| | win := true

$\mathsf{Expt}^{\mathrm{goal}\text{-}\mathrm{atk}}_{\mathsf{DS},\mathcal{A}}(1^\kappa)$ for goal $\in \{\mathrm{meuf}, \mathrm{mseuf}\}$

$(vk, sk) \leftarrow \mathsf{Gen}(1^\kappa)$
$\mathcal{Q} := \emptyset;\ \mathrm{win} := \mathsf{false}$
run $\mathcal{A}^{\mathrm{SIGN}, \mathrm{FORGE}}(vk)$
return win

$\mathrm{SIGN}(m)$ for atk $= \mathrm{cma1}$

---

if $\exists (m, \sigma) \in \mathcal{Q}$ **then**
| **return** σ
$\sigma \leftarrow \mathsf{Sign}(sk, m)$
$\mathcal{Q} := \mathcal{Q} \cup \{(m, \sigma)\}$
return σ

$\mathrm{FORGE}(m^*, \sigma^*)$ for goal $\in \{\mathrm{seuf}, \mathrm{mseuf}\}$

---

if $\mathsf{Vrfy}(vk, m^*, \sigma^*) = \mathsf{true}$ **then**
| **if** $(m^*, \sigma^*) \notin \mathcal{Q}$ **then**
| | win := true

Fig. 1. $\mathsf{Expt}^{\mathrm{goal}\text{-}\mathrm{atk}}_{\mathsf{DS},\mathcal{A}}(1^\kappa)$ for goal $\in \{\mathrm{euf}, \mathrm{seuf}, \mathrm{meuf}, \mathrm{mseuf}\}$ and atk $\in \{\mathrm{cma}, \mathrm{cma1}\}$.

$\mathsf{Expt}^{\mathrm{po}}_{\mathsf{DS},\mathcal{A}}(1^\kappa)$

$(vk, sk) \leftarrow \mathsf{Gen}(1^\kappa)$
$\mathcal{Q} := \emptyset$
run $\mathcal{A}^{|\mathrm{SIGN}\rangle, \mathrm{FORGE}}(vk)$
return $[\![\#\mathcal{Q} > q_S]\!]$

$\mathrm{FORGE}(m^*, \sigma^*)$

---

if $\mathsf{Vrfy}(vk, m^*, \sigma^*) = \mathsf{true}$ **then**
| **if** $(m^*, \sigma^*) \notin \mathcal{Q}$ **then**
| | $\mathcal{Q} := \mathcal{Q} \cup \{(m^*, \sigma^*)\}$

$\mathrm{SIGN} : |m\rangle\,|y\rangle \mapsto |m\rangle\,|y \oplus \sigma\rangle$

/generate randomness r on each query
/share r on every message
$\sigma := \mathsf{Sign}(sk, m; r)$
return σ

Fig. 2. $\mathsf{Expt}^{\mathrm{po}}_{\mathsf{DS},\mathcal{A}}(1^\kappa)$. q_S denotes the number of the signing queries.

the security game is asked to output $q + 1$ distinct valid message/signature pairs after making q quantum queries to the signing oracle. They defined it in the same spirit as the *strong* EUF security. In the original definition, the adversary outputs $q + 1$ pairs at once and stops. We introduce the oracle FORGE to the security game of the PO security since we want to consider memory tightness. The formal definition follows:

Definition 3.4 (Plus-One Security [16], adapted). *Let* $\mathsf{DS} = (\mathsf{Gen}, \mathsf{Sign}, \mathsf{Vrfy})$ *be a digital signature scheme. For any* $\mathcal{A}$, *we define its* po *advantage against* DS *as follows:*

$$\mathsf{Adv}^{\mathrm{po}}_{\mathsf{DS},\mathcal{A}}(\kappa) := \Pr[\mathsf{Expt}^{\mathrm{po}}_{\mathsf{DS},\mathcal{A}}(1^\kappa) = 1],$$

where $\mathsf{Expt}^{\mathrm{po}}_{\mathsf{DS},\mathcal{A}}(1^\kappa)$ *is an experiment described in Fig. 2. We say that* DS *is* PO-*secure if* $\mathsf{Adv}^{\mathrm{po}}_{\mathsf{DS},\mathcal{A}}(\kappa)$ *is negligible for any QPT adversary* $\mathcal{A}$.

Alagic et al. [5] introduced another new security notion concerning a quantum signing oracle and called it *blind unforgeability* (BU security). Let $\epsilon \in \{0/2^p, 1/2^p, \ldots, (2^p - 1)/2^p\}$ for some $p = p(\kappa)$ be a parameter. Let B_ϵ be a random subset of the message space $\mathcal{M}$ where each $m \in \mathcal{M}$ is independently selected with probability ϵ. Roughly speaking, an adversary is asked to output a

$\text{Expt}_{\mathsf{DS},\mathcal{A}}^{\text{sec}}(1^\kappa)$ for $\text{sec} \in \{\text{bu}, \text{sbu}\}$

$(vk, sk) \leftarrow \text{Gen}(1^\kappa)$
$B_\epsilon \leftarrow \text{Func}_{\mathcal{M}, \{0,1\}}(\text{Ber}_\epsilon)$ /bu
$B_\epsilon \leftarrow \text{Func}_{\mathcal{M} \times \mathcal{S}, \{0,1\}}(\text{Ber}_\epsilon)$ /sbu
$\text{win} := \text{false}$
$\text{run } \mathcal{A}^{|B_\epsilon \text{SIGN}\rangle, \text{FORGE}}(vk)$
return win

$\text{SIGN} : |m\rangle |y\rangle \mapsto |m\rangle |y \oplus \sigma\rangle$
/generate randomness r on each query
/share r on every message
$\sigma := \text{Sign}(sk, m; r)$
$\text{return } \sigma$

$\text{FORGE}(m^*, \sigma^*)$

$\textbf{if } \text{Vrfy}(vk, m^*, \sigma^*) = \text{true then}$
$\quad \textbf{if } m^* \in B_\epsilon \textbf{ then } \text{win} := \text{true}$ /bu
$\quad \textbf{if } (m^*, \sigma^*) \in B_\epsilon \textbf{ then } \text{win} := \text{true}$ /sbu

Fig. 3. $\text{Expt}_{\mathsf{DS},\mathcal{A},\epsilon}^{\text{bu}}(1^\kappa)$ and $\text{Expt}_{\mathsf{DS},\mathcal{A},\epsilon}^{\text{sbu}}(1^\kappa)$.

valid signature on a message in B_ϵ while it can access a quantum signing oracle that returns a signature on a message *not* in B_ϵ. The strong version is defined by a subset of the product of the message space $\mathcal{M}$ and the signature space $\mathcal{S} \subseteq \{0,1\}^\lambda$ for some $\lambda = \lambda(\kappa)$. For $f: \mathcal{M} \to \mathcal{S}$, $B \subseteq \mathcal{M}$, and $B' \subseteq \mathcal{M} \times \mathcal{S}$, we define

$$Bf(x) := \begin{cases} \bot & x \in B \\ f(x) & \text{otherwise} \end{cases} \text{ and } B'f(x) := \begin{cases} \bot & (x, f(x)) \in B' \\ f(x) & \text{otherwise.} \end{cases}$$

Remark 3.1. The quantum oracle $|Bf\rangle$ is considered as a mapping $|x\rangle |y\rangle \mapsto |x\rangle |y \oplus Bf(x)\rangle$, where $y \in \{0,1\}^{\lambda+1}$, $f(x)$ is considered as $f(x)\|0 \in \{0,1\}^{\lambda+1}$, and $\bot$ is considered as $0^\lambda \| 1 \in \{0,1\}^{\lambda+1}$.

In the security proofs, instead of choosing a random subset B_ϵ, we will consider random function $\text{RF}_B : \mathcal{M} \to \mathcal{P}$, where $\mathcal{P} = \{0, 1, \ldots, 2^p - 1\}$, and we will interpret the condition $m \in B_\epsilon$ as $\text{RF}_B(m) < \epsilon 2^p$. The cost of this procedure is denoted by $\text{Time}(B_\epsilon)$ and $\text{Mem}(B_\epsilon)$.

We again introduce the oracle FORGE to the security game and consider the multi-challenge situation. The formal definition follows:

Definition 3.5 (Blind Unforgeability [5], adapted). *Let* $\mathsf{DS} = (\text{Gen}, \text{Sign}, \text{Vrfy})$ *be a digital signature scheme. For any* $\mathcal{A}$, *any efficiently computable function* $\epsilon: \mathbb{Z}^+ \to [0, 1)$, *and* $\text{sec} \in \{\text{bu}, \text{sbu}\}$, *we define its goal-atk advantage against* DS *as follows:*

$$\text{Adv}_{\mathsf{DS},\mathcal{A}}^{\text{sec}}(\kappa) := \Pr[\text{Expt}_{\mathsf{DS},\mathcal{A},\epsilon}^{\text{sec}}(1^\kappa) = 1],$$

where $\text{Expt}_{\mathsf{DS},\mathcal{A}}^{\text{sec}}(1^\kappa)$ *is an experiment described in Fig. 3. We say that* DS *is BU-secure (sBU-secure, resp.) if* $\text{Adv}_{\mathsf{DS},\mathcal{A},\epsilon}^{\text{bu}}(\kappa)$ *(*$\text{Adv}_{\mathsf{DS},\mathcal{A},\epsilon}^{\text{sbu}}(\kappa)$, *resp.) is negligible for any QPT adversary* $\mathcal{A}$ *and any efficiently computable function* $\epsilon: \mathbb{Z}^+ \to [0, 1)$.

$$\begin{array}{lll}
\underline{\mathsf{Gen}(1^\kappa)} & \underline{\mathsf{Sign}(sk, m)} & \underline{\mathsf{Vrfy}(vk, m, \sigma)} \\
(vk, sk) \leftarrow \mathsf{Gen}'(1^\kappa) & n \leftarrow \{0,1\}^\lambda & \textbf{parse } \sigma = (\sigma', n) \\
\textbf{return } (vk, sk) & \sigma' \leftarrow \mathsf{Sign}'(sk, (m, n)) & \textbf{return } \mathsf{Vrfy}'(vk, (m, n), \sigma') \\
& \textbf{return } \sigma := (\sigma', n) &
\end{array}$$

Fig. 4. Scheme $\mathsf{DS} := \mathsf{RDS}[\mathsf{DS}', \lambda]$. We require $\mathcal{M}' = \mathcal{M} \times \{0,1\}^\lambda$.

$$\begin{array}{lll}
\underline{\mathsf{Gen}(1^\kappa)} & \underline{\mathsf{Sign}_{wz}(sk, m)/\mathsf{Sign}_{cz}(sk, m)} & \underline{\mathsf{Vrfy}_{wz}(vk, m, \sigma)} \\
(vk, sk) \leftarrow \mathsf{Gen}_{\mathsf{LID}}(1^\kappa) & k := 1;\ z := \bot & \textbf{parse } \sigma = (w, z) \\
\textbf{return } (vk, sk) & \textbf{while } z = \bot \wedge k \leq B \textbf{ do} & c := \mathsf{H}(m, w) \\
& \quad (w, s) \leftarrow \mathsf{P}_1(sk) & \textbf{return } \mathsf{V}(vk, w, c, z) \\
& \quad c := \mathsf{H}(m, w) & \\
& \quad z := \mathsf{P}_2(sk, w, c, s) & \underline{\mathsf{Vrfy}_{cz}(vk, m, \sigma)} \\
& \quad k := k + 1 & \textbf{parse } \sigma = (c, z) \\
& \textbf{if } z = \bot \textbf{ then return } \bot & w' := \mathsf{Rec}(vk, c, z) \\
& \textbf{return } \sigma := (w, z) \quad /\mathsf{Sign}_{wz} & c' := \mathsf{H}(m, w') \\
& \textbf{return } \sigma := (c, z) \quad /\mathsf{Sign}_{cz} & \textbf{return } [\![c = c']\!]
\end{array}$$

Fig. 5. Scheme $\mathsf{FS}_{B,wz}[\mathsf{LID}, \mathsf{H}] = (\mathsf{Gen}, \mathsf{Sign}_{wz}, \mathsf{Vrfy}_{wz})$ and $\mathsf{FS}_{B,cz}[\mathsf{LID}, \mathsf{H}] = (\mathsf{Gen}, \mathsf{Sign}_{cz}, \mathsf{Vrfy}_{cz})$. $\mathsf{H} \colon \mathcal{M} \times \mathcal{W} \to \mathcal{C}$ is a random oracle.

3.1 From CMA1 Security to CMA Security

Diemert et al. [24] shows the following lemma, which is the multi-challenge version of [9, Theorem 5].

Lemma 3.1 ([24, Theorem 14]). *Let DS' be a signature scheme whose message space is $\mathcal{M}' = \mathcal{M} \times \{0,1\}^\lambda$ and let DS be $\mathsf{RDS}[\mathsf{DS}', \lambda]$ in Fig. 4. Let $\mathcal{A}$ be an adversary against the $\textsc{msEUF-CMA}$ security of DS which queries to $\textsc{Sign}$ q_S times. Then, there exists an adversary $\mathcal{B}$ against the $\textsc{msEUF-CMA1}$ security of DS' such that*

$$\mathsf{Adv}_{\mathsf{DS},\mathcal{A}}^{\mathrm{mseuf\text{-}cma}}(\kappa) \leq \mathsf{Adv}_{\mathsf{DS}',\mathcal{B}}^{\mathrm{mseuf\text{-}cma1}}(\kappa) + q_S^2 \cdot 2^{-\lambda},$$

$$\mathsf{Time}(\mathcal{B}) \approx \mathsf{Time}(\mathcal{A}), \text{ and } \mathsf{Mem}(\mathcal{B}) = \mathsf{Mem}(\mathcal{A}).$$

If the signature scheme is *deterministic*, then the CMA1 security implies the CMA security [34]. Thus, if we derandomize a CMA1-secure signature scheme, the obtained scheme archives CMA security. See, e.g., [36,40] for the derandomization by PRF.[9] Unfortunately, the derandomization by PRF is sometimes annoying when we consider memory-tight reductions.

3.2 Signature from Lossy Identification

We review a signature scheme constructed from a lossy identification scheme with abort [2,34]. Let $\mathsf{LID} = (\mathsf{Gen}_{\mathsf{LID}}, \mathsf{LossyGen}_{\mathsf{LID}}, \mathsf{P}_1, \mathsf{P}_2, \mathsf{V})$ be a lossy identification

---

[9] Let K be a secret key of PRF independent of the signing key sk. Kiltz et al. [34] credited the security proof of a signature scheme derandomized by $\mathsf{PRF}(K, m)$ to Bellare et al. [9]. Unfortunately, the derandomization proposed by Bellare et al. [9] computes randomness as $\mathsf{RF}(sk\|m)$ instead of $\mathsf{PRF}(K, m)$.

scheme. The signature scheme obtained by applying a variant of the Fiat-Shamir transform $\mathsf{FS}_{B,wz}$ is depicted in Fig. 5.

One might think if the underlying LID scheme is ρ-complete, then the obtained scheme is $(1 - (1 - \rho)^B)$-complete. For the correctness of the general case, Devevey et al. [22] gave a careful analysis of the correctness of the obtained signature scheme:

Lemma 3.2 ([22, Theorem 8], adapted). *Let $\gamma > 0$ and $\beta \in (0, 1)$. Let $B > 0$. Let $\mathsf{H}\colon \mathcal{M} \times \mathcal{W} \to \mathcal{C}$ be a hash function modeled as a random oracle. Let LID be a LID scheme that is (γ, β)-correct and has (α, ϵ_m)-commitment min-entropy. Let $\mathsf{DS} = \mathsf{FS}_{B,wz}[\mathsf{LID}, \mathsf{H}]$. Then, for any message $\mu \in \mathcal{M}$, we have*

$$\Pr_{(vk,sk) \leftarrow \mathsf{Gen}(1^\kappa)} \left[\Pr[\mathsf{V}(vk, m, \mathsf{Sign}(sk, m)) = \mathsf{true}] \geq \rho'(\alpha, \beta, \gamma, B) \right] \geq 1 - \epsilon_m,$$

where the inner probability is taken over the choice of H and the coins of Sign and

$$\rho'(\alpha, \beta, \gamma, B) := \gamma \cdot \left(1 - \beta^B - \frac{2^{-\alpha}}{(1 - \beta)^3} \right).$$

For simplicity, in what follows, we just say that the signature scheme is $\rho'(\alpha, \beta, \gamma, B)$-complete with probability at least $1 - \epsilon_m$ over the choice of key.

When the underlying LID is commitment-recoverable, we can apply another variant $\mathsf{FS}_{B,cz}$ depicted in Fig. 5 whose signature is of the form (c, z), which is often shorter than (w, z). If P_1 is derandomized by PRF, say, $\mathsf{P}_1(sk; \mathsf{PRF}(K, (m, k)))$, then we call this conversion as DFS instead of FS and denote $\mathsf{DFS}[\mathsf{LID}, \mathsf{H}, \mathsf{PRF}]$. If we use RF instead of PRF, then we denote it as $\mathsf{DFS}^+[\mathsf{LID}, \mathsf{H}, \mathsf{RF}]$. If we apply RDS in Subsect. 3.1 to the obtained scheme, then we call the conversion as RFS and denote $\mathsf{RFS}[\mathsf{LID}, \mathsf{H}, \lambda]$.

In this paper, we employ $\mathsf{FS}_{B,wz}$ to capture generic case, while [24] only consider $\mathsf{FS}_{B,cz}$. We can show the security of $\mathsf{FS}_{B,cz}$ by modifying our proofs for MsEUF-CMA, sBU, and PO securities.

4   Multi-challenge Security of Signature from Lossy Identification

Theorem 4.1 (msEUF-CMA1 security of $\mathsf{FS}_{B,wz}[\mathsf{LID}, \mathsf{H}]$).   *Let $B \geq 1$. Let $\mathsf{H}\colon \mathcal{M} \times \mathcal{W} \to \mathcal{C}$ be a hash function modeled as a random oracle. Let LID be a lossy identification scheme that is (γ, β)-correct, ϵ_{zk}-HVZK, and ϵ_ℓ-lossy, and has (α, ϵ_m)-commitment min-entropy. Let $\mathsf{DS} := \mathsf{FS}_{B,wz}[\mathsf{LID}, \mathsf{H}]$ and let ρ' be the completeness of DS defined in Lemma 3.2.*

Then, for a quantum adversary $\mathcal{A}$ breaking the MsEUF-CMA1 security of DS that issues at most q_H quantum queries to the random oracle H, q_S classical queries to the signing oracle, and q_F classical queries to the forgery oracle, there exist quantum $\mathcal{F}$-oracle adversaries $\mathcal{A}_{\mathrm{cur}}$ against computationally unique response of LID and $\mathcal{A}_{\mathrm{ind}}$ against key indistinguishability of LID such that

$$\mathsf{Adv}_{\mathsf{DS},\mathcal{A}}^{\mathrm{mseuf\text{-}cma1}}(\kappa) \leq \mathsf{Adv}_{\mathsf{LID},\mathcal{A}_{\mathrm{cur}}}^{\mathrm{cur}}(\kappa) + \mathsf{Adv}_{\mathsf{LID},\mathcal{A}_{\mathrm{ind}}}^{\mathrm{ind\text{-}key}}(\kappa) + 8(q+1)^2\epsilon_\ell$$
$$+ 8(q+1)^2(1-\rho') + q_F B 2^{-\alpha} + 2q B 2^{-\frac{-\alpha-1}{2}}$$
$$+ 3\epsilon_m + \sqrt{(6q)^3 B \epsilon_{\mathrm{zk}}},$$
$$\mathsf{Time}^*(\mathcal{A}_{\mathrm{cur}}) = \mathsf{Time}(\mathcal{A}) + q \cdot O(B\mathsf{Time}(\mathsf{LID}) + B^2),$$
$$\mathsf{Mem}^*(\mathcal{A}_{\mathrm{cur}}) = \mathsf{Mem}(\mathcal{A}) + O(B\mathsf{Mem}(\mathsf{LID})),$$
$$\mathsf{Time}^*(\mathcal{A}_{\mathrm{ind}}) = \mathsf{Time}(\mathcal{A}) + q \cdot O(B\mathsf{Time}(\mathsf{LID}) + B^2),$$
$$\mathsf{Mem}^*(\mathcal{A}_{\mathrm{ind}}) = \mathsf{Mem}(\mathcal{A}) + O(B\mathsf{Mem}(\mathsf{LID})),$$

where $q = q_S + q_H + q_F$ and $\mathcal{F} = \mathsf{Func}(\mathcal{M} \times \mathcal{W}, \mathcal{C}) \times \mathsf{Func}(\mathcal{M} \times [B], \mathcal{C}) \times \mathsf{Func}(\mathcal{M} \times [B], \mathcal{R})$.

Applying Lemma 3.1, we obtain the following corollary.

Corollary 4.1 (msEUF-CMA security of $\mathsf{RFS}_{B,wz}[\mathsf{LID}, \mathsf{H}, \lambda]$). *For sufficiently large $\lambda = \omega(\kappa)$, $\mathsf{RFS}_{B,wz}[\mathsf{LID}, \mathsf{H}, \lambda]$ has a memory-tight MsEUF-CMA security proof.*

4.1   Proof of Theorem

Roadmap: We define thirteen games G_i for $i \in \{0, 1, \ldots, 12\}$ to show our theorem. Let W_i denote the event that G_i outputs true. Before describing games, we briefly give intuitions for games. In what follows, $\mathrm{TRANS}(m)$ denotes the oracle generating at most B transcripts invoked from the signing oracle. Let $(w^{(i)}, c^{(i)}, z^{(i)})$ be the i-th transcript of $\mathrm{TRANS}(m)$.

While we mainly follow the proof by Devevey et al. [22], the details are different. We consider the original game, denoted by G_0, in which the signing oracle queried on m calls $\mathrm{TRANS}(m)$ internally and uses this real transcript as a signature. After derandomizing the prover in G_2, we modify the forgery-checking oracle to output a special symbol if the signature $(w^{(k)}, z^{(k)})$ generated from $\{(w^{(i)}, c^{(i)}, z^{(i)})\}_{i \in [k]}$ output by $\mathrm{TRANS}(m^*)$ yields an *invalid* signature, which is denoted by G_3. We then remove the list $\mathcal{Q}$ and replace the condition $(m^*, (w^*, z^*)) \notin \mathcal{Q}$ with $(w^*, z^*) \neq (w^{(k)}, z^{(k)})$ in G_4 as Diemert et al. [24]. While the random oracle leaks the information of $w^{(k)}$, we can show that the min-entropy of $w^{(k)}$ is high unless m^* is queried to the signing oracle and the adversary's guessing probability is at most $B2^{-\alpha}$. In G_7, we then modify the random oracle to patch the hash value on $\mathsf{H}(m, w^{(i)})$ by $c^{(i)}$ instead of $\mathsf{RF}_\mathsf{H}(m, w^{(i)})$, where $(w^{(i)}, c^{(i)}, z^{(i)})$ is the i-th transcript of $\mathrm{TRANS}(m)$. In G_9, we further implement $\mathrm{TRANS}(m)$ by the simulator, which removes the use of sk in the following games. We then consider the case that $w^* = \tilde{w}^{(k)}$ in G_{10}, which violates the CUR property. After additional small modifications, we arrive at G_{12} in which we replace a normal verification key with a lossy verification key as in [1,34], and this replacement is justified key indistinguishability of LID. Finally, in G_{12}, the adversary wins with negligible probability as in Kiltz et al. [34] due to ϵ_ℓ-lossiness.

$$G_0, \ldots, G_{12}$$
$(vk, sk) \leftarrow \text{Gen}_{\text{LID}}(1^\kappa)$	$/G_0\text{-}G_{11}$
$vk \leftarrow \text{LossyGen}_{\text{LID}}(1^\kappa)$	$/G_{12}$
$RF_H \leftarrow \text{Func}(\mathcal{M} \times \mathcal{W}, \mathcal{C})$	
$RF'_H \leftarrow \text{Func}(\mathcal{M} \times [B], \mathcal{C})$	$/G_6\text{-}$
$RF_P \leftarrow \text{Func}(\mathcal{M} \times [B], \mathcal{R}_{P_1})$	$/G_2\text{-}G_6$
$RF_S \leftarrow \text{Func}(\mathcal{M} \times [B], \mathcal{R}_{\text{Sim}})$	$/G_7\text{-}$
$Q := \emptyset$	$/G_0\text{-}G_3$
$\text{win} := \text{false}$	

$\text{run } \mathcal{A}^{\text{SIGN},\text{FORGE},|H\rangle}(vk)$
return win

$\text{SIGN}(m)$
if $\exists(m,\sigma) \in Q$ then return σ	$/G_0\text{-}G_1$
if $\text{TRANS}(m) = \lrcorner$ then return $\lrcorner$	$/G_6\text{-}$
$(w^{(k)}, c^{(k)}, z^{(k)}) \leftarrow \text{TRANS}(m)$	$/G_0$
$\{(w^{(i)}, c^{(i)}, z^{(i)})\}_{i \in [k]} \leftarrow \text{TRANS}(m)$	$/G_1\text{-}$

if $z^{(k)} = \bot$ then
$\quad \sigma := \bot$
else
$\quad \sigma := (w^{(k)}, z^{(k)})$
$Q := Q \cup \{(m,\sigma)\}$	$/G_0\text{-}G_3$

return σ

$\text{FORGE}(m^*, \sigma^*) \text{ where } \sigma^* = (w^*, z^*)$
if $\text{TRANS}(m) = \lrcorner$ then return $\lrcorner$	$/G_6\text{-}$
$\{(\tilde{w}^{(i)}, \tilde{c}^{(i)}, \tilde{z}^{(i)})\}_{i \in [k]} \leftarrow \text{TRANS}(m^*)$	$/G_3\text{-}$
if $V(vk, \tilde{w}^{(k)}, \tilde{c}^{(k)}, \tilde{z}^{(k)}) = \text{false}$ then return $\lrcorner$	$/G_3\text{-}$

$c^* := H(m^*, w^*)$
if $V(vk, w^*, c^*, z^*) = \text{true} \wedge (m^*,\sigma^*) \notin Q$ then	$/G_0\text{-}G_3$
$\quad \text{win} := \text{true}$	$/G_0\text{-}G_3$
if $V(vk, w^*, c^*, z^*) = \text{true} \wedge (w^*,z^*) \neq (\tilde{w}^{(k)}, \tilde{z}^{(k)})$ then	$/G_4\text{-}$
$\quad \text{win} := \text{true}$	$/G_4\text{-}G_7$
$\quad \mathcal{L}_{m^*} := \{\tilde{w}^{(i)}\}_{i \in [k]}; \mathcal{L}'_{m^*} := \{\tilde{w}^{(i)}\}_{i \in [k-1]}$	$/G_8\text{-}G_{10}$
$\quad$ if $(w^* \notin \mathcal{L}_{m^*}) \vee (w^* \in \mathcal{L}'_{m^*} \wedge c^* = RF'_H(m^*, w^*))$ then win := true	$/G_8\text{-}G_9$
$\quad$ if $(w^* \notin \mathcal{L}_{m^*}) \vee (w^* \in \mathcal{L}'_{m^*} \wedge c^* = RF'_H(m^*, w^*))$ then win := true	$/G_{10}$
$\quad$ if $w^* \neq \tilde{w}^{(k)} \wedge c^* = RF'_H(m^*, w^*)$ then win := true	$/G_{11}\text{-}$

$H: |m, w\rangle |y\rangle \mapsto |m, w\rangle |y \oplus c'\rangle$
return $c' := RF_H(m, w)$	$/G_0\text{-}G_4$
if $\text{TRANS}(m) = \lrcorner$ then return $\lrcorner$	$/G_6\text{-}$
$\{(w^{(i)}, c^{(i)}, z^{(i)})\}_{i \in [k]} \leftarrow \text{TRANS}(m)$	$/G_5\text{-}$
if $\exists i : w = w^{(i)}$ then	$/G_5\text{-}$
$\quad c' := c^{(i)}$	$/G_5\text{-}$
else	$/G_5\text{-}$
$\quad c' := RF_H(m, w)$	$/G_5\text{-}$

$\text{TRANS}(m)$
$k := 1; z^{(0)} := \bot$
while $z^{(k-1)} = \bot \wedge k \leq B$ do
$\quad (w^{(k)}, s) \leftarrow P_1(sk)$	$/G_0\text{-}G_1$
$\quad (w^{(k)}, s) := P_1(sk; RF_P(m, k))$	$/G_2\text{-}G_8$
$\quad c^{(k)} := RF_H(m, w^{(k)})$	$/G_0\text{-}G_6$
$\quad c^{(k)} := RF'_H(m, k)$	$/G_7\text{-}$
$\quad z^{(k)} := P_2(sk, w^{(k)}, c^{(k)}, s)$	$/G_0\text{-}G_8$
$\quad (w^{(k)}, z^{(k)}) := \text{Sim}(vk, c^{(k)}; RF_S(m, k))$	$/G_9$
$\quad k := k + 1$	
$k := k - 1$	/cancel the last increment
if $\text{Coll}(\{w^{(i)}\}_{i \in [k]}) = \text{true}$ then return $\lrcorner$	$/G_6\text{-}$
return $(w^{(k)}, c^{(k)}, z^{(k)})$	$/G_0$
return $\{(w^{(i)}, c^{(i)}, z^{(i)})\}_{i \in [k]}$	$/G_1\text{-}$

Fig. 6. G_i for $i \in \{0, 1, \ldots, 12\}$ for MSEUF-CMA1 security.

The formal definitions of games follow.

Game G_0: This is the original game. See Fig. 6 for a concrete definition of G_0, where we expand the Sign algorithm and H is defined as RF_H. By the definition, we have $\Pr[W_0] = \text{Adv}_{\text{DS},\mathcal{A}}^{\text{mseuf-cma1}}(\kappa)$.

Game G_1: In this game, TRANS outputs *all* transcripts instead of the last one. The signing oracle also takes the last one as a candidate for a signature. See G_1 in Fig. 6 for the detail. Since this is a conceptual change, we have $G_0 = G_1$.

Game G_2: We next derandomize the prover in TRANS by RF_P as in Fig. 6. Since we consider *one-signature-per-one-message* situation, this derandomization by the random function RF_P changes nothing. We have $G_1 = G_2$.

Game G_3: We next modify the forgery checking oracle as follows: On a query (m^*, σ^*), the oracle FORGE first computes the transcripts by invoking $\text{TRANS}(m^*)$. If $(\tilde{w}^{(k)}, \tilde{z}^{(k)})$ is an *invalid* signature, then the oracle returns a special symbol $\lrcorner$. See G_3 in Fig. 6 for the details.

We note that TRANS's output yields an *invalid* signature with probability at most $1 - \rho'$ as discussed in Subsect. 3.2 (with probability at least $1 - \epsilon_m$ over the choice of the keys). Notice that the adversary can obtain this information via the oracle Sign and the random oracle H.

Lemma 4.1. *Suppose that* LID *is* (γ, β)-*correct and has* (α, ϵ_m)-*min-entropy. We have*

$$|\Pr[W_2] - \Pr[W_3]| \leq 8(q_S + q_F + q_H + 1)^2(1 - \rho') + \epsilon_m.$$

The proof will appear in the full version.

Game G_4: In this game, we replace the condition $(m^*, \sigma^*) \notin \mathcal{Q}$ with the condition $(w^*, z^*) \neq (\tilde{w}^{(k)}, \tilde{z}^{(k)})$. See G_4 in Fig. 6.

Lemma 4.2. *Suppose that* LID *has* (α, ϵ_m)-*commit min-entropy. Then, we have*

$$|\Pr[W_3] - \Pr[W_4]| \leq q_F \cdot B2^{-\alpha} + \epsilon_m.$$

Proof. Suppose that the adversary queries m^* and $\sigma^* = (w^*, z^*)$ to the oracle FORGE.

If m^* is queried to the signing oracle before, then there is no difference between the two games: The signing oracle returns $(\tilde{w}^{(k)}, \tilde{z}^{(k)})$ as a signature on m^* and, thus, the condition $(m^*, \sigma^*) \notin \mathcal{Q}$ and the condition $(w^*, z^*) \neq (\tilde{w}^{(k)}, \tilde{z}^{(k)})$ are equivalent.

If m^* is not queried to the signing oracle, then the two games might differ if the adversary queries m^* and $(w^*, z^*) = (\tilde{w}^{(k)}, \tilde{z}^{(k)})$, which implies $w^* = \tilde{w}^{(k)}$. This means that the adversary succeeds to guess $\tilde{w}^{(k)}$ on m^* without knowing it. Let Bad_i denote the event that m^* is not queried before but w^* equals to $\tilde{w}^{(k)}$ happens in G_i. We have $|\Pr[W_3] - \Pr[W_4]| \leq \Pr[\mathsf{Bad}_3]$. According to Proposition 4.1, even if we know the *whole* table of RF_H, and $\tilde{w}^{(k)} \neq \bot$ has min-entropy $\alpha - \lg(B)$ with probability $1 - \epsilon_m$ over choice of (vk, sk). Therefore, we have $\Pr[\mathsf{Bad}_3] \leq q_F \cdot B2^{-\alpha} + \epsilon_m$. □

Proposition 4.1. *Fix* (vk, sk) *and suppose that the min-entropy of* w *is at least* α. *In* G_3, *we have for any* m^*,

$$\max_{w \in \mathcal{W}} \Pr[\tilde{w}^{(k)} = w \mid H] \leq B \cdot 2^{-\alpha}.$$

Proof. To simplify the notation, we let $\mathcal{W} = [W]$. We consider the distribution of the table on $H(m^*, \cdot)$ and let $C_1, \ldots, C_W$ be random variables representing values of $H(m^*, 1), \ldots, H(m^*, W)$.

Let p_i denote the probability that $i \in [W]$ is chosen by the prover. By the definition of the min-entropy of commitment, we have $\max_{i \in [W]} p_i \leq 2^{-\alpha}$. Let $q_{i,c}$ denote the probability that the prover outputs $z = \bot$ when it chooses i as the commitment and receives c as the challenge.

Let us fix the values of the table $H(m^*, \cdot)$ as $\mathbf{c} = (c_1, \ldots, c_W) \in \mathcal{C}^W$. This fix allows us to compute the probability that the prover outputs $z = \bot$, which is $\beta_{\mathbf{c}} := \sum_{i \in [W]} p_i \cdot q_{i,c_i} \leq 1$. On each try except the last one, $\tilde{w}^{(k)} = i$ is chosen with probability $p_i(1 - q_{i,c_i})$. On the last try, $\tilde{w}^{(k)} = i$ is chosen with probability p_i. Thus, for any $B \geq 1$, we have

$$\Pr[\tilde{w}^{(k)} = i \mid \boldsymbol{C} = \boldsymbol{c}]$$

$$= p_i(1 - q_{i,c_i}) + \beta_c p_i(1 - q_{i,c_i}) + \cdots + \beta_c^{B-2} p_i(1 - q_{i,c_i}) + \beta_c^{B-1} p_i$$

$$= p_i(1 - q_{i,c_i})(1 + \beta_c + \cdots + \beta_c^{B-2}) + p_i \beta_c^{B-1}$$

$$\leq p_i(1 + \beta_c + \cdots + \beta_c^{B-1})$$

$$\leq B \cdot p_i,$$

where we use the inequality $(1 + x + x^2 + \cdots + x^{B-1}) \leq B$ for $x \in [0, 1]$. This yields that

$$\max_{i \in [W]} \Pr[\tilde{w}^{(k)} = i \mid \boldsymbol{C} = \boldsymbol{c}] \leq \max_{i \in [W]} B \cdot p_i \leq B \cdot 2^{-\alpha}$$

as we wanted. $\qquad\square$

Game G_5: We next modify the random oracle as follows: On a query (m, w), the oracle first computes the transcripts $\{(w^{(i)}, c^{(i)}, z^{(i)})\}_{i \in [k]}$. If the input w is equivalent to one of $w^{(i)}$, then it returns $c' := c^{(i)}$; otherwise, it returns $c' := \mathsf{RF}_\mathsf{H}(m, w)$. See G_5 in Fig. 6 for the details.

Since $c^{(i)}$ is defined as $\mathsf{RF}_\mathsf{H}(m, w^{(i)})$ in TRANS, this change nothing and we have $\mathsf{G}_4 = \mathsf{G}_5$.

Game G_6: We next introduce a collision check for $w^{(i)}$'s in TRANS. If TRANS finds a collision among $w^{(1)}, \ldots, w^{(k)}$, it outputs a special symbol $\lrcorner$. See G_6 in Fig. 6.

For each message, the collision probability is at most $B^2 \cdot 2^{-\alpha-1}$ if $H_\infty(w)$ is α [22, Lemma 11]. Using the one-sided O2H lemma [6], Devevey et al. showed the following lemma, where we additionally introduce ϵ_m.

Lemma 4.3. *Suppose that* LID *has* (α, ϵ_m)-*min-entropy. Then, we have*

$$|\Pr[W_5] - \Pr[W_6]| \leq 2(q_S + q_H + q_F) \cdot B \cdot 2^{\frac{-\alpha-1}{2}} + \epsilon_m.$$

Game G_7: We next modify how to compute $c^{(k)}$ in TRANS, in which it is computed as $\mathsf{RF}'_\mathsf{H}(m, k)$ instead of $\mathsf{RF}_\mathsf{H}(m, w^{(k)})$. We note that this does not change the adversary's view because RF'_H is a random function, and if $w = w^{(i)}$ for the query (m, w), then consistent $c' = c^{(i)} = \mathsf{RF}'_\mathsf{H}(m, i)$ is output by H since we already exclude the collision. Thus, we have $\mathsf{G}_6 = \mathsf{G}_7$.

Game G_8: To ease the notation, let $\mathcal{L}_{m^*} := \{w^{(i)}\}_{i \in [k]}$ which is the w parts of the transcripts generated by TRANS(m^*). We additionally define $\mathcal{L}'_{m^*} := \{w^{(i)}\}_{i \in [k-1]}$.

In G_8, FORGE additionally checks if $w^* \in \mathcal{L}'_{m^*}$ or not; if so, we additionally checks whether $c^* = \mathsf{RF}_\mathsf{H}(m^*, w^*)$ or not. See G_8 in Fig. 6 for the details.

We have the following lemma.

Lemma 4.4. *We have* $\Pr[W_7] = \Pr[W_8]$.

Proof. The two games differ if the adversary queries $w^* = w^{(i)}$ for some $i < k$ but $c^* = c^{(i)} \neq \mathsf{RF_H}(m^*, w^*)$. We call this event in G_i as Bad_i. We have

$$|\Pr[W_7] - \Pr[W_8]| \leq \Pr[\mathsf{Bad}_7] \leq |\Pr[\mathsf{Bad}_7] - \Pr[\mathsf{Bad}_6]| + \Pr[\mathsf{Bad}_6].$$

We have $\Pr[\mathsf{Bad}_6] = 0$ because $c^* = \mathsf{RF_H}(m^*, w^*)$ always holds in G_6. Since $\mathsf{G}_6 = \mathsf{G}_7$, we have $\Pr[\mathsf{Bad}_7] = \Pr[\mathsf{Bad}_6]$. Hence, we have $\Pr[W_7] = \Pr[W_8]$. $\square$

Game G_9: We next modify TRANS to use the simulation algorithm. On a query m, the oracle computes $c^{(i)} := \mathsf{RF'_H}(m, i)$ and $(w^{(i)}, z^{(i)}) := \mathsf{Sim}(vk, c^{(i)}; \mathsf{RF_S}(m, i))$. See G_9 in Fig. 6 for the details. Since the real transcript and the simulated one is ϵ_{zk}-close, each invocation of TRANS is $B\epsilon_{\mathsf{zk}}$-close. As Devevey et al. [22], we have the following lemma by using Lemma 2.1.

Lemma 4.5. *Suppose that* LID *is* ϵ_{zk}*-HVZK. Then, we have*

$$|\Pr[W_8] - \Pr[W_9]| \leq \sqrt{(6(q_S + q_H + q_F))^3 B\epsilon_{\mathsf{zk}}}.$$

Game G_{10}: We next treat the case $w^* = \tilde{w}^{(k)}$ as a special case. To do so, we replace the condition $w^* \notin \mathcal{L}'_{m^*}$ with $w^* \notin \mathcal{L}_{m^*}$. See G_{10} in Fig. 6 for the details.

Because of this modification, if the adversary queries $(m^*, (w^*, z^*))$ satisfying $(w^*, z^*) \neq (\tilde{w}^{(k)}, \tilde{z}^{(k)})$, $w^* = \tilde{w}^{(k)}$, and $\mathsf{Vrfy}(vk, w^*, c^*, z^*) = \mathsf{true}$, then two games may differ. Fortunately, this event is easily treated by the CUR property.

Lemma 4.6. *There exists a quantum $\mathcal{F}$-oracle adversary $\mathcal{A}_{\mathrm{cur}}$ such that*

$$|\Pr[W_9] - \Pr[W_{10}]| \leq \mathsf{Adv}^{\mathrm{cur}}_{\mathsf{LID}, \mathcal{A}_{\mathrm{cur}}}(\kappa),$$

$$\mathsf{Time}^*(\mathcal{A}_{\mathrm{cur}}) = \mathsf{Time}(\mathcal{A}) + (q_H + q_S + q_F) \cdot O(B\mathsf{Time}(\mathsf{LID}) + B^2),$$

$$\mathsf{Mem}^*(\mathcal{A}_{\mathrm{cur}}) = \mathsf{Mem}(\mathcal{A}) + O(B\mathsf{Mem}(\mathsf{LID})),$$

where $\mathcal{F} = \mathsf{Func}(\mathcal{M} \times \mathcal{W}, \mathcal{C}) \times \mathsf{Func}(\mathcal{M} \times [B], \mathcal{C}) \times \mathsf{Func}(\mathcal{M} \times [B], \mathcal{R}_{\mathsf{Sim}})$.

Proof. Suppose that the queried forgery is (m^*, σ^*) with $\sigma^* = (w^*, z^*)$. Consider the computation in FORGE and assume that $(w^*, z^*) \neq (\tilde{w}^{(k)}, \tilde{z}^{(k)})$ and $\mathsf{V}(vk, w^*, c^*, z^*) = \mathsf{true}$ for $c^* = \mathsf{H}(m^*, w^*)$ and the flag win is set true in G_9. We have the following two cases to analyze G_{10}:

- If $w^* \neq \tilde{w}^{(k)}$, then there are no differences because of the collision checks and the flag win is set true in G_{10} also.
- If $w^* = \tilde{w}^{(k)}$, then $c^* := \tilde{c}^{(k)}$. Since $w^* = \tilde{w}^{(k)}$, the flag win is unchanged in G_{10}. However, the check $(w^*, z^*) \neq (\tilde{w}^{(k)}, \tilde{z}^{(k)})$ forces $z^* \neq \tilde{z}^{(k)}$, and this z^* leads to break the CUR property by outputting $(w^*, c^*, z^*, \tilde{z}^{(k)})$.

Upon the above observation, we can construct a quantum $\mathcal{F}$-oracle adversary $\mathcal{A}_{\mathrm{cur}}$ straightforwardly. The analysis of advantage, running time, and memory usage in the lemma are straightforwardly obtained. $\square$

Remark 4.1. We note that $\mathsf{V}(\tilde{w}^{(k)}, \tilde{c}^{(k)}, \tilde{z}^{(k)}) = \mathsf{true}$ holds by the check we introduced in G_3 into FORGE. This check is fatal for the above proof because, if $\tilde{z}^{(k)} = \bot$ or $\mathsf{V}(\tilde{w}^{(k)}, \tilde{c}^{(k)}, \tilde{z}^{(k)}) = \mathsf{false}$, then the reduction algorithm fails to output the collision $(w^*, c^*, z^*, \tilde{z}^{(k)})$ breaking the CUR property.

Game G_{11}: We again modify the conditions in FORGE in G_{10}: FORGE checks if $V(vk, w^*, c^*, z^*) = \text{true}$ for $c^* = H(m^*, w^*)$, $(w^*, z^*) \neq (\tilde{w}^{(k)}, \tilde{z}^{(k)})$, $w^* \neq \tilde{w}^{(k)}$, and $c^* = RF_H(m^*, w^*)$ or not. If so, the flag is set as true. See G_{11} in Fig. 6 for the details.

Lemma 4.7. *We have* $G_{10} = G_{11}$.

Proof. Let us consider a forgery $(m^*, (w^*, z^*))$ satisfying $V(vk, w^*, c^*, z^*) = \text{true}$ for $c^* = H(m^*, w^*)$ and $(w^*, z^*) \neq (\tilde{w}^{(k)}, \tilde{z}^{(k)})$. Let us consider three cases:

- If $w^* \in \mathcal{L}'_{m^*}$, then there is no difference on the condition $c^* = RF_H(m^*, w^*)$ in both games.
- If $w^* = \tilde{w}^{(k)}$, then win is kept in both games.
- If $w^* \notin \mathcal{L}_{m^*}$, then FORGE sets win as true immediately in G_{10} but sets win as true if $c^* = RF_H(m^*, w^*)$ in G_{11}. We note that $c^* := RF_H(m^*, w^*)$ in FORGE since $w^* \notin \mathcal{L}_{m^*}$. Thus, FORGE in G_{11} also sets win := true and there are no differences.

Thus, both games are the same. $\qquad\square$

Game G_{12}: We finally replace a normal verification key with a lossy verification key. See G_{12} in Fig. 6 for the details.

Lemma 4.8. *There exists a quantum $\mathcal{F}$-oracle adversary $\mathcal{A}_{\text{ind}}$ such that*

$$|\Pr[W_{11}] - \Pr[W_{12}]| \leq \text{Adv}^{\text{indkey}}_{\text{LID}, \mathcal{A}_{\text{ind}}}(\kappa),$$

$$\text{Time}^*(\mathcal{A}_{\text{ind}}) = \text{Time}(\mathcal{A}) + (q_H + q_S + q_F) \cdot O(B\text{Time}(\text{LID}) + B^2),$$

$$\text{Mem}^*(\mathcal{A}_{\text{ind}}) = \text{Mem}(\mathcal{A}) + O(B\text{Mem}(\text{LID})),$$

where $\mathcal{F} = \text{Func}(\mathcal{M} \times \mathcal{W}, \mathcal{C}) \times \text{Func}(\mathcal{M} \times [B], \mathcal{C}) \times \text{Func}(\mathcal{M} \times [B], \mathcal{R}_{\text{Sim}})$.

Proof. We construct $\mathcal{A}_{\text{ind}}$ straightforwardly. The analysis of advantage, running time, and memory usage in the lemma are straightforwardly obtained. $\qquad\square$

Lemma 4.9. *Suppose that LID is ϵ_ℓ-lossy. Then, we have*

$$\Pr[W_{12}] \leq 8(q_H + q_S + q_F + 1)^2 \epsilon_\ell.$$

Since the proof is the same as that in Kiltz et al. [34], we omit it. See the proof for the full version.

5   Plus-One Unforgeability of Signature from Lossy Identification

Theorem 5.1 (PO security of $DFS_{B,wz}[\text{LID}, H, \text{PRF}]$). *Let $B \geq 1$. Let $H: \mathcal{M} \times \mathcal{W} \to \mathcal{C}$ be a hash function modeled as a random oracle. Let LID be a lossy identification scheme that is (γ, β)-correct, ϵ_{zk}-HVZK, and ϵ_ℓ-lossy, and* *has* (α, ϵ_m)-*min-entropy. Let* $\mathsf{DS} := \mathsf{DFS}_{B,\mathsf{wz}}[\mathsf{LID}, \mathsf{H}, \mathsf{PRF}]$ *and let* ρ' *be the completeness of* DS *defined in Lemma 3.2.*

Then, for a quantum adversary $\mathcal{A}$ *breaking the* PO *security of* DS *that issues at most* q_H *quantum queries to the random oracle* H, q_S *classical queries to the signing oracle, and* q_F *classical queries to the forgery oracle, there exists a quantum* $\mathcal{F}_{\mathrm{prf}}$-*oracle adversary* $\mathcal{A}_{\mathrm{prf}}$ *against pseudorandomness of* PRF *and quantum* $\mathcal{F}$-*oracle adversaries* $\mathcal{A}_{\mathrm{ind}}$ *against key indistinguishability of* LID *and* $\mathcal{A}_{\mathrm{cur}}$ *against computationally unique response of* LID *such that*

$$\mathsf{Adv}^{\mathrm{po}}_{\mathsf{DS},\mathcal{A}}(\kappa) \leq \mathsf{Adv}^{\mathrm{pr}}_{\mathsf{PRF},\mathcal{A}_{\mathrm{prf}}}(\kappa) + \mathsf{Adv}^{\mathrm{cur}}_{\mathsf{LID},\mathcal{A}_{\mathrm{cur}}}(\kappa) + \mathsf{Adv}^{\mathrm{ind\text{-}key}}_{\mathsf{LID},\mathcal{A}_{\mathrm{ind}}}(\kappa)$$

$$+ 8(q+1)^2\epsilon_\ell + 8(q+1)^2(1-\rho') + \frac{(q_S+1)}{\lfloor 2^\alpha/B \rfloor}$$

$$+ 2qB2^{-\frac{\alpha-1}{2}} + 3\epsilon_m + \sqrt{(6q)^3 B\epsilon_{\mathsf{zk}}},$$

$$\mathsf{Time}^*(\mathcal{A}_{\mathrm{prf}}) = \mathsf{Time}(\mathcal{A}) + q_S \cdot O(B\mathsf{Time}(\mathsf{LID})) + q_F \cdot O(\mathsf{Time}(\mathsf{LID})),$$

$$\mathsf{Mem}^*(\mathcal{A}_{\mathrm{prf}}) = \mathsf{Mem}(\mathcal{A}) + O(B\mathsf{Mem}(\mathsf{LID})) + q_F \cdot O(\mathsf{Mem}(\mathsf{LID})) + O(\lg(q_S)),$$

$$\mathsf{Time}^*(\mathcal{A}_{\mathrm{ind}}) = \mathsf{Time}(\mathcal{A}) + q \cdot O(B\mathsf{Time}(\mathsf{LID}) + B^2),$$

$$\mathsf{Mem}^*(\mathcal{A}_{\mathrm{ind}}) = \mathsf{Mem}(\mathcal{A}) + O(B\mathsf{Mem}(\mathsf{LID})),$$

$$\mathsf{Time}^*(\mathcal{A}_{\mathrm{cur}}) = \mathsf{Time}(\mathcal{A}) + q \cdot O(B\mathsf{Time}(\mathsf{LID}) + B^2),$$

$$\mathsf{Mem}^*(\mathcal{A}_{\mathrm{cur}}) = \mathsf{Mem}(\mathcal{A}) + O(B\mathsf{Mem}(\mathsf{LID})),$$

where $q = q_H + q_S + q_F$, $\mathcal{F}_{\mathrm{prf}} = \mathsf{Func}(\mathcal{M} \times \mathcal{W}, \mathcal{C})$, *and* $\mathcal{F} = \mathsf{Func}(\mathcal{M} \times \mathcal{W}, \mathcal{C}) \times \mathsf{Func}(\mathcal{M} \times [B], \mathcal{C}) \times \mathsf{Func}(\mathcal{M} \times [B], \mathcal{R}_{\mathsf{Sim}})$.

As a corollary, when we employ a random function RF_P directly, the above proof can be modified into a memory-tight one.

Corollary 5.1. $\mathsf{DFS}^+{}_{B,\mathsf{wz}}[\mathsf{LID}, \mathsf{H}, \mathsf{RF}_\mathsf{P}]$ *has a memory-tight proof for the* PO *security.*

5.1 Proof of Theorem

We define fourteen games G_i for $i \in \{0, 1, 2, 3, 4.0, 4.1, 5, 6, \ldots, 12\}$ to show our theorem. Let W_i denote the event that the experiment outputs true in G_i.

Roadmap: Before describing games, we briefly give intuitions for games.

In the PO security game, the game handles $\mathcal{Q}$ which contains distinct valid pairs of messages and signatures. The adversary wins if $\#\mathcal{Q} > q_S$ by submitting forgeries to the forgery-checking oracle FORGE. As in the case of MsEUF-CMA1 security, we start from the original game G_0 and go to G_3, in which the forgery-checking oracle outputs a special symbol if its own signature on m^* is invalid. We want to modify the winning condition that the adversary outputs at least $q_S + 1$ forgeries with the adversary succeeds in submitting $(m^*, (w^*, z^*))$ satisfying $(w^*, z^*) \neq (\tilde{w}^{(k)}, \tilde{z}^{(k)})$. We manage the latter condition by a flag win as in MsEUF-CMA1 security. In $\mathsf{G}_{4.0}$, we introduce this flag win and the game returns true if the adversary outputs at least $q_S + 1$ distinct valid pairs of message/signature ($\#\mathcal{Q} > q_S$) and the flag win is true. If a difference occurs between two games, then the adversary correctly guesses at least $q_S + 1$ signatures produced by TRANS on *distinct* $q_S + 1$ messages. This means that the adversary correctly guesses $q_S + 1$ commitments w on distinct $q_S + 1$ messages. According to Proposition 4.1, the min-entropy of commitments is at least $\alpha - \lg(B)$ even if we know the whole table of the random oracle. Combining this with Lemma 2.2, we can show the bound on this event. In $G_{4.1}$, we then remove $\mathcal{Q}$ by modifying the output of the game as win instead of $[\![\#\mathcal{Q} > q_S]\!] \wedge$ win. Since the adversary cannot detect this relaxation, the advantage in $G_{4.1}$ at least the advantage in $G_{4.0}$, i.e., $\Pr[W_{4.1}] \geq \Pr[W_{4.0}]$.

After that, we continue to modify the games as MSEUF-CMA1 security. Since the adversary can access the *quantum* signing oracle, there are minor differences on the bound.

Game G_0: This is the original game. See Fig. 7 for a concrete definition of G_0, where we expand the Sign algorithm. We have

$$\Pr[W_0] = \mathsf{Adv}_{\mathsf{DS},\mathcal{A}}^{\mathrm{mseuf\text{-}cma1}}(\kappa).$$

Game G_1: We then replace PRF in P_1 of GETTRANS with RF$_\mathsf{P}$. The straightforward argument shows the following lemma. Unfortunately, this part is *memory-loose* because the reduction algorithm should maintain the forgery list $\mathcal{Q}$.

Lemma 5.1. *There exists a quantum $\mathcal{F}$-oracle adversary $\mathcal{A}_{\mathrm{prf}}$ such that*

$$|\Pr[W_0] - \Pr[W_1]| \leq \mathsf{Adv}_{\mathsf{PRF},\mathcal{A}_{\mathrm{prf}}}^{\mathrm{pr}}(\kappa),$$

$$\mathsf{Time}^*(\mathcal{A}_{\mathsf{PRF}}) = \mathsf{Time}(\mathcal{A}) + q_S \cdot O(B\mathsf{Time}(\mathsf{LID})) + q_F \cdot O(\mathsf{Time}(\mathsf{LID})),$$

$$\mathsf{Mem}^*(\mathcal{A}_{\mathsf{PRF}}) = \mathsf{Mem}(\mathcal{A}) + O(B\mathsf{Mem}(\mathsf{LID})) + q_F \cdot O(\mathsf{Mem}(\mathsf{LID})) + O(\lg(q_S)),$$

where $\mathcal{F} = \mathsf{Func}(\mathcal{M} \times \mathcal{W}, \mathcal{C})$.

Game G_2: We next make TRANS output all transcripts instead of the last one. This modification does not change anything, and we have $G_1 = G_2$.

Game G_3: We next modify the forgery checking oracle as follows: Before checking the validity of submitted query (m^*, σ^*), it generates its own signature $(\tilde{w}^{(k)}, \tilde{c}^{(k)}, \tilde{z}^{(k)})$ by using TRANS(m^*). If the verification fails, that is, $\mathsf{V}(vk, \tilde{w}^{(k)}, \tilde{c}^{(k)}, \tilde{z}^{(k)}) = \mathsf{false}$, then the forge oracle returns the special symbol $\sqcup$.

The adversary differentiates between the two games G_2 and G_3 if it submits such (m^*, σ^*) on which TRANS(m^*) fails to output a valid signature. We can connect this event to the generic search problem with $\lambda = 1 - \rho'$. The proof will appear in the full version.

Lemma 5.2. *Suppose that LID is (γ, β)-correct and has (α, ϵ_m)-min-entropy. We have*

$$|\Pr[W_2] - \Pr[W_3]| \leq \Pr[\mathsf{Bad}_{m^*}] \leq 8(q_S + q_F + q_H + 1)^2(1 - \rho') + \epsilon_m.$$

```
G0, ..., G12
(vk, sk) ← Gen_LID(1^κ)                          /G0-G11
vk ← LossyGen_LID(1^κ)                           /G12
K ← {0,1}^κ                                      /G0
RF_H ← Func(M × W, C)
RF'_H ← Func(M × [B], C)                         /G6-
RF_P ← Func(M × [B], R_P1)                       /G2-G6
RF_S ← Func(M × [B], R_Sim)                      /G7-
Q := ∅                                           /G0-G4.0
win := false                                     /G4.0-
run A^{|Sign⟩, Forge, |H⟩}(vk)
return ⟦#Q > q_S⟧                                /G0-G3
return ⟦#Q > q_S⟧ ∧ win                          /G4.0
return win                                       /G4.1-

Sign: |m⟩|y⟩ ↦ |m⟩|y ⊕ σ⟩
if Trans(m) = ⊣ then return ⊣                    /G6-
(w^(k), c^(k), z^(k)) ← Trans(m)                 /G0-G1
{(w^(i), c^(i), z^(i))}_{i∈[k]} ← Trans(m)       /G2-
if z^(k) = ⊥ then
 |  σ := ⊥
else
 |  σ := (w^(k), z^(k))
Q := Q ∪ {(m, σ)}                                /G0-G4.0
return σ

H: |m, w⟩|y⟩ ↦ |m, w⟩|y ⊕ c'⟩
return c' := RF_H(m, w)                          /G0-G4.1
if Trans(m) = ⊣ then return ⊣                    /G6-
{(w^(i), c^(i), z^(i))}_{i∈[k]} ← Trans(m)       /G5-
if ∃i : w = w^(i) then                           /G5-
 |  c' := c^(i)                                  /G5-
else                                             /G5-
 |  c' := RF_H(m, w)                             /G5-

Trans(m)
k := 1; z^(0) := ⊥
while z^(k-1) = ⊥ ∧ k ≤ B do
 |  (w^(k), s) ← P1(sk; PRF(K, (m, k)))          /G0-G1
 |  (w^(k), s) := P1(sk; RF_P(m, k))             /G2-G8
 |  c^(k) := RF_H(m, w^(k))                      /G0-G6
 |  c^(k) := RF'_H(m, k)                         /G7-
 |  z^(k) := P2(sk, w^(k), c^(k), s)             /G0-G8
 |  (w^(k), z^(k)) := Sim(vk, c^(k); RF_S(m, k)) /G9
 |  k := k + 1
k := k - 1                                       /cancel the last increment
if Coll({w^(i)}_{i∈[k]}) = true then return ⊣    /G6-
return (w^(k), c^(k), z^(k))                     /G0-G1
return {(w^(i), c^(i), z^(i))}_{i∈[k]}           /G2-

Forge(m*, σ*) where σ* = (w*, z*)
if Trans(m) = ⊣ then return ⊣                                        /G6-
{(w̃^(i), c̃^(i), z̃^(i))}_{i∈[k]} ← Trans(m*)                        /G3-
if V(vk, w̃^(k), c̃^(k), z̃^(k)) = false then return ⊣                 /G3-
c* := H(m*, w*)
if V(vk, w*, c*, z*) = true ∧ (m*, σ*) ∉ Q then                      /G0-G4.0
 |  Q := Q ∪ {(m*, σ*)}                                              /G0-G4.0
if V(vk, w*, c*, z*) = true ∧ (w*, z*) ≠ (w̃^(k), z̃^(k)) then         /G4.0-
 |  win := true                                                      /G4.0-G7
 |  L_m* := {w̃^(i)}_{i∈[k]}; L'_m* := {w̃^(i)}_{i∈[k-1]}             /G8-G10
 |  if (w* ∉ L'_m*) ∨ (w* ∈ L'_m* ∧ c* = RF_H(m*, w*)) then win := true   /G8-G9
 |  if (w* ∉ L_m*) ∨ (w* ∈ L'_m* ∧ c* = RF_H(m*, w*)) then win := true    /G10
 |  if w* ≠ w̃^(k) ∧ c* = RF_H(m*, w*) then win := true                  /G11-
```

Fig. 7. G_i for $i \in \{0, 1, 2, 3, 4.0, 4.1, 5, 6, \ldots, 12\}$ for PO security.

Game $\mathsf{G}_{4.0}$*:* We replace the winning condition of $\mathcal{A}$ as follows: We introduce a flag win which is set true by FORGE when the adversary queries $(w^*, z^*) \neq (\tilde{w}^{(k)}, \tilde{z}^{(k)})$. The challenger outputs $[\![\#\mathcal{Q} > \mathsf{cnt}_s]\!] \wedge \mathsf{win}$. See $\mathsf{G}_{4.0}$ in Fig. 7.

Lemma 5.3. *Suppose that* LID *has* (α, ϵ_m)*-min-entropy. Then, we have*

$$|\Pr[W_3] - \Pr[W_{4.0}]| \leq (q_S + 1)/\lfloor 2^\alpha / B \rfloor + \epsilon_m.$$

Proof. The two games differ if the adversary queries at least $(q_S + 1)$ valid signatures on *distinct* messages to FORGE such that $(w^*, z^*) = (\tilde{w}^{(k)}, \tilde{z}^{(k)})$ on each m^*. This is because if two valid signatures share the same message, then two signatures should be equivalent.

Let Bad_i be the event that the adversary in G_i queries (q_S+1) valid signatures on *distinct* messages to FORGE such that $w^* = \tilde{w}^{(k)}$ on each m^*. By routine calculation, we have $|\Pr[W_3] - \Pr[W_{4.0}]| \leq \Pr[\mathsf{Bad}_3]$. Proposition 4.1 shows that the min-entropy of $\tilde{w}^{(k)}$ on m^* is at least $\alpha - \lg(B)$ even if we know the whole table of the random oracle H with probability $1 - \epsilon_m$ over the choice of keys. Hence, we have $\Pr[\mathsf{Bad}_3] \leq (q_S + 1)/\lfloor 2^\alpha / B \rfloor + \epsilon_m$ by invoking Lemma 2.2. □

Game $G_{4.1}$: We then replace the output of the game. In $G_{4.1}$, the game just outputs the flag win instead of $[\![\#\mathcal{Q} > \mathsf{cnt}_s]\!] \wedge \mathsf{win}$. See $G_{4.1}$ in Fig. 7. This modification allows us to forget $\mathcal{Q}$.

Since we *relax* the condition and the adversary cannot detect this modification, we have $\Pr[W_{4.0}] \leq \Pr[W_{4.1}]$.

Games $G_5, \ldots, G_{12}$: The games $G_5, \ldots, G_{12}$ are defined in Fig. 7. We omit the lemmas to upper-bound the differences between them since the proofs are essentially the same as those for the MsEUF-CMA1 security. See the full version for the details.

Acknowledgements. The author thank the anonymous reviewers of EUROCRYPT 2024 for their constructive comments and suggestions.

References

1. Abdalla, M., Fouque, P.-A., Lyubashevsky, V., Tibouchi, M.: Tightly-secure signatures from lossy identification schemes. In: Pointcheval, D., Johansson, T. (eds.) EUROCRYPT 2012. LNCS, vol. 7237, pp. 572–590. Springer, Heidelberg (2012). https://doi.org/10.1007/978-3-642-29011-4_34

2. Abdalla, M., Fouque, P.A., Lyubashevsky, V., Tibouchi, M.: Tightly secure signatures from lossy identification schemes. J. Cryptol. **29**(3), 597–631 (2016). https://doi.org/10.1007/s00145-015-9203-7

3. Alagic, G., et al.: Status report on the third round of the NIST post-quantum cryptography standardization process. Technical report, NIST (2022). https://doi.org/10.6028/NIST.IR.8413-upd1

4. Alagic, G., Majenz, C., Russell, A., Song, F.: Quantum-secure message authentication via blind-unforgeability. Cryptology ePrint Archive, Report 2018/1150 (2018). https://eprint.iacr.org/2018/1150

5. Alagic, G., Majenz, C., Russell, A., Song, F.: Quantum-access-secure message authentication via blind-unforgeability. In: Canteaut, A., Ishai, Y. (eds.) EUROCRYPT 2020, Part III. LNCS, vol. 12107, pp. 788–817. Springer, Cham (2020). https://doi.org/10.1007/978-3-030-45727-3_27

6. Ambainis, A., Hamburg, M., Unruh, D.: Quantum security proofs using semiclassical oracles. In: Boldyreva, A., Micciancio, D. (eds.) CRYPTO 2019, Part II. LNCS, vol. 11693, pp. 269–295. Springer, Cham (2019). https://doi.org/10.1007/978-3-030-26951-7_10

7. Auerbach, B., Cash, D., Fersch, M., Kiltz, E.: Memory-tight reductions. In: Katz, J., Shacham, H. (eds.) CRYPTO 2017, Part I. LNCS, vol. 10401, pp. 101–132. Springer, Cham (2017). https://doi.org/10.1007/978-3-319-63688-7_4

8. Barbosa, M., et al.: Fixing and mechanizing the security proof of Fiat-Shamir with aborts and Dilithium. In: Handschuh, H., Lysyanskaya, A. (eds.) Advances in Cryptology, CRYPTO 2023. LNCS, vol. 14085, pp. 358–389. Springer, Cham (2023). https://doi.org/10.1007/978-3-031-38554-4_12

9. Bellare, M., Poettering, B., Stebila, D.: From identification to signatures, tightly: a framework and generic transforms. In: Cheon, J.H., Takagi, T. (eds.) ASIACRYPT 2016, Part II. LNCS, vol. 10032, pp. 435–464. Springer, Heidelberg (2016). https://doi.org/10.1007/978-3-662-53890-6_15

10. Bellare, M., Rogaway, P.: Random oracles are practical: a paradigm for designing efficient protocols. In: Denning, D.E., Pyle, R., Ganesan, R., Sandhu, R.S., Ashby, V. (eds.) ACM CCS 1993, November 1993, pp. 62–73. ACM Press (1993). https://doi.org/10.1145/168588.168596

11. Bellare, M., Rogaway, P.: The exact security of digital signatures-how to sign with RSA and Rabin. In: Maurer, U. (ed.) EUROCRYPT 1996. LNCS, vol. 1070, pp. 399–416. Springer, Heidelberg (1996). https://doi.org/10.1007/3-540-68339-9_34

12. Bernstein, D.J.: Extending the Salsa20 nonce. In: SKEW 2011 (Symmetric Key Encryption Workshop 2011) (2011). https://doi.org/10.1109/SP46215.2023.10179342. See the authors' website or http://skew2011.mat.dtu.dk/program.html

13. Bhattacharyya, R.: Memory-tight reductions for practical key encapsulation mechanisms. In: Kiayias, A., Kohlweiss, M., Wallden, P., Zikas, V. (eds.) PKC 2020, Part I. LNCS, vol. 12110, pp. 249–278. Springer, Cham (2020). https://doi.org/10.1007/978-3-030-45374-9_9

14. Boneh, D., Dagdelen, Ö., Fischlin, M., Lehmann, A., Schaffner, C., Zhandry, M.: Random oracles in a quantum world. In: Lee, D.H., Wang, X. (eds.) ASIACRYPT 2011. LNCS, vol. 7073, pp. 41–69. Springer, Heidelberg (2011). https://doi.org/10.1007/978-3-642-25385-0_3

15. Boneh, D., Lynn, B., Shacham, H.: Short signatures from the Weil pairing. In: Boyd, C. (ed.) ASIACRYPT 2001. LNCS, vol. 2248, pp. 514–532. Springer, Heidelberg (2001). https://doi.org/10.1007/3-540-45682-1_30

16. Boneh, D., Zhandry, M.: Secure signatures and chosen ciphertext security in a quantum computing world. In: Canetti, R., Garay, J.A. (eds.) CRYPTO 2013, Part II. LNCS, vol. 8043, pp. 361–379. Springer, Heidelberg (2013). https://doi.org/10.1007/978-3-642-40084-1_21

17. Chatterjee, R., Chung, K.M., Liang, X., Malavolta, G.: A note on the post-quantum security of (ring) signatures. In: Hanaoka, G., Shikata, J., Watanabe, Y. (eds.) PKC 2022, Part II. LNCS, March 2022, vol. 13178, pp. 407–436. Springer, Heidelberg (2022). https://doi.org/10.1007/978-3-030-97131-1_14

18. Chatterjee, R., et al.: Compact ring signatures from learning with errors. In: Malkin, T., Peikert, C. (eds.) CRYPTO 2021, Part I. LNCS, vol. 12825, pp. 282–312. Springer, Cham (2021). https://doi.org/10.1007/978-3-030-84242-0_11

19. Chatterjee, S., Koblitz, N., Menezes, A., Sarkar, P.: Another look at tightness II: practical issues in cryptography. In: Phan, R.C.-W., Yung, M. (eds.) Mycrypt 2016. LNCS, vol. 10311, pp. 21–55. Springer, Cham (2017). https://doi.org/10.1007/978-3-319-61273-7_3

20. Chatterjee, S., Menezes, A., Sarkar, P.: Another look at tightness. In: Miri, A., Vaudenay, S. (eds.) SAC 2011. LNCS, vol. 7118, pp. 293–319. Springer, Heidelberg (2012). https://doi.org/10.1007/978-3-642-28496-0_18

21. Coron, J.-S.: On the exact security of full domain hash. In: Bellare, M. (ed.) CRYPTO 2000. LNCS, vol. 1880, pp. 229–235. Springer, Heidelberg (2000). https://doi.org/10.1007/3-540-44598-6_14

22. Devevey, J., Fallahpour, P., Passelègue, A., Stehlé, D.: A detailed analysis of Fiat-Shamir with aborts. In: Handschuh, H., Lysyanskaya, A. (eds) Advances in Cryptology, CRYPTO 2023. LNCS, vol. 14085, pp. 327–357. Springer, Cham (2023). https://doi.org/10.1007/978-3-031-38554-4_11

23. Devevey, J., Passelègue, A., Stehlé, D.: G+G: a Fiat-Shamir lattice signature based on convolved Gaussians. In: Guo, J., Steinfeld, R. (eds.) ASIACRYPT 2023, Part VII. LNCS, December 2023, vol. 14444, pp. 37–64. Springer, Heidelberg (2023). https://doi.org/10.1007/978-981-99-8739-9_2

24. Diemert, D., Gellert, K., Jager, T., Lyu, L.: Digital signatures with memory-tight security in the multi-challenge setting. In: Tibouchi, M., Wang, H. (eds.) ASIACRYPT 2021, Part IV. LNCS, vol. 13093, pp. 403–433. Springer, Cham (2021). https://doi.org/10.1007/978-3-030-92068-5_14

25. Dinur, I.: Tight time-space lower bounds for finding multiple collision pairs and their applications. In: Canteaut, A., Ishai, Y. (eds.) EUROCRYPT 2020, Part I. LNCS, vol. 12105, pp. 405–434. Springer, Cham (2020). https://doi.org/10.1007/978-3-030-45721-1_15

26. Doosti, M., Delavar, M., Kashefi, E., Arapinis, M.: A unified framework for quantum unforgeability. CoRR abs/2103.13994 (2021). https://arxiv.org/abs/2103.13994

27. Fiat, A., Shamir, A.: How To prove yourself: practical solutions to identification and signature problems. In: Odlyzko, A.M. (ed.) CRYPTO 1986. LNCS, vol. 263, pp. 186–194. Springer, Heidelberg (1987). https://doi.org/10.1007/3-540-47721-7_12

28. Gentry, C., Peikert, C., Vaikuntanathan, V.: Trapdoors for hard lattices and new cryptographic constructions. In: Ladner, R.E., Dwork, C. (eds.) STOC 2008, May 2008, pp. 197–206. ACM Press (2008). https://doi.org/10.1145/1374376.1374407

29. Ghoshal, A., Ghosal, R., Jaeger, J., Tessaro, S.: Hiding in plain sight: memory-tight proofs via randomness programming. In: Dunkelman, O., Dziembowski, S. (eds.) EUROCRYPT 2022, Part II. LNCS, May/June 2022, vol. 13276, pp. 706–735. Springer, Heidelberg (2022). https://doi.org/10.1007/978-3-031-07085-3_24

30. Ghoshal, A., Jaeger, J., Tessaro, S.: The memory-tightness of authenticated encryption. In: Micciancio, D., Ristenpart, T. (eds.) CRYPTO 2020, Part I. LNCS, vol. 12170, pp. 127–156. Springer, Cham (2020). https://doi.org/10.1007/978-3-030-56784-2_5

31. Ghoshal, A., Tessaro, S.: On the memory-tightness of hashed ElGamal. In: Canteaut, A., Ishai, Y. (eds.) EUROCRYPT 2020, Part II. LNCS, vol. 12106, pp. 33–62. Springer, Cham (2020). https://doi.org/10.1007/978-3-030-45724-2_2

32. Grilo, A.B., Hövelmanns, K., Hülsing, A., Majenz, C.: Tight adaptive reprogramming in the QROM. In: Tibouchi, M., Wang, H. (eds.) ASIACRYPT 2021, Part I. LNCS, vol. 13090, pp. 637–667. Springer, Cham (2021). https://doi.org/10.1007/978-3-030-92062-3_22

33. Jaeger, J., Kumar, A.: Memory-tight multi-challenge security of public-key encryption. In: Agrawal, S., Lin, D. (eds.) ASIACRYPT 2022, Part III. LNCS, December 2022, vol. 13793, pp. 454–484. Springer, Heidelberg (2022). https://doi.org/10.1007/978-3-031-22969-5_16

34. Kiltz, E., Lyubashevsky, V., Schaffner, C.: A concrete treatment of Fiat-Shamir signatures in the quantum random-oracle model. In: Nielsen, J.B., Rijmen, V. (eds.) EUROCRYPT 2018, Part III. LNCS, vol. 10822, pp. 552–586. Springer, Cham (2018). https://doi.org/10.1007/978-3-319-78372-7_18

35. Koblitz, N., Menezes, A.J.: Another look at "provable security". J. Cryptol. 20(1), 3–37 (2007). https://doi.org/10.1007/s00145-005-0432-z

36. Koblitz, N., Menezes, A.J.: The random oracle model: a twenty-year retrospective. Des. Codes Cryptogr. 77, 587–610 (2015). https://doi.org/10.1007/s10623-015-0094-2

37. Kosuge, H., Xagawa, K.: Probabilistic hash-and-sign with retry in the quantum random oracle model. In: PKC 2024 (2024, to appear). https://eprint.iacr.org/2022/1359

38. Lyubashevsky, V.: Fiat-Shamir with aborts: applications to lattice and factoring-based signatures. In: Matsui, M. (ed.) ASIACRYPT 2009. LNCS, vol. 5912, pp. 598–616. Springer, Heidelberg (2009). https://doi.org/10.1007/978-3-642-10366-7_35

39. Majenz, C., Manfouo, C.M., Ozols, M.: Quantum-access security of the Winternitz one-time signature scheme. In: Tessaro, S. (ed.) ITC 2021. LIPIcs, vol. 199, pp. 21:1–21:22. Schloss Dagstuhl - Leibniz-Zentrum für Informatik (2021). https://doi.org/10.4230/LIPICS.ITC.2021.21

40. M'Raïhi, D., Naccache, D., Pointcheval, D., Vaudenay, S.: Computational alternatives to random number generators. In: Tavares, S., Meijer, H. (eds.) SAC 1998. LNCS, vol. 1556, pp. 72–80. Springer, Heidelberg (1999). https://doi.org/10.1007/3-540-48892-8_6

41. Rivest, R.L., Shamir, A., Adleman, L.M.: A method for obtaining digital signatures and public-key cryptosystems. Commun. Assoc. Comput. Mach. **21**(2), 120–126 (1978). https://doi.org/10.1145/359340.359342

42. Wang, Y., Matsuda, T., Hanaoka, G., Tanaka, K.: Memory lower bounds of reductions revisited. In: Nielsen, J.B., Rijmen, V. (eds.) EUROCRYPT 2018. LNCS, vol. 10820, pp. 61–90. Springer, Cham (2018). https://doi.org/10.1007/978-3-319-78381-9_3

43. Yuan, Q., Tibouchi, M., Abe, M.: Quantum-access security of hash-based signature schemes. In: Simpson, L., Baee, M.A.R. (eds.) ACISP 2023. LNCS, July 2023, vol. 13915, pp. 343–380. Springer, Heidelberg (2023). https://doi.org/10.1007/978-3-031-35486-1_16

44. Zhandry, M.: How to construct quantum random functions. In: FOCS 2012, October 2012, pp. 679–687. IEEE Computer Society Press (2012). https://doi.org/10.1109/FOCS.2012.37

Key Exchange with Tight (Full) Forward Secrecy via Key Confirmation

Jiaxin Pan[1]([⊠]) , Doreen Riepel[2] , and Runzhi Zeng[3]

[1] University of Kassel, Kassel, Germany
`jiaxin.pan@uni-kassel.de`
[2] University of California San Diego, La Jolla, USA
`driepel@ucsd.edu`
[3] Norwegian University of Science and Technology, Trondheim, Norway
`runzhi.zeng@ntnu.no`

Abstract. Weak forward secrecy (wFS) of authenticated key exchange (AKE) protocols is a passive variant of (full) forward secrecy (FS). A natural mechanism to upgrade from wFS to FS is the use of key confirmation messages which compute a message authentication code (MAC) over the transcript. Unfortunately, Gellert, Gjøsteen, Jacobson and Jager (GGJJ, CRYPTO 2023) show that this mechanism inherently incurs a loss proportional to the number of users, leading to an overall non-tight reduction, even if wFS was established using a tight reduction.

Inspired by GGJJ, we propose a new notion, called one-way verifiable weak forward secrecy (OW-VwFS), and prove that OW-VwFS can be transformed *tightly* to FS using key confirmation in the random oracle model (ROM). To implement our generic transformation, we show that several tightly wFS AKE protocols additionally satisfy our OW-VwFS notion tightly. We highlight that using the recent lattice-based protocol from Pan, Wagner, and Zeng (CRYPTO 2023) can give us the first lattice-based tightly FS AKE via key confirmation in the classical random oracle model. Besides this, we also obtain a Decisional-Diffie-Hellman-based protocol that is considerably more efficient than the previous ones.

Finally, we lift our study on FS via key confirmation to the quantum random oracle model (QROM). While our security reduction is overall non-tight, it matches the best existing bound for wFS in the QROM (Pan, Wagner, and Zeng, ASIACRYPT 2023), namely, it is square-root-and session-tight. Our analysis is in the multi-challenge setting, and it is more realistic than the single-challenge setting as in Pan et al.

Keywords: Authenticated key exchange · forward secrecy · key confirmation · tight security · (quantum) random oracles

1 Introduction

Forward secrecy (FS) is an essential security requirement for authenticated key exchange (AKE) protocols. It states that even if an active adversary corrupts a

© International Association for Cryptologic Research 2024
M. Joye and G. Leander (Eds.): EUROCRYPT 2024, LNCS 14657, pp. 59–89, 2024.
https://doi.org/10.1007/978-3-031-58754-2_3

user's long-term secret key, all session keys agreed before should remain secret to the adversary. A weaker form of FS is called weak FS (wFS), where an adversary is not allowed to perform active attacks, namely, it does not actively interfere with the protocol transcripts of the session that it attacks.

Key confirmation is simple and arguably the most efficient way in achieving FS and has been used in many works, e.g., [10,15,24]. Essentially, it generically transforms an AKE protocol with wFS to FS. More precisely, two parties firstly run a wFS AKE protocol to agree on a session key k, and then they exchange key confirmation messages derived from k. These messages are usually message authentication codes (MAC) on the protocol transcripts using k as the MAC key. Apart from key confirmation, one can use a digital signature scheme to sign a passively secure key exchange protocol as in the signed Diffie-Hellman protocol [19,27] to provide FS. Considering that using a MAC or hash function is much more efficient than digital signatures, the signature-based approach is often inefficient and less desirable.

SECURITY MODELS FOR AKE. Defining the security for AKE protocols is a complex task, and there are many different security models for AKE (e.g., [3,7,25]). In this paper, we consider active adversaries that can modify, drop, or inject some messages. Moreover, they may adaptively corrupt users' long-term secret keys via CORR oracle and reveal session keys via REVEAL oracle. Some of the models even allow adversaries to learn ephemeral states (which are usually randomness in generating protocol messages) via REV-STATE oracle. We formalize key secrecy via TEST, where an adversary $\mathcal{A}$ chooses a *fresh* session, receives either a real or random key for it, and shall distinguish between the two. We consider the single-bit guessing, multi-challenge security, namely, $\mathcal{A}$ can query TEST multiple times and each time TEST responds using the same bit in deciding real or random. Composability for this notion was initially proven for password-based key exchange [1], and we refer to [21] for further discussion on why this is the realistic and meaningful notion. For forward secrecy, keys of these TEST-sessions must be computed before CORR is queried to either parties of a TEST-session. Depending on the type of forward secrecy, freshness is defined differently. If it is wFS, then $\mathcal{A}$ must perform only passive attacks on this fresh session. Otherwise, $\mathcal{A}$ can perform active attacks, for instance, modify or inject some messages.

SECURITY LOSS FOR FS VIA KEY CONFIRMATION. The complexity of AKE models makes it challenging to prove security of an AKE protocol, in particular, giving tight security proofs for AKE. The security of modern cryptographic protocols is often proven by reductions. A reduction $\mathcal{R}$ uses an adversary $\mathcal{A}$ against protocol Π to break the security of the underlying primitive P. By doing so, we can conclude the concrete security bound, $\varepsilon_{\mathcal{A}} \leq \ell \cdot \varepsilon_{\mathcal{R}}$, where $\varepsilon_{\mathcal{A}}$ and $\varepsilon_{\mathcal{R}}$ are the success probability of $\mathcal{A}$ and $\mathcal{R}$, respectively. ℓ is called the security loss. Assuming $\mathcal{A}$ and $\mathcal{R}$ have roughly the same running time, if ℓ is a small constant, we say protocol Π has tight security, and non-tight security, otherwise. A tight security reduction is highly desirable, since it allows protocols to be instantiated with optimal parameters without compensation for the security loss.

A natural question to ask is whether the key confirmation approach preserves the tightness of the underlying wFS AKE. Due to its high efficiency, it would be ideal to have an affirmative answer to this question, since it means that we do not need to increase the security parameter of the wFS AKE to compensate any security loss.

Intuitively, there should not be a tightness loss when going from wFS to FS, which was even falsely claimed by the work of Cohn-Gordon et al. [10] previously. At CRYPTO 2023, Gellert, Gjøsteen, Jacobsen, and Jager (GGJJ) [18] identified a flaw in [10] and proposed a fix by using a selective variant of wFS (called selective key secrecy in [18]). The selective wFS is essentially the same as wFS, except that an adversary $\mathcal{A}$ has to select a user of which $\mathcal{A}$ will not corrupt the long-term secret key. Unfortunately, when we construct a reduction $\mathcal{R}$ to prove FS based on this selective wFS, $\mathcal{R}$ has to guess the non-corrupted user, which leads to a security loss of $O(\mu)$ where μ is the maximal number of users. This security loss is proven to be inherent (and thus optimal) in [18] when starting from a wFS AKE with key indistinguishability.

However, a linear loss in the number of users is undesirable, since in the real world the number of users can be massive. According to the impossibility result in [10], it seems inherent to have this security loss. Hence, it motivates us to propose a different modularization that potentially requires strong security for the underlying wFS AKE in achieving tight FS.

1.1 Our Contribution I: Tight Forward Secrecy via Key Confirmation

We revise the security proof for the wFS-to-FS transformation.

TIGHT FS FROM VERIFIABLE WFS. We propose a new variant of wFS, called One-Wayness against key Verification attacks and weak Forward Secrecy (OW-VwFS). In the OW-VwFS security game, an adversary has the same capability as in the usual wFS game, but additionally it can verify whether a session key is the valid one of a particular session. Hence, the adversary capability of OW-VwFS is stronger than that of wFS and it is the main reason why we bypass the optimality result from Gellert et al. [18]. In terms of security goals, OW-VwFS is weaker than wFS, namely, OW-VwFS only requires an adversary cannot compute the session key of a fresh session, while wFS requires a session key to be indistinguishable from a random key.

Using key confirmation, we prove that OW-VwFS *tightly* implies FS in the random oracle model. Our transformation is the same as the standard wFS-to-FS transformation, but ours preserves the tightness of the underlying OW-VwFS protocol, and it enables tight FS in contrast to the selective notion in [18]. An important consequence of our work is that the future AKE design can aim at OW-VwFS, since its transformation to FS is the same as the standard wFS-to-FS one, but tightness-preserving. Moreover, our analysis considers security against (ephemeral) state reveals. Such a strong form of attacks was not considered in the work of Gellert et al. [18], which is why we bypass their impossibility.

CONSTRUCTING (TIGHTLY) VERIFIABLE WFS. Furthermore, we show that several tightly wFS protocols satisfy our new OW-VwFS notion tightly, in particular, the lattice-based protocol of Pan, Wagner, and Zeng [30][1]. Subsequently, this yields the *first* AKE protocol with tight FS from lattices.

Essentially, we show that a One-Way Checkable against Chosen-Ciphertext Attacks (OW-ChCCA) [30] secure key encapsulation mechanism (KEM) tightly implies a OW-VwFS AKE protocol. Once again, our analysis allows adversaries to reveal ephemeral state in the AKE protocol. Roughly speaking, the OW-ChCCA game is a multi-user, multi-challenge variant of the standard IND-CCA game: Besides the oracles provided by the standard IND-CCA security, it allows adversaries to corrupt some of the user's decryption keys and decrypt some of the challenge ciphertexts, and, most importantly, it allows an adversary to check if a key is valid with respect to a ciphertext. The adversary goal is to invert a fresh challenge ciphertext. As shown in [30], we can construct OW-ChCCA KEM tightly from the Decisional Diffie-Hellman (DDH) and Learning-With-Errors (LWE) assumptions, respectively. As a technical note, our proof requires only a slightly weaker version of OW-ChCCA, where adversaries are not allowed to ask for a decryption, but to verify whether a ciphertext can be decapsulated.

EFFICIENCY COMPARISON AMONG DDH-BASED PROTOCOLS. Besides having the first lattice-based AKE with tight FS, we also obtain the most efficient DDH-based protocol against state reveal attacks. In Table 1, we compare efficiency among well-known DDH-based AKE with tight or "optimal" tight FS (namely, with security loss $O(\mu)$) to show the practicality of our work. Our estimation focuses on communication and computation complexity for both parties to agree on a session key. For computation complexity, we only count the number of exponentiations, since they are the most costly operations. For concrete efficiency, we instantiate the protocols at 128-bit security and assume that the number of users $\mu \approx 2^{30}$. This is about the number of monthly active users in a social media app[2]. We instantiate the fully tight protocols with a NIST P256 curve and "optimal" tight ones with a NIST P384 (since they require a 158-bit hard DLog assumption). Our benchmarks for an exponentiation in a P256 and P384 are 0.5 ms and 1 ms, using Apple M1 Max, 32GB of RAM and macOS Ventura 13.3.1 (a).

We observe that the DDH-based non-committing KEM in [21] is tightly OW-ChCCA secure (cf. [30, Footnote 1]). Our analysis shows that the wFS JKRS in [21] is tightly OW-VwFS, and after adding key confirmation to the wFS JKRS in [21] we get JKRS$_{KC}$ that is tightly FS. According to Table 1, our tight security proofs allow one to implement JKRS$_{KC}$ with about 30% shorter transcripts and 50% faster speed than the one with the "optimal", non-tight proofs in [18] at 128-bit security. Considering security against State Reveals, JKRS$_{KC}$ is the

---

[1] Their lattice-based protocol is almost tight (similar to [9]), since it needs to lose a factor of $O(\lambda)$ to the LWE assumption, where λ is the security parameter. We call it tight as well, but specify the concrete loss in our theorems and proofs.

[2] Cf. https://www.statista.com/statistics/264810/number-of-monthly-active-facebook-users-worldwide/.

Table 1. Comparison of Diffie-Hellman-based AKE protocols with (tight or "optimal" tight) FS. Concrete efficiency is estimated for 128-bit security. "JKRS$_{KC}$ [18]" is transforming the implicitly authenticated JKRS [21] via key confirmation. We estimate its efficiency, according to the "optimal", non-tight security bound by Gellert et al. [18]. The last row is the same construction as the second last one, but with our tight security proof (cf. Theorem 4). In the upper arrows, schemes are using signatures, and we estimate the concrete bytes with the most efficient signature scheme in [13]. **Comm.** counts values exchanged during the protocol execution. $\mathbb{G}$ counts the number of group elements, H the number of hashes or MACs, 'Sign' the number of signatures, and 'other' the additional data in bits. **Bytes** counts total data in bytes by instantiating $\mathbb{G}$ with NIST P256 or P384 (for the non-tight JKRS$_{KC}$). **Exp.** counts the total numbers of exponentiation (which is the most costly computation in an AKE protocol) from both parties in agreeing a session key, and **Time** is the estimated time of computing those exponentiation in milliseconds.

Protocol	Comm. ($\mathbb{G}, H$, Sign, other)	Bytes	Exp.	Time (ms)	#Msg.	State Reveal	Security loss
TLS 1.3 [11,14]	$(2,2,2,512)$	384	32	16	3	no	$O(1)$
GJ [19]	$(2,1,2,0)$	288	32	16	3	no	$O(1)$
LLGW [26]	$(3,0,2,0)$	288	35	17.5	2	no	$O(1)$
JKRS [21]	$(5,1,1,0)$	288	29	14.5	2	yes	$O(1)$
PQR [27]	$(2,0,2,0)$	256	32	16	2	no	$O(1)$
CCGJJ$_{KC}$ [10]	$(2,2,0,0)$	160	8	8	3	no	$O(\mu)$
JKRS$_{KC}$ [18]	$(5,2,0,0)$	304	15	15	3	yes	$O(\mu)$
JKRS$_{KC}$ (Ours)	$(5,2,0,0)$	224	15	7.5	3	yes	$O(1)$

most efficient DDH-based protocol, due to our tight security proofs. It is worth mentioning that the CCGJJ$_{KC}$ has shorter protocol transcripts, but it is insecure under State Reveals.

Interestingly, although the signature-based JKRS uses relatively inefficient primitives as signatures, its tight security proof allows an instantiation that is slightly more efficient than the non-tight, signature-less JKRS (namely, JKRS$_{KC}$ with proofs in [18]).

RELATION TO THE WORK OF GELLERT ET AL. [18]. We circumvent the impossibility result of Gellert et al. [18] by using a different wFS notion, OW-VwFS, and random oracles. As discussed earlier, the key checking oracle makes our notion stronger. The security definition in [18] does not have such an oracle and thus their impossibility result does not apply to our proof. At the same time, we opted for the weakest definition which allows a tight reduction (i.e., one-wayness and also no Reveal oracle), which makes our definition and that of [18] incomparable (neither implies the other). Moreover, their impossibility is in the standard model, while ours is in the random oracle model. For these reasons, our results do not contradict the impossibility result in [18], but rather provides an alternative way to prove security while enabling full tightness.

1.2   Our Contribution II: Forward Secrecy via Key Confirmation in the QROM

Our second contribution is proposing the first security proof for FS via key confirmation in the quantum random oracle model (QROM) [6], where a quantum adversary can have quantum access to the hash function. Our analysis considers the KEM-based AKE protocol (via key confirmation) and assumes a Multi-User, Multi-Challenge Chosen-Ciphertext Attacks (MUC-CCA) KEM and a Multi-Challenge CCA (MC-CCA) KEM. The main reason of doing so is that we do not know how to tightly prove OW-VwFS implies FS in the QROM, since it will trigger the Oneway-to-Hiding Lemma [32] and lead to a square-root-loss such as $\sqrt{\varepsilon}$, where ε is the advantage of breaking the underlying KEM. We still think that our tight lattice-based protocol in the classical ROM is interesting, since it is the first protocol with tight FS from post-quantum assumptions. Of course, one may alternatively rephrase our analysis in the classical ROM with the suitable KEMs, but it may lower the readability. More importantly, our OW-VwFS notion is more generic and gives more freedom to designers to construct their OW-VwFS protocols that will lead to FS in a tightness-preserving manner.

Our security bound in the QROM is unfortunately non-tight. More precisely, ignoring the statistically negligible terms, **our security bound for FS** in the QROM is

$$\varepsilon_{\mathsf{FS}}^{\mathsf{our}} \leq O(\mu) \cdot \varepsilon_{\text{MC-CCA}} + O(1) \cdot \varepsilon_{\text{MUC-CCA}}. \tag{1}$$

where μ is the number of users, $\varepsilon_{\text{MC-CCA}}$ is the advantage of MC-CCA, and $\varepsilon_{\text{MUC-CCA}}$ is that of MUC-CCA. It matches the best known bound for wFS in the QROM proposed by Pan, Wagner, and Zeng (PWZ) [31]. In this sense our FS bound preserves the tightness of the KEM-based AKE protocol with wFS. It is worth mentioning that, as shown in [31], we can tightly instantiate MC-CCA and MUC-CCA from the LWE assumption in the QROM.

We also improve PWZ's analysis in the sense that their analysis considers only one single TEST query, but our security bound (as stated in Eq. (1)) is established in the context of multiple challenges, where an adversary is allowed to query TEST multiple times. The multi-challenge setting is more realistic and well-established for public-key primitives [2,10,16,17], since in the real world, an adversary usually wants to attack multiple instances of a primitives. Although the security bound of PWZ can be extended to the multi-TEST setting with a multiplicative factor t (which is the number of TEST-queries), ours does not need to lose such a factor. In practice, t can be up to the total number of established sessions, which can be much larger than the number of users. We stress that the analysis of PWZ is only for wFS, and transforming it to FS, it may lose another multiplicative factor μ by applying the analysis of GGJJ [18]. Hence, combining the analysis of PWZ and GGJJ leads to a bound for FS in the QROM as

$$\varepsilon_{\mathsf{FS}}^{\mathsf{PWZ \ \& \ GGJJ}} \leq O(\mu^2 t) \cdot \varepsilon_{\text{MC-CCA}} + O(\mu t) \cdot \varepsilon_{\text{MUC-CCA}}. \tag{2}$$

Strictly speaking, the bound above is only an estimation and not theoretically sound, since the analysis of GGJJ is in the classical setting. Their bound may change, if an adversary can query the hash function or key derivation function with a quantum state.

MORE RELATED WORK IN THE QROM. Another work on the KEM-based AKE protocol in the QROM is due to Hövelmanns, Kiltz, Schäge, and Unruh [20], and it has a square-root-loss, namely, its security bound is

$$O(S^2 + S \cdot \mu) \cdot \left(\varepsilon_{\text{CPA}} + \sqrt{Q \cdot \varepsilon_{\text{CPA}}} \right), \tag{3}$$

where S, μ, and Q are the numbers of total sessions, users, and random oracle queries, respectively, and ε_{CPA} is the advantage of breaking the underlying CPA secure PKE. Similar to the work of PWZ, Eq. (3) is only for wFS and in the single-TEST setting. Upgrading to FS in the multi-TEST setting requires an additional multiplicative loss in μt. It is usually less desirable to have the square-root-loss as in Eq. (3), since it reduces the security guarantee of the underlying PKE in half.

2 Preliminaries

For $n \in \mathbb{N}$, let $[n] = \{1, \ldots, n\}$. For a finite set $\mathcal{S}$, we denote the sampling of a uniform random element x by $x \xleftarrow{\$} \mathcal{S}$. By $[\![B]\!]$ we denote the bit that is 1 if the evaluation of the Boolean statement B is **true** and 0 otherwise.

ALGORITHMS. For an algorithm $\mathcal{A}$ which takes x as input, we denote its computation by $y := \mathcal{A}(x)$ if $\mathcal{A}$ is deterministic, and $y \leftarrow \mathcal{A}(x)$ if $\mathcal{A}$ is probabilistic. We assume all the algorithms (including adversaries) in this paper to be probabilistic unless stated differently. We denote an algorithm $\mathcal{A}$ with access to an oracle O by $\mathcal{A}^{\text{O}}$. In terms of running time, if a reduction's running time t' is dominated by that of an adversary t (more precisely, $t' = t + s$ where $s \ll t$), we write $t' \approx t$.

GAMES. We use code-based games [4] to present our definitions and proofs. We implicitly assume all Boolean flags to be initialized to 0 (**false**), numerical variables to 0, sets to $\emptyset$ and strings to $\bot$. We make the convention that a procedure terminates once it has returned an output. $G^{\mathcal{A}} \Rightarrow b$ denotes the final (Boolean) output b of game G running adversary $\mathcal{A}$, and if $b = 1$ we say $\mathcal{A}$ wins G. The randomness in $\Pr[G^{\mathcal{A}} \Rightarrow 1]$ is over all random coins in game G. More generically, we write $\Pr[\text{Event} : G]$ to denote the probability that Event happens in the game G. If the context is clear, we simply write it as $\Pr[\text{Event}]$. Within a procedure, "**abort**" means that we terminate the run of an adversary $\mathcal{A}$.

3 Three-Message Authenticated Key Exchange

We recall the AKE security model from [21] and adapt it to three-message protocols. A three-message key exchange protocol AKE := (Setup, Gen$_{\text{AKE}}$, Init$_{\text{I}}$, Init$_{\text{R}}$, Der$_{\text{I}}$, Der$_{\text{R}}$) consists of five algorithms which are executed interactively by two parties as shown in Fig. 1.

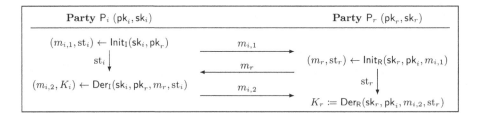

Fig. 1. Running a three-message AKE protocol between two parties.

Setup is the setup algorithm for the system parameters. We denote the party which initiates the session by P_i and the party which responds to the session by P_r. The key generation algorithm $\mathsf{Gen}_{\mathsf{AKE}}$ outputs a key pair $(\mathsf{pk}, \mathsf{sk})$ for one party. The initiator's initialization algorithm Init_I inputs the initiator's long-term secret key sk_i and the responder's long-term public key pk_r, and outputs a message $m_{i,1}$ and the initiator's state st_i. The responder's initialization algorithm Init_R inputs the responder's long-term secret key sk_r and the initiator's long-term public key pk_i, and outputs a message m_r and the responder's state st_r. The initiator's derivation algorithm Der_I takes as input $\mathsf{sk}_i, \mathsf{pk}_r$, a message m_r and the state st_i. It computes the final message $m_{i,2}$ and a session key K. The responder's derivation algorithm Der_R takes as input the $\mathsf{sk}_r, \mathsf{pk}_i$, a message $m_{i,2}$ and the state st_r. It computes the session key K. Here K can be $\perp$ meaning that the session is rejected during the execution. Correctness of an AKE protocol states that an honest execution between two parties should yield the same session key.

Definition 1 (Correctness of three-message AKE). *Let* AKE $:=$ (Setup, $\mathsf{Gen}_{\mathsf{AKE}}$, Init_I, Init_R, Der_I, Der_R) *be a three-message AKE protocol. We say* AKE *is ρ-correct if*

$$\Pr\left[K_i = K_r \neq \perp : \begin{array}{l} \mathsf{par} \leftarrow \mathsf{Setup}(1^\lambda), \\ (\mathsf{pk}_i, \mathsf{sk}_i) \leftarrow \mathsf{Gen}_{\mathsf{AKE}}(\mathsf{par}), (\mathsf{pk}_r, \mathsf{sk}_r) \leftarrow \mathsf{Gen}_{\mathsf{AKE}}(\mathsf{par}), \\ (m_{i,1}, \mathsf{st}_i) \leftarrow \mathsf{Init}_I(\mathsf{sk}_i, \mathsf{pk}_r), \\ (m_r, \mathsf{st}_r) \leftarrow \mathsf{Init}_R(\mathsf{sk}_r, \mathsf{pk}_i, m_{i,1}), \\ (m_{i,2}, K_i) \leftarrow \mathsf{Der}_I(\mathsf{sk}_i, \mathsf{pk}_r, m_r, \mathsf{st}_i), \\ K_r := \mathsf{Der}_R(\mathsf{sk}_r, \mathsf{pk}_i, m_{i,2}, \mathsf{st}_r) \end{array}\right] \geq \rho,$$

where the probability is taken over the randomness of Setup, $\mathsf{Gen}_{\mathsf{AKE}}$, Init_I, Init_R, *and* Der_I.

We give a security game written in pseudocode focusing on (full) forward secrecy, rather than implicit or explicit authentication. We refer readers to [12] for more details on different types of authentication for key exchange protocols, and their connections to forward secrecy in [18].

EXECUTION ENVIRONMENT. We consider μ parties $P_1, \ldots, P_\mu$ with long-term key pairs $(\mathsf{pk}_n, \mathsf{sk}_n)$, $n \in [\mu]$. When two parties A and B want to communicate, the initiator, say, A first creates a session. To identify this session, we increase the

Fig. 2. Games IND-FS and IND-FS-St for AKE. REV-STATE is only available in IND-FS-St. In IND-FS, $\mathcal{A}$ has access to oracles $O := \{\text{SESSION}_I, \text{SESSION}_R, \text{DER}_I, \text{DER}_R, \text{REVEAL}, \text{CORR}, \text{TEST}\}$. In IND-FS-St, $\mathcal{A}$ has access to the oracles in IND-FS and the REV-STATE oracle. Helper procedures FRESH and VALID are defined in Fig. 3. If there exists any test session which is neither fresh nor valid, the game will return b.

global identification number sID and assign the current state of sID to identify this session owned by A. The state of sID will increase after every assignment. Moreover, a message will be sent to the responder. The responder then similarly creates a corresponding session which is assigned the current state of sID. Hence each conversation includes two sessions. We then define variables in relation to the identifier sID:

- Init[sID] $\in [\mu]$ denotes the initiator of the session.
- Resp[sID] $\in [\mu]$ denotes the responder of the session.
- Type[sID] $\in \{$"In", "Re"$\}$ denotes the session's view, i. e. whether the initiator or the responder computes the session key.

$\text{FRESH}(sID^*)$

00 $\mathfrak{M}(sID^*) := \text{MATCH}(sID^*)$

01 **if** $\text{revSK}[sID^*]$ **or**

    $(\exists sID \in \mathfrak{M}(sID^*) : \text{revSK}[sID] = \textbf{true})$

02   **return false**

03 **if** $\exists sID \in \mathfrak{M}(sID^*)$ s.t. $sID \in \mathcal{S}_{\text{test}}$

04   **return false**

05 **return true**

$\text{VALID}(sID^*)$

06 $\mathfrak{M}(sID^*) := \text{MATCH}(sID^*)$

07 $\mathfrak{P}(sID^*) := \text{PARTIALMATCH}(sID^*)$

08 **if** $|\mathfrak{M}(sID^*)| > 1$ **or** $|\mathfrak{P}(sID^*)| > 1$ **return true**

09 **for** attack $\in$ Table 2 **and** attack $\in$ [28, Table 4]

10   **if** attack = **true return true**

11 **return false**

$\text{MATCH}(sID^*)$ //matching sessions

12 $\mathfrak{M}(sID^*) := \{sID \mid (\text{Init}[sID], \text{Resp}[sID]) = (\text{Init}[sID^*], \text{Resp}[sID^*]) \wedge (\text{Msg}_{\text{I},1}[sID], \text{Msg}_{\text{R}}[sID],$
    $\text{Msg}_{\text{I},2}[sID]) = (\text{Msg}_{\text{I},1}[sID^*], \text{Msg}_{\text{R}}[sID^*], \text{Msg}_{\text{I},2}[sID^*]) \wedge \text{Type}[sID] \neq \text{Type}[sID^*]\}$

13 **return** $\mathfrak{M}(sID^*)$

$\text{PARTIALMATCH}(sID^*)$ //partially matching sessions

14 $\mathfrak{P}(sID^*) := \{sID \mid (\text{Init}[sID], \text{Resp}[sID]) = (\text{Init}[sID^*], \text{Resp}[sID^*]) \wedge (\text{Msg}_{\text{I},1}[sID], \text{Msg}_{\text{R}}[sID]) =$
    $(\text{Msg}_{\text{I},1}[sID^*], \text{Msg}_{\text{R}}[sID^*]) \wedge \text{Type}[sID] \neq \text{Type}[sID^*] \wedge \text{Type}[sID] = \text{"Re"}\}$

15 **return** $\mathfrak{P}(sID^*)$

Fig. 3. Helper procedures FRESH and VALID for games IND-FS and IND-FS-St defined in Fig. 2. Procedure FRESH checks if the adversary performed some trivial attack. In procedure VALID, each attack is evaluated by the set of variables in attack tables and checks if an allowed attack was performed. The attack table for IND-FS is shown in Table 2 and the table for game IND-FS-St is given in [28, Table 4], where the latter includes session-state reveal attacks. If the values of the variables are set as in the corresponding row, the attack was performed, i.e. attack = **true**, and thus the session is valid.

- $\text{Msg}_{\text{I},1}[sID]$ denotes the first message that was computed by the initiator.
- $\text{Msg}_{\text{R}}[sID]$ denotes the message that was computed by the responder.
- $\text{Msg}_{\text{I},2}[sID]$ denotes the final message that was computed by the initiator.
- $\text{ST}[sID]$ denotes the (secret) state information, i.e. ephemeral secret keys.
- $\text{SK}[sID]$ denotes the session key. If the session terminates without a valid session key, we set this variable to the special string "reject".

To establish a session between two parties, the adversary is given access to oracles SESSION$_\text{I}$ and SESSION$_\text{R}$, where the first one starts a session of type "In" and the second one of type "Re". In order to complete a session, oracles DER$_\text{I}$ and DER$_\text{R}$ have to be queried. The adversary has also access to oracles CORR, REVEAL and REV-STATE to obtain secret information. (The latter is only available if state reveal attacks are considered.) We use the following boolean values to keep track of which queries the adversary made:

- $\text{cor}[n]$ denotes whether the long-term secret key of party P_n was given to the adversary.
- $\text{peerPreCor}[sID]$ denotes whether the peer of the session was corrupted and its long-term key was given to the adversary *before* the owner's session key was computed, which is important for forward security.
- $\text{revST}[sID]$ denotes whether the session state was given to the adversary.
- $\text{revSK}[sID]$ denotes whether the session key was given to the adversary.

The adversary can forward messages between sessions or modify them. By that, we can define the relationship between two sessions:

- **Matching Session**: Two sessions sID and sID′ *match* if the same parties are involved, the messages sent and received are the same they are of different types (cf. line 12 in Fig. 3).
- **Partially Matching Session**: A session sID has a *partially matching* session sID′ if the same parties are involved, the messages sent and received are the same without considering the last message and they are of different types, where sID′ is of type "Re" (cf. line 14 in Fig. 3).

Finally, the adversary is given access to oracle TEST which can be queried multiple times and which will return either the session key of the specified session or a uniformly random key. We use one bit b for all queries, and store test sessions in a set $\mathcal{S}_{\text{test}}$. For each test session, we require that the adversary does not issue queries such that the session key can be trivially computed. In Fig. 3 we define the properties of freshness and validity which all test sessions have to satisfy:

- **Freshness**: A (test) session is called *fresh* if the session key was not revealed. Furthermore, if there exists a matching session, we require that this session's key is not revealed and that this session is not also a test session.
- **Validity**: A (test) session is called *valid* if it is fresh and the adversary performed any attack which is defined in the security model. For game IND-FS-St, we capture this with attacks listed in our full paper [28, Table 4]. For game IND-FS, we use Table 2 to capture valid attacks.

If the protocol does not use appropriate randomness, it should not be considered secure. In this case, there can be multiple matching sessions to a test session, which an adversary can take advantage of. We capture this as part of the validity property (cf. line 08). For an honest run of the protocol, the underlying min-entropy ensures that this attack will only happen with negligible probability.

We define validity of different attack strategies in Table 2, using variables to indicate which queries the adversary may (not) make. The purpose is to make our proofs precise by listing all the possible and non-trivial attacks. Attacks covered in the IND-FS model capture *forward secrecy* (FS) and *key compromise impersonation* (KCI) attacks. We provide a more detailed description of Table 2 and the full table for IND-FS-St in our full paper [28, Appendix B]. For all test sessions, at least one attack has to evaluate to true. Then, the adversary wins if he distinguishes the session keys from uniformly random keys which he obtains through queries to the TEST oracle.

Definition 2 (Key Indistinguishability of AKE). *We define games* IND-FS *and* IND-FS-St *as in Figs. 2 and 3. We say* AKE *is* $(t, \varepsilon, \mu, S, T, Q_{\text{COR}})$-IND-FS-*secure resp.* $(t', \varepsilon', \mu, S, T, Q_{\text{COR}}, Q_{\text{ST}})$-IND-FS-St-*secure if for all adversaries* $\mathcal{A}$ *attacking the protocol in time t resp. t' with μ users, S sessions, T test queries, Q_{COR} corruptions, and Q_{ST} state reveals, we have*

$$\left| \Pr[\text{IND-FS}_{\text{AKE}}^{\mathcal{A}} \Rightarrow 1] - \frac{1}{2} \right| \leq \varepsilon \quad resp. \quad \left| \Pr[\text{IND-FS-St}_{\text{AKE}}^{\mathcal{A}} \Rightarrow 1] - \frac{1}{2} \right| \leq \varepsilon' .$$

Table 2. Table of attacks for adversaries against three-message protocols with FS. An attack is regarded as an AND conjunction of variables with specified values as shown in the each line, where "–" means that this variable can take arbitrary value and **F** means "false". This table is obtained from [28, Table 3] by excluding all trivial attacks.

	$\mathcal{A}$ gets (Initiator, Responder)	$\mathsf{cor}[i^*]$	$\mathsf{cor}[r^*]$	$\mathsf{peerPreCor}[\mathsf{sID}^*]$	$\mathsf{Type}[\mathsf{sID}^*]$	$\|\mathfrak{M}(\mathsf{sID}^*)\|$	$\|\mathfrak{R}(\mathsf{sID}^*)\|$
1	**(long-term, long-term)**	–	–	–	"In"	–	1
2	**(long-term, long-term)**	–	–	–	"Re"	1	–
5	**(long-term, long-term)**	–	–	**F**	"In"	–	0
6	**(long-term, long-term)**	–	–	**F**	"Re"	0	–

Note that if there exists a session which is neither fresh nor valid, the game outputs the bit b, which implies that $\Pr[\mathsf{IND\text{-}FS}^{\mathcal{A}}_{\mathsf{AKE}} \Rightarrow 1] = \frac{1}{2}$ or $\Pr[\mathsf{IND\text{-}FS\text{-}St}^{\mathcal{A}}_{\mathsf{AKE}} \Rightarrow 1] = \frac{1}{2}$, giving the adversary an advantage equal to 0. This captures that an adversary will not gain any advantage by performing a trivial attack.

4   Verifiable Authenticated Key Exchange

To build a tightly secure three-message AKE protocol with key confirmation from a two-message AKE protocol, we define two security notions of the two-message protocol: The first one is <u>O</u>ne-<u>W</u>ay against key <u>V</u>erification attacks and <u>w</u>eak <u>F</u>orward <u>S</u>ecrecy, or OW-VwFS for short, and the second one is OW-VwFS with <u>st</u>ate-reveal attacks, or OW-VwFS-St for short.

We define the syntax of a two-message key exchange protocol in a similar fashion as the three-message AKE. Let $\mathsf{AKE}' := (\mathsf{Setup}', \mathsf{Gen}', \mathsf{Init}'_\mathsf{I}, \mathsf{Init}'_\mathsf{R}, \mathsf{Der}'_\mathsf{I})$, where Setup', Gen' and $\mathsf{Init}'_\mathsf{I}$ are defined exactly as in the three-message protocol. instead of a state, the responder's algorithm $\mathsf{Init}'_\mathsf{R}$ computes a session key K. The initiator's algorithm Der'_I does not output a second message, but only the session key. Correctness is defined similarly to the three-message case.

Definition 3 (Correctness of two-message AKE). *Let* $\mathsf{AKE}' := (\mathsf{Setup}', \mathsf{Gen}', \mathsf{Init}'_\mathsf{I}, \mathsf{Init}'_\mathsf{R}, \mathsf{Der}'_\mathsf{I})$ *be an AKE protocol. We say* AKE' *is* ρ*-correct if*

$$
\Pr\left[K_i = K_r \neq \bot :
\begin{array}{l}
\mathsf{par}' \leftarrow \mathsf{Setup}'(1^\lambda), \\
(\mathsf{pk}_i, \mathsf{sk}_i) \leftarrow \mathsf{Gen}'(\mathsf{par}), (\mathsf{pk}_r, \mathsf{sk}_r) \leftarrow \mathsf{Gen}'(\mathsf{par}), \\
(m_i, \mathsf{st}_i) \leftarrow \mathsf{Init}'_\mathsf{I}(\mathsf{sk}_i, \mathsf{pk}_r), \\
(m_r, K_r) \leftarrow \mathsf{Init}'_\mathsf{R}(\mathsf{sk}_r, \mathsf{pk}_i, m_i), \\
K_i := \mathsf{Der}'_\mathsf{I}(\mathsf{sk}_i, \mathsf{pk}_r, m_r, \mathsf{st}_i)
\end{array}
\right] \geq \rho,
$$

where the probability is taken over the randomness of Setup', Gen', $\mathsf{Init}'_\mathsf{I}$, *and* $\mathsf{Init}'_\mathsf{R}$.

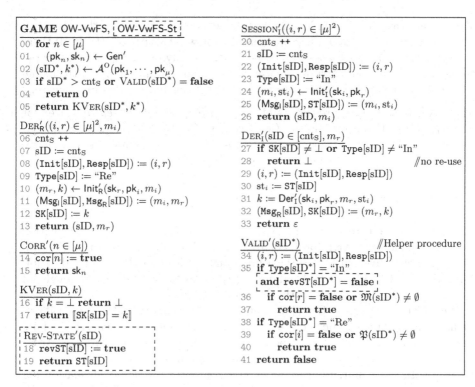

Fig. 4. Games OW-VwFS (without dashed boxes) and OW-VwFS-St (including dashed boxes) for AKE'. $\mathcal{A}$ has access to oracles $O := \{\text{SESSION}'_\text{I}, \text{DER}'_\text{R}, \text{DER}'_\text{I}, \text{CORR}', \text{KVER}\}$. In OW-VwFS-St, $\mathcal{A}$ also has access to REV-STATE'. In two-message AKE, responder sessions do not have state. So, REV-STATE'(sID) will return $\perp$ if sID is a responder session. Further, partially matching session is defined as $\mathfrak{P}(\text{sID}^*) := \{\text{sID} \mid \text{Type}[\text{sID}] = \text{"In"} \wedge (\text{Init}[\text{sID}], \text{Resp}[\text{sID}]) = (\text{Init}[\text{sID}^*], \text{Resp}[\text{sID}^*]) \wedge \text{Msg}_\text{I}[\text{sID}] = \text{Msg}_\text{I}[\text{sID}^*]\}$.

OW-VwFS is similar to the standard weak forward secrecy, but an adversary is additionally allowed to check if a key corresponds to some generated transcripts. The security notion OW-VwFS-St, based on OW-VwFS, allows the adversary to reveal session states. Moreover, these two security notions do not have REVEAL and TEST oracles. Our notion is motivated by the one-wayness against honest and key verification attacks in [27], but it is stronger in the sense that it allows active attacks. These are formally defined by Definition 4 with security games OW-VwFS and OW-VwFS-St as in Fig. 4.

Definition 4 (OW-VwFS and OW-VwFS-St security). *A two-message authenticated key exchange protocol* AKE' *is* $(t, \varepsilon, \mu, S, Q_{\text{COR}}, Q_{Ver})$-OW-VwFS *secure resp.* $(t', \varepsilon', \mu, S, Q_{\text{COR}}, Q_{Ver}, Q_{\text{ST}})$-OW-VwFS-St *secure, where* μ *is the number of users,* S *is the number of sessions,* Q_{Ver} *is the number of calls to* KVER *and* Q_{ST} *is the number of calls to* REV-STATE', *if for all adversaries* $\mathcal{A}$ *attacking the protocol in time at most* t *resp.* t', *we have*

$$\Pr[\text{OW-VwFS}^{\mathcal{A}}_{\text{AKE}'} \Rightarrow 1] \leq \varepsilon \quad resp. \quad \Pr[\text{OW-VwFS-St}^{\mathcal{A}}_{\text{AKE}'} \Rightarrow 1] \leq \varepsilon' \ .$$

Valid attacks are defined via VALID'. For the session sID^* for which the adversary aims to compute the session key, we basically allow two types of attacks: If there is a (partially) matching session, then both parties may be corrupted. Otherwise, the adversary must not corrupt the peer of the session. Additionally for the model with state reveal attacks, the state for sID^* must not be revealed in any case.

MIN-ENTROPY. We require that public keys have γ *bits of min-entropy*, i.e., for all $(\text{pk}_0, \text{sk}_0) \leftarrow \text{Gen}'$, $(\text{pk}_1, \text{sk}_1) \leftarrow \text{Gen}'$, we have $\Pr[\text{pk}_0 = \text{pk}_1] \leq 2^{-\gamma}$. Similarly, we require that messages have α *bits of min-entropy*, i.e., for all messages m' we have $\Pr[m = m'] \leq 2^{-\alpha}$, where m is output by either Init'_I or Init'_R.

5   AKE with Key Confirmation

We now build a three-message AKE protocol AKE_{KC} with key confirmation from a two-message AKE protocol AKE' and three hash functions G_I, G_R, H. An overview is given in Fig. 5. Hash functions G_I, G_R and H are defined as follows: $G_I, G_R : \{0,1\}^* \to \{0,1\}^\lambda$ and $H : \{0,1\}^* \to \mathcal{K}$, where λ is the length of key confirmation tags and $\mathcal{K}$ is the key space of AKE_{KC}.[3]

Let $\text{AKE}' = (\text{Setup}', \text{Gen}', \text{Init}'_I, \text{Init}'_R, \text{Der}'_I)$. We define AKE_{KC} as follows: $\text{Setup}, \text{Gen}_{\text{AKE}}, \text{Init}_I$ will be the same as $\text{Setup}', \text{Gen}'$ and Init'_I, respectively. Init_R first runs Init'_R to obtain the responder's message m_r and the key k of AKE', where the latter is used to derive the final session key and key confirmation messages. In particular, the responder first computes the key confirmation tag $\pi_r := G_R(k, \text{ctxt})$, where ctxt is defined as the two parties' public keys and the initial messages (cf. Fig. 5). It then also computes the expected key confirmation tag π'_i and session key K' using G_I and H on the same input. It sends (m_r, π_r) to the initiator and keeps (π'_i, K') as state. The initiator runs Der_I which is defined as follows: First, it runs Der'_I to get k and then performs the same computations as the responder to compute key confirmation tags π_i, π'_r and the final session key K. It accepts K if $\pi'_r = \pi_r$ and sends π_i as the final message. The responder's derivation algorithm Der_R checks whether the key confirmation tag is valid, i.e., $\pi_i = \pi'_i$, and if this is the case it sets the session key to K'.

Whenever an equality check fails or the underlying algorithms of AKE' return $\bot$, the parties terminate the session, i.e., they *reject*, and return $\bot$.

CORRECTNESS. The correctness of AKE_{KC} follows directly from the correctness of AKE'. In particular, if AKE' is $(1 - \delta)$-correct, then so is AKE_{KC}.

SECURITY. We prove IND-FS security of AKE_{KC} based on OW-VwFS security of AKE' and modeling G_I, G_R and H as random oracles.

Theorem 1. *Let* AKE' *be* $(1 - \delta)$-*correct and have public keys with* γ *bits of entropy and messages with* α *bits of entropy. Let* AKE_{KC} *be as defined in Fig. 5, where* $G_I, G_R : \{0,1\}^* \to \{0,1\}^\lambda$ *and* $H : \{0,1\}^* \to \mathcal{K}$

---

[3] We define three different hash functions here which allows us to model them as independent random oracles. When instantiating the hash functions with the same function, one would need to use appropriate domain separation.

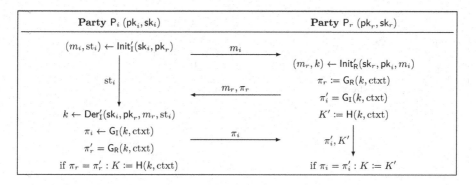

Fig. 5. AKE protocol $\mathsf{AKE_{KC}}$ from $\mathsf{AKE'}$ and key confirmation. The context is defined as $\mathrm{ctxt} := (\mathsf{pk}_i, \mathsf{pk}_r, m_i, m_r)$. $\mathsf{G_I}$, $\mathsf{G_R}$ and H are independent random oracles.

are modelled as random oracles. For every adversary $\mathcal{A}$ that breaks the $(t, \varepsilon, \mu, S, T, Q_{\mathrm{COR}})$-IND-FS-security of $\mathsf{AKE_{KC}}$, there exists an adversary $\mathcal{B}$ that breaks the $(t', \varepsilon', \mu, S, Q_{\mathrm{COR}}, Q_{Ver})$-OW-VwFS security of $\mathsf{AKE'}$ with $t' \approx t$ and

$$\varepsilon \le \varepsilon' + 2S \cdot \delta + (S + S^2) \cdot 2^{-\lambda} + \mu^2 \cdot 2^{-\gamma} + S(S + Q_{\mathsf{G_I}} + Q_{\mathsf{G_R}} + Q_{\mathsf{H}}) \cdot 2^{-\alpha} ,$$

where $Q_{\mathsf{G_I}}, Q_{\mathsf{G_R}}$ and Q_{H} are the number of queries to random oracles $\mathsf{G_I}$, $\mathsf{G_R}$ and H and $Q_{Ver} \le S + Q_{\mathsf{G_I}} + Q_{\mathsf{G_R}} + Q_{\mathsf{H}}$.

The idea of the proof is that we can simulate the key confirmation tags and session keys without knowing the key k of the underlying two-message protocol as long as it has not been queried to (one of) the random oracles. For this we have to keep track of whether the adversary trivially knows k because the session is not fresh anymore. We can handle this case and still simulate correctly using KVER oracle. The only way to win the game is to compute k for a fresh and valid session, thus breaking one-wayness of the underlying protocol. We now prove the theorem formally.

Proof. Let $\mathcal{A}$ be an adversary against IND-FS security of $\mathsf{AKE_{KC}}$. We consider the sequence of games $\mathsf{G_0}$-$\mathsf{G_3}$ in Figs. 6 and 7.

GAME $\mathsf{G_0}$. The first game $\mathsf{G_0}$ is the original IND-FS security game, however we exclude that public keys or messages collide (which means that if such events happen, then the game will abort and return a random bit). This also includes the key confirmation tags. Thus we get

$$\Pr[\mathsf{G_0^{\mathcal{A}}} \Rightarrow 1] \le \Pr[\mathsf{IND\text{-}FS^{\mathcal{A}}_{AKE_{KC}}} \Rightarrow 1] + \mu^2 \cdot 2^{-\gamma} + S^2 \cdot 2^{-\alpha} + S^2 \cdot 2^{-\lambda}.$$

Note that this means there can be at most one (partially) matching session for each session.

GAME $\mathsf{G_1}$. In game $\mathsf{G_1}$, we want to ensure that π_r, π_i and K have not been queried to the respective random oracle before they are determined. Note that

GAMES G_0-G_3		**SESSION$_I$$((i,r) \in [\mu]^2)$**	
00 **for** $n \in [\mu]$		38 cnt$_S$ ++	
01 $(\mathsf{pk}_n, \mathsf{sk}_n) \leftarrow \mathsf{Gen}'$		39 sID := cnt$_S$	
02 $b \xleftarrow{\$} \{0,1\}$		40 $(\mathtt{Init}[\mathrm{sID}], \mathtt{Resp}[\mathrm{sID}]) := (i,r)$	
03 $b' \leftarrow \mathcal{A}^O(\mathsf{pk}_1, \cdots, \mathsf{pk}_\mu)$		41 $\mathtt{Type}[\mathrm{sID}] :=$ "In"	
04 **for** sID$^* \in \mathcal{S}_{\mathsf{test}}$		42 $(m_i, \mathrm{st}_i) \leftarrow \mathsf{Init}'_I(\mathsf{sk}_i, \mathsf{pk}_r)$	
05 **if** FRESH(sID*) = **false**		43 $(\mathtt{Msg}_{I,1}[\mathrm{sID}], \mathtt{ST}[\mathrm{sID}]) := (m_i, \mathrm{st}_i)$	
or VALID(sID*) = **false**		44 $\mathtt{ctxt}[\mathrm{sID}] := (\mathsf{pk}_i, \mathsf{pk}_r, m_i, \bot)$	//G_2-G_3
06 **return** b		45 **return** (sID, m_i)	
07 **return** $[\![b = b']\!]$			
		DER$_I$(sID $\in$ [cnt$_S$], (m_r, π_r))	
SESSION$_R$$((i,r) \in [\mu]^2, m_i)$		46 **if** SK[sID] $\neq \bot$ **or** Type[sID] $\neq$ "In" **return** $\bot$	
08 cnt$_S$ ++		47 $(i,r) := (\mathtt{Init}[\mathrm{sID}], \mathtt{Resp}[\mathrm{sID}])$	
09 sID := cnt$_S$		48 $\mathrm{st}_i := \mathtt{ST}[\mathrm{sID}]$	
10 $(\mathtt{Init}[\mathrm{sID}], \mathtt{Resp}[\mathrm{sID}]) := (i,r)$		49 $\mathtt{peerPreCor}[\mathrm{sID}] := \mathtt{cor}[r]$	
11 $\mathtt{Type}[\mathrm{sID}] :=$ "Re"		50 $k := \mathsf{Der}'_I(\mathsf{sk}_i, \mathsf{pk}_r, m_r, \mathrm{st}_i)$	
12 $(m_r, k) \leftarrow \mathsf{Init}'_R(\mathsf{sk}_r, \mathsf{pk}_i, m_i)$		51 **if** $k = \bot$	
13 **if** $k = \bot$		52 SK[sID] := "reject"	
14 SK[sID] := "reject"		53 **return** $\bot$	
15 **return** $\bot$		54 **if** $\pi_r \neq \mathsf{G_R}(k, \mathsf{pk}_i, \mathsf{pk}_r, m_i, m_r)$	//G_0-G_1
16 $\pi_r := \mathsf{G_R}(k, \mathsf{pk}_i, \mathsf{pk}_r, m_i, m_r)$	//G_0	55 SK[sID] := "reject"	//G_0-G_1
17 $\pi_i := \mathsf{G_I}(k, \mathsf{pk}_i, \mathsf{pk}_r, m_i, m_r)$	//G_0	56 **return** $\bot$	//G_0-G_1
18 $K := \mathsf{H}(k, \mathsf{pk}_i, \mathsf{pk}_r, m_i, m_r)$	//G_0	57 $\pi_i := \mathsf{G_I}(k, \mathsf{pk}_i, \mathsf{pk}_r, m_i, m_r)$	//G_0-G_1
19 **if** $\exists k'$ s.t. $\mathsf{G_R}[k', \mathsf{pk}_i, \mathsf{pk}_r, m_i, m_r] \neq \bot$	//G_1-G_3	58 $K := \mathsf{H}(k, \mathsf{pk}_i, \mathsf{pk}_r, m_i, m_r)$	//G_0-G_1
or $\mathsf{G_I}[k', \mathsf{pk}_i, \mathsf{pk}_r, m_i, m_r] \neq \bot$	//G_1-G_3	59 k[sID] := k	//G_2-G_3
or $\mathsf{H}[k', \mathsf{pk}_i, \mathsf{pk}_r, m_i, m_r] \neq \bot$	//G_1-G_3	60 Replace $\bot$ in ctxt[sID] with m_r	//G_2-G_3
20 BadEntropy := **true**; **abort**	//G_1-G_3	61 **if** $\exists$sID$'$ s.t. ctxt[sID] = ctxt[sID$'$]	//G_2-G_3
21 $\pi_r \xleftarrow{\$} \{0,1\}^\lambda, \pi_i \xleftarrow{\$} \{0,1\}^\lambda, K \xleftarrow{\$} \mathcal{K}$	//G_1-G_3	62 **if** $\pi_r \neq \mathsf{G_R}(\diamond, \mathsf{pk}_i, \mathsf{pk}_r, m_i, m_r)$	//G_2-G_3
22 $\mathsf{G_R}[k, \mathsf{pk}_i, \mathsf{pk}_r, m_i, m_r] := \pi_r$	//G_1	63 SK[sID] := "reject"	//G_2-G_3
23 $\mathsf{G_I}[k, \mathsf{pk}_i, \mathsf{pk}_r, m_i, m_r] := \pi_i$	//G_1	64 **return** $\bot$	//G_2-G_3
24 $\mathsf{H}[k, \mathsf{pk}_i, \mathsf{pk}_r, m_i, m_r] := K$	//G_1	65 $\pi_i := \mathsf{G_I}(\diamond, \mathsf{pk}_i, \mathsf{pk}_r, m_i, m_r)$	//G_2-G_3
25 ctxt[sID] := $(\mathsf{pk}_i, \mathsf{pk}_r, m_i, m_r)$	//G_2-G_3	66 $K := \mathsf{H}(\diamond, \mathsf{pk}_i, \mathsf{pk}_r, m_i, m_r)$	//G_2-G_3
26 k[sID] := k	//G_2-G_3	67 **else**	
27 **if** $\exists$sID$'$ s.t. ctxt[sID$'$] = $(\mathsf{pk}_i, \mathsf{pk}_r, m_i, \bot)$		68 **if** $\mathsf{G_R}[k, \mathsf{pk}_i, \mathsf{pk}_r, m_i, m_r] = \pi_r$	//G_2-G_3
or $\mathtt{cor}[i] =$ **false**	//G_2-G_3	69 **if** $\mathtt{cor}[r] =$ **false**	//G_3
28 $\mathsf{G_R}[\diamond, \mathsf{pk}_i, \mathsf{pk}_r, m_i, m_r] := \pi_r$	//G_2-G_3	70 QueryRO := **true**; **abort**	//G_3
29 $\mathsf{G_I}[\diamond, \mathsf{pk}_i, \mathsf{pk}_r, m_i, m_r] := \pi_i$	//G_2-G_3	71 $\pi_i := \mathsf{G_I}(k, \mathsf{pk}_i, \mathsf{pk}_r, m_i, m_r)$	//G_2-G_3
30 $\mathsf{H}[\diamond, \mathsf{pk}_i, \mathsf{pk}_r, m_i, m_r] := K$	//G_2-G_3	72 $K := \mathsf{H}(k, \mathsf{pk}_i, \mathsf{pk}_r, m_i, m_r)$	//G_2-G_3
31 **else**	//G_2-G_3	73 **else**	
32 $\mathsf{G_R}[\oplus, \mathsf{pk}_i, \mathsf{pk}_r, m_i, m_r] := \pi_r$	//G_2-G_3	74 $\mathsf{G_R}[\diamond, \mathsf{pk}_i, \mathsf{pk}_r, m_i, m_r] \xleftarrow{\$} \{0,1\}^\lambda$	//G_2-G_3
33 $\mathsf{G_I}[\oplus, \mathsf{pk}_i, \mathsf{pk}_r, m_i, m_r] := \pi_i$	//G_2-G_3	75 **if** $\pi_r = \mathsf{G_R}(\diamond, \mathsf{pk}_i, \mathsf{pk}_r, m_i, m_r)$	//G_2-G_3
34 $\mathsf{H}[\oplus, \mathsf{pk}_i, \mathsf{pk}_r, m_i, m_r] := K$	//G_2-G_3	76 RandKC := **true**; **abort**	//G_2-G_3
35 $(\mathtt{Msg}_{I,1}[\mathrm{sID}], \mathtt{Msg}_R[\mathrm{sID}]) := (m_i, (m_r, \pi_r))$		77 SK[sID] := "reject"	//G_2-G_3
36 ST[sID] := (π_i, K)		78 **return** $\bot$	//G_2-G_3
37 **return** (sID, (m_r, π_r))		79 $(\mathtt{Msg}_R[\mathrm{sID}], \mathtt{Msg}_{I,2}[\mathrm{sID}]) := (m_r, \pi_i)$	
		80 SK[sID] := K	
		81 **return** π_i	

Fig. 6. Games G_0-G_3 for the proof of Theorem 1. $\mathcal{A}$ has access to oracles O := {SESSION$_I$, SESSION$_R$, DER$_I$, DER$_R$, REVEAL, CORR, TEST, G$_I$, G$_R$, H}. Helper procedures FRESH and VALID are defined in Fig. 3.

all three values will be determined in SESSION$_R$ when m_r and k are computed. Thus, whenever SESSION$_R$ is queried, we check whether there already exists a query $(k', \mathsf{pk}_i, \mathsf{pk}_r, m_i, m_r)$ to G$_R$, G$_I$ or H for some k' (line 19). If this is the case, we raise flag BadEntropy and abort. If BadEntropy is not raised, we draw fresh values for π_r, π_i and K and explicitly assign them to the corresponding

```
DERR(sID ∈ [cnts], π_i)                          G_R(k, pk_i, pk_r, m_i, m_r)
00 if SK[sID] ≠ ⊥ or Type[sID] ≠ "Re"            27 if G_R[◦, pk_i, pk_r, m_i, m_r] = π ≠ ⊥          //G₂-G₃
01   return ⊥                                     28   S := {sID | ctxt[sID] = (pk_i, pk_r, m_i, m_r)}  //G₂-G₃
02 (i, r) := (Init[sID], Resp[sID])               29   for sID ∈ S // note |S| ≤ 2                     //G₂-G₃
03 (π'_i, K') := ST[sID]                          30     if k[sID] = k                               //G₂-G₃
04 peerPreCor[sID] := cor[i]                       31       QueryRO := true; abort                    //G₃
05 if π_i ≠ π'_i                     //G₀-G₁       32     return π                                    //G₂-G₃
06   SK[sID] := "reject"             //G₀-G₁       33 elseif G_R[⊕, pk_i, pk_r, m_i, m_r] = π ≠ ⊥      //G₂-G₃
07   return ⊥                        //G₀-G₁       34   Find sID s.t. ctxt[sID] = (pk_i, pk_r, m_i, m_r) //G₂-G₃
08 K := K'                           //G₀-G₁       35   if k[sID] = k                                 //G₂-G₃
09 if ∃sID' s.t. ctxt[sID'] = ctxt[sID]  //G₂-G₃   36     Replace ⊕ with k                            //G₂-G₃
10   if π_i ≠ G_I[◦, pk_i, pk_r, m_i, m_r] //G₂-G₃ 37   return π                                      //G₂-G₃
11     SK[sID] := "reject"           //G₂-G₃       38 if G_R[k, pk_i, pk_r, m_i, m_r] = π ≠ ⊥
12     return ⊥                      //G₂-G₃       39   return π
13   K := H[◦, pk_i, pk_r, m_i, m_r] //G₂-G₃       40 π ←$ {0,1}^λ
14 else                             //G₂-G₃        41 G_R[k, pk_i, pk_r, m_i, m_r] := π
15   if G_I[k, pk_i, pk_r, m_i, m_r] = π_i //G₂-G₃ 42 return π
16     if cor[i] = false             //G₃
17       QueryRO := true; abort      //G₃          CORR(n ∈ [μ])
18       K := H(k, pk_i, pk_r, m_i, m_r) //G₂-G₃   43 cor[n] := true
19   else                            //G₂-G₃       44 return sk_n
20     G_I[◦, pk_i, pk_r, m_i, m_r] ←$ {0,1}^λ //G₂-G₃
21     if π_i = G_I[◦, pk_i, pk_r, m_i, m_r] //G₂-G₃  TEST(sID)
22       RandKC := true; abort       //G₂-G₃       45 if sID ∈ S_test return ⊥
23     SK[sID] := "reject"           //G₂-G₃       46 if SK[sID] ∈ {⊥, "reject"} return ⊥
24     return ⊥                      //G₂-G₃       47 S_test := S_test ∪ {sID}
25 (Msg_{l,2}[sID], SK[sID]) := (π_i, K)           48 K*_0 := SK[sID]
26 return ε                                        49 K*_1 ←$ K
                                                   50 return K*_b
```

Fig. 7. Oracles for games G_0-G_3 for the proof of Theorem 1. G_I and H are defined analogously to G_R.

entry of the respective random oracle (lines 21–24). We make this explicit here to prepare for the next step where we have to do a case distinction. Note that G_0 and G_1 are the same, except if BadEntropy is raised. Thus,

$$|\Pr[G_0^{\mathcal{A}} \Rightarrow 1] - \Pr[G_1^{\mathcal{A}} \Rightarrow 1]| \leq \Pr[\mathsf{BadEntropy}] \leq S(Q_{G_R} + Q_{G_I} + Q_H) \cdot 2^{-\alpha},$$

where we bound the event by the entropy of AKE′. The message m_r is computed by the game directly before we check for this event. We then use the union bound over the maximum number of sessions S.

GAME G_2. In game G_2, we want to compute π_r, π_i and K without using k explicitly and prepare for the reduction to OW-VwFS. For this, we have to make a distinction between fresh and non-fresh sessions. We add two additional variables $\mathsf{ctxt}[sID]$ and $k[sID]$ for each session which store the context and the session key of the underlying AKE′. When $\mathsf{SESSION_R}$ is queried, we no longer assign the random oracle entries $[k, pk_i, pk_r, m_i, m_r]$. Instead, we use a special placeholder symbol for the key k. In particular, if the session is still fresh and valid (i.e., there exists a session with a matching context up to this point, or the intended peer is not (yet) corrupted), we use the symbol $\diamond$ (lines 28–30). Otherwise, in case the session is not valid, we use the symbol $\oplus$ (lines 32–34). This distinction will be necessary to patch the random oracle correctly. Note that an adversary might be able to compute the correct key k for a non-valid session.

We describe how the random oracles are patched below. First, we explain how to change $\mathsf{Der_I}$ and $\mathsf{Der_R}$ accordingly. For each query to $\mathsf{Der_I}$, we first update the context with the message m_r that was used to query the oracle. Then we check whether there exists a potential partnered session with the same context (line 61). In this case we know the corresponding values π_r, π_i and K which are stored with the symbol $\diamond$. We check whether the tag π_r is correct (if not, the session rejects) and assign the session key (lines 62–66). If there is no other session with the same context, we have to make another case distinction. In the first case, we use k explicitly to check whether there has been a query to the random oracle $\mathsf{G_R}$ such that the tag π_r matches (line 68). In this case, we proceed normally. Looking ahead, this will be a critical point in the next game modification. If there exists no such query to $\mathsf{G_R}$, then the game makes the query and chooses a tag uniformly at random (line 74). If this tag is the same as the one provided by the adversary, we raise flag RandKC and abort (line 76). Otherwise, the session simply rejects. We modify $\mathrm{DER_R}$ in the exact same way, except that we are now looking at π_i (Fig. 7, lines 09–24).

Before bounding RandKC, we explain the simulation of random oracles as described in Fig. 7. We explain $\mathsf{G_R}$ in more detail. ($\mathsf{G_I}$ and H are modeled in exactly the same way). For each query $(k, \mathsf{pk}_i, \mathsf{pk}_r, m_i, m_r)$, we first check for entries with the special symbol. More specifically, if there exists an entry with the given context and the symbol $\diamond$, we look for the sID with this context. Note that there can be at most two sessions (one of type "In" and one of type "Re" which will be matching sessions), which we capture by computing a set $\mathcal{S}$ containing the corresponding sID(s) (line 29). If the key k of the random oracle query corresponds to the one stored in $\mathrm{k}[\mathrm{sID}]^4$, then $\mathsf{G_R}$ simply outputs the stored value π (line 32). We do the same for special symbol $\oplus$ (line 34, note that here sID is always unique), except that we also update the entry accordingly, i.e., replace $\oplus$ with k if $k = \mathrm{k}[\mathrm{sID}]$ (line 36). This way, the simulation is consistent with the other oracles.

Overall, the two games only differ when flag RandKC is raised. Note that we can bound the probability that a tag is valid without the random oracle being queried by the length of the tag. Union bound over S session gives us

$$|\Pr[\mathsf{G}_1^{\mathcal{A}} \Rightarrow 1] - \Pr[\mathsf{G}_2^{\mathcal{A}} \Rightarrow 1]| \leq \Pr[\mathsf{RandKC}] \leq S \cdot 2^{-\lambda} + S \cdot \delta.$$

GAME G_3. In the final game G_3, we raise flag $\mathsf{QueryRO}$ if the adversary ever queries the random oracle on a key k of a fresh session. Depending on the order of queries, this event can occur for different oracles: $\mathrm{DER_I}$ (Fig. 6, line 70), $\mathrm{DER_R}$ (Fig. 7, line 17) or one of the random oracles (Fig. 7, line 31). First, we look at sessions that do not have a matching session with the same context. For queries to oracle $\mathrm{DER_I}$ we check the validity of π_r in line 68. If the peer r is not corrupted,

---

[4] Since we cannot check correctness efficiently in the reduction which we will build in the next step, we explicitly perform the test here for all sessions in $\mathcal{S}$. However, if $\mathcal{S}$ indeed contains two sessions, then by correctness, this key (and thus the outcome) will be the same.

then the session is still fresh and valid. Thus, we raise QueryRO if there has been a query to G_R on the correct key and context such that the output is indeed π_r. We proceed similarly for responder sessions when DER_R is queried, checking for queries to G_I. This means that all sessions where the peer is uncorrupted and no session with a matching context exist will reject (or abort).

We now look at sessions that have a session with matching context and whose relevant random oracle entries are marked with $\diamond$. Whenever one of the random oracles is queried, we check whether the key matches the one stored in $k[\text{sID}]$ (as described earlier) and if this is the case, we also raise QueryRO and abort.

We claim that

$$| \Pr[G_2^{\mathcal{A}} \Rightarrow 1] - \Pr[G_3^{\mathcal{A}} \Rightarrow 1]| \leq \Pr[\text{QueryRO}] \leq \varepsilon' + S \cdot \delta.$$

Before proving the claim, note that in G_3 we have $\Pr[G_3^{\mathcal{A}} \Rightarrow 1] = 1/2$. For this, observe that all sessions must have a (partially) matching session and that random oracle H is never queried on k for any of those sessions. Thus, the session key is indistinguishable from a uniformly random key.

BOUNDING EVENT QueryRO. We now describe an adversary $\mathcal{B}$ against OW-VwFS security of the underlying AKE$'$ to bound event QueryRO. A pseudocode description is given in Fig. 8. The idea is that whenever $\mathcal{A}$ queries one of the random oracles on the underlying key k of a fresh and valid session (either in order to forge a key confirmation tag or to distinguish the actual session key), we can use this to break OW-VwFS security of AKE$'$, where the verification oracle KVER is used to simulate the random oracles consistently.

We now describe $\mathcal{B}$ in more detail. It gets as input μ public keys and forwards them to $\mathcal{A}$. $\mathcal{B}$ simulates queries to oracle SESSION$_I$ in a straightforward way by querying its own oracle SESSION$'_I$ which returns (sID, m_i). After assigning the corresponding variables, $\mathcal{B}$ forwards the output to $\mathcal{A}$. Queries to SESSION$_R$ are simulated as in game G_3. $\mathcal{B}$ first queries DER'_R to receive (sID, m_r). Instead of checking whether $k = \bot$, $\mathcal{B}$ checks whether $m_r = \bot$. If this is the case, it rejects and outputs $\bot$. Otherwise, it proceeds as described in G_3, preparing random oracle assignments by assigning fresh values to π_i, π_r and K and returning $(\text{sID}, (m_r, \pi_r))$.

When $\mathcal{A}$ queries DER_I, $\mathcal{B}$ queries DER'_I. $\mathcal{B}$ will not be able to explicitly check whether the session key was computed successfully, however, we will argue that the simulation is consistent by correctness of AKE$'$ and the validity of the key confirmation tag. Thus, $\mathcal{B}$ directly proceeds as described in G_3. Whenever there exists a session with the same context, then the key confirmation tag must be the same as the one computed by that session, up to correctness of AKE$'$. Thus the simulation is perfect except with probability $S \cdot \delta$. Whenever there exists no (partially) matching session, $\mathcal{B}$ needs to check whether G_R was already queried on the correct k. For this it checks all random oracle queries that have output π_r provided by $\mathcal{A}$. If such a query exists, it will be unique since we excluded collisions in the first game. $\mathcal{B}$ checks whether the respective key of the query is the correct key using its oracle KVER. If this is the case, we further distinguish two cases, based on whether the session still qualifies for a valid test session

$\mathcal{B}^{\text{Session}'_I, \text{Der}'_R, \text{Der}'_I, \text{Corr}', \text{KVer}}(\mathsf{pk}_1, \cdots, \mathsf{pk}_\mu)$

00 $b' \leftarrow \mathcal{A}^O(\mathsf{pk}_1, \cdots, \mathsf{pk}_\mu)$
01 **return** $\perp$

$\text{Session}_R((i,r) \in [\mu]^2, m_i)$

02 $(\text{sID}, m_r) \leftarrow \text{Der}'_R((i,r), m_i)$
03 $(\text{Init}[\text{sID}], \text{Resp}[\text{sID}]) := (i, r)$
04 $\text{Type}[\text{sID}] := \text{``Re''}$
05 **if** $m_r = \perp$
06    $\text{SK}[\text{sID}] := \text{``reject''}$
07   **return** $\perp$
08 **if** $\exists k'$ s.t. $\mathsf{G}_R[k', \mathsf{pk}_i, \mathsf{pk}_r, m_i, m_r] \neq \perp$
or $\mathsf{G}_I[k', \mathsf{pk}_i, \mathsf{pk}_r, m_i, m_r] \neq \perp$
or $\mathsf{H}[k', \mathsf{pk}_i, \mathsf{pk}_r, m_i, m_r] \neq \perp$
09   **abort**
10 $\pi_r \xleftarrow{\$} \{0,1\}^\lambda, \pi_i \xleftarrow{\$} \{0,1\}^\lambda, K \xleftarrow{\$} \mathcal{K}$
11 $\text{ctxt}[\text{sID}] := (\mathsf{pk}_i, \mathsf{pk}_r, m_i, m_r)$
12 **if** $\exists \text{sID}'$ s.t. $\text{ctxt}[\text{sID}'] = (\mathsf{pk}_i, \mathsf{pk}_r, m_i, \perp)$
or $\text{cor}[i] = \mathbf{false}$
13    $\mathsf{G}_R[\diamond, \mathsf{pk}_i, \mathsf{pk}_r, m_i, m_r] := \pi_r$
14    $\mathsf{G}_I[\diamond, \mathsf{pk}_i, \mathsf{pk}_r, m_i, m_r] := \pi_i$
15    $\mathsf{H}[\diamond, \mathsf{pk}_i, \mathsf{pk}_r, m_i, m_r] := K$
16 **else**
17    $\mathsf{G}_R[\oplus, \mathsf{pk}_i, \mathsf{pk}_r, m_i, m_r] := \pi_r$
18    $\mathsf{G}_I[\oplus, \mathsf{pk}_i, \mathsf{pk}_r, m_i, m_r] := \pi_i$
19    $\mathsf{H}[\oplus, \mathsf{pk}_i, \mathsf{pk}_r, m_i, m_r] := K$
20 $(\text{Msg}_I[\text{sID}], \text{Msg}_R[\text{sID}]) := (m_i, (m_r, \pi_r))$
21 **return** $(\text{sID}, (m_r, \pi_r))$

$\text{Reveal}(\text{sID})$

22 $\text{revSK}[\text{sID}] := \mathbf{true}$
23 **return** $\text{SK}[\text{sID}]$

$\text{Corr}(n \in [\mu])$

24 $\text{cor}[n] := \mathbf{true}$
25 $\text{sk}_n \leftarrow \text{Corr}'(n)$
26 **return** sk_n

$\text{Session}_I((i, r) \in [\mu]^2)$

27 $(\text{sID}, m_i) \leftarrow \text{Session}'_I(i, r)$
28 $(\text{Init}[\text{sID}], \text{Resp}[\text{sID}]) := (i, r)$
29 $\text{Type}[\text{sID}] := \text{``In''}$
30 $\text{Msg}_{I,1}[\text{sID}] := m_i$
31 $\text{ctxt}[\text{sID}] := (\mathsf{pk}_i, \mathsf{pk}_r, m_i, \perp)$
32 **return** (sID, m_i)

$\text{Der}_I(\text{sID}, (m_r, \pi_r))$

33 **if** $\text{SK}[\text{sID}] \neq \perp$ **or** $\text{Type}[\text{sID}] \neq \text{``In''}$
34   **return** $\perp$
35 $(i, r) := (\text{Init}[\text{sID}], \text{Resp}[\text{sID}])$
36 $\text{peerPreCor}[\text{sID}] := \text{cor}[r]$
37 $\text{Der}'_I(\text{sID}, m_r)$
38 Replace $\perp$ in $\text{ctxt}[\text{sID}]$ with m_r
39 **if** $\exists \text{sID}'$ s.t. $\text{ctxt}[\text{sID}'] = \text{ctxt}[\text{sID}]$
40   **if** $\pi_r \neq \mathsf{G}_R[\diamond, \mathsf{pk}_i, \mathsf{pk}_r, m_i, m_r]$
41      $\text{SK}[\text{sID}] := \text{``reject''}$
42   **return** $\perp$
43    $\pi_i := \mathsf{G}_I[\diamond, \mathsf{pk}_i, \mathsf{pk}_r, m_i, m_r]$
44    $K := \mathsf{H}[\diamond, \mathsf{pk}_i, \mathsf{pk}_r, m_i, m_r]$
45 **else**
46   **if** $\exists k$ s.t. $\mathsf{G}_R[k, \mathsf{pk}_i, \mathsf{pk}_r, m_i, m_r] = \pi_r$
and $\text{KVer}(k, \text{sID})$
47   **if** $\text{cor}[r] = \mathbf{false}$
48   Stop with (sID, k)
49      $\pi_i := \mathsf{G}_I(k, \mathsf{pk}_i, \mathsf{pk}_r, m_i, m_r)$
50      $K := \mathsf{H}(k, \mathsf{pk}_i, \mathsf{pk}_r, m_i, m_r)$
51   **else**
52      $\mathsf{G}_R[\diamond, \mathsf{pk}_i, \mathsf{pk}_r, m_i, m_r] \xleftarrow{\$} \{0,1\}^\lambda$
53   **if** $\pi_r = \mathsf{G}_R[\diamond, \mathsf{pk}_i, \mathsf{pk}_r, m_i, m_r]$ **abort**
54      $\text{SK}[\text{sID}] := \text{``reject''}$
55   **return** $\perp$
56 $(\text{Msg}_R[\text{sID}], \text{Msg}_{I,2}[\text{sID}]) := (m_r, \pi_i)$
57 $\text{SK}[\text{sID}] := K$
58 **return** π_i

Fig. 8. Adversary $\mathcal{B}$ against OW-VwFS. $\mathcal{A}$ has access to oracles $\text{O} := \{\text{Session}_I, \text{Session}_R, \text{Der}_I, \text{Der}_R, \text{Reveal}, \text{Corr}, \text{Test}, \mathsf{G}_I, \mathsf{G}_R, \mathsf{H}\}$. Helper procedures Fresh and Valid are defined in Fig. 3. Oracles Der_R, Test and G_R are defined in Fig. 9, and G_I, H are defined analogously.

or not. If the peer of the session has not been corrupted yet, then this is a valid session and $\mathcal{B}$ outputs (sID, k) as solution in its own game. Otherwise, it proceeds. Oracle Der_R is simulated similarly, looking at G_I instead of G_R.

Oracle Reveal and Corr can be simulated in a straightforward way. The latter requires $\mathcal{B}$ to query its own oracle Corr'. Queries to Test will always return the real session key. Note that this is a perfect simulation since session keys are perfectly hidden unless QueryRO happens in which case $\mathcal{B}$ stops because it breaks OW-VwFS security.

It remains to describe the simulation of random oracles. In Fig. 9 we give a description of G_R. G_I and H are simulated in the same way. As in G_3, $\mathcal{B}$ first checks whether there exists an entry with the special symbol $\diamond$. If this is the case, it finds the corresponding sID and uses the KVer oracle to check whether the key k provided by $\mathcal{A}$ belongs to this session. Since $\diamond$ is used to mark sessions

$\text{DER}_R(\text{sID}, \pi_i)$	$G_R(k, \text{pk}_i, \text{pk}_r, m_i, m_r)$
00 **if** SK[sID] $\neq \perp$ **or** Type[sID] $\neq$ "Re" **return** $\perp$	20 **if** $G_R[\diamond, \text{pk}_i, \text{pk}_r, m_i, m_r] = \pi \neq \perp$
01 $(i, r) := (\text{Init}[\text{sID}], \text{Resp}[\text{sID}])$	21 $S := \{\text{sID} \mid \text{ctxt}[\text{sID}] = (\text{pk}_i, \text{pk}_r, m_i, m_r)\}$
02 peerPreCor[sID] := cor[i]	22 **for** sID $\in S$
03 **if** $\exists \text{sID}'$ s.t. $\text{ctxt}[\text{sID}'] = \text{ctxt}[\text{sID}]$	23 **if** KVER(sID, k)
04 **if** $\pi_i \neq G_I[\diamond, \text{pk}_i, \text{pk}_r, m_i, m_r]$	24 Stop with (sID, k)
05 SK[sID] := "reject"	25 **elseif** $G_R[\oplus, \text{pk}_i, \text{pk}_r, m_i, m_r] = \pi \neq \perp$
06 **return** $\perp$	26 Find sID s.t. $\text{ctxt}[\text{sID}] = (\text{pk}_i, \text{pk}_r, m_i, m_r)$
07 $K := H[\diamond, \text{pk}_i, \text{pk}_r, m_i, m_r]$	27 **if** KVER(sID, k)
08 **else**	28 Replace $\oplus$ with k
09 **if** $\exists k$ s.t. $G_I[k, \text{pk}_i, \text{pk}_r, m_i, m_r] = \pi_i$	29 **return** π
and KVER(k, sID)	30 **if** $G_R[k, \text{pk}_i, \text{pk}_r, m_r] = \pi \neq \perp$
10 **if** peerPreCor[sID] = **false**	31 **return** π
11 Stop with (sID, k)	32 $\pi \stackrel{\$}{\leftarrow} \{0, 1\}^\lambda$
12 $K := H(k, \text{pk}_i, \text{pk}_r, m_i, m_r)$	33 $G_R[k, \text{pk}_i, \text{pk}_r, m_i, m_r] := \pi$
13 **else**	34 **return** π
14 $G_I[\diamond, \text{pk}_i, \text{pk}_r, m_i, m_r] \stackrel{\$}{\leftarrow} \{0, 1\}^\lambda$	
15 **if** $\pi_i = G_I[\diamond, \text{pk}_i, \text{pk}_r, m_i, m_r]$ **abort**	$\text{TEST}(\text{sID})$
16 SK[sID] := "reject"	35 **if** sID $\in S_{\text{test}}$ **return** $\perp$
17 **return** $\perp$	36 **if** SK[sID] $\in \{\perp, \text{"reject"}\}$ **return** $\perp$
18 $(\text{Msg}_{I,2}[\text{sID}], \text{SK}[\text{sID}]) := (m_{i,2}, K)$	37 $S_{\text{test}} := S_{\text{test}} \cup \{\text{sID}\}$
19 **return** ε	38 **return** SK[sID]

Fig. 9. Oracles DER_R, TEST and G_R for adversary $\mathcal{B}$. G_I and H are defined analogously to G_R.

that have a (partially) matching session, $\mathcal{B}$ can always use this key to win the OW-VwFS game. If there is no entry with $\diamond$ but one with $\oplus$, $\mathcal{B}$ again queries the KVER oracle, but this time it updates the corresponding entry with the correct key (if KVER returns **true**). This way, $\mathcal{B}$ can perfectly simulate non-test sessions. If none of these cases happen or KVER has returned **false**, then $\mathcal{B}$ proceeds as usual by lazy sampling.

This concludes the description of $\mathcal{B}$. Note that if QueryRO happens in game G_3, i.e., there exists a random oracle query for a fresh and valid session with correct key k, then $\mathcal{B}$ wins game OW-VwFS. We get $\Pr[\text{QueryRO}] \leq \varepsilon' + S \cdot \delta$.

Further, note that $\mathcal{B}$ issues at most $(S + Q_{G_I} + Q_{G_R} + Q_H)$ to KVER since we have excluded collisions of tags in the first game. The number of queries to all other oracles is preserved. This completes the proof of Theorem 1.

AKE WITH KEY CONFIRMATION AGAINST STATE REVEAL. Based on AKE_{KC}, we build a three-message AKE protocol AKE_{stKC} that is secure against state-reveal attacks (cf. Definition 2). Since AKE_{stKC} has a similar structure with AKE_{KC}, we follow the notations used in defining AKE_{KC} (cf. Fig. 5). An overview of AKE_{stKC} is given in Fig. 10.

AKE_{stKC} uses the state-encryption technique [21, 30] to protect session states. Concretely, let $G_{\text{stI}} : \{0, 1\}^\kappa \times \{0, 1\}^\kappa \rightarrow \{0, 1\}^{d_I}$ and $G_{\text{stR}} : \{0, 1\}^\kappa \times \{0, 1\}^\kappa \rightarrow \{0, 1\}^{d_R}$ be two hash functions. We assume that any initiator session state of the underlying two-message AKE protocol AKE' can be encoded as a d_I-bit string and $d_R = 2\lambda$ (the length of key confirmation tag plus the length of session key derived by AKE'). AKE_{stKC} proceeds the same as AKE_{KC} except that (1) the long-term secret key of user i in AKE_{stKC} also include a uniformly random key

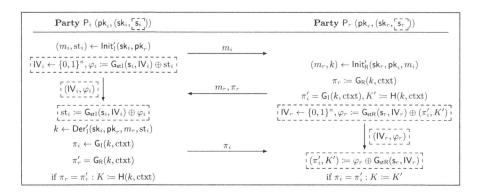

Fig. 10. AKE protocol $\mathsf{AKE_{stKC}}$ from $\mathsf{AKE'}$, key confirmation, and state encryption. The context is defined as $\mathrm{ctxt} := (\mathsf{pk}_i, \mathsf{pk}_r, m_i, m_r)$. $\mathsf{G_I}$, $\mathsf{G_R}$, and H are independent random oracles. Dashed parts show how we use the state encryption technique to protect the session states. $\mathsf{G_{stI}}$ and $\mathsf{G_{stR}}$ are independent random oracles used for state encryption.

$\mathsf{s}_i \in \{0,1\}^\kappa$, and (2) each session will sample a one-time key IV uniformly at random and encrypt the session state of $\mathsf{AKE_{KC}}$ via XORing with the one-time pad $\mathsf{G_{stI}}(\mathsf{s}_i, \mathsf{IV})$. Now the session state (that the adversary can reveal in the state-reveal AKE model) is (IV, φ). Dashed parts in Fig. 10 shows how this technique works.

CORRECTNESS. Similar to $\mathsf{AKE_{KC}}$, the correctness of $\mathsf{AKE_{stKC}}$ follows directly from the correctness of $\mathsf{AKE'}$. If $\mathsf{AKE'}$ is $(1-\delta)$-correct, then so is $\mathsf{AKE_{stKC}}$.

SECURITY. In Theorem 2, we prove IND-FS-St security of $\mathsf{AKE_{KC}}$ based on OW-VwFS-St security of $\mathsf{AKE'}$ and modeling $\mathsf{G_I}$, $\mathsf{G_R}$, H, $\mathsf{G_{stI}}$, and $\mathsf{G_{stR}}$ as random oracles. Here we sketch the proof idea. By using the state encryption technique, the adversary cannot learn the unencrypted states of the underlying two-message AKE, unless it reveals the encrypted session state and corrupts the owner of the session. But this makes the session invalid and thus, it cannot be tested. Therefore, for valid sessions, state-reveal queries do not give any advantage to the adversary, and thus we can use the proof idea of Theorem 1. The full proof of Theorem 2 is postponed to our full version [28, Appendix C].

Theorem 2. *Let $\mathsf{AKE'}$ be $(1-\delta)$-correct and have public keys with γ bits of entropy and messages with α bits of entropy. Let $\mathsf{AKE_{stKC}}$ be as defined in Fig. 5, where $\mathsf{G_I}, \mathsf{G_R} : \{0,1\}^* \to \{0,1\}^\lambda$, $\mathsf{H} : \{0,1\}^* \to \mathcal{K}$, $\mathsf{G_{stI}} : \{0,1\}^\kappa \times \{0,1\}^\kappa \to \{0,1\}^{d_I}$, and $\mathsf{G_{stR}} : \{0,1\}^\kappa \times \{0,1\}^\kappa \to \{0,1\}^{d_R}$ are modeled as random oracles. For every adversary $\mathcal{A}$ that breaks the $(t, \varepsilon, \mu, S, T, Q_{\mathrm{COR}}, Q_{\mathrm{ST}})$-IND-FS-St-security of $\mathsf{AKE_{stKC}}$, there exists an adversary $\mathcal{B}$ that breaks the $(t', \varepsilon', \mu, S, Q_{\mathrm{COR}}, Q_{Ver}, S)$-OW-VwFS-St security of $\mathsf{AKE'}$ with*

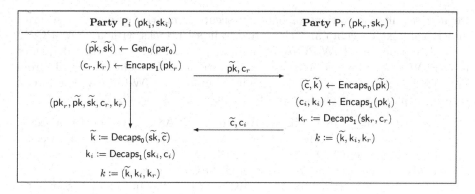

Fig. 11. AKE protocol $\mathsf{AKE}'_{\mathsf{kem}}$ from KEM schemes KEM_1, KEM_0.

$t' \approx t$ and

$$\varepsilon \leq \varepsilon' + 2S \cdot \delta + (\mu^2 + S^2 + \mu Q_{\mathsf{G_{stI}}} + 2S Q_{\mathsf{G_{stI}}}) \cdot 2^{-\kappa}$$
$$+ \mu^2 \cdot 2^{-\gamma} + (S + S^2) \cdot 2^{-\lambda} + (Q_{\mathsf{G_R}} + Q_{\mathsf{G_I}} + Q_{\mathsf{H}} + S) \cdot S \cdot 2^{-\alpha},$$

where Q_{h} is the number of queries to the respective random oracle h and $Q_{Ver} \leq S + Q_{\mathsf{G_I}} + Q_{\mathsf{G_R}} + Q_{\mathsf{H}}$.

6 Applying Our Results to Existing Protocols

We first show how to construct verifiable AKE from KEMs which gives us tight AKE with key confirmation and perfect forward secrecy from lattices and DDH. The advantage is that we do not have to consider random oracles and the proofs are comparably simpler than those of full AKE security. We then show how we can recover the optimal tightness bound for the CCGJJ protocol [10] using our modular transformation rather than that of [18].

6.1 AKE from KEMs

We provide results for KEM-based AKE secure without and with state reveal, where the former allows for weaker assumptions. The protocol, denoted by $\mathsf{AKE}'_{\mathsf{kem}}$, to which we want to apply our compiler from the previous section is given in Fig. 11. Each party holds long-term keys of a KEM scheme KEM_1 and in each session, an ephemeral key using KEM_0 is exchanged. The session key then simply consists of three KEM keys. We also denote its variant with key confirmation by $\mathsf{AKE}_{\mathsf{kem}}$ (i.e., combining Fig. 11 with Fig. 5) and the one resisting state reveals by $\mathsf{AKE}_{\mathsf{st,kem}}$ (i.e., combining Fig. 11 with Fig. 10).

ONE-WAY SECURITY OF KEM. Depending on whether the KEM is used for long-term keys or ephemeral keys and whether state reveals are allowed, we need a different variant of one-way security: multi-user one-way security under plaintext checking and ciphertext validity attacks without (OW-PCVA) or with corruptions (OW-PCVA-C), and with corruptions and reveal queries (OW-PCVA-CR). These notions are weaker variants of OW-ChCCA security from Pan, Wagner and Zeng [30] and are tightly implied by OW-ChCCA. The formal security definitions are given in our full version [28, Appendix A].

ANALYSIS OF $\mathsf{AKE}'_{\mathsf{kem}}$ AND $\mathsf{AKE}_{\mathsf{kem}}$. We prove that $\mathsf{AKE}'_{\mathsf{kem}}$ protocol is a secure verifiable AKE protocol. When not considering state reveals, we can use weaker assumptions, namely OW-PCVA and OW-PCVA-C. We also prove security with state-reveals which uses the definition of OW-PCVA-CR security. We then apply Theorem 1 resp. Theorem 2 to obtain $\mathsf{AKE}_{\mathsf{kem}}$ which has full forward secrecy.

CORRECTNESS AND ENTROPY. Let KEM_0 be $(1 - \delta_0)$-correct and have public keys with γ_0 bits of entropy and messages with α_0 bits of entropy. Let KEM_1 be $(1 - \delta_1)$-correct and have public keys with γ_1 bits of entropy and messages with α_1 bits of entropy. Then $\mathsf{AKE}'_{\mathsf{kem}}$ is $(1 - \delta_0 - 2\delta_1)$-correct. Further, $\mathsf{AKE}'_{\mathsf{kem}}$ has public keys with γ_1 bits of entropy and messages with at least $\min(\gamma_0, \alpha_0, \alpha_1 - 1)$ bits of entropy.

We now establish OW-VwFS and OW-VwFS-St security of $\mathsf{AKE}'_{\mathsf{kem}}$ and defer the proofs to our full paper [28, Appendix D.1].

Lemma 1. *For every adversary $\mathcal{A}$ that breaks the $(t, \varepsilon, \mu, S, T, Q_{\mathrm{COR}}, Q_{Ver})$-OW-VwFS security of $\mathsf{AKE}'_{\mathsf{kem}}$, there exist adversaries $\mathcal{B}_1$ and $\mathcal{B}_2$ that break $(t_1, \varepsilon_1, S, S, S, Q_{Ver})$-OW-PCVA security of KEM_0 and $(t_2, \varepsilon_2, \mu, S, S, 2Q_{Ver}, Q_{\mathrm{COR}})$-OW-PCVA-C security of KEM_1 with $t_1 \approx t_2 \approx t$ and $\varepsilon \leq \varepsilon_1 + \varepsilon_2$.*

Lemma 2. *For every adversary $\mathcal{A}$ that breaks the $(t, \varepsilon, \mu, S, T, Q_{\mathrm{COR}}, Q_{Ver}, Q_{\mathrm{ST}})$-OW-VwFS-St security of $\mathsf{AKE}'_{\mathsf{kem}}$, there exist adversaries $\mathcal{B}_1$ and $\mathcal{B}_2$ that break $(t_1, \varepsilon_1, S, S, S, Q_{Ver}, Q_{\mathrm{ST}})$-OW-PCVA-C security of KEM_0 and $(t_2, \varepsilon_2, \mu, S, S, 2Q_{Ver}, Q_{\mathrm{COR}}, Q_{\mathrm{ST}})$-OW-PCVA-CR security of KEM_1 with $t_1 \approx t_2 \approx t$ and $\varepsilon \leq \varepsilon_1 + \varepsilon_2$.*

We now add key confirmation to $\mathsf{AKE}'_{\mathsf{kem}}$ as described in Fig. 5 resp. Fig. 10. The following theorem then follows from combining Theorem 1 with Lemma 1 resp. Theorem 2 with Lemma 2.

Theorem 3. *Let KEM_0 be $(1 - \delta_0)$-correct and have public keys with γ_0 bits of entropy and messages with α_0 bits of entropy. Let KEM_1 be $(1 - \delta_1)$-correct and have public keys with γ_1 bits of entropy and messages with α_1 bits of entropy. Let $\mathsf{AKE}_{\mathsf{kem}}$ resp. $\mathsf{AKE}_{\mathsf{st,kem}}$ be defined as described above by combining Fig. 11 with Fig. 5 resp. Fig. 10, where $\mathsf{G}_\mathsf{I}, \mathsf{G}_\mathsf{R} : \{0,1\}^* \to \{0,1\}^\lambda$, $\mathsf{H} : \{0,1\}^* \to \mathcal{K}$, $\mathsf{G}_{\mathsf{stI}} : \{0,1\}^\kappa \times \{0,1\}^\kappa \to \{0,1\}^{d_\mathsf{I}}$ and $\mathsf{G}_{\mathsf{stR}} : \{0,1\}^\kappa \times \{0,1\}^\kappa \to \{0,1\}^{d_\mathsf{R}}$ are modeled as random oracles. Let Q_h be the number of queries to the respective random oracle h.*

For any $\mathcal{A}$ against the $(t, \varepsilon, \mu, S, T, Q_{\mathrm{COR}})$-IND-FS-security of $\mathsf{AKE}_{\mathsf{kem}}$, there exist adversaries $\mathcal{B}_1$ and $\mathcal{B}_2$ that break $(t_1, \varepsilon_1, S, S, S, Q_{Ver})$-OW-PCVA security

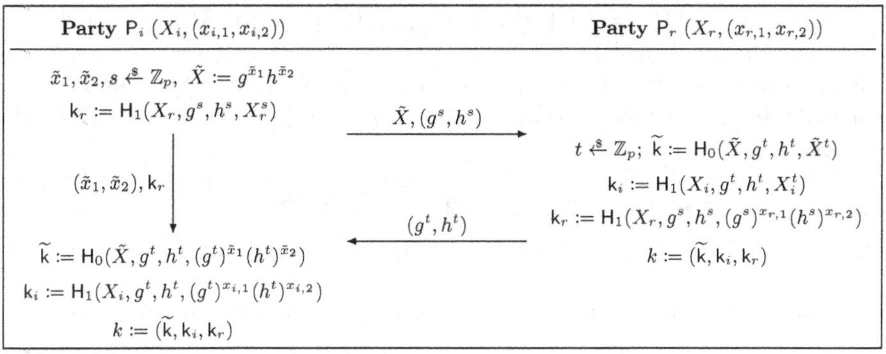

Fig. 12. AKE protocol JKRS. H_0, H_1 are independent random oracles. Protocol $\mathsf{JKRS_{KC}}$ is obtained by adding the transformation from Fig. 10.

of $\mathsf{KEM_0}$ and $(t_2, \varepsilon_2, \mu, S, S, 2Q_{Ver}, Q_{COR})$-OW-PCVA-C security of $\mathsf{KEM_1}$, where $Q_{Ver} \leq S + Q_{G_I} + Q_{G_R} + Q_H$, with $t_1 \approx t_2 \approx t$ and

$$\varepsilon \leq \varepsilon_1 + \varepsilon_2 + 2S \cdot (\delta_0 + 2\delta_1) + (S + S^2) \cdot 2^{-\lambda} + \mu^2 \cdot 2^{-\gamma_1}$$
$$+ S(S + Q_{G_I} + Q_{G_R} + Q_H) \cdot (2^{-\gamma_0} + 2^{-\alpha_0} + 2^{-\alpha_1+1}).$$

Further, for every adversary $\mathcal{A}$ that breaks the $(t, \varepsilon, \mu, S, T, Q_{COR}, Q_{ST})$-IND-FS-St-security of $\mathsf{AKE_{st,kem}}$, there exist adversaries $\mathcal{B}_1$ and $\mathcal{B}_2$ that break $(t_1, \varepsilon_1, S, S, S, Q_{Ver}, Q_{ST})$-OW-PCVA-C security of $\mathsf{KEM_0}$ and $(t_2, \varepsilon_2, \mu, S, S, 2Q_{Ver}, Q_{COR}, Q_{ST})$-OW-PCVA-CR security of $\mathsf{KEM_1}$, where $Q_{Ver} \leq S + Q_{G_I} + Q_{G_R} + Q_H$, with $t_1 \approx t_2 \approx t$ and

$$\varepsilon \leq \varepsilon_1 + \varepsilon_2 + 2S \cdot (\delta_0 + 2\delta_1) + (\mu^2 + S^2 + \mu Q_{G_{stI}} + 2SQ_{G_{stI}}) \cdot 2^{-\kappa} + \mu^2 \cdot 2^{-\gamma_1}$$
$$+ (S + S^2) \cdot 2^{-\lambda} + S(Q_{G_R} + Q_{G_I} + Q_H + S) \cdot (2^{-\gamma_0} + 2^{-\alpha_0} + 2^{-\alpha_1+1}).$$

INSTANTIATION WITH NON-COMMITTING KEM. We can use a non-committing KEM as defined in [21] to instantiate a verifiable AKE protocol very efficiently, e.g., from DDH (cf. protocol JKRS in Fig. 12). We can easily show that a non-committing KEM implies OW-PCVA-CR security of that KEM. In our full version [28, Appendix A], we recall the formal definition of NC-CCA security for KEMs from [21] and show the implication. Adding key confirmation as described in Fig. 10 then yields protocol $\mathsf{JKRS_{KC}}$.

SECURITY OF $\mathsf{JKRS_{KC}}$. We now establish security of protocol $\mathsf{JKRS_{KC}}$. Since the JKRS protocol is perfectly correct, so is $\mathsf{JKRS_{KC}}$. Further, public keys and messages have $\log(p)$ bits entropy. Security is based on the DDH assumption which asks to distinguish between (g^x, g^y, g^{xy}) and (g^x, g^y, g^z) for $x, y, z \overset{\$}{\leftarrow} \mathbb{Z}_p$.

Theorem 4. Let $\mathsf{JKRS_{KC}}$ be defined as in Fig. 12, where $\mathsf{G_I, G_R} : \{0,1\}^* \to \{0,1\}^\lambda$, $\mathsf{H} : \{0,1\}^* \to \mathcal{K}$, $\mathsf{H_0} : \{0,1\}^* \to \mathsf{KEM_0}.\mathcal{K}$, $\mathsf{H_1} : \{0,1\}^* \to \mathsf{KEM_1}.\mathcal{K}$,

$\mathsf{G_{stI}} : \{0,1\}^\kappa \times \{0,1\}^\kappa \to \{0,1\}^{d_I}$, and $\mathsf{G_{stR}} : \{0,1\}^\kappa \times \{0,1\}^\kappa \to \{0,1\}^{d_R}$ are modeled as random oracles.

For every adversary $\mathcal{A}$ that breaks the $(t, \varepsilon, \mu, S, T, Q_{\mathrm{COR}}, Q_{\mathrm{ST}})$-IND-FS-St-security of $\mathsf{JKRS_{KC}}$, there exists an adversary $\mathcal{B}$ that breaks (t', ε')-DDH with $t' \approx t$ and

$$\varepsilon \leq \varepsilon' + (\mu^2 + S^2 + \mu Q_{\mathsf{G_{stI}}} + 2SQ_{\mathsf{G_{stI}}}) \cdot 2^{-\kappa} + \mu^2 \cdot 2^{-\log(p)}$$
$$+ (S + S^2) \cdot 2^{-\lambda} + S(Q_{\mathsf{G_R}} + Q_{\mathsf{G_I}} + Q_{\mathsf{H}} + Q_{\mathsf{H_0}} + Q_{\mathsf{H_1}} + S + 1) \cdot 2^{-\log(p)} ,$$

where Q_{h} is the number of queries to the respective random oracle h.

The theorem follows from [28, Theorem 6], Lemma 2 and Theorem 2 in combination with [21, Theorem 5], where the latter deals with the optimization that only one ciphertext is sent in the second round.

INSTANTIATION FROM LATTICES. We can also instantiate the KEM-based verifiable AKE protocol using lattices assumptions. The scheme $\mathsf{KEM_{LWE}}$ described in [30, Section 3] satisfies OW-ChCCA security which implies OW-PCVA-CR security. This gives us an AKE protocol with key confirmation from LWE secure in the random oracle model.

6.2   The CCGJJ Protocol and Its Isogeny-Based Variant

It is easy to see that the core protocol from Cohn-Gordon et al. (CCGJJ) [10] is a verifiable AKE protocol, ignoring the session key hash. For completeness, we provide a formal treatment in our full paper [28, Appendix F].

ISOGENY-BASED AKE. The isogeny-based AKE protocol which was independently analyzed by de Kock, Gjøsteen and Veroni [23] and Kawashima et al. [22] follows the same blueprint as the CCGJJ protocol, relying on the group action structure of CSIDH [8] rather than prime-order groups. Thus, we also get an AKE protocol with key confirmation from isogenies, based on the same assumptions as the analysis in [22,23]. This is particularly interesting because the only group action based and tightly-secure signature scheme supporting adaptive corruptions [29] is rather inefficient.

7   KEM-Based AKE with Key Confirmation in the QROM

We analyze FS via key confirmation in the quantum random oracle model (QROM). Following [31], we use IND-CCA-secure KEMs in the multi-user, multi challenge settings as building blocks. By the key confirmation technique, we lift the result of Pan, Wagner, and Zeng [31] to FS in the QROM. The work of Pan, Wagner, and Zeng only achieves weak FS in the QROM. Our result not only preserves the security loss of their protocol, but also achieves FS and allows multiple TEST queries with single challenge bit, while [31] allows at most one single TEST query.

The MC-IND-CCA and MUC-IND-CCA security definitions of KEMs are given in our full paper [28, Appendix A]. We use notations introduced in Sect. 5 to present our protocol $\mathsf{AKE_{kem}}$. Let $\mathsf{KEM_1}$ and $\mathsf{KEM_0}$ be two KEM schemes and $\mathsf{G_I}, \mathsf{G_R} : \{0,1\}^* \to \{0,1\}^\lambda$, and $\mathsf{H} : \{0,1\}^* \to \mathcal{K}$ be hash functions, where λ is the length of key confirmation tags and $\mathcal{K}$ is the key space of $\mathsf{AKE_{kem}}$. An overview of our AKE construction $\mathsf{AKE_{kem}}$ is given in Fig. 13. $\mathsf{AKE_{kem}}$ is essentially the KEM-based AKE protocol in [31] adding key confirmation, namely, it is obtained from combining Fig. 11 and Fig. 5.

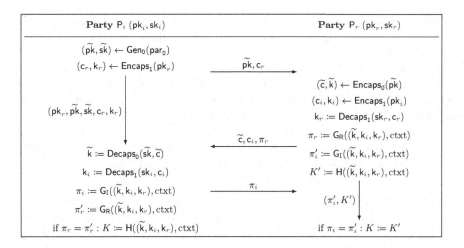

Fig. 13. AKE protocol $\mathsf{AKE_{kem}}$ from KEM schemes $\mathsf{KEM_1}$, $\mathsf{KEM_0}$, and key confirmation. The context is defined as $\mathsf{ctxt} := (\mathsf{pk}_i, \mathsf{pk}_r, \widetilde{\mathsf{pk}}, \widetilde{c}, c_i, c_r)$. $\mathsf{G_I}$, $\mathsf{G_R}$, and H are independent random oracles.

CORRECTNESS. The correctness of $\mathsf{AKE_{kem}}$ is due to $\mathsf{KEM_1}$ and $\mathsf{KEM_0}$. Each session of $\mathsf{AKE_{kem}}$ includes two ciphertexts of $\mathsf{KEM_1}$ and one ciphertext of $\mathsf{KEM_0}$. If $\mathsf{KEM_1}$ is $(1-\delta_1)$-correct and $\mathsf{KEM_0}$ is $(1-\delta_0)$-correct, then by the union bound, $\mathsf{AKE_{kem}}$ is $(1-2\delta_1-\delta_0)$-correct.

SECURITY. We prove IND-FS security of $\mathsf{AKE_{kem}}$ based on the MC-IND-CCA security of $\mathsf{KEM_1}$, the MUC-IND-CCA security of $\mathsf{KEM_0}$, and modeling $\mathsf{G_I}, \mathsf{G_R}$, and H as quantum-accessible random oracles, as stated in Theorem 5. The proof of Theorem 5 is postponed to our full version [28, Appendix E].

Theorem 5. *Let $\mathsf{KEM_0}$ be $(1-\delta_0)$-correct and have public keys with γ_0 bits of entropy and messages with α_0 bits of entropy. Let $\mathsf{KEM_1}$ be $(1-\delta_1)$-correct and have public keys with γ_1 bits of entropy and messages with α_1 bits of entropy. $\mathcal{K}_0$ and $\mathcal{K}_1$ are the KEM key spaces of $\mathsf{KEM_0}$ and $\mathsf{KEM_1}$, respectively.*

Let $\mathsf{AKE_{kem}}$ be as defined in Fig. 13, where Let $\mathsf{G_I}, \mathsf{G_R} : \{0,1\}^* \to \{0,1\}^\lambda$ and $\mathsf{H} : \{0,1\}^* \to \mathcal{K}$. For every adversary $\mathcal{A}$ that breaks the

$(t, \varepsilon, \mu, S, T, Q_{\mathrm{COR}})$-IND-FS-*security of* $\mathsf{AKE_{KC}}$, *there exists an adversary* $\mathcal{B}_0$ *that breaks the* $(t'_0, \varepsilon'_0, S, S)$-MUC-IND-CCA *security of* $\mathsf{KEM_0}$ *and an adversary* $\mathcal{B}_1$ *that breaks the* $(t'_1, \varepsilon'_1, S)$-MC-IND-CCA *security of* $\mathsf{KEM_1}$ *with* $t'_0 \approx t'_1 \approx t$ *and*

$$\varepsilon \leq 2\varepsilon'_0 + 2\mu\varepsilon'_1 + 2S(\delta_0 + \mu\delta_1) + \mu^2 2^{-\gamma_1} + \mu S 2^{-\lambda+1}$$
$$+ S^2(2^{-\alpha_1} + 2^{-\gamma_0} + 2^{-\alpha_0}) + \frac{2\mu(Q_{\mathsf{G_R}} + Q_{\mathsf{G_I}})\sqrt{S}}{\sqrt{|\mathcal{K}_1|}} + \frac{2Q_{\mathsf{H}}\sqrt{S}}{\sqrt{|\mathcal{K}_0|}},$$

where $Q_{\mathsf{G_I}}, Q_{\mathsf{G_R}}$ *and* Q_{H} *are the number of quantum-superposition queries to* $\mathsf{G_I}$, $\mathsf{G_R}$ *and* H.

Remark 1 (Implicit Rejection). Following [31], when proving Theorem 5, we assume $\mathsf{KEM_1}$ and $\mathsf{KEM_0}$ have implicit rejection [5], namely, if the input ciphertext is invalid, then the decapsulation algorithm returns a pseudorandom KEM key. We use implicit-rejection KEM because it simplifies our AKE proof.

To adapt the proof of Theorem 5 to the one that uses explicit-rejection KEMs, we can add extra codes in the games sequence to deal with explicit rejections from KEM. Concretely, upon receiving an invalid KEM ciphertext, the session oracle (e.g., $\mathrm{SESSION_R}$, $\mathrm{DER_R}$, or $\mathrm{DER_I}$) simply sets the session key as "reject" and returns $\bot$. This can be tightly simulated by MUC-IND-CCA and MC-IND-CCA secure KEMs with explicit rejection, and thus the security bound in Theorem 5 also applies to explicit-rejection KEMs.

Remark 2 (Instantiations with LWE). In [31], Pan et al. proposed lattice-based instantiations of MC-IND-CCA-secure KEM and MUC-IND-CCA-secure KEM that have (almost-)tight reduction from the well-known Learning With Errors (LWE) problem in the QROM. Here we only discuss the security loss of these KEM schemes and give the final security loss of our AKE protocol instantiated with these KEM schemes.

Let $\varepsilon_{\mathsf{lwe}}$ be the best computational advantage against LWE assumptions and λ be the security parameter (which decides the security level, the length of message, etc.). The two KEM schemes proposed in [31] have asymptotic bounds $\varepsilon'_1 \leq \Theta(\lambda) \cdot \varepsilon_{\mathsf{lwe}}$ and $\varepsilon'_0 \leq \Theta(\lambda) \cdot \varepsilon_{\mathsf{lwe}}$, where ε'_1 and ε'_0 are the computational advantages against MC-IND-CCA security and MUC-IND-CCA security of the KEM schemes in [31], respectively. By combining these bounds with the bounds given in Theorem 5, we have

$$\varepsilon \leq \Theta(\lambda) + \Theta(\mu) \cdot \Theta(\lambda) \cdot \varepsilon_{\mathsf{lwe}} = \Theta(\mu) \cdot \Theta(\lambda) \cdot \varepsilon_{\mathsf{lwe}},$$

where ε is the computational advantage against the resulting AKE protocol. This gives us a session-tight and square-root-tight (namely, does not suffer from the square-root security loss) LWE-based instantiation of AKE with full forward secrecy in the QROM.

Acknowledgements. We thank the anonymous reviewers for their valuable comments on better motivating our works and comparisons with the related work. Doreen Riepel was supported in part by Bellare's KACST grant. Jiaxin Pan was supported in part by the Research Council of Norway (RCN) under Project No. 324235, and Runzhi Zeng were supported by the same project from RCN.

References

1. Abdalla, M., Fouque, P.A., Pointcheval, D.: Password-based authenticated key exchange in the three-party setting. In: Vaudenay, S. (ed.) PKC 2005. LNCS, vol. 3386, pp. 65–84. Springer, Heidelberg (2005). https://doi.org/10.1007/978-3-540-30580-4_6

2. Bellare, M., Boldyreva, A., Micali, S.: Public-key encryption in a multi-user setting: security proofs and improvements. In: Preneel, B. (ed.) EUROCRYPT 2000. LNCS, vol. 1807, pp. 259–274. Springer, Heidelberg (2000). https://doi.org/10.1007/3-540-45539-6_18

3. Bellare, M., Rogaway, P.: Entity authentication and key distribution. In: Stinson, D.R. (ed.) CRYPTO 1993. LNCS, vol. 773, pp. 232–249. Springer, Heidelberg (1994). https://doi.org/10.1007/3-540-48329-2_21

4. Bellare, M., Rogaway, P.: The security of triple encryption and a framework for code-based game-playing proofs. In: Vaudenay, S. (ed.) EUROCRYPT 2006. LNCS, vol. 4004, pp. 409–426. Springer, Heidelberg (2006). https://doi.org/10.1007/11761679_25

5. Bernstein, D.J., Persichetti, E.: Towards KEM unification. Cryptology ePrint Archive, Report 2018/526 (2018). https://eprint.iacr.org/2018/526

6. Boneh, D., Dagdelen, Ö., Fischlin, M., Lehmann, A., Schaffner, C., Zhandry, M.: Random oracles in a quantum world. In: Lee, D.H., Wang, X. (eds.) ASIACRYPT 2011. LNCS, vol. 7073, pp. 41–69. Springer, Heidelberg (2011). https://doi.org/10.1007/978-3-642-25385-0_3

7. Canetti, R., Krawczyk, H.: Analysis of key-exchange protocols and their use for building secure channels. In: Pfitzmann, B. (ed.) EUROCRYPT 2001. LNCS, vol. 2045, pp. 453–474. Springer, Heidelberg (2001). https://doi.org/10.1007/3-540-44987-6_28

8. Castryck, W., Lange, T., Martindale, C., Panny, L., Renes, J.: CSIDH: an efficient post-quantum commutative group action. In: Peyrin, T., Galbraith, S. (eds.) ASIACRYPT 2018, Part III. LNCS, vol. 11274, pp. 395–427. Springer, Heidelberg (2018). https://doi.org/10.1007/978-3-030-03332-3_15

9. Chen, J., Wee, H.: Fully, (almost) tightly secure IBE and dual system groups. In: Canetti, R., Garay, J.A. (eds.) CRYPTO 2013, Part II. LNCS, vol. 8043, pp. 435–460. Springer, Heidelberg (2013). https://doi.org/10.1007/978-3-642-40084-1_25

10. Cohn-Gordon, K., Cremers, C., Gjøsteen, K., Jacobsen, H., Jager, T.: Highly efficient key exchange protocols with optimal tightness. In: Boldyreva, A., Micciancio, D. (eds.) CRYPTO 2019, Part III. LNCS, vol. 11694, pp. 767–797. Springer, Heidelberg (2019). https://doi.org/10.1007/978-3-030-26954-8_25

11. Davis, H., Günther, F.: Tighter proofs for the SIGMA and TLS 1.3 key exchange protocols. In: Sako, K., Tippenhauer, N.O. (eds.) ACNS 2021, Part II. LNCS, vol. 12727, pp. 448–479. Springer, Heidelberg (2021). https://doi.org/10.1007/978-3-030-78375-4_18

12. Delpech de Saint Guilhem, C., Fischlin, M., Warinschi, B.: Authentication in key-exchange: definitions, relations and composition. In: Jia, L., Küsters, R. (eds.) CSF 2020 Computer Security Foundations Symposium, pp. 288–303. IEEE Computer Society Press (2020). https://doi.org/10.1109/CSF49147.2020.00028

13. Diemert, D., Gellert, K., Jager, T., Lyu, L.: More efficient digital signatures with tight multi-user security. In: Garay, J. (ed.) PKC 2021, Part II. LNCS, vol. 12711, pp. 1–31. Springer, Heidelberg (2021). https://doi.org/10.1007/978-3-030-75248-4_1

14. Diemert, D., Jager, T.: On the tight security of TLS 1.3: theoretically sound cryptographic parameters for real-world deployments. J. Cryptol. **34**(3), 30 (2021). https://doi.org/10.1007/s00145-021-09388-x

15. Fischlin, M., Günther, F., Schmidt, B., Warinschi, B.: Key confirmation in key exchange: a formal treatment and implications for TLS 1.3. In: 2016 IEEE Symposium on Security and Privacy, pp. 452–469. IEEE Computer Society Press, May 2016. https://doi.org/10.1109/SP.2016.34

16. Freire, E.S.V., Hofheinz, D., Kiltz, E., Paterson, K.G.: Non-interactive key exchange. In: Kurosawa, K., Hanaoka, G. (eds.) PKC 2013. LNCS, vol. 7778, pp. 254–271. Springer, Heidelberg (2013). https://doi.org/10.1007/978-3-642-36362-7_17

17. Gay, R., Hofheinz, D., Kiltz, E., Wee, H.: Tightly CCA-secure encryption without pairings. In: Fischlin, M., Coron, J.S. (eds.) EUROCRYPT 2016, Part I. LNCS, vol. 9665, pp. 1–27. Springer, Heidelberg (2016). https://doi.org/10.1007/978-3-662-49890-3_1

18. Gellert, K., Gjøsteen, K., Jacobsen, H., Jager, T.: On optimal tightness for key exchange with full forward secrecy via key confirmation. In: Handschuh, H., Lysyanskaya, A. (eds.) CRYPTO 2023. LNCS, Springer, Heidelberg (2023). https://doi.org/10.1007/978-3-031-38551-3_10

19. Gjøsteen, K., Jager, T.: Practical and tightly-secure digital signatures and authenticated key exchange. In: Shacham, H., Boldyreva, A. (eds.) CRYPTO 2018, Part II. LNCS, vol. 10992, pp. 95–125. Springer, Heidelberg (2018). https://doi.org/10.1007/978-3-319-96881-0_4

20. Hövelmanns, K., Kiltz, E., Schäge, S., Unruh, D.: Generic authenticated key exchange in the quantum random oracle model. In: Kiayias, A., Kohlweiss, M., Wallden, P., Zikas, V. (eds.) PKC 2020, Part II. LNCS, vol. 12111, pp. 389–422. Springer, Heidelberg (2020). https://doi.org/10.1007/978-3-030-45388-6_14

21. Jager, T., Kiltz, E., Riepel, D., Schäge, S.: Tightly-secure authenticated key exchange, revisited. In: Canteaut, A., Standaert, F.X. (eds.) EUROCRYPT 2021, Part I. LNCS, vol. 12696, pp. 117–146. Springer, Heidelberg (2021). https://doi.org/10.1007/978-3-030-77870-5_5

22. Kawashima, T., Takashima, K., Aikawa, Y., Takagi, T.: An efficient authenticated key exchange from random self-reducibility on CSIDH. In: Hong, D. (ed.) ICISC 2020. LNCS, vol. 12593, pp. 58–84. Springer, Heidelberg (2020). https://doi.org/10.1007/978-3-030-68890-5_4

23. de Kock, B., Gjøsteen, K., Veroni, M.: Practical isogeny-based key-exchange with optimal tightness. In: Dunkelman, O., Jacobson Jr., M.J., O'Flynn, C. (eds.) SAC 2020. LNCS, vol. 12804, pp. 451–479. Springer, Heidelberg (2020). https://doi.org/10.1007/978-3-030-81652-0_18

24. Krawczyk, H.: HMQV: a high-performance secure Diffie-Hellman protocol. In: Shoup, V. (ed.) CRYPTO 2005. LNCS, vol. 3621, pp. 546–566. Springer, Heidelberg (2005). https://doi.org/10.1007/11535218_33

25. LaMacchia, B.A., Lauter, K., Mityagin, A.: Stronger security of authenticated key exchange. In: Susilo, W., Liu, J.K., Mu, Y. (eds.) ProvSec 2007. LNCS, vol. 4784, pp. 1–16. Springer, Heidelberg (Nov (2007)

26. Liu, X., Liu, S., Gu, D., Weng, J.: Two-pass authenticated key exchange with explicit authentication and tight security. In: Moriai, S., Wang, H. (eds.) ASIACRYPT 2020, Part II. LNCS, vol. 12492, pp. 785–814. Springer, Heidelberg (2020). https://doi.org/10.1007/978-3-030-64834-3_27

27. Pan, J., Qian, C., Ringerud, M.: Signed (group) Diffie-Hellman key exchange with tight security. J. Cryptol. **35**(4), 26 (2022). https://doi.org/10.1007/s00145-022-09438-y
28. Pan, J., Riepel, D., Zeng, R.: Key exchange with tight (full) forward secrecy via key confirmation. In: Cryptology ePrint Archive (2024)
29. Pan, J., Wagner, B.: Lattice-based signatures with tight adaptive corruptions and more. In: Hanaoka, G., Shikata, J., Watanabe, Y. (eds.) PKC 2022, Part II. LNCS, vol. 13178, pp. 347–378. Springer, Heidelberg (2022). https://doi.org/10.1007/978-3-030-97131-1_12
30. Pan, J., Wagner, B., Zeng, R.: Lattice-based authenticated key exchange with tight security. In: Handschuh, H., Lysyanskaya, A. (eds.) CRYPTO 2023. LNCS, Springer, Heidelberg (2023). https://doi.org/10.1007/978-3-031-38554-4_20
31. Pan, J., Wagner, B., Zeng, R.: Tighter security for generic authenticated key exchange in the QROM. In: ASIACRYPT 2023. LNCS, Springer, Heidelberg (2023). https://doi.org/10.1007/978-981-99-8730-6_13, https://eprint.iacr.org/2023/1380
32. Unruh, D.: Revocable quantum timed-release encryption. In: Nguyen, P.Q., Oswald, E. (eds.) EUROCRYPT 2014. LNCS, vol. 8441, pp. 129–146. Springer, Heidelberg (2014). https://doi.org/10.1007/978-3-642-55220-5_8

SLAP: Succinct Lattice-Based Polynomial Commitments from Standard Assumptions

Martin R. Albrecht[1]([✉]), Giacomo Fenzi[2], Oleksandra Lapiha[3], and Ngoc Khanh Nguyen[4]

[1] King's College London and SandboxAQ, London, UK
martin.albrecht@kcl.ac.uk, martin.albrecht@sandboxaq.com
[2] EPFL, Lausanne, Switzerland
giacomo.fenzi@epfl.ch
[3] Royal Holloway, University of London, London, UK
sasha.lapiha.2021@live.rhul.ac.uk
[4] King's College London, London, UK
ngoc_khanh.nguyen@kcl.ac.uk

Abstract. Recent works on lattice-based extractable polynomial commitments can be grouped into two classes: (i) non-interactive constructions that stem from the functional commitment by Albrecht, Cini, Lai, Malavolta and Thyagarajan (CRYPTO 2022), and (ii) lattice adaptations of the Bulletproofs protocol (S&P 2018). The former class enjoys security in the standard model, albeit a knowledge assumption is desired. In contrast, Bulletproof-like protocols can be made secure under falsifiable assumptions, but due to technical limitations regarding subtractive sets, they only offer inverse-polynomial soundness error. This issue becomes particularly problematic when transforming these protocols to the non-interactive setting using the Fiat-Shamir paradigm.

In this work, we propose the first lattice-based non-interactive extractable polynomial commitment scheme which achieves polylogarithmic proof size and verifier runtime (in the length of the committed message) under standard assumptions in the random oracle model. At the core of our work lies a new tree-based commitment scheme, along with an efficient proof of polynomial evaluation inspired by FRI (ICALP 2018). Natively, the interactive version of the construction is secure under a "multi-instance version" of the Power-Ring BASIS assumption (Eprint 2023/846). We then base security on the Module-SIS assumption by introducing several re-randomisation techniques which can be of independent interest.

1 Introduction

Zero-knowledge succinct non-interactive arguments of knowledge (zk-SNARKs) [Kil92,Mic94] are a cryptographic primitive that allows a prover to produce a short proof that a statement is true without revealing any information

© International Association for Cryptologic Research 2024
M. Joye and G. Leander (Eds.): EUROCRYPT 2024, LNCS 14657, pp. 90–119, 2024.
https://doi.org/10.1007/978-3-031-58754-2_4

beyond the validity of the statement itself. A particularly successful paradigm in the construction of zkSNARKs, which has been evident since the "canonical" construction of zkSNARKs [Mic94], is that of combining an *information theoretical proof system* with a *cryptographic compiler*. Originally, this was done via the combination of probabilistic checkable proof (PCPs) [BFLS91] and vector commitment schemes [Mer90]. While the zkSNARKs obtained from these ingredients were not concretely efficient (mostly due to the inefficiency of the PCP), [BCS16] iterated on this approach, introducing interactive oracle proofs (IOPs), and these efforts lead to many concretely deployed constructions (see e.g. [BBHR18b, BCRSVW19, AHIV22, GLSTW21, COS20]). Currently, some of the most efficient and widely deployed zkSNARKs are based on a similar ingredient combination, namely (i) polynomial IOPs (PIOPs) [CHMMVW20]; (ii) and polynomial commitment schemes [KZG10].

In this work, we focus on the cryptographic component of the above recipe, namely polynomial commitment schemes. A polynomial commitment scheme is a generalisation of vector commitments in which a prover is able to commit to any polynomial of bounded degree $f := \sum_{i=0}^{d-1} f_i \cdot \mathsf{X}^i$ over a ring $\mathcal{R}$, and then later produce a proof π that $f(u) = z$ for some public u, z. For the purpose of this work, we are concerned with polynomial commitment schemes that are *succinct* in both the size of the proof π and in the verification time, i.e. we wish both to be polylogarithmic in d. We aim the verification time to be polylogarithmic *without preprocessing* dependent on u, as that reflects the usage of polynomial commitment schemes in many PIOPs. Further, to obtain a SNARK, we will require that π is a *proof of knowledge*, and call a polynomial commitment scheme with this property *extractable*.

The literature on polynomial commitments [KZG10, BBBPWM18, BMMTV21, Lee21, BFS20, BHRRS21, WTsTW17] is vast, but most of the existing construction rely on classical computational assumptions, and are thus insecure against quantum adversaries. If we require post-quantum security, the only concretely and asymptotically efficient polynomial commitment schemes that are currently known are based on the FRI IOP of Proximity [BBHR18a], compiled into an argument via the BCS construction [BCS16] in the (quantum) random oracle model [CMS19].

A natural question is whether using post-quantum computational assumptions with "more structure" can lead to more efficient plausibly post-quantum secure polynomial commitment schemes. Constructions based on hard lattice problems have been successfully deployed in various areas of cryptography, as evidenced by the NIST PQC competition, which concluded by standardising lattice-based solutions for both key encapsulation mechanisms and signatures.

Constructions from Functional Commitments. Recently, a number of lattice-based polynomial commitment schemes were introduced, mostly as a result of promising work on linear functional commitments [ACLMT22, WW23b, CP23, PPS21, BCFL22, FLV23, CLM23]. At a high level, by interpreting the evaluation $f(u) = z$ as the linear relation $\langle \mathbf{f}, \mathsf{pow}(u) \rangle = z$, where $\mathsf{pow}(u) = (1, u, \ldots, u^{d-1})$, those schemes naturally lead to polynomial commitments. A significant limitation in that paradigm is that, without preprocessing, the verification cost (when performed naively[1]) is linear in d and thus not succinct. Since in most PIOPs of interest u is sampled during the interactive portion of the protocol, and thus cannot be preprocessed, this limits the applicability of those schemes. Furthermore, only [ACLMT22, BCFL22, CLM23, FLV23] offer extractability, albeit under a knowledge k-M-ISIS assumption [ACLMT22]. However, this knowledge k-M-ISIS assumption has been recently shown to be (at least "morally") broken [WW23a].

Split-and-fold Protocols. Another line of research on lattice-based (interactive) polynomial commitments with succinct verification [BCS23, CLM23] stems from the lattice adaptation [BLNS20] of the Bulletproofs interactive protocol [BBBPWM18]. Unfortunately, both constructions inherit the inverse-polynomial soundness error from [BLNS20]. Although basic parallel repetition can be applied in the interactive setting for soundness amplification [AF22], this strategy incurs a super-polynomial security loss when applying the Fiat-Shamir transformation in the random oracle model, as shown by Attema, Fehr and Klooß [AFK22].

Independently, Fenzi, Moghaddas and Nguyen [FMN23] extended a commitment scheme introduced by Wee and Wu [WW23b] to efficiently prove polynomial evaluations with a split-and-fold approach from FRI [BBHR18a]. The authors pick an exponential-sized challenge space, which results in negligible soundness error in one-shot. As a downside, due to the enormous norm growth of extracted witnesses along with slack, which has direct influence on the proof system modulus and other lattice parameters, [FMN23] only manages to achieve *quasi*-polylogarithmic proof and verifier complexity. Also, their scheme inherits several practical inefficiencies from [WW23b], i.e. a common reference string (CRS) and committing time that are undesirably large, as they are quadratic in the degree of the committed polynomial. Further, the binding property of the commitment scheme relies on the non-standard Power-Ring-BASIS (PRISIS) assumption[2], which did not feature a reduction from more well-understood lattice problems.

In this work, we iterate on this previous construction, and study the following open question.

Can we construct a non-interactive, extractable polynomial commitment scheme with polylogarithmic communication and verifier complexity; (quasi)-linear prover time; negligible knowledge soundness error and whose security relies on standard lattice assumptions?

1.1 Our Contributions

We present SLAP, the first lattice-based polynomial commitment scheme that achieves the above goals.

---

[1] The recent work of Fisch, Liu and Vesely [FLV23] manages to avoid this issue.

[2] Technically, the construction can be based either on PRISIS, or more general PowerBASIS assumption.

Merkle-PRISIS Commitment Scheme. Our starting point is the PRISIS-based commitment scheme of Fenzi, Moghaddas and Nguyen [FMN23] which is compressing and supports arbitrarily large messages. We will use it as a subroutine to build a Merkle tree. Concretely, for a message $\mathbf{f} = (f_j)_{j \in [\ell]} \in \mathcal{R}^d$ where $\ell = 2^h$, we consider vectors $\mathbf{t}_{h,j} := f_j \cdot \mathbf{e}$ to be the leaves of the Merkle tree, where $\mathbf{e} \in \mathcal{R}^n$ is a fixed vector defined later to argue binding. Then, given the i-th layer $(\mathbf{t}_{i,j})_{j \in [2^i]}$ of the tree, we commit to the pairs of the form $(\mathbf{t}_{i,2j-1}, \mathbf{t}_{i,2j}) \in \mathcal{R}^{2n}$ to obtain PRISIS commitments $(\mathbf{t}_{i-1,j})_{i \in [2^{i-1}]} \in \mathcal{R}^n$. The final commitment is the root $\mathbf{t}_{1,1} \in \mathcal{R}^n$.

An immediate advantage over the original construction of [FMN23] is a quasi-linear commitment time. Indeed, we only apply the PRISIS commitment scheme for constant-sized messages. Hence, the only non-constant cost comes from building the Merkle tree, which is quasi-linear[3]. Furthermore, since the commitment key for each layer is of constant size, the common reference string has size only polylog(d).

Security Under Module-SIS via New Re-randomisation Techniques. The binding property of our commitment scheme holds under a "multi-instance" version of the PRISIS assumption, which we call h-PRISIS. Recall that a PRISIS problem [FMN23] belongs to the class of "SIS-with-hints" problems [ACLMT22, BLNS23, WW23b], i.e. given a matrix $\mathbf{A}$ with some a hint aux, find a short non-zero vector $\mathbf{s}$ such that $\mathbf{A} \cdot \mathbf{s} = \mathbf{0}$. In the multi-instance version of "SIS-with-hints", the adversary is given $h \geq 2$ pairs of challenges $(\mathbf{A}_i, \mathsf{aux}_i)_{i \in [h]}$ generated as above, and the goal is to find a short non-zero vector such that $[\mathbf{A}_1 \mid \cdots \mid \mathbf{A}_h] \cdot \mathbf{s} = \mathbf{0}$.

In this work, we introduce new re-randomisation techniques to argue that, for a certain type of "SIS-with-hints" problems, the multi-instance version is no easier than the single-instance version. In particular, in Sect. 3.2, we give a reduction showing that h-PRISIS is no easier than PRISIS for $h = \mathsf{poly}(\lambda)$. Using the same re-randomisation strategy, we also provide a reduction in full version of the paper that Twin-k-M-ISIS [BCFL22] is no easier than $2k$-M-ISIS [ACLMT22]. These re-randomisation tricks and reductions might be of independent interest.

Finally, we apply the result from [FMN23] which says that a single-instance PRISIS for "small parameters" is no easier than Module-SIS [LS15]. Since we work with such parameters when building a Merkle tree of arity two, we conclude that the binding property of the Merkle-PRISIS commitment scheme holds under the Module-SIS assumption.

Polynomial Evaluation Protocol and Negligible Soundness. As a next step, we augment the new commitment scheme with a log d-round *interactive* polynomial evaluation proof, that applies a "split-and-fold" approach from FRI [BBHR18a]. The protocol has polylogarithmic communication and verifier complexity, while also simultaneously achieving negligible knowledge soundness error *without parallel repetition.*

---

[3] The *quasi* part comes from the fact that q is a super-polynomial in d. Hence, performing operations over $\mathcal{R}_q := \mathbb{Z}_q[X]/(X^N + 1)$ takes polylog(d) time.

The crucial difference from [FMN23] is that here we apply soundness amplification via batching, namely proving multiple statements of the form $f_i(u) = z_i$ simultaneously. We note that a similar approach was applied in the setting of groups of unknown order [BHRRS21], to argue knowledge soundness, we do not aim to find a short (right-)inverse but instead we prove that our protocol satisfies coordinate-wise special soundness [FMN23]. This results in concretely smaller blow-up in parameters. Finally, we show how to achieve zero-knowledge by applying the standard Fiat-Shamir-with-aborts paradigm for lattices [BTT22].

Our construction natively supports polynomials over the standard power-of-two cyclotomic rings $\mathcal{R}_q := \mathbb{Z}_q[X]/(X^N + 1)$. In order to make it compatible with current Polynomial IOPs, the commitment scheme should be able to commit and prove evaluations over finite fields. To this end, we apply the $\mathbb{Z}_q$-to-$\mathcal{R}_q$ transformation demonstrated by Lyubashevsky, Nguyen and Plançon [LNP22] to map a polynomial evaluation statement over $\mathbb{Z}_q$ to one over $\mathcal{R}_q$, where the polynomial in the latter case has degree N times smaller. This technique is generic and could be applied to subsequent lattice-based constructions for more efficiency.

1.2 Related Works

We provide a literature review on the existing publicly-verifiable succinct interactive proof systems from lattices. Bootle, Lyubashevsky, Nguyen and Seiler [BLNS20] introduced the first lattice-based adaptation of the Bulletproofs protocol [BCCGP16, BBBPWM18] over polynomial rings $\mathcal{R}_q = \mathbb{Z}_q[X]/(X^N + 1)$, achieving polylogarithmic proof sizes. This methodology was later improved in the context of soundness analysis [ACK21, AL21], and generalised to the bilinear module setting [BCS21].

The core protocol, unfortunately, has the following three drawbacks. First, the verification time is linear in the witness size. Second, soundness error of the protocol is only $1/\mathsf{poly}(\lambda)$, and thus soundness amplification is necessary. The reason for this limitation is a technical requirement on the challenge space, where any two distinct challenges have to be invertible over the ring, and what is more, its (scaled) inverse has to be short (such sets are called subtractive). As demonstrated in [AL21], such sets can only have polynomial size. Thirdly, we need to account for slack and a huge norm blow-up when performing knowledge extraction. In the case of lattice Bulletproofs, this boils down to inverting a 3×3 Vandermonde matrix for each round, and thus the extracted witness suffers a blow-up in the order of $\mathsf{poly}(\lambda)^{3h}$, where h is the number of rounds. Since, for security purposes, the proof system modulus q has to be larger than the norm of the extracted witness, we conclude that q must be super-polynomial.

Recently, Bootle, Chiesa and Sotiraki [BCS23] and Cini, Lai and Malavolta [CLM23] independently proposed variants of the lattice Bulletproofs protocol which achieve polylogarithmic verification time. The work of [BCS23] avoids linear-time verification via a delegation protocol inspired by Dory [Lee21]. On the other hand, [CLM23] introduces additional power structure on the Ajtai commitment [Ajt96], which enables succinct verification at the cost of a new assumption called Vanishing-SIS. The aforementioned works still inherit the latter two problems above.

Bünz and Fisch [BF22] considered a modified protocol, where instead of subtractive sets, the challenges are simply integers in the range $[0, 2^{\lambda-1})$. Then, using a new knowledge extraction strategy called "almost special soundness", the authors manage to achieve negligible soundness error – also in the non-interactive setting. However, the protocol still maintains linear-time verification and suffers from large extracted norm growth.

Fenzi, Moghaddas and Nguyen [FMN23] moved away from the lattice Bulletproofs template, and instead considered a commitment scheme based on a power variant of the BASIS assumption [WW23b]. The algebraic structure of the commitment allows proving polynomial evaluations using the FRI-type split-and-fold approach, rather than the one from Bulletproofs. An immediate consequence of this change is the norm blow-up in the order of $\mathsf{poly}(\lambda)^h$, since the knowledge extractor now only needs to account for the norm growth from inverting a 2×2 Vandermonde matrix. This comes at the cost of a trusted setup. The authors propose two concrete instantiations, which either achieve polylogarithmic verification time (using subtractive sets), or negligible soundness error (using an exponential-size challenge space) – but not both.

Beullens and Seiler [BS23] proposed an interactive proof, which successfully combines ideas from lattice-based batch arguments [BBCdGL18, NS22] with algebraic techniques from the non-interactive zero-knowledge (NIZK) framework by Lyubashevsky, Nguyen and Plançon [LNP22]. The protocol achieves asymptotically polylogarithmic proof size, and concretely $\approx 50\mathrm{KB}$ proofs for circuits of size 2^{20}. The key to achieving such small proofs in practice is proving exactly that the short witness $\mathbf{s}$ satisfies a relation $\|\mathbf{s}\| = \beta$ without any blow-up in the extracted norm. As in [LNP22], the approach is to prove that $\|\mathbf{s}\| \ll \sqrt{q}$ via an *approximate range proof* [LNS21, GHL22], and $\|\mathbf{s}\|^2 = \beta^2 \bmod q$ as a quadratic equation over $\mathbb{Z}_q$. Here, Beullens and Seiler observed that both claims are folding-friendly and can thus be proven efficiently using recursion. As a downside, the protocol does not support succinct verification due to the approximate range proof part.

In this work, we address the three limitations stated above: (i) our construction achieves polylogarithmic verification time, (ii) the protocol enjoys negligible soundness error via a batching argument, and (iii) thanks to the FRI split-and-fold structure, we suffer the norm blow-up in the order of $\mathsf{poly}(\lambda)^h$ rather than $\mathsf{poly}(\lambda)^{3h}$ as in the Bulletproofs-type protocols. Unfortunately, the algebraic structure of our commitment comes at a price of a trusted setup.

We summarise the comparison with prior works in Table 1. To estimate concrete efficiency from asymptotic statements, we estimate so-called "stretch" and "slack" of the protocols. That is, in every lattice-based proof system there is a part where the prover wants to prove knowledge of a short vector $\mathbf{s}$ such that $\mathbf{A} \cdot \mathbf{s} = \mathbf{t}$ and $\|\mathbf{s}\| \leq \beta$. However, due to technical reasons, it is the case that one can only extract a slightly larger vector $\mathbf{z}$, along with a scalar c for which

$$\mathbf{A} \cdot \mathbf{z} = c \cdot \mathbf{t} \quad \text{and} \quad \|\mathbf{z}\| \leq \gamma_{\mathsf{stretch}} \cdot \beta \quad \text{and} \quad \|c\| \leq \gamma_{\mathsf{slack}}. \tag{1}$$

In the literature, $\gamma_{\mathsf{stretch}}$ is called stretch, and c is the slack. The term $\gamma_{\mathsf{stretch}} \cdot \gamma_{\mathsf{slack}} \in \mathbb{R}_+$ often indicates how efficient the underlying protocol is, because, for security, the proof system modulus has to be larger than $(\gamma_{\mathsf{stretch}} \cdot \gamma_{\mathsf{slack}}) \cdot \beta$. For instance, [BS23] achieves $\gamma_{\mathsf{stretch}}, \gamma_{\mathsf{slack}} \in O(1)$, which results in small proof sizes.

Naturally, more efficient lattice-based constructions were proposed in the designated-verifier setting [ISW21,SSEK22], which enjoy proofs of size a few kilobytes at the cost of very large crs (in the order of tens of gigabytes). This line of works follows the template of combining Linear PCPs with a secret-key homomorphic encryption scheme [BCIOP13].

It is also worth mentioning that lattice assumptions are not only used to construct lattice-based commitments, but also to build non-interactive proof systems from the Fiat-Shamir transformation *without* requiring a random oracle. For this goal, a so-called correlation intractable hash function [CGH04] is needed, which can be built from the Learning with Errors (LWE) problem [HLR21]. Following this methodology, an exciting recent work by Choudhuri, Jain and Jin [CJJ22] showed how to obtain non-interactive succinct arguments for languages in P, assuming only the LWE problem with polynomial modulus. This result can be further applied to RAM delegation.

1.3   Technical Overview

We provide a brief overview of our techniques. First, let us introduce some notation. We write $\mathbb{Z}_2^h$ for the set of binary strings of length h, and let $\mathbb{Z}_2^{\leq h} := \cup_{0 \leq j \leq h} \mathbb{Z}_2^j$. For $\mathbf{b} = (b_1, \ldots, b_h) \in \mathbb{Z}_2^h$ and $j \in [h]$ we let $\mathbf{b}_{:j} = (b_1, \ldots, b_j) \in \mathbb{Z}_2^j$. Let λ be a security parameter, q be an odd prime, and N be a power-of-two. Define the polynomial rings $\mathcal{R} := \mathbb{Z}[X]/(X^N + 1)$ and $\mathcal{R}_q := \mathbb{Z}_q[X]/(X^N + 1)$. Letting $\delta \geq 2$ be a (fixed) base and $n \geq 1$, we define the gadget matrix as $\mathbf{G}_n := \begin{bmatrix} 1 & \delta & \cdots & \delta^{\tilde{q}} \end{bmatrix} \otimes \mathbf{I}_n \in \mathcal{R}_q^{n \times n\tilde{q}}$ where $\tilde{q} := \lfloor \log_\delta q \rfloor + 1$. For simplicity, we omit the subscript n and write $\mathbf{G} := \mathbf{G}_n$ when clear from context. In our context, a *trapdoor* for a matrix $\mathbf{B}$ is a short matrix such that $\mathbf{B} \cdot \mathbf{T} = \mathbf{G}$. In particular, knowledge of a trapdoor of $\mathbf{B}$ enables to sample (random) short preimages of $\mathbf{B}$, i.e. short $\mathbf{v}$ such that $\mathbf{B} \cdot \mathbf{v} = \mathbf{t}$ for a given image $\mathbf{t}$ [MP12]. We also let $\mathbf{e}$ be the unit vector with 1 as its first (and only) entry.

Table 1. Comparison of lattice-based publicly verifiable (interactive) polynomial commitments for polynomials of degree at most d with polylogarithmic communication complexity.

scheme	assumption	TP	soundness error	time		size		stretch × slack
				prover	verifier	crs	proof	
[BLNS20]	M-SIS	✓	$1/\text{poly}(\lambda)$	$O(d)$	$O(d)$	$O(1)$	$O(\log d)$	$O(d^{3\log N})$
[BCS23]	M-SIS	✓	$1/\text{poly}(\lambda)$	$O(d)$	$O(\log^2 d)$	$O(1)$	$O(\log^2 d)$	$O(d^{6\log N})$
[CLM23]	vSIS	✓	$1/\text{poly}(\lambda)$	$O(d)$	$O(\log d)$	$O(1)$	$O(\log d)$	$O(d^{4\log N})$
[BF22]	(M-)SIS	✓	$\text{negl}(\lambda)$	$O(d)$	$O(d)$	$O(1)$	$O(\log d)$	$O(d^{\log d+2\lambda})$
[BS23]	M-SIS	✓	$\text{negl}(\lambda)$	$O(d)$	$O(d)$	$O(1)$	$O(\log d)$	$O(1)$
[FMN23]	PowerBASIS	✗	$1/\text{poly}(\lambda)$	$O(d^2)$	$O(\log d)$	$O(d^2)$	$O(\log d)$	$O(d^{\log N})$
SLAP	M-SIS	✗	$\text{negl}(\lambda)$	$O(d)$	$O(\log^2 d)$	$O(\log d)$	$O(\log^2 d)$	$O(d^{\log N})$

We count the runtime (resp. sizes) in the number of operations (resp. elements) in $\mathcal{R}_q :=$ $\mathbb{Z}_q[X]/(X^N + 1)$, which take time (resp. size) polylog(d) each. We ignore the terms related polynomially in the security parameter λ. The "TP" column specifies whether the scheme has transparent setup. The "stretch × slack" column denotes the term $\gamma_{\text{stretch}} \cdot \gamma_{\text{slack}}$ defined in (1). For presentation, we only include the terms that are super-polynomial in d.

1.3.1   Merkle-PRISIS Commitment Schemes

A polynomial commitment scheme naturally consists of two components: (i) a commitment scheme; (ii) an evaluation protocol. In order to achieve succinct verification, the commitment scheme has to be *compressing*. Further, in order to commit to *arbitrary* polynomials, we would want the commitment scheme to work for any message over $\mathcal{R}_q$ and not only elements of small norm. Our starting point is the following two-to-one commitment scheme, whose security relies on BASIS-style assumptions introduced in [WW23b] and revisited in [FMN23]. The common reference string consists of a triple $(\mathbf{A}, w, \mathbf{T})$, where $\mathbf{T}$ is a trapdoor to the matrix $\mathbf{B} := \begin{bmatrix} \mathbf{A} & 0 & -\mathbf{G} \\ 0 & w \cdot \mathbf{A} & -\mathbf{G} \end{bmatrix}$ and $w \in \mathcal{R}_q^\times$. To commit to a vector $\mathbf{f} = (f_0, f_1) \in \mathcal{R}_q^2$, the committer sets $\mathbf{t}_b = f_b \cdot \mathbf{e}$ and uses $\mathbf{T}$ to sample short vectors $\mathbf{s}_0, \mathbf{s}_1, \hat{\mathbf{t}}$ such that

$$\mathbf{B} \cdot \begin{bmatrix} \mathbf{s}_0 \\ \mathbf{s}_1 \\ \hat{\mathbf{t}} \end{bmatrix} = \begin{bmatrix} -\mathbf{t}_0 \\ -\mathbf{t}_1 \end{bmatrix} .$$

The final commitment is then set to be $\mathbf{t} := \mathbf{G} \cdot \hat{\mathbf{t}}$. To verify an opening, which consists of $\mathbf{s}_0, \mathbf{s}_1$, the verifier simply checks whether the induced constraints are satisfied, namely by checking that the openings are short and that $w^b \cdot \mathbf{A} \cdot \mathbf{s}_b + \mathbf{t} = \mathbf{t}_b$ for $b \in \{0, 1\}$. The commitment scheme can be naturally extended to handle messages of arbitrary length, and indeed variants of this construction are at the core of the results in both [WW23b] and [FMN23]. However, these natural extensions incur some drawbacks. First, the common reference string has size *quadratic* in the message length. Second, binding holds under BASIS-style assumptions in parameter regimes that are not known to feature a reduction from standard assumptions.

Conversely, the commitment scheme that we sketched is binding under a version of the PRISIS assumption of arity 2, which was shown in [FMN23] to permit a reduction from the *standard* Module-SIS assumption. The commitment scheme that we introduce in the work, which we refer to as Merkle-PRISIS commitment, addresses both of these drawbacks by applying the sketched commitments scheme iteratively in a Merkle-tree fashion. It is compressing for messages of arbitrary length in $\mathcal{R}_q$, binding follows under the Module-SIS assumption, has polylogarithmic common reference string, and quasi-linear commitment time.

For simplicity, assume that $\ell = 2^h$. The common reference string for the Merkle-PRISIS commitment scheme (when used with messages of length ℓ) consists of h common reference strings for the base commitment scheme, which we denote as $(\mathbf{A}_i, w_i, \mathbf{T}_i)_{i \in [h]}$. To commit to a message $\mathbf{f} \in \mathcal{R}_q^\ell$, which we index by $\mathbb{Z}_2^h$, the committer applies the basic commitment scheme to $(f_{\mathbf{b},0}, f_{\mathbf{b},1}) \in \mathcal{R}_q^2$ for $\mathbf{b} \in \mathbb{Z}_2^{h-1}$, obtaining $\ell/2$ commitments $\mathbf{t}_\mathbf{b}$ (and corresponding openings). Recall that this is done by setting $\mathbf{t}_{\mathbf{b},b_h} := f_{\mathbf{b},b_h} \cdot \mathbf{e}$ and then sampling an appropriate preimage. In the next layer, we apply again the commitment scheme to these resulting commitments, *without scaling by* $\mathbf{e}$. This process is repeated h times, until a single commitment is obtained. Denoting by $\mathbf{t}$ this final commitment, and by $(\mathbf{s}_\mathbf{b})_{\mathbf{b} \in \mathbb{Z}_2^{\leq h}}$ the openings, checking a valid opening involves checking shortness of the openings and that the following equation for each of the ℓ authentication paths $\mathbf{b} \in \mathbb{Z}_2^h$

$$\sum_{j \in [h]} w_j^{b_j} \cdot \mathbf{A}_j \cdot \mathbf{s}_{\mathbf{b}_{:j}} + f_\mathbf{b} \cdot \mathbf{e} = \mathbf{t} \ .$$

It is easy to verify that the commitment scheme has the claimed efficiency properties. What might be surprising is that, despite the fact that the inner instantiations of the commitment schemes are not *individually* binding, we show that the overall scheme is binding under a multi-instance version of the PRISIS assumption, which we discuss next, and base on standard assumptions.

PRISIS.Sample$_\ell(\mathbf{A})$:

1. Sample[a] $\mathbf{a}^\top \leftarrow \mathcal{R}_q^m$ and set $\bar{\mathbf{A}} := \begin{bmatrix} \mathbf{a}^\top \\ \mathbf{A} \end{bmatrix}$. We write PRISIS$_\ell :=$ BASIS[PRISIS.Sample$_\ell$].
2. Sample $w \leftarrow \mathcal{R}_q^\times$.
3. Return

$$\mathbf{B} := \begin{bmatrix} w^0 \cdot \bar{\mathbf{A}} & & & -\mathbf{G} \\ & \ddots & & \vdots \\ & & w^{\ell-1} \cdot \bar{\mathbf{A}} & -\mathbf{G} \end{bmatrix} \quad \text{and} \quad \mathsf{aux} := w \ .$$

---
[a] This vector $\mathbf{a}$ will be used in concert with $\mathbf{e}$ to argue binding later. Refer to Section 4.1 for details.

Fig. 1. Sampling algorithm for the PRISIS assumption.

1.3.2   Power-Ring-BASIS Assumption

We first recall the BASIS family of assumptions, introduced in [WW23b]. Informally, each of the assumptions states that it should be hard for an adversary to find a short non-zero element in the kernel of a random matrix *even when given a trapdoor* to a matrix related to the target matrix.

Definition 1.1 (Informal). *Let* Samp *be an algorithm that, when given* $\mathbf{A} \in \mathcal{R}_q^{n \times m}$, *outputs* $(\mathbf{B}, \mathsf{aux}) \leftarrow$ Samp$(\mathbf{A})$. *The* BASIS[Samp] *assumption states that an efficient adversary, given access to* $(\mathbf{A}, \mathbf{B}, \mathsf{aux}, \mathbf{T})$, *where* $\mathbf{A}$ *is a random matrix and* $\mathbf{T}$ *is a trapdoor for* $\mathbf{B}$, *is not able to compute a short non-zero solution* $\mathbf{z}$ *to* $\mathbf{A} \cdot \mathbf{z} \equiv \mathbf{0} \bmod q$.

The choice of the Samp algorithm affects the hardness of the assumption. In this work, we consider the PRISIS assumption, introduced in [FMN23], which is obtained from BASIS when the sampling algorithm is defined as in Fig. 1.

As mentioned before, binding of the Merkle-PRISIS commitment scheme follows from a *multi-instance* version of the PRISIS$_2$ assumption. We give a general definition for multi-instance BASIS assumptions, in which the adversary is given a number of BASIS instances, and aims to find a short non-zero solution to the matrix obtained by concatenating the challenge matrices of the individual instances.

Definition 1.2 (Informal). *Let* Samp *be an algorithm as before. Let* $\mathbf{A}_1, \ldots, \mathbf{A}_h$ *be random matrices in* $\mathcal{R}_q$, *and suppose further that* $\mathbf{B}_i, \mathsf{aux}_i \leftarrow$ Samp$(\mathbf{A}_i)$ *and that* $\mathbf{T}_i$ *is a trapdoor for* $\mathbf{B}_i$. *The* h-BASIS[Samp] *assumption states that no efficient adversary, given* $(\mathbf{A}_i, \mathbf{B}_i, \mathsf{aux}_i, \mathbf{T}_i)_i$, *can find a short non-zero vector* $\mathbf{z}$ *such that* $[\mathbf{A}_1 | \ldots | \mathbf{A}_h] \cdot \mathbf{z} \equiv \mathbf{0} \bmod q$.

The PRISIS version is defined as h-PRISIS$_\ell := h$-BASIS[PRISIS.Sample$_\ell$]. In Sect. 3.2 we show that this multi-instance version of PRISIS is as hard as the single-instance version. Combining this with the result in [FMN23, Sec 3.1], which reduces Module-SIS to PRISIS_2, implies that binding of Merkle-PRISIS follows from standard assumption. We alternatively show a tighter reduction directly from Module-SIS to h-PRISIS_2 in Sect. 3.1.

1.3.3   Evaluation Protocol

Next, we focus on the second component of our polynomial commitment scheme, namely the evaluation protocol. First, we present a Σ-protocol, resembling that in [FMN23], that reduces checking an opening of a committed degree d polynomial to that of one of degree $d/2$. Our final protocol will apply this Σ-protocol recursively, which will suffice to achieve $\mathrm{polylog}(d)$ communication and verifier complexity.

Again for simplicity, assume that $d = 2^h - 1$, and let $(\mathbf{A}_j, w_j, \mathbf{T}_j)_{j \in [h]}$ be a Merkle-PRISIS common reference string as before. Given a public commitment $\mathbf{t}$, an evaluation point u and a claimed image z, the prover aims to show knowledge of a polynomial f of degree at most d such that $f(u) = z$, and that $\mathbf{t}$ is a commitment to f.

The protocol, as the previous work, follows a FRI-inspired split-and-fold approach. The prover will split the witness vector into odd and even components, and send over some evaluations and partial openings. The verifier will sample randomness which will be used to update the witness to a random linear combination of those components. Prover and verifier will jointly (and efficiently) updated their reference string and commitment to one of the folded polynomial. We describe the Σ-protocol in Fig. 2.

Correctness, follows easily, if not for some cumbersome notation. We index the coefficients of f, g with binary strings as before. Thus, the $\mathbf{j}$-th coefficient of g is $g_{\mathbf{j}} = \alpha_0 f_{0,\mathbf{j}} + \alpha_1 f_{1,\mathbf{j}}$ for $\mathbf{j} \in \mathbb{Z}_2^{h-1}$. Now, by expanding the verification equations, we have

$$
\begin{aligned}
g_{\mathbf{j}} \cdot \mathbf{e} = {} & (\alpha_0 \cdot f_{0,\mathbf{j}} + \alpha_1 \cdot f_{1,\mathbf{j}}) \cdot \mathbf{e} \\
= {} & \alpha_0 \cdot \left(\mathbf{t} - w_1^0 \cdot \mathbf{A}_1 \cdot \mathbf{s}_0 - \sum_{t=1}^{h-1} w_{1+t}^{j_t} \cdot \mathbf{A}_{1+t} \cdot \mathbf{s}_{0,\mathbf{j}:t} \right) \\
& + \alpha_1 \cdot \left(\mathbf{t} - w_1^1 \cdot \mathbf{A}_1 \cdot \mathbf{s}_1 - \sum_{t=1}^{h-1} w_{1+t}^{j_t} \cdot \mathbf{A}_{1+t} \cdot \mathbf{s}_{1,\mathbf{j}:t} \right) \\
= {} & \alpha_0 \cdot \left(\mathbf{t} - w_1^0 \cdot \mathbf{A}_1 \cdot \mathbf{s}_0 \right) + \alpha_1 \cdot \left(\mathbf{t} - w_1^1 \cdot \mathbf{A}_1 \cdot \mathbf{s}_1 \right) \\
& - \sum_{t=1}^{h-1} w_{1+t}^{j_t} \cdot \mathbf{A}_{1+t} \cdot \left(\alpha_0 \cdot \mathbf{s}_{0,\mathbf{j}:t} + \alpha_1 \cdot \mathbf{s}_{1,\mathbf{j}:t} \right) \\
= {} & \mathbf{t}' - \sum_{t=1}^{h-1} \cdot w_{1+t}^{j_t} \cdot \mathbf{A}_{1+t} \cdot \mathbf{z}_{\mathbf{j}:t} \ \ .
\end{aligned}
$$

Basic Σ-Protocol

Prover		Verifier
$f(\mathsf{X}) = f_0(\mathsf{X}^2) + \mathsf{X} f_1(\mathsf{X}^2)$		
$z_i := f_i(u^2)$ for $i \in \mathbb{Z}_2$	$\xrightarrow{\quad z_0, z_1, \mathbf{s}_0, \mathbf{s}_1 \quad}$	Check: $z_0 + u z_1 =_? z$; Check: $\mathbf{s}_0, \mathbf{s}_1$ short
$g(\mathsf{X}) := \alpha_0 f_0(\mathsf{X}) + \alpha_1 f_1(\mathsf{X})$	$\xleftarrow{\quad \alpha_0, \alpha_1 \quad}$	$\alpha_0, \alpha_1 \leftarrow \{\, \mathsf{X}^i : i \in \mathbb{Z} \,\}$
$\mathbf{z}_\mathsf{b} := \alpha_0 \mathbf{s}_{\mathsf{b},0} + \alpha_1 \mathbf{s}_{\mathsf{b},1}$ for $\mathbf{b} \in \mathbb{Z}_2^{\leq h-1}$	$\xrightarrow{\quad g, (\mathbf{z}_\mathsf{b})_\mathsf{b} \quad}$	$\mathsf{crs}' := (\mathbf{A}_{1+t}, w_{1+t}, \mathbf{T}_{1+t})_{t \in [h-1]}$
		$\mathbf{t}' := \alpha_0 \cdot (\mathbf{t} - w_1^0 \mathbf{A}_1 \mathbf{s}_0) + \alpha_1 \cdot (\mathbf{t} - w_1^1 \mathbf{A}_1 \mathbf{s}_1)$
		$u' := u^2$; $z' := \alpha_0 \cdot z_0 + \alpha_1 \cdot z_1$
		Check: $g(u') = z'$
		Check: $\mathsf{Open}(\mathsf{crs}', \mathbf{t}', g, (\mathbf{z}_\mathsf{b})_\mathsf{b}) = 1$

Fig. 2. Σ-protocol to check evaluations of a degree d polynomial committed under Merkle-PRISIS.

Note also that $g(u^2) = \alpha_0 \cdot f_0(u^2) + \alpha_1 \cdot f_1(u^2) = \alpha_0 \cdot z_0 + \alpha_1 \cdot z_1$. Further, the updated openings are scaled by monomials, and thus remain short. We are able to straightforwardly generalise the protocol to an arbitrary "folding factor", that we denote as k. This parameter regulates in how many components the polynomial is divided into in a round of the protocol. More concretely, the original degree d polynomial is split into 2^k polynomials of degree roughly $d/2^k$, which are then folded as in the original protocol. Applying the protocol recursively logarithmically many times (in d), we are able to obtain an interactive evaluation protocol with communication complexity and verification complexity polylogarithmic.

Knowledge soundness of the Σ protocol follows from techniques similar to those in [FMN23], inheriting the limitation that the knowledge soundness error is $\frac{2^k}{2N}$, where $N = \mathsf{poly}(\lambda)$ and thus non-negligible. In the interactive setting, we could boost this via parallel repetition, but since our aim will to construct non-interactive arguments through the Fiat-Shamir transform another approach is required.

To this end, we combine the amortisation techniques from [BBCdGL18, BHRRS21]. Rather than proving a single claim $f(u) = z$, we consider a protocol for a bundle of r claims $\{f_i(u) = z_i\}_{i \in [r]}$ (note that the evaluation points are *the same* across claims). The new Σ-protocol takes as input r polynomials of degree d, applies the same "split" strategy to obtain $r \cdot 2^k$ polynomials of degree roughly $d/2^k$. These polynomials are combined into r new ones via a redundant linear combination, which induces a new bundle of claim to be recursively proven.

We apply this new Σ-protocol ℓ times recursively, and analyse the resulting protocol using coordinate-wise special soundness. We show that the knowledge soundness error is roughly $\ell \cdot r 2^k/(2\,N)^r$. Setting r large enough, we can thus achieve negligible knowledge soundness error. Applying the Fiat-Shamir transformation is then sound, and we obtain a non-interactive protocol for proving multiple polynomial evaluations. The single polynomial case is then handled by proving the *same* claim multiple times with the resulting protocol. An appropriate setting of parameters then implies our main result.

Our protocols, as they are, natively provide evaluations proofs of polynomials over $\mathcal{R}_q$. We present a new generic technique to make use of such evaluations proof to provide evaluations proofs over $\mathbb{Z}_q$. The techniques, allow to prove evaluation of degree d polynomials over $\mathbb{Z}_q$ by making use of evaluation protocols of degree d/N in $\mathcal{R}_q$, leading to significant savings in practice. At a high level, we make use of the observation in [LNP22] that $\mathcal{R}$ has an automorphism $\sigma : \mathcal{R} \to \mathcal{R}$ such that, for $a, b \in \mathcal{R}$, the constant coefficient of $a \cdot \sigma(b)$ equals the inner product of the coefficient vectors of a and b. We then make use of this fact to "pack" the coefficients of the original polynomial in $\mathbb{Z}_q$ in one of smaller degree over $\mathcal{R}_q$, embedding the original claim in the constant coefficient of this new polynomial.

2 Preliminaries

We denote the security parameter by λ, which is implicitly given to all algorithms unless specified otherwise. Further, we write $\mathsf{negl}(\lambda)$ (resp. $\mathsf{poly}(\lambda)$) to denote a negligible function (resp. polynomial) in λ. In this work, we implicitly assume that the vast majority of the key parameters, e.g. the ring dimension, and the dimensions of matrices and vectors, are $\mathsf{poly}(\lambda)$. However, the modulus used in this work may be super-polynomial in λ.

For $a, b \in \mathbb{N}$ with $a < b$, write $[a, b] := \{a, a+1, \ldots, b\}$, $[a] := [1, a]$. For $q \in \mathbb{N}$ write $\mathbb{Z}_q$ for the integers modulo q. We denote vectors with lowercase boldface (e.g. $\mathbf{u}, \mathbf{v}$) and matrices with uppercase boldface (e.g. $\mathbf{A}, \mathbf{B}$). Given two vectors $\mathbf{u}, \mathbf{v}$, we denote by $(\mathbf{u}, \mathbf{v})$ its concatenation. Also, ε is an empty string. Given two matrices $\mathbf{A}, \mathbf{B}$ we write $[\mathbf{A} \mid \mathbf{B}]$ for their concatenation.

Norms. We define the ℓ_p norm on $\mathbb{C}^n$ as $\|\mathbf{x}\|_p = \left(\sum_i |x_i|^p\right)^{1/p}$ for $p < \infty$ and $\|\mathbf{x}\|_\infty := \max_i |x_i|$. Unless otherwise specified, we use $\|\cdot\|$ for the ℓ_2 norm.

Bits-to-Integer Conversion. Let $k \geq 1$. For a vector $\mathbf{b} \in \mathbb{Z}_2^k$, we define the bits-to-integer conversion function $\mathsf{int}(\mathbf{b}) := \sum_{i=1}^k b_i \cdot 2^{i-1} \in [0, 2^k - 1]$. Clearly, if $\mathbf{u} \in \mathbb{Z}_2^k$ and $\mathbf{v} \in \mathbb{Z}_2^l$ then $\mathsf{int}((\mathbf{u}, \mathbf{v})) = \mathsf{int}(\mathbf{u}) + 2^k \cdot \mathsf{int}(\mathbf{v})$.

Sampling Algorithms. We denote $\mathsf{TrapGen}$ and $\mathsf{SamplePre}$ the algorithms for generating a matrix with a trapdoor and for using the trapdoor to sample short preimages of target vectors respectively. We write $\mathbf{B}_\sigma^{-1}(\mathbf{v})$ for sampling a Discrete Gaussian preimage of vector $\mathbf{v}$ for matrix $\mathbf{B}$.

Due to space constraints in the main body, the remaining preliminaries are in the full version of the paper.

3   Power-Ring-BASIS Assumption

Our construction of the polynomial commitment will rely on the multi-instance version of the PRISIS (Power-Ring-BASIS) assumption [FMN23] which is a special case of the BASIS assumption introduced by Wee and Wu [WW23b].[4] Recall that $\mathbf{G}_n$ is a gadget matrix with base δ. We fix the modulus q and set $\tilde{q} := \lfloor \log_\delta q \rfloor + 1$. Here, we consider a multi-instance version of BASIS, where the adversary is given h instances $(\mathbf{A}_i, \mathbf{B}_i, \mathbf{T}_i, \mathsf{aux}_i)$ of BASIS, and it has to find a short non-zero solution to the concatenated matrix $[\mathbf{A}_1 \mid \cdots \mid \mathbf{A}_h]$.

We also analyse hardness of the h-PRISIS assumption for $h = \mathsf{poly}(\lambda)$. First, we show that for specific parameters, h-$\mathsf{PRISIS}_{n,m,\mathcal{R}_q,2,\sigma,\beta}$ is secure under the Module-SIS assumption. This implies that our polynomial commitment scheme in Sect. 5 is secure under standard assumptions. Furthermore, we prove that h-PRISIS generally has a reduction from a single instance PRISIS which can be of independent interest.

Definition 3.1 (h-BASIS). *Let $h \geq 1$ and $q, n, m, n', m', \ell, N, \sigma, \beta$ be the lattice parameters. Let Samp_ℓ be a PPT algorithm, which given a matrix $\mathbf{A} \in \mathcal{R}_q^{n \times m}$, outputs a matrix $\mathbf{B} \in \mathcal{R}_q^{n' \times m'}$ along with auxiliary information aux. We say the h-$\mathsf{BASIS}_{n,m,n',m',\mathcal{R}_q,\ell,\sigma,\beta}$ assumption holds w.r.t. Samp_ℓ if for any PPT adversary $\mathcal{A}$:*

$$
\Pr \left[\begin{array}{c|c} \begin{array}{l} [\mathbf{A}_1 \mid \cdots \mid \mathbf{A}_h] \cdot \mathbf{z} = 0 \\ 0 < \|\mathbf{z}\| \leq \beta \end{array} & \begin{array}{c} \forall j \in [h], \mathbf{A}_j \leftarrow \mathcal{R}_q^{n \times m}, \\ (\mathbf{B}_j, \mathsf{aux}_j) \leftarrow \mathsf{Samp}(\mathbf{A}_j) \\ \mathbf{T}_j \leftarrow \mathbf{B}_{j\,\sigma}^{-1}(\mathbf{G}_{n'}) \\ \mathbf{z} \leftarrow \mathcal{A}\left((\mathbf{A}_j, \mathbf{B}_j, \mathbf{T}_j, \mathsf{aux}_j)_{j \in [h]}\right) \end{array} \end{array} \right] \leq \mathsf{negl}(\lambda) \ .
$$

The PRISIS assumption is defined by the following sampling algorithm Samp.

Definition 3.2 (h-PRISIS). *The h-$\mathsf{PRISIS}_{n,m,\mathcal{R}_q,\ell,\sigma,\beta}$ assumption is an instantiation of the h-BASIS assumption with the following sampling algorithm Samp_ℓ. That is, $\mathsf{Samp}_\ell(\mathbf{A})$ samples a row $\mathbf{a}^\mathsf{T} \leftarrow \mathcal{R}_q^m$ and sets $\bar{\mathbf{A}}$ as*

$$
\bar{\mathbf{A}} := \begin{bmatrix} \mathbf{a}^\mathsf{T} \\ \mathbf{A} \end{bmatrix} \in \mathcal{R}_q^{(n+1) \times m} \ . \tag{2}
$$

Then, it samples $w \leftarrow \mathcal{R}_q^\times$, and outputs

$$
\mathbf{B} := \begin{bmatrix} w^0 \cdot \bar{\mathbf{A}} & & & -\mathbf{G}_{n+1} \\ & \ddots & & \vdots \\ & & w^{\ell-1} \cdot \bar{\mathbf{A}} & -\mathbf{G}_{n+1} \end{bmatrix} \quad and \quad \mathsf{aux} := w.
$$

---

[4] BASIS stands for Basis-Augmented Shortest Integer Solution.

3.1 h-PRISIS Assumption for $\ell = 2$

We provide an efficient reduction from MSIS to the h-PRISIS$_{n,m,\mathcal{R}_q,\ell,\sigma,\beta}$ assumption, where $\ell = 2$. Since we base security of our constructions on this case, we obtain a polynomial commitment from standard lattice assumptions. In particular, we prove the following theorem:

Theorem 3.3 (MSIS $\implies$ h-PRISIS). *Let $n > 0, m \geq n$ and denote $t = (n+1) \cdot \tilde{q}$. Let $q = \omega(N)$ satisfy $q \equiv 5 \bmod 8$. Take $\varepsilon \in (0, 1/3)$ and $\sigma_0 \geq \max(\sqrt{N \ln(8\,N \cdot q)} \cdot q^{1/2+\varepsilon}, \omega(N^{3/2} \cdot \ln^{3/2} \cdot N))$ such that $2^{10}\,N\,q^{-\lfloor \varepsilon \cdot N \rfloor}$ is negligible. Let $\tau := \max(2 \cdot (n+1), 2\,m + t)$ and*

$$\sigma_1 \geq \delta\sqrt{t \cdot N \cdot (N^2 \cdot \sigma_0^2 \cdot m + 2\,t)} \cdot \omega(\sqrt{N \cdot \log(\tau N)}) \ .$$

Then, for $h = \mathsf{poly}(\lambda)$, h-PRISIS$_{n,m,\mathcal{R}_q,2,\sigma_1,\beta}$ is hard under the MSIS$_{n,hm,\mathcal{R}_q,\beta}$ assumption.

The proof is given in the full version of the paper.

3.2 h-PRISIS Assumption for $\ell = O(1)$

In this section, we show that if PRISIS is hard then h-PRISIS is hard for $\ell \in O(1) > 2$ and $h = \mathsf{poly}(\lambda)$. In particular, we will prove the following theorem.

Theorem 3.4 (PRISIS $\implies$ h-PRISIS). *Let $n, m, \mathcal{R}_q, \ell, \sigma_T$ be PRISIS parameters. Let the ring $\mathcal{R}_q$ split into fields of superpolynomial size. Let $\ell, n \in O(1)$. Let $\sigma_x > 0$ and $\beta > 0$ be real numbers. Let δ be a gadget matrix base and set $\tilde{q} := \lfloor \log_\delta q \rfloor + 1$. Let $m \geq 2n > 0$, let $h = \mathsf{poly}(\lambda)$, let*

$$\beta' \geq 4\,h \cdot \beta \cdot N^{9/2} \cdot m^{5/2} \cdot q^{4n/m+8/(Nm)} \cdot \omega(\log N) \ ,$$

let
$$\sigma_{Ti} \geq N^{6+2\ell} \cdot \sigma_x^{2\ell} \cdot 2^{\ell+2} \cdot q^{4n/m+8/(Nm)} \cdot m^2 \cdot \delta \cdot \sigma_T$$
$$\cdot \sqrt{(m\,\ell + n\,\tilde{q}) \cdot n\,\tilde{q}\,\ell \cdot \log(m \cdot N)} \cdot \omega(\log^{3/2+\ell}(N)) \ .$$

Then h-PRISIS$_{n,m,\mathcal{R}_q,\ell,\sigma_{Ti},\beta}$ is hard under the PRISIS$_{n,m,\mathcal{R}_q,\ell,\sigma_T,\beta'}$ assumption, under the RLWE$_{\mathcal{R}_q,\mathcal{D}_{\mathcal{R},\sigma_x}}$ and the NTRU$_{\mathcal{R}_q,\mathcal{D}_{\mathcal{R},\sigma_x},\mathcal{D}_{\mathcal{R},\sigma_x}}$ assumptions.

The proof is given in the full version of the paper.

4   Merkle-PRISIS Commitment Scheme

In this section we define a new compressing commitment scheme which combines the BASIS construction [FMN23, WW23b] with Merkle trees (of arity two). This approach significantly reduces the size of the common reference string, as well as the prover running time.

Let $\ell = 2^h$ be the length of the committed message. The message space is $\mathcal{M} := \mathcal{R}_q^\ell$. We let γ be the parameter controlling the norm of the opening vectors. Further, we define the slack space to be the set $\mathcal{S} := \mathcal{R}_q^\times$. We define $\mathbf{G} := \mathbf{G}_n \in \mathcal{R}_q^{n \times t}$ and the decomposition base δ. Also, $\mathbf{e}_1 := (1, 0, \ldots, 0) \in \mathcal{R}_q^n$. The commitment scheme is presented in Fig. 3.

Merkle-PRISIS Commitment Scheme

$\underline{\mathsf{Setup}(1^\lambda)}$

1. For $j = h, \ldots, 1$:
2. $(\mathbf{A}, \mathbf{R}) \leftarrow \mathsf{TrapGen}(n, m)$.
3. $w \leftarrow \mathcal{R}_q^\times$.
4.   Let $\mathbf{R}_i := \mathbf{R} \cdot \mathbf{G}^{-1}(w^{-i} \cdot \mathbf{G})$ for $i \in [0, 1]$.
5.   Set

$$\mathbf{B} := \begin{bmatrix} \mathbf{A} & \mathbf{0} & -\mathbf{G} \\ \mathbf{0} & w \cdot \mathbf{A} & -\mathbf{G} \end{bmatrix}, \quad \tilde{\mathbf{R}} := \begin{bmatrix} \mathbf{R}_0 & \mathbf{0} \\ \mathbf{0} & \mathbf{R}_1 \\ \mathbf{0} & \mathbf{0} \end{bmatrix} .$$

6.   Sample $\mathbf{T} \leftarrow \mathsf{SamplePre}(\mathbf{B}, \tilde{\mathbf{R}}, \mathbf{G}_{2n}, \sigma_0)$
7.   Let $(\mathbf{A}_j, w_j, \mathbf{T}_j) := (\mathbf{A}, w, \mathbf{T})$.
8. Return $\mathsf{crs} := (\mathbf{A}_j, w_j, \mathbf{T}_j)_{j \in [h]}$.

$\underline{\mathsf{Commit}(\mathsf{crs}, \mathbf{f} = (f_\mathbf{b})_{\mathbf{b} \in \mathbb{Z}_2^h} \in \mathcal{R}_q^\ell)}$

1. Set $\mathbf{t}_\mathbf{b} := f_\mathbf{b} \cdot \mathbf{e}_1$ for $\mathbf{b} \in \mathbb{Z}_2^h$.
2. For $j = h, \ldots, 1$:
3.   For $\mathbf{b} \in \mathbb{Z}_2^{j-1}$:
4. $\begin{bmatrix} \mathbf{s}_{(\mathbf{b},0)} \\ \mathbf{s}_{(\mathbf{b},1)} \\ \hat{\mathbf{t}}_\mathbf{b} \end{bmatrix} \leftarrow \mathsf{SamplePre}\left(\begin{bmatrix} \mathbf{A}_j & \mathbf{0} & -\mathbf{G} \\ \mathbf{0} & w_j \cdot \mathbf{A}_j & -\mathbf{G} \end{bmatrix}, \begin{bmatrix} -\mathbf{t}_{(\mathbf{b},0)} \\ -\mathbf{t}_{(\mathbf{b},1)} \end{bmatrix}, \mathbf{T}_j, \sigma_1 \right)$
5.   Set $\mathbf{t}_\mathbf{b} := \mathbf{G} \cdot \hat{\mathbf{t}}_\mathbf{b}$.
6.   Return $(C := \mathbf{t}_\varepsilon, \mathsf{st} := (\mathbf{s}_\mathbf{b})_{\mathbf{b} \in \mathbb{Z}_2^{\leq h}})$.

$\underline{\mathsf{Open}(\mathsf{crs}, C, \mathbf{f}, \mathsf{st}, c)}$

1. Parse $C := \mathbf{t}$, $\mathbf{f} := (f_\mathbf{b})_{\mathbf{b} \in \mathbb{Z}_2^h}$, $\mathsf{st} := (\mathbf{s}_\mathbf{b})_{\mathbf{b} \in \mathbb{Z}_2^{\leq h}}$ and $c \in \mathcal{S}$.
2. Return 1 if and only if for all $\mathbf{b} \in \mathbb{Z}_2^h$,
   - $\sum_{j=1}^h w_j^{b_j} \cdot \mathbf{A}_j \cdot \mathbf{s}_{\mathbf{b}_{:j}} + f_\mathbf{b} \cdot \mathbf{e}_1 = \mathbf{t}$.
   - $\forall j \in [h], \|c \cdot \mathbf{s}_{\mathbf{b}_{:j}}\| \leq \gamma$.

Fig. 3. Merkle-PRISIS commitment scheme for arbitrary messages of length $\ell = 2^h$ over $\mathcal{R}_q$ with the slack space being $\mathcal{S} := \mathcal{R}_q^\times$.

4.1 Security Analysis

In the following, we show that the Merkle-PRISIS commitment scheme from Fig. 3 satisfies completeness, relaxed binding and hiding.

Lemma 4.1 (Completeness). *Suppose* $n, N, \beta_s \geq 1$, *define* $t := n \cdot \tilde{q}$. *Let* $m \geq t + n$, $m' := 2m + t$, $n' := 2t$ *and* $t' := \max(n', m')^5$ *and* $s > 2 N \cdot q^{\frac{n}{m-t} + \frac{2}{N \cdot (m-t)}}$. *Take*

$$\sigma_0 \geq 2 \delta s N \cdot \omega(\sqrt{t \cdot (m-t) \cdot \log(t'N)}) \quad and$$
$$\sigma_1 \geq \delta \sigma_0 N \cdot \omega(\sqrt{m' n' \cdot \log(t'N)}) .$$

If $\gamma \geq \sigma_1 \sqrt{m'N}$ *for* $j \in [h]$, *then the Merkle-*PRISIS *commitment scheme satisfies completeness.*

The proof is given in the full version of the paper.

Lemma 4.2 (Relaxed Binding). *Define* $t := n \cdot \tilde{q}$ *and let* $m \geq t + n$ *and* $n' = 2t$. *Take* $m' := 2m + t$, $n' := 2t$ *and* $t' := \max(n', m')$ *and* $s > 2 N \cdot q^{\frac{n}{m-t} + \frac{2}{N \cdot (m-t)}}$. *If* $\sigma_0 \geq 2 \delta s \cdot N \cdot \omega(\sqrt{t \cdot (m-t) \cdot \log(t'N)})$ *then under the* h-PRISIS$_{n-1, m, \mathcal{R}_q, 2, \sigma_0, 2\gamma\sqrt{h}}$ *assumption the* PowerBASIS *commitment scheme satisfies binding.*

The proof is given in the full version of the paper.

Hiding. In order to argue hiding, we first note that the underlying PRISIS commitment is hiding (see [FMN23, Lemma 4.3]), and thus the bottom non-leaf commitments $(\mathbf{t_b})_{\mathbf{b} \in \mathbb{Z}_2^{h-1}}$ look pseudo-random. Therefore, any commitments computed in higher nodes (in particular, the root) do not leak any information about the message $\mathbf{f}$. Since the methodology is folklore and we do not instantiate the hiding variant of our commitment, we leave a formal treatment out of scope of this paper.

Efficiency. If we assume that $n, m, N \in \mathsf{poly}(\lambda)$, then the common reference string contains $\log \ell \cdot \mathsf{poly}(\lambda)$ elements in $\mathcal{R}_q$, while the prover and the verifier make $\ell \cdot \mathsf{poly}(\lambda)$ ring operations.

5   Proof of Polynomial Evaluation

We use the construction in Fig. 3 to build our polynomial commitment scheme. Namely, given a polynomial $f \in \mathcal{R}_q[X]$ of degree at most $d := 2^h - 1$ over $\mathcal{R}_q$, we commit to f by committing to its coefficient vector $\mathbf{f} = (f_\mathbf{b})_{\mathbf{b} \in \mathbb{Z}_2^h} \in \mathcal{R}_q^{d+1}$ to obtain a commitment $\mathbf{t} \in \mathcal{R}_q^n$, along with the decommitment state $\mathsf{st} = (\mathbf{s_b})_{\mathbf{b} \in \mathbb{Z}_2^{\leq h}}$, where each $\mathbf{s_b} \in \mathcal{R}_q^m$. Here, we represent a polynomial f as

$$f(X) = \sum_{\mathbf{b} \in \mathbb{Z}_2^h} f_\mathbf{b} \cdot X^{\mathsf{int}(\mathbf{b})} .$$

We say that the $\mathbf{b}$-th coefficient of f is $f_\mathbf{b}$.

---

[5] Clearly, $m' \geq n'$.

An essential property of polynomial commitments is the ability to show that the committed polynomial was evaluated correctly, i.e. $f(u) = z$ for public u and z in $\mathcal{R}_q$. In other words, we consider the following relation:

$$
\mathsf{R}_{h,\beta} := \left\{ \begin{array}{c} \left((\mathbf{A}_j, w_j, \mathbf{T}_j)_{j\in[h]}, \right. \\ (\mathbf{t}, u, z), \\ \left. (f, (\mathbf{s_b})_{\mathbf{b}\in\mathbb{Z}_2^{\leq h}}) \right) \end{array} \middle| \begin{array}{c} \forall\, \mathbf{b} \in \mathbb{Z}_2^h,\ \|\mathbf{s_b}\| \leq \beta \\ \wedge \sum_{j=1}^h w_j^{b_j} \cdot \mathbf{A}_j \cdot \mathbf{s}_{\mathbf{b}_{:j}} + f_{\mathbf{b}} = \mathbf{t} \\ \wedge f(u) = z \end{array} \right\} . \tag{3}
$$

5.1   Compressed Σ-Protocol

The main intuition for proving evaluations can be described with the following Σ-protocol. First, we define $k \in [h]$ to be the folding factor and $l := h - k$.

The prover starts by splitting the polynomial f into 2^k polynomials of degree at most $d' := 2^l - 1$. Namely, we introduce a $(k+1)$-variate function $\bar{f} : \mathcal{R}_q \times \mathbb{Z}_2^k \to \mathcal{R}_q$ as follows:

$$
\bar{f}(\mathsf{X}, \mathbf{l}) := \sum_{\mathbf{j}\in\mathbb{Z}_2^l} f_{(\mathbf{l},\mathbf{j})} \cdot \mathsf{X}^{\mathsf{int}(\mathbf{j})} .
$$

Then, by construction and the fact that $\mathsf{int}((\mathbf{i},\mathbf{j})) = \mathsf{int}(\mathbf{i}) + 2^k \cdot \mathsf{int}(\mathbf{j})$:

$$
z = f(u) = \sum_{\mathbf{i}\in\mathbb{Z}_2^k} \left(\sum_{\mathbf{j}\in\mathbb{Z}_2^l} f_{(\mathbf{i},\mathbf{j})} \cdot u^{2^k \cdot \mathsf{int}(\mathbf{j})} \right) \cdot u^{\mathsf{int}(\mathbf{i})}
$$
$$
= \sum_{\mathbf{i}\in\mathbb{Z}_2^k} \bar{f}(u^{2^k}, \mathbf{i}) \cdot u^{\mathsf{int}(\mathbf{i})} = \sum_{\mathbf{i}\in\mathbb{Z}_2^k} z_{\mathbf{i}} \cdot u^{\mathsf{int}(\mathbf{i})} ,
$$

where for each $\mathbf{i} \in \mathbb{Z}_2^k$, we define $z_{\mathbf{i}} := \bar{f}(u^{2^k}, \mathbf{i}) \in \mathcal{R}_q$. The partial evaluations $(z_{\mathbf{i}})_{\mathbf{i}}$ are then sent to the verifier. The prover also outputs the partial openings $(\mathbf{s_i})_{\mathbf{i}\in\mathbb{Z}_2^{\leq k}}$ in the clear; later we will explain the meaning behind this move. After the first round, the verifier already checks whether:

$$
z = \sum_{\mathbf{i}\in\mathbb{Z}_2^k} z_{\mathbf{i}} \cdot u^{\mathsf{int}(\mathbf{i})} \quad \text{and} \quad \|\mathbf{s_i}\| \leq \beta \text{ for } \forall \mathbf{i} \in \mathbb{Z}_2^{\leq k} . \tag{4}
$$

Now, the verifier outputs the challenge vector $\boldsymbol{\alpha} = (\alpha_{\mathbf{i}})_{\mathbf{i}} \leftarrow \mathcal{X}^{2^k}$, and the prover computes the folded polynomial of degree d'

$$
g(\mathsf{X}) := \sum_{\mathbf{i}\in\mathbb{Z}_2^k} \alpha_{\mathbf{i}} \cdot \bar{f}(\mathsf{X}, \mathbf{i}) .
$$

So far, this protocol focused on proving the evaluation $f(u) = z$. We additionally need to prove knowledge of the opening Merkle-PRISIS commitment $\mathbf{t}$. Let $\mathbf{j} \in \mathbb{Z}_2^l$. Then, the $\mathbf{j}$-th coefficient of g satisfies

$$g_{\mathbf{j}} \cdot \mathbf{e}_1 = \sum_{\mathbf{i} \in \mathbb{Z}_2^k} \alpha_{\mathbf{i}} \cdot f_{(\mathbf{i},\mathbf{j})} \cdot \mathbf{e}_1$$

$$= \sum_{\mathbf{i} \in \mathbb{Z}_2^k} \alpha_{\mathbf{i}} \cdot \left(\mathbf{t} - \sum_{t=1}^{k} w_t^{i_t} \cdot \mathbf{A}_t \cdot \mathbf{s}_{\mathbf{i}:t} - \sum_{t=1}^{l} w_{k+t}^{j_t} \cdot \mathbf{A}_{k+t} \cdot \mathbf{s}_{(\mathbf{i},\mathbf{j}:t)} \right) .$$

Thus, we obtain

$$\sum_{t=1}^{l} w_{k+t}^{j_t} \mathbf{A}_{k+t} \cdot \left(\sum_{\mathbf{i} \in \mathbb{Z}_2^k} \alpha_{\mathbf{i}} \cdot \mathbf{s}_{(\mathbf{i},\mathbf{j}:t)} \right) + g_{\mathbf{j}} \mathbf{e}_1 = \sum_{\mathbf{i} \in \mathbb{Z}_2^k} \alpha_{\mathbf{i}} \cdot \left(\mathbf{t} - \sum_{t=1}^{k} w_t^{i_t} \mathbf{A}_t \cdot \mathbf{s}_{\mathbf{i}:t} \right) \quad (5)$$

where the right-hand side can be computed by the verifier given the initial commitment $\mathbf{t}$ and partial openings $\mathbf{s}_{\mathbf{i}:t}$. Hence, by setting for $\mathbf{j} \in \mathbb{Z}_2^{\leq l}$:

$$\mathbf{z_j} := \sum_{\mathbf{i} \in \mathbb{Z}_2^k} \alpha_{\mathbf{i}} \cdot \mathbf{s}_{(\mathbf{i},\mathbf{j})}, \quad \mathbf{t}' := \sum_{\mathbf{i} \in \mathbb{Z}_2^k} \alpha_{\mathbf{i}} \cdot \left(\mathbf{t} - \sum_{t=1}^{k} w_t^{i_t} \cdot \mathbf{A}_t \cdot \mathbf{s}_{\mathbf{i}:t} \right) \quad \text{and}$$

$$z' := \sum_{\mathbf{i} \in \mathbb{Z}_2^k} \alpha_{\mathbf{i}} \cdot z_{\mathbf{i}}$$

we can check that:

$$\left((\mathbf{A}_{k+t},\ w_{k+t},\ \mathbf{T}_{k+t})_{t \in [l]},\ (\mathbf{t}',\ u^{2^k},\ z'),\ (g,\ (\mathbf{z_j})_{\mathbf{j} \in \mathbb{Z}_2^{\leq l}}) \right) \in \mathsf{R}_{l,2^k\beta} .$$

Thus, in the third round the prover outputs $(g, (\mathbf{z_j})_{\mathbf{j} \in \mathbb{Z}_2^{\leq l}})$, and the verifier checks the claim above, along with (4). We highlight that the newly formed statement $(\mathbf{t}', u^{2^k}, z')$ can be constructed directly by the verifier.

Similarly as in [FMN23], one can show that the soundness error of the protocol above is $2^k/(2N)$. In order to amplify soundness, we directly consider proving r polynomial evaluations $f_\iota(u) = z_\iota$ at the same point u for $\iota = 1, \ldots, r$, where r will be the amplification parameter. Hence, in the setting of our commitment scheme, we are interested in the following ternary relation:

$$\mathsf{R}_{h,\beta}^{(r)} := \left\{ \left(\begin{array}{c} (\mathbf{A}_j,\ w_j,\ \mathbf{T}_j)_{j \in [h]}, \\ ((\mathbf{t}_\iota)_{\iota \in [r]},\ u,\ (z_\iota)_{\iota \in [r]}), \\ (f_\iota, (\mathbf{s}_{\iota,\mathbf{b}})_{\mathbf{b} \in \mathbb{Z}_2^{\leq h}})_{\iota \in [r]} \end{array} \right) \left| \begin{array}{c} \forall \iota \in [r],\ f_\iota(u) = z_\iota \wedge \forall \mathbf{b} \in \mathbb{Z}_2^h, \\ \wedge \sum_{j=1}^{h} w_j^{b_j} \mathbf{A}_j \cdot \mathbf{s}_{\iota,\mathbf{b}:j} + f_{\iota,\mathbf{b}} = \mathbf{t}_\iota \\ \wedge \forall j \in [h], \|\mathbf{s}_{\iota,\mathbf{b}:j}\| \leq \beta \end{array} \right. \right\} . \quad (6)$$

To handle proving multiple polynomial evaluations at the same point u the prover defines functions $\bar{f}_\iota$ with respect to the polynomials f_ι for $\iota \in [r]$ as before, and computes $z_{\iota,\mathbf{i}} := \bar{f}_\iota(u^{2^k}, \mathbf{i})$ for $\mathbf{i} \in \mathbb{Z}_2^k$. It outputs $(z_{\iota,\mathbf{i}})_{\iota,\mathbf{i}}$ along with the partial openings $(\mathbf{s}_{\iota,\mathbf{i}})_{\iota \in [r], \mathbf{i} \in \mathbb{Z}_2^{\leq k}}$. The verifier replies with a challenge $(\boldsymbol{\alpha}_{\iota,\mathbf{i}})_{\iota \in [r], \mathbf{i} \in \mathbb{Z}_2^k} \leftarrow (\mathcal{X}^r)^{r2^k}$ where $\boldsymbol{\alpha}_{\iota,\mathbf{i}} := (\alpha_{\iota,\mathbf{i},1}, \ldots, \alpha_{\iota,\mathbf{i},r}) \in \mathcal{X}^r$. Next, the prover computes r polynomials $g_1, \ldots, g_r$ defined as:

$$g_\kappa(\mathsf{X}) := \sum_{\iota=1}^{r} \sum_{\mathbf{i} \in \mathbb{Z}_2^k} \alpha_{\iota,\mathbf{i},\kappa} \cdot \bar{f}_\iota(\mathsf{X}, \mathbf{i}) \quad \text{for } \kappa = 1, \ldots, r.$$

Using the same strategy as in (5), we deduce that the $\mathbf{j}$-th coefficient of g_κ satisfies:

$$\sum_{t=1}^{l} w_{k+t}^{j_t} \cdot \mathbf{A}_{k+t} \cdot \left(\sum_{\iota=1}^{r} \sum_{\mathbf{i} \in \mathbb{Z}_2^k} \alpha_{\iota,\mathbf{i},\kappa} \cdot \mathbf{s}_{\iota,(\mathbf{i},\mathbf{j}_{:t})} \right) + g_{\kappa,\mathbf{j}} \cdot \mathbf{e}_1$$
$$= \sum_{\iota=1}^{r} \sum_{\mathbf{i} \in \mathbb{Z}_2^k} \alpha_{\iota,\mathbf{i},\kappa} \cdot \left(\mathbf{t}_\iota - \sum_{t=1}^{k} w_t^{i_t} \cdot \mathbf{A}_t \cdot \mathbf{s}_{\iota,\mathbf{i}_{:t}} \right) .$$

Hence, by defining for $\mathbf{j} \in \mathbb{Z}_2^{\leq l}$ and $\kappa \in [r]$:

$$\mathbf{z}_{\kappa,\mathbf{j}} := \sum_{\iota=1}^{r} \sum_{\mathbf{i} \in \mathbb{Z}_2^k} \alpha_{\iota,\mathbf{i},\kappa} \cdot \mathbf{s}_{\iota,(\mathbf{i},\mathbf{j})},$$

$$\mathbf{t}_\kappa' := \sum_{\iota=1}^{r} \sum_{\mathbf{i} \in \mathbb{Z}_2^k} \alpha_{\iota,\mathbf{i},\kappa} \cdot \left(\mathbf{t}_\iota - \sum_{t=1}^{k} w_t^{i_t} \cdot \mathbf{A}_t \cdot \mathbf{s}_{\iota,\mathbf{i}_{:t}} \right),$$

$$z_\kappa' := \sum_{\iota=1}^{r} \sum_{\mathbf{i} \in \mathbb{Z}_2^k} \alpha_{\iota,\mathbf{i},\kappa} \cdot z_{\iota,\mathbf{i}} ,$$

we obtain

$$\begin{pmatrix} (\mathbf{A}_{k+t}, w_{k+t}, \mathbf{T}_{k+t})_{t \in [l]}, \\ \left((\mathbf{t}_\kappa')_{\kappa \in [r]}, \ u^{2^k}, \ (z_\kappa')_{\kappa \in [r]} \right), \\ \left(g_\kappa, \ (\mathbf{z}_{\kappa,\mathbf{b}})_{\mathbf{b} \in \mathbb{Z}_2^{\leq l}} \right)_{\kappa \in [r]} \end{pmatrix} \in \mathsf{R}_{l,r2^k\beta}^{(r)} . \tag{7}$$

Hence, the prover sends $\left(g_\kappa, (\mathbf{z}_{\kappa,\mathbf{b}})_{\mathbf{b} \in \mathbb{Z}_2^{\leq h}} \right)_{\kappa \in [r]}$, and the verifier checks (7), and whether for all $\iota \in [r]$:

$$z_\iota = \sum_{\mathbf{i} \in \mathbb{Z}_2^k} z_{\iota,\mathbf{i}} \cdot u^{\mathrm{int}(\mathbf{i})} \quad \text{and} \quad \|\mathbf{s}_{\iota,\mathbf{i}}\| \leq \beta \text{ for } \forall \mathbf{i} \in \mathbb{Z}_2^{\leq k} . \tag{8}$$

As we will show in the more general case, soundness error of this Σ-protocol is $r2^k/(2N)^r$ which is negligible for e.g. $N = \mathsf{poly}(\lambda)$, and $r, k = O(\log d)$.

Table 2. Overview of parameters and notation.

Parameter	Explanation
q	proof system modulus
N	degree of the cyclotomic ring $\mathcal{R} := \mathbb{Z}[X]/(X^N + 1)$
d	degree of the committed polynomial $f \in \mathcal{R}_q[X]$
$\mathcal{X}$	Set of signed monomials $\pm X^i$ of $\mathcal{R}$
n, m	height and width of the matrices $\mathbf{A}_j$
$\delta, \tilde{q}$	decomposition base of the gadget matrix $\mathbf{G}$; $\lfloor \log_\delta q \rfloor + 1$
h	positive integer such that $d + 1 = 2^h$
k	folding factor of the folding protocol, divisor of h
l	$h - k$
ℓ	$\leq h/k$
β, γ	initial norm of the witness openings; extracted norm

5.2   Succinct Arguments via Recursion

In order to achieve succinct proofs and verification, we extend the Σ-protocol above as follows. Concretely, instead of checking (7) manually, the verifier recursively runs the Σ-protocol ℓ times (or until the degrees of the r committed polynomials are zero). This yields a $(2\ell + 1)$-th round protocol where $\ell \leq h/k$ (here we assume that k is divisible by h). We recall the notation in Table 2 and describe the resulting interactive proof in Fig. 4.

Security Analysis. In the following, we state completeness and coordinate-wise special soundness of the protocol in Fig. 4 and provide proofs in the appendix.

Lemma 5.1 (Completeness). *The protocol in Fig. 4 satisfies perfect completeness.*

The formal proof is in the full version of the paper which closely follows our discussion above. To argue coordinate-wise special soundness, we consider a relaxed relation:

$$\tilde{\mathsf{R}}^{(r)}_{h,\gamma,\xi} := \left\{ \left(\begin{array}{c} (\mathbf{A}_j, w_j, \mathbf{T}_j)_{j \in [h]}, \\ ((\mathbf{t}_\iota)_{\iota \in [r]}, u, (z_\iota)_{\iota \in [r]}), \\ (f_\iota, (\mathbf{s}_{\iota,\mathbf{b}})_{\mathbf{b} \in \mathbb{Z}_2^{\leq h}})_{\iota \in [r]} \end{array} \right) \middle| \begin{array}{c} \forall \iota \in [r], f_\iota(u) = z \land \forall \mathbf{b} \in \mathbb{Z}_2^h, \\ \land \sum_{j=1}^h w_j^{b_j} \mathbf{A}_j \mathbf{s}_{\iota,\mathbf{b}:j} + f_{\iota,\mathbf{b}} \mathbf{e}_1 = \mathbf{t}_\iota \\ \land \forall j \in [h], \|\xi \cdot \mathbf{s}_{\iota,\mathbf{b}:j}\| \leq \gamma \end{array} \right\} . \quad (9)$$

Let us note the difference from the original relation $\mathsf{R}^{(r)}_{h,\beta}$ in (6). Namely, we do not require the opening vectors to have norm at most β, and thus they do not need to be short anymore. One can also see the connection between the relaxed notion and the slack space of the commitment in Sect. 4. Also, we observe that $\tilde{\mathsf{R}}^{(r)}_{h,\beta,1} = \mathsf{R}^{(r)}_{h,\beta}$ which is the relation appearing in Item 4 of Fig. 4.

Interactive Protocol for $R_{h,\beta}^{(r)}$

$\mathcal{P}\left((\mathbf{A}_j, w_j, \mathbf{T}_j)_{j\in[h]}, ((\mathbf{t}_{0,\iota})_{\iota\in[r]}, u_0, (z_{0,\iota})_{\iota\in[r]}), (f_{0,\iota}, (\mathbf{s}_{0,\iota,\mathbf{b}})_{\mathbf{b}\in\mathbb{Z}_2^{\leq h}})_{\iota\in[r]}\right)$

---

1. Set $l_0 = h$.
2. For $\tau \in [\ell]$:
   (a) Set $l_\tau := l_{\tau-1} - k$.
   (b) Compute $u_\tau := u_{\tau-1}^{2^k}$.
   (c) For $\iota \in [r]$ and $\mathbf{i} \in \mathbb{Z}_2^k$:
      i. Set $\bar{f}_{\tau-1,\iota}(\mathsf{X}, \mathbf{i}) := \sum_{\mathbf{j}\in\mathbb{Z}_2^{l_\tau}} f_{\tau-1,\iota,(\mathbf{i},\mathbf{j})} \cdot \mathsf{X}^{\mathrm{int}(\mathbf{j})} \in \mathcal{R}_q[\mathsf{X}]$.
      ii. Set $z_{\tau-1,\iota,\mathbf{i}} := \bar{f}_{\tau-1,\iota}(u_\tau, \mathbf{i})$.
   (d) Send $\left((z_{\tau-1,\iota,\mathbf{i}})_{\mathbf{i}\in\mathbb{Z}_2^k}, (\mathbf{s}_{\tau-1,\iota,\mathbf{i}})_{\mathbf{i}\in\mathbb{Z}_2^{\leq k}}\right)_{\iota\in[r]}$ to the verifier.
   (e) Receive $(\boldsymbol{\alpha}_{\iota,\mathbf{i}}^{(\tau)})_{\iota\in[r],\mathbf{i}\in\mathbb{Z}_2^k} \leftarrow (\mathcal{X}^r)^{r2^k}$ from the verifier.
   (f) For $\kappa \in [r]$:
      i. Compute $f_{\tau,\kappa}(\mathsf{X}) := \sum_{\iota=1}^r \sum_{\mathbf{i}\in\mathbb{Z}_2^k} \alpha_{\iota,\mathbf{i},\kappa}^{(\tau)} \bar{f}_{\tau-1,\iota}(\mathsf{X},\mathbf{i})$
      ii. Compute $\mathbf{s}_{\tau,\kappa,\mathbf{j}} := \sum_{\iota=1}^r \sum_{\mathbf{i}\in\mathbb{Z}_2^k} \alpha_{\iota,\mathbf{i},\kappa}^{(\tau)} \mathbf{s}_{\tau-1,\iota,(\mathbf{i},\mathbf{j})}$ for $\mathbf{j} \in \mathbb{Z}_2^{\leq l_\tau}$
3. Send $((f_{\ell,\kappa}) \in \mathcal{R}_{\bar{q}}^{\leq 2^{h-k\ell}-1}[\mathsf{X}], (\mathbf{s}_{\ell,\kappa,\mathbf{i}})_{\mathbf{i}\in\mathbb{Z}_2^{\leq h-k\ell}})_{\kappa\in[r]}$ to the verifier.

$\mathcal{V}((\mathbf{A}_j, w_j, \mathbf{T}_j)_{j\in[h]}, ((\mathbf{t}_{0,\iota})_{\iota\in[r]}, u_0, (z_{0,\iota})_{\iota\in[r]}))$

---

1. Set $l_0 = h$ and $\beta_0 := \beta$.
2. For $\tau \in [\ell]$:
   (a) Set $l_\tau := l_{\tau-1} - k$.
   (b) Compute $u_\tau := u_{\tau-1}^{2^k}$.
   (c) Receive $\left((z_{\tau-1,\iota,\mathbf{i}})_{\mathbf{i}\in\mathbb{Z}_2^k}, (\mathbf{s}_{\tau-1,\iota,\mathbf{i}})_{\mathbf{i}\in\mathbb{Z}_2^{\leq k}}\right)_{\iota\in[r]}$ from the prover.
   (d) Check for $\iota \in [r]$:
      i. $z_{\tau-1,\iota} = \sum_{\mathbf{i}\in\mathbb{Z}_2^k} z_{\tau-1,\iota,\mathbf{i}} \cdot u_\tau^{\mathrm{int}(\mathbf{i})}$
      ii. $\|\mathbf{s}_{\tau-1,\iota,\mathbf{i}}\| \leq (r2^k)^{\tau-1}\beta$ for all $\mathbf{i} \in \mathbb{Z}_2^{\leq k}$
   (e) Sample $(\boldsymbol{\alpha}_{\iota,\mathbf{i}}^{(\tau)})_{\iota\in[r],\mathbf{i}\in\mathbb{Z}_2^k} \leftarrow (\mathcal{X}^r)^{r2^k}$ and send it to the prover.
   (f) For $\kappa \in [r]$:
      i. For $\iota \in [r], \mathbf{i} \in \mathbb{Z}_2^k$, $\tilde{\mathbf{t}}_{\iota,\mathbf{i},\mathbf{k}} := \mathbf{t}_{\tau-1,\iota} - \sum_{t=1}^k w_{(\tau-1)k+t}^{i_t} \mathbf{A}_{(\tau-1)k+t} \mathbf{s}_{\tau-1,\iota,\mathbf{i}:t}$
      ii. Set $\mathbf{t}_{\tau,\kappa} := \sum_{\iota=1}^r \sum_{\mathbf{i}\in\mathbb{Z}_2^k} \alpha_{\iota,\mathbf{i},\kappa}^{(\tau)} \tilde{\mathbf{t}}_{\iota,\mathbf{i},\mathbf{k}}$.
      iii. Set $z_{\tau,\kappa} := \sum_{\iota=1}^r \sum_{\mathbf{i}\in\mathbb{Z}_2^k} \alpha_{\iota,\mathbf{i},\kappa}^{(\tau)} z_{\tau-1,\iota,\mathbf{i}}$.
   (g) Set $\beta_\tau := r2^k \cdot \beta_{\tau-1}$.
3. Receive $((f_{\ell,\kappa}) \in \mathcal{R}_{\bar{q}}^{\leq 2^{h-k\ell}-1}[\mathsf{X}], (\mathbf{s}_{\ell,\kappa,\mathbf{i}})_{\mathbf{i}\in\mathbb{Z}_2^{\leq h-k\ell}})_{\kappa\in[r]}$ from the prover.
4. Check:
$$\begin{pmatrix} (\mathbf{A}_{k\ell+t}, w_{k\ell+t}, \mathbf{T}_{k\ell+t})_{t\in[h-k\ell]}, \\ ((\mathbf{t}_{\ell,\kappa})_{\kappa\in[r]}, u_\ell, (z_{\ell,\kappa})_{\kappa\in[r]}), \\ ((f_{\ell,\kappa}), (\mathbf{s}_{\ell,\kappa,\mathbf{i}})_{\mathbf{i}\in\mathbb{Z}_2^{\leq h-k\ell}})_{\kappa\in[r]} \end{pmatrix} \in R_{h-k\ell,(r2^k)^\ell\beta}^{(r)}.$$

Fig. 4. Interactive protocol for $R_{h,\beta}^{(r)}$ with notation from Table 2. Intuitively, index τ keeps track of the number of iterations of the compressed Σ-protocol, while indices ι and κ are used as in Section 5.1.

Lemma 5.2 (Coordinate-Wise Special Soundness). *Define* $\gamma^* := (2^{k+1}rN)^\ell\beta$. *If* $(r2^k+1)^\ell = \mathsf{poly}(\lambda,d)$, *then the interactive proof in Fig. 4 is* $r2^k$-*coordinate-wise special sound w.r.t. the relation* $\tilde{\mathsf{R}}^{(r)}_{h,\gamma^*,2^\ell}$.

The proof is in the full version of the paper. The result above in particular says that one can extract a relaxed opening for the Merkle-PRISIS commitment with the relaxation factor $2^{h/k-1} = 2^\ell \in \mathcal{R}_q^\times$.

Efficiency. We analyse the efficiency of the protocol in the next lemma.

Lemma 5.3 (Efficiency). *The total communication complexity of the protocol in Fig. 4 (in bits) can be bounded by*

$$\underbrace{(\ell+1)\cdot(2^k N\lceil\log q\rceil)}_{\text{partial evaluations}} + \underbrace{2^{k+1}mN\cdot\sum_{i=0}^{\ell-1}\lceil\log 2(r2^k)^i\beta\rceil}_{\text{short openings}} + \underbrace{\ell\cdot r^2 2^k\lceil\log 2N\rceil}_{\text{verifier messages}}$$

$$+ \underbrace{2^{h-k\ell}N\lceil\log q\rceil + 2^{h-k\ell+1}\lceil\log 2(r2^k)^\ell\beta\rceil}_{\text{final message}} .$$

Further, accounting both in terms of operations over $\mathcal{R}_q$, *the prover runs in time* $O(r^2md + r2^{h-k\ell})$ *and the verifier in time* $O\left(\ell\cdot 2^k n(km+r^2) + r2^{h-k\ell}\right)$.

Proof. We start with the communication complexity. Note that the size of each i-th of the first ℓ messages (counting from zero) can be naively bounded by

$$2^k\cdot N\cdot\lceil\log q\rceil + 2^{k+1}mN\cdot\lceil\log 2(r2^k)^i\beta\rceil .$$

The size of the last message can be naively bounded by

$$2^{h-k\ell}\cdot N\cdot\lceil\log q\rceil + 2^{h-k\ell+1}\cdot\lceil\log 2(r2^k)^\ell\beta\rceil .$$

Meanwhile the total size of the verifier messages is $\ell\cdot r^2 2^k\lceil\log 2N\rceil$.

Next, consider the prover runtime in a single iteration of the loop in Item 2 for some $\tau\in[\ell]$. The main bottleneck is the procedure in Item 2(f)ii which takes $r\cdot 2^{k+l_\tau+1}\cdot m = r\cdot 2^{l_\tau-1+1}\cdot m$ operations over $\mathcal{R}_q$. Since we run that line r times, we conclude that the total runtime in a single iteration of the loop is $O(r^2 m2^{l_\tau-1})$. Hence, the total prover runtime can be bounded by

$$O\left(\sum_{\tau=1}^{\ell}r^2 m2^{l_\tau-1} + r2^{h-k\ell}\right) = O\left(r^2 m\sum_{\tau=1}^{\ell}2^{h-(\tau-1)k} + r2^{h-k\ell}\right)$$

$$= O(r^2 md + r2^{h-k\ell}) .$$

As for the verifier, excluding reading the last message, the main bottleneck is computing the new $\mathbf{t}_{\tau,\kappa}$ in Item 2(f)ii. First, the verifier can compute all the necessary partial sums $\sum_{t=1}^{k}w^{i_t}_{(\tau-1)k+t}\mathbf{A}_{(\tau-1)k+t}\mathbf{s}_{\tau-1,\iota,\mathbf{i}_{:t}}$ in $O(2^k knm)$ operations over $\mathcal{R}_q$. Then, calculating $\mathbf{t}_{\tau,\kappa}$ takes $O(rn2^k)$ time. Since we compute that for every $\kappa\in[r]$, a single iteration of the loop in Item 2f takes $O(2^k n(km+r^2))$ operations. Hence, by iterating over all possible $\tau\in[\ell]$, the verifier runtime can be bounded by $O(\ell\cdot 2^k n(km+r^2) + r2^{h-k\ell})$. $\square$

Table 3. Parameters for the polynomial commitment scheme obtained from Fig. 3 and running the protocol in Fig. 4 for proofs of evaluation.

Par.	Instantiation	Par.	Instantiation
δ	$q^{1/O(1)}$	s	$> 2N \cdot q^{\frac{n}{m-t} + \frac{2}{N \cdot (m-t)}}$
t	$n\tilde{q}$	σ_0	$\geq 2\delta s N \cdot \omega(\sqrt{t(m-t)\log t'N})$
m	$\geq t + n$	σ_1	$\geq \delta\sigma_0 N \cdot \omega(\sqrt{m'n'\log t'N})$
m'	$2m + t$	β	$\geq \sigma_1\sqrt{m'N}$
n'	$2t$	γ	$(2^{k+1}rN)^\ell\beta$
t'	$\max(n', m')$	k	$O(\log\log d)$
r	$O(\log\lambda)$	ℓ	$h/k = O\left(\frac{\log d}{\log\log d}\right)$

5.3   Succinct Polynomial Commitment Scheme

Finally, by combining the results above, we obtain a polynomial commitment scheme with polylogarithmic evaluation proofs, quasi-linear prover runtime, and polylogarithmic verifier runtime.

Namely, we use the construction in Fig. 3; given a polynomial $f \in \mathcal{R}_q[X]$ of degree at most $d := 2^h - 1$ over $\mathcal{R}_q$, we commit to f by committing to its coefficient vector $\mathbf{f} = (f_\mathbf{b})_{\mathbf{b} \in \mathbb{Z}_2^h} \in \mathcal{R}_q^{d+1}$ to obtain a commitment $\mathbf{t} \in \mathcal{R}_q^n$, together with the decommitment state $\mathsf{st} = (\mathbf{s_b})_{\mathbf{b} \in \mathbb{Z}_2^{\leq h}}$. Then, the Eval protocol runs the Fiat-Shamir trasnformed protocol[6] in Fig. 4, and Verify verifies the proof. The following theorem summarises our results.

Theorem 5.4 (Polynomial Commitment Scheme). *Let* $n, m, N, d \in$ $\mathsf{poly}(\lambda)$ *be lattice parameters. Define* PC $=$ (Setup, Commit, Open, Eval, Verify) *where* Setup, Commit, Open *are as in Fig. 3 and* Eval, Verify *are defined in Fig. 4. Take the parameters from Table 3. Then,* PC *is an interactive polynomial commitment scheme which satisfies evaluation completeness and relaxed binding under the* h-$\mathsf{PRISIS}_{n-1,m,\mathcal{R}_q,2,\sigma_1,2\gamma\sqrt{h}}$ *assumption. Further,*

- *the evaluation proof consists of* $O(\log^2 d) \cdot \mathsf{poly}(\lambda)$ *elements in* $\mathcal{R}_q$,
- *running time of* Eval *is* $O(d) \cdot \mathsf{poly}(\lambda)$ *operations over* $\mathcal{R}_q$,
- *running time of* Verify *is* $O(\log^2 d) \cdot \mathsf{poly}(\lambda)$ *operations over* $\mathcal{R}_q$,
- PC *is knowledge sound in the random oracle model, with knowledge error* $O\left(\frac{\log^2 d \cdot \log\lambda}{\lambda^{\log N+1}}\right) = \mathsf{negl}(\lambda)$.

Proof. First, evaluation completeness follows from Lemmas 4.1 and 5.1. Then, relaxed binding follows from Lemma 4.2. Note that the parameter γ is chosen with respect to the extracted openings in Lemma 5.2.

---

[6] Note that the prover in Fig. 4 starts with proving r evaluations of r (not necessarily distinct) polynomials $(f_{0,\iota})_{\iota\in[r]}$ at a single point u_0, while for Eval we only require proving one evaluation for a single polynomial f. We can thus naively let Eval run $\mathcal{P}$ for $f = f_{0,1} = \ldots = f_{0,r}$.

The proof sizes and the running times of Eval and Verify come from Lemma 5.3 for $k = O(\log \log d)$, $r = O(\log \lambda)$ and $\ell = O\left(\frac{\log d}{\log \log d}\right)$. The knowledge error can be directly deduced from the lemmas above while keeping in mind that

$$(r2^k + 1)^\ell = O\left(\ell \cdot (r2^k)^\ell\right) = O\left(\frac{\log d}{\log \log d} \cdot (\log \lambda \cdot \log d)^{\frac{\log d}{\log \log d}}\right)$$
$$= O\left(\frac{\log d}{\log \log d} \cdot d^2\right) = \mathsf{poly}(d).$$

$\square$

Batching. It is easy to see that the protocol in Fig. 4 naturally supports proving multiple polynomial evaluations at a single point; indeed, we consider proving r evaluations simultaneously from the very start. Unfortunately, apart from small optimisations in the last round as in [FMN23, Section 5.4.2], we do not see how to batch polynomial evaluations proofs for multiple distinct points.

Non-interactive Polynomial Commitments. Eval, Verify can be made non-interactive using the Fiat-Shamir transformation. Fenzi, Moghaddas and Nguyen showed in [FMN23, Section 8] that coordinate-wise special sound protocols maintain knowledge soundness after performing the Fiat-Shamir transformation, with the linear reduction loss in the number of random oracle queries. Since our protocol satisfies coordinate-wise special soundness, this yields a secure non-interactive polynomial commitment scheme.

Acknowledgments. Giacomo Fenzi is partially supported by the Ethereum Foundation. Oleksandra Lapiha was supported by the EPSRC and the UK Government as part of the Centre for Doctoral Training in Cyber Security for the Everyday at Royal Holloway, University of London (EP/S021817/1). Ngoc Khanh Nguyen was supported by the Protocol Labs RFP-013: Cryptonet network grant, and most of their work was done while at EPFL. Martin Albrecht's work is supported by UKRI grant EP/Y02432X/1.

References

[ACK21]   Attema, T., Cramer, R., Kohl, L.: A compressed Σ-protocol theory for lattices. In: Malkin, T., Peikert, C. (eds.) Advances in Cryptology – CRYPTO 2021. CRYPTO 2021. LNCS, vol. 12826, pp. 549–579. Springer, Cham (2021). https://doi.org/10.1007/978-3-030-84245-1_19

[ACLMT22] Albrecht, M.R., Cini, V., Lai, R.W.F., Malavolta, G., Thyagarajan, S.A.: Lattice-based SNARKs: publicly verifiable, preprocessing, and recursively composable. In: Dodis, Y., Shrimpton, T. (eds.) Advances in Cryptology – CRYPTO 2022. CRYPTO 2022. LNCS, vol. 13508, pp. 102–132. Springer, Cham (2022). https://doi.org/10.1007/978-3-031-15979-4_4

[AF22]   Attema, T., Fehr, S.: Parallel repetition of $(k_1, \ldots, k_\mu)$-special-sound multi-round interactive proofs. In: Dodis, Y., Shrimpton, T. (eds.) Advances in Cryptology – CRYPTO 2022. CRYPTO 2022. LNCS, vol. 13507, pp. 415–443. Springer, Cham (2022). https://doi.org/10.1007/978-3-031-15802-5_15

[AFK22]   Attema, T., Fehr, S., Klooß, M.: Fiat-Shamir transformation of multi-round interactive proofs. In: Kiltz, E., Vaikuntanathan, V. (eds.) Theory of Cryptography. TCC 2022. LNCS, vol. 13747, pp. 113–142. Springer, Cham (2022). https://doi.org/10.1007/978-3-031-22318-1_5

[AHIV22]   Ames, S., Hazay, C., Ishai, Y., Venkitasubramaniam, M.: Ligero: lightweight sublinear arguments without a trusted setup. Cryptology ePrint Archive, Report 2022/1608. https://eprint.iacr.org/2022/1608 (2022)

[AL21]   Albrecht, M.R., Lai, R.W.F.: Subtractive sets over cyclotomic rings. In: Malkin, T., Peikert, C. (eds.) CRYPTO 2021. LNCS, vol. 12826, pp. 519–548. Springer, Cham (2021). https://doi.org/10.1007/978-3-030-84245-1_18

[Ajt96]   Ajtai, M.: Generating hard instances of lattice problems (extended abstract). In: 28th ACM STOC, pp. 99–108. ACM Press, May 1996. https://doi.org/10.1145/237814.237838

[BBBPWM18]   Bünz, B., Bootle, J., Boneh, D., Poelstra, A., Wuille, P., Maxwell, G.: Bulletproofs: short proofs for confidential transactions and more. In: 2018 IEEE Symposium on Security and Privacy, pp. 315–334. IEEE Computer Society Press, May 2018. https://doi.org/10.1109/SP.2018.00020

[BBCdGL18]   Baum, C., Bootle, J., Cerulli, A., del Pino, R., Groth, J., Lyubashevsky, V.: Sub-linear lattice-based zero-knowledge arguments for arithmetic circuits. In: Shacham, H., Boldyreva, A. (eds.) CRYPTO 2018. LNCS, vol. 10992, pp. 669–699. Springer, Cham (2018). https://doi.org/10.1007/978-3-319-96881-0_23

[BBHR18a]   Ben-Sasson, E., Bentov, I., Horesh, Y., Riabzev, M.: Fast reed-Solomon interactive oracle proofs of proximity. In: Chatzigiannakis, I., Kaklamanis, C., Marx, D., Sannella, D. (eds.) ICALP 2018, vol. 107. LIPIcs. Schloss Dagstuhl, July 2018, pp. 14:1–14:17 (2018). https://doi.org/10.4230/LIPIcs.ICALP.2018.14

[BBHR18b]   Ben-Sasson, E., Bentov, I., Horesh, Y., Riabzev, M.: Scalable, transparent, and post-quantum secure computational integrity. Cryptology ePrint Archive, Report 2018/046 (2018). https://eprint.iacr.org/2018/046

[BCCGP16]   Bootle, J., Cerulli, A., Chaidos, P., Groth, J., Petit, C.: Efficient zero-knowledge arguments for arithmetic circuits in the discrete log setting. In: Fischlin, M., Coron, J.-S. (eds.) EUROCRYPT 2016. LNCS, vol. 9666, pp. 327–357. Springer, Heidelberg (2016). https://doi.org/10.1007/978-3-662-49896-5_12

[BCFL22]   Balbas, D., Catalano, D., Fiore, D., Lai, R.W.: Functional Commitments for Circuits from Falsifiable Assumptions. Cryptology ePrint Archive, Report 2022/1365. https://eprint.iacr.org/2022/1365 (2022)

[BCIOP13]   Bitansky, N., Chiesa, A., Ishai, Y., Paneth, O., Ostrovsky, R.: Succinct non-interactive arguments via linear interactive proofs. In: Sahai, A. (ed.) TCC 2013. LNCS, vol. 7785, pp. 315–333. Springer, Heidelberg (2013). https://doi.org/10.1007/978-3-642-36594-2_18

[BCRSVW19] Ben-Sasson, E., Chiesa, A., Riabzev, M., Spooner, N., Virza, M., Ward, N.P.: Aurora: transparent succinct arguments for R1CS. In: Ishai, Y., Rijmen, V. (eds.) EUROCRYPT 2019. LNCS, vol. 11476, pp. 103–128. Springer, Cham (2019). https://doi.org/10.1007/978-3-030-17653-2_4

[BCS16] Ben-Sasson, E., Chiesa, A., Spooner, N.: Interactive oracle proofs. In: Hirt, M., Smith, A. (eds.) TCC 2016. LNCS, vol. 9986, pp. 31–60. Springer, Heidelberg (2016). https://doi.org/10.1007/978-3-662-53644-5_2

[BCS21] Bootle, J., Chiesa, A., Sotiraki, K.: Sumcheck arguments and their applications. In: Malkin, T., Peikert, C. (eds.) CRYPTO 2021. LNCS, vol. 12825, pp. 742–773. Springer, Cham (2021). https://doi.org/10.1007/978-3-030-84242-0_26

[BCS23] Bootle, J., Chiesa, A., Sotiraki, K.: Lattice-based succinct arguments for np with polylogarithmic-time verification. In: Handschuh, H., Lysyanskaya, A. (eds.) Advances in Cryptology – CRYPTO 2023. CRYPTO 2023. LNCS, vol. 14082, pp. 227–251. Springer, Cham (2023). https://doi.org/10.1007/978-3-031-38545-2_8

[BF22] Bünz, B., Fisch, B.: Schwartz-Zippel for multilinear polynomials mod N. Cryptology ePrint Archive, Report 2022/458. https://eprint.iacr.org/2022/458 (2022)

[BFLS91] Babai, L., Fortnow, L., Levin, L.A., Szegedy, M.: Checking computations in polylogarithmic time. In: Proceedings of the 23rd Annual ACM Symposium on Theory of Computing. STOC 1991, pp. 21–32 (1991)

[BFS20] Bünz, B., Fisch, B., Szepieniec, A.: Transparent SNARKs from DARK compilers. In: Canteaut, A., Ishai, Y. (eds.) EUROCRYPT 2020. LNCS, vol. 12105, pp. 677–706. Springer, Cham (2020). https://doi.org/10.1007/978-3-030-45721-1_24

[BHRRS21] Block, A.R., Holmgren, J., Rosen, A., Rothblum, R.D., Soni, P.: Time- and space-efficient arguments from groups of unknown order. In: Malkin, T., Peikert, C. (eds.) CRYPTO 2021. LNCS, vol. 12828, pp. 123–152. Springer, Cham (2021). https://doi.org/10.1007/978-3-030-84259-8_5

[BLNS20] Bootle, J., Lyubashevsky, V., Nguyen, N.K., Seiler, G.: A Non-PCP approach to succinct quantum-safe zero-knowledge. In: Micciancio, D., Ristenpart, T. (eds.) CRYPTO 2020. LNCS, vol. 12171, pp. 441–469. Springer, Cham (2020). https://doi.org/10.1007/978-3-030-56880-1_16

[BLNS23] Bootle, J., Lyubashevsky, V., Nguyen, N.K., Sorniotti, A.: A framework for practical anonymous credentials from lattices. In: Handschuh, H., Lysyanskaya, A. (eds.) Advances in Cryptology – CRYPTO 2023. CRYPTO 2023. LNCS, vol. 14082, pp. 384–417. Springer, Cham (2023). https://doi.org/10.1007/978-3-031-38545-2_13

[BMMTV21] Bünz, B., Maller, M., Mishra, P., Tyagi, N., Vesely, P.: Proofs for inner pairing products and applications. In: Tibouchi, M., Wang, H. (eds.) ASIACRYPT 2021. LNCS, vol. 13092, pp. 65–97. Springer, Cham (2021). https://doi.org/10.1007/978-3-030-92078-4_3

[BS23] Beullens, W., Seiler, G.: LaBRADOR: compact proofs for R1CS from module-SIS. In: Handschuh, H., Lysyanskaya, A. (eds.) Advances in Cryptology – CRYPTO 2023. CRYPTO 2023. LNCS, vol. 14085, pp.

518–548. Springer, Cham (2023). https://doi.org/10.1007/978-3-031-38554-4_17

[BTT22] Boschini, C., Takahashi, A., Tibouchi, M. MuSig-L: lattice-based multi-signature with single-round online phase. In: Dodis, Y., Shrimpton, T. (eds.) Advances in Cryptology – CRYPTO 2022. CRYPTO 2022. LNCS, vol. 13508, pp. 276–305. Springer, Cham (2022). https://doi.org/10.1007/978-3-031-15979-4_10

[CGH04] Canetti, R., Goldreich, O., Halevi, S.: The random oracle methodology, revisited. J. ACM **51**(4), 557–594 (2004)

[CHMMVW20] Chiesa, A., Hu, Y., Maller, M., Mishra, P., Vesely, N., Ward, N.: Marlin: preprocessing zkSNARKs with universal and updatable SRS. In: Canteaut, A., Ishai, Y. (eds.) EUROCRYPT 2020. LNCS, vol. 12105, pp. 738–768. Springer, Cham (2020). https://doi.org/10.1007/978-3-030-45721-1_26

[CJJ22] Choudhuri, A.R., Jain, A., Jin, Z.: SNARGs for P from LWE. In: 62nd FOCS, pp. 68–79. IEEE Computer Society Press, February 2022. https://doi.org/10.1109/FOCS52979.2021.00016

[CLM23] Cini, V., Lai, R.W.F., Malavolta, G.: Lattice-based succinct arguments from vanishing polynomials. In: Handschuh, H., Lysyanskaya, A. (eds.) Advances in Cryptology – CRYPTO 2023. CRYPTO 2023. LNCS, vol. 14082, pp. 72–105. Springer, Cham (2023). https://doi.org/10.1007/978-3-031-38545-2_3

[CMS19] Chiesa, A., Manohar, P., Spooner, N.: Succinct arguments in the quantum random oracle model. In: Hofheinz, D., Rosen, A. (eds.) TCC 2019. LNCS, vol. 11892, pp. 1–29. Springer, Cham (2019). https://doi.org/10.1007/978-3-030-36033-7_1

[COS20] Chiesa, A., Ojha, D., Spooner, N.: Fractal: post-quantum and transparent recursive proofs from holography. In: Canteaut, A., Ishai, Y. (eds.) EUROCRYPT 2020. LNCS, vol. 12105, pp. 769–793. Springer, Cham (2020). https://doi.org/10.1007/978-3-030-45721-1_27

[CP23] de Castro, L., Peikert, C.: Functional commitments for all functions, with transparent setup and from SIS. In: Hazay, C., Stam, M. (eds.) Advances in Cryptology – EUROCRYPT 2023. EUROCRYPT 2023. LNCS, vol. 14006, pp. 287–320. Springer, Cham (2023). https://doi.org/10.1007/978-3-031-30620-4_10

[FLV23] Fisch, B., Liu, Z., Vesely, P.: Orbweaver: succinct linear functional commitments from lattices. In: Handschuh, H., Lysyanskaya, A. (eds.) Advances in Cryptology – CRYPTO 2023. CRYPTO 2023. LNCS, vol. 14082, pp. 106–131. Springer, Cham (2023). https://doi.org/10.1007/978-3-031-38545-2_4

[FMN23] Fenzi, G., Moghaddas, H., Nguyen, N.K.: Lattice-Based Polynomial Commitments: Towards Asymptotic and Concrete Efficiency. Cryptology ePrint Archive, Paper 2023/846. https://eprint.iacr.org/2023/846 (2023)

[GHL22] Gentry, C., Halevi, S., Lyubashevsky, V.: Practical non-interactive publicly verifiable secret sharing with thousands of parties. In: Dunkelman, O., Dziembowski, S. (eds.) Advances in Cryptology – EUROCRYPT 2022. EUROCRYPT 2022. LNCS, vol. 13275, pp. 458–487. Springer, Cham (2022). https://doi.org/10.1007/978-3-031-06944-4_16

[GLSTW21] Golovnev, A., Lee, J., Setty, S.T., Thaler, J., Wahby, R.S.: Brakedown: linear-time and post-quantum SNARKs for R1CS. Cryptology ePrint Archive, Report 2021/1043. https://eprint.iacr.org/2021/1043 (2021)

[HLR21] Holmgren, J., Lombardi, A., Rothblum, R.D.: Fiat-Shamir via list-recoverable codes (or: parallel repetition of GMW is not zero-knowledge). In: Khuller, S., Williams, V.V. (eds.) 53rd ACM STOC, pp. 750–760. ACM Press, June 2021. https://doi.org/10.1145/3406325.3451116

[ISW21] Ishai, Y., Su, H., Wu, D.J.: Shorter and faster post-quantum designated-verifier zkSNARKs from lattices. In: Vigna, G., Shi, E. (eds.) ACM CCS 2021, pp. 212–234. ACM Press, November 2021. https://doi.org/10.1145/3460120.3484572

[KZG10] Kate, A., Zaverucha, G.M., Goldberg, I.: Constant-size commitments to polynomials and their applications. In: Abe, M. (ed.) ASIACRYPT 2010. LNCS, vol. 6477, pp. 177–194. Springer, Heidelberg (2010). https://doi.org/10.1007/978-3-642-17373-8_11

[Kil92] Kilian, J.: A note on efficient zero-knowledge proofs and arguments (extended abstract). In: 24th ACM STOC, pp. 723–732. ACM Press, May 1992. https://doi.org/10.1145/129712.129782

[LNP22] Lyubashevsky, V., Nguyen, N.K., Planc, M.: Lattice-based zero-knowledge proofs and applications: shorter, simpler, and more general. In: Dodis, Y., Shrimpton, T. (eds.) Advances in Cryptology – CRYPTO 2022. CRYPTO 2022. LNCS, vol. 13508, pp. 71–101. Springer, Cham (2022). https://doi.org/10.1007/978-3-031-15979-4_3

[LNS21] Lyubashevsky, V., Nguyen, N.K., Seiler, G.: Shorter lattice-based zero-knowledge proofs via one-time commitments. In: Garay, J.A. (ed.) PKC 2021. LNCS, vol. 12710, pp. 215–241. Springer, Cham (2021). https://doi.org/10.1007/978-3-030-75245-3_9

[LS15] Langlois, A., Stehlé, D.: Worst-case to average-case reductions for module lattices. Des. Codes Cryptogr. **75**(3), 565–599 (2015)

[Lee21] Lee, J.: Dory: efficient, transparent arguments for generalised inner products and polynomial commitments. In: Nissim, K., Waters, B. (eds.) TCC 2021. LNCS, vol. 13043, pp. 1–34. Springer, Cham (2021). https://doi.org/10.1007/978-3-030-90453-1_1

[MP12] Micciancio, D., Peikert, C.: Trapdoors for lattices: simpler, tighter, faster, smaller. In: Pointcheval, D., Johansson, T. (eds.) EUROCRYPT 2012. LNCS, vol. 7237, pp. 700–718. Springer, Heidelberg (2012). https://doi.org/10.1007/978-3-642-29011-4_41

[Mer90] Merkle, R.C.: A certified digital signature. In: Brassard, G. (ed.) CRYPTO 1989. LNCS, vol. 435, pp. 218–238. Springer, New York (1990). https://doi.org/10.1007/0-387-34805-0_21

[Mic94] Micali, S.: CS proofs (extended abstracts). In: 35th FOCS, pp. 436–453. IEEE Computer Society Press, November 1994. https://doi.org/10.1109/SFCS.1994.365746

[NS22] Nguyen, N.K., Seiler, G.: Practical sublinear proofs for R1CS from lattices. In: Dodis, Y., Shrimpton, T. (eds.) Advances in Cryptology – CRYPTO 2022. CRYPTO 2022. LNCS, vol. 13508, pp. 133–162. Springer, Cham (2022). https://doi.org/10.1007/978-3-031-15979-4_5

[PPS21] Peikert, C., Pepin, Z., Sharp, C.: Vector and functional commitments from lattices. In: Nissim, K., Waters, B. (eds.) TCC 2021. LNCS, vol.

13044, pp. 480–511. Springer, Cham (2021). https://doi.org/10.1007/978-3-030-90456-2_16

[SSEK22]   Steinfeld, R., Sakzad, A., Esgin, M.F., Kuchta, V.: Private Re-Randomization for Module LWE and Applications to Quasi-Optimal ZK-SNARKs. Cryptology ePrint Archive, Report 2022/1690. https://eprint.iacr.org/2022/1690 (2022)

[WTsTW17]   Wahby, R.S., Tzialla, I., Shelat, A., Thaler, J., Walfish, M.: Doubly-efficient zkSNARKs without trusted setup. Cryptology ePrint Archive, Report 2017/1132. https://eprint.iacr.org/2017/1132 (2017)

[WW23a]   Wee, H., Wu, D.J.: Lattice-based functional commitments: fast verification and cryptanalysis. In: Guo, J., Steinfeld, R. (eds.) Advances in Cryptology – ASIACRYPT 2023. ASIACRYPT 2023. LNCS, vol. 14442, pp. 201–235. Springer, Singapore (2023). https://doi.org/10.1007/978-981-99-8733-7_7

[WW23b]   Wee, H., Wu, D.J.: Succinct vector, polynomial, and functional commitments from lattices. In: Hazay, C., Stam, M. (eds.) Advances in Cryptology – EUROCRYPT 2023. EUROCRYPT 2023. LNCS, vol. 14006, pp. 385–416. Springer, Cham (2023). https://doi.org/10.1007/978-3-031-30620-4_13

Universal Composable Password Authenticated Key Exchange for the Post-Quantum World

You Lyu[1,2], Shengli Liu[1,2(✉)], and Shuai Han[2,3]

[1] Department of Computer Science and Engineering, Shanghai Jiao Tong University, Shanghai 200240, China
{vergil,slliu}@sjtu.edu.cn
[2] State Key Laboratory of Cryptology, P.O. Box 5159, Beijing 100878, China
[3] School of Cyber Science and Engineering, Shanghai Jiao Tong University, Shanghai 200240, China
dalen17@sjtu.edu.cn

Abstract. In this paper, we construct the *first* password authenticated key exchange (PAKE) scheme from isogenies with Universal Composable (UC) security in the random oracle model (ROM). We also construct the *first* two PAKE schemes with UC security in the quantum random oracle model (QROM), one is based on the learning with error (LWE) assumption, and the other is based on the group-action decisional Diffie-Hellman (GA-DDH) assumption in the isogeny setting.

To obtain our UC-secure PAKE scheme in ROM, we propose a generic construction of PAKE from basic lossy public key encryption (LPKE) and CCA-secure PKE. We also introduce a new variant of LPKE, named extractable LPKE (eLPKE). By replacing the basic LPKE with eLPKE, our generic construction of PAKE achieves UC security in QROM. The LPKE and eLPKE have instantiations not only from LWE but also from GA-DDH, which admit four specific PAKE schemes with UC security in ROM or QROM, based on LWE or GA-DDH.

1 Introduction

Password Authenticated Key Exchange (PAKE) enables two parties (say, a client and a server) who possess a low-entropy password pw to securely establish session keys over public networks. These session keys subsequently facilitate the establishment of secure communication channels. Unlike authenticated key exchange (AKE), which necessitates a Public Key Infrastructure (PKI) to verify the authenticity of public keys, PAKE runs with easily memorable passwords and offers enhanced convenience for deployments and applications.

Security Notions for PAKE: IND vs. UC. There are two primary security notions for PAKE, the game-based security in the Indistinguishability model (IND security) [9] and the simulation-based security under the Universally Composable framework (UC security) [16]. As shown in [16], the UC security in the UC framework implies the IND security. In contrast to the IND model which

© International Association for Cryptologic Research 2024
M. Joye and G. Leander (Eds.): EUROCRYPT 2024, LNCS 14657, pp. 120–150, 2024.
https://doi.org/10.1007/978-3-031-58754-2_5

assumes passwords uniformly distributed over a set, the UC framework permits arbitrary correlations and distributions for passwords and guarantees security amidst composition with arbitrary protocols and hence is a better security model.

PAKE with Post-Quantum Security. There are quite a few IND-secure PAKE schemes constructed from post-quantum assumptions, including lattice-based [11,19,23,24,34] and isogeny-based [3] ones.

As for UC security, there exists a generic construction for PAKE from Oblivious Transfer (OT) [15]. However, achieving UC security for PAKE requires the underlying OT protocol have adaptive UC security even in absence of authenticated channels. As far as we know, up to now such OT only has instantiations from number-theoretic assumptions like CDH or Factoring, so no instantiation from post-quantum assumptions via the OT approach is known for PAKE. There also exist frameworks of constructing PAKE from Hash Proof System (HPS) (e.g., [2]). To apply the HPS framework, one needs an HPS for language consisting of pairs of messages and commitments/ciphertexts (m, c), but as far as we know there is no suitable HPS from lattice/isogenies serving for UC-secure PAKE. A feasible approach to PAKE from post-quantum assumptions is making use of Encrypted Key Exchange [10] (EKE) and resorting to the Ideal Cipher Model (ICM) to achieve UC security. This EKE approach results in two UC-secure PAKE schemes [8,31] both of which are lattice-based. However, the ICM has two limitations and this leads to two questions.

- It is unclear how to instantiate ideal cipher from isogenies, as highlighted in [7]. Hence isogeny-based PAKE with UC security is now missing.
  Q1: Can we construct UC-secure PAKE from isogeny-based assumptions?
- ICM does not consider quantum access from adversaries and it is unclear how to exploit quantum ICM (QICM) to achieve security against quantum algorithms. But quantum random oracle model (QROM) [13] takes into account quantum-access adversaries, and is better understood than QICM [22].
  Q2: Can we construct PAKE protocols with UC security in QROM ?

Our Contribution. We answer the above two questions in this paper with the following two folds of contributions.

1. We propose a generic construction for UC-secure PAKE in the random oracle model (ROM) from two building blocks, a basic Lossy Public Key Encryption (LPKE) and a CCA-secure PKE.
   - The pivot of our generic construction is Lossy Public Key Encryption (LPKE). We identify properties for basic LPKE so that its integration with hashing function makes UC security possible for PAKE in ROM.
   - The instantiations of the basic LPKE and CCA-secure PKE yield two UC-secure PAKE schemes in ROM, one is based on the LWE assumption and the other based on the GA-DDH assumption, which leads to the *first* PAKE scheme with UC security from isogenies.
2. We upgrade UC security from ROM to QROM for our generic PAKE construction, by replacing the "basic LPKE + Hash" with an extractable LPKE.

- We define extractable LPKE by equipping it with an extracting algorithm and identify its properties to make UC security possible for PAKE in QROM. We also present a generic construction for extractable LPKE.
- The instantiations of extractable LPKE lead to the *first* two UC-secure PAKE schemes in QROM, one is based on the LWE assumption and the other based on the GA-DDH assumption in the isogeny setting.

Technique Overview. The design principle of our PAKE is to make the underlying PKE associating with passwords. To this end, we introduce a labeled lossy public key encryption LPKE, where the passwords pw are used to derive labels $b := H(pw)$ for LPKE via hash function. The labels are used to generate public keys pk and secret keys sk, i.e., $(pk, sk) \leftarrow$ LPKE.LKeyGen$(b = H(pw))$, and the encryptions also involve labels, i.e., $c \leftarrow$ LPKE.LEnc$(pk, b = H(pw), m)$. Moreover, LPKE has an algorithm named IsLossy(td, pk, b), which can use the trapdoor td to tell whether b is a lossy label for pk. If the output is 0, then b must be a normal label for pk, and hence LPKE works in normal mode, which has correctness and CPA security. Otherwise b must be a lossy label, and hence LPKE works in lossy mode. When applying FO-transformation to LPKE, it has CCA security in normal mode but has pseudo-random ciphertexts in lossy mode.

Together with another CCA-secure PKE scheme PKE, we can design a 3-round PAKE scheme which is high-level shown in Fig. 2.

If client C and server S share the same password pw, then the label used to generate pk/sk and that used in the encryption are consistent. Accordingly, LPKE works in *normal* mode and the successful decryption of c guarantees C and S share $m = r|\sigma|k$. The ciphertext $C = $ PKE.CEnc$(cpk, pw|pk|c; r)$ can be considered as a proof of server S's knowledge of pw and the authentication of transcript $pk|c$, so it plays the role of authenticating S. Moreover, client C's knowledge of σ from the decryption of c proves that C shares the same password with S, and hence the third message σ is able to authenticate C.

UC SECURITY IN ROM. To prove the UC security for our PAKE, we have to construct a simulator Sim, which has no knowledge of password pw but can simulate all the interaction transcripts for both passive attacks and active attacks. The simulations must be indistinguishable to those in the real experiment for an environment, which uses pw to control C and S, and manipulates adversaries $\mathcal{A}$ to

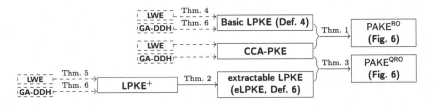

Fig. 1. Schematic overview of our PAKE constructions, where solid arrows "$\longrightarrow$" indicate generic constructions and dashed arrows "$\dashrightarrow$" indicate instantiations.

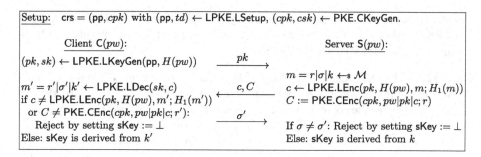

Fig. 2. Our PAKE from LPKE and PKE

interfere the interactions between C and S. Now we consider how the simulations are implemented according to the type of attacks, passive or active.

Case I: passive attacks. By requiring *pseudo-randomness of public key* for LPKE, simulator Sim can send a random pk as the simulation for the first-round message. The random pk is independent of the random label $H(pw)$ (due to random oracle), so $H(pw)$ is hardly the correct label generating pk. Then $c = \mathsf{LPKE.LEnc}(pk, H(pw), m; H_1(m))$ works in lossy mode and c is pseudo-random due to *pseudo-randomness of ciphertext under lossy labels of* LPKE. Therefore, the simulation of c in the second-round message can be accomplished with a uniformly chosen one. As a result, $m = r|\sigma|k$ are random and independent of c. Then the *CCA security* of PKE implies $C \leftarrow \mathsf{PKE.CEnc}(cpk, pw|pk|c; r) \approx_c C \leftarrow \mathsf{PKE.CEnc}(cpk, 0; r)$. So ciphertext C in the second-round message can be simulated by $C \leftarrow_\$ \mathsf{PKE.CEnc}(cpk, 0)$. Furthermore, the third-round message σ' can simply be simulated by setting $\sigma' := \sigma$ to keep consistence to the second-round message.

As for active attacks, a critical problem for Sim is that without any knowledge of pw, how to determine whether $\mathcal{A}$ implements attacks with a correct guess of pw. To solve this problem, we resort to the trapdoor td of LPKE, the algorithm IsLossy, random oracle H, and also the secret key of PKE.

Sim will generate the crs of PAKE and hold the trapdoor td of LPKE and the secret key csk of PKE to extract the possible passwords used in active attacks.

- **Password extraction from $\tilde{pk}$.** For a first-round message $\tilde{pk}$ from $\mathcal{A}$'s active attack, if $\tilde{pk}$ is associated with some password pw', then $H(pw')$ must have been queried by $\mathcal{A}$. Sim just searches all the hash queries and replies under random oracle H to find $(pw', b = H(pw'))$ s.t. $\mathsf{IsLossy}(td, \tilde{pk}, H(pw')) = 0$. If $\mathsf{IsLossy}(td, \tilde{pk}, H(pw')) = 0$ then $H(pw')$ must be a normal label used to generate $\tilde{pk}$. Meanwhile, random oracle H makes sure the uniqueness of such password. In this way, the password pw' used by $\mathcal{A}$ for generating $\tilde{pk}$, if any, is successfully extracted by Sim.
- **Password extraction from $(\tilde{c}, \tilde{C})$.** For a second-round message $(\tilde{c}, \tilde{C})$ from $\mathcal{A}$'s active attack, Sim will use the secret key csk (w.r.t. the system public key

cpk) to decrypt $\tilde{C}$ to extract the encrypted password pw'. The correctness of PKE makes sure that the password pw' used by $\mathcal{A}$ for generating $(\tilde{c}, \tilde{C})$, if any, is successfully extracted by Sim.

Case II: active attacks. With help of the above extractions of password pw', Sim can submit Testpw(pw') to the ideal functionality of $\mathcal{F}_{pake}$ to decide whether pw' is the correct one. If pw' is correct, then Sim uses the correct pw' to simulate the protocol interactions, just like the real case. If the extracted password pw' is not correct, the simulations are implemented as follows.

– For a first-round message $\tilde{pk}$ from $\mathcal{A}$'s active attack, if the extracted pw' is not correct, then the random label $H(pw)$ must be lossy for $\tilde{pk}$. The simulator can simulate the second-round message (c, C) just like the case of passive attacks.

– For a second-round message $(\tilde{c}, \tilde{C})$ from $\mathcal{A}$'s active attack,
  - if the extracted pw' is not correct, the simulator just aborts the protocol. In the real case, the correctness of PKE also leads to abort due to an incorrect password.
  - if the extracted pw' is correct, recall that in this case, pk is a random one (simulated in the passive attack), the simulator has no knowledge of sk and cannot decrypt $\tilde{c}$ with LPKE.LDec. To solve this problem, we resort to random oracle $H_1(m')$ to extract the message $m' = r'|\sigma'|k'$ such that $\tilde{c} = \text{LPKE.LEnc}(pk, H(pw), m'; H_1(m'))$, if it exists.

UC Security in QROM. Note that random oracle H plays an important role in simulator's password extracting from $\tilde{pk}$. However, H fails in QROM, because the simulating technique of storing and searching queries & hash values in a list does not apply to QRO due to the no-cloning principle.

To achieve UC security in the QROM, our solution is discarding hash function H and directly using passwords pw as labels in the generation of $\tilde{pk}$ and the encryption of m. More importantly, we augment an Extract($td, \tilde{pk}$) algorithm to LPKE which can use trapdoor td to extract password pw' from $\tilde{pk}$ directly, free of hash. In this way, LPKE is upgraded to an extractable one, namely eLPKE. The generic construction of PAKE remains the same except that we replace LPKE with eLPKE. The simulator can use Extract($td, \tilde{pk}$) to extract pw' and the rest of simulations are almost the same as that in ROM.

We can construct extractable LPKE (eLPKE) from LPKE as follows. Parse the label bit-wise $pw = (pw_1, \ldots, pw_\lambda)$. Each bit $pw_i \in \{0, 1\}$ corresponds to two public random tags v_i^0, v_i^1. Then λ invocations of $(pk_i, sk_i) \leftarrow \text{LPKE.LKeyGen}(v_i^{pw_i})$ result in public key $\boldsymbol{pk} := (pk_1, \ldots, pk_\lambda)$ and secret key $\boldsymbol{sk} := (sk_1, \ldots, sk_\lambda)$. In this way, the password pw can be extracted bit-wisely via testing IsLossy(td, pk_i, v_i^0) $\overset{?}{=} 0$ and IsLossy(td, pk_i, v_i^1) $\overset{?}{=} 0$. For encryption, the plaintext m is divided into λ shares $m_1, ..., m_\lambda$ such that $m = m_1 \oplus ... \oplus m_\lambda$ via (λ, λ)-secret sharing. The ciphertext contains sub-ciphertexts $\{c_i := \text{LPKE.LEnc}(pk_i, m_i)\}_{i \in [\lambda]}$.

There remains a subtlety to be addressed. To justify that the real pk can be replaced by a random one, the security reduction must ensure that the

Table 1. Comparison of PAKE schemes from post-quantum assumptions. In [3,11], a simultaneous flow of two round-messages is counted as 1-round while we count it as 2.

Scheme	Rounds	Security	Model	Assumption	Mutual Authentication	CRS
[11,24]	2	IND	Standard	LWE	No	Yes
[34]	2	IND	RO	LWE	No	Yes
[23]	3	IND	Standard	LWE	Yes	Yes
[19]	3	IND	RO	RLWE	Yes	No
[3]	2	IND	RO	SqInv-GA-StCDH	No	Yes
[15] + [5]	3	IND	Standard	GA-DDH	Yes	Yes
[15] + [28]	3	IND	Standard	LWE	Yes	Yes
[8,31]	2	UC	Ideal Cipher	MLWE	No	No
$\mathsf{PAKE}_{\mathsf{lwe}}^{\mathsf{RO}}$	3	UC	RO	LWE	Yes	Yes
$\mathsf{PAKE}_{\mathsf{ga}}^{\mathsf{RO}}$	3	UC	RO	GA-DDH	Yes	Yes
$\mathsf{PAKE}_{\mathsf{lwe}}^{\mathsf{QRO}}$	3	UC	QRO	LWE	Yes	Yes
$\mathsf{PAKE}_{\mathsf{ga}}^{\mathsf{QRO}}$	3	UC	QRO	GA-DDH	Yes	Yes

secret key sk is not needed for the decryption of c to get m. To solve this problem, the UC security in ROM also uses the hash list of H_1, and search the list to find the right $(m, H_1(m))$ by testing the re-encryption relation $c = \mathsf{LPKE.LEnc}(pk, pw, m; H_1(m))$. In QROM, this trick does not apply either. To solve the problem in QROM, we resort to the *on-line extraction* technique [20] so that the simulator can extract m while simulating H_1 in an indistinguishable way. Moreover, in case of active attack $(\tilde{c}, \tilde{C})$, after the simulator extracts a correct password pw, it also uses the on-line extraction technique to extract m'.

By instantiating LPKE and eLPKE in our genertic construction, we obtain PAKE schemes $\mathsf{PAKE}_{\mathsf{lwe}}^{\mathsf{RO}}$, $\mathsf{PAKE}_{\mathsf{ga}}^{\mathsf{RO}}$, $\mathsf{PAKE}_{\mathsf{lwe}}^{\mathsf{QRO}}$, $\mathsf{PAKE}_{\mathsf{ga}}^{\mathsf{QRO}}$ from LWE in lattice, from GA-DDH in the isogeny setting, in ROM, and in QROM respectively.

The schematic overview of our PAKE constructions is given in Fig. 1.

Comparison. In Table 1, we compare our PAKE schemes with the available schemes based on post-quantum assumptions. Up to now, there are only two PAKE schemes [8,31] with UC security from post-quantum assumptions, both of which are based on ICM. Note that ICM is equivalent to ROM [18]. Therefore, our work admits the *first* UC-secure PAKE schemes from isogenies, both in ROM and QROM, and the *first* UC-secure PAKE schemes from LWE in QROM. We also give more comparisons in terms of time complexity and communication complexity in the full version of our paper [25].

A recent progress on PAKE [26] shows how to compile PAKE to strong asymmetric PAKE with CSIDH assumption. Applying their compiler, our PAKE from GA-DDH can be upgraded to a strong asymmetric PAKE from isogenies.

2 Preliminaries

If x is defined by y or the value of y is assigned to x, we write $x := y$. For $\mu \in \mathbb{N}$, define $[\mu] := \{1, 2, \ldots, \mu\}$. Denote by $x \leftarrow_\$ \mathcal{X}$ the procedure of sampling x from set $\mathcal{X}$ uniformly at random. We also use "\$" to denote a random variable uniformly chosen from an implicitly known set. Let $|\mathcal{X}|$ denote the number of elements in $\mathcal{X}$. All our algorithms are probabilistic unless stated otherwise. We use $y \leftarrow \mathcal{A}(x)$ to define the random variable y obtained by executing algorithm $\mathcal{A}$ on input x. We also use $y \leftarrow \mathcal{A}(x; r)$ to make explicit the random coins r used in the probabilistic computation. The notation $\approx_s$ represents statistical indistinguishability, while $\approx_c$ denotes computational indistinguishability. We use bold lower-case letters to denote column vectors. For a vector $\mathbf{v}$, we let $\|\mathbf{v}\|$ (resp., $\|\mathbf{v}\|_\infty$) denote its ℓ_2 (resp., ℓ_∞ infinity) norm.

2.1 Hardness Assumptions

Lattice Backgrounds. A q-ary lattice defined with $\mathbf{A} \in \mathbb{Z}_q^{n \times m}$ is $\Lambda(\mathbf{A}) := \{\mathbf{A}^T \mathbf{s} \mid \mathbf{s} \in \mathbb{Z}_q^n\} + q\mathbb{Z}^m$. The Gaussian function on $\mathbb{R}^n$ centered at $\mathbf{c}$ with parameter s is defined by $\rho_{s,\mathbf{c}}(\mathbf{x}) := e^{-\pi \|\mathbf{x} - \mathbf{c}\|^2 / s^2}$. The discrete Gaussian distribution $D_{\Lambda,s,\mathbf{c}}$ over an n-dimensional lattice $\Lambda \subseteq \mathbb{R}^n$ is defined by $D_{\Lambda,s,\mathbf{c}}(\mathbf{x}) := \rho_{s,\mathbf{c}}(\mathbf{x})/\rho_{s,\mathbf{c}}(\Lambda)$ for any lattice vector $\mathbf{x} \in \Lambda$, where $\rho_{s,\mathbf{c}}(\Lambda) := \sum_{\mathbf{z} \in \Lambda} \rho_{s,\mathbf{c}}(\mathbf{z})$. The centered vector $\mathbf{c}$ is often omitted when $\mathbf{c} = \mathbf{0}$. More specifically, we use the notion $D_{\mathbb{Z}^m,r}$ to represent discrete Gaussian distribution over lattice $\Lambda := \mathbb{Z}^m$ centered at $\mathbf{c} := \mathbf{0}$ with parameter r.

Definition 1 (LWE Assumption [30]). *Let $n, m, q \in \mathbb{N}$, and χ be a distribution over $\mathbb{Z}_q$. The $\mathsf{LWE}_{n,q,m,\chi}$ assumption states that the following distributions are computationally indistinguishable: $(\mathbf{A}, \mathbf{A}^T\mathbf{s} + \mathbf{e}) \approx_c (\mathbf{A}, \mathbf{u})$, where $\mathbf{A} \leftarrow_{\$} \mathbb{Z}_q^{n \times m}, \mathbf{e} \leftarrow \chi^m, \mathbf{s} \leftarrow_{\$} \mathbb{Z}_q^n$ and $\mathbf{u} \leftarrow_{\$} \mathbb{Z}_q^m$.*

Lemma 1 ([4,27]). *There exists a PPT algorithm $\mathsf{TrapGen}$ that takes as input positive integers n, q ($q \geq 2$) and a sufficiently large $m = O(n \log q)$, outputs a matrix $\mathbf{A} \in \mathbb{Z}_q^{n \times m}$ and a trapdoor matrix $\mathbf{T_A} \in \mathbb{Z}_q^{m \times m}$ such that $\mathbf{A}$ is statistically close to the uniform distribution, $\mathbf{A} \cdot \mathbf{T_A} = \mathbf{0}$, and $\left\| \widetilde{\mathbf{T}}_\mathbf{A} \right\| \leq O(\sqrt{n \log q})$, where $\widetilde{\mathbf{T}}_\mathbf{A}$ denotes the Gram-Schmidt orthogonalization of $\mathbf{T_A}$.*

Lemma 2 ([27, Theorem 5.4]). *There exists a deterministic polynomial-time algorithm Invert that takes as inputs the trapdoor information $\mathbf{T_A}$ and a vector $\mathbf{v} := \mathbf{A}^T \cdot \mathbf{s} + \mathbf{e}$ with $\mathbf{s} \in \mathbb{Z}_q^n$ and $\|\mathbf{e}\| \leq q/(10 \cdot \sqrt{m})$, and outputs $\mathbf{s}$ and $\mathbf{e}$.*

Lemma 3 ([21]). *Let n and q be positive integers with q prime, and let $m \geq 2n \log q$. Then for all but a $2q^{-n}$ fraction of all $\mathbf{A} \in \mathbb{Z}_q^{n \times m}$ and for any $r \geq \omega(\sqrt{\log m})$, the distribution of the syndrome $\mathbf{u} = \mathbf{Ae} \bmod q$ is statistically close to uniform over $\mathbb{Z}_q^n$, where $\mathbf{e} \leftarrow D_{\mathbb{Z}^m,r}$.*

Cryptographic Group Actions. We will focus on group actions where $\mathbb{G}$ is *abelian* and the action is *regular* (we refer to the full version [25] for the definition). We recall the notion of restricted effective group actions (REGA) as follows.

Definition 2 (REGA [5]). *A group action $(\mathbb{G}, \mathcal{X}, \star)$ is a restricted effective group action (REGA) if properties 1–4 are satisfied.*

1. *The group* $\mathbb{G}$ *is finite and generated by a set* $\{g_1, \ldots, g_n\}$ *with* $n = \mathsf{poly}(\log |\mathbb{G}|)$.
2. *The set* $\mathcal{X}$ *is finite and there exist PPT algorithms for membership testing and for computing unique representation of set element.*
3. *There exists a distinguished element* $x_0 \in \mathcal{X}$, *called the origin, such that its representation is known.*
4. *There exists an efficient algorithm that given* g_i *in the generating set and any* $x \in \mathcal{X}$, *outputs* $g_i \star x$ *and* $g_i^{-1} \star x$ *where* $i \in [n]$.

With a REGA, we can use the generating set to approximate the random sampling process of $g \leftarrow_\$ \mathbb{G}$. The regularity of the $(\mathbb{G}, \mathcal{X}, \star)$ enables an efficient algorithm to sample $x \leftarrow_\$ \mathcal{X}$ uniformly.

There is a natural generalization of the DDH assumption in REGA settings.

Definition 3 (GA-DDH Assumptions). *Given a restricted effective group action* $(\mathbb{G}, \mathcal{X}, \star)$, *the Group Action DDH (GA-DDH) assumption states that the following distributions are computationally indistinguishable:*

$$\{x \leftarrow_\$ \mathcal{X}; s, t \leftarrow_\$ \mathbb{G} : (x, s \star x, t \star x, (s \cdot t) \star x)\} \approx_c \{x \leftarrow_\$ \mathcal{X}; s, t, z \leftarrow_\$ \mathbb{G} : (x, s \star x, t \star x, z \star x)\}.$$

We can instantiate REGA with isogeny-based group actions, like CSIDH. The GA-DDH assumption is believed to hold for CSIDH [17].

2.2 UC Framework for PAKE

We present a concise overview of the UC framework for PAKE. Figure 4 shows the picture of the "real world" execution of a protocol Π in environment $\mathcal{Z}$ and the "ideal world" execution with a simulator Sim in environment $\mathcal{Z}$. The environment $\mathcal{Z}$ can be considered as higher-level protocols utilizing Π as a sub-protocol ($\mathcal{Z}$ also includes the adversary that is attacking those higher-level protocols). The adversary $\mathcal{A}$ essentially models a completely insecure network and it communicates continuously with $\mathcal{Z}$. The client/server instances send and receive messages via $\mathcal{A}$, and $\mathcal{A}$ can do dropping, injecting, and modifying protocol messages at will.

In the real world, the client/server instances are executed as described in the protocol Π. They receive their inputs (passwords in PAKE) from $\mathcal{Z}$ and send their outputs (session key in PAKE) to $\mathcal{Z}$. Hash function H is modeled as a random oracle. Clients, servers and adversary may directly (quantum) access the random oracle H. However, $\mathcal{Z}$ can only access H indirectly via $\mathcal{A}$.

In the ideal world, clients/servers are "dummy" parties that pass their passwords directly from $\mathcal{Z}$ to an ideal functionality $\mathcal{F}_{pake}$, and their outputs directly from $\mathcal{F}_{pake}$ to $\mathcal{Z}$. We mainly follow the definition of $\mathcal{F}_{pake}$ by Shoup [32], which is a modified version by Canetti et al. [16]. Simulator Sim can communicate with $\mathcal{Z}$, just as $\mathcal{A}$ did in the real world. Besides, Sim can also interact with $\mathcal{F}_{pake}$. Sim has two main tasks. Firstly, it must simulate the network transcripts in a way that is indistinguishable from those generated in the real world. Secondly, Sim must provide appropriate inputs to $\mathcal{F}_{pake}$ to obtain outputs (session key) that are indistinguishable from the outputs produced by the client/server instances in the real world.

Functionality $\mathcal{F}_{pake}$

The functionality $\mathcal{F}_{pake}$ is parameterized by a security parameter λ. It interacts with a simulator Sim and a set of parties via the following queries:

Password Storage

> **Upon receiving a query** (StorePWFile, $C^{(i)}$, $S^{(j)}$, pw) **from a client** $C^{(i)}$ **or a server** $S^{(j)}$:
>
> > If there exists a record $\langle$file, $C^{(i)}$, $S^{(j)}$, $\cdot\rangle$, ignore this query. Otherwise, record $\langle$file, $C^{(i)}$, $S^{(j)}$, $pw\rangle$, and send (StorePWFile, $C^{(i)}$, $S^{(j)}$) to Sim.

Sessions

> **Upon receiving a query** (NewClient, iid, $S^{(j)}$) **from a client** $C^{(i)}$:
>
> > Retrieve the record $\langle$file, $C^{(i)}$, $S^{(j)}$, $pw\rangle$. Send (NewClient, $C^{(i)}$, iid, $S^{(j)}$) to Sim.
> > Record $(C^{(i)}, iid, S^{(j)}, pw)$ and mark it as **fresh**.
> > In this case, $S^{(j)}$ is called the intended partner of $(C^{(i)}, iid)$.
>
> **Upon receiving a query** (NewServer, iid', $C^{(i)}$) **from a server** $S^{(j)}$:
>
> > Retrieve the record $\langle$file, $C^{(i)}$, $S^{(j)}$, $pw\rangle$. Send (NewServer, $S^{(j)}$, iid', $C^{(i)}$) to Sim.
> > Record $(S^{(j)}, iid', C^{(i)}, pw)$ and mark it as **fresh**.
> > In this case, $C^{(i)}$ is called the intended partner of $(S^{(j)}, iid')$.
>
> Two instances $(C^{(i)}, iid)$ and $(S^{(j)}, iid')$ are said to be **partnered**, if there are two records $(C^{(i)}, iid, S^{(j)}, pw)$ and $(S^{(j)}, iid', C^{(i)}, pw)$ sharing the same pw.

Active Session Attacks

> **Upon receiving a query** (Testpw, P, iid, pw') from Sim:
>
> > If there is a **fresh** record $(P, iid, \cdot, pw)$:
> >
> > > If $pw' = pw$, mark the record **compromised** and reply to Sim with "correct guess".
> > > If $pw' \neq pw$, mark the record **interrupted** and reply with "wrong guess".

Key Generation

> **Upon receiving a query** (FreshKey, P, iid, sid) from Sim:
>
> > If 1) there is a **fresh** record (P, iid, Q, pw); and 2) sid has never been assigned to P's any other instance (P, iid'):
> > Pick a new random key sKey, mark the record (P, iid, Q, pw) as **completed**, assign it with sid, send $(iid, sid, sKey)$ to P, and record $(P, Q, sid, sKey)$.
>
> **Upon receiving a query** (CopyKey, P, iid, sid) from Sim:
>
> > If 1) there is a **fresh** record (P, iid, Q, pw) and a **completed** record (Q, iid^*, P, pw) s.t. (P, iid) and (Q, iid^*) are partnered; and 2) sid has never been assigned to P's any other instance (P, iid'); and 3) the partnered (Q, iid^*) is the unique one that has been assigned with sid:
> > Retrieve the record $(Q, P, sid, sKey)$, mark the record (P, iid, Q, pw) as **completed**, assign it with sid, and send $(iid, sid, sKey)$ to P.
>
> **Upon receiving a query** (CorruptKey, $P, iid, sid, sKey$) from Sim:
>
> > If 1) there is a **compromised** record (P, iid, Q, pw); and 2) sid has never been assigned to P's any other instance (P, iid'):
> > Mark the record (P, iid, Q, pw) as **completed**, assign it with sid, and send $(iid, sid, sKey)$ to P.
>
> **Upon receiving a query** (Abort, P, iid) from Sim:
>
> > mark the record $(P, iid, \cdot, pw)$ as **abort**, and send $(iid, \perp)$ to P.

Fig. 3. The ideal functionality $\mathcal{F}_{pake}$ for PAKE.

The ideal functionality $\mathcal{F}_{pake}$ is shown in Fig. 3. We stress that our ideal functionality $\mathcal{F}_{pake}$ supports *mutual authentication*, which indicates mutual explicit authentication. It is mainly captured by the first item and the last item of "Key Generation" in our ideal functionality (Fig. 3), which guarantee that if an adversary makes an unsuccessful password guess on a protocol instance, then when that instance terminates, the corresponding party will receive an abort message. Accordingly, this requires that each party can identify active attacks explicitly in the real-world protocol.

In a nutshell, we say protocol Π securely emulates ideal functionality $\mathcal{F}_{pake}$ if for any efficient adversary $\mathcal{A}$, there exists an efficient simulator Sim such that no efficient environment $\mathcal{Z}$ can effectively distinguish between the actual execution in the real world and the hypothetical execution in the ideal world.

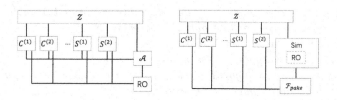

Fig. 4. The real world execution (left) and the ideal world execution (right).

2.3 ROM vs. QROM

In the Random Oracle Model (ROM), a cryptographic hash function $H : \mathcal{X} \to \mathcal{Y}$ is idealized as a truly random function $\mathsf{RF} : \mathcal{X} \to \mathcal{Y}$. And any adversary needs to query H on inputs $x \in \mathcal{X}$ to learn the hash values $H(x)$.

In the quantum world, a quantum algorithm $\mathcal{A}$ can perform superposition queries to the random oracle H, and then oracle H behaves as a unitary operation $|x\rangle|y\rangle \mapsto |x\rangle|y \oplus H(x)\rangle$. In this case, H becomes a quantum random oracle (QRO). The QRO model supports classical queries x on H, and this can be formalized as setting query register and output register to be $|x\rangle|0\rangle$, and measuring the output register after the unitary operation $|x\rangle|0\rangle \mapsto |x\rangle|0 \oplus H(x)\rangle$.

3 PAKE from Basic LPKE in ROM

In this section we present the definition of basic LPKE and show how to apply the FO-transformation to LPKE to obtain a CCA-secure KEM. Then we show the generic construction of PAKE from basic LPKE and its UC security in ROM.

3.1 Basic Lossy Public Key Encryption (LPKE)

LPKE works in two modes. If label b is a normal one, then LPKE works in normal mode and has correctness and CPA security. If label b is a lossy one, then LPKE works in lossy mode, and the ciphertexts are random. With the trapdoor, algorithm IsLossy can decide whether label b is lossy or normal for pk.

Definition 4 (Basic LPKE). *A basic Lossy Public Key Encryption scheme* LPKE = (LSetup, LKeyGen, LEnc, LDec, IsLossy) *consists of five probabilistic algorithms.*

- LSetup(1^λ) : *The setup algorithm takes as input the security parameter 1^λ, and outputs a public parameter* pp *and a trapdoor td. The parameter* pp *specifies a public key space $\mathcal{PK}$, a secret key space $\mathcal{SK}$, a label space $\mathcal{T}$, a message space $\mathcal{M}$ and a ciphertext space $\mathcal{CT}$.*
  All the remaining algorithms take pp *as input, and we omit it for simplicity.*
- LKeyGen(b) : *The key generation algorithm takes as input a label b and outputs a key pair (pk, sk).*

- LEnc(pk, b, m) : *The encryption algorithm takes as input a public key pk, a label b and a message m, and outputs a ciphertext c.*
- LDec(sk, c) : *The decryption algorithm takes as input a secret key sk and a ciphertext c, and outputs a message m.*
- IsLossy(td, pk, b) : *The algorithm takes as input a trapdoor td, a public key pk and a label b, and outputs a bit 0 or 1.*

For any $pk \in \mathcal{PK}$ and $b \in \mathcal{T}$, if IsLossy(td, pk, b) $= 1$, then label b is called a *lossy label* of public key pk. Otherwise, label b is called a *normal label* of pk.

Correctness of Basic LPKE. For all $b \in \mathcal{T}$ and $m \in \mathcal{M}$, it holds that

$$\Pr\left[\mathsf{LDec}(sk, \mathsf{LEnc}(pk, b, m)) \neq m\right] \leq \mathsf{negl}(\lambda), \Pr\left[\mathsf{IsLossy}(td, pk, b) = 1\right] \leq \mathsf{negl}(\lambda),$$

where $(pp, td) \leftarrow \mathsf{LSetup}(1^\lambda)$ and $(pk, sk) \leftarrow \mathsf{LKeyGen}(b)$.

A basic LPKE scheme LPKE should satisfy the following properties.

① **Pseudorandomness of Public Key.** For all $b \in \mathcal{T}$, it holds that

$$\left\{ \begin{array}{l} (pp, td) \leftarrow \mathsf{LSetup} \\ (pk, sk) \leftarrow \mathsf{LKeyGen}(b) \end{array} : (pp, pk) \right\} \approx_c \left\{ \begin{array}{l} (pp, td) \leftarrow \mathsf{LSetup} \\ pk \leftarrow_\$ \mathcal{PK} \end{array} : (pp, pk) \right\}.$$

② **Random Ciphertexts under Lossy Labels.** For all admissible adversary $\mathcal{A}$ which outputs (pk, b) such that IsLossy(td, pk, b) $= 1$, it holds that $(pp, pk, b, m, c) \approx_s (pp, pk, b, m, c')$, where $(pp, td) \leftarrow \mathsf{LSetup}$, $(pk, b) \leftarrow \mathcal{A}(pp)$ s.t. IsLossy(td, pk, b) $= 1$, $m \leftarrow_\$ \mathcal{M}$, $c \leftarrow \mathsf{LEnc}(pk, b, m)$ and $c' \leftarrow_\$ \mathcal{CT}$.

③ **Uniqueness of Normal Labels among Polynomial-Size Set:** For any $Q := poly(\lambda)$, it holds that

$$\Pr\left[\begin{array}{l} (pp, td) \leftarrow \mathsf{LSetup} \\ b_1, \ldots, b_Q \leftarrow_\$ \mathcal{T} \end{array} : \begin{array}{l} \exists pk \in \mathcal{PK}, i \neq j \text{ with } i, j \in [Q] \\ \mathsf{IsLossy}(td, pk, b_i) = 0 \wedge \mathsf{IsLossy}(td, pk, b_j) = 0 \end{array} \right] \leq \mathsf{negl}(\lambda).$$

④ **Lossiness of Random Labels.** For all adversary $\mathcal{A}$, it holds that

$$\Pr\left[(pp, td) \leftarrow \mathsf{LSetup}; pk \leftarrow \mathcal{A}(pp); b \leftarrow_\$ \mathcal{T} : \mathsf{IsLossy}(td, pk, b) = 0 \right] \leq \mathsf{negl}(\lambda).$$

⑤ **Ciphertext Unpredictability under Normal Labels:** For all but a negligible fraction of pp from $(pp, td) \leftarrow \mathsf{LSetup}(1^\lambda)$, for all $b \in \mathcal{T}$, all $(pk, sk) \leftarrow \mathsf{LKeyGen}(b)$, all messages $m \in \mathcal{M}$ and all ciphertexts $c \in \mathcal{CT}$, it holds that $\Pr\left[r \leftarrow_\$ \mathcal{R} : \mathsf{LEnc}(pk, b, m; r) = c \right] \leq \mathsf{negl}(\lambda)$.

⑥ **CPA Security under Normal Labels:** For all PPT $\mathcal{A}$, we have $(pp, pk, b, c_0) \approx_c (pp, pk, b, c_1)$, where $(pp, td) \leftarrow \mathsf{LSetup}$, $(b, st) \leftarrow \mathcal{A}(pp)$, $(pk, sk) \leftarrow \mathsf{LKeyGen}(b)$, $(m_0, m_1) \leftarrow \mathcal{A}(st, pk)$, $c_0 \leftarrow \mathsf{LEnc}(pk, b, m_0)$, $c_1 \leftarrow \mathsf{LEnc}(pk, b, m_1)$.

Remark 1. The concept of R-lossy PKE (R-LPKE) was introduced by Boyle et al. [14]. Our basic LPKE can be considered as a special R-LPKE with relation R simply defined as $R(K, t) := (K \overset{?}{=} t)$, but our basic LPKE is augmented with IsLossy algorithm and equipped with a different set of properties.

By leveraging the FO-transformation, LPKE under normal label b can be transformed to a labeled KEM scheme, whose encapsulation algorithm is implemented as $c \leftarrow \mathsf{LEnc}(pk, b, m; H_1(m))$ with $m \leftarrow_\$ \mathcal{M}$ and $K := H_2(m)$ (See the full version [25] for its formal description). Consequently, the CPA-security of LPKE is upgraded to CCA-security of the KEM, according to [20]. This is shown in Lemma 4. Meanwhile, the property of *random ciphertexts under lossy labels* for LPKE is inherited by that of KEM but degrades to a pseudo-random one, as shown in Lemma 5 with proof in the full version [25].

Lemma 4 (CCA Security of KEM [20]). *Suppose that* $\mathsf{LPKE} = (\mathsf{LSetup}, \mathsf{LKeyGen}, \mathsf{IsLossy}, \mathsf{LEnc}, \mathsf{LDec})$ *is a basic lossy public key encryption scheme and* H_1 *and* H_2 *are two (quantum-accessible) random oracles. For any PPT adversary* $\mathcal{A}$ *against CCA security of the KEM scheme, it holds that*

$$\mathsf{Adv}_{\mathsf{KEM}}^{\mathsf{CCA\text{-}FO}}(\mathcal{A}) := \left| \Pr\left[\mathsf{Exp}_{\mathsf{KEM}}^{\mathsf{CCA\text{-}FO\text{-}0}} \Rightarrow 1 \right] - \Pr\left[\mathsf{Exp}_{\mathsf{KEM}}^{\mathsf{CCA\text{-}FO\text{-}1}} \Rightarrow 1 \right] \right| \leq \mathsf{negl}(\lambda),$$

where $\mathsf{Exp}_{\mathsf{KEM}}^{\mathsf{CCA\text{-}FO\text{-}\beta}}$ *is defined in Fig 5.*

$\mathsf{Exp}_{\mathsf{KEM}}^{\mathsf{CCA\text{-}FO\text{-}\beta}}$: $\quad\quad\quad /\!/ \beta \in \{0,1\}$	$\mathcal{O}_{\mathrm{DEC}}(c)$:
$(\mathsf{pp}, td) \leftarrow \mathsf{LSetup}$; $(b, \mathsf{st}) \leftarrow \mathcal{A}(\mathsf{pp})$	If $c = c^*$: Return $\perp$
$(pk, sk) \leftarrow \mathsf{LKeyGen}(b)$	$K \leftarrow \mathsf{LDec}(sk, c)$
$m \leftarrow_\$ \mathcal{M}$, $c^* \leftarrow \mathsf{LEnc}(pk, b, m; H_1(m))$	Return K
$K_0^* := H_2(m)$, $K_1^* \leftarrow_\$ \mathcal{K}_{\mathsf{kem}}$	
$\beta' \leftarrow \mathcal{A}^{\mathcal{O}_{\mathrm{DEC}}(\cdot)}(\mathsf{st}, pk, c^*, K_\beta^*)$	
Return β'	

Fig. 5. CCA-security of KEM from LPKE via FO

Lemma 5 (Ciphertext Pseudo-Randomness under Lossy Labels). *Suppose that* $\mathsf{LPKE} = (\mathsf{LSetup}, \mathsf{LKeyGen}, \mathsf{IsLossy}, \mathsf{LEnc}, \mathsf{LDec})$ *is a basic lossy public key encryption scheme and* H_1 *and* H_2 *are two (quantum-accessible) random oracles. For all admissible adversary* $\mathcal{A}$ *which outputs* (pk, b) *such that* $\mathsf{IsLossy}(td, pk, b) = 1$, *it holds that* $(\mathsf{pp}, pk, b, c, K) \approx_c (\mathsf{pp}, pk, b, c' \leftarrow_\$ \mathcal{CT}, K' \leftarrow_\$ \mathcal{K})$, *where* $(\mathsf{pp}, td) \leftarrow \mathsf{LSetup}, (pk, b) \leftarrow \mathcal{A}(\mathsf{pp})$ *s.t.* $\mathsf{IsLossy}(td, pk, b) = 1$, $m \leftarrow_\$ \mathcal{M}$, $c \leftarrow \mathsf{LEnc}(pk, b, m; H_1(m))$, *and* $K := H_2(m)$.

3.2 Construction of PAKE from Basic LPKE in ROM

We propose a generic construction of 3-round PAKE scheme $\mathsf{PAKE}^{\mathsf{RO}}$ from LPKE and PKE. The underlying building blocks are as follows.

- a basic lossy public key encryption scheme $\mathsf{LPKE} = (\mathsf{LSetup}, \mathsf{LKeyGen}, \mathsf{LEnc}, \mathsf{LDec}, \mathsf{IsLossy})$ with message space $\{0,1\}^\lambda$, label space $\mathcal{T}$ and randomness space $\mathcal{R}$;
- a CCA-secure public key encryption scheme $\mathsf{PKE} = (\mathsf{CKeyGen}, \mathsf{CEnc}, \mathsf{CDec})$;
- four hash functions: $H : \mathcal{PW} \rightarrow \mathcal{T}$, $H_1 : \{0,1\}^\lambda \rightarrow \mathcal{R}$, $H_2 : \{0,1\}^\lambda \rightarrow \{0,1\}^{3\lambda}$, $H_3 : \{0,1\}^* \rightarrow \{0,1\}^\lambda$.

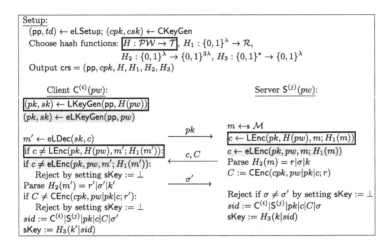

Fig. 6. Construction of PAKE^{RO} (resp. PAKE^{QRO}) from ⟨LPKE⟩ (resp. eLPKE). ⟨text⟩ only appears in PAKE^{RO} from LPKE and text only appears in PAKE^{QRO} from eLPKE.

Our generic construction of PAKE from LPKE and PKE is given in Fig. 6.

The UC security for PAKE^{RO} constructed from LPKE in ROM is shown in Theorem 1. To facilitate the proof, we define the concept of *linked to* like [32].

Definition 5 (Linked To). *In a protocol execution, a client (resp. server) instance is "linked to" a server (resp. client) instance at a specific time being if the transcript of the client (resp. server) is consistent to that of the server (resp. client), i.e., the messages received and sent by a party are exactly those messages sent and received by another party.*

Theorem 1. *If LPKE is a basic LPKE scheme, PKE is a CCA-secure PKE scheme, and H, H_1, H_2, H_3 work as random oracles, then the PAKE scheme PAKE^{RO} in Fig. 6 securely emulates $\mathcal{F}_{pake}$, hence achieving UC security in ROM.*

Proof. The main objective of the proof is to construct a PPT simulator Sim. Sim is designed to have access to the ideal functionality $\mathcal{F}_{pake}$ and interact with the environment $\mathcal{Z}$, thereby emulating the real-world PAKE protocol interactions involving the adversary $\mathcal{A}$, the parties, and the environment $\mathcal{Z}$. It is important to note that Sim *does not possess any password*.

The complete description of the simulator Sim is given in the full version [25].

Let **Real**$_{\mathcal{Z},\mathcal{A}}$ represent the real-world experiment where the environment $\mathcal{Z}$ interacts with the actual parties and adversary $\mathcal{A}$, while **Ideal**$_{\mathcal{Z},\text{Sim}}$ represents the ideal experiment where $\mathcal{Z}$ interacts with the simulator Sim.

Our goal is to demonstrate that $|\Pr[\textbf{Real}_{\mathcal{Z},\mathcal{A}} \Rightarrow 1] - \Pr[\textbf{Ideal}_{\mathcal{Z},\text{Sim}} \Rightarrow 1]|$ is negligible by employing a series of games, denoted as Game G_0-G_{11}. In this sequence, G_0 corresponds to **Real**$_{\mathcal{Z},\mathcal{A}}$, while G_{11} corresponds to **Ideal**$_{\mathcal{Z},\text{Sim}}$. We aim to show that these adjacent games are indistinguishable from the view of $\mathcal{Z}$.

Game G_0. This is the real experiment **Real**$_{\mathcal{Z},\mathcal{A}}$. In this experiment, $\mathcal{Z}$ initializes a password for each client-server pair, sees the interactions among clients, servers and adversary $\mathcal{A}$, and also obtains the corresponding session keys of protocol instances. Here $\mathcal{A}$ may implement attacks like view, modify, insert, or drop messages over the network. We have $\Pr\left[\mathbf{Real}_{\mathcal{Z},\mathcal{A}} \Rightarrow 1\right] = \Pr\left[\mathsf{G}_0 \Rightarrow 1\right]$.

Game G_1 (simulations for clients and servers with pw).
In this game, we introduce a simulator Sim who *receives passwords* from $\mathcal{Z}$. Then it simulates the clients and servers to generate transcripts for instances of the PAKE protocol. With the knowledge of *passwords*, the simulations of the behaviors of all clients and servers are perfect.

Moreover, Sim also simulates random oracles H, H_1, H_2, H_3 by maintaining four separate lists, namely $\mathcal{L}_H, \mathcal{L}_{H_1}, \mathcal{L}_{H_2}, \mathcal{L}_{H_3}$. For example, for a query x on $H(\cdot)$, if $(x,y) \in \mathcal{L}_H$, then Sim will return y as the reply. Otherwise, Sim will choose a random element y, record (x,y) in $\mathcal{L}_H$, and return y as the reply. By the ideal functionality of random oracles, Sim's simulations for oracles H, H_1, H_2, H_3 are also perfect. So we have $\Pr\left[\mathsf{G}_1 \Rightarrow 1\right] = \Pr\left[\mathsf{G}_0 \Rightarrow 1\right]$.

The following games will change the simulations of Sim step by step in an indistinguishable way so that Sim can arrive at its final form and accomplish the simulations in $\mathbf{Ideal}_{\mathcal{Z},\mathsf{Sim}}$ without passwords pw.

Game G_2 (simulation for crs). In G_2, Sim simulates the generation of $\mathsf{crs} = (\mathsf{pp}, cpk, \dots)$ with $(\mathsf{pp}, td) \leftarrow \mathsf{LSetup}$ and $(cpk, csk) \leftarrow \mathsf{CKeyGen}$, and it also records the trapdoor td of LPKE and the secret key csk of PKE. Clearly, the simulation of crs is perfect, so we have $\Pr\left[\mathsf{G}_2 \Rightarrow 1\right] = \Pr\left[\mathsf{G}_1 \Rightarrow 1\right]$.

Game G_3 (simulation of $r|\sigma|k$ for server instances and simulation of the third-round message σ' for client instances in case of passive attacks). In G_3, simulator Sim is the same as in G_2, except for the simulation of generating $r|\sigma|k$ for server instances and the corresponding simulation for client instances in case of passive attacks.

- For a server instance $(\mathsf{S}^{(j)}, iid')$ that is linked to $(\mathsf{C}^{(i)}, iid)$ when receiving a first-round message pk, simulator Sim will randomly sample $r|\sigma|k \leftarrow \{0,1\}^{3\lambda}$, rather than computing $r|\sigma|k := H_2(m)$ as did in G_2. Note that pk must have been generated for the client instance $(\mathsf{C}^{(i)}, iid)$ by Sim.
- For a client instance $(\mathsf{C}^{(i)}, iid)$ that is linked to server instance $(\mathsf{S}^{(j)}, iid')$ when receiving a second-round message (c, C), we know that (c, C) and the corresponding $r|\sigma|k$ must have been generated for $(\mathsf{S}^{(j)}, iid')$ by Sim. In this case, Sim directly sets $\mathsf{sKey} := H_3(k|sid)$ and outputs $\sigma' := \sigma$.

According to Lemma 4, $(pk, c = \mathsf{LEnc}(pk, H(pw), m; H_1(m)), r|\sigma|k := H_2(m))$ works as a CCA-secure KEM, where pk is the public key, $H(pw)$ is the normal lablel of pk, c is the ciphertext, $m \leftarrow_{\$} \mathcal{M}$ and $H_2(m) = r|\sigma|k$ is the encapsulated key. Then by the CCA-security of KEM we have

$$(pk, c \leftarrow \mathsf{LEnc}(pk, m; H_1(m)), r|\sigma|k := H_2(m)) \approx_c (pk, c \leftarrow \mathsf{LEnc}(pk, m; H_1(m)), \$)$$

for PPT adversaries access to decryption oracle. There are at most ℓ sessions, so hybrid arguments across the ℓ sessions yield

$$|\Pr[G_3 \Rightarrow 1] - \Pr[G_2 \Rightarrow 1]| \le \ell \cdot \mathsf{Adv}_{\mathsf{KEM}}^{\mathsf{CCA\text{-}FO}}(\mathcal{B}_{\mathsf{KEM}}) \le \mathsf{negl}(\lambda).$$

Game G_4 (simulation of sKey in case of passive attacks). In G_4, Sim is the same as in G_3, except for the generation of sKey for client instances and its corresponding sever instances in case of passive attacks.

- For a client instance $(C^{(i)}, iid)$ that is linked to server instance $(S^{(j)}, iid')$, when client $C^{(i)}$ receives a second-round message (c, C), simulator Sim changes the simulation of generating session key sKey for $C^{(i)}$. More precisely, Sim will not set $\mathsf{sKey} := H_3(k|sid)$ as did in G_3, but sample $\mathsf{sKey} \leftarrow_\$ \{0,1\}^\lambda$ instead. Sim stores sKey for $(C^{(i)}, iid)$. Note that (c, C) must have been generated by Sim and $r|\sigma|k$ sampled uniformly by Sim for server instance $(S^{(j)}, iid')$. For the simulation of $C^{(i)}$ outputting σ', Sim still outputs $\sigma' := \sigma$ by retrieving σ from $r|\sigma|k$, just like G_3.
- For a server instance $(S^{(j)}, iid')$ that is linked to $(C^{(i)}, iid)$, when $S^{(j)}$ receives a third-round message σ', Sim will compare σ' with σ in the transcription (pk, c, C, σ) of instance $(S^{(j)}, iid')$. If $\sigma' = \sigma$, Sim will retrieve sKey stored for $(C^{(i)}, iid)$ and set the same session key sKey for $(S^{(j)}, iid')$.

Note that in the above two cases, $(C^{(i)}, iid)$ and $(S^{(j)}, iid')$ share the same $r|\sigma|k$, where $r|\sigma|k$ is uniformly chosen and independent of the view of $\mathcal{A}$. The uniformity of k makes sure that $\mathcal{A}$ ever queries $H_3(k|sid)$ for some sid with negligible probability. As long as no query on $H_3(k|\cdot)$ is made by $\mathcal{A}$, the session key $\mathsf{sKey} := H_3(k|\cdot)$ is uniform and independent of other variables in G_3. In G_4, the session key sKey is sampled in a random and independent way. Consequently, G_4 and G_3 are the same to $\mathcal{Z}$, except that $\mathcal{A}$ ever queries $H_3(k|\cdot)$ which happens with negligible probability. So we have $|\Pr[G_4 \Rightarrow 1] - \Pr[G_3 \Rightarrow 1]| \le \mathsf{negl}(\lambda)$.

Game G_5 (simulation for client instances in case of active attacks). In G_5, simulator Sim is the same as in G_4, except that Sim will add a rejection rule in the simulations for client instances in case of active attacks. More precisely,

- For a client instance $(C^{(i)}, iid)$ that is not linked to any server instance $(S^{(j)}, iid')$ when receiving the second-round message $(\tilde{c}, \tilde{C})$, we know that $(\tilde{c}, \tilde{C})$ is NOT generated from any server instance, so it must be forged by adversary $\mathcal{A}$ (with active attacks). Let pw be the password shared between $C^{(i)}$ and $S^{(j)}$ and pk be the public key generated by Sim for instance $(C^{(i)}, iid)$. **Rejection rule:** Upon receiving the second-round message $(\tilde{c}, \tilde{C})$, Sim first extracts password pw' by invoking $pw'|pk'|c' \leftarrow \mathsf{CDec}(csk, \tilde{C})$. If
$$pw \ne pw' \quad \text{or} \quad pk'|c' \ne pk|\tilde{c}, \qquad (\star)$$
then Sim rejects $(\tilde{c}, \tilde{C})$ by setting $\mathsf{sKey} := \bot$.

G_5 and G_4 differ only when a message $(\tilde{c}, \tilde{C})$ satisfying $(\star)$ leads to rejection in G_5 but not in G_4. However, if $(\tilde{c}, \tilde{C})$ satisfies $(\star)$ then either $pw' \ne pw$ or $pk'|c' \ne pk|\tilde{c}$. If such $(\tilde{c}, \tilde{C})$ does not lead to rejection in G_4, then we have $\tilde{C} = \mathsf{CEnc}(cpk, pw|pk|\tilde{c}; r)$ and $pw'|pk'|c' = \mathsf{CDec}(csk, \tilde{C})$, but $pw'|pk'|c' \ne pw|pk|\tilde{c}$, which contradicts to the correctness of PKE. Therefore, $(\tilde{c}, \tilde{C})$ satisfying $(\star)$ must lead to rejection in G_4 except with negligible probability, and hence we have

$$|\Pr[G_5 \Rightarrow 1] - \Pr[G_4 \Rightarrow 1]| \leq \mathsf{negl}(\lambda).$$

Game G_6 (Get Rid of sk in simulation for client instances in case of active attacks). In G_6, Sim is the same as in G_5, except for the generation of m' during Sim's simulations for client instances in case of active attacks.

- For any client instance $(C^{(i)}, iid)$ that is not linked to any server instance $(S^{(j)}, iid')$ when receiving the second-round message $(\tilde{c}, \tilde{C})$, we know that $(\tilde{c}, \tilde{C})$ is NOT generated from any server instance, so it must be forged by adversary $\mathcal{A}$. When generating m' during the simulation for instance $(C^{(i)}, iid)$, Sim will not use the decryption algorithm to obtain $m' \leftarrow \mathsf{LDec}(sk, \tilde{c})$ as did in G_5. Instead, it will check whether $\exists (m', r_H) \in \mathcal{L}_{H_1}$ such that $\tilde{c} = \mathsf{LEnc}(pk, H(pw), m'; r_H)$, where pw is the password of $C^{(i)}$ and pk is the first-round message generated by Sim for $(C^{(i)}, iid)$. If there exists such pair $(m', r_H) \in \mathcal{L}_{H_1}$, then Sim retrieves m' as the decrypted plaintext. Otherwise Sim rejects $(\tilde{c}, \tilde{C})$ by setting sKey $:= \perp$.

We consider two cases.

Case I. $\exists (m', r_H) \in \mathcal{L}_{H_1}$ s.t. $\tilde{c} = \mathsf{LEnc}(pk, H(pw), m'; r_H)$. By the correctness of LPKE, we have $\mathsf{LDec}(sk, \tilde{c}) = m'$. Therefore, G_6 results in the same m' as that in G_5, and thus G_6 and G_5 are indistinguishable to $\mathcal{Z}$ in this case.

Case II. $\nexists (m', r_H) \in \mathcal{L}_{H_1}$ s.t. $\tilde{c} = \mathsf{LEnc}(pk, H(pw), m'; r_H)$. This suggests that adversary $\mathcal{A}$ does not ever query $H_1(m')$ and hence $H_1(m')$ is random. Recall that pk was generated from $\mathsf{LKeyGen}(H(pw))$, so $H(pw)$ is the normal label of pk. Then by the property of *ciphertext unpredictability under normal labels*, $\tilde{c} = \mathsf{LEnc}(pk, H(pw), m'; H_1(m'))$ hardly holds. Accordingly, Sim's simulation of $C^{(i)}$ will reject with sKey $:= \perp$ in G_5, except with negligible probability. In G_6, Sim will terminate the simulation by setting sKey $:= \perp$. Obviously, G_6 and G_5 are identical to $\mathcal{Z}$ except with negligible probability in this case.

Therefore, we have $|\Pr[G_6 \Rightarrow 1] - \Pr[G_5 \Rightarrow 1]| \leq \mathsf{negl}(\lambda)$.

We stress that now in G_6 (and hereafter), Sim's simulation for client instances does not need the secret key sk of LPKE any more, no matter dealing with active attacks or passive attacks. This helps us to proceed to the next game.

Game G_7 (simulation of generating first-round message pk without pw). In G_7, Sim is the same as in G_6, except for Sim's simulation of generating the first-round message pk for client instances.

- For any client instance $(C^{(i)}, iid)$, when generating the first-round message pk, Sim randomly samples $pk \leftarrow_{\$} \mathcal{PK}$ in G_7, rather than invoking $(pk, sk) \leftarrow \mathsf{LKeyGen}(H(pw))$ as did in G_6.

Due to the *pseudo-randomness of public key* of LPKE and by hybrid arguments across the ℓ sessions, we have $|\Pr[G_7 \Rightarrow 1] - \Pr[G_6 \Rightarrow 1]| \leq \mathsf{negl}(\lambda)$.

We note that the reduction proof for the above equation proceeds smoothly since sk is not needed any more in the simulation for client instances.

Game G_8 (simulation of generating c in second-round message). In G_8, Sim is the same as in G_7, except for Sim's simulation of generating c in the second-round message (c, C) for server instances. There are two cases.

Case 1: Passive attacks on Servers. For a server instance $(S^{(j)}, iid')$ that is linked to some client instance $(C^{(i)}, iid)$ when receiving a first-round message pk, simulator Sim will sample c by $c \leftarrow_\$ \mathcal{CT}$, rather than computing it with $c \leftarrow \mathsf{LEnc}(pk, H(pw), m; H_1(m))$ as did in G_7.

Note that $r|\sigma|k \leftarrow_\$ \{0, 1\}^{3\lambda}$ and $C \leftarrow \mathsf{CEnc}(cpk, pw|pk|c; r)$ are still computed in the same way as in G_7.

Case 2: Active attacks on Servers. For a server instance $(S^{(j)}, iid')$ that is not linked to any client instance when receiving a first-round message $\tilde{pk}$, we further consider three sub-cases.

    Case 2.1: $\nexists(pw', r_H) \in \mathcal{L}_H$ s.t. $\mathsf{IsLossy}(td, \tilde{pk}, r_H) = 0$. In this case, Sim will compute $c \leftarrow_\$ \mathcal{CT}$, $r|\sigma|k \leftarrow_\$ \{0, 1\}^{3\lambda}$, rather than computing $c \leftarrow \mathsf{LEnc}(\tilde{pk}, H(pw), m; H_1(m))$ and $r|\sigma|k := H_2(m)$ as did in G_7.

    Case 2.2: $\exists!(pw', r_H) \in \mathcal{L}_H$ s.t. $\mathsf{IsLossy}(td, \tilde{pk}, r_H) = 0$. In this case, Sim extracts this password pw' and checks whether $pw' = pw$ or not.

        – If $pw' \neq pw$, Sim simulates (c, C) just like Case 2.1.

        – If $pw' = pw$, Sim computes (c, C) just like G_7, i.e., $c \leftarrow \mathsf{LEnc}(\tilde{pk}, H(pw), m; H_1(m))$ and $C \leftarrow \mathsf{CEnc}(cpk, pw|\tilde{pk}|c; r)$.

    Case 2.3: $\exists(pw, r_H), (pw', r'_H) \in \mathcal{L}_H$ s.t. $\mathsf{IsLossy}(td, \tilde{pk}, r_H) = \mathsf{IsLossy}(td, \tilde{pk}, r'_H) = 0$. In this case, Sim just aborts the simulation directly.

In Case 1, pk is random and independent of password pw. Then $H(pw)$ is a random label w.r.t. pk. According to the *lossiness of random labels*, we have $\mathsf{IsLossy}(td, pk, H(pw)) = 1$, i.e., $H(pw)$ is a lossy label of pk. Then according to Lemma 5, the ciphertext $c := \mathsf{LEnc}(pk, H(pw), m; H_1(m))$ is pseudo-random in G_7. Therefore, we can replace c with a random one as did in G_8 in a computationally indistinguishable way.

In Case 2.1, $\mathcal{A}$ did not ever query $H(pw)$, and hence $H(pw)$ is random to $\mathcal{A}$. With a similar argument as Case 1, we can also replace c with a random one. Now that c is independent of m, then the randomness of m makes sure that $\mathcal{A}$ hardly ever queries $H_2(m)$. So, $r|\sigma|k := H_2(m)$ is uniform and independent of c.

In Case 2.2, $H(pw')$ is a normal label of pk. If pw' is not the correct password, then $H(pw)$ must be a lossy label to $\tilde{pk}$ except with a negligible probability. The reason is as follows. If $(pw, \cdot) \in \mathcal{L}_H$, then $\mathsf{IsLossy}(td, \tilde{pk}, H(pw)) = 1$ must hold, hence $H(pw)$ is a lossy label of $\tilde{pk}$. If $(pw, \cdot) \notin \mathcal{L}_H$, then $\mathcal{A}$ did not ever query $H(pw)$, so $H(pw)$ is random to $\mathcal{A}$. With a similar argument as Case 1, we can replace c with a random one in a computationally indistinguishable way.

    Case 2.3 implies $\mathsf{IsLossy}(td, \tilde{pk}, r_H) = \mathsf{IsLossy}(td, \tilde{pk}, r'_H) = 0$, which happens with negligible probability according to the property of *uniqueness of normal labels among polynomial-size set* (among the all the labels stored in $\mathcal{L}_H$).

Accounting for the above cases, we have $|\Pr[G_8 \Rightarrow 1] - \Pr[G_7 \Rightarrow 1]| \leq \mathsf{negl}(\lambda)$.

Game G_9 (simulation of generating C in the second-round message). In G_9, Sim is the same as in G_8, except for Sim's simulation of generating C in the second-round message (c, C) for client instances. We consider the same cases as in G_8. In Case 1, Case 2.1 and the sub-case $pw' \neq pw$ in Case 2.2, Sim invokes $C \leftarrow \mathsf{CEnc}(cpk, 0; r)$ rather than $C \leftarrow \mathsf{CEnc}(cpk, pw|pk|c; H_1(m))$ as did in G_8.

Note that r is random and independent of $pw|pk|c$. According to the CCA security of PKE and hybrid arguments over the (at most) ℓ ciphertexts, we have

$$|\Pr[G_9 \Rightarrow 1] - \Pr[G_8 \Rightarrow 1]| \leq \ell \cdot \mathsf{Adv}_{\mathsf{PKE}}^{\mathsf{cca}}(\mathcal{B}_{\mathsf{PKE}}) \leq \mathsf{negl}(\lambda).$$

Game G_{10} (simulation of dealing with the third-round message $\tilde{\sigma}$ for Server Instances in Case of Active Attacks). In G_{10}, Sim is the same as in G_9, except for Sim's simulation of generating sKey upon receiving the third-round message $\tilde{\sigma}$. Consider the same cases defined in G_9 (also G_8). In Case 1, Case 2.1 and the sub-case $pw' \neq pw$ in Case 2.2, Sim sets sKey $:= \perp$ directly in G_{10} regardless of whether $\sigma = \tilde{\sigma}$ or not.

G_{10} is the same as G_9 except that $\sigma = \tilde{\sigma}$ happens in these cases in G_9. However, σ is uniformly chosen and independent of other variables, and hence $\mathcal{A}$ can present a correct guess of σ with negligible probability. So we have

$$|\Pr[G_{10} \Rightarrow 1] - \Pr[G_9 \Rightarrow 1]| \leq \mathsf{negl}(\lambda).$$

Now Sim does not use pw anymore except for the comparison $pw' \overset{?}{=} pw$ in Case 2.2 for server instances and in the rejection rule $(\star)$ for client instances.

Game G_{11} (Integration of Sim with $\mathcal{F}_{pake}$). G_{11} is the same as G_{10}, except that Sim accesses $\mathcal{F}_{pake}$ by issuing $\mathsf{Testpw}(pw')$ to decide $pw' \overset{?}{=} pw$ for Case 2.2 and $(\star)$. (The detail of G_{11} and analysis is shown in the full version [25].) Note that $\mathsf{Testpw}(pw')$ and $pw' \overset{?}{=} pw$ has the same functionality, so

$$\Pr[G_{11} \Rightarrow 1] = \Pr[G_{10} \Rightarrow 1].$$

Now that Sim completely gets rid of pw in the simulation, it finally arrives at its final form and G_{11} is exactly $\mathbf{Ideal}_{\mathcal{Z},\mathsf{Sim}}$.

Finally, by combining all the statements across G_0-G_{11}, we know that

$$|\Pr[\mathbf{Real}_{\mathcal{Z},\mathcal{A}}] - \Pr[\mathbf{Ideal}_{\mathcal{Z},\mathsf{Sim}}]| \leq \mathsf{negl}(\lambda).$$

$\square$

Remark 2. For our UC-secure PAKE construction in ROM, it is possible for us to remove the CCA-secure encryption C in the second-round message, resulting in a more efficient PAKE scheme without affecting its UC security. Note that C was originally used to extract password pw in the proof. Benefiting from the RO model, now the simulator can accomplish the extraction of pw without C using a new strategy: the simulator checks if there exists a query $(pw, H(pw))$ and a query $(m, H_1(m))$ s.t. $c = \mathsf{LPKE.Enc}(pk, H(pw), m; H_1(m))$ so as the password pw and the encrypted message m can be extracted from the ciphertext c. However, for our UC-secure PAKE construction in QROM, the new strategy does not work and we still need the CCA encryption of C for the extraction.

4   PAKE from Extractable LPKE in QROM

When considering post-quantum security in QROM, we have to consider a quantum adversary $\mathcal{A}$ making quantum superposition access to the random oracle. The proving technique of keeping hash query lists and searching for all queries in the lists in ROM does not apply any more, since the no-cloning principle makes impossible to maintain a query list.

In order to achieve UC security in QROM, we have to adjust the four hash functions H, H_1, H_2, H_3 in our PAKE construction to avoid keeping hash lists for them in the proof.

- In PAKE^{RO}, hash function H_1 helps LPKE to achieve CCA security as a KEM. According to [20], the FO-transformation works well in QROM.
- In PAKE^{RO}, the hash list of H_1 is also used for decryptions of c without secret key sk. To eliminate hash list of H_1, we resort to the online-extractability technique due to Don et al. [20]. With this technique, we can construct a simulator $\mathcal{S} = (\mathcal{S}.RO, \mathcal{S}.E)$ who not only extracts the decrypting result m from $c = \mathsf{LEnc}(pk, b, m; H_1(m)) = f_{pk,b}(m, H_1(m))$ with $\mathcal{S}.E$, but also simulates H_1 with $\mathcal{S}.RO$ in QROM. Note that the unpredictability of ciphertexts and the correctness of LPKE ensure not too many y's satisfy $f_{pk,b}(m, y) = c$, which is a necessary condition for online-extractability to apply.
- In PAKE^{RO}, hash function H_2 and H_3 are used as PRF. Applying the O2H lemma enables us to prove the pseudo-randomness of $r|\sigma|k := H_2(m)$ and $\mathsf{sKey} := H_3(k|sid)$ in QROM, when m and k are uniform.
- In PAKE^{RO}, hash list of H is used to extract password pw from the first-round message pk in the security proof in ROM. However, when formalizing H as a quantum accessible random oracle in $pk = \mathsf{LKeyGen}(H(pw); r)$, an obstacle comes in the way: The O2H lemma does not apply because $\mathsf{LKeyGen}(H(pw); r)$ is not in the form of $H(k|\cdot)$. The online-extractability does not apply either, since the simulator is not able to obtain the randomness r sampled by $\mathcal{A}$ and hence cannot determine the function f to be extracted. To eliminate the obstacle, we discard hash function H and replace the building block LPKE with an "extractable" one named eLPKE. To accomplish password extraction from pk in QROM, eLPKE directly uses pw as its label and uses an extra algorithm Extract to extract pw from pk with the help of trapdoor.

In Subsect. 4.1, we introduce the concept of extractable LPKE. In Subsect. 4.2, we show how to construct extractable LPKE from LPKE. In Subsect. 4.3, we show the generic construction of PAKE and prove its UC security in QROM.

4.1 Definition of Extractable LPKE (eLPKE)

When augmenting an extracting algorithm to a basic LPKE, we obtain *extractable LPKE* (eLPKE in short). An eLPKE scheme additionally requires *lossiness of random public keys* and *extractability of the unique normal label*, besides the properties of ①②⑤⑥ as per basic LPKE (see Sect. 3.1).

Definition 6. *An extractable LPKE scheme* eLPKE = (eLSetup, eLKeyGen, eLEnc, eLDec, eIsLossy, Extract) *consists of six algorithms, where* (eLSetup, eLKeyGen, eLEnc, eLDec, eIsLossy) *are defined in the same way as the five algorithms* (LSetup, LKeyGen, LEnc, LDec, IsLossy) *in* LPKE *(cf. Def.4). Algorithm* Extract *is defined below.*

- Extract(td, pk) : *The extracting algorithm takes as input a trapdoor td and a public key pk, and outputs a label b.*

Correctness of eLPKE. It has the same correctness requirement as LPKE.

An extractable LPKE scheme eLPKE should satisfy the following properties and security requirements.

① **Pseudorandomness of Public Keys.** Same as ① of LPKE. (cf. Def. 4)
② **Random Ciphertexts under Lossy Labels.** Same as ② of LPKE.
③ **Extractablity of the Unique Normal Label.** For every $\mathcal{A}$, it holds that

$$\Pr\left[\begin{array}{c}(\mathsf{crs}, td) \leftarrow \mathsf{eLSetup} \\ pk \leftarrow \mathcal{A}(\mathsf{crs}); b \leftarrow \mathsf{Extract}(td, pk)\end{array} : \exists b' \neq b, \mathsf{eIsLossy}(td, pk, b') = 0\right] \leq \mathsf{negl}(\lambda).$$

④ **Lossiness of Random Public Keys.** For every adversary $\mathcal{A}$, it holds that

$$\Pr\left[\begin{array}{c}(\mathsf{crs}, td) \leftarrow \mathsf{eLSetup} \\ b \leftarrow \mathcal{A}(\mathsf{crs}), pk \leftarrow_\$ \mathcal{PK}\end{array} : \mathsf{eIsLossy}(td, pk, b) = 0\right] \leq \mathsf{negl}(\lambda).$$

⑤ **Ciphertext Unpredictability under Normal Labels.** Same as ⑤ of LPKE. (cf. Def. 4)
⑥ **CPA Security under Normal Label.** Same as ⑥ of LPKE. (cf. Def. 4)

Remark 3. Propery ③ means that for adversary's choice of pk, either there exists no normal label for pk or Extract(td, pk) can extract a unique normal label for pk. In fact, Property ③ along with correctness of eLPKE imply that if $(pk, sk) \leftarrow$ eLKeyGen(b) then Extract(td, pk) outputs the unique normal label b of pk.

4.2 Construction of eLPKE from LPKE$^+$

Given a basic LPKE = (LSetup, LKeyGen, LEnc, LDec, IsLossy) with message space $\{0,1\}^\lambda$ and label space $\mathcal{T}$, we construct an extractable LPKE scheme eLPKE with message space $\{0,1\}^\lambda$ and label space $\{0,1\}^\lambda$. See Fig. 7 for eLPKE construction.

We will prove the property of eLPKE if the underlying basic LPKE not only satisfies property ①②③⑤⑥ (cf. Definition 4) but also two additional properties ④ (cf. Def. 6) and ⑦, where ⑦ is defined below.

eLSetup(1^λ) :	eLDec($\boldsymbol{sk} = (sk_1, ..., sk_\lambda), \boldsymbol{c} = (c_1, ..., c_\lambda))$:
$(pp', td') \leftarrow$ LSetup	For $i := 1$ to λ : $z_i \leftarrow$ LDec(sk_i, c_i)
For $i := 1$ to λ : $v_i^0, v_i^1 \leftarrow_\$ \mathcal{T}$	Return $m := z_1 \oplus ... \oplus z_\lambda$
Return ($pp := (pp', \{v_i^0, v_i^1\}_{i \in [\lambda]}), td := td'$)	elsLossy($td, \boldsymbol{pk}, \boldsymbol{b} = b_1 ... \| b_\lambda \in \{0,1\}^\lambda$) :
eLKeyGen($\boldsymbol{b} = b_1 ... \| b_\lambda \in \{0,1\}^\lambda$):	Parse $\boldsymbol{pk} = (pk_1, ..., pk_\lambda)$
For $i := 1$ to λ :	For $i := 1$ to λ :
$\quad (pk_i, sk_i) \leftarrow$ LKeyGen($v_i^{b_i}$)	$\quad$ If IsLossy($td, pk_i, v_i^{b_i}$) = 1:
Return $\boldsymbol{pk} := (pk_1, ..., pk_\lambda), \boldsymbol{sk} := (sk_1, ..., sk_\lambda)$	$\quad\quad$ Return 1
eLEnc($\boldsymbol{pk}, \boldsymbol{b} = b_1 ... \| b_\lambda \in \{0,1\}^\lambda, m \in \{0,1\}^\lambda$) :	Return 0
Parse $\boldsymbol{pk} := (pk_1, ..., pk_\lambda)$	Extract($td, \boldsymbol{pk} = (pk_1, ..., pk_\lambda)$):
For $i := 1$ to $\lambda - 1$: $z_i \leftarrow_\$ \{0,1\}^\lambda$	For $i := 1$ to λ :
$z_\lambda := m \oplus z_1 \oplus ... \oplus z_{\lambda-1}$	$\quad$ If IsLossy(td, pk_i, v_i^0) = 0: $b_i := 0$
For $i := 1$ to λ : $c_i \leftarrow$ LEnc($pk_i, v_i^{b_i}, z_i$)	$\quad$ Else: $b_i := 1$
Return $\boldsymbol{c} := (c_1, ..., c_\lambda)$	Return $\boldsymbol{b} := b_1 ... \| b_\lambda$

Fig. 7. Construction of eLPKE from LPKE$^+$.

⑦ **Ciphertext Randomness in case of Random Messages for LPKE.** For all $(pp, td) \leftarrow$ LSetup(1^λ), every (possibly malformed) public key pk, every label $b \in \mathcal{T}$ (no matter whether IsLossy(td, pk, b) = 1 or not), it holds that $c \approx_s \$$, where $m \leftarrow_\$ \{0,1\}^\lambda$ and $c \leftarrow$ LEnc(pk, b, m).

We designate such a LPKE as LPKE$^+$ if it satisfies ①②③④⑤⑥⑦.

Theorem 2. *For the construction of eLPKE in Fig. 7, if the underlying LPKE is a LPKE$^+$ scheme, i.e., it satisfies* ①②③④⑤⑥⑦, *then the resulting eLPKE scheme has the properties of* ①②③④⑤⑥ *and supports label space* $\{0,1\}^\lambda$.

Proof. For eLPKE, its properties of ①④⑤⑥ follow directly from ①④⑤⑥ of the underlying LPKE$^+$. Now we prove ②③ for eLPKE.

② **Random Ciphertexts under Lossy Labels:** We aim to show $(pp, \boldsymbol{pk}, \boldsymbol{b}, m, \boldsymbol{c}) \approx_s (pp, \boldsymbol{pk}, \boldsymbol{b}, m, \$)$, where $(pp, td) \leftarrow$ eLSetup, $(\boldsymbol{pk}, \boldsymbol{b}) \leftarrow \mathcal{A}(pp)$ s.t. elsLossy($td, \boldsymbol{pk}, \boldsymbol{b}$) = 1, $m \leftarrow_\$ \{0,1\}^\lambda$, $z_i \leftarrow_\$ \{0,1\}^\lambda$ for $i \in [\lambda - 1]$, $z_\lambda := m \oplus z_1 \oplus ... \oplus z_{\lambda-1}$, $c_i \leftarrow$ LEnc($pk_i, v_i^{b_i}, z_i$) for $i \in [\lambda]$ and $\boldsymbol{c} = c_1 | ... | c_\lambda$. Given elsLossy($td, \boldsymbol{pk}$) = 1, there must exist a position j such that IsLossy($td, pk_j, v_j^{b_j}$) = 1. Then we can replace c_j in $\boldsymbol{c}$ with a random $c_j \leftarrow_\$ \mathcal{CT}$ by the property of "② *random ciphertexts under lossy labels*" of the underlying LPKE$^+$ scheme.

Now m and $\{z_i\}_{i \in [\lambda]}$ can be sampled in an equivalent way: $m \leftarrow_\$ \{0,1\}^\lambda$, $z_i \leftarrow_\$ \{0,1\}^\lambda$ for $i \in [\lambda] \setminus \{j\}$, and set $z_j := m \oplus \bigoplus_{i=1, i \neq j}^\lambda z_i$. Note that plaintexts $\{z_i\}_{i \in [\lambda] \setminus \{j\}}$ encrypted in $\{c_i\}_{i \in [\lambda] \setminus \{j\}}$ are independent of message m. Therefore, by "⑦ *ciphertext randomness in case of random messages*" of underlying LPKE$^+$ scheme, we can replace c_i with a random $c_i \leftarrow_\$ \mathcal{CT}$ for each $i \in [\lambda] \setminus \{j\}$. Together with the random ciphertext c_j, we arrive at the right side in a statistical indistinguishable way.

③ **Extractablity of the Unique Normal Label:** Suppose toward contradiction, there is a $\boldsymbol{b}'$ such that $\boldsymbol{b}' \neq \boldsymbol{b}$ and elsLossy($td, \boldsymbol{pk}, \boldsymbol{b}'$) = 0, where $(pp, td) \leftarrow$ eLSetup, $pk \leftarrow \mathcal{A}(pp)$, $\boldsymbol{b} \leftarrow$ Extract(td, pk).

Given $\boldsymbol{b}' \neq \boldsymbol{b}$, there must exist a position $j \in [\lambda]$ s.t. $b_j' \neq b_j$. Given elsLossy($td, \boldsymbol{b}', \boldsymbol{pk}$) = 0, it holds that IsLossy($td, pk_i, v_i^{b_i'}$) = 0 for $i \in [\lambda]$. Now we have $b'_j \neq b_j$ and $\mathsf{IsLossy}(td, pk_j, v_j^{b'_j}) = 0$. According to the specification of $b \leftarrow \mathsf{Extract}(td, \mathbf{pk})$, we know that $b_j = 0$ if and only if $\mathsf{IsLossy}(td, pk_j, v_j^0) = 0$. We consider two cases according to the value of b_j.

Case 1: $b_j = 0$ (so $b'_j = 1$). In this case, we have $\mathsf{IsLossy}(td, pk_j, v_j^0) = \mathsf{IsLossy}(td, pk_j, v_j^1) = 0$, which contradicts to property ③ of the LPKE$^+$.
Case 2: $b_j = 1$ (so $b'_j = 0$). In this case, we have $\mathsf{IsLossy}(td, pk_j, v_j^0) \neq 0$ which contradicts to the fact that $\mathsf{IsLossy}(td, pk_j, v_j^{b'_j}) = \mathsf{IsLossy}(td, pk_j, v_j^0) = 0$. □

Remark 4. With the FO-transformation, we can construct a KEM scheme KEM$'$ from eLPKE. Note that Lemma 4 and Lemma 5 remain applicable to eLPKE since eLPKE has properties of ②⑤⑥. Therefore, KEM$'$ has both CCA-security and ciphertext pseudo-randomness under lossy labels.

4.3   Construction of PAKE from eLPKE in QROM

Replacing the building block of basic LPKE with eLPKE, we obtain the generic construction of PAKE from eLPKE. The resulting PAKE scheme PAKE^{QRO} is shown in Fig. 6 and its UC security proof in QROM is shown in Theorem 3.

Theorem 3. *If* eLPKE *is an extractable LPKE scheme,* PKE *is a CCA-secure PKE, and* H_1, H_2, H_3 *are quantum-accessible random oracles, then scheme* PAKE^{QRO} *in Fig. 6 securely emulates* $\mathcal{F}_{pake}$, *hence achieving UC security in QROM.*

The proof outline is similar to that of Theorem 1, where $\mathsf{G}'_1, \mathsf{G}'_2, \mathsf{G}'_5, \mathsf{G}'_7, \mathsf{G}'_9\text{-}\mathsf{G}'_{11}$ are the same as $\mathsf{G}_1, \mathsf{G}_2, \mathsf{G}_5, \mathsf{G}_7, \mathsf{G}_9\text{-}\mathsf{G}_{11}$. Note that the simulator will not keep the hash lists. The differences lie in $\mathsf{G}'_3, \mathsf{G}'_4, \mathsf{G}'_6, \mathsf{G}'_8$, for which we give a brief overview.

G'_3 & G'_8. We do not maintain hash list for $H_2(\cdot)$ to compute $r|\sigma|k$ as did in G_3 & G_8. Instead, we make use of Lemma 4 & Lemma 5 to argue $r|\sigma|k := H_2(m)$ is pseudo-random.
G'_4. We do not maintain hash list for $H_3(\cdot)$ to compute sKey as did in G_4. Instead, we make use of O2H Lemma [6] to argue sKey $:= H_3(k|sid)$ is pseudorandom.
G'_6. For client instances, we have to eliminate the usage of sk of eLPKE so that the first round message pk can be replaced with a random one in G'_7. We do not use the hash list for $H_1(\cdot)$, as did in G_6. Instead we resort to the online-extractability technique and make use of the corresponding simulator $\mathcal{S} = (\mathcal{S}.RO, \mathcal{S}.E)$ to simulates random oracle $H_1(\cdot)$ and extract the decryption result of $\mathsf{eLDec}(sk, c)$.
G'_8. For server instances receiving the first-round message pk in an active attack, we do not maintain the hash list for $H(\cdot)$ and search the list to find the correct password pw (if exists). Instead we use $\mathsf{Extract}(td, pk)$ to extract pw.

The full description of the proof is shown in the full version [25].

5   Instantiations

In our generic PAKE constructions, one building block is a CCA-secure PKE scheme, which can be easily obtained from CPA-secure PKE via FO-transformation in (quantum) ROM [33]. For example, by applying FO-transformation to the Regev PKE [30] or ElGamal-like PKE from GA-DDH (Sect. 7.1 in [12]), we can obtain CCA-secure PKE from the LWE or GA-DDH assumption. Therefore, to obtain specific PAKE schemes, we only consider the instantiations of LPKE.

In Subsect. 5.1 and 5.2, we give the instantiations of LPKE and LPKE$^+$, from LWE and GA-DDH respectively. The instantiations of CCA-secure PKE and LPKE yield four specific post-quantum UC-secure PAKE schemes, two in ROM and the other two in QROM, as shown in Subsect. 5.3.

5.1   LPKE and LPKE$^+$ Schemes from LWE

We present LWE-based LPKE scheme $\mathsf{LPKE_{lwe}}$ and LPKE$^+$ scheme $\mathsf{LPKE'_{lwe}}$. Before presenting our scheme $\mathsf{LPKE_{lwe}}$, we recall some technical tools including an important algorithm called $\mathsf{IsMessy}$ introduced in [21].

– **Statistical distance** $\delta_{q,r}(\mathbf{A}, \mathbf{x})$. Given $\mathbf{A} \in \mathbb{Z}_q^{n \times m}$ and $\mathbf{x} \in \mathbb{Z}_q^m$, define

$$\delta_{q,r}(\mathbf{A}, \mathbf{x}) := \Delta((\mathbf{Ae}, \mathbf{x}^T \mathbf{e}), (\mathbf{u}, u)), \tag{1}$$

where $\mathbf{e} \leftarrow D_{\mathbb{Z}^m, r}$, $\mathbf{u} \leftarrow_\$ \mathbb{Z}_q^n$, $u \leftarrow_\$ \mathbb{Z}_q$ and Δ is the statistical distance.
– **Algorithm** $\mathsf{IsMessy}(\mathbf{T_A}, \mathbf{A}, \mathbf{x})$. It takes as input a matrix $\mathbf{A} \in \mathbb{Z}_q^{n \times m}$, $\mathbf{A}$'s trapdoor $\mathbf{T_A}$, and a vector $\mathbf{x} \in \mathbb{Z}_q^m$ and outputs "messy" or "not sure".

Lemma 6 (Proposition 7.8 in [28]). *Let* $m \geq 2(n+1)\log q$ *and let* $r \geq \sqrt{qm} \cdot \log^2 m$. *Suppose that* $(\mathbf{A}, \mathbf{T_A})$ *are generated by* $\mathsf{TrapGen}$ *(c.f. Lemma 1). Then the PPT algorithm* $\mathsf{IsMessy}(\mathbf{T_A}, \mathbf{A}, \mathbf{x})$ *satisfying the following statements.*

(a) *With overwhelming probability over the choice of* $\mathbf{A}, \mathbf{T_A}$, *for all but an at most* $(1/2\sqrt{q})^m$ *fraction of vectors* $\mathbf{x} \in \mathbb{Z}_q^m$, $\mathsf{IsMessy}(\mathbf{T_A}, \mathbf{A}, \mathbf{x})$ *outputs "messy" with overwhelming probability (over its own randomness).*
(b) *There exists* $\epsilon(\lambda) = \mathsf{negl}(\lambda)$ *such that if* $\delta_{q,r}(\mathbf{A}, \mathbf{x}) > 2\epsilon(\lambda)$, *then* $\mathsf{IsMessy}(\mathbf{T_A}, \mathbf{A}, \mathbf{x}) = $ *"not sure", with overwhelming probability (over its own randomness). (In other words, if* $\mathsf{IsMessy}(\mathbf{T_A}, \mathbf{A}, \mathbf{x}) = $ *"messy", then* $\delta_{q,r}(\mathbf{A}, \mathbf{x}) = \mathsf{negl}$ *with overwhelming probability.)*

Our basic LPKE scheme $\mathsf{LPKE_{lwe}}$ is described as follows.

$\mathsf{LSetup}(1^\lambda):$	$\mathsf{LDec}(sk = \mathbf{s}, ct = (\mathbf{u}_1|...|\mathbf{u}_\lambda, c_1|...|c_\lambda)):$
$\quad (\mathbf{A}, \mathbf{T_A}) \leftarrow \mathsf{TrapGen}(1^\lambda)$	$\quad$ For $i := 1$ to λ:
$\quad$ Return $(pp := \mathbf{A}, td := \mathbf{T_A})$	$\qquad d_i := c_i - \mathbf{s}^T \mathbf{u}_i$
$\mathsf{LKeyGen}(\mathbf{v} \in \mathbb{Z}_q^m):$	$\qquad$ If $d_i \in [q/4, 3q/4] : m_i := 1$
$\quad \mathbf{s} \leftarrow_{\$} \mathbb{Z}_q^n, \ \mathbf{e} \leftarrow D_{\mathbb{Z}^m, \sigma}$	$\qquad$ Else $m_i := 0$
$\quad$ Return $(pk := \mathbf{A}^T \mathbf{s} + \mathbf{e} - \mathbf{v}, sk := \mathbf{s})$	$\quad$ Return $m := m_1|...|m_\lambda$
$\mathsf{LEnc}(pk, \mathbf{v}, m \in \{0,1\}^\lambda):$	
$\quad \mathbf{p} := pk + \mathbf{v}$	$\mathsf{IsLossy}(td = \mathbf{T_A}, pk, \mathbf{v}):$
$\quad$ For $i := 1$ to λ:	$\quad$ If $\mathsf{IsMessy}(\mathbf{T_A}, \mathbf{A}, pk + \mathbf{v}) = $"messy":
$\qquad \mathbf{e}_i \leftarrow D_{\mathbb{Z}^m, r}, \ \mathbf{u}_i := \mathbf{A}\mathbf{e}_i$	$\qquad$ Return 1
$\qquad c_i := \mathbf{p}^T \mathbf{e}_i + m_i \cdot \frac{q}{2}$	$\quad$ Else: Return 0
$\quad$ Return $ct := (\mathbf{u}_1|...|\mathbf{u}_\lambda, c_1|...|c_\lambda)$	

Fig. 8. The basic LPKE scheme $\mathsf{LPKE}_{\mathsf{lwe}}$.

Theorem 4. *If $q > 4r\sigma m \log^2 n$, $m > 2(n+1)\log q$, and $r > \sqrt{qm}\log^2 m$, then $\mathsf{LPKE}_{\mathsf{lwe}}$ is a basic LPKE scheme satisfying properties ①-⑥ based on $\mathsf{LWE}_{n,q,m,D_{\mathbb{Z}^m,\sigma}}$ assumption.*

Proof. We prove that $\mathsf{LPKE}_{\mathsf{lwe}}$ has correctness and the corresponding properties. By the tail bound, $\|\mathbf{e}\| \leq \omega(\sqrt{\log n}) \cdot \sigma\sqrt{m}$ and $\|\mathbf{e}_i\| \leq \omega(\sqrt{\log n}) \cdot r\sqrt{m}$. The correctness follows from $|\mathbf{e}^T \mathbf{e}_i| \leq \|\mathbf{e}\| \|\mathbf{e}_i\| \leq r\sigma m \cdot \omega(\log n) < q/4$.

① **Pseudorandomness of Public Key:** According to Lemma 1, the matrix $\mathbf{A}$ outputted from $\mathsf{TrapGen}$ is statistically close to a uniform distribution. Then *pseudorandomness of public key* follows from the LWE assumption.

② **Random Ciphertext under Lossy Labels:** By statement (b) of Lemma 6 and (1), we know $(\mathbf{Ae}_i, \mathbf{p}^T\mathbf{e}_i) \approx_s (\$, \$)$ and independent of $(\mathbf{A}, pk, \mathbf{v})$ for $i \in [\lambda]$. So we have $(\mathbf{A}, pk, \mathbf{v}, m, \{\mathbf{Ae}_i, \mathbf{p}^T\mathbf{e}_i + m_i \cdot \frac{q}{2}\}_{i \in [\lambda]}) \approx_s (\mathbf{A}, pk, \mathbf{v}, m, \{\$, \$\}_{i \in [\lambda]})$.

③ **Uniqueness of Normal Labels among Polynomial-Size Set:** According to statement (a) of Lemma 6, we know that there are $1 - \mathsf{negl}(\lambda)$ fraction of matrices $\mathbf{A}$ (and $\mathbf{T_A}$) such that $\Pr[\mathbf{x} \leftarrow_{\$} \mathbb{Z}_q^m : \mathsf{IsMessy}(\mathbf{T_A}, \mathbf{A}, \mathbf{x}) = $"messy"$] \geq 1 - \mathsf{negl}(\lambda)$. Let $\mathbf{A}$ (and $\mathbf{T_A}$) be such a fixed matrix, and define set $\mathcal{S} := \{\mathbf{x} \in \mathbb{Z}_q^m \mid \mathsf{IsMessy}(\mathbf{T_A}, \mathbf{A}, \mathbf{x}) = $"messy"$\}$. Then $\Pr[\mathbf{x} \leftarrow_{\$} \mathbb{Z}_q^m : \mathbf{x} \notin \mathcal{S}] \leq (1/2\sqrt{q})^m$.
Further fixing a public key $pk = \mathbf{p} \in \mathbb{Z}_q^m$, we have

$$\Pr\left[\mathbf{x}_0, \mathbf{x}_1 \leftarrow_{\$} \mathbb{Z}_q^m : \mathbf{p} + \mathbf{x}_0 \notin \mathcal{S} \wedge \mathbf{p} + \mathbf{x}_1 \notin \mathcal{S}\right] = \left(\Pr\left[\mathbf{x} \leftarrow_{\$} \mathbb{Z}_q^m : \mathbf{x} \notin \mathcal{S}\right]\right)^2 \leq (1/4q)^m.$$

By a union bound over $Q(Q-1)/2 (\leq Q^2)$ possible pairs of $(\mathbf{x}_i, \mathbf{x}_j)$, we have

$$\Pr\left[\mathbf{x}_1, ..., \mathbf{x}_Q \leftarrow_{\$} \mathbb{Z}_q^m : \exists i \neq j, i, j \in [Q], \mathbf{p} + \mathbf{x}_i \notin \mathcal{S} \wedge \mathbf{p} + \mathbf{x}_j \notin \mathcal{S}\right] \leq Q^2 \cdot (1/4q)^m.$$

If $\mathbf{x}_1, ..., \mathbf{x}_Q \leftarrow_{\$} \mathbb{Z}_q^m$, then with a union bound over all q^m possible $pk = \mathbf{p} \in \mathbb{Z}_q^m$, we have $\Pr\left[\exists \mathbf{p} \in \mathbb{Z}_q^m, \exists i \neq j, \mathbf{p} + \mathbf{x}_i \notin \mathcal{S} \wedge \mathbf{p} + \mathbf{x}_j \notin \mathcal{S}\right] \leq Q^2 \cdot (1/4)^m \leq \mathsf{negl}(\lambda)$, so $\Pr\left[\exists \mathbf{p} \in \mathbb{Z}_q^m, \exists i \neq j, \mathsf{IsLossy}(\mathbf{T_A}, \mathbf{p}, \mathbf{x}_i) = 0 \wedge \mathsf{IsLossy}(\mathbf{T_A}, \mathbf{p}, \mathbf{x}_j) = 0\right] \leq \mathsf{negl}(\lambda)$.

④ **Lossiness of Random Labels:** It follows directly from (b) of Lemma 6.
⑤ **Ciphertext Unpredictability under Normal Labels:** According to Lemma 3, we know that $\mathbf{Ae}$ is statistically close to a uniform distribution, hence the probability that a ciphertext output from the encryption algorithm collides with a fixed ciphertext should be negligible.
⑥ **CPA Security under Normal Labels:** Indeed, the encryption scheme under a normal label is a variant of the Regev public key encryption scheme [30]. So it naturally inherits the CPA security from the Regev cryptosystem. □

Remark 5. Our basic LPKE scheme is adapted from the LWE-based dual-mode PKE scheme [28] but with the following differences.

- **Different label space.** The dual-mode PKE [28] only supports a simple label space $\{0, 1\}$, while our $\mathsf{LPKE}_{\mathsf{lwe}}$ has label space $\mathbb{Z}_q^m$, which is compatible to the hash value $H(pw)$ of password in the PAKE scheme.
- **Different syntax.** In [28], the CRS consists of two fixed vectors corresponding to label 0 and label 1 respectively. And there are two indistinguishable ways for generating CRS to determine the normal mode or the messy mode. In our $\mathsf{LPKE}_{\mathsf{lwe}}$, the CRS only has one mode and the public key together with a label determine the encryption is in a normal mode or a lossy mode.
- **Different security requirements.** Due to the different syntax and different applications, we also have different security requirements for $\mathsf{LPKE}_{\mathsf{lwe}}$.

Parameters. Set $n = \Theta(\lambda)$, $m = \Theta(\lambda \log \lambda)$, $q = \Theta(\lambda^5 \log^3 \lambda)$, $r = \Theta(\lambda^{3.5})$, and $\sigma = \Theta(\sqrt{\lambda})$. Such parameters satisfy the requirements in Theorem 4.

$\mathsf{LPKE}_{\mathsf{lwe}}$ is not a LPKE^+ scheme since it does not satisfy "⑦ *ciphertext randomness in case of random messages*". Recall that the ciphertext element $c_i = \mathbf{p}^T \mathbf{e}_i + m_i \cdot \frac{q}{2}$. We can consider $k_i := \mathbf{p}^T \mathbf{e}_i \in \mathbb{Z}_q$ as an ephemeral key used to hide the bit $m_i \in \{0, 1\}$. However, the uniformity of one bit $m_i \in \{0, 1\}$ is not sufficient to fully randomize $c_i \in \mathbb{Z}_q$. To solve this problem, we introduce the novel round function $R(\cdot)$ parameterized by T from [11] to result in $k_i := R(\mathbf{p}^T \mathbf{e}_i) \in \{0, 1\}$ so that $c_i := k_i \oplus m_i \in \{0, 1\}$. In this way, property ⑦ is achieved. However, CPA-security is lost since $R(\mathbf{p}^T \mathbf{e}_i)$ is not pseudo-random. To fix that, we add multiple $R(\mathbf{p}^T \mathbf{e}_{ij})$ to get $k_i := \bigoplus_{j \in [\lambda]} R(\mathbf{p}^T \mathbf{e}_{ij})$. By the LWE assumption and leftover hash lemma, $\mathbf{p}^T \mathbf{e}_{ij}$ can be replaced by a uniform element $\mathbf{u}_{ij}$. Then the rounding function R makes $R(\mathbf{u}_{ij})$ follow a Bernoulli distribution with parameter about $\frac{1}{3}$. By the piling-up lemma [1], $k_i := \bigoplus_{j \in [\lambda]} R(\mathbf{u}_{ij})$ is statistically to the uniform distribution, thus achieving CPA-security.

$$
\begin{array}{|ll|}
\hline
\textsf{LSetup}(1^\lambda): & \textsf{LDec}(sk=\mathbf{s},ct): \\
\quad (\mathbf{A},\mathbf{T_A}) \leftarrow \textsf{TrapGen}(1^n,1^m,q) & \quad \text{Parse } ct=(\{\mathbf{c}_{ij}\}_{i,j\in[\lambda]},\{\beta_i\}_{i\in[\lambda]}). \\
\quad \text{Return } (pp:=\mathbf{A},td:=\mathbf{T_A}) & \quad \text{For } i:=1 \text{ to } \lambda: \\
\textsf{LKeyGen}(\mathbf{v}\in\mathbb{Z}_q^m): & \qquad m_i := \bigoplus_{j\in[\lambda]} R(\mathbf{s}^T\mathbf{c}_{ij})\oplus\beta_i \\
\quad \mathbf{s}\leftarrow_\$\mathbb{Z}_q^n,\ \mathbf{e}\leftarrow_\$ D_{\mathbb{Z}^m,t} & \quad \text{Return } m=m_1|...|m_\lambda \\
\quad \text{Return } (pk:=\mathbf{A}^T\mathbf{s}+\mathbf{e}-\mathbf{v},sk:=\mathbf{s}) & \\
\textsf{LEnc}(pk,m=m_1|...|m_\lambda\in\{0,1\}^\lambda,\mathbf{v}): & \textsf{IsLossy}(td=\mathbf{T_A},pk,\mathbf{v}): \\
\quad \mathbf{p}:=pk+\mathbf{v} & \quad \mathbf{p}:=pk+\mathbf{v} \\
\quad \text{For } i:=1 \text{ to } \lambda: & \quad (\mathbf{s},\mathbf{e})\leftarrow \textsf{Invert}(\mathbf{T_A},\mathbf{A},\mathbf{p}) \\
\quad\quad \text{For } j:=1 \text{ to } \lambda: & \qquad /\!/\text{See Lemma 2 for Invert} \\
\quad\quad\quad \mathbf{e}_{ij}\leftarrow D_{\mathbb{Z}^m,r},\ \mathbf{c}_{ij}:=\mathbf{A}\mathbf{e}_{ij} & \quad \text{If } ||\mathbf{e}||\le q/8\sqrt{m}: \text{Return } 0 \\
\quad\quad \beta_i:=\big(\bigoplus_{j\in[\lambda]}R(\mathbf{p}^T\mathbf{e}_{ij})\big)\oplus m_i & \quad \text{Else: Return } 1 \\
\quad \text{Return } ct=(\{\mathbf{c}_{ij}\}_{i,j\in[\lambda]},\{\beta_i\}_{i\in[\lambda]}) & \\
\hline
\end{array}
$$

Fig. 9. LPKE$^+$ scheme LPKE$'_\textsf{lwe}$.

Our LPKE$^+$ scheme LPKE$'_\textsf{lwe}$ is adapted from [11,29] and shown in Fig. 9. The security of LPKE$'_\textsf{lwe}$ shown in Theorem 5 is proved in the full version [25]

Theorem 5. *If* $r > n\log n$, $trm/q = \textsf{negl}(\lambda)$, $T/q = \textsf{negl}(\lambda)$, $m = \Theta(n\log n)$, *and* $\frac{\sqrt{m}}{r}(\frac{nq}{T})^2 < \Theta(\sqrt{m})$, *then* LPKE$'_\textsf{lwe}$ *in Fig. 9 is a LPKE$^+$ scheme based on the* $\textsf{LWE}_{n,q,m,D_{\mathbb{Z}^m,t}}$ *assumption.*

Parameters. Set $n = \Theta(\lambda)$, $q = 2^\lambda$, $m = \Theta(\lambda^2)$, $t = \tilde{O}(\lambda^{3/2})$, $T = 2^{\frac{2\lambda}{3}}$, $k = \Theta(\lambda)$, and $r = \Omega(\lambda^4 \cdot 2^{\frac{2\lambda}{3}})$. Such parameters satisfy the requirements in Theorem 5.

5.2 LPKE and LPKE$^+$ Scheme from Group Actions

The second LPKE scheme LPKE$_\textsf{ga}$ is based on restricted effective group actions (REGA). It is adapted from the construction of the dual-mode PKE from group actions in [5]. Our LPKE$_\textsf{ga}$ vs. the dual-mode PKE from group actions in [5] is analogous to LPKE$_\textsf{lwe}$ vs. the dual-mode PKE from LWE in [28](See Remark 5).

Let $(\mathbb{G},\mathcal{X},\star)$ be a REGA, $\mathcal{H} = \{\mathsf{H}:\mathcal{X}^\ell \to \{0,1\}\}$ be a family of pairwise independent universal hash functions. Scheme LPKE$_\textsf{ga}$ is described in Fig. 10.

$$
\begin{array}{|ll|}
\hline
\textsf{LSetup}(1^\lambda): & \textsf{LKeyGen}(pp,g\in\mathbb{G}): \\
\quad x\leftarrow_\$\mathcal{X},\ t\leftarrow_\$\mathbb{G},\ \bar{x}\leftarrow t\star x,\ \mathsf{H}\leftarrow_\$\mathcal{H} & \quad s\leftarrow_\$\mathbb{G} \\
\quad \text{Return } (pp:=(x,\bar{x},\mathsf{H}),td:=t) & \quad \text{Return } (pk:=(s\star x,(g\cdot s)\star\bar{x}),sk:=s) \\
& \\
\textsf{LEnc}(pk=(y,\bar{y}),g\in\mathbb{G},m=m_1|...|m_\lambda\in\{0,1\}^\lambda): & \textsf{LDec}(sk=s,ct): \\
\quad \text{For } i:=1 \text{ to } \lambda: & \quad \text{Parse } ct=(\mathbf{c}_1,b_1),...,(\mathbf{c}_\lambda,b_\lambda) \\
\quad\quad \mathbf{r}_i=(r_{i1},...,r_{i\ell})\leftarrow_\$\mathbb{G}^\ell & \quad \text{For } i:=1 \text{ to } \lambda: \\
\quad\quad \mathbf{b}_i=(b_{i1},...,b_{i\ell})\leftarrow_\$\{0,1\}^\ell & \quad\quad \mathbf{z}_i:=(s\star\mathbf{c}_i)=(s\star c_{i1},...,s\star c_{i\ell}) \\
\quad\quad \text{For } j:=1 \text{ to } \ell: & \quad\quad m_i:=b_i\oplus\mathsf{H}(\mathbf{z}_i) \\
\quad\quad\quad \text{If } b_{ij}=0: c_{ij}:=r_{ij}\star x,\ c'_{ij}:=r_{ij}\star(g^{-1}\star\bar{y}) & \quad \text{Return } m:=m_1|...|m_\lambda \\
\quad\quad\quad \text{Else } c_{ij}:=r_{ij}\star\bar{x},\ c'_{ij}:=r_{ij}\star y & \\
\quad\quad \mathbf{c}_i:=(c_{i1},...,c_{i\ell})\in\mathcal{X}^\ell,\ \mathbf{c}'_i:=(c'_{i1},...,c'_{i\ell})\in\mathcal{X}^\ell & \textsf{IsLossy}(td=t\in\mathbb{G},pk=(y,\bar{y},g\in\mathbb{G})): \\
\quad\quad ct_i:=(\mathbf{c}_i,\mathsf{H}(\mathbf{c}'_i)\oplus m_i) & \quad \text{If } \bar{y}=(t\cdot g)\star y: \text{Return } 0 \\
\quad \text{Return } ct:=(ct_1,...,ct_\lambda) & \quad \text{Else: Return } 1 \\
\hline
\end{array}
$$

Fig. 10. LPKE and LPKE$^+$ scheme LPKE$_\textsf{ga}$.

Theorem 6. *If* $(\mathbb{G}, \mathcal{X}, \star)$ *is a REGA, then* $\mathsf{LPKE}_{\mathsf{ga}}$ *in Fig. 10 is both a LPKE scheme and a LPKE$^+$ scheme based on GA-DDH assumption.*

Proof. The proofs are similar to [5], so we only provide a concise overview.

① **Pseudorandomness of Public Keys:** We need to show that

$$(x, t \star x, s \star x, (g \cdot s \cdot t) \star x) \approx_c (x, t \star x, u_1, u_2) \tag{2}$$

for all $g \in \mathbb{G}$ provided by adversary $\mathcal{A}$, where $s, t \leftarrow_\$ \mathbb{G}$ and $u_1, u_2 \leftarrow_\$ \mathcal{X}$. The GA-DDH assumption requires $(x, s \star x, t \star x, (s \cdot t) \star x) \approx_c (x, s \star x, t \star x, z \star x)$, where $s, t, z \leftarrow_\$ \mathbb{G}$. Let g act on the last term, we have $(x, s \star x, t \star x, g \star ((s \cdot t) \star x)) \approx_c (x, s \star x, t \star x, g \star (z \star x))$. Note that $g \star ((s \cdot t) \star x)) = (g \cdot s \cdot t) \star x$, and the uniformity and independence of x and z guarantees that $s \star x$ and $g \star (z \star x))$ are uniformly and independently distributed. So we obtain (2).

② **Random Ciphertexts under Lossy Labels:** Recall that $\mathsf{pp} = (x, \bar{x} = t \star x, \mathsf{H}), pk = (y, \bar{y})$. Given a lossy label $g \in \mathbb{G}$ from $\mathcal{A}$, we have $\mathsf{IsLossy}(td, pk, g) = 1$, i.e., $\bar{y} \neq (t \cdot g) \star y$. When writing $\bar{y} = (t \cdot g') \star y$, we have $g \neq g'$. Now the encryption scheme using label g becomes

$$c_j = \begin{cases} (r_j \cdot t) \star x & \text{if } b_j = 0 \\ r_j \star x & \text{if } b_j = 1 \end{cases} \quad, \quad c'_j = \begin{cases} (r_j \cdot (g^{-1} \cdot g') \cdot t) \star y & \text{if } b_j = 0 \\ r_j \star y & \text{if } b_j = 1 \end{cases}.$$

Conditioned on pp, pk, g, c_j, bit b_j is perfectly hidden in c_j thanks to the randomness of r_j. Suppose $y = s \star x$. Then given $(x, t \star x, y, (t \cdot g') \star y, g, m, c_j)$, we know either $c'_j = s \star (g^{-1} \cdot g') \star c_j$ in case of $b_j = 0$ or $c'_j = s \star c_j$ in case of $b_j = 1$. Now that $g \neq g'$, so c'_j has one bit entropy and hence $\mathbf{c}'$ has ℓ bits entropy.

As a result, the vector $\mathbf{c}' = (c'_1, \ldots, c'_\ell)$ has ℓ bit entropy and by the leftover hash lemma, $\mathsf{H}(\mathbf{c}')$ is close to uniform distribution, thus hiding m_i statistically.

③ **Uniqueness of Normal Labels among Polynomial-Size Set:** By the regularity of the group action, we have

$$\Pr\left[\begin{array}{c} x \leftarrow_\$ \mathcal{X}, t \leftarrow_\$ \mathbb{G}, \bar{x} := t \star x \\ g_1, \ldots, g_Q \leftarrow_\$ \mathbb{G} \end{array} : \begin{array}{c} \exists (y, \bar{y}) \in \mathcal{X} \times \mathcal{X}, \ i \neq j \\ \bar{y} = (t \cdot g_i) \star y \wedge \bar{y} = (t \cdot g_j) \star y \end{array}\right]$$
$$= \Pr\left[g_1, \ldots, g_Q \leftarrow_\$ \mathbb{G} : \exists i \neq j, g_i = g_j\right] \leq Q^2/|\mathbb{G}| = \mathsf{negl}(\lambda).$$

④&④' **Lossiness of Random Labels/Random Public Keys:** By the regularity of the group action, we have $\Pr\left[g \leftarrow_\$ \mathbb{G} : \bar{y} = (t \cdot g) \star y\right] \leq 1/|\mathbb{G}| = \mathsf{negl}(\lambda)$ for any fixed $y, \bar{y} \in \mathcal{X}$ and $t \in \mathbb{G}$, and prove ④. For any fixed $g \in \mathbb{G}$ and $t \in \mathbb{G}$, we have $\Pr\left[y, \bar{y} \leftarrow_\$ \mathcal{X} : \bar{y} = (t \cdot g) \star y\right] \leq 1/|\mathcal{X}| = \mathsf{negl}(\lambda)$ that proves ④'.

⑤ **Ciphertext Unpredictability under Normal Labels:** For any fixed pp, pk, b, m, c, by the regularity of the group action, we have

$$\Pr\left[r \leftarrow_\$ \mathcal{R} : \mathsf{LEnc}(pk, b, m; r) = c\right] \leq \Pr\left[r \leftarrow_\$ \mathbb{G} : r \star x = c\right] \leq 1/|\mathbb{G}| = \mathsf{negl}(\lambda).$$

⑥ **CPA Security under Normal Labels:** The proof begins with changing public key to a random one by property ①. Then with overwhelming probability, the label is a lossy one of the random public key. Finally, the property of *random ciphertexts under lossy labels* guarantees the CPA security.

⑦ **Ciphertext Randomness in case of Random Messages:** Note that for each component $ct_i = (\mathbf{c}_i, \mathsf{H}(\mathbf{c}'_i) \oplus m_i)$ of the ciphertext, the first part $\mathbf{c}_i$ is uniformly distributed in $\mathcal{X}$. Moreover, the random message bit m_i is independent of $\mathbf{c}_i, \mathbf{c}'_i$, so $\mathsf{H}(\mathbf{c}'_i) \oplus m$ is uniform and independent of $\mathbf{c}_i$. □

Remark 6. When instantiating REGA with CSIDH, any group element $g \in \mathbb{G}$ will be sampled with randomness $r_1 \in \mathcal{R}_1, ..., r_n \in \mathcal{R}_n$ such that $g = g_1^{r_1} \cdot g_2^{r_2} \cdot ... \cdot g_n^{r_n}$ and g is described by $g = [r_1, \ldots, r_n]$, where $\{g_1, \ldots, g_n\}$ is a generating set of $\mathbb{G}$. In fact, we need to use the exponents $r_1, \ldots, r_n$ to implement the group action. In $\mathsf{PAKE}_{\mathsf{ga}}^{\mathsf{RO}}$, the hash function H is implemented with $H(pw) := [r_1, \ldots, r_n] \in \mathcal{R}_1 \times \ldots \times \mathcal{R}_n$. We stress that knowing the exponents $[r_1, \ldots, r_n]$ does not lead to any gain to adversary $\mathcal{A}$. For example, ① of $\mathsf{LPKE}_{\mathsf{ga}}$ holds even if $g = [r_1, \ldots, r_n]$ is provided or chosen by adversary $\mathcal{A}$ since $\mathcal{A}$ does not know the representation of t and s and the GA-DDH assumption holds. Similarly, for $\mathsf{PAKE}_{\mathsf{ga}}^{\mathsf{QRO}}$, there is no harm to issue the exponent representation of the labels $\{v_i^0 = [r_{i1}^0, \ldots, r_{in}^0], v_i^1 = [r_{i1}^1, \ldots, r_{in}^1]\}_{i \in [\lambda]}$ in pp to adversary.

5.3 Instantiations of PAKE

With the instantiations of LPKE and LPKE$^+$, we obtain four PAKE schemes in ROM and QROM, namely $\mathsf{PAKE}_{\mathsf{lwe}}^{\mathsf{RO}}, \mathsf{PAKE}_{\mathsf{ga}}^{\mathsf{RO}}$, $\mathsf{PAKE}_{\mathsf{lwe}}^{\mathsf{QRO}}, \mathsf{PAKE}_{\mathsf{ga}}^{\mathsf{QRO}}$.

Corollary 1. *By plugging the $\mathsf{LPKE}_{\mathsf{lwe}}$ in Fig. 8 (resp. $\mathsf{LPKE}_{\mathsf{ga}}$ in Fig. 10) scheme in the generic PAKE construction (cf. Fig. 6), we obtain a specific PAKE scheme $\mathsf{PAKE}_{\mathsf{lwe}}^{\mathsf{RO}}$ (resp. $\mathsf{PAKE}_{\mathsf{ga}}^{\mathsf{RO}}$), which UC-realizes the $\mathcal{F}_{pake}$ functionality based on the LWE (resp. GA-DDH) assumption in ROM.*

Corollary 2. *By plugging the LPKE$^+$ scheme $\mathsf{LPKE}'_{\mathsf{lwe}}$ in Fig. 9 (resp. $\mathsf{LPKE}_{\mathsf{ga}}$ in Fig. 10) in the construction of eLPKE in Fig. 7, we obtain eLPKE from the LWE (resp. GA-DDH) assumption in the QROM. Moreover, by plugging the resulting eLPKE scheme in the generic PAKE construction in Fig. 6, we obtain a specific PAKE scheme $\mathsf{PAKE}_{\mathsf{lwe}}^{\mathsf{QRO}}$ (resp. $\mathsf{PAKE}_{\mathsf{ga}}^{\mathsf{QRO}}$), which UC-realizes the $\mathcal{F}_{pake}$ functionality based on the LWE (resp. GA-DDH) assumption in QROM.*

Acknowledgements. We would like to thank the reviewers for their valuable comments. This work was partially supported by National Natural Science Foundation of China under Grant 61925207 and Grant 62372292, Guangdong Major Project of Basic and Applied Basic Research (2019B030302008), and the National Key R&D Program of China under Grant 2022YFB2701500.

References

1. https://en.wikipedia.org/wiki/Piling-up_lemma
2. Abdalla, M., Benhamouda, F., Blazy, O., Chevalier, C., Pointcheval, D.: SPHF-friendly non-interactive commitments. In: Sako, K., Sarkar, P. (eds.) ASIACRYPT 2013, Part I. LNCS, vol. 8269, pp. 214–234. Springer, Heidelberg (2013). https://doi.org/10.1007/978-3-642-42033-7_12
3. Abdalla, M., Eisenhofer, T., Kiltz, E., Kunzweiler, S., Riepel, D.: Password-authenticated key exchange from group actions. In: Dodis, Y., Shrimpton, T. (eds.) CRYPTO 2022, Part II. LNCS, vol. 13508, pp. 699–728. Springer, Heidelberg (2022). https://doi.org/10.1007/978-3-031-15979-4_24
4. Ajtai, M.: Generating hard instances of lattice problems (extended abstract). In: 28th ACM STOC, pp. 99–108. ACM Press (1996). https://doi.org/10.1145/237814.237838
5. Alamati, N., De Feo, L., Montgomery, H., Patranabis, S.: Cryptographic group actions and applications. In: Moriai, S., Wang, H. (eds.) ASIACRYPT 2020, Part II. LNCS, vol. 12492, pp. 411–439. Springer, Cham (2020). https://doi.org/10.1007/978-3-030-64834-3_14
6. Ambainis, A., Hamburg, M., Unruh, D.: Quantum security proofs using semi-classical oracles. In: Boldyreva, A., Micciancio, D. (eds.) CRYPTO 2019, Part II. LNCS, vol. 11693, pp. 269–295. Springer, Cham (2019). https://doi.org/10.1007/978-3-030-26951-7_10
7. Azarderakhsh, R., Jao, D., Koziel, B., LeGrow, J.T., Soukharev, V., Taraskin, O.: How not to create an isogeny-based PAKE. In: Conti, M., Zhou, J., Casalicchio, E., Spognardi, A. (eds.) ACNS 2020, Part I. LNCS, vol. 12146, pp. 169–186. Springer, Cham (2020). https://doi.org/10.1007/978-3-030-57808-4_9
8. Beguinet, H., Chevalier, C., Pointcheval, D., Ricosset, T., Rossi, M.: Get a CAKE: generic transformations from key encapsulation mechanisms to password authenticated key exchanges. In: Tibouchi, M., Wang, X. (eds.) ACNS 2023, Part II. LNCS, vol. 13906, pp. 516–538. Springer, Cham (2023). https://doi.org/10.1007/978-3-031-33491-7_19
9. Bellare, M., Pointcheval, D., Rogaway, P.: Authenticated key exchange secure against dictionary attacks. In: Preneel, B. (ed.) EUROCRYPT 2000. LNCS, vol. 1807, pp. 139–155. Springer, Heidelberg (2000). https://doi.org/10.1007/3-540-45539-6_11
10. Bellovin, S.M., Merritt, M.: Encrypted key exchange: password-based protocols secure against dictionary attacks. In: 1992 IEEE Symposium on Security and Privacy, pp. 72–84. IEEE Computer Society Press (1992). https://doi.org/10.1109/RISP.1992.213269 1109/RISP.1992.213269
11. Benhamouda, F., Blazy, O., Ducas, L., Quach, W.: Hash proof systems over lattices revisited. In: Abdalla, M., Dahab, R. (eds.) PKC 2018, Part II. LNCS, vol. 10770, pp. 644–674. Springer, Cham (2018). https://doi.org/10.1007/978-3-319-76581-5_22
12. Beullens, W., Dobson, S., Katsumata, S., Lai, Y.F., Pintore, F.: Group signatures and more from isogenies and lattices: generic, simple, and efficient. In: Dunkelman, O., Dziembowski, S. (eds.) EUROCRYPT 2022, Part II. LNCS, vol. 13276, pp. 95–126. Springer, Heidelberg (2022). https://doi.org/10.1007/978-3-031-07085-3_4
13. Boneh, D., Dagdelen, Ö., Fischlin, M., Lehmann, A., Schaffner, C., Zhandry, M.: Random oracles in a quantum world. In: Lee, D.H., Wang, X. (eds.) ASIACRYPT 2011. LNCS, vol. 7073, pp. 41–69. Springer, Heidelberg (2011). https://doi.org/10.1007/978-3-642-25385-0_3

14. Boyle, E., Segev, G., Wichs, D.: Fully leakage-resilient signatures. In: Paterson, K.G. (ed.) EUROCRYPT 2011. LNCS, vol. 6632, pp. 89–108. Springer, Heidelberg (2011). https://doi.org/10.1007/978-3-642-20465-4_7
15. Canetti, R., Dachman-Soled, D., Vaikuntanathan, V., Wee, H.: Efficient password authenticated key exchange via oblivious transfer. In: Fischlin, M., Buchmann, J., Manulis, M. (eds.) PKC 2012. LNCS, vol. 7293, pp. 449–466. Springer, Heidelberg (2012). https://doi.org/10.1007/978-3-642-30057-8_27
16. Canetti, R., Halevi, S., Katz, J., Lindell, Y., MacKenzie, P.: Universally composable password-based key exchange. In: Cramer, R. (ed.) EUROCRYPT 2005. LNCS, vol. 3494, pp. 404–421. Springer, Heidelberg (2005). https://doi.org/10.1007/11426639_24
17. Castryck, W., Lange, T., Martindale, C., Panny, L., Renes, J.: CSIDH: an efficient post-quantum commutative group action. In: Peyrin, T., Galbraith, S. (eds.) ASIACRYPT 2018, Part III. LNCS, vol. 11274, pp. 395–427. Springer, Cham (2018). https://doi.org/10.1007/978-3-030-03332-3_15
18. Coron, J.-S., Patarin, J., Seurin, Y.: The random oracle model and the ideal cipher model are equivalent. In: Wagner, D. (ed.) CRYPTO 2008. LNCS, vol. 5157, pp. 1–20. Springer, Heidelberg (2008). https://doi.org/10.1007/978-3-540-85174-5_1
19. Ding, J., Alsayigh, S., Lancrenon, J., RV, S., Snook, M.: Provably secure password authenticated key exchange based on RLWE for the post-quantum world. In: Handschuh, H. (ed.) CT-RSA 2017. LNCS, vol. 10159, pp. 183–204. Springer, Cham (2017). https://doi.org/10.1007/978-3-319-52153-4_11
20. Don, J., Fehr, S., Majenz, C., Schaffner, C.: Online-extractability in the quantum random-oracle model. In: Dunkelman, O., Dziembowski, S. (eds.) EUROCRYPT 2022, Part III. LNCS, vol. 13277, pp. 677–706. Springer, Heidelberg (2022). https://doi.org/10.1007/978-3-031-07082-2_24
21. Gentry, C., Peikert, C., Vaikuntanathan, V.: Trapdoors for hard lattices and new cryptographic constructions. In: Ladner, R.E., Dwork, C. (eds.) 40th ACM STOC, pp. 197–206. ACM Press (2008).https://doi.org/10.1145/1374376.1374407
22. Hosoyamada, A., Yasuda, K.: Building quantum-one-way functions from block ciphers: Davies-Meyer and Merkle-Damgård constructions. In: Peyrin, T., Galbraith, S. (eds.) ASIACRYPT 2018, Part II. LNCS, vol. 11272, pp. 275–304. Springer, Cham (2018). https://doi.org/10.1007/978-3-030-03326-2_10
23. Jiang, S., Gong, G., He, J., Nguyen, K., Wang, H.: PAKEs: new framework, new techniques and more efficient lattice-based constructions in the standard model. In: Kiayias, A., Kohlweiss, M., Wallden, P., Zikas, V. (eds.) PKC 2020, Part I. LNCS, vol. 12110, pp. 396–427. Springer, Cham (2020). https://doi.org/10.1007/978-3-030-45374-9_14
24. Katz, J., Vaikuntanathan, V.: Smooth projective hashing and password-based authenticated key exchange from lattices. In: Matsui, M. (ed.) ASIACRYPT 2009. LNCS, vol. 5912, pp. 636–652. Springer, Heidelberg (2009). https://doi.org/10.1007/978-3-642-10366-7_37
25. Lyu, Y., Liu, S., Han, S.: Universal composable password authenticated key exchange for the post-quantum world. Cryptology ePrint Archive (2024). https://eprint.iacr.org/2024/374
26. McQuoid, I., Xu, J.: An efficient strong asymmetric Pake compiler instantiable from group actions. Cryptology ePrint Archive, Paper 2023/1434 (2023). https://eprint.iacr.org/2023/1434

27. Micciancio, D., Peikert, C.: Trapdoors for lattices: simpler, tighter, faster, smaller. In: Pointcheval, D., Johansson, T. (eds.) EUROCRYPT 2012. LNCS, vol. 7237, pp. 700–718. Springer, Heidelberg (2012). https://doi.org/10.1007/978-3-642-29011-4_41

28. Peikert, C., Vaikuntanathan, V., Waters, B.: A framework for efficient and composable oblivious transfer. In: Wagner, D. (ed.) CRYPTO 2008. LNCS, vol. 5157, pp. 554–571. Springer, Heidelberg (2008). https://doi.org/10.1007/978-3-540-85174-5_31

29. Quach, W.: UC-secure OT from LWE, revisited. In: Galdi, C., Kolesnikov, V. (eds.) SCN 2020. LNCS, vol. 12238, pp. 192–211. Springer, Cham (2020). https://doi.org/10.1007/978-3-030-57990-6_10

30. Regev, O.: On lattices, learning with errors, random linear codes, and cryptography. In: Gabow, H.N., Fagin, R. (eds.) 37th ACM STOC, pp. 84–93. ACM Press (2005). https://doi.org/10.1145/1060590.1060603

31. Santos, B.F.D., Gu, Y., Jarecki, S.: Randomized half-ideal cipher on groups with applications to UC (a)PAKE. In: Hazay, C., Stam, M. (eds.) EUROCRYPT 2023, Part V. LNCS, vol. 14008, pp. 128–156. Springer, Heidelberg (2023). https://doi.org/10.1007/978-3-031-30589-4_5

32. Shoup, V.: Security analysis of $SPAKE2+$. In: Pass, R., Pietrzak, K. (eds.) TCC 2020, Part III. LNCS, vol. 12552, pp. 31–60. Springer, Cham (2020). https://doi.org/10.1007/978-3-030-64381-2_2

33. Zhandry, M.: How to record quantum queries, and applications to quantum indifferentiability. In: Boldyreva, A., Micciancio, D. (eds.) CRYPTO 2019. LNCS, vol. 11693, pp. 239–268. Springer, Cham (2019). https://doi.org/10.1007/978-3-030-26951-7_9

34. Zhang, J., Yu, Yu.: Two-round PAKE from approximate SPH and instantiations from lattices. In: Takagi, T., Peyrin, T. (eds.) ASIACRYPT 2017, Part III. LNCS, vol. 10626, pp. 37–67. Springer, Cham (2017). https://doi.org/10.1007/978-3-319-70700-6_2

Asymptotics and Improvements
of Sieving for Codes

Léo Ducas[1,2(✉)], Andre Esser[3], Simona Etinski[2],
and Elena Kirshanova[3,4]

[1] Centrum Wiskunde & Informatica, Amsterdam, Netherlands
leo.ducas@cwi.nl
[2] Leiden University, Leiden, Netherlands
simona.etinski@cwi.nl
[3] Technology Innovation Institute, Abu Dhabi, United Arab Emirates
{andre.esser,elena.kirshanova}@tii.ae
[4] Immanuel Kant Baltic Federal University, Kaliningrad, Russia

Abstract. A recent work of Guo, Johansson, and Nguyen (Eprint'23) proposes a promising adaptation of sieving techniques from lattices to codes, in particular claiming concrete cryptanalytic improvements on various schemes. The core of their algorithm reduces to a Near Neighbor Search (NNS) problem, for which they devise an ad-hoc approach. In this work, we aim for a better theoretical understanding of this approach. First we provide an asymptotic analysis which is not present in the original paper. Second, we propose a more systematic use of known NNS machinery, namely Locality Sensitive Hashing and Filtering (LSH/F), an approach that has been applied very successfully in the case of sieving over lattices. We establish the first baseline for the sieving approach with a decoding complexity of $2^{0.117n}$ for the conventional worst parameters (full distance decoding, complexity maximized over all code rates). Our cumulative improvements, eventually enable us to lower the hardest parameter decoding complexity for SievingISD algorithms to $2^{0.101n}$. While this outperforms the BJMM algorithm (Eurocrypt'12) it falls yet behind the most advanced conventional ISD approach by Both and May (PQCrypto'18). As for lattices, we found the Random-Spherical-Code-Product (RPC) gives the best asymptotic complexity. Moreover, we also consider an alternative that seems specific to the Hamming Sphere, which we believe could be of practical interest, as they plausibly hide less subexponential overheads than RPC.

1 Introduction

One of the central problems in coding theory is, given a linear code, finding a small codeword in this code. Concretely, given a parity check matrix $\mathbf{H} \in \mathbb{F}^{(n-k) \times n}$ of a code of dimension k, length n, defined over a field $\mathbb{F}$, find $\mathbf{e} \in \mathbb{F}^n$ such that

$$\mathbf{He} = 0 \quad \text{and} \quad |\mathbf{e}| < w$$

for some bound $0 \le w \le n$ and $|\cdot|$ is a metric defined over $\mathbb{F}$. In this work, we focus on the case where $\mathbb{F} = \mathbb{F}_2$ and $|\cdot|$ is the Hamming metric. Thus, we are

© International Association for Cryptologic Research 2024
M. Joye and G. Leander (Eds.): EUROCRYPT 2024, LNCS 14657, pp. 151–180, 2024.
https://doi.org/10.1007/978-3-031-58754-2_6

interested in finding small Hamming weight codewords in a binary linear code. Specifically, we consider the case of random binary linear codes, i.e., $\mathbf{H}$ is chosen uniformly at random from $\mathbb{F}_2^{(n-k) \times n}$.

The problem of finding small Hamming weight codewords is a building block in all known efficient decoding algorithms for random linear codes: Information Set Decoding (ISD) algorithms [24,30] construct such codewords by cleverly enumerating them, while the Statistical Decoding approach [5] requires an oracle that returns a set of small weight codewords. To instantiate the oracle, [5] uses the above-mentioned ISD algorithms.

In the world of Euclidean lattices, a very similar problem occurs, namely the problem of finding a short lattice vector in the Euclidean metric. For finding those short vectors there exist (at least) two different established approaches. Concretely, *enumeration* based algorithms [15,19] are challenged by *sieving* algorithms [1,21,27], where the latter, instead of carefully pruning the enumeration space, saturate the space with many lattice vectors to the point where pairwise sums start producing short vectors. Drawing inspiration from sieving-based techniques in lattices, one can naturally ask:

Is there a sieving-type algorithm for finding small-weight codewords?

Given how natural this question is, it seems fair to assume that it has been investigated by various experts over the years. However, it was not until recently that the first satisfying answer was given by Guo, Johansson, and Nguyen [17] (GJN) in the form of their sieving-style ISD algorithm.

Any sieving algorithm (either for codes or for lattices) starts by generating a (large) list of vectors (either codewords or lattice vectors). A sieving step consists of finding a pair $\mathbf{e}, \mathbf{e}'$ from the list such that their sum produces a short(-er) vector. Codes resp. lattices are closed under addition, hence the newly produced vector is a codeword resp. a lattice vector, and is qualitatively better than the original elements from the list.

The sieving-style ISD approach from [17] now uses two key ingredients that differ from the lattice setting and make the sieving especially effective for finding short codewords. First, instead of applying the sieving technique to the full code, it is applied only to a subcode within the conventional ISD framework [16]. Essentially, the enumeration routine of the ISD procedure is substituted with a sieving-style algorithm for finding small codewords. The second main difference to the lattice setting is that, instead of starting with large codewords which become shorter through the sieving steps, the weight is kept equal throughout all sieving iterations. However, the "quality" of elements improves in each step as lists contain codewords from supercodes, where the codimension increases in each step until codewords eventually belong to the input code.

The fundamental task of finding a pair $\mathbf{e}, \mathbf{e}'$ that produces a short sum is called *the near neighbor problem* and has been extensively studied in various settings [1,8,18,25,28]. More specifically, let us denote by $\mathcal{S}_w^n \subset \mathbb{F}_2^n$ the set of binary vectors of weight w. The near neighbor search problem we are interested in is formulated as follows.

Definition 1.1 (*w*-Nearest Neighbor Search (informal)). *Given a list of vectors $L \subset S_w^n$ of weight w, find all pairs $\mathbf{x}, \mathbf{y} \in L^2$ s.t. $|\mathbf{x} + \mathbf{y}| = w$.*

Interestingly, this problem variant, where the input vectors all lie on the sphere S_w^n, has not attracted much attention yet. It was studied in the context of *different input distributions* in [12]. It was shown there that the fastest known algorithms for a uniformly random list $L \subset \mathbb{F}_2^n$, without further tweaks, do not perform well in the case of fixed-weight input vectors. Recent works [4,10] studied a slightly more general version of the problem, where the input and output weight can differ. Esser [10] shows that advanced algorithms for this problem have the potential to improve the state of the art of ISD algorithms and provide a first algorithm for solving the problem. Carrier [4] provides advanced algorithms by showing how to efficiently adapt the concepts from the uniformly random input list case to the sphere. Most recently, in the context of the introduction of sieving-style ISD, GJN [17] specified a new algorithm for solving the w-near neighbor search used as a subroutine in the sieving step.

Here we see room for improvement and systematization: lattice sieving has benefited greatly from the Locality-Sensitive Filtering (LSF) framework, both in terms of clarity and efficiency. We study the translation of this framework to the Hamming case resulting in improved algorithms for nearest neighbor search and, consequently, in improved SievingISD instantiations.

1.1 Our Contributions

The contribution of this work is twofold. First, motivated by the relevance of the w-near neighbor search in the context of SievingISD [17] and in general ISD algorithms [10], we provide improved algorithms solving the problem from Definition 1.1. As this problem might be of independent interest, we provide those results in their full generality, allowing application in an arbitrary context. Our second contribution is to provide improved SievingISD instantiations based on these new near neighbor routines. In this context, we initiate the asymptotic study of the SievingISD framework and establish the asymptotic complexity exponent of the GJN algorithm. Further, we show that the new algorithms significantly improve the GJN running time and provide a comparison to the state-of-the-art of conventional ISD algorithms.

Near Neighbor Algorithms. To construct new algorithms solving the w-near neighbor search, we formulate the Locality-Sensitive-Filtering framework in the Hamming metric; this framework is a generic method for solving the near neighbor problem and was originally proposed in the context of lattices [1] as a generalization of Locally-Sensitive-Hashing techniques [20]. We show how to adapt it to the Hamming metric and provide several concrete instantiations of this framework.

We obtain the GJN algorithm as one of those instantiations. In this context, we establish the asymptotic complexity of the GJN near neighbor algorithm, later serving as a foundation when analyzing its use in the SievingISD framework. We then give a series of algorithms resulting in significantly improved asymptotic complexities. The asymptotically fastest algorithm uses the most recent techniques based on Random Product Codes (RPCs). We were only recently pointed to an existing analysis of RPCs for the Hamming sphere in the Thesis of Carrier [4]. Because Carrier's Thesis [4] is only available in French we preferred to leave our analysis in Sect. 4.2, but original credit should go to [4].

Moreover, we give an additional algorithm (HASH-OPT) particular to the Hamming case which has high potential in practice: paying only a slight asymptotic penalty in comparison to RPC, it improves hidden sub-exponential factors considerably. In Fig. 1 we illustrate the complexity exponent ϑ, where the time complexity of the algorithms is equal to $|L|^\vartheta$, for varying weight and fixed list size. We compare the previous approaches of GJN (GJN) and Esser (ESSER) against the fastest instantiation RPC-OPT and the more practical instantiation HASH-OPT, as well as a quadratic search baseline, corresponding to $\vartheta = 2$. It can be observed that the new algorithms improve the running time significantly for all weights.

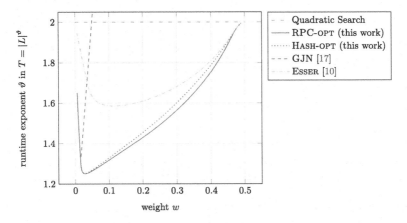

Fig. 1. Comparison of the running time of different algorithms solving the w-nearest neighbor search for fixed list size $|L| = 2^{0.05n}$.

SievingISD Instantiations. We study the asymptotics of SievingISD algorithms. We focus on the worst-case complexity in the full-distance decoding setting, the established measure for comparing the performance of decoding procedures. We establish the asymptotic worst-case complexity of the GJN SievingISD algorithm as $2^{0.117n}$. This shows that the algorithm improves on Prange's original ISD algorithm [29] but, as opposed to initial assumptions [17], falls behind the modern ISD algorithm by May, Meurer and Thomae (MMT) [24]. The new SievingISD instantiations based on RPC-OPT and HASH-OPT improve significantly by decreasing worst case complexity to $2^{0.1001n}$ and $2^{0.1007n}$ respectively. As illustrated in Fig. 2, this improvement is larger than the improvement made by any previous ISD algorithm over its predecessor.[1] Moreover, RPC-OPT and

---

[1] Due to the chosen precision, Fig. 2 shows equality between SISD-RPC-OPT and SISD-HASH-OPT. However, in higher precision and for fixed rate SISD-RPC-OPT outperforms SISD-HASH-OPT.

HASH-OPT improve drastically over the MMT algorithm and even slightly over the ISD algorithm by Becker, Joux, May, Meurer (BJMM) [2].

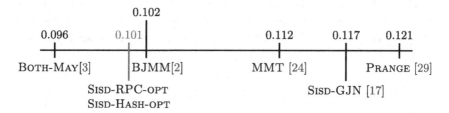

Fig. 2. Comparison of the asymptotic worst-case runtime exponent c in the full distance setting for different SievingISD and conventional ISD algorithms. Runtime is of the form 2^{cn}.

Note that the conventional ISD algorithm by Both and May [3], which incorporates the algorithmic refinements of more than a decade, still has the lowest runtime exponent. However, we show that the recently introduced framework of SievingISD allows for competitive instantiations, already coming close to the best conventional ISD procedures. Moreover, practical applications usually resort to the MMT algorithm [13,14] due to lower overheads. We propose a practical SievingISD variant SISD-HASH-OPT which has a strong potential to lead to more efficient implementations, as it improves significantly on the MMT runtime.

In practical scenarios, memory is often limited, which puts a burden on ISD algorithms, SievingISD as well as conventional ISD, which require a high amount of memory for their enumeration subroutines. However, those algorithms can reduce the enumeration effort and with it the memory requirements at the cost of an increased runtime, resulting in a better time-memory trade-off. In the extreme case of only a polynomial amount of memory being available, they interpolate to the running time of the original ISD algorithm by Prange. In Fig. 3, we compare the resulting time-memory trade-offs of SISD-HASH-OPT and SISD-RPC-OPT against those of SISD-GJN and BOTH-MAY. Additionally, we compare against two recently proposed improvements of the MMT and BJMM trade-offs due to Esser and Zweydinger [14], labeled EZ-MMT and EZ-BJMM respectively.

We observe that the new SievingISD instantiations outperform SISD-GJN for all memory parameters. Moreover, the SISD-RPC-OPT trade-off behavior comes close to the one of BOTH-MAY for moderate amounts of memory. In terms of practical instantiations, we find that SISD-HASH-OPT outperforms the recent trade-offs by Esser and Zweydinger for any memory larger than $2^{0.015n}$ (EZ-MMT) or $2^{0.035n}$ (EZ-BJMM), respectively, further supporting its practical potential.

On heuristics. Our LSF algorithms, which perform the nearest neighbor search, do not rely on any heuristics. We rely on heuristics only when we apply these algorithms to solve the decoding problem. Note that, in the application to ISD, the input vectors to a near neighbor routine are not independent since they are constructed as pairwise sums of (potentially non-independent) vectors in the previous

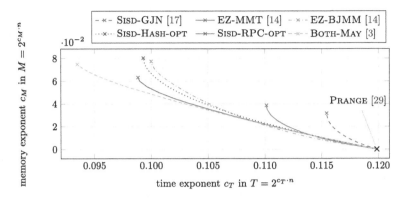

Fig. 3. Time-memory trade-off curves of SievingISD instantiations in comparison to conventional ISD trade-offs ($k = 0.5n$, full distance, i.e., $w \approx 0.11n$).

sieving step. Roughly speaking, we assume that the input list elements provided at any step behave like uniformly random and independent vectors from the sphere $S_w^n \subset \mathbb{F}_2$ (for a more formal statement see Heuristic 6). However, we show in extensive experiments that this building of iterative sums does not negatively influence the output list distribution. We note that the same situation occurs in lattices: LSF-based near neighbor search techniques enjoy provable correctness and runtime [1], but efficient lattice sieving algorithms that rely on these LSF routines are heuristic. Moreover, similar assumptions arose in other contexts [11, 22, 31], which have later been substantiated by the corresponding proofs [7, 23, 26].

1.2   Technical Overview

This section aims to provide an intuition and a simpler description of the algorithms following the LSF framework in the Hamming metric to solve the problem from Definition 1.1. Therefore, we omit some technical details (including Landau notations) for the sake of clarity. Rigorous descriptions and proofs are presented later in the main chapters.

The input is a list $L \subset S_w^n$ of uniform random and independent vectors and $|L| = N$. We call any pair $\mathbf{x}, \mathbf{y} \in L$ with $|\mathbf{x} + \mathbf{y}| = w$ a solution to the nearest neighbor search. Notice that $|\mathbf{x} \wedge \mathbf{y}| = w/2$ for $\mathbf{x}, \mathbf{y} \in S_w^n$, implies that $\mathbf{x}, \mathbf{y}$ is a solution to the near neighbor search,[2] where $\wedge$ is applied coordinate-wise. Therefore, we can also search for pairs with a predefined coordinate-wise AND.

The idea of LSF is to apply a certain relation to list vectors such that if two vectors collide under this relation, they are likely to be a solution. Specifically, in LSF we create a set $C_f \subset \mathbb{F}_2^n$ of *filters* or *centers*[3] $\mathbf{c}$ which divides the Hamming

---

[2] Precisely, those pairs are guaranteed to be of distance *smaller* or equal to w. However, the overwhelming fraction is of distance exactly w.

[3] We use those terms interchangeably and even sometimes use the term *filter centers* to refer to the elements from the set C_f.

space into (possibly overlapping) regions. Each element $\mathbf{x} \in L$ is assigned to a filter $\mathbf{c}$ if and only if $|\mathbf{x} \wedge \mathbf{c}| = \alpha$ for some integer α. List elements assigned to the same $\mathbf{c}$ form a *bucket*:

$$\text{Bucket}_{\alpha,\mathbf{c}} = \{\mathbf{x} \in L \colon |\mathbf{x} \wedge \mathbf{c}| = \alpha\}.$$

Note that if two uniform random vectors $\mathbf{x}, \mathbf{y}$ happen to be assigned to the same bucket, they have a certain (large) overlap in support (positions of 1's) with $\mathbf{c}$, so they are more likely to have overlap in support with each other. This principle lies at the heart of Algorithm 1, which is a simplified version of the more formal Algorithm 4, specified later. To ease the description of the algorithm we introduce $\mathcal{B}_{\alpha,\mathbf{x}}$ – the set of *valid filters* to which a fixed $\mathbf{x}$ was assigned.

$$\mathcal{B}_{\alpha,\mathbf{x}} := \{\mathbf{c} \in \mathcal{C}_f \colon |\mathbf{x} \wedge \mathbf{c}| = \alpha\}.$$

With that, the near neighbor search in Algorithm 1 consists of two steps: bucketing, which assigns each $\mathbf{x}$ to $\text{Bucket}_{\alpha,\mathbf{c}}$ for $\mathbf{c} \in \mathcal{B}_{\alpha,\mathbf{x}}$, and checking, which for each $\mathbf{x}$ searches for a matching element in $\text{Bucket}_{\alpha,\mathbf{c}}$ for all $\mathbf{c} \in \mathcal{B}_{\alpha,\mathbf{x}}$.

Algorithm 1: Nearest Neighbor Search (simplified)

Input : $L \subseteq \mathcal{S}_w^n$,
$\quad\quad\quad$ $\mathcal{C}_f$ set of filter centers,
$\quad\quad\quad$ α – parameter
Output: list L' containing pairs $\mathbf{x}, \mathbf{y} \in L^2$ with $|\mathbf{x} + \mathbf{y}| = w$

BUCKETING PHASE:
1 **for** $\mathbf{x} \in L$ **do**
2 $\quad$ Put $\mathbf{x}$ into $\text{Bucket}_{\alpha,\mathbf{c}} \; \forall c \in \mathcal{B}_{\alpha,\mathbf{x}}$

CHECKING PHASE:
3 **for** $\mathbf{x} \in L$ **do**
4 $\quad$ **for** $\mathbf{c} \in \mathcal{B}_{\alpha,\mathbf{x}}$ **do**
5 $\quad\quad$ **for** $\mathbf{y} \in \text{Bucket}_{\alpha,\mathbf{c}}$ **do**
6 $\quad\quad\quad$ **if** $|\mathbf{x} \wedge \mathbf{y}| = w/2$ **then**
7 $\quad\quad\quad\quad$ store $(\mathbf{x}, \mathbf{y})$ in L'

8 **return** L'

Notice that Algorithm 1 does not specify how $\mathcal{C}_f$ should be chosen, nor the parameter α that determines the bucketing phase. By specifying these two inputs, we obtain an instantiation of Algorithm 1. Interestingly, the recent GJN approach [17] can be obtained as an instantiation of Algorithm 1 as we detail below. However, as we show next, other choices of $\mathcal{C}_f$ and α lead to faster routines. In all the instantiations that we describe below, the following notations should be kept in mind

⬦ $N = |L|$ s.t. the expected number of solutions is N,
⬦ $F = |\mathcal{S}_\alpha^n| = \binom{n}{\alpha}$,
⬦ $P = |\mathcal{S}_\alpha^w| = \binom{w}{\alpha}$,
⬦ $D = \mathbb{E}\big[|\mathcal{B}_{\alpha,\mathbf{x}} \cap \mathcal{B}_{\alpha,\mathbf{y}}|\big]$ for some fixed pair $\mathbf{x}, \mathbf{y}$ s.t. $|\mathbf{x} + \mathbf{y}| = w$.

We describe the improvements in a progressive manner for didactic reasons starting with the GJN approach. In the later rigorous analysis in Sect. 4 we then skip certain, less effective variants. Whenever a variant has a counterpart in that section we specify the corresponding statement in parenthesis for fast reference.

Sieving by Guo-Johansson-Nguyen (Lemma 4.2). The main idea of the GJN sieving algorithm is to exploit the fact that for $\mathbf{x}, \mathbf{y} \in \mathcal{S}_w^n$ satisfying $|\mathbf{x} + \mathbf{y}| = w$, there exists a $\mathbf{c}$ of weight $w/2$ such that $|\mathbf{x} \wedge \mathbf{c}| = |\mathbf{y} \wedge \mathbf{c}| = w/2$. Moreover, given two vectors $\mathbf{x}, \mathbf{y}$ of weight w, the existence of such a $\mathbf{c}$ implies that $|\mathbf{x} + \mathbf{y}| \leq w$. The GJN algorithm enumerates all those $\mathbf{c}$ and assigns $\mathbf{x}$ to a filter $\mathbf{c}$ if $|\mathbf{x} \wedge \mathbf{c}| = w/2$. In the context of Algorithm 1 this means the set of filters contains all vectors on the Hamming sphere of radius $w/2$, i.e., $\mathcal{C}_f = \mathcal{S}_{w/2}^n$, and the bucketing parameter is chosen as $\alpha = w/2$. This implies that there are $|\mathcal{C}_f| = F = \binom{n}{w/2}$ filters, while any vector $\mathbf{x} \in L$ is stored within $P = \binom{w}{w/2}$ buckets.

Let us now consider the runtime of this instantiation. From the above, the cost for the bucketing phase amounts to NP. For the cost of the checking phase, we note that this parametrization gives (almost) no false positives and no false negatives. Put differently, a pair of vectors found in the same bucket is (almost always)[4] of distance w and each pair of distance w is found. Furthermore, those pairs are found exactly once, i.e., there are no duplicate pairs, since the valid $\mathbf{c}$ is unique as $\mathbf{c} = \mathbf{x} \wedge \mathbf{y}$. This implies that the cost of the checking phase is exactly the number of solutions, which, due to our choice of N, is N, giving time and memory

$$T = NP \quad \text{and} \quad M = T = NP.$$

Sieving with False Positives. While the GJN algorithm fits the LSF framework, this LSF instantiation is just too restrictive. In particular, efficient LSF instantiations try to balance the cost of the bucketing and checking phases to minimize the time complexity. Usually, those instantiations give rise to false positives, that is, pairs ending up in the same bucket, but not being as close as desired. Those are then simply discarded during the checking phase.

To implement this idea, we change the parameters of the filters from having weight $w/2$ to any smaller value. In particular, we choose the centers $\mathbf{c}$ now on the α-sphere for $\alpha < w/2$, i.e., $\mathcal{C}_f = \mathcal{S}_\alpha^n$. Note that this changes the amount of filters to $|\mathcal{C}_f| = F = \binom{n}{\alpha}$, while each element $\mathbf{x} \in L$ can be found in $P = \binom{w}{\alpha}$ buckets. Finding all centers associated with a vector $\mathbf{x}$, i.e., all $\mathbf{c} \in \mathcal{C}_f$ such that $|\mathbf{x} \wedge \mathbf{c}| = \alpha$ remains efficient, by simple subset enumeration.

Therefore, the bucketing phase has cost NP as before (now for updated P) and on expectation, there are NP/F elements in each bucket as the probability that $\mathbf{x}$ lands in a certain bucket is P/F. The checking phase iterates for every

---

[4] The *almost* is related to the fact that $|\mathbf{x} \wedge \mathbf{y}| = w/2$ implies $|\mathbf{x} + \mathbf{y}| \leq w$.

list element. over all elements in the associated buckets, which gives a total of $NP \cdot (NP/F) = (NP)^2/F$ checks. The overall complexity is summarized as

$$T = NP + (NP)^2/F \quad \text{and} \quad M = NP.$$

Note that this instantiation still does not allow for any false negative, meaning all pairs of distance w are detected. Each such pair is detected by exactly $\binom{w/2}{\alpha}$ many centers.

Sieving with False-Negatives. While it is optimal if every pair of distance w is detected exactly once, the previous instantiation detects any such pair $D = \binom{w/2}{\alpha}$ times. In the following, we therefore discard most of the bucket centers $\mathbf{c}$ randomly, only keeping a $1/D$ fraction of them. Then on expectation, every pair is still detected in one of the non-discarded buckets. This can be realized by defining the set $\mathcal{C}_f$ to only include those centers for which $\mathcal{H}(\mathbf{c}) = 0$ for some random function $\mathcal{H}: S_\alpha^n \to [D]$.

Since still every list element $\mathcal{H}$ has to be evaluated for all P possible centers to determine which centers are valid, the cost of the bucketing phase remains unchanged. However, since the expected amount of considered filters is now only $|\mathcal{C}_f| = F/D$, every element is found in only $P/D = \binom{w}{\alpha}/D$ different buckets, which reduces the cost of the checking phase and the memory consumption by a factor of D, resulting in

$$T = NP + (NP)^2/(DF) \quad \text{and} \quad M = NP/D. \tag{1}$$

Faster Sieving with False-Negatives (Theorem 4.3). Next, we mitigate the necessity of looping over all P possible centers to decide which centers belong to $\mathcal{C}_f$ by specially crafting $\mathcal{H}$. Precisely, we craft $\mathcal{H}$ such that for a given $\mathbf{x}$ the set of valid centers $\mathcal{B}_{\alpha,\mathbf{x}}$ (of expected size P/D) can be computed in time less than P. For our concrete construction, consider a random binary linear code $\mathcal{C}_\mathcal{H}$ (independent from the original input code) with co-dimension $r \approx \log D$. With this code, define the hash function as follows

$$\mathcal{H}(\mathbf{c}) = 0 \iff \mathbf{c} \in \mathcal{C}_\mathcal{H}.$$

In turn, we expect only $1/2^r \approx 1/D$ random centers to evaluate to zero under this hash function.

Determining a valid center boils down to finding weight-α codewords in a random binary code. It might appear that we came back to the original problem of finding small-weight codewords, but it turns out that the effective length of the code $\mathcal{C}_\mathcal{H}$ is much smaller than n, hence the search for small-weight codewords is easier. In particular, denoting by T_{decode} the running time of finding weight-α codewords in $\mathcal{C}_\mathcal{H}$, the overall complexity of this sieving subroutine is

$$T = N \cdot (P/D + T_{\mathsf{decode}}) + (NP)^2/(DF) \quad \text{and} \quad M = NP/D. \tag{2}$$

Later in our formal analysis, we use Prange's algorithm [29] to instantiate a decoder for $\mathcal{C}_\mathcal{H}$.

Repeating Faster Sieving with False-Negatives (Corollary 4.1). To improve the memory of the above algorithm, we do not consider all filters at once but rather repeat bucketing and checking phases for smaller sets of size $|\mathcal{C}_f| = F/(D \cdot R)$, for a repetition parameter R. Each run then uses less time and memory while after R repetitions we expect to find all the solutions. Concretely, we reduce the size of $|\mathcal{C}_f|$ by choosing smaller codes $\mathcal{C}_\mathcal{H}$, with co-dimension $r \approx \log(DR)$, for the construction of $\mathcal{H}$. Since in each run we consider only a $1/R$ fraction of the filters, the relevant expectations are reduced by that factor, leading to a time and memory complexity of

$$T = R \cdot \left(N \cdot (P/(DR) + T'_{\text{decode}}) + (NP)^2/(DRF) \right) \quad \text{and} \quad M = NP/(DR)$$
$$= N \cdot (P/D + R \cdot T'_{\text{decode}}) + (NP)^2/(DF) \quad \text{and} \quad M = NP/(DR). \qquad (3)$$

Here T'_{decode} denotes the time complexity to determine the set $\mathcal{B}_{\alpha,\mathbf{x}}$ for a given $\mathbf{x}$, corresponding to finding weight-α codewords in the, now smaller, code $\mathcal{C}_\mathcal{H}$. Note that interestingly this technique also allows decreasing the time complexity in comparison to Eq. (2), since by tweaking the code parameters we can ensure that over all executions we still reduce the overhead for finding valid centers, i.e., we ensure $R \cdot T'_{\text{decode}} < T_{\text{decode}}$.

Sieving with Random Product Codes (RPC). Finally, we describe a technique that does not introduce any asymptotic overhead for finding valid centers, i.e., we construct the set $\mathcal{B}_{\alpha,\mathbf{x}}$ for any element $\mathbf{x}$ in time $|\mathcal{B}_{\alpha,\mathbf{x}}|$. The way we achieve this is by using *random product spherical codes*. We construct $\mathcal{C}_f = \mathcal{C}_f^{(1)} \times \mathcal{C}_f^{(2)} \times \ldots \times \mathcal{C}_f^{(t)}$ as the Cartesian product of t sets (or non-linear codes) $\mathcal{C}_f^{(i)}$. The sets themselves contain a random selection of vectors of length n/t on the α/t-sphere, i.e., $\mathcal{C}_f^{(i)} \subset \mathcal{S}_{\alpha/t}^{n/t}$. The cardinality of each set is $|\mathcal{C}_f^{(i)}| = \sqrt[t]{F/D}$, such that overall $|\mathcal{C}_f| = F/D$ centers are considered.

A list element $\mathbf{x} = (\mathbf{x}_1, \ldots, \mathbf{x}_t)$ is now stored in the bucket associated with $\mathbf{c} = (\mathbf{c}_1, \ldots, \mathbf{c}_t)$. Interestingly, bucketing remains efficient because of the product structure. For an element $\mathbf{x} \in L$ first all partial centers $\mathbf{c}_1$ of $\mathcal{C}_f^{(1)}$ are found that can be extended to valid bucket center, i.e., those with $|\mathbf{x}_1 \wedge \mathbf{c}_1| = \alpha/t$. Then the algorithm iteratively proceeds with the next partial center. Once all partial centers have been found, those are again combined product-wise to determine all buckets in which $\mathbf{x}$ has to be stored. Using this strategy together with a careful selection of parameters allows to decrease the cost of the bucketing phase to NP/D. In total the complexities become

$$T = NP/D + (NP)^2/(DF) \quad \text{and} \quad M = NP/D.$$

Smaller RPCs with Repetitions. We again apply the technique of repeating the algorithm R times on smaller initial sets $|\mathcal{C}_f| = F/(DR)$. However, since in comparison to Eq. (3) there is no overhead in finding valid centers involved, we fix the repetition amount to $R = P/D$ which leads to an optimal memory complexity that is linear in the initial list size N, while maintaining the same time complexity, giving

$$T = NP/D + (NP)^2/(DF) \quad \text{and} \quad M = N.$$

Artifacts. The source code for our experiments on heuristics as well as the scripts used for the numerical optimization of the SievingISD instantiations are available at https://github.com/setinski/Sieving-For-Codes.

2   Preliminaries

We use non-bold letters for scalars, small bold letters for vectors, and capital bold letters for matrices. We denote by $\mathbb{F}_2$ the binary finite field and by $\mathbb{F}_2^n$ the corresponding vector space of dimension n. We use standard Landau notation, where $\tilde{\mathcal{O}}(\cdot)$ omits polylogarithmic factors. All logarithms are base 2. We define $H(\omega) := -\omega \log(\omega) - (1 - \omega) \log(1 - \omega)$ to be the binary entropy function. For a vector $\mathbf{x}$ we denote by $|\mathbf{x}| := |\{x_i \mid x_i \neq 0\}|$ the Hamming weight of $\mathbf{x}$, which counts the number of non-zero coordinates in $\mathbf{x}$. The sphere of radius w in $\mathbb{F}_2^n$ is defined as $\mathcal{S}_w^n := \{\mathbf{x} \in \mathbb{F}_2^n \mid |\mathbf{x}| = w\}$, which is of size $|\mathcal{S}_w^n| = \binom{n}{w}$.

Coding theory. A binary linear $[n, k]$ code $\mathcal{C}$ is a k-dimensional subspace of $\mathbb{F}_2^n$, where n is called its length and k its dimension. Such a code can be represented efficiently via a *parity-check matrix* $\mathbf{H} \in \mathbb{F}_2^{(n-k) \times n}$. The code $\mathcal{C}$ is then given as

$$\mathcal{C} := \{\mathbf{c} \in \mathbb{F}_2^n \mid \mathbf{Hc} = \mathbf{0}\}.$$

We make use of common transformations referred to as puncturing and shortening of codes.

Definition 2.1 (Code puncturing). *For a linear $[n, k]$ code $\mathcal{C}$ and a binary vector $\mathbf{x} \in \mathbb{F}_2^n$ with $|\mathbf{x}| = n'$ we define by $\pi_\mathbf{x} : \mathbf{c} \mapsto \mathbf{c} \wedge \mathbf{x}$ the puncturing function relative to the support of $\mathbf{x}$, and $\pi_\mathbf{x}(\mathcal{C})$ to be the corresponding punctured code.*

Note that if the support of $\mathbf{x}$ is an information set of $\mathcal{C}$, $\pi_\mathbf{x}$ is bijective (when implicitly restricted to $\mathcal{C}$), in which case we can define $\pi_\mathbf{x}^{-1}$ to return the unique pre-image in $\mathcal{C}$.

Definition 2.2 (Code shortening). *For a linear $[n, k]$ code $\mathcal{C}$ and a binary vector $\mathbf{x} \in \mathbb{F}_2^n$ with $|\mathbf{x}| = n'$ we define by $\sigma_\mathbf{x}(\mathcal{C}) := \{\mathbf{c} \in \mathcal{C} \mid \mathbf{c} \wedge \bar{\mathbf{x}} = \mathbf{0}\}$, the code shortened in the coordinates where $\mathbf{x}$ has support. Here $\bar{\mathbf{x}} := \mathbf{1} + \mathbf{x}$ is the bitwise complement of $\mathbf{x}$.*

A central problem in coding theory underlying the security of many code-based primitives is the syndrome decoding problem, defined as follows.

Definition 2.3 (Syndrome Decoding Problem (SDP)). *Let $\mathcal{C} \subseteq \mathbb{F}_2^n$ be a linear $[n, k]$ code given via a parity check matrix $\mathbf{H} \in \mathbb{F}_2^{(n-k) \times n}$. Given a weight $w \in \mathbb{N}$ and a syndrome $\mathbf{s} \in \mathbb{F}_2^{n-k}$, find a vector $\mathbf{e} \in \mathcal{S}_w^n$ satisfying $\mathbf{He} = \mathbf{s}$.*

In the remainder of this work, we study the problem of codeword finding instead, given in the following definition.

Definition 2.4 (Codeword Finding Problem (CFP)). *Let $\mathcal{C} \subseteq \mathbb{F}_2^n$ be a linear $[n, k]$ code. Given a fixed weight $w \in \mathbb{N}$, find a vector $\mathbf{e} \in \mathcal{S}_n^w \cap \mathcal{C}$.*

We consider w to be linear in n, concretely for our asymptotic results, we choose w to match the Gilbert-Varshamov bound, i.e., $w = H^{-1}(1-k/n)n$, where $H^{-1}(\cdot)$ is the inverse of the binary entropy function on the interval $[0, 0.5]$. This guarantees that for both the SDP as well as the CFP the solution is unique. Note that the two problems are equivalent under weight, length, and dimension preserving[5] polynomial reductions, implying that our results translate one-to-one to the SDP case. Observe that any solution $\mathbf{e}$ to codeword finding satisfies $\mathbf{H}\mathbf{e} = 0$ and, hence, forms a solution to SDP for syndrome $\mathbf{s} = 0$. Now, any SDP instance with solution $\mathbf{e}'$ defined by $\mathbf{H}, \mathbf{s}$ can be transformed into an instance $(\mathbf{H}', \mathbf{s}' = 0)$, by letting $\mathbf{H}' = (\mathbf{H} \mid \mathbf{s})$. This forms a CFP instance with increased weight $w + 1$, length $n + 1$, and solution $(\mathbf{e}', 1)$.

To solve those problems, ISD algorithms can be applied. The following lemma states the complexity of the original ISD algorithm by Prange to find all codewords of weight w in a given code.

Lemma 2.1 (Prange, [29]). *Given a binary linear $[n, k]$ code $\mathcal{C}$. Then for $w \leq n - k$, Prange's algorithm returns all weight w codewords in $\mathcal{C}$ in time $T = \tilde{\mathcal{O}}\left(\binom{n}{w}/\binom{n-k}{w}\right)$ and memory $M = \tilde{\mathcal{O}}(1)$.*

3   The Information Set Decoding (ISD) Framework

The information set decoding (ISD) framework consists of the following 3 steps. The first step samples $\mathbf{x} \in \mathcal{S}_{n'}^n$ and verifies if the dimension of the punctured code $\pi_{\mathbf{x}}(\mathcal{C})$ is equal to k. If that is the case, the support of $\mathbf{x}$ contains an information set of $\mathcal{C}$, and the algorithm continues.[6] In the second step, the algorithm computes N weight w' codewords of the punctured code $\pi_{\mathbf{x}}(\mathcal{C})$ using a sieving oracle. In the third and final step, the algorithm checks if any of these codewords (from the punctured code) yields a codeword of weight w in the original code when lifted using $\pi_{\mathbf{x}}^{-1}$. The procedure is detailed in Algorithm 2.

Theorem 3.1 (Complexity of SievingISD). *Let $\mathcal{C}$ be an $[n, k]$ code and $w \leq H^{-1}(1 - k/n)n$ be an integer. Let T_{O} and M_{O} be the expected time and the expected memory complexities of the oracle O used in Algorithm 2. Then Algorithm 2 returns a weight-w codeword in $\mathcal{C}$, if such exists, in expected time and memory*

$$T = \tilde{\mathcal{O}}\left((p_1 p_2)^{-1} \cdot T_{\mathsf{O}}\right) \quad and \quad M = M_{\mathsf{O}},$$

---

[5] Precisely, either length and weight or dimension increase by one depending on the chosen reduction.

[6] This happens at least with constant probability [6] so it will be omitted from the asymptotic analysis of the running time of the algorithm.

Algorithm 2: SievingISD

Input : An $[n, k]$ code $\mathcal{C}$, parameters w and $n' > k$. An oracle O returning N distinct uniformly random weight-w' codewords in a given code.

Output: $\mathbf{e} \in \mathcal{C}$ such that $|\mathbf{e}| = w$

1 **repeat**

2 | Choose random $\mathbf{x} \in \mathbb{F}_2^n$ with $|\mathbf{x}| = n'$ and $\dim(\pi_\mathbf{x}(\mathcal{C})) = k$

3 | $L \leftarrow \mathrm{O}(\pi_\mathbf{x}(\mathcal{C}), w')$

4 | **if** $\exists\, \mathbf{y} \in L \colon |\pi_\mathbf{x}^{-1}(\mathbf{y})| = w$ **then**

5 | | **return** $\pi_\mathbf{x}^{-1}(\mathbf{y})$

---

for any n', w' ensuring $p_2 \leq 1$, where

$$p_1 := \binom{n'}{w'}\binom{n - n'}{w - w'} \Big/ \binom{n}{w} \quad and \quad p_2 := N \cdot 2^{n'-k} \Big/ \binom{n'}{w'}.$$

Proof. Note that $\mathbf{x}$ is chosen randomly and as long as $\mathbf{y}' := \pi_\mathbf{x}(\mathbf{e}) = w'$, we have $\mathbf{y}' \in \pi_\mathbf{x}(\mathcal{C}) \cap \mathcal{S}_{w'}^{n'}$, which implies that $\mathbf{y}'$ can be contained in L. Further, as long as $\dim(\pi_\mathbf{x}(\mathcal{C})) = k$, $\pi_\mathbf{x}$ is bijective which reveals $\mathbf{e} = \pi_\mathbf{x}^{-1}(\mathbf{y}')$, once $\mathbf{y}'$ is found.

Regarding the success probability of the algorithm, first, it must be the case that $\mathbf{e}$ has weight w' when projected onto the support of $\mathbf{x}$, that is $|\mathbf{e} \wedge \mathbf{x}| = w'$. This happens with probability

$$p_1 = \binom{n'}{w'}\binom{n - n'}{w - w'} \Big/ \binom{n}{w}$$

If this first condition is fulfilled, we need to consider whether $\mathbf{e} \wedge \mathbf{x}$ is included in L. Note that there are on expectation $\binom{n'}{w'}/2^{n'-k}$ codewords of weight w' in $\pi_\mathbf{x}(\mathcal{C})$. The probability that $\mathbf{e} \wedge \mathbf{x}$ is included in a list of size N sampled uniformly at random from the set of small codewords is therefore

$$p_2 = 1 - \left(1 - 2^{n'-k} \Big/ \binom{n'}{w'}\right)^N = \Theta\left(N \cdot 2^{n'-k} \Big/ \binom{n'}{w'}\right). \tag{4}$$

Here, the last equality follows from the fact that for the oracle to be feasible it must hold

$$N \leq \binom{n'}{w'} \cdot 2^{k-n'}, \tag{C 1}$$

i.e., there must exist N distinct codwords of weight w' in $\pi_\mathbf{x}(\mathcal{C})$. Note that this inequality translates to $p_2 \leq 1$.

The time complexity of the algorithm is the time per iteration divided by the success probability. We already saw that the success probability is $p_1 p_2$, while one iteration is dominated by the time it takes to query the oracle, which is T_O, resulting in the claimed running time. Besides the list L, the algorithm stores only elements of polynomial size, therefore the memory complexity is equal to the memory complexity of the oracle, which is at least N. □

The Sieving Subroutine. Algorithm 2 has access to an oracle O returning N distinct weight-w' codewords for a given code. In our work, the oracle is instantiated using the *sieving* routine detailed in Algorithm 3.

Algorithm 3: O: Sieving

Input   : $[n', k]$-code $\mathcal{C}'$, N and w'.
Output: set $L = \{\mathbf{e} \in \mathcal{C}' : |\mathbf{e}| = w'\}$ with $|L| = N$

1 Choose a tower of codes $\mathbb{F}_2^{n'} = \mathcal{C}_0 \subset \mathcal{C}_1 \subset \cdots \subset \mathcal{C}_{n'-k} = \mathcal{C}'$, with dimension decrements of 1.

2 Choose N random distinct vectors of $\mathbb{F}_2^{n'}$ of weight w' as initial set L

3 **for** $i = 1$ *to* $n' - k$ **do**

4 | $L \leftarrow \{\mathbf{x} + \mathbf{y} \text{ s.t. } |\mathbf{x} + \mathbf{y}| = w' \text{ and } (\mathbf{x}, \mathbf{y}) \in L^2\} \cap \mathcal{C}_i$

5 | Discard some elements if $|L| > N$

6 Return L

This routine starts with an arbitrary list of small-weight words of length n', i.e., a list $L \subset \mathbb{F}_2^{n'} = \mathcal{C}_0$. Note that choosing small-weight words from $\mathcal{C}_0$ is efficient. The algorithm proceeds iteratively using a tower of codes $\mathcal{C}_0 \subset \mathcal{C}_1 \subset \ldots \subset \mathcal{C}_{n'-k} = \mathcal{C}'$. In each iteration i a new list of short codewords belonging to code $\mathcal{C}_i$ is constructed from sums of elements of the current list; until in iteration $n' - k$ the constructed list finally contains codewords from $\mathcal{C}' = \mathcal{C}_{n'-k}$. A possible choice for the tower of codes is, for example, $\mathcal{C}_i$'s whose parity-check matrix consists of the first i rows of the parity-check matrix from $\mathcal{C}'$.

For constructing the list in iteration i we first apply a *nearest neighbor* subroutine, which finds all words of weight w' that can be constructed via pairwise sums from the current list; after which we filter the list for codewords belonging to the current code $\mathcal{C}_i$.

Maintaining the list size. Note that, since all used codes $\mathcal{C}_i$ are linear and two subsequent codes' dimension differs by one, the filtering discards on expectation half of the constructed elements. Through all iterations, we aim at maintaining a steady list size of N, by discarding elements if necessary. Therefore, the list L must be large enough so that at least N many pairs $(\mathbf{x}, \mathbf{y}) \in L^2$ sum to short vectors. Accounting for a loss of half of the vectors, since on expectation $\#\mathcal{C}_i/\#\mathcal{C}_{i+1} = 2$, and for the fact that we take every pair twice, this requires

$$N \geq 4 \cdot \frac{\binom{n'}{w'}}{\binom{w'}{w'/2}\binom{n'-w'}{w'/2}}. \tag{C 2}$$

In the following, we choose N up to a constant factor equal to this lower bound.

Finding Short Sums. In the application of the nearest neighbor routine to ISD we rely on a certain heuristic, common to the sieving setting. Informally, we treat elements contained in the lists in each iteration as independently and uniformly sampled from the w'-sphere $\mathcal{S}_{w'}^{n'}$. This allows us to study algorithms that solve the w-*nearest neighbor search* to construct L. This problem is defined as follows.

Definition 3.1 (w-Nearest Neighbor Search). *Given a list of uniformly and independently distributed vectors $L \subset \mathcal{S}_w^n$ of weight w with $|L| = N$, find a $(1 - o(1))$-fraction of pairs $\mathbf{x}, \mathbf{y} \in L^2$ s.t. $|\mathbf{x} + \mathbf{y}| = w$. We refer to this problem as* $\mathtt{NNS}(N, n, w)$ *while we refer to (L, n, w) as an instance of the problem.*

More precisely, our heuristic assumption is that the time and memory complexity of algorithms solving the w-nearest neighbor search is only mildly affected by the dependencies between list elements if constructed as pairwise sums over multiple iterations as in Algorithm 3. We formalize this in the following heuristic.

Binary-Sieve Heuristic. *Let $n' \in \mathbb{N}$, κ, ω, λ be positive constants. Let $k = \kappa n'$, $w' = \omega n'$ and $|L| = N = 2^{\lambda n'}$ satisfying Constraints Eq. (C 1) and Eq. (C 2). Then, we assume that:*

1. *The running time and memory complexity of any algorithm applied to the nearest neighbor search instance (L, n', w') for L from Line 4 of Algorithm 3 is at most affected by a factor of $2^{o(n')}$ in comparison to L being sampled uniformly and independently from $\mathcal{S}_{w'}^{n'}$.*
2. *The probability of any element being present in the finally returned list L in Line 6 of Algorithm 3 is up to a $2^{o(n')}$ factor equal to the probability that $L \subset C' \cap \mathcal{S}_{w'}^{n'}$ is drawn uniformly at random. Formally, $\Pr\left[\mathbf{c} \in L \mid \mathbf{c} \in C' \cap \mathcal{S}_{w'}^{n'}\right] \geq p_2/2^{o(n')}$ for p_2 from Eq. (4).*

The first part of the heuristic ensures that we can use algorithms solving the w-nearest neighbor search to construct the list L in each iteration. The second part is necessary to ensure that the success probability (see Eq. (4)) of Algorithm 2 is not significantly impacted and the runtime statement of Theorem 3.1 remains valid when instantiating the oracle with Algorithm 3.

Note that an analogous heuristic is used by lattice sieving algorithms [1, Section 7]. Also in the binary case, heuristics about the mild effect of stochastic dependencies from iterative sums are commonly used as, for example, in the context of Learning Parity with Noise (LPN) [11,22], the generalized birthday problem (GBP) [31] or even by other ISD algorithms [2,24,25]. Those heuristics have been put to the test experimentally [11,13] and most of them have been proven in later works [7,23,26]. In addition, we provide experiments verifying the heuristic in our precise context in the full version of the paper given in [9].

Relying on this heuristic, the running time of the oracle (Algorithm 3) is asymptotically equal to the time required to solve the w-nearest neighbor search. We summarize this in the following theorem.

Theorem 3.2 (Complexity of the Sieving Oracle). *Let $n' \in \mathbb{N}$, κ, ω, λ be positive constants. Let $k = \kappa n'$, $w' = \omega n'$ and $|L| = N = 2^{\lambda n'}$ satisfying Constraints Eq. (C 1) and Eq. (C 2). Further, let T_{NNS} and M_{NNS} be the time* *and memory complexities to solve the* NNS(N, n', w'). *Then, under the* Binary-Sieve Heuristic *the time and memory complexity of Algorithm 3 is*

$$T_O = \tilde{\mathcal{O}}(T_{\text{NNS}}) \quad and \quad M_O = \tilde{\mathcal{O}}(M_{\text{NNS}}).$$

Proof. Note that N is exponential in n'. Therefore, the running time of Algorithm 3 is dominated by the construction of the list in Line 4. Under the Binary-Sieve Heuristic the running time to construct this list is $\tilde{\mathcal{O}}(T_{\text{NNS}})$ and the memory needed is $\tilde{\mathcal{O}}(M_{\text{NNS}})$. $\qquad\square$

Theorem 3.2 motivates the further study of algorithms to solve the w-nearest neighbor search problem in the following section. Later in Sect. 5 we study the performance of SievingISD, i.e., Algorithm 2 in combination with Algorithm 3, instantiated using those nearest neighbor search routines.

4   Nearest Neighbor Search in the Hamming Metric

In this section, we present different algorithms solving the w-near neighbor search from Definition 3.1. We first recall the general locality-sensitive hashing (LSH) or locality-sensitive filter (LSF) framework for near neighbor search - a framework that forms the basis for many of the best known algorithms to find near neighbors [1,12,25]. We then show that the recently presented algorithm by Guo-Johansson-Nguyen [17] already falls into this framework. We proceed by presenting and analyzing different improvements.

Let us first define a set $\mathcal{C}_f \subset \mathbb{F}_2^n$ of filter vectors $\mathbf{c}$ that divide the Hamming space into regions. Concretely, for an integer α let

$$\text{Region}_{\mathbf{c},\alpha} = \{\mathbf{x} \in \mathbb{F}_2^n \ : \ |\mathbf{x} \wedge \mathbf{c}| = \alpha\}. \tag{5}$$

Notice that for a sufficiently large α, two vectors that lie in the same region have large overlapping support with a fixed vector $\mathbf{c}$, hence their sum has a high chance of being of small Hamming weight.

A *bucket* associated to center $\mathbf{c}$ is defined as $\text{Bucket}_{\mathbf{c},\alpha} = \text{Region}_{\mathbf{c},\alpha} \cap L$. Since the role of α does not change, we conveniently write $\text{Bucket}_{\mathbf{c}}$ and $\text{Region}_{\mathbf{c}}$ in the following. The idea of LSH/F is to assign all vectors from L to $\text{Bucket}_{\mathbf{c}}, \forall \mathbf{c} \in \mathcal{C}_f$. Therefore, for all $\mathbf{x} \in L$ we first find all *valid filters* defined as the set

$$\mathcal{B}_{\alpha,\mathbf{x}} := \{\mathbf{c} \in \mathcal{C}_f \colon |\mathbf{x} \wedge \mathbf{c}| = \alpha\}.$$

For a fixed $\mathbf{x}$ the procedure determining and returning those valid filters is called ValidFilters in Algorithm 4. We denote the step of assigning all elements to each of its buckets as *bucketing phase*. Subsequently, the search for close pairs is carried out only within each $\text{Bucket}_{\mathbf{c}}$, which we refer to as *checking phase*.

Complexity of Algorithm 4. Let us give a general lemma stating the complexity and correctness of Algorithm 4 to which we refer in our later analyses.

Algorithm 4: Nearest Neighbor Search

Input : NNS(L, n, w) instance where $L \subseteq \mathcal{S}_w^n$, description of the set $\mathcal{C}_f$ of
bucket centers $\mathbf{c}$, bucketing parameter α

Output: list L' containing pairs $\mathbf{x}, \mathbf{y} \in L^2$ with $|\mathbf{x} + \mathbf{y}| = w$

1 BUCKETING PHASE:
2 **for** $\mathbf{x} \in L$ **do**
3   **for** $\mathbf{c} \in \mathtt{ValidFilters}(\mathcal{C}_f, \mathbf{x}, \alpha)$ **do**
4   store $\mathbf{x}$ in Bucket$_\mathbf{c}$

5 CHECKING PHASE:
6 $L' = \emptyset$
7 **for** $\mathbf{x} \in L$ **do**
8   **for** $\mathbf{c} \in \mathtt{ValidFilters}(\mathcal{C}_f, \mathbf{x}, \alpha)$ **do**
9   **for** $\mathbf{y} \in$ Bucket$_\mathbf{c}$ **do**
10   **if** $|\mathbf{x} \wedge \mathbf{y}| = w/2$ **then**
11   store $(\mathbf{x}, \mathbf{y})$ in L'

12 **return** L'

Lemma 4.1 (Complexity of Algorithm 4). *Let* $\mathbf{x}, \mathbf{y}$ *be s.t.* $|\mathbf{x}| = |\mathbf{y}| = |\mathbf{x} + \mathbf{y}| = w$ *and* $T_{\mathtt{ValidFilters}}$ *denote the time to compute the set* $\mathcal{B}_{\alpha, \mathbf{x}}$ *for any given* $\mathbf{x} \in L$. *Then Algorithm 4 returns a list containing* $\mathbf{x}, \mathbf{y}$ *in expected time* T *and expected memory* M, *where*

$$T = \tilde{\mathcal{O}}\left(N \cdot \left(T_{\mathtt{ValidFilters}} + \mathbb{E}\big[|\mathcal{B}_{\alpha, \mathbf{x}}|\big] \cdot \mathbb{E}\big[|\text{Bucket}_\mathbf{c}|\big]\right)\right) \; and$$

$$M = \tilde{\mathcal{O}}\left(N \cdot \mathbb{E}\big[|\mathcal{B}_{\alpha, \mathbf{x}}|\big]\right)$$

with probability $q := \Pr\left[\exists \mathbf{c} \in \mathcal{C}_f : \mathbf{c} \in \mathcal{B}_{\alpha, \mathbf{x}} \cap \mathbf{c} \in \mathcal{B}_{\alpha, \mathbf{y}}\right]$ *whenever* $\mathbb{E}\big[|\mathcal{B}_{\alpha, \mathbf{x}}|\big] \geq 1$.

Proof. Note that the algorithm recovers a w-close pair $\mathbf{x}, \mathbf{y}$ whenever there is a $\mathbf{c} \in \mathcal{C}_f$ for which $\mathbf{c}$ is a valid filter for both, $\mathbf{x}$ and $\mathbf{y}$, or more formally if $\exists \mathbf{c} \in \mathcal{C}_f : \mathbf{c} \in \mathcal{B}_{\alpha, \mathbf{x}}$ and $\mathbf{c} \in \mathcal{B}_{\alpha, \mathbf{y}}$. Since, in that case, $\mathbf{x}$ is stored in Bucket$_\mathbf{c}$ in the bucketing phase, while $\mathbf{y}$ checks Bucket$_\mathbf{c}$ in the checking phase for close pairs.

The running time of the algorithm is dominated by the checking phase. The bucketing can be performed in the expected time

$$T_{\text{Bucket}} = \tilde{\mathcal{O}}\left(N \cdot T_{\mathtt{ValidFilters}}\right),$$

where $T_{\mathtt{ValidFilters}}$ is the expected time to retrieve the set $\mathcal{B}_{\alpha, \mathbf{x}}$ for a fixed $\mathbf{x}$ via the $\mathtt{ValidFilters}$ function. The checking phase performs the same identification of valid centers. Additionally, for all returned valid centers it explores the corresponding bucket to find w-close pairs. Note that this exploration can be performed in time linear in the size of the bucket. Hence, we have

$$T_{\text{Check}} = T_{\text{Bucket}} + \tilde{\mathcal{O}}\left(N \cdot \mathbb{E}\big[|\mathcal{B}_{\alpha, \mathbf{x}}|\big] \cdot \mathbb{E}\big[|\text{Bucket}_\mathbf{c}|\big]\right).$$

Note that the expected bucket size is given by

$$\mathbb{E}\big[|\text{Bucket}_{\mathbf{c}}|\big] = \frac{N \cdot \mathbb{E}\big[|\mathcal{B}_{\alpha,\mathbf{x}}|\big]}{|\mathcal{C}_{\mathsf{f}}|}, \tag{6}$$

since there are expected $N \cdot \mathbb{E}\big[||\mathcal{B}_{\alpha,\mathbf{x}}||\big]$ elements stored among all buckets and the probability of any of those elements being located in a specific bucket is $1/|\mathcal{C}_{\mathsf{f}}|$. The total running time of Algorithm 4 therefore amounts to

$$T = T_{\text{Bucket}} + T_{\text{Check}} = \tilde{\mathcal{O}}\big(N \cdot (T_{\texttt{ValidFilters}} + \mathbb{E}\big[|\mathcal{B}_{\alpha,\mathbf{x}}|\big] \cdot \mathbb{E}\big[|\text{Bucket}_{\mathbf{c}}|\big])\big),$$

while the expected memory is given by

$$M = \tilde{\mathcal{O}}\big(N\big(1 + \mathbb{E}\big[|\mathcal{B}_{\alpha,\mathbf{x}}|\big]\big)\big) = \tilde{\mathcal{O}}\big(N \cdot \mathbb{E}\big[|\mathcal{B}_{\alpha,\mathbf{x}}|\big]\big),$$

as long as $\mathbb{E}\big[|\mathcal{B}_{\alpha,\mathbf{x}}|\big] \geq 1$. $\qquad\qquad\square$

The main differences of all following instantiations of Algorithm 4 lies in the precise choice of $\mathcal{C}_{\mathsf{f}}$ and the definition of the `ValidFilters` function.

The GJN Algorithm. We first show that the GJN algorithm already falls into the framework of Algorithm 4 and establish its asymptotic complexity for a later classification of our improvements. The main idea of the GJN nearest neighbor algorithm is to exploit the fact that for $\mathbf{x}, \mathbf{y}$ satisfying $|\mathbf{x}| = |\mathbf{y}| = w$ and $|\mathbf{x} + \mathbf{y}| = w$, there exists a $\mathbf{c}$ of weight $w/2$ such that $|\mathbf{x} \wedge \mathbf{c}| = |\mathbf{y} \wedge \mathbf{c}| = w/2$. Moreover, given two vectors $\mathbf{x}, \mathbf{y}$ of weight w, the existence of such a $\mathbf{c}$ implies that $|\mathbf{x} + \mathbf{y}| \leq w$.

In the context of Algorithm 4 the GJN algorithm chooses $\mathcal{C}_{\mathsf{f}} = \mathcal{S}^n_{w/2}$ and $\alpha = w/2$. For a given $\mathbf{x}$ the valid centers $\mathbf{c}$ are found by simple enumeration of all weight $w/2$ words restricted to the support of $\mathbf{x}$. That is the function `ValidFilters` is defined as

$$\texttt{ValidFilters}(\mathcal{S}^n_{w/2}, \mathbf{x}, w/2) \quad \text{returns} \quad \mathcal{B}_{\mathcal{S}^n_{w/2}, w/2, \mathbf{x}} := \{\mathbf{c} \in \mathcal{S}^n_{w/2} : |\mathbf{x} \wedge \mathbf{c}| = w/2\}. \tag{7}$$

Note that this set can be efficiently enumerated in time $|\mathcal{B}_{\mathcal{S}^n_{w/2}, w/2, \mathbf{x}}| = \binom{w}{w/2}$.

Lemma 4.2 (LSF via GJN). *Let $n, w \in \mathbb{N}$, $w < n$. Further, let $\mathcal{C}_{\mathsf{f}} := \mathcal{S}^n_{w/2}$, $\alpha := w/2$ and `ValidFilters` as defined in (7). Then Algorithm 4 solves the $\text{NNS}(N, n, w)$ using expected time T and expected memory M, where*

$$T = M = \tilde{\mathcal{O}}\left(N \cdot \binom{w}{w/2}\right).$$

Proof. Note that for any w-close pair $\mathbf{x}, \mathbf{y}$ with $|\mathbf{x}| = |\mathbf{y}| = w$, it holds that $\mathbf{c}^* = \mathbf{x} \wedge \mathbf{y}$ is of weight $|\mathbf{c}^*| = w/2$. Also it implies $|\mathbf{x} \wedge \mathbf{c}^*| = |\mathbf{y} \wedge \mathbf{c}^*| = w/2$. Therefore we have $\mathbf{c}^* \in \mathcal{B}_{\mathcal{S}^n_{w/2}, w/2, \mathbf{x}}$ as well as $\mathbf{c}^* \in \mathcal{B}_{\mathcal{S}^n_{w/2}, w/2, \mathbf{y}}$ implying that any such pair $\mathbf{x}, \mathbf{y}$, is recovered with probability $q = 1$ (compare to Lemma 4.1). The `ValidFilters` function can be computed in time

$$T_{\texttt{ValidFilters}} = \tilde{\mathcal{O}}\left(|\mathcal{B}_{\mathcal{S}^n_{w/2}, w/2, \mathbf{x}}|\right) = \tilde{\mathcal{O}}\left(\binom{w}{w/2}\right),$$

while the expected bucket size is given (compare to Eq. (6)) as

$$\mathbb{E}\big[|\mathrm{Bucket}_{\mathbf{c}}|\big] = \frac{N \cdot \mathbb{E}\big[|\mathcal{B}_{\mathcal{S}^n_{w/2}, w/2, \mathbf{x}}|\big]}{|\mathcal{S}^n_{w/2}|} = \frac{N \cdot \binom{w}{w/2}}{\binom{n}{w}}.$$

The expected time complexity therefore becomes (see Lemma 4.1)

$$T = \tilde{\mathcal{O}}\left(N\binom{w}{w/2} \cdot \left(1 + \frac{\binom{w}{w/2}}{\binom{n}{w}}\right)\right) = \tilde{\mathcal{O}}\left(N\binom{w}{w/2}\right),$$

while the expected memory amounts to the same value, since $M = \tilde{\mathcal{O}}\left(N \cdot \mathbb{E}\big[|\mathcal{B}_{\mathcal{S}^n_{w/2}, w/2, \mathbf{x}}|\big]\right) = \tilde{\mathcal{O}}\left(N\binom{w}{w/2}\right)$. □

Improved Instantiations of the Framework. While the GJN algorithm chooses the set $\mathcal{C}_{\mathsf{f}} = \mathcal{S}^n_{w/2}$ to be all vectors on the $w/2$-sphere, our following algorithms choose $\mathcal{C}_{\mathsf{f}} \subset \mathcal{S}^n_v$ with $v < w/2$. Note that choosing the subset $\mathcal{C}_{\mathsf{f}}$ too small might lead to false negatives, i.e., close pairs that never fall into the same bucket and, hence, remain undetected. On the other hand, we aim at choosing $\mathcal{C}_{\mathsf{f}}$ of minimal size, while still detecting all pairs, to optimize the running time.

To determine this lower bound on $|\mathcal{C}_{\mathsf{f}}|$, we analyze the number of centers on the v-sphere that can identify a given close pair, which we call D in the following (analogous to Sect. 1.2). We then show that a $1/D$ fraction of all centers, i.e. $|\mathcal{C}_{\mathsf{f}}| \geq |\mathcal{S}^n_v|/D$, is sufficient to identify all pairs.

Aligned with the lattice sieving literature, our analysis uses a geometric interpretation of the algorithm. Therefore note that the previously defined regions (compare to Eq. (5)) can also be interpreted as half-spaces $\mathcal{H}_{\mathbf{c},v} := \mathrm{Region}_{\mathbf{c},v} = \{\mathbf{x} \in \mathbb{F}^n_2 : |\mathbf{x} \wedge \mathbf{c}| = \alpha\}$. Moreover, let us define a *spherical cap* as the intersection of the sphere with such a half-space.

Definition 4.1 (Spherical cap). *For $\mathbf{c} \in \mathcal{S}^n_w$, integers $0 \leq \alpha, w \leq n$, a spherical cap is defined by $\mathcal{C}_{\mathbf{c},w,\alpha} = \mathcal{S}^n_w \cap \mathcal{H}_{\mathbf{c},\alpha} = \{\mathbf{x} \in \mathcal{S}^n_w : |\mathbf{x} \wedge \mathbf{c}| = \alpha\}$.*

The volume of a cap is defined as the number of elements included in the cap and can be computed as follows.

Theorem 4.1 (Cap volume). *Fix integers $0 \leq \alpha \leq w \leq n$ and fix $\mathbf{c} \in \mathcal{S}^n_v$. Then the volume of $\mathcal{C}_{\mathbf{c},w,\alpha}$ is $\mathscr{C}^n_{v,w,\alpha} := \mathrm{Vol}(\mathcal{C}_{\mathbf{c},w,\alpha}) = \binom{v}{\alpha} \cdot \binom{n-v}{w-\alpha}$.*

Proof. The first binomial in the product defines the number of possible placements of α-many 1's in $\mathbf{x} \in \mathcal{C}_{\mathbf{c},w,\alpha}$ that we should put in the support of $\mathbf{c}$. The second binomial defines the number of possible placements of the remaining $(w - \alpha)$-many 1's of $\mathbf{x}$ in the 0-positions of $\mathbf{c}$. □

Note that the spherical cap $C_{\mathbf{c},w,\alpha}$ includes all values $\mathbf{x}$ on the w-sphere which are associated with the bucket center $\mathbf{c}$. In turn $C_{\mathbf{x},v,\alpha} = \mathcal{B}_{\mathcal{S}_v^n,\alpha,\mathbf{x}}$ describes the set of bucket centers $\mathbf{c}$ on the v-sphere to which a fixed element $\mathbf{x}$ is associated. Therefore, the set of bucket centers that can identify a fixed pair of distance w, is formed as the intersection of two spherical caps, which we call a *spherical wedge* in the following.

Definition 4.2 (Spherical wedge). *Fix integers $0 \le \alpha, v \le n$. For $\mathbf{x}, \mathbf{y} \in \mathbb{F}_2^n$ of weight w a (spherical) wedge is defined as*

$$\mathcal{W}_{\mathbf{x},\mathbf{y},v,\alpha}^n = C_{\mathbf{x},v,\alpha} \cap C_{\mathbf{y},v,\alpha} = \mathcal{S}_v^n \cap \mathcal{H}_{\mathbf{x},\alpha} \cap \mathcal{H}_{\mathbf{y},\alpha} = \{\mathbf{c} \in \mathcal{S}_v^n : |\mathbf{c} \wedge \mathbf{x}| = |\mathbf{c} \wedge \mathbf{y}| = \alpha\}.$$

Now the number of centers able to identify a fixed pair $\mathbf{x}, \mathbf{y}$ is the number of elements in $\mathcal{W}_{\mathbf{x},\mathbf{y},v,\alpha}^n$, or its volume $\mathrm{Vol}(\mathcal{W}_{\mathbf{x},\mathbf{y},v,\alpha}^n)$. The following lemma specifies this volume for a fixed pair $\mathbf{x}, \mathbf{y}$ of distance w.

Theorem 4.2 (Wedge volume). *Fix integers $0 \le \alpha, v \le n$. For $\mathbf{x}, \mathbf{y} \in \mathbb{F}_2^n$ of weight w s.t. $|\mathbf{x} + \mathbf{y}| = w$ it holds that*

$$\mathscr{W}_{w,v,\alpha}^n := \mathrm{Vol}(\mathcal{W}_{\mathbf{x},\mathbf{y},v,\alpha}^n) = \sum_{e=0}^{w/2} \binom{w/2}{e} \binom{w/2}{\alpha - e}^2 \binom{n - 3w/2}{v - 2\alpha + e}$$

Proof. The statement of the theorem follows from counting the possibilities to place the v ones in $\mathbf{c}$ on the positions where either $\mathbf{x}$ or $\mathbf{y}$ have support, none of them has support or both of them have support.

Concretely, denote the number of 1-entries of $\mathbf{c}$ on the positions where $\mathbf{x}$ and $\mathbf{y}$ have support by e. We have $e \in [0, w/2]$, since $|\mathbf{x} \wedge \mathbf{y}| = w/2$. Since $\mathbf{c} \in \mathcal{W}_{\mathbf{x},\mathbf{y},v,\alpha}^n$ implies that $\mathbf{c}$ overlaps with the support of $\mathbf{x}$ (resp. $\mathbf{y}$) in exactly α positions there must be additional $\alpha - e$ ones in $\mathbf{c}$ among the $w/2$ positions where only $\mathbf{x}$ (resp. $\mathbf{y}$) has support. The remaining $v - 2\alpha + e$ ones of $\mathbf{c}$ then have to be placed among the $n - 3w/2$ positions where neither $\mathbf{x}$ nor $\mathbf{y}$ have support. $\square$

The volume of the wedge describes how often a close pair is identified considering all bucket centers $\mathbf{c}$ on $\mathcal{S}_v$. Throughout this quantity is labeled D. The following remark shows how to obtain the previous value of D from Theorem 4.2.

Remark 4.1 (Obtain D via Theorem 4.2). Note that for $\alpha = v$ it follows that the only e for which the term of the sum in Theorem 4.2 is well defined is $e = v$. This in turn gives $\mathrm{Vol}(\mathcal{W}_{\mathbf{x},\mathbf{y},v,\alpha}^n) = \binom{w/2}{v}$ which exactly matches the previously stated value of D in Sect. 1.2.

Note that asymptotically $\mathscr{W}_{w,v,\alpha}^n$ is equal to the maximal addend of the sum in Theorem 4.2. The following remark shows how to obtain the value of e for which the term in the sum is maximized numerically.

Remark 4.2 (Maximal addend in Theorem 4.2). The value of e for which the addend in the sum of Theorem 4.2 becomes maximized does not seem to have a compact representation. However, it can be computed numerically. In particular, approximating the binomials via $\binom{a}{b} \approx 2^{aH(b/a)}$ and then taking the partial derivative wrt. e, leads to the following cubic

$$e\left(w'/2 + \alpha - e\right)^2 (v - 2\alpha + e) = (w'/2 - e)(\alpha - 2)^2(n - 3w'/2 - v + 2\alpha - e). \quad (8)$$

A similar equation appears in the Thesis of Carrier [4, Eq. 8.10]. This cubic has one real and two imaginary roots. The real root gives the maximal addend. To obtain the integer solution the value can be rounded up or downwards, depending on which one is larger.

In the next lemma, we formalize that choosing the size of $\mathcal{C}_f$ to be larger than $\mathrm{Vol}(S_v^n)/D = \mathrm{Vol}(S_v^n)/\mathscr{W}_{w,v,\alpha}^n$ indeed guarantees to identify every w-close pair with overwhelming probability.

Lemma 4.3 (Amount of Filters). *Let $n \in N$ be sufficiently large, $w, \alpha, v = \Theta(n)$ be integers. Let $\mathbf{x}, \mathbf{y} \in S_w^n$ satisfy $|\mathbf{x} \wedge \mathbf{y}| = w$. Further, let $\mathcal{C}_f \subset S_v^n$ be a random subset of size $|\mathcal{C}_f| \geq \mathrm{poly}(n) \cdot \frac{\mathrm{Vol}(S_v^n)}{\mathrm{Vol}(\mathcal{W}_{\mathbf{x},\mathbf{y},v,\alpha}^n)} = \frac{\mathrm{poly}(n) \cdot \binom{n}{v}}{\mathscr{W}_{w,v,\alpha}^n}$. Then we have*

$$q = \Pr\left[\exists \mathbf{c} \in \mathcal{C}_f : \mathbf{c} \in \mathcal{B}_{\alpha,\mathbf{x}} \cap \mathcal{B}_{\alpha,\mathbf{y}}\right] = \Pr\left[\exists \mathbf{c} \in \mathcal{C}_f : \mathbf{c} \in \mathcal{W}_{\mathbf{x},\mathbf{y},v,\alpha}^n\right] \geq 1 - \mathrm{negl}(n).$$

Proof. We have

$$q = 1 - \left(1 - \frac{\mathscr{W}_{w,v,\alpha}^n}{\mathrm{Vol}(S_v^n)}\right)^{|\mathcal{C}_f|} \geq 1 - \left(1 - \frac{\mathscr{W}_{w,v,\alpha}^n}{\mathrm{Vol}(S_v^n)}\right)^{\frac{\mathrm{poly}(n) \cdot \mathrm{Vol}(S_v^n)}{\mathscr{W}_{w,v,\alpha}^n}} \geq 1 - \exp(-\mathrm{poly}(n))$$

$\square$

4.1 LSF via Coded Hashing

Our first improved version relies on a hash function to select the random subset $\mathcal{C}_f$. While not leading to the asymptotically fastest variant, it already comes close and has comparably low overhead and therefore might be well suited for practical settings.

Note that we can define a random hash function $\mathcal{H}: S_v^n \to [2^r]$ and a set $\mathcal{C}_f := \{\mathbf{c} \in S_v^n \mid \mathcal{H}(\mathbf{c}) = 0\}$ to select a random subset of filters $\mathcal{C}_f \subset S_v^n$ of size $\mathrm{Vol}(S_v^n)/2^r$. Put differently, we discard all filters $\mathbf{c} \in S_v^n$ with $\mathcal{H}(\mathbf{c}) \neq 0$. However, without further tweaks, this would require looping over all possible filters in S_v^n and evaluating $\mathcal{H}$ to decide if the respective filter should be discarded or not. In turn, this would only improve the checking phase, but not the bucketing phase.

To overcome this problem we design a hash function that allows for any given $\mathbf{x} \in L$ to more efficiently identify the valid centers $\mathbf{c} \in \mathcal{B}_{\alpha,\mathbf{x}}$. This hash function is instantiated via a random binary linear code $\mathcal{C}_\mathcal{H}$ of length n and dimension $n - r$. Note that for such a code any filter $\mathbf{c} \in \mathcal{C}_f$ is contained as a codeword with probability $\Pr[\mathbf{c} \in \mathcal{C}_\mathcal{H}] = \frac{1}{2^r}$. The hash function outputs 0 if and only if $\mathbf{c} \in \mathcal{C}_\mathcal{H}$. Therefore the problem of identifying valid bucket centers reduces to finding codewords of weight v in $\mathcal{C}_\mathcal{H}$.

In the following, we choose $\alpha = v$ where $\mathcal{C}_f \subset \mathcal{S}_v^n$. Therefore, for a given list element $\mathbf{x} \in L$, the support of valid bucket centers $\mathbf{c} \in \mathcal{B}_{\alpha,\mathbf{x}}$ overlaps entirely with the support of $\mathbf{x}$, i.e. $\mathbf{x} \wedge \mathbf{c} = \mathbf{c}$. This implies that for $\mathbf{c} \in \mathcal{B}_{\alpha,\mathbf{x}}$ we have

$$\mathcal{H}(\mathbf{c}) = \mathbf{0} \Leftrightarrow \mathbf{c} \in \mathcal{C}_{\mathcal{H}} \Leftrightarrow \mathbf{c} \in \sigma_{\mathbf{x}}(\mathcal{C}_{\mathcal{H}}).$$

This means we only need to find short codewords in $\sigma_{\mathbf{x}}(\mathcal{C}_{\mathcal{H}})$, which is presumably easier. We detail the procedure to identify valid bucket centers for a given list element $\mathbf{x}$ in Algorithm 5.

Algorithm 5: ValidFilters (coded hashing)

    Input   : $\mathcal{S}_v^n$ and random $[n, n-r]$ code $\mathcal{C}_{\mathcal{H}}$ describing $\mathcal{C}_f = \mathcal{S}_v^n \cap \mathcal{C}_{\mathcal{H}}$, list
               element $\mathbf{x} \in \mathcal{S}_w^n$, bucketing parameter v
    Output: $\mathcal{B}_{v,\mathbf{x}} := \{\mathbf{c} \in \mathcal{C}_f : |\mathbf{x} \wedge \mathbf{c}| = v\}$

1 **return** $\{\sigma_{\mathbf{x}}^{-1}(\mathbf{c}) \mid \mathbf{c} \in \sigma_{\mathbf{x}}(\mathcal{C}_{\mathcal{H}})$ with $|\mathbf{c}| = v\}$

Lemma 4.4 (ValidFilters for Coded Hashing). *Let $\mathcal{C}_{\mathcal{H}}$ be a $[n, n-r]$ code and $\mathcal{C}_f = \mathcal{S}_v^n \cap \mathcal{C}_{\mathcal{H}}$, $v \in N$. Then Algorithm 5 returns the set $\mathcal{B}_{v,\mathbf{x}}$ in time $\binom{w}{v}/\binom{r}{v}$.*

Proof. Note that by the above argumentation the sets

$$\mathcal{B}_{v,\mathbf{x}} := \{\mathbf{c} \in \mathcal{S}_v^n \cap \mathcal{C}_{\mathcal{H}} : |\mathbf{x} \wedge \mathbf{c}| = v\} \quad \text{and} \quad \{\mathbf{c} \in \sigma_{\mathbf{x}}(\mathcal{C}_{\mathcal{H}}) : |\mathbf{c}| = v\}$$

are identical, implying the correctness of the algorithm. We use Prange's algorithm to find all short codewords in $\sigma_{\mathbf{x}}(\mathcal{C}_{\mathcal{H}})$. Note that $\sigma_{\mathbf{x}}(\mathcal{C}_{\mathcal{H}})$ has an effective length of $|\mathbf{x}| = w$ and dimension $w - r$. The asymptotic cost of Prange's algorithm to find all weight v codewords in $\sigma_{\mathbf{x}}(\mathcal{C}_{\mathcal{H}})$ is, as per Lemma 2.1, $\binom{w}{v}/\binom{r}{v}$. □

The following theorem establishes the running time using our approach of a coded hash function.

Theorem 4.3 (LSF via Coded Hashfunction). *Let $n \in \mathbb{N}$, $w, v = \Theta(n)$. Further let $\alpha := v$, $\mathcal{C}_{\mathcal{H}}$ be a random binary $[n, n-r]$ code for $r := \log\binom{w/2}{v} - \log n$, $\mathcal{C}_f = \mathcal{S}_v^n \cap \mathcal{C}_{\mathcal{H}}$ and ValidFilters as defined in Algorithm 5. Then Algorithm 4 solves the NNS(N, n, w) using expected time T and expected memory M, where*

$$T = \tilde{\mathcal{O}}\left(N \cdot \binom{w}{v} \cdot \left(\binom{r}{v}^{-1} + \frac{N\binom{w}{v}}{\binom{n}{v} \cdot 2^r}\right)\right) \quad \text{and} \quad M = \tilde{\mathcal{O}}\left(N \cdot \binom{w}{v}/\binom{w/2}{v}\right).$$

Proof. Note that $|\mathcal{C}_f| = \mathcal{S}_v^n \cap \mathcal{C}_{\mathcal{H}} = \{\mathbf{c} \in \mathcal{C}_{\mathcal{H}} : |\mathbf{c}| = v\}$. Therefore we have

$$\mathbb{E}\left[|\mathcal{C}_f|\right] = \frac{\binom{n}{v}}{2^r} = \frac{n \cdot \mathrm{Vol}(\mathcal{S}_v^n)}{\binom{w/2}{v}} = \frac{n \cdot \mathrm{Vol}(\mathcal{S}_v^n)}{\mathscr{W}_{w,v,\alpha}},$$

where the last equality follows from the fact that $\alpha = v$ (compare to Remark 4.1). Assuming that this construction of $\mathcal{C}_f$ via a random linear code resembles a random subset of $\mathcal{S}_v^n$ of size $\mathbb{E}[|\mathcal{C}_f|]$, we can apply Lemma 4.3, which ensures that every close pair is stored in the same bucket at least once with overwhelming probability. The correctness now follows from the correctness of the `ValidFilters` function (see Lemma 4.4) and Algorithm 4 (see Lemma 4.1).

Note that the set of valid filters is of size

$$\mathbb{E}[|\mathcal{B}_{v,\mathbf{x}}|] = \mathbb{E}[|\{\mathbf{c} \in \sigma_{\mathbf{x}}(\mathcal{C}_{\mathcal{H}}) \colon |\mathbf{c}| = v\}|] = \binom{w}{v}/2^r = \tilde{\Theta}\left(\binom{w}{v}\Big/\binom{w/2}{v}\right).$$

Therefore the condition $\mathbb{E}[|\mathcal{B}_{v,\mathbf{x}}|] \geq 1$ of Lemma 4.1 is satisfied. Due to Lemma 4.4 the set $\mathcal{B}_{v,\mathbf{x}}$ can be computed in time $T_{\texttt{ValidFilters}} = \binom{w}{v}/\binom{r}{v}$. The expected bucket size is given by

$$\mathbb{E}[|\text{Bucket}_{\mathbf{c}}|] = \frac{N \cdot \mathbb{E}[|\mathcal{B}_{v,\mathbf{x}}|]}{|\mathcal{C}_f|} = \frac{N\binom{w}{v}}{\binom{n}{v}}.$$

Eventually, by plugging in those quantities into the time complexity given by Lemma 4.1 we obtain the claim, namely

$$T = \tilde{\mathcal{O}}\left(N \cdot \left(\binom{w}{v}/\binom{r}{v} + \frac{N\binom{w}{v}^2}{\binom{n}{v} \cdot 2^r}\right)\right) \quad \text{and} \quad M = \tilde{\mathcal{O}}\left(N \cdot \binom{w}{v}/2^r\right).$$

$\square$

We also explored the use of more advanced ISD algorithms for the `ValidFilters` definition from Algorithm 5, however, this resulted only in very small improvements, which is why we stayed with the simple Prange formula here.

Saving Memory Through Repetitions. To ensure a high success probability we only need to classify the input elements according to enough filters $\mathcal{C}_f$ (see Lemma 4.3). Thereby, it is possible to interleave the bucketing and checking phases. We can, for example, first execute the bucketing phase for half of the filters, perform the checking phase, and then repeat the process for the second half of the filters. Note that the size of all buckets is halved (on expectation) in the repeated execution. Hence, as long as the buckets dominate the memory consumption, we obtain a memory improvement with such modification.

More generally, in the following, we execute the algorithm on an initial set of filters $\mathcal{C}_f'$ of size $|\mathcal{C}_f'| = |\mathcal{C}_f|/2^d$. We compensate for the reduced size of the filter set by repeating the algorithm 2^d times. Overall, this improves the memory complexity by a factor of 2^d as formalized in the following corollary.

Corollary 4.1 (LSF via Coded Hashfunction with Repetitions). *Let $n \in \mathbb{N}$, $w, v = \Theta(n)$. Further let, $\alpha := v$, $\mathcal{C}_{\mathcal{H}}$ be a random binary $[n, n-r]$ code for $\log\binom{w}{v} - \log n \geq r \geq \log\binom{w/2}{v} - \log n$, $\mathcal{C}_f = \mathcal{S}_v^n \cap \mathcal{C}_{\mathcal{H}}$ and* `ValidFilters` *as defined* *in Algorithm 5. Define $d := r - (\log \binom{w/2}{v} - \log n)$. Then 2^d sequential repetitions of Algorithm 4 on fresh randomness solve the* NNS(N, n, w) *using expected time T and expected memory M, where*

$$T = \tilde{\mathcal{O}}\left(2^d \cdot N \cdot \binom{w}{v} \cdot \left(\binom{r}{v}^{-1} + \frac{N\binom{w}{v}}{\binom{n}{v} \cdot 2^r}\right)\right) \quad and \quad M = \tilde{\mathcal{O}}\left(N \cdot \binom{w}{v}/2^r\right).$$

Proof. Over all 2^d iterations, the list elements are still classified with respect to

$$2^d \cdot \mathbb{E}\big[|\mathcal{C}_f|\big] = \frac{2^d \binom{n}{v}}{2^r} = \frac{n \cdot \mathrm{Vol}(\mathcal{S}_v^n)}{\binom{w/2}{v}} = \frac{n \cdot \mathrm{Vol}(\mathcal{S}_v^n)}{\mathscr{W}_{w,v,\alpha}},$$

filters as required by Lemma 4.3. Note that the time of the algorithm and the memory consumption remain the same as before, now for potentially updated r. Overall, the running time suffers an additional 2^d factor due to the sequential repetitions.   □

Interestingly, as we show in Sect. 5, this repetition approach also leads to an improvement in the time complexity, due to the more optimal choice of r for the decoding routine used within the ValidFilters function.

4.2   LSF via Random Product Codes

Our fastest instantiation of Algorithm 4 uses random product codes (RPC) to define the set of centers $\mathcal{C}_f$. Similarly to the Coded Hashing algorithm, LSF with RPC also comes with a memory-optimal version. In the later section, we refer to these algorithms as RPC and RPC-OPT for the usual and memory optimal versions respectively. Their description is deferred to the full version of the paper given in [9].

5   Results and Performance Comparisons

Each of the presented algorithms to solve the w-nearest neighbor search from Sect. 4 leads to an instantiation of the SievingISD algorithm (Algorithm 2) via the machinery presented in Sect. 3. The SievingISD framework dictates specific parameters for the w-nearest neighbor search problem NNS(N, n', w') solved within the ISD routine. While n' and w' are optimization parameters chosen to minimize the running time, N is chosen equal to the lower bound given in Constraint (C 2), to ensure that there are again N close vectors.

Note that algorithms solving the w-nearest neighbor search might be of independent interest for a broader range of parameters. Therefore, to allow for a more general categorization, we compare the performance of the nearest neighbor search algorithms for a wider range of parameters first, independent of the choices in SievingISD. However, this comparison already allows us to draw conclusions on possible speedups obtained via those algorithms in the context of the SievingISD framework. Subsequently, we study the resulting SievingISD instantiations in more detail.

5.1   Performance of Nearest Neighbor Algorithms

In the comparison of algorithms to solve the w-near neighbor search we refer to the algorithms as GJN ([17], Lemma 4.2), HASH (Theorem 4.3), HASH-OPT (Corollary 4.1), RPC and RPC-OPT for the random product code and its memory optimal version, resp. Additionally, we compare those algorithms against a quadratic search baseline that naively computes all list pairs to find those that are close, and against an algorithm recently proposed by Esser [10].

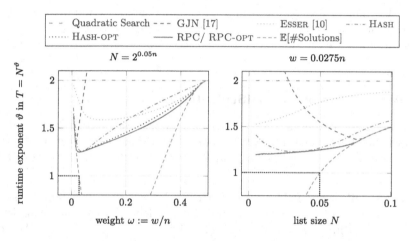

Fig. 4. Comparison of the running time of different algorithms solving the w-nearest neighbor search for fixed list size (left) and fixed weight (right).

On the left in Fig. 4 we compare the running time of the different algorithms for different relative weights $\omega := w/n$ and fixed list size $N = 2^{0.05n}$. A choice that roughly corresponds to the list sizes encountered in the later SievingISD application. All algorithms, except for GJN, outperform the quadratic-search baseline for all weights $\omega < 0.5$. Furthermore, the fastest algorithms presented in this work outperform the previous approaches, GJN and ESSER, for all weights. Note that RPC and RPC-OPT obtain the same running time since RPC-OPT corresponds to a pure memory improvement. Interestingly, the same repetition approach leads to a significant time improvement in the context of HASH-OPT over HASH. This is because the extra degree of freedom allows optimizing the code parameters to reduce the overhead for finding valid bucket centers in HASH-OPT via Lemma 4.4.

Additionally, the graph depicts the expected amount of solutions, $\mathbb{E}[\#\text{Solutions}] = \binom{n}{w}/2^{n-k}$, as an orange dashed line. It can be observed that all algorithms, except ESSER, obtain a running time that is (roughly) linear in the number of existing solutions for very small weights. For larger weights the complexities diverge, while all algorithms (except GJN) converge to the quadratic search baseline for weight $\omega = 0.5$.

In the ISD application, we are interested in the performance of the algorithms when the amount of solutions is equal to the list size, i.e., the point on the dashed orange line at $\vartheta = 1$. This is the case for $\omega \approx 0.02748$, which is highlighted by a black dotted line in the plot. We find that the new algorithm from Sect. 4.1 significantly improves on GJN in that regime, indicating an improved SievingISD algorithm. On the other hand, all new algorithms obtain similar complexities in that regime, implying that they show similar performance within the SievingISD framework. The algorithm by Esser performs worse than GJN in that regime indicating no improvement in the SievingISD context.

On the right in Fig. 4 we consider for completeness the running time of the algorithms for fixed weight and variable list size. Again, the SievingISD relevant instantiation, where the amount of solutions is equal to the list size, is highlighted via a black dotted line.

5.2 Performance of SievingISD Instantiations

In this section, we detail the performance of the SievingISD instantiations obtained via the w-nearest neighbor search algorithms from Sect. 4. We then compare the obtained complexities against the state of the art of ISD algorithms.

Obtaining Different ISD Instantiations. Recall, that Theorem 3.1 states the running time of any ISD algorithm in dependence on the time complexity of an oracle to find short codewords of weight w' in a given code. We then instantiate this oracle via a sieving routine (see Algorithm 3). Under the Binary-Sieve Heuristic (Heuristic 6) the complexity of this sieving algorithm is equal to the complexity of solving the w'-nearest neighbor search.

We now obtain different SievingISD algorithms, by instantiating the nearest neighbor search routine used within the sieving routine with the different algorithms from Sect. 4. Note that the nearest neighbor search instance solved within the sieving routine corresponds to the $\texttt{NNS}(N, n', w')$ problem, for N matching Eq. (C 2), and n', w' as defined in Theorem 3.1. We obtain the different instantiations by using the different statements about T_{NNS} from Theorem 3.2. More precisely, we refer to the obtained instantiations as: SISD-GJN (Lemma 4.2), SISD-HASH (Theorem 4.3), SISD-HASH-OPT (Corollary 4.1), SISD-RPC and SISD-RPC-OPT from the full version.

To compare the complexities of these different instantiations, we follow the common practice of modeling the running time and memory as $2^{c(k,w)n}$, where c is a constant that depends on k and w. Therefore, we approximate all binomial coefficients via the upper bound. Note that this leads to at most a polynomial divergence, asymptotically subsumed by the fact that we always round the constant $c(k, w)$ upwards. We then consider $k = \kappa n$, $w = \omega n$, for constants κ, ω and model any additional optimization parameter o_i, such as n' and w', as $o_i = \hat{o}_i n$. Then for given κ, ω we perform a numerical minimization of the running time over the choice of the $\hat{o}_i$, resulting in the complexity exponent $c(k, w)$, or $c(\kappa, \omega)$, as the constant only depends on κ and ω.

Table 1. Worst case running time $2^{c_T(\kappa,\omega)n}$ and corresponding memory usage $2^{c_M(\kappa,\omega)n}$ for different ISD algorithms. Running time is maximized for given κ using $\omega = H^{-1}(1 - \kappa)$ equal to the Gilbert-Varshamov bound.

Type	Algorithm	κ	$c_T(\kappa,\omega)$	$c_M(\kappa,\omega)$
SievingISD	SISD-GJN [17]	0.44	0.1169	0.0279
	SISD-HASH	0.44	0.1007	0.0849
	SISD-HASH-OPT	0.44	0.1007	0.0830
	SISD-RPC	0.44	0.1001	0.0852
	SISD-RPC-OPT	0.44	0.1001	0.0636
Conventional ISD	PRANGE [29]	0.45	0.1207	0.0000
	MMT [24]	0.45	0.1116	0.0541
	BJMM [2]	0.43	0.1020	0.0728
	BOTH-MAY [3]	0.42	0.0951	0.0754

Worst-Case Complexities. A common measure to compare the performance of algorithms to solve the syndrome decoding problem is their worst-case complexity. Therefore one considers $w = \omega n$ matching the Gilbert-Varshamov bound, i.e., $\omega = H^{-1}(1 - \kappa)$, with H^{-1} being the inverse of the binary entropy function in the interval $[0, 0.5]$. The worst-case running time is then obtained by maximizing the constant $c(\kappa, \omega)$ over all possible choices of the rate κ. Table 1 states the worst-case running times for the different SievingISD instantiations in comparison to the best known ISD algorithms.[7]

We observe that the new SievingISD instantiations obtain a significant improvement over the running time of the original SISD-GJN proposal from [17]. Still, they do not yet reach the best time complexity exponent for conventional ISD algorithms, given by the Both-May algorithm [3][8]. However, the new algorithms yield the first improvement over the running time of the BJMM algorithm, which does not follow the conventional ISD paradigm. Furthermore, our more practical instantiations SISD-HASH and SISD-HASH-OPT, still slightly outperform the BJMM algorithm, while significantly improving on the MMT algorithm, which is usually the preferred choice in practice [13,14].

In Fig. 5 we compare the running time exponent of the different SievingISD instantiations, SISD-GJN, SISD-HASH-OPT, and SISD-RPC-OPT for all rates κ against conventional ISD procedures. We find that the SISD-GJN instantiation falls between the running times of PRANGE and of MMT.

The improved SievingISD instantiations offer BJMM comparable running times. We observe that for rates $\kappa \leq 0.6$ our best SievingISD instantiations even outperform the BJMM algorithm. It can also be observed that our more practical SISD-HASH-OPT instantiation generally suffers only a slight overhead

---

[7] For obtaining the numerical exponents of conventional ISD procedures we use the code available at https://github.com/Memphisd/Revisiting-NN-ISD.

[8] See [5,10] for a correction of the initial result.

in terms of time complexity compared to our best Sisd-RPC-opt variant, as it was also suggested by the comparison in Sect. 5.1.

In the full version, we give a detailed discussion on the time-memory trade-off potential of the different instantiations.

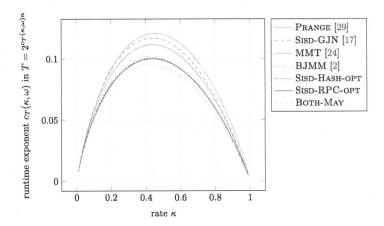

Fig. 5. Runtime exponent for different ISD and SievingISD variants as a function of the rate κ using $\omega := H^{-1}(1 - \kappa)$.

Acknowledgments. Andre Esser is supported by the Deutsche Forschungsgemeinschaft (DFG, German Research Foundation) - Project-ID MA 2536/12. Léo Ducas and Simona Etinski are supported by ERC Starting Grant 947821 (ARTICULATE). Elena Kirshanova is supported by Russian Science Foundation grant N 22-41-04411, https://rscf.ru/project/22-41-04411/.

References

1. Becker, A., Ducas, L., Gama, N., Laarhoven, T.: New directions in nearest neighbor searching with applications to lattice sieving. In: Krauthgamer, R. (ed.) 27th SODA, pp. 10–24. ACM-SIAM (2016). https://doi.org/10.1137/1.9781611974331.ch2
2. Becker, A., Joux, A., May, A., Meurer, A.: Decoding random binary linear codes in $2^{n/20}$: how $1 + 1 = 0$ improves information set decoding. In: Pointcheval, D., Johansson, T. (eds.) EUROCRYPT 2012. LNCS, vol. 7237, pp. 520–536. Springer, Heidelberg (2012). https://doi.org/10.1007/978-3-642-29011-4_31
3. Both, L., May, A.: Decoding linear codes with high error rate and its impact for LPN security. In: Lange, T., Steinwandt, R. (eds.) PQCrypto 2018. LNCS, vol. 10786, pp. 25–46. Springer, Cham (2018). https://doi.org/10.1007/978-3-319-79063-3_2
4. Carrier, K.: Recherche de presque-collisions pour le décodage et la reconnaissance de codes correcteurs. Ph.D. thesis, Sorbonne université (2020)

5. Carrier, K., Debris-Alazard, T., Meyer-Hilfiger, C., Tillich, J.P.: Statistical decoding 2.0: reducing decoding to LPN. In: Agrawal, S., Lin, D. (eds.) ASIACRYPT 2022, Part IV. LNCS, vol. 13794, pp. 477–507. Springer, Heidelberg (2022). https://doi.org/10.1007/978-3-031-22972-5_17

6. Cooper, C.: On the distribution of rank of a random matrix over a finite field. Random Struct. Algorithms **17**(3–4), 197–212 (2000)

7. Devadas, S., Ren, L., Xiao, H.: On iterative collision search for LPN and subset sum. In: Kalai, Y., Reyzin, L. (eds.) TCC 2017. LNCS, vol. 10678, pp. 729–746. Springer, Cham (2017). https://doi.org/10.1007/978-3-319-70503-3_24

8. Dubiner, M.: Bucketing coding and information theory for the statistical high-dimensional nearest-neighbor problem. IEEE Trans. Inf. Theory **56**(8), 4166–4179 (2010)

9. Ducas, L., Esser, A., Etinski, S., Kirshanova, E.: Asymptotics and improvements of sieving for codes. In: IACR Cryptology ePrint Archive, p. 1577 (2023). https://eprint.iacr.org/2023/1577

10. Esser, A.: Revisiting nearest-neighbor-based information set decoding. In: IMA International Conference on Cryptography and Coding, pp. 34–54. Springer (2023). https://doi.org/10.1007/978-3-031-47818-5_3

11. Esser, A., Heuer, F., Kübler, R., May, A., Sohler, C.: Dissection-BKW. In: Shacham, H., Boldyreva, A. (eds.) CRYPTO 2018. LNCS, vol. 10992, pp. 638–666. Springer, Cham (2018). https://doi.org/10.1007/978-3-319-96881-0_22

12. Esser, A., Kübler, R., Zweydinger, F.: A faster algorithm for finding closest pairs in hamming metric. In: Bojanczyk, M., Chekuri, C. (eds.) 41st IARCS Annual Conference on Foundations of Software Technology and Theoretical Computer Science, FSTTCS 2021, December 15-17, 2021, Virtual Conference. LIPIcs, vol. 213, pp. 20:1–20:21. Schloss Dagstuhl - Leibniz-Zentrum für Informatik (2021).https://doi.org/10.4230/LIPIcs.FSTTCS.2021.20

13. Esser, A., May, A., Zweydinger, F.: McEliece needs a break - solving McEliece-1284 and quasi-cyclic-2918 with modern ISD. In: Dunkelman, O., Dziembowski, S. (eds.) EUROCRYPT 2022, Part III. LNCS, vol. 13277, pp. 433–457. Springer, Heidelberg (2022).https://doi.org/10.1007/978-3-031-07082-2_16

14. Esser, A., Zweydinger, F.: New time-memory trade-offs for subset sum: improving ISD in theory and practice. In: Hazay, C., Stam, M. (eds.) EUROCRYPT 2023, Part V. LNCS, vol. 14008, pp. 360–390. Springer, Heidelberg (2023). https://doi.org/10.1007/978-3-031-30589-4_13

15. Fincke, U., Pohst, M.: A procedure for determining algebraic integers of given norm. In: van Hulzen, J.A. (ed.) Computer Algebra, pp. 194–202 (1983)

16. Finiasz, M., Sendrier, N.: Security bounds for the design of code-based cryptosystems. In: Matsui, M. (ed.) ASIACRYPT 2009. LNCS, vol. 5912, pp. 88–105. Springer, Heidelberg (2009). https://doi.org/10.1007/978-3-642-10366-7_6

17. Guo, Q., Johansson, T., Nguyen, V.: A new sieving-style information-set decoding algorithm. Cryptology ePrint Archive, Report 2023/247 (2023). https://eprint.iacr.org/2023/247

18. Indyk, P., Motwani, R.: Approximate nearest neighbors: towards removing the curse of dimensionality. In: 30th ACM STOC, pp. 604–613. ACM Press (1998). https://doi.org/10.1145/276698.276876

19. Kannan, R.: Improved algorithms for integer programming and related lattice problems. In: Proceedings of the Fifteenth Annual ACM Symposium on Theory of Computing, pp. 193–206. STOC '83 (1983). https://doi.org/10.1145/800061.808749

20. Laarhoven, T.: Sieving for shortest vectors in lattices using angular locality-sensitive hashing. In: Gennaro, R., Robshaw, M. (eds.) CRYPTO 2015. LNCS, vol. 9215, pp. 3–22. Springer, Heidelberg (2015). https://doi.org/10.1007/978-3-662-47989-6_1

21. Laarhoven, T., de Weger, B.: Faster sieving for shortest lattice vectors using spherical locality-sensitive hashing. In: Lauter, K., Rodríguez-Henríquez, F. (eds.) LATINCRYPT 2015. LNCS, vol. 9230, pp. 101–118. Springer, Cham (2015). https://doi.org/10.1007/978-3-319-22174-8_6

22. Levieil, É., Fouque, P.-A.: An improved LPN algorithm. In: De Prisco, R., Yung, M. (eds.) SCN 2006. LNCS, vol. 4116, pp. 348–359. Springer, Heidelberg (2006). https://doi.org/10.1007/11832072_24

23. Liu, H., Yu, Y.: A non-heuristic approach to time-space tradeoffs and optimizations for BKW. In: Agrawal, S., Lin, D. (eds.) ASIACRYPT 2022, Part III. LNCS, vol. 13793, pp. 741–770. Springer, Heidelberg (2022). https://doi.org/10.1007/978-3-031-22969-5_25

24. May, A., Meurer, A., Thomae, E.: Decoding random linear codes in $\tilde{\mathcal{O}}(2^{0.054n})$. In: Lee, D.H., Wang, X. (eds.) ASIACRYPT 2011. LNCS, vol. 7073, pp. 107–124. Springer, Heidelberg (2011). https://doi.org/10.1007/978-3-642-25385-0_6

25. May, A., Ozerov, I.: On computing nearest neighbors with applications to decoding of binary linear codes. In: Oswald, E., Fischlin, M. (eds.) EUROCRYPT 2015. LNCS, vol. 9056, pp. 203–228. Springer, Heidelberg (2015). https://doi.org/10.1007/978-3-662-46800-5_9

26. Minder, L., Sinclair, A.: The extended k-tree algorithm. J. Cryptol. **25**(2), 349–382 (2012). https://doi.org/10.1007/s00145-011-9097-y

27. Nguyen, P.Q., Vidick, T.: Sieve algorithms for the shortest vector problem are practical. J. Math. Cryptol. **2**(2), 181–207 (2008). https://doi.org/10.1515/JMC.2008.009

28. Pagh, R.: Locality-sensitive hashing without false negatives. In: Krauthgamer, R. (ed.) 27th SODA, pp. 1–9. ACM-SIAM (2016). https://doi.org/10.1137/1.9781611974331.ch1

29. Prange, E.: The use of information sets in decoding cyclic codes. IRE Trans. Inf. Theory **8**(5), 5–9 (1962)

30. Stern, J.: A method for finding codewords of small weight. In: Cohen, G., Wolfmann, J. (eds.) Coding Theory 1988. LNCS, vol. 388, pp. 106–113. Springer, Heidelberg (1989). https://doi.org/10.1007/BFb0019850

31. Wagner, D.: A generalized birthday problem. In: Yung, M. (ed.) CRYPTO 2002. LNCS, vol. 2442, pp. 288–304. Springer, Heidelberg (2002). https://doi.org/10.1007/3-540-45708-9_19

Isogeny Problems with Level Structure

Luca De Feo[1]([✉])(iD), Tako Boris Fouotsa[2](iD), and Lorenz Panny[3]

[1] IBM Research Europe, Zurich, Switzerland
`eurocrypt24@defeo.lu`
[2] EPFL, Lausanne, Switzerland
`tako.fouotsa@epfl.ch`
[3] Technische Universität München, Munich, Germany
`lorenz@yx7.cc`

Abstract. Given two elliptic curves and the degree of an isogeny between them, finding the isogeny is believed to be a difficult problem—upon which rests the security of nearly any isogeny-based scheme. If, however, to the data above we add information about the behavior of the isogeny on a large enough subgroup, the problem can become easy, as recent cryptanalyses on SIDH have shown.

Between the restriction of the isogeny to a full N-torsion subgroup and no "torsion information" at all lies a spectrum of interesting intermediate problems, raising the question of how easy or hard each of them is. Here we explore *modular isogeny problems* where the torsion information is masked by the action of a group of 2×2 matrices. We give reductions between these problems, classify them by their difficulty, and link them to security assumptions found in the literature.

Keywords: Isogenies · Post-quantum · Security reductions

1 Introduction

Isogeny-based cryptography is a fast-changing field, with new schemes and assumptions appearing at a sustained pace and, recently, a series of powerful attacks shaking its foundations. It may be difficult for an outsider to make sense of the scores of different assumptions, and understand what level of security they actually offer. Luckily, in parallel with the accumulation of new assumptions, works on security reductions have helped somewhat systematize the landscape and reduce the amount of hypotheses to keep track of [40,58,65,66]. Also worth mentioning is the project "Is SIKE broken yet?"[1], which tries to collect most isogeny assumptions and track the best reductions and attacks known on them.

The goal of this work is to add another layer to our understanding of isogeny-based cryptography by giving a framework that encompasses several seemingly

---

[1] https://issikebrokenyet.github.io/.

Author list in alphabetical order; see https://ams.org/profession/CultureStatement04.pdf. Date of this document: 2024-02-29.

M. Joye and G. Leander (Eds.): EUROCRYPT 2024, LNCS 14657, pp. 181–204, 2024.
https://doi.org/10.1007/978-3-031-58754-2_7

unrelated assumptions and proving reductions between them. We start from two well-known problems: on one hand SIDH [49], also known as the Computational Supersingular Isogeny (CSSI) problem, which was recently solved quite efficiently and in fair generality [15,55,62]; on the other hand the generic (fixed-degree) isogeny problem, for which no general classical or quantum algorithm better than exponential is known, and which is the foundation of all isogeny-based cryptography. SIDH has sometimes been described as an isogeny problem *with torsion-point information* [59], but what is known as "torsion-point information" in the cryptographic community has long been known as a special type of *level structure* among mathematicians. By generalizing the SIDH problem to other types of level structures, we obtain a family of problems, some easy, some hard, which happen to have reductions to/from isogeny problems that had previously appeared in the literature without apparent connection. Along the way, we extend the SIDH attacks to a more general setting, we prove that, somewhat ironically, some proofs of knowledge based on SIDH are *at least as hard* as CSIDH [18], and we improve on the best generic algorithms to compute isogenies of ordinary curves [35].

Torsion-Point Information, a.k.a. Level Structures. In the generic fixed-degree isogeny problem, one is given a pair of curves E, E' isogenous of exponentially large degree d, and is tasked with finding a d-isogeny $\phi : E \to E'$, for instance by exhibiting a generator for $\ker \phi$. In SIDH and variants, next to E, E' we add an (ordered) basis (P, Q) of $E[N]$ for some fixed parameter $N \approx d$ coprime to d (typically $N = 2^a$ or $N = 3^b$) and its image $(\phi(P), \phi(Q))$ under the secret isogeny. The goal is again to find ϕ.

The extra information provided by $(P, Q, \phi(P), \phi(Q))$ has been called *torsion-point information* in [59] and follow-ups. It is precisely this information that is exploited by the attacks on SIDH [15,55,62]; its absence in the generic isogeny problem is the reason why the rest of isogeny-based cryptography still stands.

A curve E together with a basis (P, Q) of $E[N]$ is called a *full level structure of level N* in the literature on modular curves. More generally, a level structure of level N is a basis of $E[N]$ *up to change of basis* by some group of matrices $\Gamma \leq \mathrm{GL}_2(\mathbb{Z}/N\mathbb{Z})$. So, for example, when Γ is the group of diagonal matrices a Γ-level structure is the set of bases (aP, bQ) for all $a, b \in \mathbb{Z}/N\mathbb{Z}$ such that ab is invertible, and when $\Gamma = \mathrm{GL}_2$ the associated level structure is the set of all possible bases.

Once we interpret SIDH as a generic isogeny problem between curves with full level structure, it becomes natural to define isogeny problems with Γ-level structures for arbitrary subgroups Γ. The interpretation is that we are given tuples (E, P, Q) and (E', P', Q'), with the promise that there exists an isogeny $\phi : E \to E'$ mapping (P, Q) to one of the bases in the orbit of (P', Q') by Γ. Thus, when Γ is the diagonal group, the Γ-SIDH problem is to find ϕ knowing that $\phi(P) = aP'$ and $\phi(Q) = bQ'$ for some unknown $a, b \in \mathbb{Z}/N\mathbb{Z}$ such that ab is invertible. The GL_2-SIDH problem is simply the generic isogeny problem.

Related Work. Level structures were first considered in the context of isogeny-based cryptography by Arpin [3], who studied the relation between supersingular isogeny graphs with level structure and Eichler orders in a quaternion algebra. In [6] it is proved that supersingular isogeny graphs with *Borel level structure* have the Ramanujan property, which is then used to construct a proof of isogeny knowledge with statistical zero-knowledge. The follow-up work [25] proves similar expansion properties for graphs with other level structures.

Level structures in disguise appeared in isogeny schemes quickly after SIDH was broken: the key exchange M-SIDH [42] is a variant of SIDH using the group of scalar matrices to mask the torsion point information, thus blocking the attacks; the trapdoor one-way function FESTA [8] uses a diagonal matrix as a trapdoor to mask a standard SIDH problem. Recent attacks against special instances of M-SIDH and FESTA [21] function by, essentially, reducing the Γ-SIDH problem to a plain SIDH problem.

This work was prompted by a question raised at the Leuven Isogeny Days 2022: is it possible to solve the "SIDH with only one point" problem in polynomial time, i.e., the problem where one is only given (E, P) and $(E', \phi(P))$ with P of order N? We answered in the affirmative when N contains a large smooth square factor, thus, in particular, when $N = 2^a$ or $N = 3^b$, by giving a reduction to the standard SIDH problem (see Corollary 12). This result having been circulated privately for more than a year, it has already been used to break some *ad hoc* instances of class group actions on ordinary curves [16, §6], and to extend the attacks on overstretched FESTA [21, Remark 5].

Contributions. We generalize the SIDH problem to isogeny problems with arbitrary level structures. In doing so, we:

- Identify several interesting types of level structures which correspond to problems related to M-SIDH, FESTA, CSIDH, proofs of isogeny knowledge [33,36], etc., which had not previously been known to be connected;
- Give our main technical contribution: a polynomial-time reduction between different level structures (Corollary 10);
- As a special case, show an attack against "SIDH with only one point" (Corollary 12), which has already been weaponized in [16,21];
- As another special case, prove that breaking SIDH-based proofs of isogeny knowledge [33] is at least as hard as breaking CSIDH (Corollary 13 and Lemma 14);
- Improve upon the best generic algorithm [35] to compute isogenies between ordinary curves (Sect. 5.6).

Limitations. We stress that it is rare that the security of a cryptographic scheme reduces to a Γ-SIDH problem as stated here. For example, the security of key exchange schemes typically depends on DDH- or CDH-like assumptions which are usually stronger than the corresponding Γ-SIDH one. In the interest of conciseness, we also avoid discussing decisional variants of Γ-SIDH, with the only exception of Sect. 5.5.

Some high profile schemes that fit quite badly in our framework are SQIsign and its variants [22,30,37], whose security reduces to a distinguishing problem on isogeny walks generated according to an *ad-hoc* distribution. Pre-quantum schemes such as verifiable delay functions [38] and delay encryption [13] are also out of the scope of this work.

Despite all this, it is often the case that the best known attack against any isogeny-based scheme consists in solving an instance of a Γ-SIDH problem, thus our classification is especially valuable for cryptanalysts. In what follows whenever we mention "breaking a cryptosystem", we mean finding its secrets, rather than just breaking the assumption.

Ultimately, we hope that our framework will help better systematize and assess the landscape of assumptions in isogeny-based cryptography.

Outline. We formally define level structures in Sect. 2. In Sect. 3 we define the isogeny problem with level structure, and discuss how the inputs and the outputs of the problem are represented. We give our main technical contribution in Sect. 4: a polynomial-time reduction between isogeny problems with different level structures. We conclude in Sect. 5 with a review of isogeny problems with level structure that have previously appeared in the literature, and spell out the consequences of our reduction.

Notation. We will work with several groups of 2×2 matrices. We will use asterisks $*$ to denote entries of matrices that can take arbitrary values, and leave zero entries blank, thus $\left(\begin{smallmatrix} * & *\ell \\ & * \end{smallmatrix}\right)$ represents any upper-triangular matrix whose upper right coefficient is divisible by ℓ. We will use the same notation to mean the group of all matrices having a certain form.

GL_2 denotes the group of invertible 2×2 matrices and SL_2 its subgroup of determinant-1 matrices. We write $\Gamma \leq \Delta$ to indicate that Γ is a subgroup of Δ.

Lower-case Greek letters ϕ, ψ, χ will be used to denote isogenies. To reduce clutter, we will write ϕP instead of $\phi(P)$ for the value of ϕ at a point P.

Throughout the document, p is a prime, q a power of p, N an integer coprime to p, and d coprime to N. We write $\tilde{O}(x)$ as a shorthand for $O(x \operatorname{polylog}(x))$.

2   Level Structures

In this section we consider an elliptic curve E defined over some finite field $\mathbb{F}_q$. In the cases of cryptographic interest which motivated this work, E is supersingular and the finite field is either a prime field $\mathbb{F}_p$ or a quadratic extension $\mathbb{F}_{p^2}$, but the main results of this work apply in general.

Let N be a positive integer coprime to q. The torsion subgroup $E[N]$, i.e., the group of points of order dividing N, taken over the algebraic closure of $\mathbb{F}_q$, is isomorphic to $(\mathbb{Z}/N\mathbb{Z})^2$. We call a *basis* of $E[N]$ any ordered pair of points (P, Q) that generate $E[N]$. Denote by $\mathcal{B}_E(N)$ the set of all bases of $E[N]$.

The group $\mathrm{GL}_2(\mathbb{Z}/N\mathbb{Z})$ of 2×2 invertible matrices with coefficients modulo N acts on $\mathcal{B}_E(N)$ on the left by

$$\begin{pmatrix} a & b \\ c & d \end{pmatrix} \cdot (P, Q) = (aP + bQ, cP + dQ).$$

Consider a subgroup $\Gamma \leq \mathrm{GL}_2$ (from now on all matrix groups will implicitly have coefficients in $\mathbb{Z}/N\mathbb{Z}$). If (P, Q) is a basis, we write $\Gamma \cdot (P, Q)$ for its Γ-*orbit*, that is the set

$$\{\gamma \cdot (P, Q) \mid \gamma \in \Gamma\}.$$

The Γ-*level structures (of level N)* on E are precisely the Γ-orbits of the bases of $E[N]$, forming a partition of $\mathcal{B}_E(N)$. We write $\mathcal{B}_E(\Gamma)$ for the set of Γ-level structures on E.

Said otherwise, a Γ-level structure is a basis of $E[N]$, up to transformation by elements of $\Gamma \leq \mathrm{GL}_2$. So, for example, when $\Gamma = \{(\begin{smallmatrix} 1 & 0 \\ 0 & 1 \end{smallmatrix})\}$ the Γ-level structures are just the bases of $E[N]$.

A pair (P, Q) of points in $E[N]$ forms a basis of $E[N]$ if and only if the Weil pairing $e_N(P, Q)$ is a primitive N-th root of unity. If $\gamma \in \mathrm{GL}_2$, by the alternating property of the Weil pairing,

$$e_N\big(\gamma \cdot (P, Q)\big) = e_N(P, Q)^{\det \gamma}.$$

Hence, the action of SL_2 partitions $\mathcal{B}_E(N)$ into $\varphi(N)$ orbits, each corresponding to one value of the pairing. We will chiefly be interested in subgroups $\Gamma \leq \mathrm{SL}_2$, so that it makes sense to talk about the value of the Weil pairing on a Γ-level structure. If $S \in \mathcal{B}_E(\Gamma)$ is one such level structure, we write $e_N(S)$ for the value of the Weil pairing.

3   Modular Isogeny Problems

Let E, E' be isogenous elliptic curves over $\mathbb{F}_q$, so that $\#E(\mathbb{F}_q) = \#E'(\mathbb{F}_q)$. From now on we let $\phi : E \to E'$ be an isogeny of degree d defined over $\mathbb{F}_q$.

Suppose $\gcd(d, N) = 1$; then ϕ defines a bijection between $\mathcal{B}_E(N)$ and $\mathcal{B}_{E'}(N)$. Let $\Gamma \leq \mathrm{GL}_2$ and let $S \in \mathcal{B}_E(\Gamma)$ be a level structure. The image $\phi(S)$ of S under ϕ is a Γ-level structure on E'.

We can now define generalizations of the classic SIDH problem.

Definition 1 (Γ-SIDH).   *Fix coprime integers d and N and a subgroup $\Gamma \leq \mathrm{GL}_2(\mathbb{Z}/N\mathbb{Z})$.*

Let E, E' be elliptic curves defined over $\mathbb{F}_q$ such that there exists an $\mathbb{F}_q$-rational isogeny $\phi : E \to E'$ of degree d. Assuming $\gcd(N, q) = 1$, let $S \in \mathcal{B}_E(\Gamma)$ be a Γ-level structure.

The (d, Γ)-modular isogeny problem (of level N) asks, given $(E, S, E', \phi(S))$ to compute ϕ. When d is clear from context, we call this the Γ-SIDH problem.

Although the S in SIDH stands for "supersingular", we consider these problems for ordinary and supersingular elliptic curves alike. For groups Γ of special interest, we will also give other names.

Remark 2. When d and N have common factors, the image $\phi(S)$ is not well defined, however the problem of computing ϕ given some information on how it behaves on $E[N]$ is still meaningful. This problem, though, is usually much easier to solve: If ℓ is a prime dividing d, either $\phi(E[\ell])$ is trivial, in which case ϕ factors as $\phi' \circ [\ell]$ with $\deg \phi' = d/\ell^2$, or $\phi(E[\ell])$ is the kernel of an ℓ-isogeny $\psi : E' \to E''$ such that $\phi = \widehat{\psi} \circ \phi'$ with $\deg \phi' = d/\ell$. By repeatedly removing common factors of d and N in this way, we reduce to a Γ-SIDH problem.

Remark 3. The isogeny ϕ may not be unique. In this case we just ask for any isogeny that satisfies the statement.

Alternatively, one may be given a tuple (E, S, E', S') and be asked whether there exists a d-isogeny such that $E' = \phi(E)$ and $S' = \phi(S)$. Variations on this decisional problem occur in cryptography, and we will point to them where relevant.

We were purposefully vague on the data structures involved in the definition of Γ-SIDH. Indeed the meaning of "given S" and "compute ϕ" may vary depending on context. It shall be understood that elliptic curves are represented by some projective model (e.g., a Weierstrass equation), and points by their coordinates in the model. We shall assume that the factorization of N is known, and that the modular groups Γ have some simple description, e.g., through a set of generators, or implicitly such as in "Γ_0, the subgroup of triangular matrices of determinant 1". The representation of level structures and isogenies is subtler.

Representing Isogenies. "Computing an isogeny" is usually understood as "computing a generator of its kernel". From this data, we can use Vélu's formulas to evaluate the isogeny at any point. However, in some cases of interest the points of the kernel may be defined over prohibitively large field extensions, or the isogeny may have large prime degree preventing the use of Vélu's formulas.

Instead, following [54,66], we will say that an algorithm (efficiently) *represents* an isogeny $\phi : E \to E'$ if, given any point $P \in E(\mathbb{F}_{q^k})$ as input, it outputs $\phi(P)$ in time $\mathrm{poly}(k \log(q))$. The goal of the Γ-SIDH problem will thus be to output a representation of ϕ, for instance as an arithmetic circuit.

Representing Level Structures. A level structure may be exponentially large, so representing it by the list of its bases is out of question. As a first attempt, we may represent $S \in \mathcal{B}_E(\Gamma)$ through an arbitrary basis in S and the group Γ, but even this representation may turn out to be prohibitively expensive. We now illustrate different ways of representing level structures through two examples.

Example 4. For supersingular curves, one never needs to look far to complete a basis. Indeed, if $P \in E(\mathbb{F}_q)$ is a point of order N, then a point Q such that (P, Q) forms a basis of $E[N]$ is always defined over an extension of $\mathbb{F}_q$ of degree at most 6 (or even 2, when $j(E) \neq 0, 1728$). It is thus possible to represent a level structure by an arbitrary basis (P, Q) and the group Γ at little extra cost.

Familiar examples are SIDH [49] and B-SIDH [27] public keys: these are triples (E, P, Q) where E is a supersingular curve over $\mathbb{F}_{p^2}$, and (P, Q) is a basis of $E[N]$, defined over $\mathbb{F}_{p^2}$ in SIDH's case, or over $\mathbb{F}_{p^4}$ in B-SIDH's case. In both cases Γ is the trivial group.

When N factors into primes as $N = \ell_1^{e_1} \cdots \ell_r^{e_r}$, it may be more advantageous to use the decomposition

$$E[N] = E[\ell_1^{e_1}] \oplus \cdots \oplus E[\ell_r^{e_r}]$$

and use a pair (P_i, Q_i) of generators of $E[\ell_i^{e_i}]$ for each factor. Indeed the fields of definition of each $E[\ell_i^{e_i}]$ will tend to be much smaller than their compositum, the field of definition of $E[N]$. The group Γ will then act on $E[\ell_i^{e_i}]$ in a similar way as $\Gamma \bmod \ell_i^{e_i}$.

Example 5. Ordinary curves behave differently: even when a point of order N is defined over some field $\mathbb{F}_q$, a full basis of $E[N]$ is, in general, only defined over an extension of degree $O(N)$. However some level structures may be appropriately described by a single point of order N. For example, given a basis (P, Q), its orbit under the group of upper-triangular matrices consists of all the bases $(aP + bQ, cQ)$, i.e., all the bases whose second generator lies in $\langle Q \rangle$. Such a level structure may thus simply be encoded by an arbitrary generator of $\langle Q \rangle$, or even by some implicit definition, such as "the unique subgroup of order N defined over the extension of degree n of $\mathbb{F}_q$".

The case where N is a power of a prime is well-known to be related to the theory of *isogeny volcanoes* [43,51]. These are graphs with elliptic curves for nodes and ℓ-isogenies for edges. The nodes are arranged into levels, corresponding to the endomorphism rings of the curves: At the top level, the *crater*, lie the curves with the largest endomorphism ring; at the bottom, the *floor* lie the curves with smallest endomorphism ring; from one level to the next the endomorphism ring grows or shrinks by a factor ℓ. ℓ-isogenies between curves on the same level are only possible on the crater, at every other level ℓ-isogenies can only go up or down one level. On the other hand, isogenies of degree d coprime to ℓ are only possible between curves on the same levels of the respective ℓ-isogeny volcanoes.

Miret, Sadornil, Tena, Tomàs, Rosana, and Valls [56] show that the structure of the ℓ-*Sylow* of $E(\mathbb{F}_q)$, i.e. of the largest subgroup of $E(\mathbb{F}_q)$ of order a power of ℓ, is controlled by the level in the volcano. At the floor of the volcano, the ℓ-Sylow is cyclic and is thus naturally identified with a ($*\atop*$)-level structure of level, say, ℓ^e; however a basis of the full $E[\ell^e]$ will only be defined over an extension of degree $O(\ell^e)$. At the other end, on the crater, the ℓ-Sylow may be isomorphic to $(\mathbb{Z}/\ell^{e/2}\mathbb{Z})^2$ and thus all bases of $E[\ell^{e/2}]$ would be defined, but we would have trouble representing any meaningful level structure of level $\ell^e \gg \ell^{e/2}$.

Because d is coprime to ℓ, the isogeny ϕ must be between curves on the same level of their respective ℓ-isogeny volcanoes, and thus preserve the structure of the ℓ-Sylows. Therefore, whichever representation of Γ-level structures works for E also works for E'.

As the examples show, there is not a single "good way" of representing level structures. In what follows we will enunciate algorithms assuming all points of $E[N]$ are always defined over the base field, for coherence with the most cryptographically relevant cases. The reader is left with the task of adjusting the algorithms to other representations where appropriate.

Restricting to SL₂. In most cases it makes sense to restrict to Γ-SIDH problems for $\Gamma \leq \mathrm{SL}_2$. Indeed, provided we can solve discrete logarithms in the subgroup of N-th roots of unity of $\overline{\mathbb{F}}_q$, we can reduce any Γ-SIDH problem to a $(\Gamma \cap \mathrm{SL}_2)$-SIDH as follows.

Lemma 6. *Let $\Gamma \leq \mathrm{GL}_2(\mathbb{Z}/N\mathbb{Z})$ and denote by $\mu_N \subset \mathbb{F}_{q^r}^\times$ the subgroup of N-th roots of unity. Given an oracle to solve discrete logarithms in μ_N, there exists a reduction from Γ-SIDH to $(\Gamma \cap \mathrm{SL}_2)$-SIDH with complexity polynomial in r, $\log(q)$ and $\log(N)$.*

Proof. Let (E, S, E', S') be a Γ-SIDH problem. If $E(\mathbb{F}_q)$ has order divisible by N, then by assumption $E[N] \subset E(\mathbb{F}_{q^{2r}})$. We can thus choose a representative (P, Q) of S and compute its order-N Weil pairing $\zeta := e_N(P, Q) \in \mathbb{F}_{q^r}$. Let $\overline{S} = (\Gamma \cap \mathrm{SL}_2) \cdot (P, Q)$; in other words, $\overline{S}$ is the set of bases obtained by acting on the basis (P, Q) with matrices in Γ having determinant 1. Thanks to the compatibility of the Weil pairing with isogenies,

$$e_N(\phi(\overline{S})) = e_N(\overline{S})^{\deg \phi} = \zeta^d.$$

Choose now a representative (P', Q') of $\phi(S)$ and compute its Weil pairing $\xi := e_N(P', Q')$. Use the oracle to compute the discrete logarithm x of ζ^d to base ξ and find a matrix $\gamma \in \Gamma$ with $\det \gamma = x$. Define $\overline{S}' = (\Gamma \cap \mathrm{SL}_2) \cdot \gamma \cdot (P', Q')$; then $\overline{S}' = \phi(\overline{S})$. Hence, $(E, \overline{S}, E', \overline{S}')$ is an instance of $(\Gamma \cap \mathrm{SL}_2)$-SIDH and has the same solutions as the original problem. $\square$

In the next sections we shall focus our attention on groups $\Gamma \leq \mathrm{SL}_2$, which happen to be the most common in cryptography.

4   A Reduction

We come to the main technical result of this work: a reduction between the Γ-SIDH problems for different modular groups Γ.

For ℓ an integer dividing N, define the subgroup

$$\Gamma_0(\ell) = \left\{ \left(\begin{smallmatrix} a & b \\ c \cdot \ell & d \end{smallmatrix} \right) \right\} \leq \mathrm{SL}_2(\mathbb{Z}/N\mathbb{Z}).$$

For $\Gamma \leq \Gamma_0(\ell)$, define its ℓ-*conjugate* as

$$\Gamma^* = \left\{ \left(\begin{smallmatrix} a & b \cdot \ell \\ c' & d \end{smallmatrix} \right) \mid \left(\begin{smallmatrix} a & b \\ c \cdot \ell & d \end{smallmatrix} \right) \in \Gamma \text{ and } c' \equiv c \pmod{N/\ell} \right\};$$

it is easily verified that Γ^* is a subgroup of SL_2.

The main subroutine of the reduction is Algorithm 1, which constructs from a curve E with Γ-level structure an ℓ-isogenous curve E' with Γ^*-level structure.

The correctness of Algorithm 1 follows from the following lemma:

Lemma 7. *Let N, ℓ be positive integers with $\ell \mid N$. Let E be an elliptic curve and (P, Q) a basis of $E[N]$. Let $\psi : E \to E'$ be an ℓ-isogeny with kernel $\langle (N/\ell) \cdot Q \rangle$ and let $\widehat{\psi}$ be its dual. A point $Q' \in E'[N]$ satisfies $\widehat{\psi} Q' = Q$ if and only if $e_N(\psi P, Q') = e_N(P, Q)$ and $\ell Q' = \psi Q$. In that case, the pair $(\psi P, Q')$ forms a basis of $E'[N]$.*

Algorithm 1: Changing from Γ-level structure to Γ^*-level structure.

Input: Integers N and $\ell \,|\, N$, a subgroup $\Gamma \leq \Gamma_0(\ell) \leq \mathrm{SL}_2(\mathbb{Z}/N\mathbb{Z})$,
      an elliptic curve E with Γ-level structure S.

Output: An elliptic curve E' with Γ^*-level structure S' and an ℓ-isogeny
      $\psi \colon E \to E'$ such that $\widehat{\psi}Q' \in \langle Q \rangle$ for all $(\_, Q) \in S$ and $(\_, Q') \in S'$.

1 Pick an arbitrary basis $(P, Q) \in S$;
2 Let $K := (N/\ell) \cdot Q$;
3 Compute an isogeny $\psi : E \to E'$ with kernel $\langle K \rangle$;
4 Let $P' := \psi P$ and $Q'' := \psi Q$;
5 Compute Q' such that $\ell Q' = Q'' = \psi Q$ and $e_N(P', Q') = e_N(P, Q)$;
6 Let $S' := \Gamma^* \cdot (P', Q')$ and **return** (E', S', ψ).

Proof. Let Q' be such that $\widehat{\psi}Q' = Q$, then, by the properties of the Weil pairing

$$e_N(\psi P, Q') = e_N(P, \widehat{\psi}Q') = e_N(P, Q). \tag{1}$$

Moreover $\psi Q = \psi \widehat{\psi}Q' = \ell Q'$.

Conversely, let Q' be a point satisfying Eq. (1) and such that $\ell Q' = \psi Q$. By the non-degeneracy of the Weil pairing we have $\widehat{\psi}Q' \in Q + \langle P \rangle$. Writing $\widehat{\psi}Q' = Q + xP$ for some $x \in \mathbb{Z}/N\mathbb{Z}$, we have

$$\ell Q' = \psi \widehat{\psi}Q' = \psi Q + x\psi P = \ell Q' + x\psi P,$$

hence $x = 0$ because ψP has order N.

In either case, because the Weil pairing from Eq. (1) has maximal order, $(\psi P, Q')$ must be a basis of $E'[N]$. $\qquad\square$

We are now ready to present a reduction from Γ-SIDH to Γ^*-SIDH. The idea underlying the algorithm is visualized in the diagram below, where the vertical arrows represent the ℓ-isogenies constructed by Algorithm 1: The key point is that all matrices in Γ are upper-triangular modulo ℓ, hence by construction the isogenies ψ, χ are parallel with respect to ϕ, i.e., $\ker \chi = \phi(\ker \psi)$, which implies the existence of ϕ'.

$$
\begin{array}{ccc}
E_0, \left(P_0, Q_0 \right) & \overset{\phi}{\dashrightarrow} & E_1, \left(P_1, Q_1 \right) \\[2mm]
\psi \Big\downarrow\Big\uparrow \widehat{\psi} & & \widehat{\chi}\Big\uparrow\Big\downarrow \chi \\[2mm]
\frac{E_0}{\langle N/\ell \cdot Q_0 \rangle}, \left(\psi P_0, \widehat{\psi}^{-1} Q_0 \right) & \overset{\phi'}{\dashrightarrow} & \frac{E_1}{\langle N/\ell \cdot Q_1 \rangle}, \left(\chi P_1, \widehat{\chi}^{-1} Q_1 \right)
\end{array}
$$

Theorem 8. *Let $\phi : E \to E'$ be an isogeny of degree d coprime to N, and let N be coprime to the characteristic. Let ℓ divide N and let $\Gamma \leq \Gamma_0(\ell)$. Given an instance of a Γ-SIDH problem with solution ϕ, Algorithm 2 outputs an instance of a Γ^*-SIDH problem with solution $\phi' = \chi \phi \widehat{\psi}/\ell$.*

Algorithm 2: Γ-SIDH to Γ^*-SIDH reduction.

Input: Integers N and $\ell \mid N$, a subgroup $\Gamma \le \Gamma_0(\ell) \le \mathrm{SL}_2(\mathbb{Z}/N\mathbb{Z})$,
　　　　a Γ-SIDH instance $(E_0, S, E_1, \phi(S))$.
Output: A Γ^*-SIDH instance $(E_0', S', E_1', \phi'(S'))$ together with ℓ-isogenies
　　　　$\psi: E_0 \to E_0'$, $\chi: E_1 \to E_1'$ such that $\chi \circ \phi = \phi' \circ \psi$.
1 Run Algorithm 1 with input (E_0, S) and let (E_0', S', ψ) be the result;
2 Run Algorithm 1 with input $(E_1, \phi(S))$ and let $(E_1', \phi'(S'), \chi)$ be the result;
3 **Return** $(E_0', S', E_1', \phi'(S'))$ *and* (ψ, χ).

Proof. Fix $(P_0, Q_0) \in S$, $(P_1, Q_1) \in \phi(S)$, $(P_0', Q_0') \in S'$, and $(P_1', Q_1') \in \phi'(S')$.

By definition of Γ-SIDH, there exists a matrix $\gamma = \left(\begin{smallmatrix} a & b \\ c \cdot \ell & d \end{smallmatrix} \right) \in \Gamma$ such that $\gamma \cdot (P_1, Q_1) = (\phi P_0, \phi Q_0)$. Thus we have $d(N/\ell) \cdot Q_1 = (N/\ell) \cdot \phi Q_0$, implying that $\ker \chi = \phi(\ker \psi)$ and therefore $\chi \phi \widehat{\psi}(E_0'[\ell]) = \chi \phi(\ker \psi) = \chi(\ker \chi) = \{0\}$. This proves that $\phi' := \chi \phi \widehat{\psi}/\ell$ is a well-defined isogeny.

Lemma 7 shows that (P_0', Q_0') and (P_1', Q_1') form bases of the respective N-torsion subgroups, and that $\widehat{\psi} Q_0' = Q_0$ and $\widehat{\chi} Q_1' = Q_1$. Using the properties of the dual isogeny, we readily see that $\widehat{\psi} P_0' = \ell P_0$ and $\widehat{\chi} P_1' = \ell P_1$.

To each of the isogenies in the diagram, we associate a matrix representing its action (on the left) on the N-torsion, with respect to the bases (P_0, Q_0), (P_1, Q_1), (P_0', Q_0') and (P_1', Q_1'). Thus, ϕ acts like γ^t, ψ and χ act like $\left(\begin{smallmatrix} 1 & \\ & \ell \end{smallmatrix} \right)$, and $\widehat{\psi}$ and $\widehat{\chi}$ act like $\left(\begin{smallmatrix} \ell & \\ & 1 \end{smallmatrix} \right)$. Writing $\left(\begin{smallmatrix} x & y \\ w & z \end{smallmatrix} \right)^t$ for the matrix of ϕ', we obtain the relations

$$\left(\begin{smallmatrix} 1 & \\ & \ell \end{smallmatrix} \right) \left(\begin{smallmatrix} a & c \cdot \ell \\ b & d \end{smallmatrix} \right) \equiv \left(\begin{smallmatrix} x & w \\ y & z \end{smallmatrix} \right) \left(\begin{smallmatrix} 1 & \\ & \ell \end{smallmatrix} \right) \pmod{N}; \qquad \text{\footnotesize [from } \chi \circ \phi = \phi' \circ \psi \text{]}$$

$$[.5ex] \left(\begin{smallmatrix} a & c \cdot \ell \\ b & d \end{smallmatrix} \right) \left(\begin{smallmatrix} \ell & \\ & 1 \end{smallmatrix} \right) \equiv \left(\begin{smallmatrix} \ell & \\ & 1 \end{smallmatrix} \right) \left(\begin{smallmatrix} x & w \\ y & z \end{smallmatrix} \right) \pmod{N}. \qquad \text{\footnotesize [from } \phi \circ \widehat{\psi} = \widehat{\chi} \circ \phi' \text{]}$$

Whence

$$x \equiv a, \quad y \equiv b\ell, \quad w\ell \equiv c\ell, \quad z \equiv d \pmod{N},$$

thus ϕ' acts like $\left(\begin{smallmatrix} a & b \cdot \ell \\ c' & d \end{smallmatrix} \right)^t$ for some $c' \equiv c \pmod{N/\ell}$.

Applying the same reasoning to all matrices $\gamma \in \Gamma$, we conclude that

$$\left(E_0', (P_0', Q_0'), E_1', (P_1', Q_1') \right)$$

is an instance of a Γ^*-SIDH problem with solution ϕ'. □

Example 9. Going back to Example 5, Algorithm 2 can be understood as moving up and down the volcano. For example, suppose one is given curves E_0, E_1 on the floor of their respective ℓ-volcanoes and seeks to compute an isogeny $\phi : E_0 \to E_1$. The ℓ-Sylows of E_0 and E_1 are cyclic, say of order ℓ^e, and are mapped one onto the other. Thus ϕ is solution to an instance of a Γ_0-SIDH problem of level ℓ^e.

There are unique rational ℓ-isogenies $\psi : E_0 \to E_0'$ and $\chi : E_1 \to E_1'$, both ascending, and their target curves E_0', E_1' have ℓ-Sylows isomorphic to $\mathbb{Z}/\ell\mathbb{Z} \times \mathbb{Z}/\ell^{e-1}\mathbb{Z}$. Algorithm 2 reduces the Γ_0-problem between E_0 and E_1 to a $\left(\begin{smallmatrix} * & *\ell \\ *\ell^{e-1} & * \end{smallmatrix} \right)$-problem between E_0' and E_1', matching the structure of the ℓ-Sylows.

To finish the reduction, we need to show that from a solution to the Γ^*-SIDH problem we can efficiently construct a solution to the original Γ-SIDH problem. This task essentially consists in evaluating the fractional isogeny $\phi = \widehat{\chi}\phi'\psi/\ell$; see the proof below for details.

A small difficulty arises when analyzing the complexity of Algorithm 1: Indeed during the computation of $\widehat{\psi}^{-1}Q$ in Step 5, it is possible that Q' is only defined over an extension field of $\mathbb{F}_q$. This cannot happen if we assume that $E[N]$ is defined over $\mathbb{F}_q$ for all curves in the isogeny class, as is the case for supersingular curves. We will only analyze the cost in this case, but note that the ordinary case can be handled by simply using Q'' as a representation for $\widehat{\psi}^{-1}Q$.

Corollary 10. *Γ-SIDH reduces to Γ^*-SIDH, with a polynomial overhead in ℓ, $\log(N)$ and $\log(q)$.*

Proof. Given an instance of Γ-SIDH, we apply Algorithm 2 and pass the result to a Γ^*-SIDH oracle, obtaining a representation of $\phi' : E_0' \to E_1'$. We use ϕ' to build a representation of ϕ as follows. Let P be a point of E_0 of which we want to know the image ϕP. Compute R such that $\ell R = P$, then $\phi P = \ell\phi R$. Now observe that $\ell\phi = \widehat{\chi}\phi'\psi$, hence $\phi P = \widehat{\chi}\phi'\psi R$.

We now analyze the cost of Algorithm 1 in terms of field operations. The choice of the basis (P, Q) is assumed to be free. The scalar multiplication in Step 2 costs $O(\log(N))$. Evaluating ψ costs $O(\ell)$ operations using Vélu's formulas. We can compute Q' by finding a preimage to Q'', using a root finding algorithm such as Cantor–Zassenhaus [14], which costs $\tilde{O}(\ell\log(q))$.

The cost of Algorithm 2 is that of running Algorithm 1 twice. Finally the additional cost of evaluating ϕP amounts to a division by ℓ and a few ℓ-isogeny evaluations, thus the same cost as Algorithm 2. $\square$

For an example of how the reduction in this section can be applied concretely, see Sect. 5.4 below.

5 Γ-SIDH Problems in the Wild

We finally review the occurrences of Γ-SIDH problems in the literature, and use the reduction of Sect. 4 to reveal some new connections. As previously stated, we only consider subgroups $\Gamma \leq \mathrm{SL}_2$. Fig. 1 gives an overview of this section: The table on the left lists groups Γ, the best known attack against the generic Γ-SIDH problem, and some schemes whose security is "based" on it; the diagram on the right shows reductions between the problems.

5.1   The Generic Isogeny Problem

When $\Gamma = \mathrm{SL}_2$, a level structure is just the set of all bases of $E[N]$ with a given value of the Weil pairing. Assuming we can solve discrete logarithms in μ_N, an arbitrary such basis can be computed from E using the technique described in

Γ	Best attack	Schemes
$\begin{pmatrix} 1 & \\ & 1 \end{pmatrix}$	poly	SIDH
$\begin{pmatrix} 1 & * \\ & 1 \end{pmatrix}$	poly	[16,21]
$\begin{pmatrix} \lambda & \\ & \lambda \end{pmatrix}$	exp	M-SIDH
$\begin{pmatrix} * & \\ & * \end{pmatrix}$	exp	FESTA, binSIDH, CSIDH, SCALLOP
$\begin{pmatrix} * & * \\ & * \end{pmatrix}$	exp	SIDH PoKs
SL_2	exp	generic

Fig. 1. Γ-SIDH problems, their difficulty and reductions. The *Schemes* column lists schemes that can be broken by solving the corresponding Γ-SIDH problem. Note these are not security reductions: some schemes may have better attacks (e.g., quantum subexponential time against CSIDH and SCALLOP). The reduction diagram uses dashed arrows to signify trivial inclusions and continuous arrows to represent reductions following from Theorem 10: The latter are between a Γ-SIDH problem of level n^2 and a Γ'-SIDH problem of level n; the filled arrow tip points towards the problem of level n.

Lemma 6. Thus SL_2-SIDH is simply the generic fixed-degree isogeny problem: given isogenous curves E, E', find $\phi : E \to E'$ of degree d.

The best generic algorithms to solve this problem have complexity polynomial in d, and are not much more advanced than plain exhaustive search. When $d = d_1 d_2$, a meet-in the middle approach [1,28] improves slightly over exhaustive search by intersecting the list of all curves d_1-isogenous to E with the list of all curves d_2-isogenous to E'.

When E and E' are supersingular, it is known that the generic isogeny problem is equivalent to the endomorphism ring problem (computing a quaternion representation of $\mathrm{End}(E)$ and $\mathrm{End}(E'))$ [40,66][2]. These are considered to be the most fundamental problems in isogeny-based cryptography, and a solution to them would compromise almost all known schemes. The best algorithms known take $\tilde{O}(\sqrt{p})$ classical time [39,41,44] or $\tilde{O}(\sqrt[4]{p})$ quantum time [11]. The generic fixed-degree isogeny problem is only known to be equivalent to the endomorphism ring problem when d is at least $O(p^3)$ [5,9].

In the ordinary case, the theory of isogeny volcanoes applies and yields an improvement over generic algorithms when d is large enough. The first step is to ascend to the craters of the ℓ-isogeny volcanoes for each ℓ dividing the conductors of $\mathrm{End}(E)$ and $\mathrm{End}(E')$, which has cost polynomial in the largest such ℓ. The second step is a collision-search algorithm in the isogeny class of the maximal order, taking $O(\sqrt{C})$ classical operations [45], or a hidden shift algorithm taking $O(\exp(\sqrt{\log(C)}))$ quantum operations [52,53,60], where C is the size of the isogeny class.[3] The final step evaluates the actual isogeny of degree d and can be done in $O(\exp(\sqrt{\log(C)}))$ classical and quantum time [24,50]. The same theory

---

[2] When d contains a large prime factor, the reduction is only quantum [23].

[3] The isogeny class of a random curve over $\mathbb{F}_q$ has size $O(\sqrt{q})$, however some curves (e.g., pairing-friendly curves) may be specially constructed with a small isogeny class.

also applies to supersingular curves defined over a prime field as in CSIDH [18], or more generally to *oriented* supersingular curves [34]. We shall come back to these cases when discussing $(^*_*)$-SIDH in Sect. 5.6.

5.2   The SIDH Problem

Appearance: SIDH key exchange and derivatives [48,49], B-SIDH [27], Séta [31].
Best attacks: polynomial time when N is smooth [15,55,62].

On the opposite end of the spectrum we have $\Gamma = \{(\begin{smallmatrix} 1 & 0 \\ 0 & 1 \end{smallmatrix})\}$, which is none else than (a minimal generalization of) the well-known SIDH problem: we are given d-isogenous curves E, E', points P, Q generating $E[N]$ and their images, and we want to find the isogeny.

The standard SIDH/SIKE setting [48,49] has $d = 2^n \approx 3^m = N$ and the (supersingular) curves are chosen so that $E[dN] \subset E(\mathbb{F}_{p^2})$. In some variants [27, 31] d and N are coprime smooth integers, and $E[dN] \subset E(\mathbb{F}_{p^4})$. The attacks on SIDH [15,55,62] show that in all these instances the SIDH problem can be solved in polynomial time. More generally, Robert proves the following theorem.

Theorem 11. *Let E be an elliptic curve over a finite field $\mathbb{F}_q$. Let $N \in \mathrm{poly}(q)$ be a polylog(q)-smooth integer, let $S \in \mathcal{B}_E(N)$, and suppose that S can be represented over an extension of $\mathbb{F}_q$ of size polylog(q).*

If $\phi : E \to E'$ is an isogeny of degree $d < N^2$, the instance $(E, S, E', \phi(S))$ of the SIDH problem can be solved in time polylog(q).

In more detail, in [61, Theorem 1.2] Robert provides an algorithm that, given $(E, S, E', \phi(S))$ and a point $R \in E(\mathbb{F}_{q^k})$, outputs ϕR. The only minor difference with the statement above is a stronger condition $d < N$, however this can be relaxed to $d < N^2$ using the technique described in [62, § 6.4].

Note that, when d is smooth too, one can recover a more traditional representation of ϕ as an isogeny walk by evaluating ϕ on $E[d]$.

In conclusion, the only instances where the (generalized) SIDH problem still appears to be hard are those where N contains a large prime factor, or where points of $E[N]$ cannot be represented over small extensions of $\mathbb{F}_q$.

5.3 $(^\lambda{}_\lambda)$-SIDH a.k.a. M-SIDH

Appearance: Masked-torsion SIDH [42].
Reduces to: SIDH, when N has few distinct prime factors.
Best attacks: exponential time [42], polynomial time for "special" supersingular curves [42] and for curves over $\mathbb{F}_p$ [21].

Acting by the group $\{(^\lambda{}_\lambda)\}$ of determinant-1 scalar matrices has been proposed as a countermeasure against the SIDH attacks. The key exchange scheme M-SIDH [42] (short for Masked-torsion SIDH) works exactly like SIDH, however, before publishing the images of the basis (P, Q) of $E[N]$, it masks them by a random scalar λ. That is, an M-SIDH public key is a triple $(E', \lambda\phi P, \lambda\phi Q)$.

By definition $\lambda^2 = 1$, so a straightforward way to solve M-SIDH is to try and guess λ, thus reducing to an SIDH problem. To protect against this, M-SIDH chooses N to have r distinct prime factors, so that there are 2^r possible solutions for λ, rendering the attack infeasible.

In [42] it is shown how to solve M-SIDH when the starting curve E is supersingular and has small endomorphisms. In [21] it is shown how to solve it when E is defined over a prime field $\mathbb{F}_p$ or when E is connected to its Galois conjugate by a small-degree isogeny. In the general case, the best known attacks consist in guessing $\lambda \bmod N'$ where N' is a divisor of N with the minimal number of prime factors such that $d \leq N'^2$. As before, the correct guess for $\lambda \bmod N'$ allows a reduction to an SIDH problem. The degree d and the integer N are chosen such that any such N' has r distinct prime factors, where r depends on the desired security level ($r = 128, 192, 256$ for example), so that the complexity of this attack is at least 2^r.

5.4 $(\begin{smallmatrix}1 & * \\ 1\end{smallmatrix})$-SIDH a.k.a. Unipotent SIDH a.k.a. Γ_1-SIDH a.k.a. SIDH$_1$

> **Appearance:** weak instances of class-group actions [16], flawed implementations of proofs of knowledge [33].
> **Reduces to:** SIDH, when N contains a large smooth square factor.

The next group we consider is Γ_1, the group of unitriangular matrices $(\begin{smallmatrix}1 & * \\ & 1\end{smallmatrix})$, a.k.a. the unipotent subgroup of SL_2. If $(P, Q) \in \mathcal{B}_E(N)$, its orbit $\Gamma_1 \cdot (P, Q)$ consists of all bases (R, Q) such that $e_N(R, Q) = e_N(P, Q)$, i.e., after fixing a value for the Weil pairing, Γ_1-level structures are in one-to-one correspondence with points of order N. Hence, Γ_1-SIDH is the variant of SIDH where, instead of the image of two generators of $E[N]$, only the image of a single point of order N is known. Because the notation of Γ_1 for the unipotent subgroup is standard in the theory of modular forms, we like to dub this the SIDH$_1$ problem.

Applying the reduction of Sect. 4, we prove a reduction from SIDH$_1$ to SIDH whenever N contains a large square smooth factor, e.g., when $N = \ell^e$ for some small prime ℓ.

Corollary 12. *Let n be an integer and ℓ its largest prime factor. The SIDH$_1$ problem of level n^2 reduces to the SIDH problem of level n in* $\mathrm{poly}(\ell)$-*time.*

Proof. Using Algorithm 2 repeatedly for each prime factor of n, we reduce SIDH$_1$ to Γ-SIDH with $\Gamma = \{(\begin{smallmatrix}1 & n* \\ n* & 1\end{smallmatrix})\}$. But $\Gamma \bmod n$ is the trivial subgroup of $\mathrm{SL}_2(\mathbb{Z}/n\mathbb{Z})$, thus, restricting the level structure to the n-torsion (i.e., multiplying the basis generators by n), we obtain an instance of SIDH of level n. □

Even if N is not exactly a square, the corollary above gives a strategy to attack SIDH$_1$. Indeed, if $N = sn^2$ with a small squarefree factor s, we can simply ignore s and restrict to the SIDH$_1$ problem of level n^2, which reduces to

SIDH of level n. Should this not be sufficient, we can add a small exhaustive search on s to reduce to SIDH of level sn.

To the best of our knowledge, SIDH_1 has not appeared in the literature as a security assumption, however we are aware of at least two instances where it showed up somewhat unexpectedly.

The first instance is in variants of the Couveignes–Rostovtsev–Stolbunov group action [29, 63] designed to be vulnerable precisely to Corollary 12 [16]. These isogeny classes are set up so that a large power $\ell^e > \sqrt{d}$ divides the discriminant. A self-pairing is then used to guess the image by ϕ of a point of order ℓ^e, leading to an SIDH_1 problem. Finally, our reduction is used to reduce to an SIDH problem that is solved using Robert's technique. Although this construction is artificial and not meant as a basis for cryptography, it shows that some isogeny-based group actions are less strong than originally thought.

The second instance is in proofs of knowledge of isogenies à la SIDH as seen in [33, 36]. Both papers claim computational zero-knowledge based on the decisional variant of Γ_0-SIDH, however an implementation mistake makes them actually reliant on Γ_1-SIDH, and thus broken. We shall give more details on this in the next section.

5.5 $(\begin{smallmatrix} * & * \\ * \end{smallmatrix})$-SIDH a.k.a. Borel SIDH a.k.a. Γ_0-SIDH a.k.a. SIDH_0

> **Appearance:** Proofs of Knowledge (decisional) [6, 33, 36].
> **Reduces to:** $(\begin{smallmatrix} * & * \end{smallmatrix})$-SIDH, when N contains a large smooth square factor.
> **Best attacks:** generic.

Γ_0 is the group of determinant-1 upper-triangular matrices, the *Borel subgroup* of SL_2. The associated level structures correspond to cyclic subgroups of order N with a given value for the Weil pairing, and are sometimes called *Borel level structures* [6, 25]. Again, we shorten Γ_0-SIDH into SIDH_0.

Using the reduction of Sect. 4, we prove that it is in fact equivalent to $(\begin{smallmatrix} * & * \end{smallmatrix})$-SIDH. We are told this isomorphism between level structures is folklore among experts in modular curves (see [25, § 2.5]), but the algorithmic aspect appears to be new.

Corollary 13. *Let n be an integer and ℓ its largest prime factor. The SIDH_0 problem of level n^2 and the $(\begin{smallmatrix} * & * \end{smallmatrix})$-SIDH problem of level n are* $\text{poly}(\ell)$-*time-equivalent.*

Proof. Using Algorithm 2 repeatedly for each prime factor of n, we reduce SIDH_0 to Γ-SIDH with $\Gamma = \{(\begin{smallmatrix} * & n* \\ n* & * \end{smallmatrix})\}$. Reducing modulo n we obtain a $(\begin{smallmatrix} * & * \end{smallmatrix})$-SIDH problem of level n.

Conversely, let (E_0, S_0, E_1, S_1) be an instance of $(\begin{smallmatrix} * & * \end{smallmatrix})$-SIDH. Pick arbitrary bases $(P_0, Q_0) \in S$ and $(P_1, Q_1) \in S_1$. Lift (P_0, Q_0) to a basis (P_0', Q_0') of $E_0[n^2]$ such that $nP_0' = P_0$ and $nQ_0' = Q_0$. Similarly lift (P_1, Q_1) to a basis (P_1', Q_1') of $E_1[n^2]$, with the additional constraint $e_{n^2}(P_1', Q_1') = e_{n^2}(P_0', Q_0')^d$, by solving a discrete logarithm for each factor ℓ of n, as in Lemma 6. Then

$(E_0, (P'_0, Q'_0), E_1, (P'_1, Q'_1))$ is an $\left(\begin{smallmatrix} * & n* \\ n* & * \end{smallmatrix}\right)$-SIDH instance of level n^2. Now apply Algorithm 2 to reduce to $\left(\begin{smallmatrix} * & \\ & * \end{smallmatrix}\right)$-SIDH and transpose to reduce to SIDH$_0$.   □

SIDH$_0$ arises naturally in proofs of knowledge of isogenies *à la SIDH* [33,36]. To prove knowledge of an N-isogeny $\psi : E_0 \to E_1$ between supersingular curves, these schemes eventually produce an N-isogeny $\psi' : E_2 \to E_3$ such that $\ker \psi' = \phi(\ker \psi)$ for some secret isogeny ϕ of degree d. $\ker \psi = \langle Q \rangle$ and $\ker \psi' = \phi(\langle Q \rangle) = \langle Q' \rangle$ are cyclic groups of order N, thus, completing them to bases $(P, Q) = E_0[N]$ and $(P', Q') = E_1[N]$, we see that $\phi(P, Q) \in \Gamma_0 \cdot (P', Q')$. Hence, recovering ϕ from ψ and ψ' is naturally an SIDH$_0$ problem.

In fact, the zero-knowledge property of these schemes reduces to the decisional version of SIDH$_0$: the game is to distinguish $(E_0, \ker \psi, E_2, \phi(\ker \psi))$ from $(E_0, \ker \psi, E_2, G)$ where G is a random cyclic group of order N. This problem was named Decisional Supersingular Product (DSSP) in [36]. Recently, DSSP was proven undecidable when $\deg \phi \to \infty$, and even statistically undecidable as soon as $d \in O((pN)^c)$ for an explicit constant c depending on N, using the theory of *supersingular isogeny graphs with level structure* [6].

When implementing these schemes, it is a common mistake to encode $\ker \psi$ by some particular generator Q, and $\ker \psi'$ by $\phi(Q)$ rather than by some arbitrary generator of $\phi(\langle Q \rangle)$. However, in doing so the tuple $(E_0, Q, E_2, \phi(Q))$ becomes an instance of SIDH$_1$ rather than SIDH$_0$, and may thus be solved in polynomial time depending on the relative sizes of d and N. The fix is to multiply $\phi(Q)$ by a random scalar to hide the exact image of Q. The bug is present in [36] and [33], although the latter has been fixed in the online version [32].[4]

5.6 $\left(\begin{smallmatrix} * & \\ & * \end{smallmatrix}\right)$-SIDH a.k.a. Diagonal SIDH

> **Appearance:** FESTA [8], CSIDH [18], SCALLOP [34], binSIDH [7].
> **Reduces to:** $\left(\begin{smallmatrix} * & * \\ & * \end{smallmatrix}\right)$-SIDH, when N contains a large smooth square factor.
> **Best attacks:** generic.

The last group we consider is the diagonal group $\{\left(\begin{smallmatrix} * & \\ & * \end{smallmatrix}\right)\}$, whose associated level structures are pairs of cyclic subgroups of order N, sometimes called *split Cartan level structures* (see [25]). Corollary 13 shows that $\left(\begin{smallmatrix} * & \\ & * \end{smallmatrix}\right)$-SIDH is equivalent to SIDH$_0$ when N has a large square smooth factor.

The supersingular version of this problem appears in the security analysis of the FESTA encryption scheme [8], where it is called the Computational Isogeny with Scaled Torsion (CIST) problem. Solving CIST breaks FESTA, however the IND-CCA security of the scheme reduces to a "double" variant of CIST named CIST^2. The $\left(\begin{smallmatrix} * & \\ & * \end{smallmatrix}\right)$-SIDH problem also appears in binSIDH [7] where it is referred to as the Artificially Oriented Isogeny Problem.

---

[4] We heard rumors that the same bug was at some point also present in the source code for [6], but, looking at https://github.com/trusted-isogenies/SECUER-pok, it appears to have been fixed.

$(*_*)$-SIDH also naturally appears in the theory of isogeny volcanoes, and thus in all "group action" schemes such as Couveignes–Rostovtsev–Stolbunov (CRS) [29,63], CSIDH [18] and SCALLOP [34].

When $\mathcal{O}$ is an imaginary-quadratic order, an $\mathcal{O}$-*oriented curve* [26] is an elliptic curve E together with an injection $\iota : \mathcal{O} \hookrightarrow \mathrm{End}(E)$. Thus, ordinary curves are $\mathrm{End}(E)$-oriented, curves in CSIDH are $\mathbb{Z}[\sqrt{-p}]$-oriented, and curves in SCALLOP are oriented by an order of large prime conductor inside $\mathbb{Z}[\sqrt{-1}]$.

To an ideal $\mathfrak{a}$ of $\mathcal{O}$ of norm coprime to q, we associate a subgroup

$$E[\mathfrak{a}] = \bigcap_{\alpha \in \mathfrak{a}} \{P \in E \mid \iota(\alpha)(P) = 0\}$$

and an isogeny $\phi_{\mathfrak{a}} : E \to E/E[\mathfrak{a}]$. A prime ℓ splits in $\mathcal{O}$ if the ideal $\ell\mathcal{O}$ factors as a product of two distinct ideals $\mathfrak{l}\bar{\mathfrak{l}}$, and in this case any $\mathcal{O}$-oriented curve has two distinguished cyclic groups of order ℓ, namely $E[\mathfrak{l}]$ and $E[\bar{\mathfrak{l}}]$.

For the key-recovery problem in the group-action setting, we are given two $\mathcal{O}$-oriented curves $E, E'/\mathbb{F}_q$; the goal is to find an ideal $\mathfrak{a}$ such that $\phi_{\mathfrak{a}} : E \to E'$. This problem is known as the Group Action Inverse Problem (GAIP).

Lemma 14. *Let $\mathcal{O}$ be an imaginary-quadratic order of discriminant $-\Delta$ and suppose that all but $O(\log\log\Delta)$ prime factors of Δ are bounded by $\mathrm{polylog}(\Delta)$. Under heuristics on the distribution of ideal classes, the GAIP with respect to $\mathcal{O}$ reduces to a $(*_*)$-SIDH problem in time polynomial in $\log(q)$ and $\log(\Delta)$.*

Proof. Let E, E' be a pair of $\mathcal{O}$-oriented curves. We assume access to an algorithm that solves the $(*_*)$-SIDH problem; using this, we seek to compute an ideal $\mathfrak{a}$ such that $\phi_{\mathfrak{a}} : E \to E'$.

The main heuristic concerns the fact that the norm of $\mathfrak{a}$ is an input to the $(*_*)$-SIDH oracle; however, this quantity is a priori unknown in the GAIP problem. We bypass this issue by sampling a "default degree" d from a distribution which heuristically yields a valid guess for the degree at a $1/\mathrm{polylog}(\Delta)$ rate. The distribution is designed to work around two major obstructions: First, genus theory for binary quadratic forms implies that a suitable d must have the correct values for the *genus characters* of $\mathcal{O}$. We may recover the correct symbols for all characters of moduli lying in $\mathrm{polylog}(\Delta)$ using the DDH attack of [17,20] and randomly guess the remaining $O(\log\log\Delta)$ symbols; the chance of being correct is thus $1/\mathrm{polylog}(\Delta)$. Second, a much more elementary constraint is that if d has ω prime factors, then there are at most 2^ω distinct $\mathcal{O}$-ideals of norm d; hence, any d covering all ideal classes in some genus must necessarily have many prime factors. Absent any unforeseen further obstructions, it should therefore suffice to choose d as a product of a set of $\tilde{\Omega}(\log\Delta)$ random split primes of size $\mathrm{polylog}(\Delta)$, such that the chosen values for the genus characters are satisfied.[5]

---

[5] Evidence (conditional on GRH) in support of this heuristic are (1) Bach's proof that ideals of norm up to $6\log(\Delta)^2$ generate the class group [4]; and (2) results in a line of work initiated by Landau and Bernays, see [10, part II, § 3] or for instance [57, § 5], which bound the density of integers represented by *all* quadratic forms in a given genus; however, those results are asymptotic and only become meaningful far beyond the sizes (relative to Δ) that are required for our purposes.

Now, assume that the degree d is known. Let E and E' be two $\mathcal{O}$-oriented curves and let $\mathfrak{a} \subset \mathcal{O}$ be an ideal of norm d such that $\phi_\mathfrak{a} : E \to E'$. For any positive integer e and any split prime $\ell = \mathfrak{l}\bar{\mathfrak{l}}$ not dividing d, we must have $\phi_\mathfrak{a}(E[\mathfrak{l}^e]) = E'[\mathfrak{l}^e]$ and $\phi_\mathfrak{a}(E[\bar{\mathfrak{l}}^e]) = E'[\bar{\mathfrak{l}}^e]$. Thus, one can always determine the images under $\phi_\mathfrak{a}$ of two disjoint cyclic groups of arbitrarily large powersmooth order $N = \ell_1^{e_1} \cdots \ell_r^{e_r}$, coprime to d, where each ℓ_i splits. Note that the choice of N as powersmooth ensures that the $\ell_i^{e_i}$-torsion points are defined over extension fields of polynomial degree. Hence, recovering $\phi_\mathfrak{a}$ of degree d is an $(^*_*)$-SIDH problem of level N, which we can pass to the $(^*_*)$-SIDH oracle.

There is one more caveat: In the supersingular setting, solving the constructed $(^*_*)$-SIDH problem may in fact produce a generic isogeny that fails to respect the orientation. In that case, to complete the reduction, we make use of known reductions between the supersingular endomorphism ring problem and the GAIP problem due to [19,65]: We first generate any $\mathcal{O}$-oriented supersingular curve E_0 of known endomorphism ring and apply the reduction above to both (E_0, E) and (E_0, E'). The resulting knowledge of smooth-degree isogenies $E_0 \to E$ and $E_0 \to E'$ thus reveals the endomorphism rings of E and E', respectively. This puts us into a position to invoke the reduction and finally recover an $\mathcal{O}$-ideal connecting E and E', as desired.   □

In all existing isogeny group actions (CRS, CSIDH, SCALLOP), the discriminant of the order $\mathcal{O}$ in play has very few prime factors. Hence, by Lemma 14, the respective GAIPs in isogeny group actions reduce to the corresponding $(^*_*)$-SIDH problem, which in turn is equivalent to SIDH$_0$, as previously shown.

Improved Algorithm for Isogenies Between Ordinary Curves. The fact that computing isogenies between oriented curves reduces to an $(^*_*)$-SIDH problem is well-known, and was already used in [35] in the context of the SEA point-counting algorithm [64]. The goal here is to compute an isogeny $\phi : E \to E'$ between ordinary curves, for a moderately large $d = \deg \phi$.

The algorithm in [35] finds a small split prime ℓ not dividing d and assumes that E and E' are on the craters of the respective ℓ-volcanoes (see Examples 5 and 9 for more background). Then it computes a *horizontal* basis B of $E[\ell^e]$ for $\ell^e > 2\sqrt{d}$, i.e., a basis (P, Q) such that $\langle P \rangle = \ker \phi_{\mathfrak{l}^e}$ and $\langle Q \rangle = \ker \phi_{\bar{\mathfrak{l}}^e}$. Then it computes a horizontal basis B' for $E'[\ell^e]$, so that $\phi(B) = \gamma \cdot B'$ for some matrix $\gamma \in \mathrm{GL}_2$. It finally finds γ by exhaustive search: for each choice it computes $\gamma \cdot B'$ and tries to compute ϕ by interpolation, halting when this succeeds. Since there are $O(\ell^{2e})$ diagonal matrices, and each interpolation step costs $\tilde{O}(d)$ operations, the total complexity is in $\tilde{O}(d^2)$.

We can give a first improvement using the technique of Lemma 6: choose B' so that $e_{\ell^e}(B') = e_{\ell^e}(B)^d$, then it is sufficient to go through the diagonal matrices in SL_2, which only number $O(\ell^e)$, leading to an algorithm with complexity $\tilde{O}(d^{1.5})$. Yet another improvement has recently become possible: instead of interpolation, we can use the algorithm of Theorem 11—whose dependency in d is only $\mathrm{polylog}(d)$—to test whether ϕ maps B to $\gamma \cdot B'$. Hence, we can find γ in $\tilde{O}(\sqrt{d})$ operations. In principle, we could stop here and use the isogeny representation returned by Theorem 11, however the goal of [35] is to compute ϕ as a rational fraction, which we can now do by interpolation using $\tilde{O}(d)$ operations, which is quasi-optimal.

When E and E' are not on the crater, the paper reduces to this case by walking up the volcano. However one can again improve the algorithm as follows. Say the curves are at depth h, the ℓ-Sylows of E and E' will typically contain a unique cyclic subgroup of maximal order, at least ℓ^{2h} (see [56] for details). These two groups must be mapped one onto the other by ϕ, thus they define a $(\begin{smallmatrix}*&*\end{smallmatrix})$-SIDH problem. Using Corollary 13 we reduce this to a $(\begin{smallmatrix}*&*\end{smallmatrix})$-SIDH problem of level (at least) ℓ^h, call it (F, S_1, F', S_1').

Now we proceed like before and compute horizontal bases of $F[\ell^h]$ and $F'[\ell^h]$, which define a second $(\begin{smallmatrix}*&*\end{smallmatrix})$-SIDH problem, call it (F, S_2, F', S_2'). As argued above, S_2 (and S_2') consists of all possible bases (P, Q) such that $\langle P \rangle = \ker \phi_{\ell^h}$ and $\langle Q \rangle = \ker \phi_{\hat\ell^h}$. However S_1 (and S_1') consists of all bases (P, R) such that $\langle P \rangle = \ker \phi_{\ell^h}$ and $\langle R \rangle$ generates the kernel of the ℓ^h-isogeny descending back towards E.

Combining both constraints with the one coming from the Weil pairing, all degrees of freedom are removed and we are left with a pure SIDH problem. In the extreme case where $\ell^{2h} > 4d$, we can directly compute ϕ without trial-and-error; otherwise the number of trials will be divided by ℓ^h.

In conclusion, we have a generic algorithm with quasi-optimal complexity in d for computing isogenies of known degree between ordinary curves, albeit with large constants hidden inside the $O()$. This was previously only known in the case where the characteristic is larger than $2d$ and the curve models are *normalized* [12].

This new algorithm asymptotically beats all previously known approaches to the so called "Elkies step" of the SEA algorithm in the regime where characteristic and extension degree both grow polynomially, and may be useful in practice for solving some large point counting problems (likely outside cases of cryptographic interest). Note, however, that the overall complexity of SEA is dominated by other steps, thus we do not have an asymptotic improvement on point counting.

6   Conclusion

We introduced a new framework to study assumptions in isogeny-based cryptography. We hope that it will help classify and relate seemingly distant isogeny assumptions.

An important consequence of our main theorem is that the image of a single point of large-enough order is in general sufficient to recover an isogeny. Understanding how far these attacks can be pushed is a fundamental question for isogeny-based cryptography.

We also showed that CSIDH reduces to Diagonal SIDH, which is equivalent to SIDH$_0$, and is thus no harder than breaking SIDH-like proofs of knowledge. While this may lend more credibility to the security of these proofs of knowledge, we warn against using the reduction to set parameters. Indeed the best quantum attacks against CSIDH are subexponential, whereas the best quantum attacks against SIDH-like proofs of knowledge are exponential, thus the reduction is void if one uses the best possible parameters. Conversely, it is an interesting question whether or not $SIDH_0$ and Diagonal SIDH can be solved in quantum subexponential time.

Acknowledgments. Luca De Feo acknowledges support from the Swiss National Science Foundation through grant no. 213766, CryptonIs. This research project was initiated at the Isogeny Days 2022 workshop organized with support from the ERC grant no. 101020788, ISOCRYPT. At the time, Lorenz Panny was a postdoc at Academia Sinica, Taiwan, funded by Academia Sinica Investigator Award AS-IA-109-M01.

We would like to thank Wouter Castryck, Antonin Leroux, Christophe Petit, Fréderik Vercauteren and Benjamin Wesolowski for the fruitful discussions, and the anonymous referees for their useful suggestions.

Disclosure of Interests. The authors have no competing interests to declare that are relevant to the content of this article.

References

1. Adj, G., Cervantes-Vázquez, D., Chi-Domínguez, J.J., Menezes, A., Rodríguez-Henríquez, F.: On the cost of computing isogenies between supersingular elliptic curves. In: Cid, C., Jacobson Jr:, M.J. (eds.) SAC 2018. LNCS, vol. 11349, pp. 322–343. Springer, Heidelberg (2019). https://doi.org/10.1007/978-3-030-10970-7_15
2. Agrawal, S., Lin, D. (eds.): ASIACRYPT 2022, Part II, LNCS, vol. 13792. Springer, Heidelberg (2022)
3. Arpin, S.: Adding level structure to supersingular elliptic curve isogeny graphs (2023). https://doi.org/10.48550/arXiv.2203.03531
4. Bach, E.: Analytic methods in the analysis and design of number-theoretic algorithms. MIT Press Cambridge (1985)
5. Basso, A., et al.: Exploring SIDH-based signature parameters. Cryptology ePrint Archive, Paper 2023/1906 (2023). https://link.springer.com/chapter/10.1007/978-3-031-54770-6_17
6. Basso, A., et al.: Supersingular curves you can trust. In: Hazay, C., Stam, M. (eds.) EUROCRYPT 2023, Part II. LNCS, vol. 14005, pp. 405–437. Springer, Heidelberg (2023). https://doi.org/10.1007/978-3-031-30617-4_14
7. Basso, A., Fouotsa, T.B.: New SIDH countermeasures for a more efficient key exchange. In: Guo and Steinfeld [46], pp. 208–233. https://doi.org/10.1007/978-981-99-8742-9_7
8. Basso, A., Maino, L., Pope, G.: FESTA: fast encryption from supersingular torsion attacks. In: Guo and Steinfeld [46], pp. 98–126. https://doi.org/10.1007/978-981-99-8739-9_4
9. Benčina, B., Kutas, P., Merz, S.P., Petit, C., Stopar, M., Weitkämper, C.: Improved algorithms for finding fixed-degree isogenies between supersingular elliptic curves. Cryptology ePrint Archive, Paper 2023/1618 (2023). https://eprint.iacr.org/2023/1618
10. Bernays, P.: Über die Darstellung von positiven, ganzen Zahlen durch die primitiven, binären quadratischen Formen einer nicht-quadratischen Diskriminante. Ph.D. thesis, Georg-August-Universität, Göttingen (1912)

11. Biasse, J.F., Jao, D., Sankar, A.: A quantum algorithm for computing isogenies between supersingular elliptic curves. In: Meier, W., Mukhopadhyay, D. (eds.) INDOCRYPT 2014. LNCS, vol. 8885, pp. 428–442. Springer, Heidelberg (2014). https://doi.org/10.1007/978-3-319-13039-2_25

12. Bostan, A., Morain, F., Salvy, B., Schost, É.: Fast algorithms for computing isogenies between elliptic curves. Math. Comput. **77**(263), 1755–1778 (2008)

13. Burdges, J., De Feo, L.: Delay encryption. In: Canteaut, A., Standaert, F.X. (eds.) EUROCRYPT 2021, Part I. LNCS, vol. 12696, pp. 302–326. Springer, Heidelberg (2021). https://doi.org/10.1007/978-3-030-77870-5_11

14. Cantor, D.G., Zassenhaus, H.: A new algorithm for factoring polynomials over finite fields. Math. Comput. **36**, 587–592 (1981)

15. Castryck, W., Decru, T.: An efficient key recovery attack on SIDH. In: Hazay and Stam [47], pp. 423–447. https://doi.org/10.1007/978-3-031-30589-4_15

16. Castryck, W., Houben, M., Merz, S.P., Mula, M., van Buuren, S., Vercauteren, F.: Weak instances of class group action based cryptography via self-pairings. In: Handschuh, H., Lysyanskaya, A. (eds.) CRYPTO 2023. LNCS, vol. 14083, pp. 762–792. Springer, Cham (2023). https://doi.org/10.1007/978-3-031-38548-3_25

17. Castryck, W., Houben, M., Vercauteren, F., Wesolowski, B.: On the decisional Diffie-Hellman problem for class group actions on oriented elliptic curves. Cryptology ePrint Archive, Report 2022/345 (2022). https://doi.org/10.1007/s40993-022-00399-6

18. Castryck, W., Lange, T., Martindale, C., Panny, L., Renes, J.: CSIDH: an efficient post-quantum commutative group action. In: Peyrin, T., Galbraith, S. (eds.) ASIACRYPT 2018, Part III. LNCS, vol. 11274, pp. 395–427. Springer, Heidelberg (2018). https://doi.org/10.1007/978-3-030-03332-3_15

19. Castryck, W., Panny, L., Vercauteren, F.: Rational isogenies from irrational endomorphisms. In: Canteaut, A., Ishai, Y. (eds.) EUROCRYPT 2020, Part II. LNCS, vol. 12106, pp. 523–548. Springer, Heidelberg (2020). https://doi.org/10.1007/978-3-030-45724-2_18

20. Castryck, W., Sotáková, J., Vercauteren, F.: Breaking the decisional Diffie-Hellman problem for class group actions using genus theory. In: Micciancio, D., Ristenpart, T. (eds.) CRYPTO 2020, Part II. LNCS, vol. 12171, pp. 92–120. Springer, Heidelberg (2020). https://doi.org/10.1007/978-3-030-56880-1_4

21. Castryck, W., Vercauteren, F.: A polynomial time attack on instances of M-SIDH and FESTA. In: Guo and Steinfeld [46], pp. 127–156. https://doi.org/978-981-99-8739-9_5

22. Chavez-Saab, J., et al.: SQIsign. Tech. rep., National Institute of Standards and Technology (2023). https://csrc.nist.gov/Projects/pqc-dig-sig/round-1-additional-signatures

23. Chen, M., Imran, M., Ivanyos, G., Kutas, P., Leroux, A., Petit, C.: Hidden stabilizers, the isogeny to endomorphism ring problem and the cryptanalysis of pSIDH. In: Guo and Steinfeld [46], pp. 99–130. https://doi.org/978-981-99-8727-6_4

24. Childs, A., Jao, D., Soukharev, V.: Constructing elliptic curve isogenies in quantum subexponential time. J. Math. Cryptol. **8**(1), 1–29 (2014). https://doi.org/10.1515/jmc-2012-0016

25. Codogni, G., Lido, G.: Spectral theory of isogeny graphs (2023). https://doi.org/10.48550/arXiv.2308.13913

26. Colò, L., Kohel, D.: Orienting supersingular isogeny graphs. J. Math. Cryptol. **14**(1), 414–437 (2020)

27. Costello, C.: B-SIDH: supersingular isogeny Diffie-Hellman using twisted torsion. In: Moriai, S., Wang, H. (eds.) ASIACRYPT 2020, Part II. LNCS, vol. 12492, pp. 440–463. Springer, Heidelberg (2020). https://doi.org/10.1007/978-3-030-64834-3_15

28. Costello, C., Longa, P., Naehrig, M., Renes, J., Virdia, F.: Improved classical cryptanalysis of SIKE in practice. In: Kiayias, A., Kohlweiss, M., Wallden, P., Zikas, V. (eds.) PKC 2020, Part II. LNCS, vol. 12111, pp. 505–534. Springer, Heidelberg (2020). https://doi.org/10.1007/978-3-030-45388-6_18

29. Couveignes, J.M.: Hard homogeneous spaces. Cryptology ePrint Archive, Report 2006/291 (2006). https://eprint.iacr.org/2006/291

30. Dartois, P., Leroux, A., Robert, D., Wesolowski, B.: SQISignHD: new dimensions in cryptography. In: EUROCRYPT 2024. LNCS, Springer (2024). https://eprint.iacr.org/2023/436

31. De Feo, L., et al.: Séta: supersingular encryption from torsion attacks. In: Tibouchi, M., Wang, H. (eds.) ASIACRYPT 2021, Part IV. LNCS, vol. 13093, pp. 249–278. Springer, Heidelberg (2021). https://doi.org/10.1007/978-3-030-92068-5_9

32. De Feo, L., Dobson, S., Galbraith, S.D., Zobernig, L.: SIDH proof of knowledge. Cryptology ePrint Archive, Report 2021/1023 (2021). https://eprint.iacr.org/2021/1023

33. De Feo, L., Dobson, S., Galbraith, S.D., Zobernig, L.: SIDH proof of knowledge. In: Agrawal and Lin [2], pp. 310–339. https://doi.org/10.1007/978-3-031-22966-4_11

34. De Feo, L., et al.: SCALLOP: scaling the CSI-FiSh. In: Boldyreva, A., Kolesnikov, V. (eds.) PKC 2023, Part I. LNCS, vol. 13940, pp. 345–375. Springer, Heidelberg (2023). https://doi.org/10.1007/978-3-031-31368-4_13

35. De Feo, L., Hugounenq, C., Plût, J., Schost, E.: Explicit isogenies in quadratic time in any characteristic. LMS J. Comput. Mat. **19**(A), 267-282 (2016). https://doi.org/10.1112/s146115701600036x

36. De Feo, L., Jao, D., Plût, J.: Towards quantum-resistant cryptosystems from supersingular elliptic curve isogenies. J. Math. Cryptol. **8**(3), 209–247 (2014). https://doi.org/10.1515/jmc-2012-0015

37. De Feo, L., Kohel, D., Leroux, A., Petit, C., Wesolowski, B.: SQISign: compact post-quantum signatures from quaternions and isogenies. In: Moriai, S., Wang, H. (eds.) ASIACRYPT 2020, Part I. LNCS, vol. 12491, pp. 64–93. Springer, Heidelberg (2020). https://doi.org/10.1007/978-3-030-64837-4_3

38. De Feo, L., Masson, S., Petit, C., Sanso, A.: Verifiable delay functions from supersingular isogenies and pairings. In: Galbraith, S.D., Moriai, S. (eds.) ASIACRYPT 2019, Part I. LNCS, vol. 11921, pp. 248–277. Springer, Heidelberg (2019). https://doi.org/10.1007/978-3-030-34578-5_10

39. Delfs, C., Galbraith, S.D.: Computing isogenies between supersingular elliptic curves over $\mathbb{F}_p$. Des. Codes Crypt. **78**(2), 425–440 (2016). https://doi.org/10.1007/s10623-014-0010-1

40. Eisenträger, K., Hallgren, S., Lauter, K.E., Morrison, T., Petit, C.: Supersingular isogeny graphs and endomorphism rings: Reductions and solutions. In: Nielsen, J.B., Rijmen, V. (eds.) EUROCRYPT 2018, Part III. LNCS, vol. 10822, pp. 329–368. Springer, Heidelberg (2018). https://doi.org/10.1007/978-3-319-78372-7_11

41. Eisenträger, K., Hallgren, S., Leonardi, C., Morrison, T., Park, J.: Computing endomorphism rings of supersingular elliptic curves and connections to path-finding in isogeny graphs. Open Book Series **4**(1), 215–232 (2020)

42. Fouotsa, T.B., Moriya, T., Petit, C.: M-SIDH and MD-SIDH: countering SIDH attacks by masking information. In: Hazay and Stam [47], pp. 282–309. https://doi.org/10.1007/978-3-031-30589-4_10

43. Fouquet, M., Morain, F.: Isogeny volcanoes and the SEA algorithm. In: Fieker, C., Kohel, D.R. (eds.) Algorithmic Number Theory Symposium. LNCS, vol. 2369, pp. 47–62. Springer, Berlin (2002). https://doi.org/10.1007/3-540-45455-1_23

44. Fuselier, J., Iezzi, A., Kozek, M., Morrison, T., Namoijam, C.: Computing supersingular endomorphism rings using inseparable endomorphisms (2023). https://doi.org/10.48550/arXiv.2306.03051

45. Galbraith, S.D., Hess, F., Smart, N.P.: Extending the GHS Weil descent attack. In: Knudsen, L.R. (ed.) EUROCRYPT 2002. LNCS, vol. 2332, pp. 29–44. Springer, Heidelberg (2002). https://doi.org/10.1007/3-540-46035-7_3

46. Guo, J., Steinfeld, R. (eds.): ASIACRYPT 2023. LNCS, Springer (2023)

47. Hazay, C., Stam, M. (eds.): EUROCRYPT 2023, Part V, LNCS, vol. 14008. Springer, Heidelberg (2023)

48. Jao, D., et al.: SIKE. Tech. rep., National Institute of Standards and Technology (2022). https://csrc.nist.gov/Projects/post-quantum-cryptography/round-4-submissions

49. Jao, D., De Feo, L.: Towards quantum-resistant cryptosystems from supersingular elliptic curve isogenies. In: Yang, B.Y. (ed.) Post-Quantum Cryptography - 4th International Workshop, PQCrypto 2011, pp. 19–34. Springer, Heidelberg (2011). https://doi.org/10.1007/978-3-642-25405-5_2

50. Jao, D., Soukharev, V.: A subexponential algorithm for evaluating large degree isogenies. Algorithmic Number Theory, pp. 219-233 (2010). https://doi.org/10.1007/978-3-642-14518-6_19

51. Kohel, D.: Endomorphism rings of elliptic curves over finite fields. Ph.D. thesis, University of California at Berkeley (1996). https://i2m.univ-amu.fr/perso/david.kohel/pub/thesis.pdf

52. Kuperberg, G.: A subexponential-time quantum algorithm for the dihedral hidden subgroup problem. SIAM J. Comput. 35(1), 170–188 (2005). https://doi.org/10.1137/S0097539703436345

53. Kuperberg, G.: Another Subexponential-time Quantum Algorithm for the Dihedral Hidden Subgroup Problem. In: Severini, S., Brandao, F. (eds.) 8th Conference on the Theory of Quantum Computation, Communication and Cryptography (TQC 2013). Leibniz International Proceedings in Informatics (LIPIcs), vol. 22, pp. 20–34. Schloss Dagstuhl–Leibniz-Zentrum fuer Informatik, Dagstuhl, Germany (2013). https://doi.org/10.4230/LIPIcs.TQC.2013.20

54. Leroux, A.: A new isogeny representation and applications to cryptography. In: Agrawal and Lin [2], pp. 3–35. https://doi.org/10.1007/978-3-031-22966-4_1

55. Maino, L., Martindale, C., Panny, L., Pope, G., Wesolowski, B.: A direct key recovery attack on SIDH. In: Hazay and Stam [47], pp. 448–471. https://doi.org/10.1007/978-3-031-30589-4_16

56. Miret, J.M., Sadornil, D., Tena, J., Tomàs, R., Valls, M.: Volcanoes of ℓ-isogenies of elliptic curves. Publicacions Matemàtiques, pp. 165–180 (2007). https://www.raco.cat/index.php/PublicacionsMatematiques/article/download/69987/387563

57. Odoni, R.: A new equidistribution property of norms of ideals in given classes. Acta Arith 33(1), 53–63 (1977)

58. Page, A., Wesolowski, B.: The supersingular endomorphism ring and one endomorphism problems are equivalent. In: Joye, M., Leander, G. (eds.) EUROCRYPT 2024, Part VI. LNCS, vol. 14656, pp. 388–417. Springer, Heidelberg (2024). https://doi.org/10.1007/978-3-031-58751-1_14

59. Petit, C.: Faster algorithms for isogeny problems using torsion point images. In: Takagi, T., Peyrin, T. (eds.) ASIACRYPT 2017, Part II. LNCS, vol. 10625, pp. 330–353. Springer, Heidelberg (2017). https://doi.org/10.1007/978-3-319-70697-9_12

60. Regev, O.: A subexponential time algorithm for the dihedral hidden subgroup problem with polynomial space. arXiv:quant-ph/0406151 (Jun 2004)

61. Robert, D.: Evaluating isogenies in polylogarithmic time. Cryptology ePrint Archive, Report 2022/1068 (2022). https://eprint.iacr.org/2022/1068

62. Robert, D.: Breaking SIDH in polynomial time. In: Hazay and Stam [47], pp. 472–503. https://doi.org/10.1007/978-3-031-30589-4_17

63. Rostovtsev, A., Stolbunov, A.: Public-Key Cryptosystem Based on Isogenies. Cryptology ePrint Archive, Report 2006/145 (2006). https://eprint.iacr.org/2006/145

64. Schoof, R.: Counting points on elliptic curves over finite fields. Journal de théorie des nombres de Bordeaux **7**(1), 219–254 (1995). http://www.numdam.org/item/JTNB_1995__7_1_219_0/

65. Wesolowski, B.: Orientations and the supersingular endomorphism ring problem. In: Dunkelman, O., Dziembowski, S. (eds.) EUROCRYPT 2022, Part III. LNCS, vol. 13277, pp. 345–371. Springer, Heidelberg (2022). https://doi.org/10.1007/978-3-031-07082-2_13

66. Wesolowski, B.: The supersingular isogeny path and endomorphism ring problems are equivalent. In: 62nd FOCS. pp. 1100–1111. IEEE Computer Society Press (Feb 2022). https://doi.org/10.1109/FOCS52979.2021.00109

Key Recovery Attack on the Partial Vandermonde Knapsack Problem

Dipayan Das[1]([⊠])[iD] and Antoine Joux[2][iD]

[1] NTT Social Informatics Laboratories, Tokyo, Japan
dipayan.das@ntt.com
[2] CISPA Helmholtz Center for Information Security, Saarbrücken, Germany
joux@cispa.de

Abstract. The Partial Vandermonde (PV) Knapsack problem is an algebraic variant of the low-density inhomogeneous SIS problem. The problem has been used as a building block for various lattice-based constructions, including signatures (ACNS'14, ACISP'18), encryptions (DCC'15,DCC'20), and signature aggregation (Eprint'20). At Crypto'22, Boudgoust, Gachon, and Pellet-Mary proposed a key distinguishing attack on the PV Knapsack exploiting algebraic properties of the problem. Unfortunately, their attack doesn't offer key recovery, except for worst-case keys.

In this paper, we propose an alternative attack on the PV Knapsack problem which provides key recovery for a much larger set of keys. Like the Crypto'22 attack, it is based on lattice reduction and uses a dimension reduction technique to speed-up the underlying lattice reduction algorithm and enhance its performance. As a side bonus, our attack transforms the PV Knapsack problem into uSVP instances instead of SVP instances in the Crypto'22 attack. This also helps the lattice reduction algorithm, both from a theoretical and practical point of view.

We use our attack to re-assess the hardness of the concrete parameters used in the literature. It appears that many contain a non-negligible fraction of weak keys, which are easily identified and extremely susceptible to our attack. For example, a fraction of 2^{-19} of the public keys of a parameter set from ACISP'18 can be solved in about 30 hours on a moderate server using off-the-shelf lattice reduction. This parameter set was initially claimed to have a 129-bit security against key recovery attack. Its security was reduced to 87-bit security using the distinguishing attack from Crypto'22. Similarly, the ACNS'14 proposal also includes a parameter set containing a fraction of 2^{-19} of weak keys; those can be solved in about 17 hours.

1 Introduction

The PV Knapsack problem, previously called the partial Fourier recovery problem, was introduced in [11] as a new lattice-based assumption for post-quantum cryptography. The efficiency and rich algebraic properties underlying the PV Knapsack problem make it an attractive choice. As a result, the problem has

© International Association for Cryptologic Research 2024
M. Joye and G. Leander (Eds.): EUROCRYPT 2024, LNCS 14657, pp. 205–225, 2024.
https://doi.org/10.1007/978-3-031-58754-2_8

been used as a building block for various primitives, such as encryptions [5,12], signatures [11,14], and aggregatable signatures [9].

Let $\mathcal{R}_q := \mathbb{Z}_q[x]/(g(x))$ be a quotient polynomial ring, where g splits linearly over $\mathbb{Z}_q$ for some prime q. In the literature, g is commonly either $x^n - 1$ with prime n or $x^n + 1$ with power-of-two n. In the rest of the paper, we assume that g corresponds to one of these choices. Denote by Ω the set of all the primitive roots of g over $\mathbb{Z}_q$. Consider Ω_t, a uniformly selected random subset of Ω of size t. The PV Knapsack problem (informally) states the following:

It is hard to recover a uniform ternary $f(x) \in \mathcal{R}_q$, given only the evaluations of $f(x)$ at $\omega \in \Omega_t$ when $t \approx \lfloor n/2 \rfloor$.

The PV Knapsack problem also has a decisional version, which asks to distinguish between the evaluations of arbitrary $f(x)$ and ternary $f(x)$ at $\omega \in \Omega_t$.

The main approach to solving the problem has been the lattice reduction algorithms [11]. Recently, the authors of [4] proposed an algebraic method that reduces the cost of the lattice reduction for solving the decisional problem.

The distinguishing attack of [4] doesn't lead to a key recovery attack in general. In Sect. 5 of [4], key recovery is only obtained for a small number of worst-case keys. Furthermore, their paper states: *We note however that this does not fully invalidate the claim made in [14], since the 128 bit-security is claimed against search attackers, and not distinguishing attackers.*

This quote is the starting motivation for this work. Indeed, it might be worthwhile – from an attacker's viewpoint – to find a search attack against the PV Knapsack. As far as we know, there are some lattice-based assumptions where the search problem remains intractable, even though the decision problem is easy; one example is the FFI problem [8].

2   Preliminaries

2.1   Notations

For any integer $N > 1$, we write $\mathbb{Z}_N$ to denote the ring of integers modulo N and $\mathbb{Z}_N^*$ to denote the multiplicative subgroup of its units. In particular, when q is prime, $\mathbb{Z}_q$ is the finite field with q elements. We assume that q is odd and, in that case, we represent elements of $\mathbb{Z}_q$ by the unique representative belonging to the interval $[-(q-1)/2, (q-1)/2]$.

We let $\mathcal{R}_q = \mathbb{Z}_q[x]/(g)$ denote the quotient polynomial ring of $\mathbb{Z}_q[x]$ by $g(x)$, where $g(x)$ is either $x^n - 1$ with n a prime or $x^n + 1$ with n a power of two. We insist that g splits into linear factors over $\mathbb{Z}_q$. We denote by Ω the set of all primitive roots of g in $\mathbb{Z}_q$. When n is a prime, Ω contains all roots of g except 1; when n is a power of two, Ω contains all roots of g. In both cases, for any $\omega \in \Omega$ and any root ω' of g in $\mathbb{Z}_q$, ω' can be written as a power of ω, say $\omega^{i_{\omega'}}$. In particular, when n is prime $1 = \omega^0$ in $\mathbb{Z}_q$. Note that for a prime value of n, the exponent $i_{\omega'}$ can take all values in $\mathbb{Z}_n$. When n is a power of two, the exponent $i_{\omega'}$ takes all odd values in $\mathbb{Z}_{2n}$. As a consequence, if we exclude the non-primitive root 1, the exponents $i_{\omega'}$ belong to $\mathbb{Z}_n^*$ when n is prime and $\mathbb{Z}_{2n}^*$ when n is a power of two. To lighten notations, we use $U(n)$ as a shorthand for $\mathbb{Z}_n^*$ when n is prime and $\mathbb{Z}_{2n}^*$ when n is a power of two.

As a consequence, it is convenient to choose an arbitrary primitive root ω_1 of g in $\mathbb{Z}_q$ and write:

$$\Omega = \{\omega_i = \omega_1^i \mid i \in U(n)\}.$$

Remark 1. The condition that g splits in $\mathbb{Z}_q$ implies that $q = 1 \bmod n$ when n is prime and that $q = 1 \bmod 2n$ when n is a power of two.

To represent polynomial in $\mathcal{R}_q$, we use the polynomial basis $\{1, x, \ldots, x^{n-1}\}$. Since we are working modulo g, for any polynomial f in $\mathcal{R}_q$, we can interpret $f(1/x)$ as a polynomial. More precisely, if $f(x) = f_0 + f_1 x + \cdots + f_{n-1} x^{n-1}$, we define:

$$f(1/x) = \begin{cases} f_0 + f_1 x^{n-1} + \cdots + f_{n-1} x & \text{when } n \text{ is prime} \\ f_0 - f_1 x^{n-1} - \cdots - f_{n-1} x & \text{when } n \text{ is a power of two} \end{cases}$$

It is easy to verify that for any root ω of g, the evaluation of $f(x)$ at ω^{-1} coincides with the evaluation of $f(1/x)$ at ω, thus justifying our definition.

Since we have specified a basis for polynomials in $\mathcal{R}_q$, we can identify a polynomial with the vector of its coefficients in this basis. We use this identification extensively in the descriptions of the various attacks. For any vector v (or polynomial using the vector identification), we write $\|v\|$ (resp. $\|v\|_\infty$) to denote the ℓ_2 norm (resp. ℓ_∞ norm) of v. We also write $A = (A_1 \mid A_2)$ to denote the concatenation of two matrices A_1 and A_2, with the same number of rows.

2.2   The PV Knapsack Problem

Let Ω_t be a subset of $t \leq \lfloor n/2 \rfloor$ distinct random elements from Ω. Let $f(x)$ be a polynomial in $\mathcal{R}_q$ whose coefficients are sampled uniformly at random from the set $\{-1, 0, 1\}$.

Definition 1 (PV Knapsack problem). *Given $\mathcal{R}_q$ and $\{(\omega, f(\omega)) \mid \omega \in \Omega_t\}$, recover $f(x)$.*

Instead of identifying a PV Knapsack instance by Ω_t, it is often simpler to identify it by the corresponding index set $S_t \subset U(n)$. The PV Knapsack instance then becomes $\{(i, f(\omega_1^i) \mid i \in S_t\}$ for some arbitrary primitive root ω_1 of g.

Remark 2. When n is prime, we have to assume the evaluation of f at 1 is never included, as this provides a simple distinguishing attack on the PV Knapsack problem. This explains why we choose Ω to only contain primitive roots.

2.3   Lattice Reduction

Any (full rank) matrix $B \in \mathbb{Z}^{n \times n}$ generates a lattice $\mathcal{L}$ of dimension n, which is the set $\mathcal{L}(B) = \{Bz : z \in \mathbb{Z}^n\}$. A lattice is called q-ary when it contains $q\mathbb{Z}^n$ as a sublattice. The volume of the lattice $\mathcal{L}(B)$ is defined as $\mathsf{Vol} = |\det(B)|$.

The key computational problem involving lattices is to find the shortest non-zero vector (SVP) in the lattice $\mathcal{L}$. Minkowski's theorem yields the following upper bounds on the norms of the shortest non-zero vector $\boldsymbol{v}$ of any lattice of dimension n and volume Vol:

$$\|\boldsymbol{v}\|_\infty \le \mathsf{Vol}^{1/n} \quad \text{and} \quad \|\boldsymbol{v}\| \le \sqrt{n}\,\mathsf{Vol}^{1/n}.$$

Definition 2 (q-ary Kernel lattice). *Let $\boldsymbol{A} \in \mathbb{Z}_q^{t\times n}$ be any (full rank) matrix with $n > t$. We define the q-ary Kernel lattice of $\boldsymbol{A}$ as*

$$\mathcal{L}_{\boldsymbol{A},q}^\perp = \{\boldsymbol{v} \in \mathbb{Z}^n : \boldsymbol{A}\boldsymbol{v} = 0 \bmod q\}.$$

If we write $\boldsymbol{A} = (\boldsymbol{A}_1|\boldsymbol{A}_2)$, where $\boldsymbol{A}_1 \in \mathbb{Z}_q^{t\times t}$, $\boldsymbol{A}_2 \in \mathbb{Z}_q^{t\times n-t}$, then assuming that $\boldsymbol{A}_1$ is invertible, $\mathcal{L}_{\boldsymbol{A},q}^\perp$ has a basis

$$\begin{pmatrix} q\boldsymbol{I}_t & -\boldsymbol{A}_1^{-1}\boldsymbol{A}_2 \\ \boldsymbol{0} & \boldsymbol{I}_{n-t} \end{pmatrix}.$$

If $\boldsymbol{A}_1$ is not invertible, we can simply re-order the columns to make $\boldsymbol{A}$ start with a $t \times t$ invertible matrix. The lattice $\mathcal{L}_{\boldsymbol{A},q}^\perp$ has dimension n and volume q^t. Finding a short vector in this lattice, i.e., a short element in the kernel of $\boldsymbol{A}$, is usually referred to as the short integer solution (SIS) problem.

Let λ_i denotes the smallest radius of a closed ball containing at least i linearly independent vectors in the lattice $\mathcal{L}$. If $\lambda_2 > \gamma\lambda_1$ for some $\gamma \ge 1$, then the lattice contains a γ-unique SVP (uSVP) solution.

Definition 3 (uSVP$_\gamma$ problem). *Given a lattice $\mathcal{L}$, with the promise that $\lambda_2 > \gamma\lambda_1$ for $\gamma \ge 1$, the uSVP$_\gamma$ problem asks to find $\boldsymbol{v}$ such that $\|\boldsymbol{v}\| = \lambda_1$. The γ is referred to as the uniqueness gap of the uSVP problem.*

In order to find short solutions in a lattice, we rely on the lattice reduction algorithms. LLL [13] is a polynomial time algorithm, but only gives an exponential approximation solution. For cryptanalysis, it is often required for better solutions, which is done using stronger (and so slower) lattice reduction algorithms. For our purpose, we use the implementation of the Blockwise Korkine-Zolotarev (BKZ) algorithm [16] given in the fplll software [17].

According to the analysis of [10], the uSVP problem, with uniqueness gap γ in dimension n, can be solved using a lattice reduction algorithm that achieves a root Hermite factor close to $\delta = \gamma^{1/n}$. In particular, when γ is large enough, the value of δ becomes achievable with practical lattice reduction [1,3]. With high enough values of δ, the uSVP problem becomes efficiently solvable.

3   Previous Attacks

In this section, we briefly describe the attacks that were considered in prior works. Based on the approach of the attacks, we can characterise them as primal and dual attacks in the context of the PV Knapsack problem.

3.1 Direct Primal Attack [11]

The problem can be expressed as a structured variant of the low-density inhomogeneous SIS (or LWE) problem by expressing the evaluation $f(\omega)$ in terms of powers of ω, which is stated below.

Given a (partial) Vandermonde matrix $V \in \mathbb{Z}_q^{t \times n}$ (with rows generated by powers of ω for $\omega \in \Omega_t$) and $b \in \mathbb{Z}_q^t$ (with elements $f(\omega)$), find f with $\|f\|_\infty \leq 1$ such that

$$Vf = b \bmod q, \tag{1}$$

The authors proposed the strategy of finding the uSVP solution (following Kannan's embedding [15]) on the kernel lattice

$$\mathcal{L}_{V',q}^{\perp} = \{v \in \mathbb{Z}^{n+1} : V'v = 0 \bmod q\}$$

where $V' = (V|b)$. Note that, $(f| - 1)^T$ is a vector in the lattice $\mathcal{L}_{V'q}^{\perp}$, which is a solution to the uSVP problem[1]. In practice, this direct attack is used as a baseline to choose the parameters, with the understanding that they should be selected to ensure that finding the uSVP solution remains intractable both on classical and quantum computers.

3.2 Dual Attack [4]

Here, we give a simplified version of the attack proposed in [4]. For this purpose, we need to restate the PV Knapsack problem as an instance of the Bounded Distance Decoding (BDD) problem in the following manner. Let $z \in \mathbb{Z}^n$ be any solution to the system of linear equations satisfying $Vz = b \bmod q$, then the PV Knapsack problem asks to find $u \in \mathcal{L}_{V,q}^{\perp}$ (i.e., $Vu = 0 \bmod q$) such that $\|u - z\|_\infty \leq 1$, i.e., the vector $u - z = f$. Algebraically, the element $u(x)$ belongs to the ideal I_{Ω_t} of $\mathcal{R}_q$, where $I_{\Omega_t} = \prod_{\omega \in \Omega_t}(x - \omega)$. So, the PV Knapsack problem can be considered a BDD problem in the ideal I_{Ω_t}.

Let $u'(x)$ be an element in the ideal $I_{\Omega \setminus \Omega_t} = \prod_{\omega' \in \Omega \setminus \Omega_t}(x - \omega')$ with "somewhat" small norm.[2] Then the product $u'(x)z(x) = u'(x)f(x)$ in $\mathcal{R}_q$ is expected to be small[3] (with coefficients $< q/4$) for a PV Knapsack instance – a highly unlikely event for a uniform instance. This gives a key distinguishing attack.

---

[1] The ternary choice of f makes the vector $(f| - 1)^T$ extremely short in the lattice $\mathcal{L}_{V',q}^{\perp}$. As a consequence, with high probability, it is significantly shorter than any vector that should normally occur in a lattice with this dimension and volume, which justifies the uniqueness assumption on the shortest vector.

[2] The elements of the ideal $I_{\Omega \setminus \Omega_t}$ correspond to the vectors of the q-ary Kernel lattice generated by the Vandermonde matrix with rows powers of ω' for $\omega' \in \Omega \setminus \Omega_t$. Note that the lattice doesn't contain any unusually short vector, so we can expect the shortest vector to have a norm predicted by Minkowski's theorem.

[3] Note that, the product $uu' = 0$ in $\mathcal{R}_q$. For the prime n case, we need to include the factor $(x - 1)$ in the product $u'(x)z(x)$ to make $uu' = 0$ in $\mathcal{R}_q$. Furthermore, the choice of g (sparse with small coefficient) leads to $O(n)$ coefficient growth of the product $u'(x)f(x)$.

The cost of the dual attack depends on finding the small $\boldsymbol{u}'(x)$, which can be improved using the algebraic methods.

Let Ω_{2t_1} be the largest subset of Ω_t that remains invariant under the computation of inverses. In other words, Ω_{2t_1} contains t_1 pairs (ω, ω^{-1}) with both ω and ω^{-1} in Ω_t. This set Ω_{2t_1} is easily constructed by removing any element of Ω_t whose inverse is not in Ω_t. Thus, $2t_1 \leq t$ and $t_1 \leq \lfloor t/2 \rfloor$. By our choice of $\boldsymbol{g}$, all the roots in Ω can be paired with their inverse. As a consequence, the complement set $\Omega \setminus \Omega_{2t_1}$ is also made of such pairs.

This symmetry can be leveraged to find a small element in the ideal $I_{\Omega \setminus \Omega_{2t_1}}$, by looking for a small polynomial $\boldsymbol{u}'(\boldsymbol{x}) \in I_{\Omega \setminus \Omega_{2t_1}}$ with the extra requirement that:

$$\text{for all } \omega \in \Omega \; : \quad \boldsymbol{u}'(\omega) = \boldsymbol{u}'(\omega^{-1}).$$

This is easily achieved by creating $\boldsymbol{u}'(\boldsymbol{x})$ using a basis of halved dimension obtained from the symmetrisation of $\{1, \boldsymbol{x}, \ldots, \boldsymbol{x}^{\lfloor n/2 \rfloor}\}$. For such a polynomial, when $\boldsymbol{x}$ is a root, so is $1/\boldsymbol{x}$. Thus we can guarantee that $\boldsymbol{u}'$ vanishes on Ω_{2t_1} using only t_1 linear conditions. As a consequence, a small $\boldsymbol{u}'(\boldsymbol{x})$ can be found using lattice reduction in a (Kernel) lattice of reduced dimension.

Furthermore, if t_1 is not too small, the PV Knapsack problem still reduces to a BDD problem in the ideal $I_{\Omega_{2t_1}}$. The condition of t_1 not being too small comes from considering the volume of the lattice, which decreases with t_1 and needs to be large enough for the reduction to BDD work. When t_1 is sufficient, considering the product $\boldsymbol{u}'(\boldsymbol{x}) \boldsymbol{z}(\boldsymbol{x})$ again gives a distinguishing attack. The authors of [4] (experimentally) show that this occurs with non-negligible probability and thus improves the cost of solving the decisional PV Knapsack problem.

As an extension of this attack, and for some choices of n, one can also aim at exploiting higher order symmetries to reduce to a lattice problem of even smaller dimension. Unfortunately, in general, this reduces the number of evaluations at the roots after symmetrisation too much. So the reduction to BDD no longer works. However, if Ω_t can be adversarially chosen, we obtain a degraded version of the PV Knapsack problem. This is called a *worst-case* Ω_t in [4]. In this worst-case, Ω_t contains a large subset Ω_{rt_0}, which remains invariant under a symmetry of order r (instead of 2). [4] With such a forced symmetry inside, this allows the PV Knapsack to remain a BDD instance in the ideal $I_{\Omega_{rt_0}}$.

Like before, the set $\Omega \setminus \Omega_{rt_0}$ also remains invariant under the transformation, so the problem of finding a short solution $\boldsymbol{u}'$ in the ideal $I_{\Omega/\Omega_{rt_0}}$ can be reduced to a lattice of (very) small dimension. Since finding an SVP solution is known in such a small dimension, e.g., using LLL lattice reduction algorithm, then, (hopefully) the product $\boldsymbol{u}'(\boldsymbol{x}) \boldsymbol{z}(\boldsymbol{x}) \in \mathcal{R}_q$ has all coefficients $< q/2$ in absolute value (i.e., no wrap-around modulo q happens for the product polynomial), which also gives a key recovery attack.

Because of this worst-case, it appears that the uniformly random choice of Ω_t makes more sense in the definition of the PV Knapsack problem. This approach

---

[4] For example, the power of two n allows the use of a subgroup of maximal order $r = n/2$, while the prime n of the form $n - 1 = 0 \bmod 3$ from the parameters of [11] allows the use of a subgroup of order up to $r = (n - 1)/3$.

is used in [5,14], while [11] doesn't explicitly mention the choice of Ω_t. In the rest of the paper, we concentrate on the key recovery attack for a uniformly random Ω_t.

4   Our Contribution

Our main goal is to find an alternative dimension reduction strategy working with the primal attack instead of the dual attack. Indeed, the primal attack corresponds to a uSVP instance, which is believed to be comparatively easier to solve than an SVP instance, both in theory [15], and in practice [1,3,10].

We achieve this goal by proposing a new dimension reduction primal attack on the PV Knapsack problem. For this, we exploit the symmetries of the ring $\mathcal{R}_q$ in a new way. This allows us to solve several PV Knapsack instances from the literature in a reasonable time, faster than what was previously thought to be possible.

As in [4], we consider the largest subset Ω_{2t_1} of Ω_t that remains invariant under the computation of inverses. For any ω in Ω_{2t_1}, we know the evaluation of f both at ω and ω^{-1}. Hence we can compute $f(\omega) \pm f(\omega^{-1})$. This gives t_1 distinct evaluations of the two polynomials $f(x) \pm f(1/x)$ at $\omega \in \Omega_{2t_1}$. We aim to recover $f(x) \pm f(1/x)$ as uSVP solutions from lattices of smaller dimensions and do the linear algebra to recover the secret $f(x)$.

Let $\psi_+(x) = f(x) + f(1/x)$ and $\psi_-(x) = f(x) - f(1/x)$. The polynomials $\psi_+(x)$, and $\psi_-(x)$ can be generated by a basis of order $n_+ = \lceil n/2 \rceil$ and $n_- = \lfloor n/2 \rfloor$, respectively. These bases are easy to compute from the polynomial basis. Also, if $f(x)$ has coefficients in the set $\{-1, 0, 1\}$, $\psi_\pm(x)$ has coefficients in the set $\{-2, -1, 0, 1, 2\}$. Then the PV Knapsack problem reduces to two independent problems of finding $\psi_\pm(x)$ from t_1 evaluations. This can be achieved by recovering uSVP solutions in lattices of dimensions $n_\pm$.

There are a few important observations from the above attack.

1. The cost of recovering $\psi_\pm$ as a uSVP solution (using lattice reduction algorithm) depends on the volume of the lattice in reduced dimension. The volume is proportional to the number of distinct evaluations t_1, which makes the problem easier as t_1 increases. When Ω_t is randomly chosen, the value of t_1 is randomised. If the system is used by many users, each one with its own set Ω_t, some of them will pick weak keys, i.e., weak sets Ω_t, which are easier to attack because of their larger value of t_1. To analyse our attack, two ingredients are needed: an attack that works when t_1 is large enough and a probability analysis of this weak-key event.
2. Note that, when a PV Knapsack instance is given, an adversary can compute t_1 easily. This only requires reading Ω_t to detect pairs of the form (ω, ω^{-1}). As a consequence, the adversary can focus on the keys that are easy enough to attack with lattice techniques. This can be done, for example, by using LWE estimators [2,7] before starting the attack.

3. Since the two uSVP problems for finding $\psi_\pm$ are independent, the corresponding lattice reductions can be performed in parallel. Hence, the running time of the attack is directly obtained by estimating the cost of the largest of the two uSVP instances.
4. We also study symmetries of order > 2 and their application to a direct attack to solve PV Knapsack. Unfortunately, for random choices of Ω_t, it turns out that the symmetry of order 2 is optimal for the parameters proposed in the literature.

In Sect. 5, we formally describe the attack sketched above. In Sect. 6, we provide experimental results that indicate that several proposed instances of the PV Knapsack problem can be solved in practice. In Sect. 7, we give a generalized version of the attack using symmetries of higher order. We hope that despite their inefficiency for the random case, their analysis can be of independent interest.

5   Proposed Attack

In this section, we propose a new key recovery attack on the PV Knapsack problem. The key idea is to use symmetry in a new way, thanks to the following lemma.

Lemma 1. *Let $f(x)$ be any polynomial in $\mathcal{R}_q$, then $\psi_\pm(x) = f(x) \pm f(1/x)$ can be generated by a basis of order $n_\pm$, where $n_+ = \lceil n/2 \rceil$ and $n_- = \lfloor n/2 \rfloor$. Moreover, if the coefficients of $f(x)$ are sampled uniformly at random from the set $\{-1, 0, 1\}$, then the expected squared-norm of $\psi_\pm(x)$ is upper-bounded by $4n_\pm/3$ in the new basis representation.*

Proof. The mapping

$$x^i \rightarrow x^i + 1/x^i \text{ for } 0 \le i \le \lfloor n/2 \rfloor$$

is well-defined. Hence, by linearity, the polynomial $\psi_+(x) = f(x) + f(1/x)$ can be generated by a basis of order n_+, as required. In particular, for prime n, since $1/x = x^{n-1}$, $\psi_+(x)$ is generated by the basis

$$\{2, (x + x^{n-1}), \ldots, (x^{\lfloor n/2 \rfloor} + x^{\lfloor n/2 \rfloor + 1})\}$$

For power of two n, since $1/x = -x^{n-1}$, $\psi_+(x)$ is generated by the basis

$$\{2, (x - x^{n-1}), \ldots, (x^{(n/2-1)} - x^{(n/2+1)})\}$$

Similarly, the mapping

$$x^i \rightarrow x^i - 1/x^i \text{ for } 1 \le i \le \lfloor n/2 \rfloor$$

is well-defined. Hence, by linearity, the polynomial $\psi_-(\boldsymbol{x}) = \boldsymbol{f}(\boldsymbol{x}) - \boldsymbol{f}(1/\boldsymbol{x})$ can be generated by a basis of order n_-, as required. In particular, for prime n, $\psi_-(\boldsymbol{x})$ is generated by the basis

$$\{(\boldsymbol{x} - \boldsymbol{x}^{n-1}), \ldots, (\boldsymbol{x}^{\lfloor n/2 \rfloor} - \boldsymbol{x}^{\lfloor n/2 \rfloor + 1})\}$$

For power of two n, $\psi_-(\boldsymbol{x})$ is generated by the basis

$$\{(\boldsymbol{x} + \boldsymbol{x}^{n-1}), \ldots, (\boldsymbol{x}^{n/2-1} + \boldsymbol{x}^{n/2+1}), 2\boldsymbol{x}^{n/2}\}$$

If individual coefficients of $\boldsymbol{f}$ are uniformly sampled from $\{-1, 0, 1\}$, then sums of symmetric coefficients $f_i + f_{n-i}$ are in $\{-2, -1, 0, 1, 2\}$ and follow the probability distribution given in Table 1.

Table 1. Probability distribution of $f_i + f_{n-i}$

$f_i + f_{n-i}$	0	1	−1	2	−2
Prob	3/9	2/9	2/9	1/9	1/9

Now, if $\boldsymbol{f}(\boldsymbol{x})$ is sampled uniformly with ternary coefficients, most coefficients of $\psi_\pm(\boldsymbol{x})$ follow the distribution of $f_i + f_{n-i}$. The exceptions being the special coefficients associated to 2 and $2\boldsymbol{x}^{n/2}$ which follow the initial uniform distribution in $\{-1, 0, 1\}$ and have a lower expectation of their squares. Hence, by linearity of expectations, the expected squared-norm of $\psi_\pm$ in the new basis representation is upper-bounded by $4n_\pm/3$.

This allows us to design a new low-density inhomogeneous SIS problem corresponding to the evaluation of $\psi_\pm$ at t_1 values. In order to do this, let us create a matrix $\boldsymbol{W}_\pm$ with t_1 rows and $n_\pm$ columns, whose entries are the evaluations of each of the $n_\pm$ monomials at an arbitrary choice of t_1 representatives for the pairs (ω, ω^{-1}) that occur in Ω_{2t_1}. We also create a vector $\boldsymbol{b}_\pm$ whose coefficients are the known evaluations of $\psi_\pm$ at each of the representative. With these notations, we look for a solution of:

$$\boldsymbol{W}_\pm \psi_\pm = \boldsymbol{b}_\pm \bmod q. \tag{2}$$

Following the same strategy as in the direct primal attack, we search for a short vector in the kernel lattice:

$$\mathcal{L}^\perp_{\boldsymbol{W}'_\pm, q} = \{\boldsymbol{v} \in \mathbb{Z}^{n+1} : \boldsymbol{W}'_\pm \boldsymbol{v} = \boldsymbol{0} \bmod q\}$$

where $\boldsymbol{W}'_\pm = (\boldsymbol{W}_\pm | \boldsymbol{b}_\pm)$. As before, $(\psi_\pm | -1)^T$ is a very short vector in the lattice and we expect that it yields a uSVP solution.

5.1   Analysis of the New Attack

As we already mentioned, to analyse the attack, we need two ingredients. First, given t_1, the number of pairs in Ω_t, we need to estimate the cost of successfully conducting the uSVP computation. Second, for a random set Ω_t, we need to compute the probability of occurrence of a given value of t_1. Since from a public key, t_1 can be computed extremely efficiently, this probability directly corresponds to the fraction of users that can be attacked with the corresponding uSVP problem.

Cost of the uSVP resolution. Thanks to the analysis of [10], we know that the cost of solving a uSVP problem mostly depends on the root Hermite factor that can be computed from the uniqueness gap γ. We recall that this factor is $\delta = \gamma^{1/n}$.

In our attack, we do not really have a promise problem. However, since the lattices we consider come from a cryptographic problem, we can follow a standard heuristic approach and assume that they behave as randomly as it can. More precisely, both for the direct primal attack of [11] and for our new attack with dimension reduction, we consider a lattice in which a vector of short length is guaranteed. The heuristic we use is to consider that other (linearly independent) vectors in the lattice have a length which can be estimated from Minkowski's bound. In other words, given its volume V and dimension d, we estimate the value of λ_2 to be $\sqrt{d}\,V^{1/d}$. To estimate λ_1, we use the square-root of the expected squared-norm. Putting the two estimations together, it just remains to compute $\gamma = \lambda_2/\lambda_1$ and take its d-th root to obtain the corresponding δ.

Recall, in the (full) primal attack, the PV Knapsack gives a uSVP instance in dimension $n+1$, and volume q^t. We also have a short vector of expected squared-norm $2n/3+1$. As a consequence, the corresponding root Hermite factor can be estimated by:

$$\delta_{\text{full}} = \left(\frac{\sqrt{n+1}\,q^{t/(n+1)}}{\sqrt{2n/3+1}} \right)^{1/(n+1)}.$$

Similarly, in our attack, we get two lattices of dimensions $n_\pm + 1$ and volume q^{t_1}. In that case, the expected squared-norm of the shortest vector is $4n_\pm/3+1$. Thus, we get an estimation of:

$$\delta_{\pm\text{new}} = \left(\frac{\sqrt{n_\pm + 1}\,q^{t_1/(n_\pm+1)}}{\sqrt{4n_\pm/3+1}} \right)^{1/(n_\pm+1)}.$$

Following [10], we need to compare δ_{full} and $\delta_{\pm\text{new}}$ to know when the new attack beats the full primal attack. To do the comparison, we slightly simplify the expression, replacing $n_\pm$ by $n/2$ and any instance of $n+1$ by n or $n_\pm + 1$ by $n_\pm$. After the simplification, we expect the new attack to become faster as soon as:

$$\left(\sqrt{3/2}\,q^{t/n} \right)^{1/n} < \left(\sqrt{3/4}\,q^{2t_1/n} \right)^{2/n}.$$

Ignoring the small constants, this happens when $4t_1 > t$.

This estimation is somewhat pessimistic. Indeed, the dimension of the lattice also counts when using lattice reduction, so even when the root Hermite factors are equal, the newer lattice should be easier to reduce due to its smaller dimension.

Distribution of t_1. To study the probability distribution of t_1, we perform a standard combinatorial analysis. The total number of sets Ω_t of t elements chosen from the primitive roots is:

$$\binom{2\lfloor n/2\rfloor}{t}.$$

When t_1 is a fixed integer in $[0, \lfloor t/2\rfloor]$, to choose a set of size t with exactly t_1 pairs, we need to take t_1 pairs from the $\lfloor n/2\rfloor$, followed by $t - 2t_1$ unpaired elements in the remaining pairs. Thus, the total number of possibilities is:

$$\binom{\lfloor n/2\rfloor}{t_1}\binom{\lfloor n/2\rfloor - t_1}{t - 2t_1}2^{t-2t_1}.$$

As a consequence, the probability of getting t_1 for a random Ω_t is:

$$\pi_1(t_1) = \frac{\binom{\lfloor n/2\rfloor}{t_1}\binom{\lfloor n/2\rfloor - t_1}{t-2t_1}2^{t-2t_1}}{\binom{2\lfloor n/2\rfloor}{t}}.$$

When $t = n/2$, the distribution of the values of t_1 is strongly concentrated around $t/4$, which is precisely the tipping point between the direct primal attack and our new attack. This is illustrated by Fig. 1. However, we see that for this typical case, t_1 can deviate from $t/4$. This explains the existence of weak instances vulnerable to our attack.

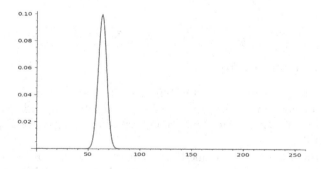

Fig. 1. $\pi_1(t_1)$ for $n = 512, t = 256$

6   Experimental Results

In this section, we analyse the effect of our attack on the concrete hardness of the problem used in the literature. We ran all our experiments on an Intel Xeon CPU E5-2683 v4 @ 2.10GHz 1200 MHz processor. The attack only depends on the value of t_1, and not on the choice of elements in Ω_{2t_1}. So to perform experiments on our attack, we first fix a value of t_1. Then we sample a uniform primitive root ω_1 of g and characterise Ω_{2t_1} by a random index set $S_{t_1} \subset U(n)$ of size t_1 (distinct up to negation). The lattice reduction algorithms are performed in parallel with fplll software [17].

The running time of a BKZ lattice reduction algorithm is exponential on the blocksize. In [6], the authors experimentally observed that most of the progress is made in the initial rounds of the BKZ reductions for the (relatively) large blocksize. In our experiments, the running time is the time taken by the lattice reduction algorithm to discover the secret.

Since it is not feasible to run lattice reductions for every parameter, following the common practice, we use LWE estimators [2, 7] to predict the running time of several instances. The LWE estimators heuristically predict the lattice reduction strength (which is characterised by the block size of the BKZ algorithm) required to find the secret in the primal attack.

Table 2. Parameters: PASS_RS [11]

	HPSSW1	HPSSW2	HPSSW3	HPSSW4
n	433	577	769	1153
t	200	280	386	600
q	775937	743177	1047379	968521
λ	$<< 62$	$<< 80$	76	≥ 130
λ^*	47	52	63	87

6.1   PASS_RS Signature from [11]

In this paper, the authors proposed PASS_RS signature scheme following the Fiat-Shamir with aborts strategy on the hardness of the PV Knapsack problem. The scheme is defined for the prime n case of the problem. The proposed parameters are given in Table 2.

The λ in the Table is the claimed bit security in the proposal. The λ^* is the re-evaluated bit security in the direct primal attack using the LWE estimator [2],[5] except for HPSSW1.

For HPSSW1, the bit security is achieved experimentally; we recovered the secret within 25 h (2^{47}-bits operation) using BKZ block size 55. For this reason, we have excluded it in our attack analysis.

---

[5] As asked in [2], we include the commit value used in this paper, which is fd4a460.

Table 3. Experimental results of our attack on the weak keys of HPSSW2.

Direct primal attack: $\lambda^* = 52$, BKZ block size 73				
t_1	Prob	Running time (in hrs)	BKZ block size	Bits operation
82	2^{-11}	115	65	2^{50}
84	2^{-13}	54	60	2^{49}
86	2^{-16}	51	60	2^{48}
88	2^{-19}	17	60	2^{46}
90	2^{-23}	6	58	2^{45}

Table 4. Predicted cost of our attack on the weak keys of HPSSW3 using the LWE estimator [2].

Direct primal attack: $\lambda^* = 63$, BKZ block size 112			
t_1	Prob	BKZ block size	Bits operation
110	2^{-8}	112	2^{61}
113	2^{-12}	106	2^{60}
115	2^{-13}	103	2^{59}
117	2^{-16}	100	2^{58}
120	2^{-19}	95	2^{56}
125	2^{-27}	87	2^{54}
127	2^{-32}	84	2^{53}
130	2^{-37}	80	2^{52}

We ran experiments of our attack on the HPSSW2 weak keys. The experimental results are given in Table 3. For the other parameters, we use the LWE estimator from [2], the details are given in Table 4 and Table 5.

Table 5. Predicted cost of our attack on the weak keys of HPSSW4 using the LWE estimator [2].

Direct primal attack: $\lambda^* = 87$, BKZ block size 200			
t_1	Prob	BKZ block size	Bits operation
167	2^{-6}	196	2^{85}
170	2^{-7}	191	2^{83}
172	2^{-8}	188	2^{82}
177	2^{-12}	180	2^{80}
182	2^{-17}	172	2^{78}
187	2^{-23}	165	2^{76}
192	2^{-30}	158	2^{74}
198	2^{-39}	151	2^{72}

Table 6. Parameters: Signature scheme [14]

	LZA1	LZA2
n	512	1024
t	256	512
q	$2^{16}+1$	$2^{16}+1$
λ	129	198
λ^*	54	99

6.2 Signature Scheme from [14]

In this paper, the authors proposed a signature scheme on the hardness of the PV Knapsack problem following the $PASS_{RS}$ signature scheme, but for the power-of-two n case. The proposed parameters are given in Table 6. The λ^* is computed using the LWE estimator [2].

Remark 3. Because of the huge difference between λ and λ^*, it is important to look for the source of the discrepancy. The best explanation we found is that the analysis in [14] apparently considers the dimension of the lattice in the direct primal attack as $n + t + 1$ (Sect. 4 [14]), instead of $n + 1$.

We ran experiments of our attack on the LZA1 weak keys. The experimental results are given Table 7. For LZA2, we use the LWE estimator from [2], the details are given in Table 8.

Table 7. Experimental results of our attack on the weak keys of LZA1.

Direct primal attack: $\lambda^* = 54$, BKZ block size 83				
t_1	Prob	Running time (in hrs)	BKZ block size	Bits operation
80	2^{-15}	117	70	2^{50}
83	2^{-19}	30	60	2^{48}
85	2^{-23}	9.5	60	2^{46}
88	2^{-30}	8	60	2^{45}
90	2^{-34}	7.5	57	2^{45}

6.3 PASSEncrypt, PVRegevEncrypt Schemes from [5]

In this paper, the authors proposed PASSEncrypt, PVRegevEncrypt encryption schemes based on the hardness of the PV Knapsack problem. The schemes are defined for the power-of-two n case of the problem. While PASSEncrypt is a modified version of the encryption scheme proposed in [12], PVRegevEncrypt is a (partial) Vandermonde variant of the Regev-style encryption scheme. The proposed parameters are given in Table 9.

Table 8. Predicted cost of our attack on the weak keys of LZA2 using the LWE estimator [2].

Direct primal attack: $\lambda^* = 99$, BKZ block size 243			
t_1	Prob	BKZ block size	Bits operation
142	2^{-8}	237	2^{97}
146	2^{-11}	233	2^{94}
148	2^{-13}	228	2^{93}
151	2^{-15}	222	2^{91}
154	2^{-19}	216	2^{90}
157	2^{-23}	210	2^{88}
163	2^{-31}	199	2^{85}
166	2^{-37}	194	2^{84}

Table 9. Parameters: PASSEncrypt, PVRegevEncrypt [5]

	BSS1	BSS2
n	1024	2048
t	512	1024
q	12289	12289
$\lambda_Q = \lambda_Q^*$	79	188

The concrete hardness of the parameters is computed using the LWE Leaky estimator [7]. The BKZ algorithm with block size β uses an SVP oracle in dimension β; the running time is evaluated using the core SVP hardness, which is only the cost of one call to an SVP oracle in dimension β. They further considered one SVP call cost $2^{0.265\beta}$ using a quantum algorithm. We also used the same estimation model for analysing the hardness of the weak keys. The details are given in Table 10 and Table 11.

7   Symmetries of Higher Order

In this section, we illustrate a generalized version of our attack to symmetries of higher order by going to order 3. It is straightforward to go to other orders. The case of order 3 naturally arises from the concrete parameters of [11]. Indeed, they use a prime n satisfying $n - 1 = 0 \bmod 3$ to do the fast Fourier transformation.

Lemma 2. *Let n be a prime satisfying $n - 1 = 0 \bmod 3$, and let θ be an element of order 3 in $U(n)$, i.e., $\theta^3 = 1$ in $U(n)$. For any polynomial $\boldsymbol{f}(\boldsymbol{x}) \in \mathcal{R}_q = \mathbb{Z}_q[\boldsymbol{x}]/(\boldsymbol{x}^n - 1)$, $\boldsymbol{\psi}_1(\boldsymbol{x}) = \boldsymbol{f}(\boldsymbol{x}) + \boldsymbol{f}(\boldsymbol{x}^\theta) + \boldsymbol{f}(\boldsymbol{x}^{\theta^2})$ can be generated by a basis of order $n_\theta = \lceil n/3 \rceil$. Moreover, if the coefficients of $\boldsymbol{f}(\boldsymbol{x})$ are sampled uniformly at random from the set $\{-1, 0, 1\}$, then the expected squared-norm of $\boldsymbol{\psi}_1(\boldsymbol{x})$ is upper-bounded by $2n_\theta$ in the new basis representation.*

Table 10. Predicted cost of our attack on the weak keys of BSS1 using the LWE Leaky estimator [7].

Direct primal attack: $\lambda_Q = \lambda_Q^* = 79$, BKZ block size 298			
t_1	Prob	BKZ block size	Quantum core SVP cost
144	2^{-9}	290	2^{77}
148	2^{-13}	280	2^{74}
150	2^{-14}	276	2^{73}
153	2^{-18}	269	2^{71}
155	2^{-20}	264	2^{70}
158	2^{-24}	258	2^{68}
162	2^{-30}	250	2^{66}
165	2^{-35}	244	2^{64}

Table 11. Predicted cost of our attack on the weak keys of BSS2 using the LWE Leaky estimator [7].

Direct primal attack: $\lambda_Q = \lambda_Q^* = 188$, BKZ block size 710			
t_1	Prob	BKZ block size	Quantum core SVP cost
266	2^{-5}	692	2^{183}
270	2^{-6}	682	2^{180}
276	2^{-8}	668	2^{177}
282	2^{-12}	653	2^{173}
288	2^{-15}	640	2^{169}
296	2^{-22}	622	2^{164}
300	2^{-26}	614	2^{162}
304	2^{-30}	605	2^{160}
308	2^{-35}	597	2^{158}

Proof. Let a be any primitive element of the group $U(n)$ (i.e., a generator of $U(n)$). Note that there are $\phi(\phi(n))$ many such elements, where $\phi(.)$ is Euler phi-function; we can pick any of those. Let $k = (n-1)/3$ and $\theta = a^k \in U(n)$. Then θ is an element of order 3.

Note that the mapping

$$x^{a^i} \rightarrow x^{a^i} + x^{a^i\theta} + x^{a^i\theta^2} \quad \text{for } 0 \le i \le k-1$$

is well-defined, since $U(n)$ is a disjoint union of:

$$\{a^i \mid 0 \le i \le k-1\}, \quad \{a^i\theta \mid 0 \le i \le k-1\}, \quad \text{and } \{a^i\theta^2 \mid 0 \le i \le k-1\}.$$

Hence, by linearity, the polynomial $\psi_1(x) = f(x) + f(x^\theta) + f(x^{\theta^2})$ is generated by the basis $\{3, x^{a^i} + x^{a^i\theta} + x^{a^i\theta^2}\}$ for $0 \le i \le k-1$ of order $n_\theta = 1 + k$, as claimed.

If individual coefficients of $\boldsymbol{f}$ are uniformly sampled from $\{-1, 0, 1\}$, then sums of symmetric coefficients $f_{a^i} + f_{a^i\theta} + f_{a^i\theta^2}$ are in $\{-3, -2, -1, 0, 1, 2, 3\}$ and follow the probability distribution given in Table 12. So the coefficients of $\boldsymbol{\psi}_1(\boldsymbol{x})$ follow the distribution of $f_{a^i} + f_{a^i\theta} + f_{a^i\theta^2}$, except for the special coefficient associated to 3, which has a lower expectation of the square. Hence, by linearity of expectations, the expected squared-norm of $\boldsymbol{\psi}_1$ in the new basis representation is upper-bounded by $2n_\theta$.

Table 12. Probability distribution of $f_{a^i} + f_{a^i\theta} + f_{a^i\theta^2}$

$f_{a^i} + f_{a^i\theta} + f_{a^i\theta^2}$	0	1	-1	2	-2	3	-3
Prob	7/27	6/27	6/27	3/27	3/27	1/27	1/27

However, this only gives us one polynomial $\boldsymbol{\psi}_1$ in reduced dimension, which is essentially the equivalent of $\boldsymbol{\psi}_+$ in the order 2 attack. We cannot directly construct an equivalent of $\boldsymbol{\psi}_-$, so we use a different approach to get two other polynomials in reduced dimension.

Let us define $\boldsymbol{f}_2(\boldsymbol{x}) = \boldsymbol{x}\boldsymbol{f}(\boldsymbol{x})$, $\boldsymbol{f}_3(\boldsymbol{x}) = \boldsymbol{x}^2\boldsymbol{f}(\boldsymbol{x})$, and $\boldsymbol{\psi}_2(\boldsymbol{x}) = \boldsymbol{f}_2(\boldsymbol{x}) + \boldsymbol{f}_2(\boldsymbol{x}^\theta) + \boldsymbol{f}_2(\boldsymbol{x}^{\theta^2})$, $\boldsymbol{\psi}_3(\boldsymbol{x}) = \boldsymbol{f}_3(\boldsymbol{x}) + \boldsymbol{f}_3(\boldsymbol{x}^\theta) + \boldsymbol{f}_3(\boldsymbol{x}^{\theta^2})$. Then, if the coefficients of $\boldsymbol{f}(\boldsymbol{x})$ are sampled uniformly at random from the ternary set, each $\boldsymbol{\psi}_i$ has an expected squared-norm bounded by $2n_\theta$ in the new basis representation. Indeed, the choice of $\boldsymbol{g}$ makes the coefficients of $\boldsymbol{f}$, $\boldsymbol{f}_2$, and $\boldsymbol{f}_3$ only different shifts in the polynomial basis representation. As a result, by linearity and from the distribution of the sums of symmetric coefficients, each $\boldsymbol{\psi}_i$ provides the same expected squared-norm in the new basis representation.

For the PV Knapsack problem, let Ω_{3t_2} is the largest subset of Ω_t that remains invariant under the transformation of θ. In other words, Ω_{3t_2} contains t_2 triplets $(\omega, \omega^\theta, \omega^{\theta^2})$ with all ω, ω^θ, and ω^{θ^2} in Ω_t, where $t_2 \leq \lfloor t/3 \rfloor$. For any ω in Ω_{3t_2}, we know the evaluations of $\boldsymbol{f}$ at ω, ω^θ, and ω^{θ^2}. Hence we can compute t_2 distinct evaluations of each of the polynomials $\boldsymbol{\psi}_i(\boldsymbol{x})$ at $\omega \in \Omega_{3t_2}$. This follows by writing $\boldsymbol{\psi}_2(\boldsymbol{x}) = \boldsymbol{x}\boldsymbol{f}(\boldsymbol{x}) + \boldsymbol{x}^\theta \boldsymbol{f}(\boldsymbol{x}^\theta) + \boldsymbol{x}^{\theta^2}\boldsymbol{f}(\boldsymbol{x}^{\theta^2})$ and $\boldsymbol{\psi}_3(\boldsymbol{x}) = \boldsymbol{x}^2\boldsymbol{f}(\boldsymbol{x}) + \boldsymbol{x}^{2\theta}\boldsymbol{f}(\boldsymbol{x}^\theta) + \boldsymbol{x}^{2\theta^2}\boldsymbol{f}(\boldsymbol{x}^{\theta^2})$.

This also allows to design a low-density inhomogeneous SIS problems to solve PV Knapsack problem. We create a matrix $\boldsymbol{W}_\theta$ with t_2 rows and n_θ columns, whose entries are the evaluations of each of the n_θ monomials at an arbitrary choice of t_2 representatives for the triplets in Ω_{3t_2}. We create a vector $\boldsymbol{b}_i$ whose coefficients are the known evaluations of $\boldsymbol{\psi}_i$ at each representative. We look for a solution of:

$$\boldsymbol{W}_\theta \boldsymbol{\psi}_i = \boldsymbol{b}_i \bmod q. \tag{3}$$

Like before, we search for a short vector in the Kernel lattice

$$\mathcal{L}_{\boldsymbol{W}_i', q}^\perp = \{\boldsymbol{v} \in \mathbb{Z}^{n+1} : \boldsymbol{W}_i'\boldsymbol{v} = \boldsymbol{0} \bmod q\}$$

where $W_i' = (W_\theta | b_i)$, and we expect $(\psi_i| -1)^T$ yields a uSVP solution. The knowledge of each ψ_i gives n_θ (independent) linear equations of the (unknown) coefficients of $f(x)$. So by doing linear algebra, we recover $f(x)$.

Distribution of t_2. The total number of sets Ω_t of t elements chosen from the primitive roots is:

$$\binom{3\lfloor n/3 \rfloor}{t}.$$

When t_2 is a fixed integer in $[0, \lfloor t/3 \rfloor]$, to choose a set of size t with exactly t_2 triplets, we need to take t_2 triplets from the set of $\lfloor n/3 \rfloor$ triplets, followed by $t - 3t_2$ non-triplets from the remaining triplets. Now, a non-triplet element can come as a combination of both pair and unpair. Thus, the total number of possibilities is:

$$\binom{\lfloor n/3 \rfloor}{t_2} \sum_{i=0}^{s} \binom{\lfloor n/3 \rfloor - t_2}{i} \binom{\lfloor n/3 \rfloor - t_2 - i}{t - 3t_2 - 2i} 3^{t-3t_2-i}.$$

where $s = \min\{\lfloor (t - 3t_2)/2 \rfloor, \lfloor n/3 \rfloor - t_2\}$. So the probability of getting t_2 for a random Ω_t is:

$$\pi_2(t_2) = \frac{\binom{\lfloor n/3 \rfloor}{t_2} \sum_{i=0}^{s} \binom{\lfloor n/3 \rfloor - t_2}{i} \binom{\lfloor n/3 \rfloor - t_2 - i}{t - 3t_2 - 2i} 3^{t-3t_2-i}}{\binom{3\lfloor n/3 \rfloor}{t}}.$$

Comparison with Symmetries of Order 2. We first would like to note that the worst-case keys, which are fully symmetric of higher order, clearly outperforms the order 2 symmetry attack. This is even clearer if one adversarially selects a key with symmetry of order 3 but no symmetry of order 2.

We keep this in mind; we now aim to compare the higher order symmetry with the order 2 symmetry for randomly selected keys. Let us start by comparing concrete examples of the attacks with symmetries of order 2 and 3.

For HPSSW2, when the value of $t_2 = 42$, we have $\pi_2(t_2) = 2^{-26}$. In this case, we recovered the secret in 111 h (2^{49}-bits operation) using BKZ block size 68. With $\pi_1(t_1) = 2^{-26}$, we get the value of $t_1 = 92$. In this case, we recovered the secret in 6.5 h (2^{45}-bits operation) using BKZ block size 58. Unfortunately, we never recovered the secret for a smaller value of t_2 running lattice reductions for 7 days.

Similarly, we can do a comparison for HPSSW3, HPSSW4 by using the LWE estimator [2], it is shown in Fig. 2.

On these three examples, it is clear that the order 2 attack performs better than the order 3 version. To understand why, let us consider a variant of the PV Knapsack problem, where the number of evaluation points t is close to pn, instead of $n/2$. Here p is an element in $(0, 1)$.

In that case, the direct attack involves a lattice of dimension $n+1$ and volume q^{pn}. For the order 2 attack, we estimate the average of pairs to be $p^2 n/2$. As a consequence, the attack involves a lattice of dimension $\lceil n/2 \rceil + 1$ and volume

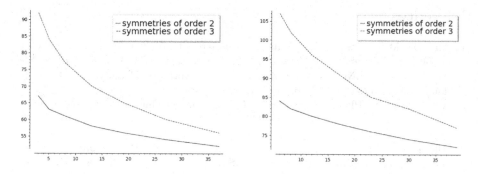

Fig. 2. Comparison: Predicted bits operation vs $\pi_i(t_i)^{-1}$ (in $\log_2$ scale) for the weak keys of HPSSW3 and HPSSW4.

$q^{p^2 n/2}$. For the order 3, we estimate the average of triplets to be $p^3 n/3$ and get an attack involving dimension $\lceil n/3 \rceil + 1$ and volume $q^{p^3 n/3}$. Ignoring constants, we can compare the root Hermite factors of the three attacks by looking at the three numbers:

$$p, \quad 2p^2, \quad \text{and} \quad 3p^3.$$

The case $p = 1/2$ that we previously considered is the crossover point between the direct attack and the order 2 symmetry attack. Similarly, the crossover point between the direct attack and the order 3 symmetry attack is $p = 1/\sqrt{3} \approx 0.58$. Finally, the crossover point between the order 2 and order 3 attacks is $p = 2/3 \approx 0.67$.

As a consequence, the higher symmetries only become worthwhile for random keys when the number of evaluation points in the PV Knapsack problem is much larger than what appears in practical parameters. We also see that by reducing the number of evaluation points below $n/2$, one can circumvent the gain provided by our main attack with symmetries of order 2.

Yet, since checking for symmetries is really fast, it cannot hurt a dedicated adversary to check their existence before launching the lattice reduction part of the attack.

Acknowledgements. The main part of this work was done while Dipayan Das was affiliated with CISPA. This work has been supported by the European Union's H2020 Programme under grant agreement number ERC-669891.

References

1. Albrecht, M.R., Göpfert, F., Virdia, F., Wunderer, T.: Revisiting the expected cost of solving uSVP and applications to LWE. In: Takagi, T., Peyrin, T. (eds.) ASIACRYPT 2017. LNCS, vol. 10624, pp. 297–322. Springer, Cham (2017). https://doi.org/10.1007/978-3-319-70694-8_11

2. Albrecht, M.R., Player, R., Scott, S.: On the concrete hardness of learning with errors. J. Math. Cryptol. **9**(3), 169–203 (2015). https://doi.org/10.1515/jmc-2015-0016

3. Alkim, E., Ducas, L., Pöppelmann, T., Schwabe, P.: Post-quantum key exchange - a new hope. In: Holz, T., Savage, S. (eds.) 25th USENIX Security Symposium, USENIX Security 16, Austin, TX, USA, 10–12 August 2016, pp. 327–343. USENIX Association (2016). https://www.usenix.org/conference/usenixsecurity16/technical-sessions/presentation/alkim

4. Boudgoust, K., Gachon, E., Pellet-Mary, A.: Some easy instances of ideal-SVP and implications on the partial Vandermonde Knapsack problem. In: Dodis, Y., Shrimpton, T. (eds.) CRYPTO 2022, Part II. Lecture Notes in Computer Science, vol. 13508, pp. 480–509. Springer, Cham (2022). https://doi.org/10.1007/978-3-031-15979-4_17

5. Boudgoust, K., Sakzad, A., Steinfeld, R.: Vandermonde meets Regev: public key encryption schemes based on partial Vandermonde problems. Des. Codes Cryptogr. **90**(8), 1899–1936 (2022). https://doi.org/10.1007/s10623-022-01083-7

6. Chen, Y., Nguyen, P.Q.: BKZ 2.0: better lattice security estimates. In: Lee, D.H., Wang, X. (eds.) ASIACRYPT 2011. LNCS, vol. 7073, pp. 1–20. Springer, Heidelberg (2011). https://doi.org/10.1007/978-3-642-25385-0_1

7. Dachman-Soled, D., Ducas, L., Gong, H., Rossi, M.: LWE with side information: attacks and concrete security estimation. In: Micciancio, D., Ristenpart, T. (eds.) CRYPTO 2020, Part II. LNCS, vol. 12171, pp. 329–358. Springer, Cham (2020). https://doi.org/10.1007/978-3-030-56880-1_12

8. Das, D., Joux, A.: On the hardness of the finite field isomorphism problem. In: Hazay, C., Stam, M. (eds.) EUROCRYPT 2023, Part V. Lecture Notes in Computer Science, vol. 14008, pp. 343–359. Springer, Cham (2023). https://doi.org/10.1007/978-3-031-30589-4_12

9. Doröz, Y., Hoffstein, J., Silverman, J.H., Sunar, B.: MMSAT: a scheme for multimessage multiuser signature aggregation. IACR Cryptology ePrint Archive (2020). https://eprint.iacr.org/2020/520

10. Gama, N., Nguyen, P.Q.: Predicting lattice reduction. In: Smart, N. (ed.) EUROCRYPT 2008. LNCS, vol. 4965, pp. 31–51. Springer, Heidelberg (2008). https://doi.org/10.1007/978-3-540-78967-3_3

11. Hoffstein, J., Pipher, J., Schanck, J.M., Silverman, J.H., Whyte, W.: Practical signatures from the partial fourier recovery problem. In: Boureanu, I., Owesarski, P., Vaudenay, S. (eds.) ACNS 2014. LNCS, vol. 8479, pp. 476–493. Springer, Cham (2014). https://doi.org/10.1007/978-3-319-07536-5_28

12. Hoffstein, J., Silverman, J.H.: Pass-encrypt: a public key cryptosystem based on partial evaluation of polynomials. Des. Codes Cryptogr. **77**(2–3), 541–552 (2015). https://doi.org/10.1007/s10623-015-0089-z

13. Lenstra, A.K., Lenstra, H.W., Lovász, L.: Factoring polynomials with rational coefficients. Mathematische annalen **261**(ARTICLE), 515–534 (1982)

14. Lu, X., Zhang, Z., Au, M.H.: Practical signatures from the partial Fourier recovery problem revisited: a provably-secure and gaussian-distributed construction. In: Susilo, W., Yang, G. (eds.) ACISP 2018. LNCS, vol. 10946, pp. 813–820. Springer, Cham (2018). https://doi.org/10.1007/978-3-319-93638-3_50
15. Luzzi, L., Stehlé, D., Ling, C.: Decoding by embedding: correct decoding radius and DMT optimality. IEEE Trans. Inf. Theory **59**(5), 2960–2973 (2013). https://doi.org/10.1109/TIT.2012.2236144
16. Schnorr, C.P., Euchner, M.: Lattice basis reduction: improved practical algorithms and solving subset sum problems. In: Budach, L. (ed.) FCT 1991. LNCS, vol. 529, pp. 68–85. Springer, Heidelberg (1991). https://doi.org/10.1007/3-540-54458-5_51
17. The FPLLL Development Team: FPLLL, a lattice reduction library, Version: 5.4.5 (2023). https://github.com/fplll/fplll

Cryptanalysis of Rank-2 Module-LIP in Totally Real Number Fields

Guilhem Mureau[1](✉), Alice Pellet-Mary[1], Georgii Pliatsok[2,3], and Alexandre Wallet[3]

[1] Univ Bordeaux, CNRS, Inria, Bordeaux INP, IMB, UMR 5251, Talence, France
{guilhem.mureau,alice.pellet-mary}@math.u-bordeaux.fr
[2] Insitute of Mathematics, NAS of Ukraine, Kyiv, Ukraine
georgiipliatsok@icloud.com
[3] Univ Rennes, Inria, CNRS, Irisa, UMR 6074, Rennes, France
alexandre.wallet@inria.fr

Abstract. We formally define the Lattice Isomorphism Problem for module lattices (module-LIP) in a number field K. This is a generalization of the problem defined by Ducas, Postlethwaite, Pulles, and van Woerden (Asiacrypt 2022), taking into account the arithmetic and algebraic specificity of module lattices from their representation using pseudo-bases. We also provide the corresponding set of algorithmic and theoretical tools for the future study of this problem in a module setting. Our main contribution is an algorithm solving module-LIP for modules of rank 2 in K^2, when K is a totally real number field. Our algorithm exploits the connection between this problem, relative norm equations and the decomposition of algebraic integers as sums of two squares. For a large class of modules (including $\mathcal{O}_K^2$), and a large class of totally real number fields (including the maximal real subfield of cyclotomic fields) it runs in classical polynomial time in the degree of the field and the residue at 1 of the Dedekind zeta function of the field (under reasonable number theoretic assumptions). We provide a proof-of-concept code running over the maximal real subfield of cyclotomic fields.

Keywords: Module Lattices · Lattice Isomorphism Problem · Cryptanalysis

1 Introduction

The Lattice Isomorphism Problem (LIP) is an algorithmic problem recently introduced in cryptography [2,14]. In its search version, LIP asks to find a linear *isometry*, that is, a distance-preserving linear transformation, mapping a lattice L_1 onto an *isomorphic* lattice L_2.[1] The decisional variant asks, given two lattices L_1 and L_2, to determine whether they are isomorphic. Algorithms for solving

---

[1] Lattices are geometric objects, so an isomorphism between lattices should respect the group structure *and* the geometry.

© International Association for Cryptologic Research 2024
M. Joye and G. Leander (Eds.): EUROCRYPT 2024, LNCS 14657, pp. 226–255, 2024.
https://doi.org/10.1007/978-3-031-58754-2_9

either variant of the problems have been studied independently of cryptography first [18], with more recent cryptanalytic works since then [6,11,12,23]. For the search variant, the best known algorithm to solve LIP is due to Haviv and Regev [18] and it runs in time $n^{O(n)}$ where n is the dimension of the space. It requires to enumerate (possibly many) short vectors in both lattices and solving a Graph Isomorphism Problem to reconstruct a linear isometry. Therefore, to our current understanding, the hardness of LIP seems to hinge on the one of SVP.

An algebraic variant of LIP (named module-LIP) was introduced in 2023 in [13], and used to construct the scheme Hawk, currently in evaluation in NIST's additional call[2] for digital post-quantum signature. The security of the scheme relies on the hardness to find a given isomorphism to $\mathcal{O}_K^2$, where $\mathcal{O}_K$ is the ring of integers of a power-of-two cyclotomic field. The authors of [13] provided some analysis on the security of this new variant, based on the algorithms solving LIP in the unstructured case. In other words, so far, the only algorithms we know for solving the module-LIP variant from [13] consist in forgetting about the algebraic structure, treating the instance as a non-structured one. Generally, the cryptographic novelty of the problem means that there are few tools for cryptanalysts to understand it. The main goal of this work is to initiate the development of these tools, motivated by the following question:

Is it possible to exploit the algebraic structure of module-LIP to solve it more efficiently than LIP?

Contributions. Our first contribution is to formalize the framework for the module-LIP problem. The definition from [13] was restricted to free modules over a CM number field (see preliminaries for the definition of a CM field). Our extended definition covers any module M and any number field, using the notion of pseudo-bases [9]. While our formulation is slightly different from the one in [13], with our definition, forging a signature against Hawk reduces to solving the module-LIP instance defined by the public key. During the exposition of our framework, we provide tools and security foundations for the future study of this problem. This extends standard tools for the unstructured case to the module setting, such as a worst-case to average-case reduction and algorithms such as the Cholesky decomposition.

Our main technical contribution is an algorithm solving module-LIP when the module $M \subset K^2$ has rank-2 and when the number field K is a totally real number field.[3] An important family of totally real fields is $K = \mathbb{Q}(\zeta + \zeta^{-1})$, with ζ a primitive root of unity, which is a degree 2 subfield of the cyclotomic field $\mathbb{Q}(\zeta)$, called its maximal totally real subfield. The precise complexity of our algorithm is related to arithmetic properties of the module. Informally, when the "gap" between the ideal generated by the coordinates of vectors in the module and the ideal generated by the norms of these vector is small, our algorithm

---

[2] https://csrc.nist.gov/Projects/pqc-dig-sig/round-1-additional-signatures.

[3] Our algorithm relies on arithmetic properties of the module, and does *not* extend to modules $M \subset K_{\mathbb{R}}^2$, where $K_{\mathbb{R}} := K \otimes_{\mathbb{Q}} \mathbb{R}$.

runs in polynomial time. This is the case for the important module $M = \mathcal{O}_K^2$ for which the result is stated in Corollary 4.7.

The general complexity statement of the algorithm (for any totally real field K and any module $M \subset K^2$) is provided in Corollary 4.8. We want to stress that this result *does not* break the Hawk signature scheme. Indeed, our algorithm only works for totally real number fields, whereas the Hawk scheme is defined over a power-of-two cyclotomic field. However, our algorithm rules out a large class of possibly interesting fields, showing that using them for instantiations could result in an insecure scheme.

We provide a proof-of-concept implementation of our algorithm using a mix of Sagemath [29] and PARI/GP [28]. The code is available at https://gitlab.inria.fr/capsule/code-for-module-lip. We were able to run our algorithm successfully on module lattice isomorphic to $\mathcal{O}_K^2$, when K is the maximal totally real subfield of a cyclotomic field up to conductor 256 (which means that the lattices involved have dimension 128)—see also Table 1

Technical Details. A central tool for our definition of module-LIP is the notion of pseudo-Gram matrices. Modules usually do not admit bases but only pseudo-bases, as defined by Cohen in [9]. A pseudo-basis B of a module M consists of a matrix $B \in K^{\ell \times \ell}$ and a list of ℓ fractional ideals $I_1, \ldots, I_\ell$, such that $M = \{\sum_i x_i \boldsymbol{b}_i \mid x_i \in I_i\}$, where $\boldsymbol{b}_i$ are the columns of B. In a natural way, we define the pseudo-Gram matrix associated to the pseudo-basis B to be $G = (B^*B, (I_i)_{1 \le i \le \ell})$.

In the same way that a Gram matrix-based formulation is the better fit in the unstructured case, this basic ingredient leads us to a well-defined version of the module-LIP problem. Let B, C be two pseudo-bases of a module M, and let G be the pseudo-Gram matrix of C (the pseudo-basis B is fixed, and will be a parameter of the problem). The module-LIP problem with parameter B (wc-smodLIP$_K^B$) is, given as input G, to recover a pseudo-basis C' of M such that its Gram matrix is G (C is a solution to this problem, but it may not be unique).[4] Let us explain briefly why this definition of the module-LIP problem includes the problem underlying the security of Hawk. In Hawk, the secret key is a basis C of $\mathcal{O}_K^2$, and the public key contains the Gram matrix $G = C^*C$. Since $\mathcal{O}_K^2$ is free, no ideals are involved. The secret key C is then a solution of the module-LIP problem with parameter I_2 (the trivial basis of $\mathcal{O}_K^2$), on input G. It can be checked that any other solution C' to this problem can be used to forge valid signatures.

The tools that we provide in Sect. 3 for manipulating module-LIP are generalization of the results known for non-structured lattices. This extension is easy once the formal framework is set up. For example, the worst-case to average-case reduction (in the full version of this paper [25]) is the adaptation to the module context of the reduction provided in [14]. The latter used a standard algorithm in lattice theory, which computes a short basis of a lattice L given as input short linearly independent vectors and a (potentially large) basis of L. A

---

[4] This definition is not formulated exactly in the same way as Definition 3.11 below, but both are equivalent.

module variant of this algorithm was provided in [16], and we used it to complete our reduction.

Algorithm for Module-LIP. We now explain how our algorithm for module-LIP works, when K is totally real. To simplify the description in this introduction, we will restrict ourselves to the case where the problem is parameterized by the module $\mathcal{O}_K^2$ (with basis $B = I_2$), and where the input of the problem is a Gram matrix G (instead of a pseudo-Gram matrix $\boldsymbol{G}$). In other words, we are given as input $G \in M_2(\mathcal{O}_K)$ are we are asked to compute $C \in \mathrm{GL}_2(\mathcal{O}_K)$ a basis of $\mathcal{O}_K^2$ such that $C^*C = C^TC = G$. We are thus looking for $u, v, r, t \in \mathcal{O}_K^2$ such that

$$\begin{pmatrix} u & v \\ r & t \end{pmatrix} \cdot \begin{pmatrix} u & r \\ v & t \end{pmatrix} = \begin{pmatrix} u^2 + v^2 & ur + vt \\ ur + vt & r^2 + v^2 \end{pmatrix} = G.$$

The diagonal coefficients of G must hence be the sum of two squares in $\mathcal{O}_K$. Sums of two squares $x^2 + y^2 = a$ over $\mathbb{Z}$ are the topic of Fermat's two-squares theorem. Algorithms such as Cornacchias's allow to find all solutions of this equation efficiently, and the equation usually does not have too many solutions (this depends on the number of prime factors of a). A similar situation happens when $\mathbb{Z}$ is changed to the ring of integers $\mathcal{O}_K$ of a totally real field K.

Let us explain the principles behind the algorithm solving equations of the form $x^2 + y^2 = a$ (with unknowns $x, y \in \mathcal{O}_K$). As K is totally real, it contains no square roots of -1. Thus there is a quadratic extension $L = K(i)$ where i is such that $i^2 = -1$. To any solution (x, y) of our equation corresponds the element $z := x + iy \in \mathcal{O}_L$. By definition of L, the relative norm $\mathcal{N}_{L|K}(z)$ of this element is precisely $z\bar{z} = x^2 + y^2 = a$. Hence, two-squares decompositions reduces to the computation of all solutions $z \in \mathcal{O}_L$ of $z\bar{z} = a$.[5]

To solve this norm equation $\mathcal{N}_{L|K}(z) = a$, we use the Gentry-Szydlo algorithm, as described by Lenstra and Silverberg in [21]. Given $a = z\bar{z} \in \mathcal{O}_K$ and $I = z\mathcal{O}_L$, the Gentry-Szydlo algorithms recovers z in polynomial time. To apply it in our setting, we then need to compute the ideal $I = z\mathcal{O}_L$ for all possible solutions z. To do so, we observe that $I \cdot \bar{I} = z\bar{z}\mathcal{O}_L = a\mathcal{O}_L$ is known. Hence, the ideals I we are looking for are *principal* divisors of the ideal $a\mathcal{O}_L$. It then only remains to factor the ideal $a\mathcal{O}_L$ and test all possible divisors I of it. The number of such divisors is exponential in the number of prime factors of $a\mathcal{O}_L$, so our algorithm is, also, exponential in the number of prime factors of $a\mathcal{O}_L$. These two steps are handled by our provided code.

Combining everything, we obtain an algorithm which finds all the matrices $C \in M_2(\mathcal{O}_K)$ such that $C^TC = G$ (so it solves module-LIP), but whose complexity is, for the moment, exponential in the number of prime factors of the diagonal coefficients q_1 and q_2 of the Gram matrix G. To make this algorithm polynomial time, we re-randomize the matrix G (by computing $G' = U^{-1}GU$

---

[5] The set of $z \in \mathcal{O}_L$ with $z\bar{z} = a$ might be strictly larger than the set of solutions, since we may have $\mathcal{O}_K + i\mathcal{O}_K \subsetneq \mathcal{O}_L$, but we can easily check, given a $z = x + iy$ if (x, y) is a solution to our equation.

with $U \in \mathrm{GL}_2(\mathcal{O}_K)$, which transforms C into $C' = CU$), until its two diagonal coefficients q_1 and q_2 are prime. Under some heuristic (formalised in Assumption 1), we expect to find a good re-randomized matrix G' in polynomial time polynomial in the input size and in ρ_K, the residue of the Dedekind zeta function of K at 1.

2   Preliminaries

Notations. Vectors are by default column vectors, and are denoted by bold lower case letters (e.g., v). Matrices are denoted by non-bold upper case letters (e.g., B), and pseudo-matrices by bold upper case letters (e.g., $\boldsymbol{B}$). For a ring R, we write $\mathrm{GL}_n(R)$ the set of $n \times n$ matrices whose determinant is an invertible element of R. We let $\mathcal{O}_n(\mathbb{R})$ be the set of orthogonal real matrices, $\mathcal{U}_n(\mathbb{C})$ be the set of unitary complex matrices, $\mathcal{S}_n^{>0}(\mathbb{R})$ be the set of real symmetric positive definite matrices, and $\mathcal{H}_n^{\geq 0}(\mathbb{C})$ be the set of complex Hermitian positive definite matrices. For vectors v in $\mathbb{R}^n$ or in $\mathbb{C}^n$, we let $\|v\|$ (resp. $\|v\|_\infty$, $\|v\|_1$) denote their ℓ_2 (resp. ℓ_∞, ℓ_1) norm. For a matrix $B \in \mathbb{C}^{n \times m}$ with column vectors $b_1, \ldots, b_m$, we use the notation $\|B\| := \max_i \|b_i\|$. For a field K and a subset S of a K-vector space H, we write $\mathrm{Span}_K(S)$ for the K-vector subspace of H spanned by S. We use $\log$ to refer to the natural logarithm (in base e).

2.1   Lattices

We call lattice any set of the form $L = \sum_{1 \leq i \leq r} b_i \cdot \mathbb{Z}$, where $b_1, \ldots, b_n \in \mathbb{R}^m$ are $\mathbb{R}$-linearly independent vectors. It is a discrete additive subgroup of $\mathbb{R}^m$. The integer n is called the rank of L, when $n = m$ we say that the lattice has full rank. The matrix $B = (b_1 | \ldots | b_n)$ is called a basis of L and all bases of L are obtained by multiplication on the right by a unimodular matrix $U \in \mathrm{GL}_n(\mathbb{Z})$. For a given matrix $B \in \mathrm{GL}_n(\mathbb{R})$, we write $L(B)$ the lattice spanned by B. The determinant (or volume) of a lattice L is $\det(L) := \sqrt{\det(B^T \cdot B)}$ for any basis B of L. For $1 \leq i \leq n$, the i-th successive minimum $\lambda_i(L)$ of the lattice L is the smallest real number $r > 0$ such that the set $\{v \in L \,|\, \|v\| \leq r\}$ spans a real vector space of dimension at least i. We define analogously the successive minima of L in the ℓ_∞-norm. Minkowski's first theorem states that $\lambda_1^{(\infty)}(L) \leq \det(L)^{1/n}$ and $\lambda_1(L) \leq \sqrt{n} \cdot \det(L)^{1/n}$. The dual of a lattice L is the lattice $L^* = \{x \in \mathrm{Span}_\mathbb{R}(L) \,|\, \langle x, v \rangle \in \mathbb{Z}, \forall\, v \in L\}$.

The Lattice Isomorphism Problem. Two lattices L, L' (with respective bases B, B') are said *isomorphic* if there exists an orthogonal transformation O such that $L' = O \cdot L$. In terms of matrices, $L(B)$ and $L(B')$ are isomorphic if and only if there exists a unimodular transformation $U \in \mathrm{GL}_n(\mathbb{Z})$ such that $B' = OBU$. The search version of the problem is precisely to find either such O or U.

Definition 2.1 (wc-sLIP^B). *For a matrix $B \in \mathrm{GL}_n(\mathbb{R})$, the worst-case search Lattice Isomorphism Problem with parameter B (wc-sLIP^B) is, given a basis $B' \in \mathrm{GL}_n(\mathbb{R})$ of a lattice $L' \subset \mathbb{R}^n$ isomorphic to $L(B)$, to find $O \in \mathcal{O}_n(\mathbb{R})$ or $U \in \mathrm{GL}_n(\mathbb{Z})$ such that $B' = OBU$.*

For convenience, we restate LIP in terms of quadratic forms. The Gram matrix associated to a basis $B \in \mathrm{GL}_n(\mathbb{R})$ is the definite positive quadratic form $G = B^T B \in \mathcal{S}_n^{>0}(\mathbb{R})$. Two quadratic forms $Q, Q' \in \mathcal{S}_n^{>0}(\mathbb{R})$ are said *congruent* if there exists $U \in \mathrm{GL}_n(\mathbb{Z})$ such that $Q' = U^T Q U$.

Definition 2.2 (wc-sLIP^Q). *For a quadratic form $Q \in \mathcal{S}_n^{>0}(\mathbb{R})$, the worst-case search LIP problem with parameter Q (wc-sLIP^Q) is, given any quadratic form $Q' \in \mathcal{S}_n^{>0}(\mathbb{R})$ congruent to Q, to find a unimodular transformation $U \in \mathrm{GL}_n(\mathbb{Z})$ such that $Q' = U^T Q U$.*

The two problems are polynomial-time equivalent, thanks to the Cholesky decomposition for quadratic forms.

Discrete Gaussian Distributions. The Gaussian function over $\mathbb{R}^m$ with parameter $s \in \mathbb{R}_{>0}$ is $\rho_s(\boldsymbol{v}) = \exp(-\pi \cdot \|\boldsymbol{v}\|^2/s^2)$ for all $\boldsymbol{v} \in \mathbb{R}^m$. For a rank-$n$ lattice $L \subset \mathbb{R}^m$, the discrete Gaussian distribution $\mathcal{D}_{L,s}$ over L with parameter s (and center 0) is the probability distribution defined over L by

$$\Pr_{X \sim \mathcal{D}_{L,s}}(X = \boldsymbol{v}) = \frac{\rho_s(\boldsymbol{v})}{\rho_s(L)},$$

for all $\boldsymbol{v} \in L$, where $\rho_s(L) = \sum_{\boldsymbol{v} \in L} \rho_s(\boldsymbol{v})$.

For $\varepsilon > 0$ and L a rank-n lattice, the smoothing parameter $\eta_\varepsilon(L)$ is the smallest real number $s > 0$ such that $\rho_{1/s}(L^* \setminus \{0\}) \le \varepsilon$. Instantiating [24, Lemma 3.3] with $\varepsilon = 1/2$, we obtain the following upper bound, for any rank-n lattice L

$$\eta_{1/2}(L) \le \sqrt{\frac{\log(6n)}{\pi}} \cdot \lambda_n(L). \tag{1}$$

Lemma 2.3 (Proof of [24, Lemma 4.4]). *Let L be a rank-n lattice, $\varepsilon > 0$ and $s \ge \eta_\varepsilon(L)$, then*

$$\rho_s(L) \in [1 - \varepsilon, 1 + \varepsilon] \cdot \frac{s^n}{\det(L)}.$$

One can efficiently sample discrete Gaussian distributions over lattices, provided the parameter s is large enough.

Lemma 2.4 (Weakening of [5, Lemma 2.3]). *There is a probabilistic polynomial time algorithm `DiscreteGaussian` (B, s) that takes as input a basis B of an n-dimensional lattice and a parameter $s \ge \sqrt{\log(2n + 4)/\pi} \cdot \max_i \|\boldsymbol{b}_i\|$ (where $\boldsymbol{b}_i$ are the columns of B) and returns a sample from $\mathcal{D}_{L,s}$.*

Note that the lower bound on s, in our statement above, is slightly larger than the one provided in [5, Lemma 2.3] (it involves the euclidean norm of the column vectors of B, instead of the Gram-Schmidt orthogonalization of B), but this will be sufficient for our purposes in this article.

Lemma 2.5 ([15, Lemma A.5]). *For any rank-n lattice L with basis $B =$* *$(\boldsymbol{b}_i)_{1 \leq i \leq n}$, if $s \geq \sqrt{n} \cdot \max_i \|\boldsymbol{b}_i\|$, then for any $\varepsilon \in (0,1]$ it holds that*

$$\Pr_{\boldsymbol{v} \sim \mathcal{D}_{L,s}} \left(\|\boldsymbol{v}\| > s\sqrt{4n + \log(1/\varepsilon)} \right) \leq \varepsilon.$$

2.2 Number Fields

A number field K is a finite extension of the field of rational numbers $\mathbb{Q}$. Any such K is isomorphic to $\mathbb{Q}[X]/(P)$ for an irreducible monic polynomial $P \in \mathbb{Q}[X]$. The degree of P is exactly the degree of the extension. Furthermore, any extension K of degree d comes naturally with d embeddings $K \to \mathbb{C}$, sending the class of X to a complex root of P. An embedding $\sigma : K \to \mathbb{C}$ such that $\sigma(K) \subset \mathbb{R}$ is called a real embedding. An embedding σ which is not real is called complex. In this case, it can be composed with complex conjugation and gives another distinct complex embedding $\overline{\sigma}$. We denote by d_1 the number of real embeddings and d_2 the number of complex embeddings up to complex conjugation, so that $d = d_1 + 2d_2$. We order the embeddings $\sigma_1, \cdots, \sigma_d$ such that σ_i is a real embedding for $1 \leq i \leq d_1$ and $\sigma_{i+d_2} = \overline{\sigma_i}$ for $d_1 < i \leq d_1 + d_2$. When $d_1 = d$ (resp. $2d_2 = d$), we say that the extension $K|\mathbb{Q}$ is totally real (resp. totally imaginary). The proofs of the lemmas from this section are available in the full version of the article [25].

The Space $K_\mathbb{R}$. The $\mathbb{R}$-algebra $K_\mathbb{R} := K \otimes_\mathbb{Q} \mathbb{R}$ is a real vector space of dimension d. If $K \sim \mathbb{Q}[X]/(P)$, then we have an identification $K_\mathbb{R} \sim \mathbb{R}[X]/(P)$. The embeddings of K can be uniquely extended to $K_\mathbb{R}$, which leads to the so-called canonical embedding $\sigma(x) = (\sigma_1(x), \ldots, \sigma_d(x)) \in \mathbb{C}^d$. This map defines a ring homomorphism from $K_\mathbb{R}$ to $\sigma(K_\mathbb{R})$, which is the d-dimensional real vector space

$$\sigma(K_\mathbb{R}) := \left\{ z = (z_i)_i \in \mathbb{C}^d \mid z_1, \ldots, z_{d_1} \in \mathbb{R}, \ \overline{z_{d_1+i}} = z_{d_1+d_2+i}, \ 1 \leq i \leq d_2 \right\}.$$

To any $z \in K_\mathbb{R}$ we associate its complex conjugate $\overline{z} := \sigma^{-1}(\overline{\sigma(z)}) \in K_\mathbb{R}$, where $\overline{\sigma(z)}$ consists in taking the complex conjugation of $\sigma(z) \in \mathbb{C}^d$ coordinatewise. We let $K_\mathbb{R}^+$ (resp. $K_\mathbb{R}^{++}$) be the subset of $K_\mathbb{R}$ corresponding to elements with all non-negative (resp. positive) embeddings (in particular, the complex embeddings are all real numbers). The norm map defined over $K_\mathbb{R}$ is $\mathcal{N}_K(z) = \prod_i \sigma_i(z)$, and extends the well-known notion of algebraic norm for elements of K. Similarly, the trace map is $\mathrm{Tr}_K(z) = \sum_i \sigma_i(z)$. When there is no ambiguity, we drop the subscript. If $z \in K$ (resp. $\mathcal{O}_K$), then $\mathcal{N}(z), \mathrm{Tr}(z) \in \mathbb{Q}$ (resp. $\mathbb{Z}$). Another important notion of size for $K_\mathbb{R}$ is the corresponding "T_2-norm" $\|z\|^2 :=$ $\|\sigma(z)\|^2 = \mathrm{Tr}(z\overline{z}) \in \mathbb{R}^+$.

We extend the canonical embedding to vectors of $K_\mathbb{R}^k$ and matrices in $K_\mathbb{R}^{k \times k'}$ by applying it coordinate-wise. We say that r vectors $\boldsymbol{b}_1, \cdots, \boldsymbol{b}_r$ in $K_\mathbb{R}^k$ are ($K_\mathbb{R}$-)linearly independent if there exists no non-zero r-tuple $\boldsymbol{x} = (x_1, \cdots, x_r) \in K_\mathbb{R}^r \setminus \{\boldsymbol{0}\}$ such that $\sum_i x_i \boldsymbol{b}_i = 0$. Note that, since $K_\mathbb{R}$ is not a field, this notion can be interesting even for $r = 1$ vector: a vector $\boldsymbol{b} \in K_\mathbb{R}^k$ is linearly independent if and only if $\sigma_i(\boldsymbol{b}) \neq \boldsymbol{0}$ for all embeddings σ_i. For a matrix $B \in K_\mathbb{R}^{k \times k'}$, we let $B^* = \overline{B}^T$; this covers vectors (k or k' is 1). We let $\mathcal{U}_k(K_{\mathbb{R}})$ denote the group of unitary matrices of $K_{\mathbb{R}}$, that is the matrices $B \in \mathrm{GL}_k(K_{\mathbb{R}})$ such that $B^* \cdot B = I_k$. Thanks to the injectivity of the canonical embedding, it holds that B is in $\mathcal{U}_k(K_{\mathbb{R}})$ if and only if $\sigma_i(B) \in \mathcal{U}_k(\mathbb{C})$ for all embeddings σ_i. For $\boldsymbol{v} = (v_i)_i$ and $\boldsymbol{w} = (w_i)_i \in K_{\mathbb{R}}^k$ (for some $k \geq 1$), we define

$$\langle \boldsymbol{v}, \boldsymbol{w} \rangle_{K_{\mathbb{R}}} := \boldsymbol{v}^* \boldsymbol{w} = \sum_i \overline{v_i} \cdot w_i \in K_{\mathbb{R}}.$$

This extends the T_2-norm to $K_{\mathbb{R}}^k$ as $\|\boldsymbol{v}\|^2 := \mathrm{Tr}\,\langle \boldsymbol{v}, \boldsymbol{v} \rangle_{K_{\mathbb{R}}} = \sum_i \mathrm{Tr}(v_i \overline{v_i}) = \|\sigma(\boldsymbol{v})\|^2$.

Ring of Integers. We denote by $\mathcal{O}_K$ the ring of integers of a number field K. The ring $\mathcal{O}_K$ is a free $\mathbb{Z}$-module of rank d. The discriminant of K is defined by $(\det(\sigma_i(e_j))_{i,j})^2 \in \mathbb{Z}$, where $(e_i)_{1 \leq i \leq d}$ is any $\mathbb{Z}$-basis of $\mathcal{O}_K$ (this does not depend on the choice of the basis). Its absolute value is denoted Δ_K. There exists some absolute constant c such that $\Delta_K \geq c^d$ for all number fields K. In particular, we always have $d = \mathrm{poly}(\log \Delta_K)$.

A special case that will be of interest for us in Sect. 4.3 is when K is totally real and $L = K[X]/(X^2 + 1)$. In this case, we have $\Delta_L \mid 4^d \Delta_K^2$. This can be obtained using the formula $\Delta_L = N_K(\Delta_{L|K}) \cdot \Delta_K^{[L:K]}$ and the fact that $\Delta_{L|K}$ divides $\mathrm{disc}(X^2 + 1) \cdot \mathcal{O}_K = 4 \cdot \mathcal{O}_K$ (see [27, III, §4, Proposition 8] and [27, III, §2, Corollary to Proposition 5] with lattices $X = \mathcal{O}_L$ and $X' = \mathcal{O}_K[i]$). In particular for these extensions we always have $\log \Delta_L = \mathrm{poly}(\log \Delta_K)$. Moreover, we also know how to compute $\mathcal{O}_L$ efficiently from $\mathcal{O}_K$, as stated in the following lemma.

Lemma 2.6 (Specialization of [8, Theorem 1.2]). *Let K be a totally real number field and $L := K[X]/(X^2 + 1)$. There exists a polynomial time algorithm $\mathcal{A}$ that, given as input a $\mathbb{Z}$-basis B_K of $\mathcal{O}_K$, computes a $\mathbb{Z}$-basis B_L of $\mathcal{O}_L$.*

Residue. We write ρ_K the residue of the zeta function of K at $s = 1$. This is a positive number, which is always $\leq O(\log \Delta_K)^d$ [22, Theorem 1]. In some number fields, such as when K is a cyclotomic fields, we have better bounds, and we know that $\rho_K = \mathrm{poly}(d)$ [4, Theorem A.5]. Unfortunately, we are not aware of a proven polynomial bound for the maximal totally real subfield of a cyclotomic field (for these fields, the best bound we found was $\rho_K = O(1.31^d)$ [30, Lemma 11.5]). However, in practice, in all our experiments with maximal totally real subfield of a cyclotomic field, we observed that the residue ρ_K was quite small.

Ideals. An integral ideal $\mathfrak{a}$ is an additive subgroup of $\mathcal{O}_K$ such that $x \cdot \mathfrak{a} \subset \mathfrak{a}$ for all $x \in \mathcal{O}_K$. Equivalently, it is an $\mathcal{O}_K$-module contained in $\mathcal{O}_K$.[6] An ideal

---

[6] Note that $\mathcal{O}_K$ is a Dedekind ring. In particular, it is Noetherian, so all ideals are finitely generated as $\mathcal{O}_K$-module.

generated by a single element a is called principal, and is denoted by $a\mathcal{O}_K$. A fractional ideal I of K is any additive subgroup of K of the form $x \cdot \mathfrak{a}$ where $x \in K \setminus \{0\}$ and $\mathfrak{a} \subset \mathcal{O}_K$ is an integral ideal. We use fraktur lower-case letters for integral ideals (e.g., $\mathfrak{a}$, $\mathfrak{b}$) and upper-case letters for fractional ideals (e.g., I, J). The product of two fractional ideals I and J is the smallest ideal containing all products xy for $x \in I$ and $y \in J$, denoted by IJ. This operation turns the set of non-zero fractional ideals into a multiplicative group. Given two fractional ideals I and J, we have that $I \subseteq J$ if and only if there exists an integral ideal $\mathfrak{a}$ such that $I = J \cdot \mathfrak{a}$. When this is the case, we say that J divides I, and we may write $J|I$. An integral ideal $\mathfrak{p}$ is prime when $\mathfrak{p} \neq \{0\}$ and $ab \in \mathfrak{p}$ implies $a \in \mathfrak{p}$ or $b \in \mathfrak{p}$ — such ideals are maximal in $\mathcal{O}_K$. We have unique factorization of integral ideals into prime ideals (up to permutation of the factors).

The algebraic norm of an integral ideal is $\mathcal{N}(\mathfrak{a}) = |\mathcal{O}_K/\mathfrak{a}|$. It is multiplicative, extends to fractional ideals as $\mathcal{N}(I) = \mathcal{N}(dI)/\mathcal{N}(d)$ for any d such that dI is integral. If $I = a\mathcal{O}_K$ is principal, then $\mathcal{N}(I) = |\mathcal{N}(a)|$.

Modules. In this article, an $(\mathcal{O}_K\text{-})$module M will refer to a subset of $K_{\mathbb{R}}^{\ell}$ of the form $\boldsymbol{b}_1 I_1 + \cdots + \boldsymbol{b}_r I_r$, where the I_i are non-zero fractional ideals of K and $(\boldsymbol{b}_1, \ldots, \boldsymbol{b}_r)$ are $K_{\mathbb{R}}$-linearly independent vectors of $K_{\mathbb{R}}^{\ell}$, for some $\ell > 0$. The integer r is called the rank of the module. When $r = \ell$, we say that the module has full rank. When $M \subset (\mathcal{O}_K)^{\ell}$ (resp. $M \subset K^{\ell}$), we say M is an integer module (resp. a rational module). We say that $\boldsymbol{B} = (B, \{I_i\}_{1 \leq i \leq r})$ is a pseudo-basis for M, where $B \in K_{\mathbb{R}}^{\ell \times r}$ is the matrix whose columns are the $\boldsymbol{b}'_i s$. Two pseudo-bases $\boldsymbol{B} = (B, \{I_i\}_{1 \leq i \leq r})$ and $\boldsymbol{B}' = (B', \{J_i\}_{1 \leq i \leq r})$ represent the same module if and only if there exists $U = (u_{i,j})_{1 \leq i,j \leq r} \in \mathrm{GL}_r(K)$ such that $B' = BU$ and $u_{i,j} \in I_i J_j^{-1}$, $v_{i,j} \in J_i I_j^{-1}$, where $V = (v_{i,j})_{1 \leq i,j \leq l} = U^{-1}$.[7] Given a module M and a non-zero fractional ideal J, we define $J \cdot M$ to be the smallest module containing all $\alpha \cdot \boldsymbol{v}$ for $\alpha \in J$ and $\boldsymbol{v} \in M$. If $\boldsymbol{B} = (B, \{I_i\}_{1 \leq i \leq r})$ is a pseudo-basis of M, then $\boldsymbol{B}' = (B, \{J \cdot I_i\}_{1 \leq i \leq r})$ is a pseudo-basis of $J \cdot M$.

If $M \subset K_{\mathbb{R}}^{\ell}$ is a module of rank r, then the set $\sigma(M) := \{\sigma(\boldsymbol{v}) \,|\, \boldsymbol{v} \in M\}$ is a *module lattice*, that is, a lattice of rank dr in the real space $\sigma(K_{\mathbb{R}})^{\ell}$ equipped with the (extended) T_2-norm. Since we always use the canonical embedding to view modules as lattices in this work, we will simplify notations and write $\lambda_i(M)$ and $\det(M)$ instead of $\lambda_i(\sigma(M))$ and $\det(\sigma(M))$.

A special case of module lattices is when $M = I$ is a non-zero fractional ideal of K. In this case, we know that $\det(I) = \sqrt{\Delta_K} \cdot \mathcal{N}(I)$ (see e.g., [26, Chapter I. Proposition 5.2]). We also know that the successive minima of $\sigma(I)$ cannot be very unbalanced. More precisely, we have

$$\lambda_d(I) \leq \Delta_K^{1/d} \cdot \lambda_1(I) \leq \sqrt{d} \cdot \Delta_K^{3/(2d)} \cdot \mathcal{N}(I)^{1/d}. \tag{2}$$

The second inequality follows from Minkowski's first theorem, and the equality $\det(I) = \Delta_K^{1/2} \cdot \mathcal{N}(I)$. This first inequality can be obtained by choosing $x \in I$

---

[7] When $M \subset K^l$ is a rational module, these are the conditions for U to be a pseudo-base change matrix, see [9].

reaching $\lambda_1(I)$ (i.e., such that $\|\sigma(x)\| = \lambda_1(I)$) and $\{\alpha_1, \ldots, \alpha_d\}$ linearly independent elements of $\mathcal{O}_K$ reaching the successive minima in infinity norm (i.e., such that $\|\sigma(\alpha_i)\|_\infty = \lambda_i^{(\infty)}(\mathcal{O}_K)$). Then $\{\alpha_1 x, \ldots, \alpha_d x\}$ are $\mathbb{Z}$-linearly independent elements of I thus $\lambda_d(I) \leq \max_i \|\sigma(\alpha_i x)\| \leq \|\sigma(x)\| \cdot \lambda_d^\infty(\mathcal{O}_K)$. The desired upper bound is then obtained by the fact that $\lambda_d^{(\infty)}(\mathcal{O}_K) \leq \Delta_K^{1/d}$ (see [3] for the asymptotic result and [4, Theorem A.4] for the upper bound with an explicit constant).

In the general case, the volume of a module M of rank r with pseudo-basis $(B, (I_i)_i)$ is $\det(M)^2 = \Delta_K^r \cdot \det(B^*B) \cdot \prod_{i=1}^r \mathcal{N}(I_i)^2$.

CM Extensions. A CM (complex multiplication) extension is any quadratic extension $L|K$ of number fields such that K is totally real and L is totally imaginary. In the rest of this article, we will always use the convention that the degree of K is d, and the degree of L is $2d$. A typical example to keep in mind is when L is a cyclotomic field and K is its maximal totally real subfield.

Any CM extension $L|K$ is Galois, and so L has two field automorphisms fixing K point-wise, namely the identity and another automorphism which we will call τ. The automorphism τ somehow plays the role of a complex conjugation on L, as can be seen in the following lemma.

Lemma 2.7. *Let $L|K$ be a CM extension of number fields and σ_i be an embedding of L in $\mathbb{C}$. Then $\sigma_i(\tau(x)) = \overline{\sigma_i(x)}$ for all $x \in L$.*

For an element $x \in L$, the relative norm of x is defined as $\mathcal{N}_{L|K}(x) := x \cdot \tau(x)$, which is an element of K (since it is fixed by τ). We also define similarly the relative norm of a fractional ideal I of L: $\mathcal{N}_{L|K}(I) := I \cdot \tau(I) \cap K$, where $\tau(I) := \{\tau(x) \mid x \in I\}$ is also a fractional ideal of L. Finally, if $I = x\mathcal{O}_L$ is a principal ideal, then it holds that $\mathcal{N}_{L|K}(I) = \mathcal{N}_{L|K}(x) \cdot \mathcal{O}_K$.

Splitting of prime ideals in CM extensions. Let $\mathfrak{p}$ be a prime ideal in $\mathcal{O}_K$. Then, $\mathfrak{p}\mathcal{O}_L$ is an integral ideal of $\mathcal{O}_L$ and one of the three situations holds for its factorization into prime ideals (see *e.g.*, [26, Chap 2. Proposition 8.2])

$$\mathfrak{p}\mathcal{O}_L = \begin{cases} \mathfrak{q} & \text{with } \mathfrak{q} \text{ prime and } \mathcal{N}_{L|K}(\mathfrak{q}) = \mathfrak{p}^2 \text{ (inert case)}, \\ \mathfrak{q}_1\mathfrak{q}_2 & \text{with } \mathfrak{q}_1 \neq \mathfrak{q}_2 \text{ prime and } \mathcal{N}_{L|K}(\mathfrak{q}_i) = \mathfrak{p} \text{ (split case)}, \\ \mathfrak{q}^2 & \text{with } \mathfrak{q} \text{ prime and } \mathcal{N}_{L|K}(\mathfrak{q}) = \mathfrak{p} \text{ (ramified case)}. \end{cases} \quad (3)$$

This implies in particular the following result.

Lemma 2.8. *Let $\mathfrak{q}$ be a prime ideal of $\mathcal{O}_L$ and $\mathfrak{p}$ be a prime ideal of $\mathcal{O}_K$. If $\mathfrak{p}$ divides $\mathcal{N}_{L|K}(\mathfrak{q})$, then $\mathfrak{q}$ divides $\mathfrak{p}\mathcal{O}_L$.*

2.3   Algorithmic Considerations

This section collects various computational results. In this article, we assume a model of computation where computers have access to infinite precision real numbers. Most of the time, we will work with elements of K which we can represent with rational numbers, and for which we define a notion of size. When we need to work with complex numbers, we assume that we have enough precision so that all computations are correct. The missing proofs of the lemmas from this section are available in the full version of the article [25].

Representation of Ideals and Modules. We assume in this article that we are always given an LLL reduced basis $\alpha_1, \ldots, \alpha_d$ of $\mathcal{O}_K$, i.e., such that $(\sigma(\alpha_i))_i$ is an LLL-reduced basis of $\mathcal{O}_K$. Elements in K (resp. $K_{\mathbb{R}}$) are represented by their coordinates in the basis $(\alpha_1, \ldots, \alpha_d)$, which is a vector in $\mathbb{Q}^d$ (resp $\mathbb{R}^d$). For $x \in K$ represented by the vector $(x_1, \ldots, x_d) \in \mathbb{Q}^d$, we define $\text{size}(x) := \sum_i \text{size}(x_i)$, where the size of a rational number a/b with a and b coprime is $\lceil \log_2 |a| \rceil + \lceil \log_2 |b| \rceil$. Since $(\alpha_i)_i$ is LLL-reduced for the canonical embedding, [16, Lemma 2] states that if $x = \sum_i x_i \alpha_i \in K$, then $\max_i |x_i| \leq 2^{3d/2} \cdot \|\sigma(x)\|$. This implies in particular that for any integral $x \in \mathcal{O}_K$, $\text{size}(x) = \text{poly}(d, \|\sigma(x)\|)$. Inversely, we have $\|\sigma(x)\| \leq \sum_i |x_i| \cdot \|\sigma(\alpha_i)\| \leq d^{3/2} \cdot 2^d \cdot \Delta_K^{1/d} \cdot \max_i |x_i|$ (where we used the fact that $\lambda_d(\mathcal{O}_K) \leq \sqrt{d} \cdot \Delta_K^{1/d}$). This implies that for any rational $x \in K$, we have $\|\sigma(x)\| \leq \text{poly}(\log \Delta_K, \text{size}(x))$.

A fractional ideal I is represented by a $\mathbb{Z}$-basis $(y_1, \ldots, y_d)$ of the ideal, such that $(\sigma(y_i))_i$ is an LLL-reduced basis of $\sigma(I)$. In particular, we have

$$\|\sigma(y_i)\| \leq 2^d \cdot \lambda_d(I) \leq \sqrt{d} \cdot 2^d \cdot \Delta_K^{3/(2d)} \cdot \mathcal{N}(I)^{1/d}, \tag{4}$$

where we used Inequality (2). We define $\text{size}(I) := \sum_i \text{size}(y_i)$. If $\mathfrak{a}$ is an integral ideal, then (4) shows that $\text{size}(\mathfrak{a}) = \text{poly}(\log \Delta_K, \log \mathcal{N}(\mathfrak{a}))$. By default, in the rest of this article, whenever an algorithm takes as input, manipulates, or returns an ideal, we implicitly assume that the ideal is represented as described above.

For vectors and matrices with coefficients in K, we define their size as the sum of the size of their coordinates. Modules in K^ℓ are represented by a pseudo-basis $\boldsymbol{B} = (B, (I_i))$, where B is a matrix with coefficients in K and the I_i's are fractional ideals, represented by LLL-reduced bases as discussed above. We define $\text{size}(\boldsymbol{B}) := \text{size}(B) + \sum_i \text{size}(I_i)$.

Basic Algorithms for Number Fields. If $x, y \in K$, then $\text{size}(x \cdot y) \leq \text{poly}(\text{size}(x), \text{size}(y), \log(\Delta_K))$, where we used the relations between $\text{size}(x)$ and $\|\sigma(x)\|$ mentioned above, and the fact that $\|\sigma(x \cdot y)\| \leq \|\sigma(x)\| \cdot \|\sigma(y)\|$. Such a product can be computed in time $\text{poly}(\text{size}(x), \text{size}(y), \log(\Delta_K))$.

With the representation of ideals as described above, one can multiply two ideals I and J in time $\text{poly}(\text{size}(I), \text{size}(J), \log \Delta_K)$. Indeed, if $(x_i)_i$ is an LLL reduced basis of I and $(y_i)_i$ is an LLL reduced basis of J, then $(x_i \cdot y_j)_{i,j}$ is a generating set of $I \cdot J$, and one can run the LLL algorithm on this generating set to extract an LLL-reduced basis from it.

Lemma 2.9. *Let $\boldsymbol{B} = (B, \{I_i\}_i)$ be a pseudo-basis of a rank r module M in K^ℓ. Then one can compute in polynomial time a basis $C \in \mathbb{C}^{d\ell \times dr}$ of $\sigma(M)$ such that the column vectors $\boldsymbol{c}_i$ of C satisfy*

$$\|c_i\| \le \sqrt{d} \cdot 2^d \cdot \Delta_K^{3/(2d)} \cdot \max_{1 \le j \le r} \left(\|\sigma(b_j)\| \cdot \mathcal{N}(I_j)^{1/d} \right),$$

where b_j is the j-th column of B.

The computation of roots of unity is handled by the following lemma.

Lemma 2.10 (Factoring Polynomials Over a Number Field [1]). *There is a polynomial time algorithm that given a number field K and a polynomial $P \in K[X]$, factorizes P in K.*

Corollary 2.11 (Computing Roots of Unity in a Number Field). *Let K be a degree d number field. Then, K has at most $2d^2$ roots of unity and there is a polynomial time algorithm that given a basis of $\mathcal{O}_K$, computes the roots of unity in K.*

Factoring Ideals. Given a prime integer $p \in \mathbb{Z}$, we can compute all prime ideals of $\mathcal{O}_K$ above p. This can be done using Buchmann-Lenstra's algorithm [7], whose detailed analysis can be found in Cohen's book [10, Section 6.2.5].

Lemma 2.12 ([10, Section 6.2.5]). *There exists a polynomial time algorithm that takes as input any prime integer $p \in \mathbb{Z}$ and a basis of the ring of integers $\mathcal{O}_K$ of a number field K, and computes all the prime ideals of $\mathcal{O}_K$ dividing $p \cdot \mathcal{O}_K$.*

As a corollary of this lemma, we have the following two algorithms, to test primality of ideals, and factor them.

Corollary 2.13. *There is a polynomial time algorithm* `PrimalityTest(a)` *that takes as input any integral ideal a and decides whether a is a prime ideal or not.*

There is a polynomial time algorithm `FactorIdeal(a)` *that takes as input an integral ideal a and the factorization of $\mathcal{N}(a) \in \mathbb{Z}$, and returns the factorisation of a into prime ideals.*

Let us write $T_{\text{factor}}(N)$ is the time needed to factor an integer $N \in \mathbb{Z}_{>0}$. Then Algorithm `FactorIdeal` can be used to factor an integral ideal a in time $\text{poly}(\text{size}(a)) + T_{\text{factor}}(\mathcal{N}(a))$.

Norm Equations in CM Fields. Let us first consider a simple case of norm equation, which will be useful later on.

Lemma 2.14. *Let $L|K$ be a CM extension of number fields with K of degree d. The units $u \in \mathcal{O}_L^\times$ that satisfy $\mathcal{N}_{L|K}(u) = 1$ are exactly the roots of unity in L.*

The Gentry-Szydlo algorithm [17] was originally presented in a cyclotomic field K and allows one to recover in polynomial-time an element $x \in K$, given as input a basis of the ideal $x\mathcal{O}_K$ and the element $x\bar{x}$.[8] A generalization of this algorithm to CM-fields (and more generally CM-orders) was proposed by Lenstra and Silverberg in [21].

---

[8] The element x is recovered up to a root of unity.

Theorem 2.15 (Specialization of [21, Theorem 1.3]). *There exists a deterministic polynomial time algorithm* `GentrySzydlo` *such that the following holds. Let $L|K$ be a CM extension of number fields, $w \in L$ and I be a fractional ideal of L. Given as input a basis of $\mathcal{O}_L$, the ideal I and the element w, algorithm* `GentrySzydlo` *decides whether there exists $v \in \mathcal{O}_L$ such that $I = v \cdot \mathcal{O}_L$ and $v\bar{v} = w$, and if so computes such an element v.*

We note that Theorem 1.3 from [21] is stated for an arbitrary CM order A. We specialized the statement to $A = \mathcal{O}_L$, which is a CM order (see Example 3.7 (i) from [21]). With this specialization, the $\mathbb{Q}$-algebra $A_{\mathbb{Q}}$ (using the notations from [21]) is the field L, and the set $(A_{\mathbb{Q}}^+)_{\gg 0}$ is the set $L \cap L_{\mathbb{R}}^{++}$. In the original statement from [21], the element w is taken in this set $(A_{\mathbb{Q}}^+)_{\gg 0}$. We note that in our case, if $w \in L$ does not have all its embeddings real and positive, then we know that there is no solution to the equation $v\bar{v} = w$, and so this case is easily discarded. For this reason, we did not restrict the statement to specific elements w. Similarly, we did not impose in the statement that the ideal I satisfies $I\bar{I} = w\mathcal{O}_L$, because this condition can be tested in polynomial time, and the two equations $I = v \cdot \mathcal{O}_L$ and $v\bar{v} = w$ can be satisfied only if $I\bar{I} = (v\bar{v})\mathcal{O}_L = w\mathcal{O}_L$.

With this theorem, we obtain the following algorithm (Algorithm 2.1), which solves norm equations in CM extensions. This is a generalization to any CM field extensions of an algorithm by Howgrave-Graham and Szydlo [19] which solves relative norm equations in some cyclotomic number fields (over their totally real subfields). A result similar to Theorem 2.16 below and its proof are provided in [20, Theorem 14]. Since the latter article does not seem to be published, we provide a proof for completeness below.

Algorithm 2.1. Solve relative norm equations (`NormEquation`)

Input: A basis of $\mathcal{O}_K$ and $\mathcal{O}_L$, an element $q \in \mathcal{O}_K$, the prime factorization of $|\mathcal{N}_K(q)|$.
Output: All elements $z \in \mathcal{O}_L$ such that $\mathcal{N}_{L|K}(z) = q$.
1: Compute the roots of unity $\mathbb{U}_L$ in L, using Corollary 2.11.
2: Factor $q \cdot \mathcal{O}_K = \prod_{i=1}^r \mathfrak{p}_i^{\alpha_i}$, using Corollary 2.13.
3: $\mathfrak{J}_0 \leftarrow \{\mathfrak{q} \subset \mathcal{O}_L \text{ prime ideal} \mid \exists i \in \{1, \ldots, r\}, \mathfrak{q} \mid \mathfrak{p}_i\mathcal{O}_L\}$
4: $\mathfrak{J} \leftarrow \{\mathfrak{a} = \mathfrak{q}_1 \ldots \mathfrak{q}_s \mid s > 0, \mathfrak{q}_i \in \mathfrak{J}_0, \mathcal{N}_{L|K}(\mathfrak{a}) = q \cdot \mathcal{O}_K\}$
5: $S \leftarrow \{\}$
6: **for** $\mathfrak{a} \in \mathfrak{J}$ **do**
7:    $z_{\mathfrak{a}} \leftarrow$ `GentrySzydlo`$(\mathcal{O}_L, \mathfrak{a}, q)$ (see Theorem 2.15)
8:    **if** `GentrySzydlo` did not fail **then**
9:        $S \leftarrow S \cup \{\zeta \cdot z_{\mathfrak{a}} \mid \zeta \in \mathbb{U}_L\}$
10:   **end if**
11: **end for**
12: **return** S

Theorem 2.16. *Let $L|K$ be a CM extension of number fields and $q \in \mathcal{O}_K$. Given as input a basis of $\mathcal{O}_K$, a basis of $\mathcal{O}_L$, the element $q \in \mathcal{O}_K$, and the factorization of $|\mathcal{N}_K(q)|$ over $\mathbb{Z}$, Algorithm 2.1 (`NormEquation`) computes the list of all elements $z \in \mathcal{O}_L$ such that $\mathcal{N}_{L|K}(z) = q$. Moreover, the algorithm runs* *in time* $\text{poly}(\log \Delta_L, \log |\mathcal{N}_K(q)|) \cdot (1 + \log |\mathcal{N}_K(q)|)^r$, *where r is the number of distinct prime factors of the ideal $q \cdot \mathcal{O}_K$.*

Note that the size of the output of the algorithm, and so in particular the number of solutions to the equation $\mathcal{N}_{L|K}(z) = q$, is bounded by the running time of the algorithm.

Proof. Correctness. Let us first show that the set $\mathfrak{J}$ from Step 4 contains all integral ideals of $\mathcal{O}_L$ with relative norm $q \cdot \mathcal{O}_K$. To do so, consider an integral ideal $\mathfrak{b} \subset \mathcal{O}_L$ with relative norm $q \cdot \mathcal{O}_K$ and write down its factorization $\mathfrak{b} = \prod_{j=1}^s \mathfrak{q}_j^{\beta_j}$ in $\mathcal{O}_L$. Since the relative norm is multiplicative, we have $\prod_{j=1}^s \mathcal{N}_{L|K}(\mathfrak{q}_j)^{\beta_j} = q \cdot \mathcal{O}_K = \prod_{i=1}^r \mathfrak{p}_i^{\alpha_i}$ (using the notations from Step 1). By uniqueness of the factorization into prime ideals, we deduce that for any $j \in \{1, \ldots, s\}$, there exists $i_j \in \{1, \ldots, r\}$ such that $\mathfrak{p}_{i_j}$ divides $\mathcal{N}_{L|K}(\mathfrak{q}_j)$. By Lemma 2.8, this implies that $\mathfrak{q}_j \mid \mathfrak{p}_{i_j}$. This means that $\mathfrak{b}$ has all its prime factors in $\mathfrak{J}_0$, and so $\mathfrak{b}$ is in $\mathfrak{J}$ (by definition of $\mathfrak{J}$), as desired. In particular, for any $z \in \mathcal{O}_L$ such that $z\bar{z} = q$, the corresponding principal ideal $z\mathcal{O}_L$ is in $\mathfrak{J}$.

In Step 7, the Gentry-Szydlo algorithm outputs, when it exists, a generator of $\mathfrak{a}$ with relative norm q for an ideal $\mathfrak{a} \in \mathfrak{J}$ (it always succeeds when a solution exists). Let us fix a principal ideal $\mathfrak{a}$ that has a generator $z_\mathfrak{a}$ of relative norm q. Let $z'_\mathfrak{a}$ be another generator with the same relative norm, so there is a unit u such that $z_\mathfrak{a} = u z'_\mathfrak{a}$. But then we have $\mathcal{N}_{L|K}(u) = q/q = 1$. By Lemma 2.14, we conclude that $u \in \mathbb{U}_L$ is a root of unity. Conversely, for any root of unity $\zeta \in \mathbb{U}_L$, one can check that $z_\mathfrak{a} \cdot \zeta$ is a generator of $\mathfrak{a}$ with relative norm q. We then conclude that the generators of $\mathfrak{a}$ whose relative norm is q are exactly the elements $\{\zeta \cdot z_\mathfrak{a} \mid \zeta \in \mathbb{U}_L\}$. This concludes the correctness of the algorithm.

Complexity. The roots of unity $\mathbb{U}_L$ can be computed in polynomial time thanks to Corollary 2.11. Recall that the factorization of $\mathcal{N}_K(q)$ is known. For Step 2 of the Algorithm, one can use `FactorIdeal` from Corollary 2.13 to factor the ideal $q\mathcal{O}_K$ in polynomial time, thanks to the knowledge of the factorization of $\mathcal{N}_K(q)$. In Step 3, computing all the prime ideals dividing $\mathfrak{p}_i\mathcal{O}_L$ for a fixed prime ideal $\mathfrak{p}_i$ can be done in time polynomial in $\log \mathcal{N}(\mathfrak{p}_i)$ and $\log \Delta_L$ thanks to Lemma 2.12. Note that each prime factor $\mathfrak{p}_i$ of $q\mathcal{O}_K$ has its algebraic norm bounded by $|\mathcal{N}_K(q)|$. Moreover, there are at most $\log_2 |\mathcal{N}_K(q)|$ distinct prime ideals $\mathfrak{p}_i$ dividing $q\mathcal{O}_K$. Hence, in Step 3, the set $\mathfrak{J}_0$ can be computed in time $\text{poly}(\log \Delta_L, \log |\mathcal{N}_K(q)|)$.

Recall that, above each prime ideal $\mathfrak{p}$ of $\mathcal{O}_K$ are at most two prime ideals of $\mathcal{O}_L$. More precisely, for each $\mathfrak{p}_i$ appearing in the prime decomposition of $q \cdot \mathcal{O}_K$, either $\mathfrak{p}_i\mathcal{O}_L$ is inert (and thus stays prime), splits into $\mathfrak{q}_i$ and $\tau(\mathfrak{q}_i)$ or ramifies as $\mathfrak{q}_i^2$. The respective relative norm ideals are then $\mathcal{N}_{L|K}(\mathfrak{p}_i\mathcal{O}_L) = \mathfrak{p}_i^2$, $\mathcal{N}_{L|K}(\mathfrak{q}_i) = \mathcal{N}_{L|K}(\tau(\mathfrak{q}_i)) = \mathfrak{p}_i$ or $\mathcal{N}_{L|K}(\mathfrak{q}_i) = \mathfrak{p}_i$. To build the set $\mathfrak{J}$ from the set of prime ideals $\mathfrak{q}_{i,j}$, we proceed as follows. Let $\mathfrak{p}_i$ be a prime factor of $q \cdot \mathcal{O}_K$. Any ideal $\mathfrak{a} \in \mathfrak{J}$ is divisible by a prime ideal above $\mathfrak{p}_i$ (recall the correctness part of the proof). From the condition on the norm of $\mathfrak{a}$ and the computation of the $\mathcal{N}_{L|K}(\mathfrak{q}_{i,j})$, we can enumerate all the possibilities for the prime factors of $\mathfrak{a}$.

Keeping the notation of the algorithm, if $\mathfrak{p}_i\mathcal{O}_L$ is inert, then α_i is an even number and $\mathfrak{a}$ must be divisible by $\mathfrak{q}_{i,0}^{\alpha_i/2}$. If $\mathfrak{p}_i\mathcal{O}_L$ ramifies as $\mathfrak{q}_i^2$, then $\mathfrak{a}$ must be divisible by $\mathfrak{q}_i^{\alpha_i}$. Lastly, if $\mathfrak{p}_i \mathcal{O}_L$ splits as $\mathfrak{q}_i$ and $\tau(\mathfrak{q}_i)$, then there exists $0 \leq a \leq \alpha_i$ such that $\mathfrak{q}_i^a \tau(\mathfrak{q}_i)^{\alpha_i - a}$ divides $\mathfrak{a}$. This number is bounded by $(\log_2 |\mathcal{N}_K(q)| + 1)$ so we get at most $(\log_2 |\mathcal{N}_K(q)| + 1)^r$ different ways to choose the prime factors of $\mathfrak{a}$. This is a bound for the cardinal of $\mathfrak{J}$, and one can construct the set $\mathfrak{J}$ (by following the procedure described above) in time $\mathrm{poly}(\log \Delta_L, \log |\mathcal{N}_K(q)|) \cdot |\mathfrak{J}|$.

The last part of the algorithm consists in repeating $|\mathfrak{J}|$ times Steps 7 to 10. These steps can be performed in time $\mathrm{poly}(\log \Delta_L, \log |\mathcal{N}_K(q)|)$ (using Theorem 2.15). The upper bound on the size of $\mathfrak{J}$ gives us the desired upper bound on the running time, which concludes the proof. □

3   Definition of Module-LIP

In this section, we extend the definition of the module-LIP problem from [13], to any number fields and any modules. We also provide some tools which are the analogue in the module settings of standard results in the unstructured case (such as Cholesky decomposition). We believe that these basic tools may be useful for further study of the module-LIP problem. Finally, at the end of the section, we compare our new definition of module-LIP with the one from [13], and we explain why breaking the module-LIP problem that we define in Definition 3.11 allows to break the Hawk scheme.

3.1   Pseudo-Gram Matrices

By applying the canonical embedding coordinate-wise to vectors and matrices, many well-known matrix decompositions and operations also extends *mutatis mutandis* to matrices over $K_{\mathbb{R}}$ — another expression of the algebraic structure. This happens since field embeddings preserves linear (and even polynomial) combinations, and we will follow this intuition in this section. The proofs of the lemmas from this section are available in the full version of the article [25].

Definition 3.1. *A matrix $G \in M_\ell(K_{\mathbb{R}})$ is said to be Hermitian definite positive[9] if it satisfies $G^* = G$ and $\boldsymbol{x}^* G \boldsymbol{x} \in K_{\mathbb{R}}^{++}$ for any linearly independent vector $\boldsymbol{x} \in K_{\mathbb{R}}^\ell$ (i.e., such that $\sigma_i(\boldsymbol{x}) \neq \boldsymbol{0}$ for all embeddings σ_i, see preliminaries). The set of Hermitian definite positive forms is denoted $\mathcal{H}_\ell^{>0}(K_{\mathbb{R}})$, and $\mathcal{H}_\ell^{>0}(K)$ when restricted to matrices with entry in K.*

Basic Properties. Below we give some standard results on Hermitian definite positive matrices in $K_{\mathbb{R}}$. The key ingredient is to observe that a matrix G is in $\mathcal{H}_\ell^{>0}(K_{\mathbb{R}})$ if and only if for all embeddings σ_i, the complex matrix $\sigma_i(G)$ is in $\mathcal{H}_\ell^{>0}(\mathbb{C}) = \{A \in M_\ell(\mathbb{C}) \,|\, A^* = A, \ x^* A x > 0, \ \forall x \in \mathbb{C}^\ell \setminus \{\boldsymbol{0}\}\}$. One can then apply the known results over complex Hermitian definite positive matrices and lift them to $\mathcal{H}_\ell^{>0}(K_{\mathbb{R}})$.

---

[9] In prior literature, this is sometimes called *Humbert forms*.

Lemma 3.2. *A matrix $G \in M_\ell(K_\mathbb{R})$ is in $\mathcal{H}_\ell^{>0}(K_\mathbb{R})$ if and only if $\sigma_i(G) \in \mathcal{H}_\ell^{>0}(\mathbb{C})$ for all embeddings σ_i of K.*

Proposition 3.3. *Let $B \in \mathrm{GL}_\ell(K_\mathbb{R})$, then $B^*B \in \mathcal{H}_\ell^{>0}(K_\mathbb{R})$.*

Proposition 3.4 (Cholesky Factorization). *Let $G \in \mathcal{H}_\ell^{>0}(K_\mathbb{R})$, then there exists a unique lower triangular matrix $L \in \mathrm{GL}_\ell(K_\mathbb{R})$ with diagonal coefficients in $K_\mathbb{R}^{++}$ such that $G = LL^*$. Moreover, this matrix L can be computed from G in polynomial time.*

Proposition 3.5. *Let B and $C \in \mathrm{GL}_\ell(K_\mathbb{R})$ be such that $B^*B = C^*C$. Then there exists $O \in \mathcal{U}_\ell(K_\mathbb{R})$ such that $B = O \cdot C$.*

Pseudo-Gram Matrices. We define an analog of quadratic forms and Gram matrices for module lattices, namely the pseudo-Gram matrices.

Definition 3.6. *Let $\boldsymbol{B} = (B, (I_i)_i)$ be a pseudo-basis of a rank-ℓ module M in $K_\mathbb{R}^k$. The pseudo-Gram matrix associated to $\boldsymbol{B}$ is $\boldsymbol{G} := (G, (I_i)_i)$, where $G = B^*B \in \mathcal{H}_\ell^{>0}(K_\mathbb{R})$.*

Using the Cholesky decomposition that we reviewed above, one can see that for any Hermitian positive definite matrix $G \in \mathcal{H}_\ell^{>0}(K_\mathbb{R})$ and any non-zero fractional ideals $I_1, \ldots, I_\ell$, there always exists a pseudo-basis $\boldsymbol{B} = (B, (I_i)_i)$ whose pseudo-Gram matrix is $\boldsymbol{G} = (G, (I_i)_i)$. Note however that Cholesky only guarantees the existence of such pseudo-basis in $K_\mathbb{R}$ (the matrix B is in $M_\ell(K_\mathbb{R})$). Even when $G \in M_\ell(K)$, there may not exist a pseudo-basis in K (with $B \in M_\ell(K)$) whose pseudo-Gram matrix is $\boldsymbol{G}$.

Definition 3.7. *Let $\boldsymbol{G} = (G, (I_i)_{1 \leq i \leq \ell})$ and $\boldsymbol{G}' = (G', (J_i)_{1 \leq i \leq \ell})$ be two pseudo-Gram matrices (with G and G' in $\mathcal{H}_\ell^{>0}(K_\mathbb{R})$). They are said congruent if there exists $U = (u_{i,j})_{1 \leq i,j \leq \ell} \in \mathrm{GL}_\ell(K)$ such that $G' = U^*GU$ and $u_{i,j} \in I_i J_j^{-1}$, $v_{i,j} \in J_i I_j^{-1}$, where $V = (v_{i,j})_{1 \leq i,j \leq \ell} := U^{-1}$. Such U is called a congruence matrix between $\boldsymbol{G}$ and $\boldsymbol{G}'$. This defines an equivalence relation $\sim$ on the set of pseudo-Gram matrices.[10] The class of $\boldsymbol{G}$ is denoted by $[\boldsymbol{G}]$.*

Sampling (Implicit) Gaussian Vectors. As in the case of standard (non-structured) lattices, it is possible to sample vectors from a discrete Gaussian distribution in an implicit module M given as input a pseudo-Gram matrix G of this module. The proof of the following lemma is available in the full version of this paper [25].

---

[10] For the transitivity ; let $\boldsymbol{G} = (G, (I_i)_{1 \leq i \leq \ell})$, $\boldsymbol{G}' = (G', (J_i)_{1 \leq i \leq \ell})$, $\boldsymbol{G}'' = (G'', (L_i)_{1 \leq i \leq \ell})$ and U (resp. U') a congruence matrix between $\boldsymbol{G}$ and $\boldsymbol{G}'$ (resp. between $\boldsymbol{G}'$ and $\boldsymbol{G}''$), then $U'' := U \cdot U'$ satisfies $G'' = U''^* \cdot G \cdot U''$ and has coefficients $U''_{i,j} = \sum_{k=1}^{\ell} u_{i,k} \cdot u'_{k,j}$. All terms of the sum are in $I_i J_j^{-1}$ by definition. The same observation for $(U'')^{-1}$ finally gives $\boldsymbol{G} \sim \boldsymbol{G}''$.

Lemma 3.8. *There is a probabilistic polynomial time algorithm* GaussianGram *such that the following holds. Let* $\boldsymbol{B} = (B, (I_i)_{1 \leq i \leq \ell})$ *be a pseudo-basis of a rank-ℓ module M in $K_{\mathbb{R}}^{\ell}$, and $\boldsymbol{G} = (G, (I_i)_{1 \leq i \leq \ell})$ be the pseudo-Gram matrix of $\boldsymbol{B}$. Let $s > 0$ be a real number satisfying*

$$s \geq \sqrt{\frac{d \cdot \log(2d\ell + 4)}{\pi}} \cdot 2^d \cdot \Delta_K^{3/(2d)} \cdot \max_{1 \leq j \leq r} \left(\|\sigma(g_{j,j})^{1/2}\| \cdot \mathcal{N}(I_j)^{1/d} \right),$$

where $G = (g_{i,j})_{1 \leq i,j \leq \ell}$ and the square-root is applied coordinate-wise to $\sigma(g_{j,j}) \in \mathbb{C}^d$. On input $\boldsymbol{G}$ and s, GaussianGram$(\boldsymbol{G}, s)$ outputs $\boldsymbol{z} \in I_1 \times \cdots \times I_{\ell}$ such that $\boldsymbol{v} := \boldsymbol{B} \cdot \boldsymbol{z}$ follows a discrete Gaussian distribution of parameter s in M (i.e., $\sigma(\boldsymbol{v}) \sim D_{\sigma(M),s}$).

3.2   Module-LIP

We are now ready to define the module-LIP problem for any number field K and any module M. Using the formalism of pseudo-bases and pseudo-Gram matrices, the situations for module lattices and non-structured lattices become quite similar. Consequently, the definitions in this subsection will be very reminiscent of the ones from preliminaries. We start by introducing the notion of isomorphism for module lattices.

Definition 3.9. *Let $M, M' \subset K_{\mathbb{R}}^{\ell}$ be two modules of rank ℓ. We say that M, M' are isomorphic as module lattices if there exists a unitary transformation $O \in \mathcal{U}_{\ell}(K_{\mathbb{R}})$ such that $M' = O \cdot M$.*

Note that if M and M' are isomorphic as module lattices, then the lattices $\sigma(M)$ and $\sigma(M')$ are isomorphic for the standard (non-structured) definition of lattice isomorphism. In the case of module lattice isomorphism, we restrict ourselves to specific lattices (the ones of the form $\sigma(M)$ for M a module) *and* specific orthogonal transformations (they should be K-linear on the modules).

   Isomorphism of module lattices can be restated in terms of pseudo-bases or pseudo-Gram matrices.

Lemma 3.10. *Let $M, M' \subset K_{\mathbb{R}}^{\ell}$ be two modules of rank ℓ with respective pseudo-bases $\boldsymbol{B} = (B, (I_i)_{1 \leq i \leq \ell})$ and $\boldsymbol{B}' = (B', (J_i)_{1 \leq i \leq \ell})$. Let $\boldsymbol{G}$ (resp. $\boldsymbol{G}'$) be the pseudo-Gram matrix associated to $\boldsymbol{B}$ (resp $\boldsymbol{B}'$). Then, the three following assertions are equivalent*

(1) M and M' are isomorphic as module lattices;
(2) there exists $O \in \mathcal{U}_{\ell}(K_{\mathbb{R}})$ and $U \in \mathrm{GL}_{\ell}(K)$ with $u_{i,j} \in I_i J_j^{-1}$ and $v_{i,j} \in J_i I_j^{-1}$ (where $U = (u_{i,j})_{1 \leq i,j \leq \ell}$ and $U^{-1} = (v_{i,j})_{1 \leq i,j \leq \ell}$) such that $B' = OBU$;
(3) $\boldsymbol{G}$ and $\boldsymbol{G}'$ are congruent (see Definition 3.7).

Proof. We prove that $(1) \Rightarrow (2) \Rightarrow (3) \Rightarrow (1)$. Assume that M and M' are isomorphic as module lattices. By definition, there exists $O \in \mathcal{U}_{\ell}(K_{\mathbb{R}})$ such that $M' = O \cdot M$. A pseudo-basis of OM is given by $(OB, (I_i)_i)$. Since B' is also a pseudo-basis of $O \cdot M$, there must exist a matrix $U \in \mathrm{GL}_\ell(K)$ such that $u_{i,j} \in I_i J_j^{-1}$ and $v_{i,j} \in J_i I_j^{-1}$ and $B' = (OB)U$, as desired.

Let us now assume that $B' = OBU$. Then $G' = U^*GU$ and this means that G and G' are congruent.

Finally, let us assume that G and G' are congruent. By definition, there exists $U \in \mathrm{GL}_\ell(K)$ (with $u_{i,j} \in I_i J_j^{-1}$ and $v_{i,j} \in J_i I_j^{-1}$) such that $G' = U^*GU$. Let us consider $C = (BU, (J_i)_i)$. Thanks to the condition on U, we know that C and B are both pseudo-bases of the same module M. Moreover, the pseudo-Gram matrix of C is exactly G'. Using Proposition 3.5, we conclude that there exists $O \in \mathcal{U}_\ell(K_\mathbb{R})$ such that $B' = OBU$, i.e., $M' = O \cdot M$. $\qquad\square$

Let us now define the module Lattice Isomorphism Problem (module-LIP), in its worst-case variant. As in the unstructured case, we could define two variants, one using the formalism of pseudo-bases and another one using the formalism of pseudo-Gram matrices. Instead, we decided to introduce only one variant, which uses both pseudo-bases and pseudo-Gram matrices. More precisely, we define a collection of problems parametrized by the field K and a pseudo-basis B of a module M, and whose input is a pseudo-Gram matrix G' (of a different pseudo-basis B' of M). This variant is tailored to fit our attack in the next section, but we also believe that it makes sense for itself. Indeed, so far, the instantiations of LIP and module-LIP in cryptography have been parameterized by very specific (module) lattices, for which a good (pseudo-)basis was known (e.g., in Hawk, the module lattice is $\mathcal{O}_K^2$).[11] On the other hand, the algorithm then usually manipulates only (pseudo-)Gram matrices, and so an attacker would get as input such a (pseudo-)Gram matrix and not a (pseudo-)basis of an isomorphic (module) lattice.

Definition 3.11 (wc-smodLIP$_K^B$). *For B a pseudo-basis of a module-lattice $M \subset K_\mathbb{R}^\ell$ with associated pseudo-Gram matrix G, the worst-case search module-Lattice Isomorphism Problem with parameter K and B denoted by wc-smodLIP$_K^B$ is, given as input any pseudo-Gram matrix $G' \sim G$ (see Definition 3.7), to find a congruence matrix between G and G'.*

When we say that the problem is parameterized by K and B, we mean that this is a collection of algorithmic problems, one for each choice of (K, B).[12] In particular, the number field K and pseudo-basis B are known to an adversary.

A definition of module-LIP was also provided in [13, Definition 7], which differs slightly from ours. There are three main differences between the two definitions: [13, Definition 7] defines module-LIP for free modules M (with $B =$

---

[11] By good, we mean here a (pseudo)-basis with rational coefficients. This will be needed for our attack, and we do not know how to recover it efficiently from the (pseudo-)Gram matrix since Cholesky decomposition only provides a basis with coefficients in $\mathbb{R}$ (or $K_\mathbb{R}$).

[12] The same terminology is used for, e.g., the LWE problem. We usually say that n, m, q are parameters of the problem, which means that for each choice of (n, m, q), we have a different algorithmic problem.

$(B, (\mathcal{O}_K)_{1 \leq i \leq 2})$ a *basis* of the module), over a CM number field, and restricts G' to be the Gram-matrix of a *basis* $B' = (B', (\mathcal{O}_K)_{1 \leq i \leq 2})$ of M, and such that the determinant of B' is the same as the one of B. On the other hand, Definition 3.11 above holds for any module M (and any pseudo-basis B), any number field, and the input G' of the problem is the Gram-matrix of any pseudo-basis B' of M. Note that even if one takes K a CM field, and B a basis of a free module M, then our problem wc-smodLIP$_K^B$ from Definition 3.11 is still not exactly the same as the problem defined in [13, Definition 7]. Indeed, in our definition, the input of the problem can be any Gram-matrix G' congruent to G, whereas in [13, Definition 7] the input is restricted to specific congruent Gram-matrices G'.

Hawk and Module-LIP. In the case of Hawk [13], the authors consider a power-of-two cyclotomic field K and the free rank-2 module-lattice $M = \mathcal{O}_K^2$. The secret key consists in a short basis U of M and the public key is the Gram matrix $G' = U^*U \in \mathcal{H}_2^{>0}(K)$.[13] With the formalism we introduced in the previous paragraph, U is a congruence matrix between $I_2 = (I_2^*I_2, (\mathcal{O}_K)_{1 \leq i \leq 2})$ and $G' = (G', (\mathcal{O}_K)_{1 \leq i \leq 2})$. We now recall how (uncompressed) Hawk proceeds (Sect. 3.1, [13]).

Given a message m to sign, first hash m together with a salt r to a point $h \in \{0,1\}^{2d}$, which is interpreted as an element of $\mathcal{O}_K^2$ thanks to the following bijective map, called coefficient embedding $K \to \mathbb{Q}^d$; $(\sum_i a_i X^i) \mapsto (a_0, \ldots, a_{d-1})^T$. Then, a vector $x \in \mathcal{O}_K^2 + \frac{1}{2}U \cdot h$ close to 0 is sampled using Gaussian samples in $\mathbb{Z}$ and $\frac{1}{2}\mathbb{Z}$ (the identification between $\mathcal{O}_K^2$ and $\mathbb{Z}^{2d}$ being possible via coefficient embedding). Finally, the signer computes $s := \frac{1}{2}h - U^{-1} \cdot x$. The (uncompressed) signature consists of the pair $sig = (r, s)$.

A verifier receiving sig computes the hash h and checks if $\|\frac{1}{2}h - s\|_{G'}$ is smaller than a fixed security parameter (here, $\|z\|_{G'} := \|z^*G'z\|$ for any $z \in K^2$). It also checks that $s \in \mathcal{O}_K^2$. If both tests succeed, it accepts the signature. Using the fact that $\|\frac{1}{2}h - s\|_{G'} = \|U \cdot (\frac{1}{2}h - s)\| = \|x\|$, one can check that the first verification test must be satisfied when the signature is honestly generated. For the second one, writing $x = y + \frac{1}{2}U \cdot h$ with $y \in \mathcal{O}_K^2$, one can see that $s = U^{-1}y$. The fact that $s \in \mathcal{O}_K^2$ follows from the fact that $U \in GL_2(\mathcal{O}_K)$ (since U is a basis of $\mathcal{O}_K^2$).

Lemma 3.12. *With the notations of the previous paragraph, finding any congruence matrix V between I_2 and the public key G' allows to forge signatures in Hawk. In other words, if one can solve the wc-smodLIP$_K^{I_2}$ problem, then one can forge signatures in Hawk, given only the public key.*

Proof. By definition, a congruence matrix V between G and G' satisfies $V \in GL_2(\mathcal{O}_K)$ and $G' = V^*V$. We show that any such matrix can be used to produce valid signatures : let (r, s) be a signature produced by Hawk with input basis

---

[13] Here M is a free module so it has a basis (equivalently, the coefficient ideals are equal to $\mathcal{O}_K$) so the authors use bases (resp. Gram-matrices) instead of pseudo-bases (resp. pseudo-Gram matrices).

V. Then $\boldsymbol{x} = \boldsymbol{y} + \frac{1}{2}V \cdot h$ is small, with $\boldsymbol{y} \in \mathcal{O}_K^2$, and $\boldsymbol{s} = \frac{1}{2}h - V^{-1}\boldsymbol{x} = V^{-1}\boldsymbol{y}$. Since $V \in \mathrm{GL}_2(\mathcal{O}_K)$, the vector $\boldsymbol{s}$ is in $\mathcal{O}_K^2$ as desired. Moreover, $\|\frac{1}{2}h - \boldsymbol{s}\|_{G'} = \|V \cdot (\frac{1}{2}h - \boldsymbol{s})\| = \|\boldsymbol{x}\|$, since $G' = V^*V$, which means that the latter norm is small the pair $(\boldsymbol{r}, \boldsymbol{s})$ is then accepted by the verifier. $\square$

The previous lemma underlines that, to forge signatures in Hawk it is enough to recover *any* congruence matrix V and not specifically the secret key U. Therefore, the problem of signature forgery in Hawk reduces to solving wc-smodLIP$_K^{I_2}$, as defined in Definition 3.11.

4   An Algorithm for Module-LIP in Rank 2 over Totally Real Fields

We now present our main algorithm, which solves wc-smodLIP$_K^B$ for totally real fields K and when the module generated by the pseudo-basis $\boldsymbol{B}$ lives in K^2 (see Algorithm 4.2 when the module is in $\mathcal{O}_K^2$ and Algorithm 4.3 for the general case). At a high level, it is based on the observation that, when the module is in $\mathcal{O}_K^2$, a diagonal element q in the pseudo-Gram matrix $\boldsymbol{G} = \boldsymbol{B}^*\boldsymbol{B} = \boldsymbol{B}^T\boldsymbol{B}$ can be written as $q = x^2 + y^2$ with $x, y \in \mathcal{O}_K$, that is, a *sum of two squares*. Already when $K = \mathbb{Q}$, a common way to find such sums is to go through a quadratic imaginary extension $L := K(i)$, where i is a root of $X^2 + 1$ over K. Indeed, all solutions to a 2-square decompositions are also solutions of a *relative norm equation* $q = \mathcal{N}_{L|K}(a) = a^*a$, which we can solve algorithmically thanks to Lenstra-Silverberg's algorithm. Our algorithm will thus use the procedure NormEquation (from preliminaries) to solve the latter, then restrict to solutions of the former in another algorithm named TwoSquares. From these solutions, we will be able to build the set of all congruence matrices to solve wc-smodLIP$_K^B$, when the module generated by $\boldsymbol{B}$ is in $\mathcal{O}_K^2$. For rational modules in K^2, we then simply multiply by a common denominator, to reduce to the situation where the module is in $\mathcal{O}_K^2$.

An apparently unavoidable component of NormEquation is the factorization of the ideal $q \cdot \mathcal{O}_K$, so there is no hope to obtain a classical polynomial-time algorithm this way. Therefore, we use a re-randomization procedure to generate random vectors $\boldsymbol{z} = (z_1, z_2)$ until $\boldsymbol{z}^*G\boldsymbol{z}$ generates a prime ideal (for the rest of this paragraph, we say that $\boldsymbol{z}$ is a "good vector" when this is the case). Primality testing can be done in polynomial time for ideals as well, and if we let $\boldsymbol{B} \cdot (z_1, z_2)^T = (x, y)^T$, then $\boldsymbol{z}^*G\boldsymbol{z} = x^2 + y^2$ is again a sum of two squares. This allows us to avoid the potentially costly factorization. With two linearly independent good vectors, we can then use a two-square decomposition algorithm together with some linear algebra to solve the module-LIP instance. Estimating the probability of finding a good vector relies on a heuristic assumption, supported by standard (but non-trivial) number-theoretic arguments: the discussion and justifications are the topic of Sect. 4.2.

4.1   Gram Ideal

In order to describe our results in this section for all modules of rank 2 in K^2, we introduce the Gram ideal and the relative Gram ideal of a module $M \subset K^\ell$ of rank ℓ. From now on, we will consider the arithmetic properties of the coefficients of vectors in M, and hence restrict ourselves to modules in K^ℓ (as opposed to $K_{\mathbb{R}}^\ell$ which we considered so far). The proofs of the lemmas from this section are available in the full version of the article [25].

Definition 4.1. *Let K be a totally real number field and $M \subset K^\ell$ be a module of rank ℓ. Let $\mathbf{B} = ((B_{i,j})_{i,j}, (J_i)_i)$ be a pseudo-basis of M and $\mathbf{G} = ((G_{i,j})_{i,j}, (J_i)_i)$ be the associated pseudo-Gram matrix. We define the following fractional ideals*

$$\mathcal{G}(M) := \sum_{1 \leq i \leq l} G_{i,i} \cdot J_i^2 + \sum_{1 \leq i < j \leq l} 2 \cdot G_{i,j} \cdot J_i \cdot J_j$$

$$\mathcal{C}(M) := \sum_{1 \leq i,j \leq l} B_{i,j} \cdot J_j \quad ; \quad \mathcal{RG}(M) := \mathcal{G}(M)/\mathcal{C}(M)^2.$$

We call $\mathcal{G}(M)$ the Gram ideal and $\mathcal{RG}(M)$ the relative Gram ideal of M.

The first two ideals correspond respectively to the ideal generated by the (squared) norm of vectors of M, and the ideal generated by the coordinates of the vectors of M. We show below that these ideals indeed depend only on the module lattice M and not on the pseudo-basis $\mathbf{B}$.

Lemma 4.2. *Let K be totally real and $M \subset K^\ell$ be a module of rank ℓ. Let $\mathbf{B}$ be a pseudo-basis of M with associated pseudo-Gram matrix $\mathbf{G}$. Then $\mathcal{G}(M)$ is the smallest ideal (for inclusion) containing the set $\{\langle \boldsymbol{v}, \boldsymbol{v} \rangle_{K_{\mathbb{R}}} \mid \boldsymbol{v} \in M\}$, and $\mathcal{C}(M)$ is the smallest ideal containing the set $\{v_j \mid \boldsymbol{v} = (v_i)_i \in M, 1 \leq j \leq \ell\}$. In particular, they do not depend on the choice of the pseudo-basis $\mathbf{B}$ of M.*

Corollary 4.3. *The relative Gram ideal $\mathcal{RG}(M)$ is integral, and do not depend on the choice of the pseudo-basis $\mathbf{B}$ of M.*

The Gram ideal and relative Gram ideal of a module M can be computed in polynomial time from any pseudo-basis $\mathbf{B}$ of M (directly from Definition 4.1). A simple but important case is when $M = \mathcal{O}_K^\ell$, e.g., in Hawk. In this case, we have $\mathcal{G}(M) = \mathcal{C}(M) = \mathcal{RG}(M) = \mathcal{O}_K$. In the following we prove that the relative Gram ideal is invariant when scaling the module (by a scalar, or even a fractional ideal).

Lemma 4.4. *Let K be totally real, $M \subset K^\ell$ be a module of rank ℓ, and J be a fractional ideal. Then,*

(1) $\mathcal{G}(J \cdot M) = J^2 \cdot \mathcal{G}(M)$.
(2) $\mathcal{C}(J \cdot M) = J \cdot \mathcal{C}(M)$.
(3) $\mathcal{RG}(J \cdot M) = \mathcal{RG}(M)$.
(4) $\mathcal{C}(M)^{-1} \cdot M \subset \mathcal{O}_K^\ell$ is an integer module lattice not contained in $\mathfrak{p}^\ell$ for any prime ideal $\mathfrak{p}$.

We will later use Lemma 4.4 to scale our input module M, in order to make it integer, but as small as possible (with respect to its determinant) among all the scaled variants of M included in $\mathcal{O}_K^\ell$.

4.2 The Assumption

In this section, we formalize the assumption that will be used by our algorithm in Sect. 4.3. This assumption essentially states that, when sampling a random vector $\boldsymbol{u}$ in an integer rank-2 module $M \subseteq \mathcal{O}_K^2$, the probability that the ideal $\langle \boldsymbol{u}, \boldsymbol{u} \rangle_{K_{\mathbb{R}}} \cdot \mathcal{O}_K$ is prime is not too small. Of course, we need to exclude the cases where this assumption is obviously false, for instance if $M = 2\mathcal{O}_K^2$, then $\langle \boldsymbol{u}, \boldsymbol{u} \rangle_{K_{\mathbb{R}}}$ will always be divisible by 4. More generally, we need to exclude the cases where the Gram ideal $\mathcal{G}(M)$ is not $\mathcal{O}_K$. We provide in the full version both theoretical and experimental justifications in favor of our assumption.

Assumption 1. *There exists some absolute polynomial P (with non-negative coefficients) such that the following holds. Let K be a totally real number field of degree d, $M \subseteq \mathcal{O}_K^2$ be a module of rank 2, and $s > 0$ be a real number such that $s \geq \eta_{1/2}(M)$. Let $I = \mathcal{G}(M)$ be the Gram ideal of the module M. Let $(z_1, z_2)^T \leftarrow D_{M,s}$ and $q = z_1^2 + z_2^2$. Then*

$$\Pr(q \cdot I^{-1} \text{ is prime }) \geq \frac{1}{\rho_K \cdot \log(s/\mathcal{N}(I)^{1/d}) \cdot P(d)},$$

where ρ_K is the residue of the Dedekind zeta function of K at 1.

Note that the ideal $q \cdot I^{-1}$ in our assumption is always an integral ideal. Indeed, thanks to Lemma 4.2, we know that the ideal I contains all square norms of vectors of M, hence it contains in particular $\langle \boldsymbol{z}, \boldsymbol{z} \rangle_{K_{\mathbb{R}}} = q$ (where $\boldsymbol{z} = (z_1, z_2)^T$), which implies $qI^{-1} \subseteq II^{-1} = \mathcal{O}_K$.

4.3 The Algorithm

Before describing the algorithm for module-LIP, let us start with an algorithm, called `TwoSquares`, which solves sum of two squares equations in $\mathcal{O}_K$ for a totally real number field K (i.e., equations of the form $x^2 + y^2 = q$ where $q \in \mathcal{O}_K$ is given and $x, y \in \mathcal{O}_K$ are the unknown). Algorithm `TwoSquares` works by reformulating this as a relative norm equation in some well chosen CM extension L of K, and then applying Algorithm `NormEquation` from preliminaries (Algorithm 2.1).

Algorithm 4.1. Finding sums of two squares in totally real fields (`TwoSquares`)

Input: A basis B_K of $\mathcal{O}_K$, an element $q \in \mathcal{O}_K$, the factorization of $|\mathcal{N}_K(q)|$.
Output: All elements $(x, y) \in \mathcal{O}_K^2$ such that $q = x^2 + y^2$.
1: Define $L \leftarrow K[X]/(X^2 + 1)$.
2: Compute $B_L \leftarrow$ a basis of $\mathcal{O}_L$, using Lemma 2.6.
3: $S \leftarrow \texttt{NormEquation}(B_K, B_L, q, \text{the factorization of } |\mathcal{N}_K(q)|)$.
4: Cast elements of S from L into K^2 (via the map $a + bX \in L \mapsto (a, b) \in K^2$)
5: **return** $S \cap \mathcal{O}_K^2$

Lemma 4.5. *Let K be a totally real number field and $q \in \mathcal{O}_K$. Given as input a basis of $\mathcal{O}_K$, the element $q \in \mathcal{O}_K$ and the factorization of $|\mathcal{N}_K(q)|$, Algorithm 4.1 (TwoSquares) computes all $(x, y) \in \mathcal{O}_K^2$ such that $q = x^2 + y^2$. Moreover, the algorithm runs in time $\mathrm{poly}\left(\log \Delta_K, (\log |\mathcal{N}_K(q)|)^r\right)$, where r is the number of distinct prime factors of the ideal $q \cdot \mathcal{O}_K$.*

Proof. Correctness. The field $L = K[X]/(X^2+1)$ is a totally imaginary quadratic extension of K, and so $L|K$ is a CM extension as desired. Moreover, the non-trivial automorphism τ of L fixing K is the map sending X to $-X$. Hence, for any element $z = a + bX \in L$, we have that $\mathcal{N}_{L|K}(z) = z \cdot \tau(z) = a^2 + b^2$. To any solution (x, y) of the sum of two squares equation $x^2 + y^2 = q$, we can then associate a solution $z = x + y \cdot X \in \mathcal{O}_L$ to the relative norm equation $\mathcal{N}_{L|K}(z) = q$. By correctness of the NormEquation algorithm (see Theorem 2.16), the set S contains all solutions to this relative norm equation. Note that not all of them provide a solution to the sum of two squares equations, since some $z = x + y \cdot X \in S$ may have x or y not belonging to $\mathcal{O}_K$ (the set $\{a + bX \mid a, b \in \mathcal{O}_K\}$ is included in $\mathcal{O}_L$, but the inclusion may be strict). This is why we intersect the set S with the set $\{a + bX \mid a, b \in \mathcal{O}_K\}$.

Complexity. A basis of $\mathcal{O}_L$ can be computed in polynomial time from a basis of $\mathcal{O}_K$, using Lemma 2.6, which proves that Step 2 can be run in polynomial time. For Step 3, we know from Theorem 2.16 that it can be run in time $\mathrm{poly}(\log \Delta_L, (\log |\mathcal{N}_K(q)|)) \cdot (1 + \log |\mathcal{N}_K(q)|)^r = \mathrm{poly}\left(\log \Delta_L, (\log |\mathcal{N}_K(q)|)^r\right)$. Recall from the preliminaries that $\log \Delta_L = \mathrm{poly}(\log \Delta_K)$, hence the previous quantity is also $\mathrm{poly}\left(\log \Delta_K, (\log |\mathcal{N}_K(q)|)^r\right)$. Finally, testing whether an element $x + y \cdot X$ in S satisfies $(x, y) \in \mathcal{O}_K^2$ can be done in polynomial time using the basis B_K. $\square$

We now describe our main algorithm, which solves wc-smodLIP$_K^B$ when K is a totally real number field and $\boldsymbol{B}$ is a pseudo-basis of a rank-2 module in $\mathcal{O}_K^2$. The general case follows as a by-product in Algorithm 4.3, thanks to the coordinate ideal $\mathcal{C}(M)$. Once a preliminary factorization of $\mathcal{G}(M)$ is done, the algorithm tries to find two "nice" vectors for the input instance $\boldsymbol{G}' = (G', (I_1', I_2'))$. By nice, we mean that we sample random vectors until we obtain somewhat short and linearly independent $\boldsymbol{v}, \boldsymbol{v}'$, such that both $q = \boldsymbol{v}^*G'\boldsymbol{v}$ and $q' = \boldsymbol{v}'^*G'\boldsymbol{v}$ generate a prime multiple of $\mathcal{G}(M)$ (recall that $q, q' \in \mathcal{G}(M)$, so the ideals they generate have to be a multiple of $\mathcal{G}(M)$). As mentioned in the beginning of this section, we will call the TwoSquares algorithm for q, q', which requires to know the factorization of $\mathcal{N}_K(q)$ and $\mathcal{N}_K(q')$. Computing these factorizations can be done efficiently once we know the factorization of $\mathcal{N}(\mathcal{G}(M))$, since we ensured that $q/\mathcal{G}(M)$ and $q'/\mathcal{G}(M)$ are prime ideals. Pairing these two-square decompositions gives as many linear equations as there are entries in B: some of them must lead to congruence matrices (others may be non-integral). We actually prove that we find them all this way.

Theorem 4.6 (Assumption 1). *Let K be a totally real number field and $M \subset \mathcal{O}_K^2$ an integer module lattice of rank 2 with pseudo-basis $\boldsymbol{B} = (B, I_1, I_2)$ and associated pseudo-Gram matrix $\boldsymbol{G}$. Algorithm 4.2 takes as input a basis of*

Algorithm 4.2. Finding all congruence matrices for integer rank-2 modules.

Input: A basis B_K of $\mathcal{O}_K$, a pseudo-basis $\boldsymbol{B} = (B, (I_1, I_2))$ of $M \subseteq \mathcal{O}_K^2$ with pseudo-Gram matrix $\boldsymbol{G}$, and $\boldsymbol{G}' = (G', (I_1', I_2')) \sim \boldsymbol{G}$ an instance of wc-smodLIP$_K^B$.

Output: All congruence matrices between $\boldsymbol{G}$ and $\boldsymbol{G}'$.

1: $I \leftarrow \mathcal{G}(M);\ \alpha = \rho_K \cdot P(d)$ *(with $P(d)$ from Assumption 1)*
2: Factor $\mathcal{N}(I) = \prod_j q_j^{f_j}$.
    Generating two "nice" instances of TwoSquares
3: $q \leftarrow 0;\ (u, v) \leftarrow (0, 0);\ s \leftarrow 4^d \cdot \Delta_K^{3/(2d)} \cdot \max_{1 \leq j \leq 2}(\|\sigma(g_{j,j}')^{1/2}\| \cdot \mathcal{N}(I_j')^{1/d})$
    (where $G' = (g_{i,j}')_{1 \leq i, j \leq 2}$)
4: **while** $\sqrt{\|\sigma(q)\|_1} > s \cdot \sqrt{8d + \log(4\alpha \log(s))}$ **or** $q \cdot I^{-1}$ is not a prime ideal **do**
5:     $I_1' \times I_2' \ni (u, v)^T \leftarrow \texttt{GaussianGram}(\boldsymbol{G}', s)$.
6:     $q \leftarrow (u, v) \cdot G' \cdot (u, v)^T$.
7: **end while**
8: $q' \leftarrow 0;\ (u', v') \leftarrow (0, 0);\ s' = 144 \cdot d \cdot \Delta_K^{1/d} \cdot \max(\alpha^2, 1) \cdot s^4$.
9: **while** $(u', v') \in \mathrm{Span}_K((u, v))$ **or** $\sqrt{\|\sigma(q)\|_1} > s' \cdot \sqrt{8d + \log(4\alpha \log(s'))}$ **or** $q' I^{-1}$
    is not a prime ideal **do**
10:     $I_1' \times I_2' \ni (u', v')^T \leftarrow \texttt{GaussianGram}(\boldsymbol{G}', s')$.
11:     $q' \leftarrow (u', v') \cdot G' \cdot (u', v')^T$.
12: **end while**
    Solving the two instances of TwoSquares
13: Factor $\mathcal{N}(qI^{-1}) = p^e$ and $\mathcal{N}(q'I^{-1}) = (p')^f$
14: $S_1 \leftarrow \texttt{TwoSquares}(B_K, q, p^e \cdot \prod_j q_j^{f_j});\ S_2 \leftarrow \texttt{TwoSquares}(B_K, q', (p')^f \cdot \prod_j q_j^{f_j})$
    Recovering the congruence matrices from the solutions to TwoSquares
15: $S \leftarrow \emptyset$.
16: **for** $((t_1, t_2), (t_1', t_2')) \in S_1 \times S_2$ **do**
17:     $D \leftarrow \begin{pmatrix} t_1 & t_1' \\ t_2 & t_2' \end{pmatrix} \cdot \begin{pmatrix} u & u' \\ v & v' \end{pmatrix}^{-1}$
18:     $V \leftarrow B^{-1} \cdot D$
19:     **if** V is a congruence matrix between $\boldsymbol{G}$ and $\boldsymbol{G}'$ **then**
20:       $S \leftarrow S \cup \{V\}$.
21:     **end if**
22: **end for**
23: **return** S.

$\mathcal{O}_K$, the pseudo-matrix $\boldsymbol{B}$ and $\boldsymbol{G}' = (G', I_1', I_2')$ an instance of wc-smodLIP$_K^B$ and finds all congruence matrices between $\boldsymbol{G}$ and $\boldsymbol{G}'$. Under Assumption 1, the algorithm runs in expected polynomial time in the size of its input and in

$$\left(\mathrm{poly}(\rho_K, \log \Delta_K, \mathrm{size}(\boldsymbol{G}')) \right)^r + T_{factor}(\mathcal{N}(\mathcal{G}(M))),$$

where ρ_K is the residue of the Dedekind zeta function of K at 1, and r is the number of distinct prime ideals dividing the Gram ideal $\mathcal{G}(M)$.

At Step 13, we actually do not need to factorize again, since standard primality tests will give us both the prime and its valuation. Note that Algorithm 4.2 solves wc-smodLIP$_K^B$ on input $\boldsymbol{G}'$, but it does even more than this, since it finds all congruence matrices between G and G', when wc-smodLIP$_K^B$ only asks to find one such congruence matrix.

Proof. Correctness. First, note that thanks to the if condition in Steps 19 of the algorithm, all matrices V that are output by our algorithm are indeed congruence matrices between G and G'.

Conversely, let us fix $U \in \mathrm{GL}_2(K_\mathbb{R})$ a congruence matrix between G and G' and show that $U \in S$ at the end of the algorithm. Let $C = B \cdot U$. By definition of congruence matrices, we know that $C = (C, I'_1, I'_2)$ is another pseudo-basis of the module M. Moreover, we also know that $U^*GU = G' = C^*C$. This means that G' is the pseudo-Gram matrix of the pseudo-basis C of M.

Let us define $z = (z_1, z_2)^T := C \cdot (u, v)^T$ (where u and v are as in the algorithm, after exiting the while loop in Step 7). Since s satisfies the constraints from Lemma 3.8 (see the discussion below for the choice of s), the algorithm GaussianGram is correct, and so we have $u \in I'_1$ and $v \in I'_2$. This implies that $z \in M$. Moreover, we have that $q := (u, v) \cdot G' \cdot (u, v)^T = z^*z = z_1^2 + z_2^2$. Since $M \subset \mathcal{O}_K^2$, the pair (z_1, z_2) thus gives a sum of two squares for q. By Lemma 4.5, TwoSquares finds them all so the pair (z_1, z_2) must belong to the set S_1 computed in Step 14. A similar argument works for $z' = (z'_1, z'_2)^T = C \cdot (u', v')^T$ and S_2.

From this, we know that during the for loop of Step 16, there must be one iteration where $(t_1, t_2) = (z_1, z_2)$ and $(t'_1, t'_2) = (z'_1, z'_2)$. When this is the case, then the matrix D computed in Step 17 must be equal to C. Note that this computation makes sense since (u, v) and (u', v') are linearly independent. This finally implies that the corresponding matrix V from Step 18 is equal to U, and so $U \in S$ at the end of the algorithm. Overall, this proves that, if the algorithm terminates, then S contains all the congruence matrices between G and G'.

Complexity. We have seen that the Gram ideal $\mathcal{G}(M)$ can be computed in polynomial time from the knowledge of G'. At Step 2, the norm of the Gram ideal is factored, which takes time $T_{factor}(\mathcal{N}(\mathcal{G}(M)))$ (note that since $M \subseteq \mathcal{O}_K^2$, its Gram ideal $\mathcal{G}(M)$ is integral, and so $\mathcal{N}(\mathcal{G}(M)) \in \mathbb{Z}$).

We discuss the choice of the parameters s and s' for the sampling algorithm. To work under our Assumption 1, they must be chosen above the smoothing parameter $\eta_{1/2}(\sigma(M))$ of the module lattice $\sigma(M)$. Equation (1) tells us that it is enough to take s larger than $\sqrt{\log(12d)/\pi} \cdot \lambda_{2d}(\sigma(M))$. Now, we know from Lemma 2.9 that there exists a basis of $\sigma(M)$ whose vectors are all smaller than $\sqrt{d} \cdot 2^d \cdot \Delta_K^{3/(2d)} \cdot \max_{1 \leq j \leq 2} \left(\|\sigma(g'_{j,j})^{1/2}\| \cdot \mathcal{N}(I'_j)^{1/d} \right)$, so this must be an upper bound on $\lambda_{2d}(\sigma(M))$. Since $2^d \geq \sqrt{d \log(12d)/\pi}$ for all $d \geq 1$, we conclude that $s' \geq s \geq \eta_{1/2}(\sigma(M))$ as needed to apply Assumption 1 and Lemma 3.8.

As a consequence, Lemma 3.8 ensures that steps 5 and 10 run in polynomial time. Moreover, by correctness of the GaussianGram algorithm, we know that $\sigma(z) \sim D_{\sigma(M),s}$ and $\sigma(z') \sim D_{\sigma(M),s'}$, where $z = C \cdot (u, v)^T$ and $z' = C \cdot (u', v')$, as before.

Now we estimate the number of trials before satisfying the conditions on Step 4. By Lemma 2.5 applied to $\varepsilon = (4\alpha \log s)^{-1}$, we have $\|\sigma(z)\| > s \cdot \sqrt{8d + \log(4\alpha \log(s))}$ with probability at most ε. Recall that $q = z_1^2 + z_2^2$, so we have that $\|\sigma(q)\|_1 = \|\sigma(z)\|^2$. This implies that the first condition in the while loop is satisfied with probability $\geq 1 - \varepsilon$. For the second condition in the while loop, we have seen that Assumption 1 applies, so qI^{-1} is prime with probability at least $(\alpha \log(s/\mathcal{N}(I)^{1/d}))^{-1} \geq (\alpha \log s)^{-1}$ (recall that $\alpha = \rho_K \cdot P(d)$ and that $M \subseteq \mathcal{O}_K^2$ so that $\mathcal{N}(I) := \mathcal{N}(\mathcal{G}(M)) \geq 1$).

Overall, the probability to exit the first `while` loop in Step 4 is larger than $(\alpha \log s)^{-1} - \varepsilon \geq (2\alpha \log s)^{-1}$, using the definition of ε.[14] The expected number of iterations of the `while` loop is then $\leq 2\alpha \log s = \text{poly}(\log \Delta_K, \rho_K, \text{size}(\boldsymbol{G}'))$.

To conclude on this first while loop, note that all the operations performed during one iteration of the while loop (including the two tests in Step 4) can be performed in time $\text{poly}(\log \Delta_K, \rho_K, \text{size}(\boldsymbol{G}'))$ (for the test that qI^{-1} is prime, we use Corollary 2.13, and we apply it only when the first test passes, which ensures that $\mathcal{N}(qI^{-1}) \leq \mathcal{N}_K(q) \leq \|\sigma(q)\|_1^d$ is not too big).

The reasoning for the second while loop is similar, except that we now also want that (u', v') be non-colinear with (u, v). This is equivalent to asking that $\boldsymbol{z}'$ is not colinear to $\boldsymbol{z}$. In other words, we want $\boldsymbol{z}'$ to avoid the rank-1 submodule $N := M \cap \text{Span}_K(\boldsymbol{z})$. Again, Lemma 3.8 tells us that $\boldsymbol{z}' \sim D_{M,s'}$, hence we want to upper bound

$$\Pr_{\boldsymbol{y} \sim \mathcal{D}_{M,s'}} (\boldsymbol{y} \in N) = \frac{\rho_{s'}(N)}{\rho_{s'}(M)}.$$

To estimate $\rho_{s'}(N)$ and $\rho_{s'}(M)$ we would like to apply Lemma 2.3 (with $\varepsilon = 1/2$). We have already seen that $s \geq \eta_{1/2}(M)$ and by definition $s' \geq s$, so this handles the denominator. Since N has rank 1, observe that $\lambda_d(N) \leq \lambda_d^{(\infty)}(\mathcal{O}_K) \cdot \lambda_1(N) \leq \Delta_K^{1/d} \cdot \|\boldsymbol{z}\|$. Using the upper bound on $\|\boldsymbol{z}\| = \sqrt{\|q\|_1}$ and Equation (1), one can check that $s' \geq \eta_{1/2}(N)$ as desired. We can then apply Lemma 2.3 and use the fact that $\det(N) \geq 1$ since $N \subset \mathcal{O}_K^2$ to obtain

$$\Pr_{\boldsymbol{y} \sim \mathcal{D}_{M,s'}} (\boldsymbol{y} \in N) \leq 3/2 \cdot \frac{\det(M)}{(s')^{2d}} \cdot 2 \cdot \frac{(s')^d}{\det(N)} \leq \frac{3\det(M)}{(s')^d}$$

$$\leq \frac{(s')^{d/2}}{4\alpha \cdot (s')^d} \leq \frac{1}{4\alpha \cdot (\sqrt{s'})^d} \leq \frac{1}{4\alpha \log(s')},$$

where the last inequality follows from the fact that $s' \geq 1$ (so that $(\sqrt{s'})^d \geq \log(s')$) and on the second line we used the fact that $\sqrt{s'} \geq (12\alpha \det(M))^{1/d}$ by choice of s'. Indeed, replacing s' by its value, the latter inequality is equivalent to having $12 \cdot \sqrt{d} \cdot \Delta_K^{1/2d} \cdot \max(\alpha, 1) \cdot s^2 \geq (12\alpha \det(M))^{1/d}$ which is implied by $s^2 \geq (\det(M))^{1/d}$. We know that $\det(M) \leq \lambda_{2d}(M)^{2d}$ (this holds in any lattice), so it is sufficient to prove that $s \geq \lambda_{2d}(M)$, which we have already proved since this was required for the Gaussian sampling algorithm `GaussianGram` (see Lemma 3.8).

Similarly to the first `while` loop, we have that, under Assumption 1, the probability that $q'I^{-1}$ is prime is $\geq (\alpha \log(s'))^{-1}$. The probability that $\sqrt{\|q\|_1} =$

---

[14] Here we also use the general fact that for two events A and B, we can upper bound $\Pr(A \cap B) = \Pr(A) - \Pr(A \cap \neg B) \geq \Pr(A) - \Pr(\neg B)$..

$\|z'\|$ is larger than the bound in the condition is $\leq (4\alpha\log(s'))^{-1}$ (the argument is again similar to the first loop). Combining everything, the probability to exit the second while loop is at least

$$\frac{1}{\alpha\log(s')} - \frac{1}{4\alpha\log(s')} - \frac{1}{4\alpha\log(s')} = \frac{1}{2\alpha\log(s')}.$$

We conclude that the expected number of iterations of the second while loop is $\mathrm{poly}(\log\Delta_K, \rho_K, \mathrm{size}(G'))$. Similarly to the first while loop, all the operations performed during one execution of the while loop can be done in time $\mathrm{poly}(\log\Delta_K, \rho_K, \mathrm{size}(G'))$.

Step 13 can be done in polynomial time since $\mathcal{N}(qI^{-1})$ and $\mathcal{N}(q'I^{-1})$ are prime powers. The two calls to the TwoSquares algorithm in Step 14 can be performed in time $\mathrm{poly}\left(\log\Delta_K, (\log|\mathcal{N}_K(q)|)^{r+1}\right) = \mathrm{poly}(\log\Delta_K, \rho_K, \mathrm{size}(G'))^r$. Here we used the fact that $q\mathcal{O}_K$ and $q'\mathcal{O}_K$ have at most $r + 1$ distinct prime factors since $I = \mathcal{G}(M)$ has r distinct prime factors and qI^{-1} and $q'I^{-1}$ are prime ideals. We also used the the fact that $\log|\mathcal{N}_K(q)|$ and $\log|\mathcal{N}_K(q')|$ are $\mathrm{poly}(\log\Delta_K, \rho_K, \mathrm{size}(G'))$, thanks to the conditions on $\|\sigma(q)\|_1$ and $\|\sigma(q')\|_1$ in the while loops.

Finally, let us consider the final for loop from Step 16. Each step in this loop can be done in polynomial time. For the number of iterations of the loop, the proof of Theorem 2.16 gives $|S_1| \leq d^2(\log(|\mathcal{N}_K(q)|) + 1)^{r+1}$ and the same holds for $|S_2|$. Hence, the number of iterations of the loop is upper bounded by $\mathrm{poly}(\log\Delta_K, \rho_K, \mathrm{size}(G'))^r$. This concludes the analysis of the running time of the algorithm. $\qquad\square$

Before extending the previous result to modules in K^2, we focus a little bit on the particular case when $M = \mathcal{O}_K^2$ and K is the maximal totally real subfield of a cyclotomic field $L = \mathbb{Q}(\zeta_m)$. In this case, the Gram ideal is simply $\mathcal{O}_K$, leading to a polynomial complexity in d (the degree of K), the residue ρ_K and the size of the input.

Corollary 4.7 (Assumption 1, ERH). *Let K be the maximal totally real subfield of a cyclotomic field, and define $I_2 = (I_2, (\mathcal{O}_K)_{1\leq i \leq 2})$ (this is a pseudo-basis of the rank-2 module $\mathcal{O}_K^2$). Under Assumption 1, there exists a probabilistic algorithm solving wc-smodLIP$_K^{I_2}$ in expected polynomial time in the degree d of K, the residue ρ_K, and in the size of the input.*

Corollary 4.8 (Assumption1). *Let K be a totally real number field and $M \subset K^2$ a module lattice of rank 2 with pseudo-basis $B = (B, I_1, I_2)$ and associated pseudo-Gram matrix G. There exists a probabilistic algorithm (Algorithm 4.3) that takes as input a basis of $\mathcal{O}_K$, the pseudo-basis B, and $G' = (G', I_1', I_2')$ an instance of wc-smodLIP$_K^B$ and finds all congruence matrices between G and G'. Under Assumption 1, the algorithm runs in expected time polynomial in its input size and in*

$$\left(\mathrm{poly}(\rho_K, \log\Delta_K, \mathrm{size}(G'))\right)^r + T_{factor}(\mathcal{N}(\mathcal{RG}(M))),$$

Algorithm 4.3. Finding all congruence matrices for rank-2 modules.

Input: A basis of $\mathcal{O}_K^2$, a pseudo-basis $\boldsymbol{B} = (B, (I_1, I_2))$ of $M \subset K^2$, with pseudo-Gram matrix $\boldsymbol{G}$, and $\boldsymbol{G}' = (G, (I_1', I_2')) \sim \boldsymbol{G}$ an instance of wc-smodLIP$_K^B$.
Output: All congruence matrices between $\boldsymbol{G}$ and $\boldsymbol{G}'$.
 1: $J \leftarrow \mathcal{C}(M)^{-1}$
 2: $\boldsymbol{B}_J \leftarrow (B, \{J \cdot I_i\}_{i=1,2})$; $\boldsymbol{G}_J \leftarrow (G, \{J \cdot I_i\}_{i=1,2})$; $\boldsymbol{G}_J' \leftarrow (G', \{J \cdot I_i'\}_{i=1,2})$
 3: $S \leftarrow$ Run Algorithm 4.2 with $\boldsymbol{B}_J, \boldsymbol{G}_J$ and $\boldsymbol{G}_J'$
 4: **return** S.

---

where r is the number of distinct prime ideals dividing the relative Gram ideal $\mathcal{RG}(M)$.

5   Implementation of the Algorithm

We have implemented a proof-of-concept of our algorithm mixing Sagemath and PARI/GP, for the totally real (maximal) subfield K of cyclotomic fields $L = \mathbb{Q}(\zeta_m)$. The current version of the code only works for fields with conductor $m = 4k$: this ensures that L contains a primitive 4-th root of unity (equivalently $L = K[X]/(X^2 + 1)$), which simplifies the code and covers the cryptographic relevant case where $m = 2^t$. This also allows us to use our implementation of the Gentry-Szydlo algorithm as in this case, $K[X]/(X^2 + 1) = L$ is a cyclotomic field. For other conductors or more general CM-extensions, a previous version of the code worked on toy-sized examples as a proof-of-concept, but we did not push more in this direction.

Our approach follows the structure of Algorithm 4.2. We give more details in the full version of this paper [25], and refer to our code in our public repository. Nonetheless, we briefly report some experimental results and observations. In our experiments, we selected instances (Q, B), with B a basis of $\mathcal{O}_K^2$ and $Q = B^T \cdot B$, where B had a quite short column (to emulate the situation in Hawk) but usually the second column would be much bigger. Our values of choice for m included the power-of-two case but also various other of the form $4k$ (see Table 1) below.

Table 1. Times in seconds for attacks over various maximal totally real subfields of cyclotomic fields with conductors $m = 4k$, averaged over 5 instances. The upper table are powers-of-two (so $m = 2d$). Experiments performed on a MacBook Pro (Apple M2), with Sagemath 10.2 and Pari/GP 2.15.5.

m	64	128	256
Time	2	25	850

(m, d)	(124, 60)	(204, 64)	(228, 72)	(276, 88)	(260, 96)	(232, 112)	(340, 128)	(296, 144)
Time	33	53	74	195	434	652	2980	4205

Acknowledgments. We are grateful to Aurel Page and Bill Allombert for their help with the implementation of the Gentry-Szydlo algorithm, Sébastien Labbé, Xavier Caruso and Vincent Delecroix for organizing the Sage Days 125, where a significant part of the implementation took place. Thanks to Paul Kirchner and Thomas Espitau for their preliminary implementation of Gentry-Szydlo that helped for proof-of-concepts. Finally we thank Koen de Boer and Wessel van Woerden for enlightening discussions.

Guilhem Mureau and Alice Pellet-Mary were supported by the CHARM ANR-NSF grant (ANR-21-CE94-0003). All the authors were supported by the PEPR quantique France 2030 programme (ANR-22-PETQ-0008). Alice Pellet-Mary was supported by the TOTORO ANR (ANR-23-CE48-0002).

Disclosure of Interests. Nothing to report.

References

1. Belabas, K., van Hoeij, M., Klüners, J., Steel, A..: Factoring polynomials over global fields. Journal de théorie des nombres de Bordeaux **21**(1), 15–39 (2009). https://doi.org/10.5802/jtnb.655
2. Bennett, H., Ganju, A., Peetathawatchai, P., Stephens-Davidowitz, N.: Just how hard are rotations of $\mathbb{Z}^n$? algorithms and cryptography with the simplest lattice. In: Hazay, C., Stam, M. (eds.) Advances in Cryptology. EUROCRYPT 2023. LNCS, vol. 14008, pp. 252–281. Springer, Cham (2023). https://doi.org/10.1007/978-3-031-30589-4_9
3. Bhargava, M., Shankar, A., Taniguchi, T., Thorne, F., Tsimerman, J., Zhao, Y.: Bounds on 2-torsion in class groups of number fields and integral points on elliptic curves. J. Am. Math. Soc. **33**(4), 1087–1099 (2020)
4. Boer, K.D.: Random walks on Arakelov class groups. Ph.D. thesis, Leiden University (2022)
5. Brakerski, Z., Langlois, A., Peikert, C., Regev, O., Stehlé, D.: Classical hardness of learning with errors. In: Proceedings of the Forty-Fifth Annual ACM Symposium on Theory of Computing, pp. 575–584 (2013)
6. Bruin, P.J., Ducas, L., Gibbons, S.: Genus distribution of random q-ary lattices. Cryptology ePrint Archive (2022)
7. Buchmann, J.A., Lenstra, H.W.: Computing maximal orders and factoring over $\mathbb{Z}_p$. Preprint (1994)
8. Buchmann, J.A., Lenstra, H.W.: Approximatting rings of integers in number fields. Journal de théorie des nombres de Bordeaux **6**(2), 221–260 (1994)
9. Cohen, H.: Advanced Topics in Computational Number Theory, vol. 193. Springer, New York (2012). https://doi.org/10.1007/978-1-4419-8489-0
10. Cohen, H.: A Course in Computational Algebraic Number Theory, vol. 138. Springer, Heidelberg (2013). https://doi.org/10.1007/978-3-662-02945-9
11. Ducas, L.: Provable lattice reduction of $\mathbb{Z}^n$ with blocksize n/2. Cryptology ePrint Archive (2023)
12. Ducas, L., Gibbons, S.: Hull attacks on the lattice isomorphism problem. In: Boldyreva, A., Kolesnikov, V. (eds.) Public-key cryptography. PKC 2023. LNCS, vol. 13940, pp. 177–204. Springer, Cham (2023). https://doi.org/10.1007/978-3-031-31368-4_7

13. Ducas, L., Postlethwaite, E.W., Pulles, L.N., Woerden, W.V.: HAWK: module LIP makes lattice signatures fast, compact and simple. In: Agrawal, S., Lin, D. (eds.) Advances in Cryptology. ASIACRYPT 2022. LNCS, vol. 13794, pp. 65–94. Springer, Cham (2023). https://doi.org/10.1007/978-3-031-22972-5_3

14. Ducas, L., van Woerden, W.: On the lattice isomorphism problem, quadratic forms, remarkable lattices, and cryptography. In: Dunkelman, O., Dziembowski, S. (eds.) Advances in Cryptology. EUROCRYPT 2022. LNCS, vol. 13277, pp. 643–673. Springer, Cham (2022). https://doi.org/10.1007/978-3-031-07082-2_23

15. Felderhoff, J., Pellet-Mary, A., Stehlé, D., Wesolowski, B.: Ideal-SVP is hard for small-norm uniform prime ideals. In: Rothblum, G., Wee, H. (eds.) Theory of Cryptography. TCC 2023. LNCS, vol. 14372, pp. 63–92. Springer, Cham (2023). https://doi.org/10.1007/978-3-031-48624-1_3

16. Fieker, C., Stehlé, D.: Short bases of lattices over number fields. In: Hanrot, G., Morain, F., Thomé, E. (eds.) Algorithmic Number Theory. ANTS-IX. LNCS, vol. 6197, pp. 157–173. Springer, Heidelberg (2010). https://doi.org/10.1007/978-3-642-14518-6_15

17. Gentry, C., Szydlo, M.: Cryptanalysis of the revised NTRU signature scheme. In: Knudsen, L.R. (ed.) Advances in Cryptology. EUROCRYPT 2002. LNCS, vol. 2332, pp. 299–320. Springer, Heidelberg (2002). https://doi.org/10.1007/3-540-46035-7_20

18. Haviv, I., Regev, O.: On the lattice isomorphism problem. In: Proceedings of the Twenty-Fifth Annual ACM-SIAM Symposium on Discrete Algorithms, pp. 391–404. SIAM (2014)

19. Howgrave-Graham, N., Szydlo, M.: A method to solve cyclotomic norm equations $f * \bar{f}$. In: Buell, D. (ed.) Algorithmic Number Theory. LNCS, vol. 3076, pp. 272–279. Springer, Heidelberg (2004). https://doi.org/10.1007/978-3-540-24847-7_20

20. Kirchner, P.: Algorithms on ideal over complex multiplication order. arXiv preprint arXiv:1602.09037 (2016)

21. Lenstra, H.W., Jr., Silverberg, A.: Testing isomorphism of lattices over cm-orders. SIAM J. Comput. 48(4), 1300–1334 (2019)

22. Louboutin, S.: Explicit bounds for residues of dedekind zeta functions, values of l-functions at s= 1, and relative class numbers. J. Num. Theory 85(2), 263–282 (2000)

23. Mehta, S.K., Rajasree, M.S.: On the bases of z n lattice. In: 2022 24th International Symposium on Symbolic and Numeric Algorithms for Scientific Computing (SYNASC), pp. 100–107. IEEE (2022)

24. Micciancio, D., Regev, O.: Worst-case to average-case reductions based on gaussian measures. SIAM J. Comput. 37(1), 267–302 (2007)

25. Mureau, G., Pellet-Mary, A., Pliatsok, G., Wallet, A.: Cryptanalysis of rank-2 module-lip in totally real number fields. Cryptology ePrint Archive (2024)

26. Neukirch, J.: Algebraic Number Theory, vol. 322. Springer, New York (2013). https://doi.org/10.1007/978-1-4612-0853-2

27. Serre, J.P.: Local Fields, vol. 67. Springer, New York (2013). https://doi.org/10.1007/978-1-4757-5673-9

28. The PARI Group. Univ. Bordeaux: PARI/GP version 2.16.2 (2024). http://pari.math.u-bordeaux.fr/

29. The Sage Developers. SageMath, the Sage Mathematics Software System (Version 10.3.0) (2024). https://www.sagemath.org

30. Washington, L.C.: Introduction to Cyclotomic Fields, vol. 83. Springer, New York (1997). https://doi.org/10.1007/978-1-4612-1934-7

Provable Dual Attacks on Learning with Errors

Amaury Pouly[1] and Yixin Shen[2(✉)]

[1] Centre National de la Recherche Scientifique (CNRS), Paris, France
amaury.pouly@cnrs.fr
[2] King's College London, London, UK
yixin.shen@kcl.ac.uk

Abstract. Learning with Errors (LWE) is an important problem for post-quantum cryptography (PQC) that underlines the security of several NIST PQC selected algorithms. Several recent papers [7,25], [16,32] have claimed improvements on the complexity of so-called dual attacks on LWE. These improvements make dual attacks comparable to or even better than primal attacks in certain parameter regimes. Unfortunately, those improvements rely on a number of untested and hard-to-test statistical assumptions. Furthermore, a recent paper [20] claims that the whole premise of those improvements might be incorrect.

The goal of this paper is to improve the situation by proving the correctness of a dual attack without relying on any statistical assumption. Although our attack is greatly simplified compared to the recent ones, it shares many important technical elements with those attacks and can serve as a basis for the analysis of more advanced attacks. We provide some rough estimates on the complexity of our simplified attack on Kyber using a Monte Carlo Markov Chain discrete Gaussian sampler.

Our main contribution is to clearly identify a set of parameters under which our attack (and presumably other recent dual attacks) can work. Furthermore, our analysis completely departs from the existing statistics-based analysis and is instead rooted in geometry. We also compare the regime in which our algorithm works to the "contradictory regime" of [20]. We observe that those two regimes are essentially complementary.

Finally, we give a quantum version of our algorithm to speed up the computation. The algorithm is inspired by [10] but is completely formal and does not rely on any heuristics.

Keywords: Learning with Errors · Dual attack · Lattice-based cryptography · Quantum algorithm

1 Introduction

The Learning With Errors (LWE) problem [40] has become central to the security of several cryptosystems. Most notably, Kyber (public-key encryption) and Dilithium (signature) have been selected by the NIST for the Post-Quantum Cryptography (PQC) Standardization and rely on algebraic version of LWE for

© International Association for Cryptologic Research 2024
M. Joye and G. Leander (Eds.): EUROCRYPT 2024, LNCS 14657, pp. 256–285, 2024.
https://doi.org/10.1007/978-3-031-58754-2_10

their security proofs. Other advanced cryptographic primitives such as FHE can be built with LWE [15]. This makes LWE security estimates critical for the future of PQC. The *search* LWE *problem* asks to recover the secret $\mathbf{s}$ given $(\mathbf{A}, \mathbf{b})$ where $\mathbf{b} = \mathbf{As} + \mathbf{e}$, $\mathbf{A}$ is a matrix chosen uniformly at random and $\mathbf{e}$ has small entries (more details in Sect. 2.1).

There are two main approaches to attack the LWE problem: so-called primal and dual attacks. In this paper, we will exclusively focus on dual attacks which have recently attracted some interest due to significant claimed improvements in their complexity. Both primal and dual attacks rely on the BKZ lattice reduction algorithm [43] to obtain short vectors in lattices. The fundamental idea of dual attacks is to use short vectors in the dual of the lattice to detect whether points are close to the lattice or not, an idea that can be traced back to [5]. This allows us to solve the *distinguishing* LWE *problem* where one is asked to detect whether a sample comes from an LWE distribution, or a uniform distribution [35]. In conjunction with some guessing step, this allows one to recover part of the secret by trying several values until we get a point close to the lattice. By repeating this operation a couple of times, we can solve the search LWE problem.

Originally, the main limiting factor (on the complexity) of dual attacks was the need to compute one short vector (a very expensive operation) for every few LWE samples (more details in Sect. 3) and compute a score for each secret guess. Since then, a series of improvements have found their way into these attacks. First, a series of works on lattice sieving have shown [13,36,38] that those algorithms produce not only one but in fact exponentially many short vectors "for free". [11] suggested that this idea could be used in dual attacks but it appears that [23] was the first paper to try to analyze it. Independently, [7] used a "re-randomization" technique to produce many short vectors from a single BKZ reduced basis. All those techniques claim to reduce the complexity of attacks although the correctness relies on an unproven assumption about the quality of those many short vectors. Then [25] noted that instead of computing the score for each secret guess separately, all the scores can be computed at once using a discrete Fourier transform (DFT), essentially reducing the cost to that of a single guess. Following this work, a technical report by the MATZOV group [32] has claimed further improvements by the use of a "modulus switching" technique[1] that significantly reduces the size of the DFT. Two recent work have modified this attack to include a quantum [10] and lattice coding [16] speed up.

One issue with the papers above is that the number of statistical assumptions that are necessary to justify the correctness of the algorithms has grown significantly, notably in [32]. While certain assumptions could probably be justified (almost) formally, others are subject to more controversy [20]. In particular, the most controversial aspect of [25,32] is that the attack only uses a few LWE samples and that all the (exponentially-many) short vectors are derived from those samples which therefore are not statistically independent. When using a small number of LWE samples, the problem becomes very close to the *Bounded Dis-*

---

[1] A modulus switching technique was also suggested in [25] but it is unclear to us how it compares to [32], and [20] suggests that they are different.

tance Decoding which has been extensively studied. The status of [7] is unclear because it computes exponentially many short vectors from exponentially many samples, but the ratio of the number of short vectors to the number of samples is also exponential so the issue of the statistical independence remains but it does not seem as problematic. This makes it unclear whether an argument like that of [20] applies to such a case.

The purpose of this paper is to encourage a more rigorous analysis of dual attacks on LWE to better understand under what set of parameters they provably work. We note in that regard that a recently accepted paper at TCC 2023 [33] has focused on similar problems in statistical decoding/"dual attacks" in coding theory. The authors claim in the conclusion that at least part of their results apply to lattice dual attack. We believe that it would indeed be interesting to see what this approach yields for lattices, however we point out that the notion of dual attack that the authors have in mind looks quite different from the one in this paper. In short, and with our notations, the "dual attack" of [33] would be akin to splitting $\mathbf{A}$ horizontally instead of vertically. This splitting would not correspond anymore to a decomposition of $L_q(\mathbf{A})$ as $L_q(\mathbf{A}_{\text{guess}}) + L_q(\mathbf{A}_{\text{dual}})$ and therefore looks incompatible with existing works on dual attacks on LWE. Furthermore, our understanding of [33] is that generating parity check vectors $\mathbf{h}$ corresponds to generating many short dual vectors in $L_q^{\perp}(\mathbf{A})$, independently of the splitting of $\mathbf{A}$. This is completely at odds with lattice dual attacks where we split $\mathbf{A}$ to generate dual vectors in $L_q^{\perp}(\mathbf{A}_{\text{dual}})$ which is much cheaper. Overall it looks like [33] might be a completely different kind of dual attack. See [39, Appendix A] for more details.

1.1   Contributions

The main contribution of this paper is to provide a *completely formal, non-asymptotic analysis* of a simplified dual attack. To simplify the presentation, we do not include elements such as the guessing complexity and modulus switching[2] to focus on the most controversial element, namely the fact that the attack only uses m LWE samples (with m not much bigger than the dimension n of the samples) and that all the short vectors are derived from those m samples.

Our approach completely departs from the existing statistics-based attacks and is instead rooted in geometry. This allows us to obtain a relatively short proof and leverage existing results on the geometry of lattices.

One of the most important technical contribution of this paper is to make completely clear (Theorem 5) under what choice of parameters the attack works, without any statistical assumption. As far as we are aware, no other dual attack has been formally analyzed in this way. We believe that this is important since virtually all algorithms in the literature rely on statistical assumptions that clearly cannot hold for all parameter regimes but without a proper analysis, it is impossible to tell when and why they hold.

---

[2] See Sect. 7 for more details about modulus switching.

We also provide some new results on random q-ary lattices in a similar spirit to that of Siegel, Rogers and Macbeath [31,41,44]. This allows us to obtain some sharper bounds on λ_1 for random q-ary lattices and show that the Gaussian Heuristic is quite tight for such lattices. This heuristic is usually considered valid for "random" lattices and has been extensively tested. Up to our knowledge, the only formal analysis of λ_1 for random q-ary lattice is in [47, Lemma 7.9.2] which only analyzes the expected value and therefore provides a much weaker bound on λ_1. We refer to Sect. 2.3 for more details.

Finally, we give a quantum version of our algorithm to speed up the computation. The algorithm is inspired by [10] and reuses some technical lemmas to speed up the computation of sums of cosines that appear in the algorithm. Similarly to our classical algorithm, we prove that our quantum algorithm is correct without relying on any heuristics.

1.2 Comparison with [20]'s Contradictory Regime

A recent paper [20] has claimed that virtually all recent dual attacks rely on an incorrect statistical assumption and that they are, therefore, probably incorrect. They do so by formalizing what they claim to be the key statistical assumption of those paper, and show that for the parameter regime of the attacks, it falls into what they call the "contradictory regime", a regime where this assumption can be proven not to hold.

As a byproduct of our analysis, we are able to compare the regime in which our analysis works with the contradictory regime of [20]. Interestingly, the two are essentially complementary with a small gap inbetween. This suggests that our analysis and that of [20] are quite tight and provide an almost complete characterization of when dual attacks work in our simplified setting. However, we nuance this conclusion by noting that the statistical model used in [20] to argue about the contradiction does not seem to match what happens in our algorithm. We refer to Sect. 6 for more details.

1.3 Organisation of the Paper

In Sect. 2, we introduce the various technical elements that are necessary to analyse the dual attack. In Sect. 3, we first present a basic dual attack whose purpose is to introduce the reader to the ideas of dual attacks without overwhelming them with technical details. This dual attack is very naive and computes one short vector per LWE sample, in the spirit of [5]. We emphasize that this attack and Theorem 4 are not new but that our analysis is significantly simpler than in previous papers. In Sect. 4, we introduce our simplified dual attack in the spirit of [32] and formally analyse its correctness without assumption. We provide some rough estimates on the complexity of our attack on Kyber using a Monte Carlo Markov Chain discrete Gaussian sampler. In Sect. 5, we give a quantum version of the algorithm from Sect. 4 and prove its correctness. In Sect. 6, we compare our regime with that of [20]. Finally, in Sect. 7, we describe what we believe is the main obstacle to develop a formal analysis of the full algorithm in [32].

2   Preliminaries

We denote vectors and matrices in bold case. We denote by $\mathbf{x}^T$ the transpose of the (column) vector $\mathbf{x}$, which is therefore a row vector. We denote by $\mathbf{I}_n$ the identity matrix of size $n \times n$. For any vector $\mathbf{x} \in \mathbb{R}^n$, we denote by $\|\mathbf{x}\|$ its Euclidean norm. We denote by $\langle \mathbf{x}, \mathbf{y} \rangle$ the scalar product between two vectors $\mathbf{x}$ and $\mathbf{y}$. For any function $f : \mathbb{R}^n \to \mathbb{C}$, we denote by $\widehat{f}$ its Fourier transform over $\mathbb{R}^n$ defined by $\widehat{f}(\mathbf{x}) = \int_{\mathbb{R}^n} f(\mathbf{y}) e^{-2i\pi \langle \mathbf{x}, \mathbf{y} \rangle} \, d\mathbf{x}$. For any $n \in \mathbb{N}$ and $R > 0$, we denote by $B_n(R)$ (resp. $\overline{B}_n(R)$) the open (resp. closed) ball of radius R in $\mathbb{R}^n$. We also let $B_n^{\mathbb{Z}}(R) = B_n(R) \cap \mathbb{Z}^n$ be the set of integers points in this ball, and similarly for $\overline{B}_n^{\mathbb{Z}}(R)$. For any two distributions P and Q, we denote by $d_{\mathrm{TV}}(P, Q)$ the statistical distance (or total variation distance) between P and Q. For any finite set X, we denote by $\mathcal{U}(X)$ the uniform distribution over X.

2.1   LWE

Let $n, m, q \in \mathbb{N}$ and let χ_e be a distribution over $\mathbb{Z}_q$, which we call the *noise distribution*. For every vector $\mathbf{s} \in \mathbb{Z}_q^n$, we denote by $\mathrm{LWE}(m, \mathbf{s}, \chi_e)$ the probability distribution on $\mathbb{Z}_q^{m \times n} \times \mathbb{Z}_q^m$ obtained by sampling a matrix $\mathbf{A} \in \mathbb{Z}_q^{m \times n}$ uniformly at random, sampling a vector $\mathbf{e} \in \mathbb{Z}_q^m$ according to χ_e^m, and outputting $(\mathbf{A}, \mathbf{b})$ where $\mathbf{b} := \mathbf{A}\mathbf{s} + \mathbf{e}$. This is the "matrix form" for the LWE distribution where each pair $(\mathbf{A}, \mathbf{b})$ encodes m LWE samples $\mathbf{b}_i = \langle \mathbf{A}_i, \mathbf{s} \rangle + \mathbf{e}_i$ in the sense of [40]. We have chosen this formalism because it is simpler for dual attacks. The value of m is typically in the order of n and depends on the cryptosystem.

The search LWE problem is to find $\mathbf{s}$ given oracle access to a sampler for $\mathrm{LWE}(m, \mathbf{s}, \chi_e)$. The decision LWE problem is to decide, given oracle access to either $\mathrm{LWE}(m, \mathbf{s}, \chi_e)$ or $\mathcal{U}(\mathbb{Z}_q^{m \times n} \times \mathbb{Z}_q^m)$, which one it is. In practical scenarios, the attacker may not have access to the sampler but rather only possess a limited number LWE samples. In this case, the search LWE problem asks, given those LWE samples, to recover $\mathbf{s}$ if possible.

The LWE secret $\mathbf{s}$ is usually generated according to a distribution χ_s over $\mathbb{Z}_q^n$. One can therefore, in principle, analyse the success probability of an algorithm for search/decision LWE on a distribution $\mathrm{LWE}(m, \mathbf{s}, \chi_e)$ where $\mathbf{s} \leftarrow_\$ \chi_s^n$. In this paper, we will not need to make any assumption on the distribution of the secret since our algorithms work for every secret.

2.2   Discrete Gaussian Distribution

Let $n \in \mathbb{N}$ and $s > 0$. For any $\mathbf{x} \in \mathbb{R}^n$, we let $\rho_s(\mathbf{x}) := e^{-\pi \|\mathbf{x}\|^2 / s^2}$. As usual, we extend to ρ_s to sets by $\rho_s(X) = \sum_{\mathbf{x} \in X} \rho_s(\mathbf{x})$ for any set X. For any lattice $L \subset \mathbb{R}^n$, we denote the *discrete Gaussian distribution* over L by $D_{L,s}(\mathbf{x}) = \frac{\rho_s(\mathbf{x})}{\rho_s(L)}$ for any $\mathbf{x} \in L$. We denote $D_{L,1}$ by D_L for simplicity.

In general, the smaller s is, the harder it is to construct a sampler for $D_{L,s}$. The notion of smoothing parameter [34] captures the idea that sampling for a valuer of s above this threshold is significantly easier than sampling below because the distribution looks more like a continuous Gaussian. There are many algorithms to sample above the smoothing parameter [14,24,28], including a time-space trade-off [3]. Sampling below the smoothing parameter is much more challenging and usually inefficient [4]. At the extreme, sampling for sufficiently small values of s allows one to solve the Shortest Vector problem (SVP) [4] which is known to be NP-hard under randomized reduction [6]. The Monte Carlo Markov Chain based algorithm of [46] works for all values of s but the complexity significantly depends on s. We will use this algorithm in this paper.

Theorem 1 ([46, **Theorem 1, (8), (23) and (24)**^{3}]). *There is an algorithm that given a basis* $\mathbf{B}$ *of a lattice* $L \subset \mathbb{R}^n$, *any* $\varepsilon > 0$ *and any* $s > 0$, *returns a sample according to some distribution* $\mathcal{D}_{L,s,\varepsilon}$ *such that* $\mathrm{d}_{\mathrm{TV}}(\mathcal{D}_{L,s,\varepsilon}, \mathcal{D}_{L,s}) \leqslant \varepsilon$. *This algorithm runs in time* $\ln\left(\frac{1}{\varepsilon}\right) \cdot \frac{1}{\Delta} \cdot \mathrm{poly}(n)$ *where* $\frac{1}{\Delta} = \frac{\prod_{i=1}^n \rho_s/\|\tilde{\mathbf{b}}_i\|^{(\mathbb{Z})}}{\rho_s(L)}$ *and* $\tilde{\mathbf{b}}_1, \ldots, \tilde{\mathbf{b}}_n$ *are the Gram-Schmidt vectors of* $\mathbf{B}$.

For any $q \in \mathbb{N}$, we denote by $D_{\mathbb{Z}_q^n,s}$ the *modular discrete Gaussian distribution* over $\mathbb{Z}_q^n$ defined by $D_{\mathbb{Z}_q^n,s}(\mathbf{x}) = \frac{\rho_s(\mathbf{x}+q\mathbb{Z}^n)}{\rho_s(\mathbb{Z}^n)}$ for any $\mathbf{x} \in \mathbb{Z}_q^n$. We define the periodic Gaussian function $f_{L,s} : \mathbb{R}^n \to \mathbb{R}$ by $f_{L,s}(\mathbf{t}) = \frac{\rho_s(L+\mathbf{t})}{\rho_s(L)}$. We have $f_{L/s,1}(\mathbf{t}/s) = f_{L,s}(\mathbf{t})$. In the following, we denote $f_{L,1}$ as f_L.

Lemma 1 ([17, **Lemma 2.14**]). *For any* L, $s > 0$, $\mathbf{x} \in \mathbb{R}^n$, $f_{L,s}(\mathbf{x}) \geqslant \rho_s(\mathbf{x})$.

Lemma 2 ([12, **Lemma 7**], see also [45, **Theorem 1.3.4**]). *For any lattice* $L \subset \mathbb{R}^n$, $\mathbf{x} \in \mathbb{R}^n$ *and* $u \geqslant 1/\sqrt{2\pi}$, $\rho_s((L - \mathbf{x}) \setminus B_n(us\sqrt{n})) \leqslant \left(u\sqrt{2\pi e}e^{-\pi u^2}\right)^n \rho_s(L)$.

Corollary 1 ([45, **Corollary 1.3.5**]). *For any lattice* $L \subset \mathbb{R}^n$, $\mathbf{t} \in \mathbb{R}^n$ *and* $r \geqslant \delta := s\sqrt{n/2\pi}$, $\rho_s((L - \mathbf{t}) \setminus B_n(r)) \leqslant \rho_s(r - \delta)\rho_s(L)$.

Lemma 3 ([5, **Claim 4.1**]). *For any lattice* L *and* $s > 0$, *we have* $\widehat{f_{L,s}} = D_{\widehat{L},1/s}$ *which is a probability measure over the dual lattice* $\widehat{L}$.

2.3 Lattices

We denote by $\widehat{L} = \{\mathbf{x} \in \mathrm{span}(L) : \forall \mathbf{y} \in L, \langle \mathbf{y}, \mathbf{x} \rangle \in \mathbb{Z}\}$ the dual of a lattice $L \subset \mathbb{R}^n$. We denote by $L^* = L \setminus \{\mathbf{0}\}$ the set of nonzero vectors of a lattice L. We denote by $\lambda_1(L)$ the length a shortest nonzero vector in L.

Let $n \in \mathbb{N}$, $1 \leqslant k \leqslant n$ and q be a prime power. We say that a lattice L is a n-dimensional q-ary lattice if $q\mathbb{Z}^n \subseteq L \subseteq \mathbb{Z}^n$. Given a matrix $\mathbf{A} \in \mathbb{Z}^{n \times k}$, we consider the following n-dimensional q-ary lattices:

$$L_q(\mathbf{A}) = \{\mathbf{x} \in \mathbb{Z}^n : \exists \mathbf{s} \in \mathbb{Z}^k, \mathbf{As} = \mathbf{x} \bmod q\},$$
$$L_q^\perp(\mathbf{A}) = \{\mathbf{x} \in \mathbb{Z}^n : \mathbf{A}^T\mathbf{x} = \mathbf{0} \bmod q\}.$$

We refer the reader to [22], [47, Section 2.5.1] or [35] for more details on those constructions. Note that, equivalently, we can write $L_q(\mathbf{A}) = \mathbf{A}\mathbb{Z}_q^k + q\mathbb{Z}^n$. It is well-know that for any q-ary lattice L, there exists $\mathbf{A}$ and $\mathbf{B}$ such that $L = L_q(\mathbf{A}) =$

---

^{3} [46] uses the normal distribution $e^{-\|\mathbf{x}\|^2/2\sigma^2}$ so $s = \sqrt{2\pi}\sigma$ with our notations.

$L_q^{\perp}(\mathbf{B})$, and that $\widehat{L_q^{\perp}(\mathbf{A})} = \frac{1}{q} L_q(\mathbf{A})$. Furthermore $\det(L_q(\mathbf{A})) = q^{n-\mathrm{rk}\,\mathbf{A}} \geqslant q^{n-k}$ and therefore $\det(L_q^{\perp}(\mathbf{A})) = q^{\mathrm{rk}\,\mathbf{A}} \leqslant q^k$. Finally, since $\mathbb{Z}_q$ is a field, a random matrix $\mathbf{A} \in \mathbb{Z}_q^{n\times k}$ has full rank (equal to k) with probability at least $1 - kq^{k-1-n}$. We will consider the distributions $\mathcal{L}_{n,k,q}$ and $\mathcal{L}_{n,k,q}^{\perp}$ of q-ary lattices defined over the set of integer lattices by

$$\mathcal{L}_{n,k,q}(L) = \Pr_{\mathbf{A} \,\leftarrow\!\!\$\, \mathcal{U}(\mathbb{Z}_q^{n\times k})}[L = L_q(\mathbf{A})],$$

$$\mathcal{L}_{n,k,q}^{\perp}(L) = \Pr_{\mathbf{A} \,\leftarrow\!\!\$\, \mathcal{U}(\mathbb{Z}_q^{n\times(n-k)})}\left[L = L_q^{\perp}(\mathbf{A})\right].$$

In other words, the distribution is obtained by taking a matrix $\mathbf{A} \in \mathbb{Z}_q^{n\times k}$ with uniform and i.i.d entries, and looking at the q-ary lattice generated by $\mathbf{A}$; and similarly for the orthogonal version. Note that contrary to the Loeliger ensemble $\mathbb{L}_{n,k,q,1}$, we do not have the rescaling factor $q^{1-k/n}$, see e.g. [47, Definition 7.9.2]. It will be more convenient to use $\mathcal{L}_{n,k,q}^{\perp}$ for proofs, but we often want to apply them for $\mathcal{L}_{n,k,q}$. Whenever neither k nor $n - k$ are too small, those two distributions are very close. The following lemma was inspired by [19, Lemma 2] which does not contain any proof.

Lemma 4 ([39, Appendix C.1]). *Let $n \in \mathbb{N}$, $1 \leqslant k \leqslant n$ and q be a prime power. Then $\mathrm{d_{TV}}(\mathcal{L}_{n,k,q}^{\perp}, \mathcal{L}_{n,k,q}) \leqslant \mathsf{poly}(n,k)\, q^{-\min(k,n-k)}$.*

Those distributions satisfy good uniformity properties when q goes to infinity. In particular, the following theorem shows that we can compute statistical properties of lattices sampled according to $\mathcal{L}_{n,k,q}^{\perp}$. The first part of this theorem is close to [30, Theorem 1]. This result is in some sense the q-ary version of the result by Siegel on random (real) lattices and its generalization by Rogers and Macbeath [31, 41, 44].

Theorem 2 ([39, Appendix C.2]). *Let $n \in \mathbb{N}$, $1 \leqslant k \leqslant n$ and q be a prime power. Let $1 \leqslant p \leqslant n$ and $f : (\mathbb{Z}_q^n)^p \to \mathbb{R}$, then*

$$\mathbb{E}_{L \,\leftarrow\!\!\$\, \mathcal{L}_{n,k,q}^{\perp}}\left[\sum_{\mathbf{x}_1,\ldots,\mathbf{x}_p \in L} f(\mathbf{x}_1,\ldots,\mathbf{x}_p)\right] = \sum_{\mathbf{x}_1,\ldots,\mathbf{x}_p \in \mathbb{Z}^n} q^{(k-n)r(\mathbf{x}_1,\ldots,\mathbf{x}_p)} f(\mathbf{x}_1,\ldots,\mathbf{x}_p)$$

where $r(\mathbf{x_1},\ldots,\mathbf{x_p}) := \mathrm{rk}_{\mathbb{Z}_q^n}(\mathbf{x}_1,\ldots,\mathbf{x}_p)$ is the rank of the $\mathbf{x}_i \bmod q$ over $\mathbb{Z}_q^n$.

We can apply this theorem to bound the expected number of lattice points in a ball, and therefore obtain bounds on λ_1.

Theorem 3 ([39, Appendix C.3]). *Let $n \in \mathbb{N}$, $1 \leqslant k \leqslant n$ and q be a prime power. For any $0 < r \leqslant q$,*

$$\mathbb{E}_{L \,\leftarrow\!\!\$\, \mathcal{L}_{n,k,q}^{\perp}}[|L^* \cap B_n(r)|] = q^{k-n}\left(|B_n^{\mathbb{Z}}(r)| - 1\right),$$

$$\mathbb{V}_{L \,\leftarrow\!\!\$\, \mathcal{L}_{n,k,q}^{\perp}}[|L^* \cap B_n(r)|] \leqslant q^{k-n}(q-1)(|B_n^{\mathbb{Z}}(r)| - 1).$$

In particular, if $|B_n^{\mathbb{Z}}(r)| \leqslant q^{n-k}$, then $\Pr_{L \,\leftarrow\!\!\$\, \mathcal{L}_{n,k,q}^{\perp}}[\lambda_1(L) \leqslant r] \leqslant q^{1+k-n}|B_n^{\mathbb{Z}}(r)|.$

Recall that the *Gaussian heuristic* says that for a "random" lattice L, $\lambda_1(L)$ is approximately

$$\text{GH}(L) := \left(\frac{\text{vol}(B_n)}{\det(L)}\right)^{-1/n} = \frac{\det(L)^{1/n}\Gamma(1+\frac{n}{2})^{1/n}}{\sqrt{\pi}} \approx \det(L)^{1/n}\sqrt{\frac{n}{2\pi e}}.$$

This heuristic is usually considered valid for "random" lattices and has been extensively tested. Up to our knowledge, the only formal analysis of λ_1 for random q-ary lattice is in [47, Lemma 7.9.2] which only analyzes the expected value and not the variance. The following corollary shows that this heuristic is indeed very sharp for random q-ary lattices.

Corollary 2 (Informal, [39, Appendix C.4]). *Let* $n \in \mathbb{N}$, $1 \leqslant k \leqslant n$ *and* q *be a prime power. Let* $\alpha \in [0,1]$ *and* $r = q^{1-k/n}\text{vol}(B_n)^{-1/n}$. *Under the assumption that* $|B_n^{\mathbb{Z}}(\alpha r)| \approx \text{vol}(B_n(\alpha r))$, *which holds when* $\alpha r \gg \sqrt{n}$, *we have*

$$\Pr_{L \leftarrow_\$ \mathcal{L}_{n,k,q}}[\lambda_1(L) \leqslant \alpha\text{GH}(L)] \lesssim q\alpha^n.$$

Lemma 5 (The Pointwise Approximation Lemma [5, Lemma 1.3]), modified). *Let* $L \subset \mathbb{R}^n$ *be a lattice, and* $h : \mathbb{R}^n \to \mathbb{R}$ *a* L*-periodic function whose Fourier series* $\hat{h}$ *is a probability measure over* $\widehat{L}$. *Let* $N \in \mathbb{N}$, $\delta > 0$ *and* $X \subseteq \mathbb{R}^n$ *a finite set. Let* $W = (\mathbf{w}_1, \cdots, \mathbf{w}_N)$ *be a list of vectors in the dual lattice chosen randomly and independently from the distribution* $\hat{h}$. *Then with probability at least* $1 - |X|2^{-\Omega(N\delta^2)}$, $h_W(\mathbf{x}) := \frac{1}{N}\sum_{i=1}^N \cos(2\pi \langle \mathbf{w}_i, \mathbf{x}\rangle)$ *satisfies that* $|h_W(\mathbf{x}) - h(\mathbf{x})| \leqslant \delta$ *for all* $\mathbf{x} \in L + X$.

Proof. The proof is the one in [5] with the following modifications. Let $\delta > 0$. For any $\mathbf{x} \in \mathbb{R}^n$, Hoeffding's inequality guarantees that the mean of N samples is not within a window of δ of the correct expectation with probability at most $2^{-\Omega(N\delta^2)}$. Since f is periodic over the lattice L, it suffices to check that the inequality that we want holds for all $\mathbf{x} \in X$. Hence, by a union bound, the probability that the approximation is within a window δ of the correct expectation for all $\mathbf{x} \in X$ simultaneously is at least $1 - |X|2^{-\Omega(N\delta^2)}$. $\qquad\square$

2.4   Short Vector Sampling

For the purpose of this paper, we will only need to know that there is a way to sample relatively short vectors (SV) in a lattice and we will treat such an algorithm as a black box. Since such an algorithm would typically be parametrized (see below), we introduce an integer parameter β to capture this fact.

Black Box 1. *For any integers* $n \leqslant m$, β *and prime power* q, *there exists a deterministic algorithm* $\mathcal{B}$ *and two functions* T_{SV} *and* ℓ_{SV} *such that when* $\mathcal{B}$ *is given* $\mathbf{A} \in \mathbb{Z}_q^{m \times n}$, *it returns a nonzero vector in* $L_q^\perp(\mathbf{A})$ *in time* $T_{\text{SV}}(m, \beta, q^n)$ *and* $\mathbb{E}_{\mathbf{A} \leftarrow_\$ \mathbb{Z}_q^{m \times n}}\left[\|\mathcal{B}(\mathbf{A})\|^2\right] \leqslant \ell_{\text{SV}}(m, \beta, q^n)^2$.

One way to implement this black box is to use lattice reduction algorithms such as BKZ: they provide a very flexible way to take a basis of lattice and compute relatively short vectors in this lattice. Since the literature on this topic is quite extensive and there are many cost models associated to that task, we refer the reader to e.g. [25] for more details. For simplicity, we assume that the algorithm is deterministic but we could make it probabilistic by adding random coins to the input of the algorithm and take those into account in the expected value. In the case of BKZ, the parameter β is the block size.

3   Basic Dual Attack

In this section, we present a basic dual attack whose purpose is to introduce the reader to the ideas of dual attacks without overwhelming them with technical details. This dual attack is very naive and assumes that we access to essentially an unlimited number of samples. It computes one short vector per m LWE samples, in the spirit of [5]. We emphasize that this attack and Theorem 4 are not new but that our analysis is significantly simpler than in previous papers.

Fix $\mathbf{s} \in \mathbb{Z}_q^n$ an unknown secret and $(\mathbf{A}, \mathbf{b})$ some LWE samples. Recall that $\mathbf{b} = \mathbf{A}\mathbf{s} + \mathbf{e}$ for some unknown $\mathbf{e} \in \mathbb{Z}_q^m$. We split the secret $\mathbf{s}$ into two parts $\mathbf{s}_{\text{guess}} \in \mathbb{Z}_q^{n_{\text{guess}}}$ and $\mathbf{s}_{\text{dual}} \in \mathbb{Z}_q^{n_{\text{dual}}}$ where $n = n_{\text{guess}} + n_{\text{dual}}$. The matrix $\mathbf{A} \in \mathbb{Z}_q^{m \times n}$ is correspondingly split into two parts:

$$\mathbf{A} = \begin{bmatrix} \mathbf{A}_{\text{guess}} \ \mathbf{A}_{\text{dual}} \end{bmatrix}, \qquad \mathbf{s} = \begin{bmatrix} \mathbf{s}_{\text{guess}} \\ \mathbf{s}_{\text{dual}} \end{bmatrix}. \tag{1}$$

Therefore, $\mathbf{b} = \mathbf{A}_{\text{guess}}\mathbf{s}_{\text{guess}} + \mathbf{A}_{\text{dual}}\mathbf{s}_{\text{dual}} + \mathbf{e}$. The algorithm now makes a guess $\tilde{\mathbf{s}}_{\text{guess}} \in \mathbb{Z}_q^{n_{\text{guess}}}$ on the value of $\mathbf{s}_{\text{guess}}$ and tries to check whether this guess is correct. Consider the lattice

$$L_q^{\perp}(\mathbf{A}_{\text{dual}}) = \{\, \mathbf{x} \in \mathbb{Z}^m : \mathbf{x}^T \mathbf{A}_{\text{dual}} = \mathbf{0} \bmod q \,\}. \tag{2}$$

By the inequalities of Sect. 2.3, we have that $\det(L_q^{\perp}(\mathbf{A}_{\text{dual}})) \leqslant q^{n_{\text{dual}}}$. Check that for any $\mathbf{x} \in L_q^{\perp}(\mathbf{A}_{\text{dual}})$,

$$\mathbf{x}^T \mathbf{b} = \mathbf{x}^T \mathbf{A}_{\text{guess}}\mathbf{s}_{\text{guess}} + \mathbf{x}^T \mathbf{A}_{\text{dual}}\mathbf{s}_{\text{dual}} + \mathbf{x}^T \mathbf{e} = \mathbf{x}^T \mathbf{A}_{\text{guess}}\mathbf{s}_{\text{guess}} + \mathbf{x}^T \mathbf{e} \pmod{q}.$$

Therefore, $\mathbf{x}^T(\mathbf{b} - \mathbf{A}_{\text{guess}}\tilde{\mathbf{s}}_{\text{guess}}) = \mathbf{x}^T \mathbf{A}_{\text{guess}}(\mathbf{s}_{\text{guess}} - \tilde{\mathbf{s}}_{\text{guess}}) + \mathbf{x}^T \mathbf{e} \pmod{q}$. The main observation is now that:

- if the guess is correct ($\tilde{\mathbf{s}}_{\text{guess}} = \mathbf{s}_{\text{guess}}$) then $\mathbf{x}^T(\mathbf{b} - \mathbf{A}_{\text{guess}}\tilde{\mathbf{s}}_{\text{guess}}) = \mathbf{x}^T \mathbf{e}$ (mod q) follows roughly a modular Gaussian distribution,
- if the guess is incorrect ($\tilde{\mathbf{s}}_{\text{guess}} \neq \mathbf{s}_{\text{guess}}$) then it follows a uniform distribution because $\mathbf{x} \neq \mathbf{0}$ and $\mathbf{A}$ was chosen uniformly at random.

A crucial ingredient in the reasoning above is the length of $\mathbf{x}$. Indeed, the scalar product $\mathbf{x}^T \mathbf{e}$ will follow a modular Gaussian whose deviation is proportional to $\|\mathbf{x}\|$. This is where the BKZ lattice reduction algorithm usually comes in: from a basis of $L_q^{\perp}(\mathbf{A}_{\text{dual}})$, we compute a short vector $\mathbf{x}$ using Black box 1.

The algorithm for this attack is described in Algorithm 1. We group many LWE samples in N tuples of m samples which we write in matrix form. We then compute one dual vector for each tuple of m LWE samples as explained above. In this attack, the value of m can be chosen arbitrarily and there usually is an optimal value of m that can be computed based on the complexity of computing a short vector, *i.e.* it depends on the specific instantiation of Black box 1.

While this kind of attack is already known to be correct, we reprove it for several reasons. First, we are not satisfied with the informal treatement of the proof in the literature. Second, our proof does not use any assumption whereas most papers in the literature use the Central Limit Theorem or approximate sums of Gaussian as a Gaussian at some point (see [39, Section 2.4]). Figure 1 gives a high level view of the variable involved and their dependencies.

Theorem 4 ([39, **Appendix B**]). *Let n, m, β be integers, q be a prime power, $n_{\text{guess}} + n_{\text{dual}} = n$, $\mathbf{s} \in \mathbb{Z}_q^n$, $\sigma_e > 0$ and $N \in \mathbb{N}$. Let $0 < \delta < \varepsilon$ where $\varepsilon := \exp\left(-\pi\sigma_e^2 \ell_{\text{SV}}(m, \beta, q^{n_{\text{dual}}})^2/q^2\right)$ and ℓ_{SV} comes from Black box 1. Let $(\mathbf{A}^{(1)}, \mathbf{b}^{(1)}), \ldots, (\mathbf{A}^{(N)}, \mathbf{b}^{(N)})$ be samples from $\text{LWE}(m, \mathbf{s}, D_{\mathbb{Z}_q, \sigma_e})$, then Algorithm 1 on $(m, n_{\text{guess}}, n_{\text{dual}}, q, \delta, N, (\mathbf{A}^{(i)}, \mathbf{b}^{(i)})_i)$ runs in time $\text{poly}(m, n) \cdot (N \cdot T_{\text{SV}}(m, \beta, q^n) + q^{n_{\text{guess}}})$ and returns $\mathbf{s}_{\text{guess}}$ with probability at least $1 - \exp\left(-\frac{N(\varepsilon-\delta)^2}{2}\right) - (q^{n_{\text{guess}}} - 1)\exp\left(-\frac{N\delta^2}{2}\right)$ over the choice of the $(\mathbf{A}^{(i)}, \mathbf{b}^{(i)})$.*

Remark 1. As expected, we recover the well-known fact that for the attack to succeed with constant probability, we can take $\delta = \varepsilon/2$ and then we need at least $N = \frac{8n_{\text{guess}}\log(q) + \Omega(1)}{\varepsilon^2}$ samples. Furthermore, a careful look at the proof shows that Black box 1 can be weakened even further to only require an inequality on the moment-generating function of $\|\mathcal{B}(\mathbf{A})\|^2$.

Algorithm 1: Basic dual attack

Input: m, $n = n_{\text{guess}} + n_{\text{dual}}$ (see (1)), q prime power, $\delta > 0$ and $N \in \mathbb{N}$.
Input: list of N LWE samples $(\mathbf{A}^{(1)}, \mathbf{b}^{(1)}), \ldots, (\mathbf{A}^{(N)}, \mathbf{b}^{(N)})$.
Output: (Guess of) the first n_{guess} coordinates of the secret or $\perp$.

1 **for** j *from* 1 *to* N **do**
2   Compute a basis of $L_q^\perp(\mathbf{A}_{\text{dual}}^{(j)})$;
3   Compute a short vector $\mathbf{x}_j \in L_q^\perp(\mathbf{A}_{\text{dual}}^{(j)})$ using Black box 1 ;
4 **for** $\tilde{\mathbf{s}}_{\text{guess}} \in \mathbb{Z}_q^{n_{\text{guess}}}$ **do**
5   Compute the list $y_1, \ldots, y_N$ where $y_j = \mathbf{x}_j^T(\mathbf{b}^{(j)} - \mathbf{A}_{\text{guess}}^{(j)}\tilde{\mathbf{s}}_{\text{guess}})$;
6   **if** $\frac{1}{N}\sum_{j=1}^N \cos(2\pi y_j/q) \geqslant \delta$ **then return** $\tilde{\mathbf{s}}_{\text{guess}}$;
7 **return** $\perp$

---

4 Modern Dual Attack

The main limitation of the basic dual attack is the requirement to compute one short vector for each tuple of m LWE samples. Looking at Fig. 1, this is necessary to ensure the statistical independence of the variables that go into

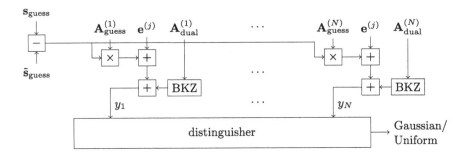

Fig. 1. Conceptual representation of the variables involved in Algorithm 1.

the distinguisher. However, computing a short vector is an expensive operation that we have to repeat many times. Another issue is that the attack requires an exponential number of LWE samples, something which is not always realistic.

As explained in the introduction, a series of work have progressively introduced the idea of generating *all short vectors* from a limited number of LWE sample, *i.e.* a single $(\mathbf{A}, \mathbf{b})$. This is the case in [7,23,25], and [32] and it dramatically reduces the complexity of the attack. Unfortunately, the statistical analysis of these attacks has been lacking in the literature: [7,23][4] and [25] offer no real proof of correctness to speak of. Only [32] tries to provide a complete proof of correctness, which is very detailed, but has to rely on statistical assumptions. Those assumptions have been called into question [20], and more importantly are extremely difficult to verify. Stepping back, we believe that the reason for this situation is that they try to analyse their attacks using a similar proof strategy to that of our basic dual attack (Sect. 3). However, the basic dual attack requires the independence of many variables to work. Since those variables become dependent in their attack, these papers inevitably have to assume or prove that non-independent quantities are "independent enough".

In this section, we start completely from scratch: we design and analyze without any assumption a modern dual attack. Our proof scheme is completely different from the basic one and shows that those attacks do work. The main outcome of this proof is that we can finally understand the constraints on the various parameters that are necessary for the attack to work.

4.1 Intuition

Fix $\mathbf{s} \in \mathbb{Z}_q^n$ an unknown secret and $(\mathbf{A}, \mathbf{b})$ some LWE samples. Recall that $\mathbf{b} = \mathbf{A}\mathbf{s} + \mathbf{e}$ for some unknown $\mathbf{e} \in \mathbb{Z}_q^m$. As in the basic dual attack, we split the secret $\mathbf{s}$ into two parts $\mathbf{s}_{\text{guess}} \in \mathbb{Z}_q^{n_{\text{guess}}}$ and $\mathbf{s}_{\text{dual}} \in \mathbb{Z}_q^{n_{\text{dual}}}$ where $n = n_{\text{guess}} + n_{\text{dual}}$. The matrix $\mathbf{A} \in \mathbb{Z}_q^{m \times n}$ is correspondingly split into two parts:

$$\mathbf{A} = \begin{bmatrix} \mathbf{A}_{\text{guess}} & \mathbf{A}_{\text{dual}} \end{bmatrix}, \qquad \mathbf{s} = \begin{bmatrix} \mathbf{s}_{\text{guess}} \\ \mathbf{s}_{\text{dual}} \end{bmatrix}. \tag{3}$$

---

[4] Part of [23] formally analyzes a similar attack to our basic attack. This paragraph only applies to the rest that relies on sieving to produce many short vectors.

The algorithm now makes a guess $\tilde{\mathbf{s}}_{\text{guess}} \in \mathbb{Z}_q^{n_{\text{guess}}}$ on the value of $\mathbf{s}_{\text{guess}}$ and tries to check whether this guess is correct. Check that

$$\mathbf{b} - \mathbf{A}_{\text{guess}} \cdot \tilde{\mathbf{s}}_{\text{guess}} = \mathbf{A}_{\text{guess}} \cdot (\mathbf{s}_{\text{guess}} - \tilde{\mathbf{s}}_{\text{guess}}) + \mathbf{A}_{\text{dual}} \cdot \mathbf{s}_{\text{dual}} + \mathbf{e}. \quad (4)$$

Consider the lattice

$$L_q^{\perp}(\mathbf{A}_{\text{dual}}) = \{\, \mathbf{x} \in \mathbb{Z}^m : \mathbf{x}^T \mathbf{A}_{\text{dual}} = \mathbf{0} \bmod q \,\}. \quad (5)$$

Fix $N \in \mathbb{N}$ and $s > 0$, and let $W = (\mathbf{w}_1, \ldots, \mathbf{w}_N) \in L_q^{\perp}(\mathbf{A}_{\text{dual}})^N$ be sampled according to $D_{L_q^{\perp}(\mathbf{A}_{\text{dual}}),qs}^N$. For any $\mathbf{x} \in \mathbb{R}^m$, define

$$g_W(\mathbf{x}) = \frac{1}{N} \sum_{j=1}^{N} \cos(2\pi \langle \mathbf{x}, \mathbf{w}_j \rangle / q) \quad (6)$$

for all $\mathbf{x} \in \mathbb{R}^m$. We will evaluate g_W at $\mathbf{b} - \mathbf{A}_{\text{guess}} \cdot \tilde{\mathbf{s}}_{\text{guess}}$ for all $\tilde{\mathbf{s}}_{\text{guess}} \in \mathbb{Z}_q^{n_{\text{guess}}}$ and keep the highest value. We now explain the intuition for this. Let $L = L_q(\mathbf{A}_{\text{dual}})$ to simplify notations. Recall that in Sect. 2.2, we have defined the standard periodic Gaussian function $f_{L,1/s}(\mathbf{x}) = \frac{\rho_{1/s}(\mathbf{x}+L)}{\rho_{1/s}(L)}$ for any $\mathbf{x} \in \mathbb{R}^m$ and $s > 0$. The important fact is that for large N, with high probability on the choice of the $\mathbf{w}_j$, g_W and $f_{L,1/s}$ are close everywhere *for integer vectors* (Lemma 6). This fact essentially comes from [5]. Therefore, it suffices to analyse the behaviour of $f_{L,1/s}$. For this, we rely on standard Gaussian tailbounds (Lemma 7) to get that for any $s > 0$ and $\mathbf{x} \in \mathbb{R}^m$, we essentially have

$$f_{L,1/s}(\mathbf{x}) \approx \rho_{1/s}(\text{dist}(\mathbf{x}, L)). \quad (7)$$

In other words, $f_{L,1/s}$ measures the *distance to the lattice* L.

We are now ready to see what makes the attack work. The intuition is that *for most choices* of $\mathbf{A}$ and $\mathbf{e}$, for all $\tilde{\mathbf{s}}_{\text{guess}} \in \mathbb{Z}_q^{n_{\text{guess}}} \setminus \{\mathbf{s}_{\text{guess}}\}$,

$$\text{dist}(\mathbf{b} - \mathbf{A}_{\text{guess}} \cdot \mathbf{s}_{\text{guess}}, L) < \text{dist}(\mathbf{b} - \mathbf{A}_{\text{guess}} \cdot \tilde{\mathbf{s}}_{\text{guess}}, L) \quad (8)$$

and therefore

$$f_{L,1/s}(\mathbf{b} - \mathbf{A}_{\text{guess}} \cdot \mathbf{s}_{\text{guess}}) > f_{L,1/s}(\mathbf{b} - \mathbf{A}_{\text{guess}} \cdot \tilde{\mathbf{s}}_{\text{guess}})$$

and the same will be true for g_W, which means that the algorithm will correctly output $\mathbf{s}_{\text{guess}}$. This is the main idea of our analysis but making it formal requires some care. The first step (Lemma 8) is to show that essentially

$$\text{if } 2\|\mathbf{e}\| < \lambda_1(L_q(\mathbf{A})) \text{ then } f_{L,\frac{1}{s}}(\mathbf{e}) > f_{L,\frac{1}{s}}(\mathbf{e}+\mathbf{x}) \text{ for all } \mathbf{x} \in L_q(\mathbf{A}_{\text{guess}}) \setminus L. \quad (9)$$

This requires some explanations. Going back to (8), we have that

$$\begin{aligned}
\text{dist}(\mathbf{b} - \mathbf{A}_{\text{guess}} \cdot \mathbf{s}_{\text{guess}}, L) &= \text{dist}(\mathbf{e} + \mathbf{A}_{\text{dual}} \cdot \mathbf{s}_{\text{dual}}, L) \\
&= \text{dist}(\mathbf{e}, L) && \text{since } \mathbf{A}_{\text{dual}} \cdot \mathbf{s}_{\text{dual}} \in L \\
&= \|\mathbf{e}\| && \text{if } \|\mathbf{e}\| < \lambda_1(L)/2.
\end{aligned}$$

On the other hand, if $\tilde{\mathbf{s}}_{\text{guess}} \neq \mathbf{s}_{\text{guess}}$ then

$$
\begin{aligned}
\text{dist}(\mathbf{b} - \mathbf{A}_{\text{guess}} \cdot \tilde{\mathbf{s}}_{\text{guess}}, L) &= \text{dist}(\mathbf{e} + \mathbf{A}_{\text{dual}} \cdot \mathbf{s}_{\text{dual}} + \mathbf{A}_{\text{guess}}(\mathbf{s}_{\text{guess}} - \tilde{\mathbf{s}}_{\text{guess}}), L) \\
&= \text{dist}(\mathbf{e} + \mathbf{A}_{\text{guess}}(\mathbf{s}_{\text{guess}} - \tilde{\mathbf{s}}_{\text{guess}}), L) \quad \text{since } \mathbf{A}_{\text{dual}} \cdot \mathbf{s}_{\text{dual}} \in L \\
&= \text{dist}(\mathbf{e} + \mathbf{x}, L)
\end{aligned}
$$

where

$$
\mathbf{x} = \mathbf{A}_{\text{guess}}(\mathbf{s}_{\text{guess}} - \tilde{\mathbf{s}}_{\text{guess}}) \in L_q(\mathbf{A}_{\text{guess}}).
$$

Assume for now that $\mathbf{x} \in L_q(\mathbf{A}_{\text{guess}}) \setminus L$ which we will see below is not always true but holds with probability exponentially close to 1 over the choice of $\mathbf{A}$. Then

$$
\begin{aligned}
\text{dist}(\mathbf{b} - \mathbf{A}_{\text{guess}} \cdot \tilde{\mathbf{s}}_{\text{guess}}, L) &= \text{dist}(\mathbf{e} + \mathbf{x}, L) = \min \left\{ \|\mathbf{e} + \mathbf{x} + \mathbf{z}\| : \mathbf{z} \in L \right\} \\
&\geqslant \min \left\{ \|\mathbf{e} + \mathbf{y} + \mathbf{z}\| : \mathbf{z} \in L, \mathbf{y} \in L_q(\mathbf{A}_{\text{guess}}) \setminus L \right\} \\
&\geqslant \min \left\{ \|\mathbf{y} + \mathbf{z}\| : \mathbf{z} \in L, \mathbf{y} \in L_q(\mathbf{A}_{\text{guess}}) \setminus L \right\} - \|\mathbf{e}\| \\
&\geqslant \lambda_1(L + L_q(\mathbf{A}_{\text{guess}})) - \|\mathbf{e}\| .
\end{aligned}
$$

The last step holds because $\mathbf{y} + \mathbf{z} \neq \mathbf{0}$ for all $\mathbf{z} \in L$ and $\mathbf{y} \in L_q(\mathbf{A}_{\text{guess}}) \setminus L$. This is where our assumption that $\mathbf{x} \in L_q(\mathbf{A}_{\text{guess}}) \setminus L$ is crucial. The condition in (8) now becomes

$$
\|\mathbf{e}\| < \lambda_1(L + L_q(\mathbf{A}_{\text{guess}})) - \|\mathbf{e}\|
$$

and this gives us (9) because $L + L_q(\mathbf{A}_{\text{guess}}) = L_q(\mathbf{A}_{\text{dual}}) + L_q(\mathbf{A}_{\text{guess}}) = L_q(\mathbf{A})$.

Now that we have (9), the second step is to apply it to $\mathbf{A}$. Recall that we made a crucial assumption above: it only applies to $\mathbf{e} + \mathbf{x}$ for $\mathbf{x} \in L_q(\mathbf{A}_{\text{guess}}) \setminus L$ where $\mathbf{x} = \mathbf{A}_{\text{guess}}(\mathbf{s}_{\text{guess}} - \tilde{\mathbf{s}}_{\text{guess}})$ and $\mathbf{s}_{\text{guess}} \neq \tilde{\mathbf{s}}_{\text{guess}}$. This condition is equivalent to $\mathbf{x} \notin \mathbf{A}_{\text{dual}}\mathbb{Z}_q^{n_{\text{dual}}} + q\mathbb{Z}^m$ since $L = L_q(\mathbf{A}_{\text{dual}})$. A sufficient condition for this to hold is that $\mathbf{A}$ has full rank over $\mathbb{Z}_q$ which happens with probability exponentially close to 1 over the choice of $\mathbf{A}$. This allows us to conclude (Theorem 5) that Algorithm 2, which essentially performs the steps highlighted above, works for almost all $\mathbf{A}$ and $\mathbf{e}$ that satisfy roughly $2\|\mathbf{e}\| < \lambda_1(L_q(\mathbf{A}))$. At this point, one can make two interesting observations:

- It tells us that if $2\|\mathbf{e}\| < \lambda_1(L_q(\mathbf{A}))$ then we can distinguish $\mathbf{e}$ from any $\mathbf{e} + \mathbf{x}$ by using $f_{L,1/s}$. This makes intuitive sense since this condition guarantees that $\mathbf{e}$ is the closest vector to $\mathbf{0}$ in $L_q(\mathbf{A})$ which is a *necessary condition* for the algorithm to work unconditionally[5]

- Even though we take short vectors in the dual lattice $L_q(\mathbf{A}_{\text{dual}})$, it looks like only the length of the shortest vectors in $\mathbf{A}$ matters for the analysis! This is just a result of the simplifications that we have made above to give the intuition. The length of the dual vectors does play a role in Lemma 8 and the subsequent lemmas.

---

[5] This condition could be relaxed if we allow the algorithm to fail for a small fraction of $\mathbf{e}$ but this is out of the scope of this article.

4.2 Formal Analysis

This section gives a formal analysis of the intuitions from the previous section. We will reuse the notation defined there. Our first lemma formalizes that g_W, defined in (6) and used in the algorithm to compute the "score" of a guess, is very close to the periodic Gaussian function $f_{L_q(\mathbf{A}_{\text{dual}})}$.

Lemma 6. *Let* $\mathbf{B} \in \mathbb{Z}_q^{m \times n}$, $s, \delta > 0$ *and* $N \in \mathbb{N}$. *With probability at least* $1 - q^m \cdot 2^{-\Omega(N\delta^2)}$ *over the choice of* $W = (\mathbf{w}_1, \ldots, \mathbf{w}_N)$ *from* $D_{L_q^{\perp}(\mathbf{B}), qs}^N$, *we have* $|g_W(\mathbf{x}) - f_{L_q(\mathbf{B}), 1/s}(\mathbf{x})| \leqslant \delta$ *for all* $\mathbf{x} \in \mathbb{Z}^m$, *where* g_W *is defined in* (6) *and* $f_{L_q(\mathbf{B})}$ *is defined in Sect.* 2.2.

Proof. Let $L = L_q(\mathbf{B})$ and for any j, let $\mathbf{w}'_j = \frac{1}{q}\mathbf{w}_j$ and $W' = (\mathbf{w}'_j)_j$. Since $\widehat{L} = \frac{1}{q}L_q^{\perp}(\mathbf{B})$ and $D_{L_q(\mathbf{B}), qs} = D_{q\widehat{L}, qs} = D_{\widehat{L}, s}$, we indeed have that W' is sampled from $D_{\widehat{L}, s}^N$ which is a probability distribution over $\widehat{L}$. Let $h = f_{L, 1/s}$ which is L-periodic, then $\widehat{h} = D_{\widehat{L}, s}$ by Lemma 3. For any $\mathbf{x} \in \mathbb{R}^m$, $g_W(\mathbf{x}) = h_{W'}(\mathbf{x})$ where h_W is defined in Lemma 5. Apply Lemma 5 to h with $X = \{0, \ldots, q-1\}^m$ to get that with probability at least $1 - |X|2^{-\Omega(N\delta^2)}$ over the choice of W', we have $|h(\mathbf{x}) - h_{W'}(\mathbf{x})| \leqslant \delta$ for all $\mathbf{x} \in L + X$. But $L = L_q(\mathbf{B})$ is a q-ary lattice, *i.e.* $q\mathbb{Z}^m \subset L$ so $L + X \supset q\mathbb{Z}^m + \{0, \ldots, q-1\}^m = \mathbb{Z}^m$ which concludes. □

The next lemma formalizes the idea that the periodic Gaussian function f_L estimates the distance of its argument and the lattice L.

Lemma 7. *Let* $L \subset \mathbb{R}^m$ *and* $s > 0$, *then for any* $\mathbf{x} \in \mathbb{R}^m$:

- $f_{L, 1/s}(\mathbf{x}) \geqslant \rho_{1/s}(\text{dist}(\mathbf{x}, L))$,
- *if* $\text{dist}(\mathbf{x}, L) \geqslant \tau := \frac{1}{s}\sqrt{m/2\pi}$ *then* $f_{L, 1/s}(\mathbf{x}) \leqslant \rho_{1/s}(\text{dist}(\mathbf{x}, L) - \tau)$.

Proof. The first fact is a direct consequence of Lemma 1. Indeed, write $\mathbf{x} = \mathbf{z} + \mathbf{t}$ where $\mathbf{z} \in L$ and $\mathbf{t} \in \mathbb{R}^m$ are such that $\text{dist}(\mathbf{x}, L) = \|\mathbf{t}\|$. Since $f_{L, 1/s}$ is L-periodic and $\mathbf{z} \in L$, $f_{L, 1/s}(\mathbf{x}) = f_{L, 1/s}(\mathbf{x} - \mathbf{z}) = f_{L, 1/s}(\mathbf{t}) \geqslant \rho_{1/s}(\mathbf{t}) = \rho_{1/s}(\|\mathbf{t}\|)$. For the second fact, let $\ell = \text{dist}(\mathbf{x}, L)$ and observe that by definition $(L - \mathbf{x}) \setminus B_m(\ell) = L - \mathbf{x}$. By assumption, $\ell \geqslant \tau := \frac{1}{s}\sqrt{m/2\pi}$, so we can apply Corollary 1 to get that $\rho_{1/s}((L - \mathbf{x}) \setminus B_m(\ell)) \leqslant \rho_{1/s}(\ell - \tau)\rho_{1/s}(L)$ and therefore

$$f_{L, 1/s}(\mathbf{x}) = \frac{\rho_{1/s}(L - \mathbf{x})}{\rho_{1/s}(L)} = \frac{\rho_{1/s}((L - \mathbf{x}) \setminus B_m(\ell))}{\rho_{1/s}(L)} \leqslant \rho_{1/s}(\ell - \tau).$$

□

Lemma 8. *Let* $\mathbf{B} \in \mathbb{Z}_q^{m \times n}$, $L \subset \mathbb{Z}^m$ *a lattice*, $\mathbf{e} \in \mathbb{Z}^m$, $s, \delta > 0$ *and* $N \in \mathbb{N}$. *Let* $\tau = \frac{1}{s}\sqrt{m/2\pi}$ *and* $\eta \geqslant 0$ *and assume that* $\lambda_1(L + L_q(\mathbf{B})) \geqslant \tau + \|\mathbf{e}\|$ *and*

$$\rho_{1/s}(\mathbf{e}) - \rho_{1/s}(\lambda_1(L + L_q(\mathbf{B})) - \|\mathbf{e}\| - \tau) > 2\delta + \eta.$$

Then, with probability at least $1 - q^m \cdot 2^{-\Omega(N\delta^2)}$ over the choice of $W = (\mathbf{w}_1, \ldots, \mathbf{w}_N)$ from $D^N_{L^\perp_q(\mathbf{B}), qs}$, we have

$$g_W(\mathbf{e}) \geqslant \rho_{1/s}(\mathbf{e}) - \delta > \rho_{1/s}(\lambda_1(L + L_q(\mathbf{B})) - \|\mathbf{e}\| - \tau) + \delta + \eta \geqslant g_W(\mathbf{e} + \mathbf{x}) + \eta$$

for all $\mathbf{x} \in L \setminus L_q(\mathbf{B})$, where g_W is defined in (6).

Proof. Apply Lemma 6 to get that with probability at least $1 - q^m \cdot 2^{-\Omega(N\delta^2)}$ over the choice of $\mathbf{w}_1, \ldots, \mathbf{w}_N$ i.i.d. from $D_{L^\perp_q(\mathbf{B}), qs}$, we have $|g_W(\mathbf{y}) - f_{L_q(\mathbf{B}), 1/s}(\mathbf{y})| \leqslant \delta$ for all $\mathbf{y} \in \mathbb{Z}^m$. By Lemma 7, we have $g_W(\mathbf{e}) \geqslant f_{L_q(\mathbf{B}), 1/s}(\mathbf{e}) - \delta \geqslant \rho_{1/s}(\mathbf{e}) - \delta$.

Let $\mathbf{x} \in L \setminus L_q(\mathbf{B})$, then $\mathbf{z} - \mathbf{x} \in L + L_q(\mathbf{B})$ and $\mathbf{z} - \mathbf{x} \neq \mathbf{0}$ for any $\mathbf{z} \in L_q(\mathbf{B})$. As a result, $L_q(\mathbf{B}) - \mathbf{x} \subseteq (L + L_q(\mathbf{B})) \setminus \{\mathbf{0}\}$. Hence,

$$\text{dist}(\mathbf{x}, L_q(\mathbf{B})) = \min_{\mathbf{z} \in L_q(\mathbf{B})} \|\mathbf{x} + \mathbf{z}\| \geqslant \min_{\mathbf{y} \in (L + L_q(\mathbf{B})) \setminus \{\mathbf{0}\}} \|\mathbf{y}\| = \lambda_1(L + L_q(\mathbf{B})) \geqslant \tau + \|\mathbf{e}\|. \tag{10}$$

But then

$$\text{dist}(\mathbf{e} + \mathbf{x}, L_q(\mathbf{B})) \geqslant \text{dist}(\mathbf{x}, L_q(\mathbf{B})) - \|\mathbf{e}\| \geqslant \tau. \tag{11}$$

We can therefore apply Lemma 7 to get that for any $\mathbf{x} \in L \setminus \{\mathbf{0}\}$,

$$g_W(\mathbf{e} + \mathbf{x}) \leqslant f_{L_q(\mathbf{B}), 1/s}(\mathbf{e} + \mathbf{x}) + \delta \leqslant \rho_{1/s}(\text{dist}(\mathbf{e} + \mathbf{x}, L_q(\mathbf{B})) - \tau) + \delta.$$

Since $\rho_{1/s} : [0, \infty) \to \mathbb{R}$ is decreasing, and reusing (10) and (11) we further have

$$\rho_{1/s}(\text{dist}(\mathbf{e} + \mathbf{x}, L_q(\mathbf{B})) - \tau) \leqslant \rho_{1/s}(\text{dist}(\mathbf{x}, L_q(\mathbf{B})) - \|\mathbf{e}\| - \tau)$$
$$\leqslant \rho_{1/s}(\lambda_1(L + L_q(\mathbf{B})) - \|\mathbf{e}\| - \tau).$$

Putting everything together, and using our assumption, we have

$$g_W(\mathbf{e}) - g_W(\mathbf{e} + \mathbf{x}) \geqslant \rho_{1/s}(\mathbf{e}) - \rho_{1/s}(\lambda_1(L + L_q(\mathbf{B})) - \|\mathbf{e}\| - \tau) - 2\delta > \eta$$

$\square$

We can now state our main result by putting everything together. It will be useful to note that $L_q(\mathbf{A}_{\text{guess}}) + L_q(\mathbf{A}_{\text{dual}}) = L_q(\mathbf{A})$ which is readily verified.

Algorithm 2: Modern dual attack

Input: m, $n = n_{\text{guess}} + n_{\text{dual}}$ (see (1)), q prime power, $N \in \mathbb{N}$
Input: LWE sample $(\mathbf{A}, \mathbf{b})$, list $W = (\mathbf{w}_1, \ldots, \mathbf{w}_N)$ of vectors in
    $L^\perp_q(\mathbf{A}_{\text{dual}})$.
Output: (Guess of) the first n_{guess} coordinates of the secret, or $\perp$.

1   $\mathbf{s}_{\text{guess}} \leftarrow \perp$; $S_{\max} \leftarrow 0$;
2   **for** $\tilde{\mathbf{s}}_{\text{guess}} \in \mathbb{Z}_q^{n_{\text{guess}}}$ **do**
3   Compute the list $y_1, \ldots, y_N$ where $y_j = \mathbf{w}_j^T(\mathbf{b} - \mathbf{A}_{\text{guess}}\tilde{\mathbf{s}}_{\text{guess}})$;
4      $S \leftarrow \sum_{j=1}^N \cos(2\pi y_j/q)$;
5   **if** $S \geqslant S_{\max}$ **then** $S_{\max} \leftarrow S$; $\mathbf{s}_{\text{guess}} \leftarrow \tilde{\mathbf{s}}_{\text{guess}}$;
6   **return** $\mathbf{s}_{\text{guess}}$

Theorem 5. *Let* $\mathbf{A} \in \mathbb{Z}_q^{m \times n}$, $\mathbf{e} \in \mathbb{Z}^m$, $\mathbf{s} \in \mathbb{Z}_q^n$, $s, \delta > 0$ *and* $N \in \mathbb{N}$. *Let* $\tau = \frac{1}{s}\sqrt{m/2\pi}$. *Assume that* $m \geqslant n$, $\mathbf{A}$ *has full rank,* $\lambda_1(L_q(\mathbf{A})) \geqslant \tau + \|\mathbf{e}\|$, *and*

$$\rho_{1/s}(\mathbf{e}) - \rho_{1/s}(\lambda_1(L_q(\mathbf{A})) - \|\mathbf{e}\| - \tau) > 2\delta.$$

Let $\mathbf{b} = \mathbf{As} + \mathbf{e} \bmod q$. *Let* $W = (\mathbf{w}_1, \ldots, \mathbf{w}_N)$ *be samples from* $D^N_{L_q^\perp(\mathbf{A}_{\mathrm{dual}}), qs}$, *then Algorithm 2 on* $(m, n_{\mathrm{guess}}, n_{\mathrm{dual}}, q, N, (\mathbf{A}, \mathbf{b}), W)$ *runs in time* $\mathrm{poly}(m, n) \cdot (N + q^{n_{\mathrm{guess}}})$ *and returns* $\mathbf{s}_{\mathrm{guess}}$ *with probability at least* $1 - q^m \cdot 2^{-\Omega(N\delta^2)}$ *over the choice of* W.

Proof. Let $\mathbf{B} = \mathbf{A}_{\mathrm{dual}}$ and $L = L_q(\mathbf{A}_{\mathrm{guess}})$. Then $L + L_q(\mathbf{B}) = L_q(\mathbf{A})$. Our assumptions are therefore exactly that of Lemma 8 for $\eta = 0$ which we can apply to get that with probability at least $1 - q^m \cdot 2^{-\Omega(N\delta^2)}$ over the choice of $W = (\mathbf{w}_1, \ldots, \mathbf{w}_N)$ from $D^N_{L_q^\perp(\mathbf{B}), qs} = D^N_{L_q^\perp(\mathbf{A}_{\mathrm{dual}}), qs}$, we have

$$g_W(\mathbf{e}) > g_W(\mathbf{e} + \mathbf{x}) \tag{12}$$

for all $\mathbf{x} \in L \setminus L_q(\mathbf{A}_{\mathrm{dual}})$, where g_W is defined in (6). Furthermore, $\mathbf{A}$ has full rank and $m \geqslant n$ so its columns are linearly independent over $\mathbb{Z}_q$ and

$$L \setminus L_q(\mathbf{A}_{\mathrm{dual}}) = L_q(\mathbf{A}_{\mathrm{guess}}) \setminus L_q(\mathbf{A}_{\mathrm{dual}}) = L_q(\mathbf{A}_{\mathrm{guess}}) \setminus q\mathbb{Z}^m. \tag{13}$$

Assume that we are in the case where W satisfies the above inequalities and consider the run of Algorithm 2 on $(m, n_{\mathrm{guess}}, n_{\mathrm{dual}}, q, N, (\mathbf{A}, \mathbf{b}), W)$. The algorithm tests all possible values of $\tilde{\mathbf{s}}_{\mathrm{guess}} \in \mathbb{Z}_q^{n_{\mathrm{guess}}}$ and returns the one that maximizes S. Let $\tilde{\mathbf{s}}_{\mathrm{guess}} \in \mathbb{Z}_q^{n_{\mathrm{guess}}}$ and $\Delta\tilde{\mathbf{s}}_{\mathrm{guess}} = \mathbf{s}_{\mathrm{guess}} - \tilde{\mathbf{s}}_{\mathrm{guess}}$. First note that

$$\mathbf{b} - \mathbf{A}_{\mathrm{guess}}\tilde{\mathbf{s}}_{\mathrm{guess}} = (\mathbf{As} + \mathbf{e} \bmod q) - \mathbf{A}_{\mathrm{guess}}\tilde{\mathbf{s}}_{\mathrm{guess}}$$
$$= \mathbf{A}_{\mathrm{dual}}\mathbf{s}_{\mathrm{dual}} + \mathbf{A}_{\mathrm{guess}}\Delta\tilde{\mathbf{s}}_{\mathrm{guess}} + \mathbf{e} \bmod q.$$

For any j, let $y_j(\tilde{\mathbf{s}}_{\mathrm{guess}})$ be the value computed at Line 3. Note that

$$y_j(\tilde{\mathbf{s}}_{\mathrm{guess}}) = \mathbf{w}_j^T(\mathbf{b} - \mathbf{A}_{\mathrm{guess}}\tilde{\mathbf{s}}_{\mathrm{guess}})$$
$$= \mathbf{w}_j^T\mathbf{A}_{\mathrm{dual}}\mathbf{s}_{\mathrm{dual}} + \mathbf{w}_j^T(\mathbf{A}_{\mathrm{guess}}\Delta\tilde{\mathbf{s}}_{\mathrm{guess}} + \mathbf{e}) \bmod q$$

but $\mathbf{w}_j \in L_q^\perp(\mathbf{A}_{\mathrm{dual}})$ so $\mathbf{w}_j^T\mathbf{A}_{\mathrm{dual}} = \mathbf{0} \bmod q$, hence

$$= \mathbf{w}_j^T(\mathbf{A}_{\mathrm{guess}}\Delta\tilde{\mathbf{s}}_{\mathrm{guess}} + \mathbf{e}) \bmod q.$$

Let $S(\tilde{\mathbf{s}}_{\mathrm{guess}})$ be the value computed at Line 4 and check that

$$S(\tilde{\mathbf{s}}_{\mathrm{guess}}) = \sum_{j=1}^N \cos(2\pi y_j(\tilde{\mathbf{s}}_{\mathrm{guess}})/q)$$
$$= \sum_{j=1}^N \cos(2\pi \mathbf{w}_j^T(\mathbf{A}_{\mathrm{guess}}\Delta\tilde{\mathbf{s}}_{\mathrm{guess}} + \mathbf{e})/q) \qquad \text{by periodicity of } \cos$$
$$= N g_W(\mathbf{A}_{\mathrm{guess}}\Delta\tilde{\mathbf{s}}_{\mathrm{guess}} + \mathbf{e}).$$

There are two cases to distinguish:

- If $\tilde{\mathbf{s}}_{\text{guess}} = \mathbf{s}_{\text{guess}}$ then $S(\tilde{\mathbf{s}}_{\text{guess}}) = Ng_W(\mathbf{e})$.
- If $\tilde{\mathbf{s}}_{\text{guess}} \neq \mathbf{s}_{\text{guess}}$ then $S(\tilde{\mathbf{s}}_{\text{guess}}) = Ng_W(\mathbf{e} + \mathbf{x})$ where $\mathbf{x} = \mathbf{A}_{\text{guess}}\Delta\tilde{\mathbf{s}}_{\text{guess}} \in L_q(\mathbf{A}_{\text{guess}}) = L$. But $\mathbf{A}$ (and hence $\mathbf{A}_{\text{guess}}$) has full rank by assumption and $\Delta\tilde{\mathbf{s}}_{\text{guess}} \neq \mathbf{0}$ so $\mathbf{x} \neq \mathbf{0} \bmod q$. It follows by (13), $\mathbf{x} \in L_q(\mathbf{A}_{\text{dual}}) \setminus q\mathbb{Z}^m = L \setminus L_q(\mathbf{A}_{\text{dual}})$. Hence, by (12), $S(\tilde{\mathbf{s}}_{\text{guess}}) < Ng_W(\mathbf{e}) = S(\mathbf{s}_{\text{guess}})$.

This shows that $S(\mathbf{s}_{\text{guess}}) > S(\tilde{\mathbf{s}}_{\text{guess}})$ for all $\tilde{\mathbf{s}}_{\text{guess}} \neq \mathbf{s}_{\text{guess}}$. Therefore, Algorithm 2 correctly returns $\mathbf{s}_{\text{guess}}$. Note that the entire argument was under the assumption that (12) holds for W, which we already argued holds with probability at least $1 - q^m \cdot 2^{-\Omega(N\delta^2)}$.

The naive analysis of the complexity is straightforward and gives $q^{n_{\text{guess}}} \cdot \text{poly}(m, n) \cdot N$. By using the DFT trick as we did in the proof of Theorem 4 we can improve the running time to $\text{poly}(m, n) \cdot (N + q^{n_{\text{guess}}})$.

4.3 Informal Application

Choosing the parameters in order to apply Theorem 5 is not immediately obvious. In this section, we explain how to do so in a concrete case of interest. In order to simplify things, we will neglect some factors and point out the various lemmas that can be used to make this reasoning completely formal.

Fix n, m and let q be a prime power. Let $\mathbf{s} \in \mathbb{Z}_q^n$ be a secret and $\sigma_e > 0$. Let $(\mathbf{A}, \mathbf{b})$ be sampled from $\text{LWE}(m, \mathbf{s}, D_{\mathbb{Z}_q, \sigma_e})$, and $\mathbf{e}$ so that $\mathbf{b} = \mathbf{As} + \mathbf{e}$. By Corollary 1, we have

$$\|\mathbf{e}\| \lesssim \sigma_e \sqrt{m/2\pi} \tag{14}$$

with high probability. Let $s > 0$ to be defined later. We choose δ to be quite smaller than the smallest possible value $\rho_{1/s}(\|\mathbf{e}\|)$, for example

$$\delta = \tfrac{1}{100}\rho_{1/s}(\sigma_e\sqrt{m/2\pi}) = \tfrac{1}{100}e^{-ms^2\sigma_e^2/2}. \tag{15}$$

We choose N accordingly so that the success probability is very high, *i.e.*

$$N = \frac{\text{poly}(m) + n\log_2(q)}{\delta^2}. \tag{16}$$

$\mathbf{A}$ has full rank with high probability and therefore $\det(L_q(\mathbf{A})) = q^{m-n}$. By Theorem 3, and the informal Corollary 2, we have

$$\lambda_1(L_q(\mathbf{A})) \gtrsim GH(L_q(\mathbf{A})) = \text{vol}(B_m)^{-1/n}q^{1-m/n} \approx \sqrt{\frac{m}{2\pi e}}q^{1-n/m}.$$

Let $\tau = \tfrac{1}{s}\sqrt{m/2\pi}$. In order to apply Theorem 5, we need to satisfy the conditions

$$\lambda_1(L_q(\mathbf{A})) \geq \tau + \|\mathbf{e}\| \quad \text{and} \quad \rho_{1/s}(\mathbf{e}) - \rho_{1/s}(\lambda_1(L_q(\mathbf{A})) - \|\mathbf{e}\| - \tau) > 2\delta.$$

Since we have chosen δ to be very small compared to $\rho_{1/s}(\mathbf{e})$, those inequalities can be shown (see [39, Appendix D]) to be essentially equivalent to

$$\lambda_1(L_q(\mathbf{A})) \geq \tau + 2\|\mathbf{e}\|.$$

This condition will be satisfied when $\sqrt{\frac{m}{2\pi e}}q^{1-n/m} \geqslant \frac{1}{s}\sqrt{m/2\pi} + 2\sigma_e\sqrt{m/2\pi}$ that is

$$q^{1-n/m} \geqslant (\tfrac{1}{s} + 2\sigma_e)\sqrt{e}. \tag{17}$$

In other words, we have a lower bound on s. We observe that there is a trade-off between the cost of sampling from $D_{L_q^\perp(\mathbf{A}_{\mathrm{dual}}),qs}$ and the cost of running Algorithm 2 since a large value of s:

- makes it easy to sample from $D_{L_q^\perp(\mathbf{A}_{\mathrm{dual}}),qs}$,
- but makes $\delta = \frac{1}{100}\rho_{1/s}(\sigma_e\sqrt{m/2\pi})$ small and therefore $N = \Omega(\delta^{-2})$, and the complexity, gigantic.

We note that the total complexity of the attack, including the cost of generating the small dual vectors, is a highly nontrivial function of the parameters. Consequently, it is not at all clear that the optimal choice of s is the lower bound identified above. We will analyze the complexity in greater detail in the next section.

4.4   Complexity Estimates

In this section, we describe how to concretely estimate the complexity of the attack described in Sect. 4 and provide numbers for Kyber. We continue with the setup from the previous section (Sect. 4.3) which we do not repeat. Recall that by Theorem 5, the complexity of the attack, to which we add the cost $T_{\mathrm{sampling}}(N, qs)$ of sampling N independent Gaussian vectors according to $D_{L_q^\perp(\mathbf{A}_{\mathrm{dual}}),qs}$ is

$$\mathsf{poly}(m, n) \cdot (N + q^{n_{\mathrm{guess}}}) + T_{\mathrm{sampling}}(N, qs) \tag{18}$$

and it succeeds with very high probabability given the choice of the parameters above. For the sampling of the dual vectors, we propose the following approach: given a block size $2 \leqslant \beta \leqslant m$,

1. compute a basis of $L_q^\perp(\mathbf{A}_{\mathrm{dual}})$,
2. run BKZ with block size β on this basis to obtain a reduced basis $\mathbf{B}$,
3. use the Markov chain Monte Carlo (MCMC) based Gaussian sampler from [46] (Theorem 1) for parameter qs with basis $\mathbf{B}$ to generate N independent samples.

The complexity of this procedure is

$$T_{\mathrm{sampling}}(N) = T_{\mathrm{BKZ}}(m, \beta) + N \cdot T_{\mathrm{MCMC}}(L_q^\perp(\mathbf{A}_{\mathrm{dual}}), qs) \tag{19}$$

where $T_{\mathrm{BKZ}}(m, \beta)$ is the cost of BKZ and $T_{\mathrm{MCMC}}(L, s)$ is the cost of producing one sample from $D_{L,s}$. We apply Theorem 1 to get that

$$T_{\mathrm{MCMC}}(L_q^\perp(\mathbf{A}_{\mathrm{dual}}), qs) = \ln\left(\tfrac{1}{\varepsilon}\right) \cdot \tfrac{1}{\Delta} \cdot \mathsf{poly}(n), \qquad \Delta = \frac{\rho_{qs}(L_q^\perp(\mathbf{A}_{\mathrm{dual}}))}{\prod_{i=1}^n \rho_{qs/\|\tilde{\mathbf{b}}_i\|}(\mathbb{Z})} \tag{20}$$

where $\widetilde{\mathbf{b}}_1, \ldots, \widetilde{\mathbf{b}}_n$ are the Gram-Schmidt vectors of the BKZ-β-reduced basis $\mathbf{B}$ of $L_q^\perp(\mathbf{A}_{\text{dual}})$ and $\varepsilon > 0$. Note that the output distribution of the algorithm is ε-close to the discrete Gaussian. Since we are going to use N samples, and by the data processing inequality, this translates into a failure probability of $N\varepsilon$ for the algorithm, so we need to choose ε to be quite small, e.g. $\varepsilon \ll 1/N$. Putting (18) and (19) together we get that the total complexity of the attack is

$$\text{poly}(m,n) \cdot (N + q^{n_{\text{guess}}}) + T_{\text{BKZ}}(m,\beta) + N \cdot T_{\text{MCMC}}(L_q^\perp(\mathbf{A}_{\text{dual}}), qs) \quad (21)$$

subject to the constraints (14), (15), (16), (17) which we summarize below:

$$\delta = \tfrac{1}{100} e^{-ms^2 \sigma_e^2 / 2}, \qquad N = \frac{\text{poly}(m) + n \log_2(q)}{\delta^2},$$

$$q^{1-n/m} \geqslant (\tfrac{1}{s} + 2\sigma_e)\sqrt{e}, \qquad \|\mathbf{e}\| \lesssim \sigma_e \sqrt{m/2\pi},$$

$$\varepsilon \ll 1/N.$$

In practice, computing Δ with (20) is nontrivial. One can show that (see [39, Appendix E])

$$\frac{1}{\Delta} \leqslant \prod_{i=1}^m \rho_{\|\widetilde{\mathbf{b}}_i\|/qs}(\mathbb{Z}) \quad (22)$$

which is easier to estimate but still requires to estimate the $\left\|\widetilde{\mathbf{b}}_i\right\|$. For this, we can assume that the Geometric Series Assumption (GSA) [42] holds for BKZ-β reduced basis. The GSA is known to be reasonably accurate when $\beta \ll m$ and $\beta \gg 50$ which is the case in our experiments, but it does not correctly model what happens in the last $m - \beta$ coordinates [1]. For our purpose, we consider the GSA to be enough to obtain credible estimates on the complexity.

Independently of the GSA, however, formula (22) is expensive to compute due the product of m terms. Indeed, we will need to compute this quantity many times in our optimizer to find a good set of parameters (see below). For the estimates below, we use (22) and the GSA to compute the final complexity estimate but we use the approximate formula below in the parameter optimizer which is very cheap to compute:

$$\text{if} \quad \|\mathbf{b}_1\| \leqslant 2qs \quad \text{then} \quad \frac{1}{\Delta} \lesssim \exp\left(\log\left(1 + 2e^{-\pi\alpha}\right) + \frac{2}{\ln(H_\beta^4)} E_1(\pi\alpha)\right) \quad (23)$$

where $\alpha = (qs)^2/\|\mathbf{b}_1\|^2$, E_1 is the generalized exponential integral and H_β is the Hermite factor for BKZ-β reduced basis. See [39, Appendix E] for more details.

In order to find a good set of parameters, we wrote an optimizer that tries all reasonable values of m, β and n_{guess}, and sets s to

$$s = \max\left(\frac{\sqrt{e}}{q^{1-n/m} - 2\sqrt{e}\sigma_e}, \frac{\|\mathbf{b}_1\|}{2q}\right)$$

so that we can use (23). We also limit the range of m to $[\tfrac{3}{2}n, 2n]$ so that the ratio m/n is not too close to 0 and 1.

In Table 1, we give the complexity estimates of our algorithm, computed by our optimizer. The first set of columns corresponds to the algorithm analyzed above, including the use of the GSA to estimate the complexity of the Gaussian sampling as described in [39, Appendix E]. To estimate the complexity of BKZ, we use the cost estimates in [8, 32] using [13] as the sieving oracle; specifically, we rely on the "lattice estimator" of [9].

Those cost are not competitive with the state of the art because our algorithm does not include modulus switching. Modulus switching is a critical component to reduce the complexity but its formal analysis is nontrivial and therefore we decided not to include it in this paper. In order to get an idea of what our algorithm extended with modulus switching would give, we include a second set of columns where we simply replace $q^{n_{\text{guess}}}$ by $2^{n_{\text{guess}}}$ in (21) which would correspond to switching the modulus to 2 in the guessing part. We emphasize that this is only a very rough estimate and not a formal analysis. The real complexity with modulus switching will most likely be higher than what we report. Furthermore, all our complexity estimates ignore the polynomial factors.

Table 1. Dual attack cost estimates and their parameters as described in Sect. 4.4. All costs are logarithms in base two. Note that the cost of attacks with modulus switching are estimates of what an algorithm with modulus switching could give if the algorithm of Sect. 4 was extended with modulus switching.

Scheme	No modulus switching						With modulus switching					
	attack	m	n_{guess}	n_{dual}	β	s	attack	m	n_{guess}	n_{dual}	β	s
Kyber512	185	1013	15	497	550	0.200	141	763	141	371	390	0.170
Kyber768	273	1469	23	745	870	0.260	202	1169	201	567	610	0.240
Kyber1024	376	2025	31	993	1230	0.270	279	1575	261	763	890	0.260

5 Quantum Dual Attack

In this section, we present a quantum version of Algorithm 2 and show that we can obtain a speed-up on the complexity. The technique is inspired by [10] which was never published and is a quantum variant of [32].

5.1 Algorithm and Analysis

We will need a quantum algorithm which estimates the mean value of $\cos(2\pi(\langle \mathbf{w}_i, \mathbf{b} \rangle)/q)$ where the $\mathbf{w}_i$ are vectors accessible via a quantum oracle. This mean value can be used to compute the DFT sums in the algorithm much faster than with a classical computer. The idea is inspired by [2, Theorem 47] and can be seen as a special case of quantum speedup of Monte Carlo methods [37]. For more background on quantum algorithms, we refer the readers to [10, Sections 2.4 and 4].

Theorem 6 ([10, **Theorem 5**]). *Let N be a positive integer and W be a list of N vectors in $\mathbb{Z}^n$: $\mathbf{w}_0, \ldots, \mathbf{w}_{N-1}$. Let $f_W(\mathbf{b}) = \frac{1}{N} \sum_{i=0}^{N-1} \cos(2\pi(\langle \mathbf{w}_i, \mathbf{b} \rangle)/q)$, where $\mathbf{b} \in \mathbb{Z}_q^n$. Let $\mathcal{O}_W$ be defined by $\mathcal{O}_W : |j\rangle|0\rangle \mapsto |j\rangle|\mathbf{w}_j\rangle$. For any $\epsilon, \delta > 0$, there exists a quantum algorithm $\mathcal{A}$ that given $\mathbf{b} \in \mathbb{Z}_q^n$ and oracle access to $\mathcal{O}_W$ outputs $\mathcal{A}^{\mathcal{O}_W}(\mathbf{b})$ which satisfies $|\mathcal{A}^{\mathcal{O}_W}(\mathbf{b}) - f_W(\mathbf{b})| \le \epsilon$ with probability $1 - \delta$. The algorithm makes $\mathcal{O}(\epsilon^{-1} \cdot \log \frac{1}{\delta})$ queries to $\mathcal{O}_W$, and requires $O(\log(\frac{1}{\epsilon}) + \mathrm{poly}(\log(n)))$ qubits.*

We will have to search for a minimum element in a collection but the oracle that computes the value of each element is probabilistic and may return a wrong result with small probability. We say that a (probabilistic) real function f has bounded error if there exists $x \in \mathbb{R}$ such that $f()$ returns x with probability at least $9/10$. The problem of finding the minimum in a collection (without errors) has been studied in [21, Theorem 1]. On the other hand, the problem of searching for a marked element in a collection with bounded-error oracle has been studied in [26]. This idea can easily be used to adapt the algorithm of [21] to bounded-error oracles. Indeed, the algorithm in [21] simply performs a constant number of Grover searches by marking nodes that are bigger than the current value. Therefore it suffices to replace this Grover search by the algorithm of [26].

Theorem 7 ([26]+[21]). *Given n algorithms, quantum or classical, each computing some real value with bounded error probability, there is a quantum algorithm that makes an expected $O(\sqrt{n})$ queries and with probability at least $9/10$ returns the index of the minimum among the n values. This algorithm uses $\mathrm{poly}(\log(n))$ qubits.*

Algorithm 3: Quantum modern dual attack

    Input: m, $n = n_{\text{guess}} + n_{\text{dual}}$ (see (1)), q prime power, $N \in \mathbb{N}$, $\eta > 0$.
    Input: LWE sample $(\mathbf{A}, \mathbf{b})$.
    Input: Oracle $\mathcal{O}_W$ for a list $W = (\mathbf{w}_1, \ldots, \mathbf{w}_N)$ of vectors in $L_q^{\perp}(\mathbf{A}_{\text{dual}})$.
    Output: (Guess of) the first n_{guess} coordinates of the secret, or $\perp$.
1 Use Theorem 6 to create an algorithm $\mathcal{A}$ with $\delta = \frac{1}{10}$, $\varepsilon = \eta$ and q ;
2 **create oracle** $\hat{\mathcal{O}}(\tilde{\mathbf{s}}_{\text{guess}})$:
3 | **return** $\mathcal{A}^{\mathcal{O}_W}(\mathbf{b} - \mathbf{A}_{\text{guess}} \tilde{\mathbf{s}}_{\text{guess}})$
4 Use Theorem 7 to find $\tilde{\mathbf{s}}_{\text{guess}}$ such that $\hat{\mathcal{O}}(\tilde{\mathbf{s}}_{\text{guess}})$ is maximum ;
5 **return** $\tilde{\mathbf{s}}_{\text{guess}}$

Theorem 8 ([39, **Appendix F.1**]). *Let $\mathbf{A} \in \mathbb{Z}_q^{m \times n}$, $\mathbf{e} \in \mathbb{Z}^m$, $\mathbf{s} \in \mathbb{Z}_q^n$, $s, \delta > 0$ and $N \in \mathbb{N}$. Let $\tau = \frac{1}{s}\sqrt{m/2\pi}$ and $\eta > 0$. Assume that $m \geqslant n$, $\mathbf{A}$ has full rank, $\lambda_1(L_q(\mathbf{A})) \geqslant \tau + \|\mathbf{e}\|$, and*

$$\rho_{1/s}(\mathbf{e}) - \rho_{1/s}(\lambda_1(L_q(\mathbf{A})) - \|\mathbf{e}\| - \tau) > 2\delta + \eta.$$

Let $\mathbf{b} = \mathbf{As} + \mathbf{e} \bmod q$. Let $W = (\mathbf{w}_1, \ldots, \mathbf{w}_N)$ be samples from $D^N_{L^\perp_q(\mathbf{A}_{\mathrm{dual}}),qs}$ and $\mathcal{O}_W$ an oracle for W in the sense of Theorem 6. Then Algorithm 3 on $m, n_{\mathrm{guess}}, n_{\mathrm{dual}}, q, N, \eta/2, (\mathbf{A}, \mathbf{b}), \mathcal{O}_W$ makes an expected $O\left(\eta^{-1} \cdot q^{n_{\mathrm{guess}}/2}\right)$ calls to $\mathcal{O}_W$ and returns $\mathbf{s}_{\mathrm{guess}}$ with probability at least $1 - q^m \cdot 2^{-\Omega(N\delta^2)}$ over the choice of W. The algorithm uses $O(\log(\eta^{-1}) + \mathsf{poly}(\log(N)))$ qubits.

In terms of proofs, the correctness of the quantum algorithm is very similar to the classical one. The main difference is that we use Theorem 6 to compute g_W which only returns an approximation. This adds an additional error term that we can take into account in Lemma 8 using η.

5.2 Applications

In order to apply Theorem 8, one needs to provide an oracle $\mathcal{O}_W$ to access the samples. The implementation of this oracle has a significant impact on the complexity since it is queried an exponential number of times by the algorithm. We outline two possible implementations. Before that, note that in practice we will usually choose η to be a small value compared to δ in Theorem 8, say $\eta = \delta/100$. This way, η has almost no influence on the maximum length of the errors $\mathbf{e}$ that we can handle.

BKZ Preprocessing with a Quantum Klein Sampler. For a value of s that is not too small, one can first compute a basis $L^\perp_q(\mathbf{A}_{\mathrm{dual}})$ of the dual lattice and reduce it using BKZ with block size β to obtain a new basis $\mathbf{M}$. One then creates a quantum circuit that implements the Klein sampler [24] with $\mathbf{M}$ hard-coded in the circuit. This circuit will be the oracle $\mathcal{O}_W$. In the details, the Klein sampler is a probabilistic algorithm so we can view it as a deterministic algorithm that takes random coins (and $\mathbf{M}$) as input. We can see the input j of the oracle as the value of the random coins so that the outputs $\mathbf{w}_1, \ldots, \mathbf{w}_N$ that correspond to inputs $1, \ldots, N$ are distributed according to the Gaussian distribution. Since the Klein sampler runs in polynomial time, each call to $\mathcal{O}_W$ takes polynomial time. The BKZ preprocessing is purely classical and done only once before the quantum algorithm runs. This means that the total runtime will be[6], per Theorem 8

$$T_{\mathrm{BKZ}}(\beta) + \sqrt{N} \cdot q^{n_{\mathrm{guess}}/2} \cdot \mathsf{poly}(\log(m)).$$

This is always better than the classical complexity since $\sqrt{N \cdot q^{n_{\mathrm{guess}}}} \leqslant N + q^{n_{\mathrm{guess}}}$. Note that when using a Klein sampler, the value of s is a function of the quality of the basis $\mathbf{M}$ and therefore depends on β. Furthermore, it is impossible for s to be smaller than the smoothing parameter of the lattice this way. Alternatively, one could also use the MCMC sampler that we used in Sect. 4.4: although its running time is not polynomial, it only uses polynomial memory so it would still only require a polynomial number of qubits, and it allows one to

---

[6] We chose $\eta = \delta/100$ and we explained in Sect. 4.3 that we need to choose $N = 1/\delta^2$ up to polynomial factors so $\eta^{-1} = \mathsf{poly}(\log(m)) \cdot \sqrt{N}$.

choose smaller values of s which seems to be quite beneficial. Note that in both cases (Klein and MCMC), we get no quantum speed up on the sampling.

Classical Sampler with a Quantum Memory. A feature of the Klein sampler is that it can output an arbitrary number of samples and the running time is proportional to the number of samples. This is not the case of all samplers. For example, [4] describes Gaussian samplers that works for smaller values of s than the smoothing parameter and produces $2^{n/2}$ samples but runs in time 2^n, even if we only require one sample. [3] contains another such algorithm with a time-space trade-off. Using such samplers with our quantum algorithm is problematic because the samples are produced and stored in a classical memory, but the algorithm requires quantum oracle access to those samples. We have two options:

- We can assume that we have access to a QRACM (classical memory with quantum random access) [29]. A QRACM of size N is a special quantum memory holding N classical values but providing $O(\log(N))$-time quantum access to those values. Such a QRACM directly implements the oracle $\mathcal{O}_W$ so the total execution time becomes

$$T_{\text{sampler}} + \sqrt{N} \cdot q^{n_{\text{guess}}/2} \cdot \log(N) \cdot \text{poly}\left(\log(m)\right).$$

  We note however that practical realizability of QRACM is debated and is potentially a strong assumption. We refer the readers to [27] for more details.
- We can replace $\mathcal{A}$ in the algorithm by a very large circuit containing all N hard-coded samples that computes the sum g_W in a naive way (without Theorem 6). This circuit will take time $N\text{poly}\left(\log(m)\right)$ to evaluate, therefore the total complexity will be

$$T_{\text{sampler}} + N \cdot q^{n_{\text{guess}}/2} \cdot \text{poly}\left(\log(m)\right).$$

  Note that this might be worse than the classical algorithm if the value of N is larger than $q^{n_{\text{guess}}/2}$.

Finally, we note that presently samplers such as [3] are still too expensive to be useful in dual attacks but future samplers might get more efficient.

6   Comparison with [20]'s Contradictory Regime

In [20], the authors claim that [32] falls into what they call the "contradictory regime" and conclude that the result is most likely incorrect. They similarly conclude the recent derivative works [10,16], as well as [25] are flawed. They do so by reconstructing the key heuristic claim of [32] and showing, both by theoretical arguments and experiments, that this heuristic is incorrect. We copy this heuristic below, slightly adjusted to our notations. In the heuristic, the function f_W is the same as h_W in Lemma 5, which is the same as g_W defined in (6) up to a factor $1/q$ in the cosine.

Heuristic 1 ([20, Heuristic Claim 3]). *Let $\Lambda \subseteq \mathbb{R}^n$ be a random lattice of determinant 1, $\mathcal{W} \subseteq \hat{\Lambda}$ be the set consisting of the $N = (4/3)^{n/2}$ shortest vectors of $\hat{\Lambda}$. For some $\sigma > 0$ and $T \geqslant 1$, consider $\mathbf{t}_{BDD} \leftarrow_\$ \mathcal{N}(0, \sigma^2)^n$ and i.i.d $\mathbf{t}_{unif}^{(i)} \leftarrow_\$ \mathcal{U}(\mathbb{R}^n / \Lambda)$ where $i \in \{1, \ldots, T\}$. Let[7] $\ell = \sqrt{4/3} \cdot \mathrm{GH}(n)$, $\varepsilon = \exp(-2\pi^2\sigma^2\ell^2)$. If $\ln T \leqslant N\varepsilon^2$,*

$$\Pr\left[f_{\mathcal{W}}(\mathbf{t}_{BDD}) > f_{\mathcal{W}}(\mathbf{t}_{unif}^{(i)}) \text{ for all } i \in \{1, \ldots, T\}\right] \geqslant 1 - O\left(\frac{1}{\sqrt{\ln T}}\right)$$

where $\mathcal{N}(0, \sigma^2)$ denotes the normal distribution.

There are several obvious (minor) problems about this heuristic since [32] works with integer lattices and discrete Gaussians. As a first step, we rewrite this heuristic in a way that is closer to [32] and we also change the notations to ours (see [39, Appendix G.1] for details about the rewrite).

Heuristic 2 ([20, Heuristic Claim 3] adapted). *Let $\mathbf{A} \in \mathbb{Z}_q^{m \times n}$ with i.i.d. coefficients. Let $L = L_q(\mathbf{A}) \subseteq \mathbb{Z}^m$ and $W \subseteq L_q^\perp(\mathbf{A})$ be the set consisting of the $N = (4/3)^{d/2}$ shortest vectors of $L_q^\perp(\mathbf{A})$. For some $\sigma_e > 0$ and $T \geqslant 1$, consider $\mathbf{e} \leftarrow_\$ D_{\mathbb{Z}_q, \sigma_e}^n$ and i.i.d $\mathbf{t}_{unif}^{(i)} \leftarrow_\$ \mathcal{U}(\mathbb{Z}^m / L)$ where $i \in \{1, \ldots, T\}$. Let $\ell = \sqrt{4/3} \cdot \mathrm{GH}(L)$, $\varepsilon = \exp(-\pi\sigma_e^2\ell^2)$. If $\ln T \leqslant N\varepsilon^2$,*

$$\Pr\left[g_W(\mathbf{e}) > g_W(\mathbf{t}_{unif}^{(i)}) \text{ for all } i \in \{1, \ldots, T\}\right] \geqslant 1 - O\left(\frac{1}{\sqrt{\ln T}}\right).$$

In [20, Section 4.2 and 4.3], the authors argue by theoretical arguments that Heuristic 1 does not hold. Although [20] did not define what they mean by "random lattice" in the heuristic, they in fact use random q-ary lattices in their experiments and also the theoretical properties of "random lattices" that they use hold for q-ary lattices. Therefore, their analysis holds also for Heuristic 2.

Their reasoning is as follows: assume that we have a large number of random candidates (the $\mathbf{t}_{unif}^{(i)}$) and one point close to the lattice L (the point $\mathbf{e}$), then Heuristic 2 says that we can always distinguish $\mathbf{e}$ from the candidates (since it has maximum value of g_W). The contradiction comes from the fact that in reality, for T large enough, many of candidates will be closer to L than $\mathbf{e}$ and therefore no algorithm can distinguish them [18]. This gives rise to what [20] calls the "contradictory regime" where an algorithm would somehow be able to distinguish indistinguishable distributions.

We first compare this regime to that of our algorithm and we then discuss the statistical model chosen by [20] in Heuristic 1.

---

[7] We overload the notation GH: in [20], $\mathrm{GH}(m)$ corresponds to our $\mathrm{GH}(L)$ for L of volume 1, that is $\mathrm{vol}(B_m)^{-1/m}$.

6.1 Almost Complementary Regimes

In Sect. 4.3, we have applied our main theorem to a concrete instance and derived that[8] for a typical LWE problem where the ratio m/n is fixed (and not too close to 0 or 1), q is large and the error follows a discrete Gaussian of parameter σ_e, our algorithm works as soon as

$$q^{1-n/m} \geqslant (\tfrac{1}{s} + 2\sigma_e)\sqrt{e} \tag{24}$$

where

$$N = \frac{\mathsf{poly}\,(m) + n\log_2(q)}{\delta^2}, \qquad \delta = \tfrac{1}{10}e^{-ms^2\sigma_e^2/2}.$$

In our attack, T is the number of guesses that the algorithm makes, that is $T = q^{n_{\mathrm{guess}}}$. In order to match [20, page 21], we will choose s so that $\ln T = N\varepsilon^2$:

$$
\begin{aligned}
\ln T = N\varepsilon^2 \quad &\Leftrightarrow \quad n_{\mathrm{guess}}\ln(q) = \frac{\mathsf{poly}\,(m) + n\log_2(q)}{\delta^2}\varepsilon^2 \\
&\Leftrightarrow \quad n_{\mathrm{guess}}\ln(q) = (\mathsf{poly}\,(m) + n\log_2(q))100e^{2ms^2\sigma_e^2/2}e^{-2\pi\sigma_e^2\ell^2} \\
&\Leftrightarrow \quad \frac{n_{\mathrm{guess}}\ln(q)}{100(\mathsf{poly}\,(m) + n\log_2(q))} = e^{(ms^2 - 2\pi\ell^2)\sigma_e^2}.
\end{aligned}
$$

Note that $n_{\mathrm{guess}} < n < m$ so for large enough value of m, the left-hand side of this expression is smaller than 1 (recall that $\mathsf{poly}\,(m)$ comes from the choice of N so we can always make it slightly bigger to artificially increase the denominator if we want). It follows that we can always choose s such that $\ln T = N\varepsilon^2$ in such a way that (24) holds (see [39, Appendix G.2]) and therefore Theorem 5 ensures that our algorithm works in this regime.

We will now compare this with [20]'s contradictory regime. This regime, defined in [20, page 21] is when[9]

$$r\,\mathrm{GH}(L_q(\mathbf{A}_{\mathrm{dual}})) < \sqrt{\frac{m}{2\pi}}\sigma_e, \qquad \text{where } r = T^{-1/m}. \tag{25}$$

Note here that the lattice is $\mathbf{A}_{\mathrm{dual}}$ because [20] modularizes the algorithm by separating the lattice in which dual-distinguishing is done, with the part of the lattice that is enumerated over (see Sect. 6.2). Indeed, this regime comes from Heuristic 1 and the lattice in question is the one where dual vectors are generated.

Recall that for the algorithm to work, $\mathbf{A}$ and therefore $\mathbf{A}_{\mathrm{dual}}$ must have full rank, so $\det(L_q(\mathbf{A}_{\mathrm{dual}})) = q^{m-n_{\mathrm{dual}}}$. Now observe that

$$\frac{r\,\mathrm{GH}(L_q(\mathbf{A}_{\mathrm{dual}}))}{\sqrt{\frac{m}{2\pi}}\sigma_e} = \frac{T^{-1/m}\sqrt{\frac{m}{2\pi e}}q^{1-n_{\mathrm{dual}}/m}}{\sqrt{\frac{m}{2\pi}}\sigma_e} = \frac{q^{-n_{\mathrm{guess}}/m}q^{1-n_{\mathrm{dual}}/m}}{\sqrt{e}\sigma_e}.$$

---

[8] Under some mild technical simplification to make the computation easier.

[9] Recall that because of the difference between the normal distribution and the discrete Gaussian, we have $\sigma = \sigma_e/\sqrt{2\pi}$ in our analysis, see [39, Appendix G.1].

Recall that $n = n_{\mathrm{dual}} + n_{\mathrm{guess}}$ so the contradictory regimes corresponds to

$$q^{1-n/m} < \sigma_e \sqrt{e}. \tag{26}$$

Comparing between the working regime (24) and the contradictory one (26), and recalling that we can choose s as large as we want, we observe that they do not overlap and the bounds only differ by a factor of two. This suggest that, for our algorithm, the "theoretically working" regime and the contradictory regime almost characterize whether the dual attack will work or not. However, the next section will explain that those regimes are based on different distributions of targets.

6.2   On the Distribution of Targets

The authors of [20] decided to modularize the algorithm by separating the lattice in which dual-distinguishing is done ($L_q(\mathbf{A}_{\mathrm{dual}})$) from the part of the lattice that is enumerated over ($L_q(\mathbf{A}_{\mathrm{guess}})$). In fact, Heuristic 1 only mentions the dual-distinguishing and not the enumeration. This however, poses a difficulty because it is clear that the "targets" ($\mathbf{b} - \mathbf{A}_{\mathrm{guess}}\tilde{\mathbf{s}}_{\mathrm{guess}}$ in our terminology, $\mathbf{t}^{(i)}_{unif}$ in Heuristic 1) are not arbitrary but have some structure.

The authors of [20] decided to model the statistics of the targets in a way that is independent of the actual choice of $\mathbf{A}_{\mathrm{guess}}$: they chose the uniform distribution over the fundamental domain of $L_q(\mathbf{A}_{\mathrm{dual}})$. In the case of [32] and our algorithm, the algorithm exclusively works over integers which is why we propose Heuristic 2 as an integer-version of Heuristic 1. This means that we now have two different settings:

- In Heuristic 2, $\mathbf{t}^{(i)}_{unif}$ is sampled uniformly in $\mathbb{Z}^m/L$.
- In reality, $\mathbf{t}^{(i)}_{unif} = \mathbf{e} + \mathbf{x}^{(i)}$ where $\mathbf{x}^{(i)}$ can be any vector in $L' \setminus q\mathbb{Z}^m$ where L' is another random q-ary lattice, chosen independently of L but fixed in the algorithm. In our algorithm, $L = L_q(\mathbf{A}_{\mathrm{dual}})$ and $L' = L_q(\mathbf{A}_{\mathrm{guess}})$.

Indeed, a key point in the proof of Theorem 5 is to show that points of the form $\mathbf{e} + \mathbf{x}^{(i)}$ as described are always far away from L, a fact that does not hold for completely uniform targets. As a result, with high probability over the choice of $\mathbf{A}$, the targets (except for the correct guess) are *all bounded away* from 0 in the dual lattice. For uniform targets, the argument of [20] is statistical in nature: while there can be very short vectors, they are unlikely and the contradiction comes from the fact that if we try too many targets, we will eventually find a short one and get a false-positive. On the other hand, our algorithm and analysis is not statistical: for the vast majority of choices of $\mathbf{A}$, all targets satisfy the bound unconditionally and we can safely look at all targets without the risk of any false-positive.

In conclusion of this section, it seems that the contradictory regime of [20] nicely complements the working regime of our algorithm. On the other hand, the statistical model that underlines this contradictory regime and what happens in our algorithm are different. We leave it as an open question to explain exactly why the two regimes seem to align perfectly.

7   Open Questions

We have analysed formally a dual attack in the spirit of [32]. However, as noted in [20], the algorithm used by [32] produces many short dual vectors *in a sublattice* L'' of $L_q^{\perp}(\mathbf{A}_{\text{dual}})$ (instead of the entire $L_q^{\perp}(\mathbf{A}_{\text{dual}})$). In other words, W is roughly the set of vectors of L'' in a ball and therefore g_W does not exactly measure the distance to L but rather to a more complicated lattice. This fact makes the analysis of g_W considerably more challenging and we believe that more research is needed to understand how this affects the choice of the parameters.

Another issue that we have avoided is that of modulus switching. Indeed, while [32] claims that this techniques bring significant improvements in the complexity, [20] claims that geometric arguments contradicts this statement. We leave as an open problem the study of a modification of our algorithm that would include modulus switching. We believe that a formal analysis would be the best way to resolve this issue. A priori, we do not see any major reason why this could not be analysed formally but it may prove to be a nontrivial technical challenge due to the effects of rounding modulo p on the uniform distribution modulo q. We note in this direction that the approach of [16] of using lattice codes instead of modulus switching might be a better fit for a formal analysis.

Finally, we have analyzed the case where the algorithm has access to m LWE samples in dimension n, and our algorithm typically requires $m \approx 2n$ to have a good complexity. In practice, however, it is common to only have n samples, something that our algorithm cannot handle. While there is a standard technique to deal with this, namely sampling in the lattice

$$\{(\mathbf{x}, \mathbf{y}) \in \mathbb{Z}^m \times \mathbb{Z}^{n_{\text{dual}}} : \mathbf{x}^T \mathbf{A}_{\text{dual}} = \mathbf{y} \bmod q\},$$

we leave it as future work to include this improvement to our analysis.

Acknowledgments. We thank the anonymous TCC reviewers for pointing out an error in a previous version of this paper where we misunderstood the contradictory regime of [20]. We thank Martin Albrecht for his helpful comments on a previous version of this paper. We thank Léo Ducas for helpful discussions on the statistical model of [20]. We thank the anonymous EUROCRYPT reviewers for valuable comments and suggestions. Y.S. is supported by EPSRC grant EP/W02778X/2.

References

1. Lattice Attacks on NTRU and LWE: A History of Refinements, p. 15-40. London Mathematical Society Lecture Note Series, Cambridge University Press (2021)
2. Aggarwal, D., Chen, Y., Kumar, R., Shen, Y.: Improved classical and quantum algorithms for the shortest vector problem via bounded distance decoding (2020). https://arxiv.org/abs/2002.07955
3. Aggarwal, D., Chen, Y., Kumar, R., Shen, Y.: Improved (provable) algorithms for the shortest vector problem via bounded distance decoding. In: Bläser, M., Monmege, B. (eds.) 38th International Symposium on Theoretical Aspects of Computer Science, STACS 2021, Saarbrücken, Germany, 16–19 March 2021 (Virtual

Conference). LIPIcs, vol. 187, pp. 4:1–4:20. Schloss Dagstuhl - Leibniz-Zentrum für Informatik (2021). https://doi.org/10.4230/LIPIcs.STACS.2021.4

4. Aggarwal, D., Dadush, D., Regev, O., Stephens-Davidowitz, N.: Solving the shortest vector problem in 2^n time using discrete gaussian sampling: Extended abstract. In: Servedio, R.A., Rubinfeld, R. (eds.) Proceedings of the Forty-Seventh Annual ACM on Symposium on Theory of Computing, STOC 2015, Portland, OR, USA, 14–17 June 2015, pp. 733–742. ACM (2015). https://doi.org/10.1145/2746539.2746606

5. Aharonov, D., Regev, O.: Lattice problems in np ∩ conp. J. ACM **52**(5), 749–765 (2005). https://doi.org/10.1145/1089023.1089025

6. Ajtai, M.: The shortest vector problem in L2 is NP-hard for randomized reductions (extended abstract). In: Proceedings of the Thirtieth Annual ACM Symposium on Theory of Computing, STOC 1998, pp. 10–19. Association for Computing Machinery, New York (1998). https://doi.org/10.1145/276698.276705

7. Albrecht, M.R.: On dual lattice attacks against small-secret LWE and parameter choices in HElib and SEAL. In: Coron, J.-S., Nielsen, J.B. (eds.) EUROCRYPT 2017. LNCS, vol. 10211, pp. 103–129. Springer, Cham (2017). https://doi.org/10.1007/978-3-319-56614-6_4

8. Albrecht, M.R., Gheorghiu, V., Postlethwaite, E.W., Schanck, J.M.: Estimating quantum speedups for lattice sieves. In: Moriai, S., Wang, H. (eds.) ASIACRYPT 2020. LNCS, vol. 12492, pp. 583–613. Springer, Cham (2020). https://doi.org/10.1007/978-3-030-64834-3_20

9. Albrecht, M.R., Player, R., Scott, S.: On the concrete hardness of learning with errors. J. Math. Cryptol. **9**(3), 169–203 (2015). http://www.degruyter.com/view/j/jmc.2015.9.issue-3/jmc-2015-0016/jmc-2015-0016.xml

10. Albrecht, M.R., Shen, Y.: Quantum augmented dual attack. Cryptology ePrint Archive, Paper 2022/656 (2022). https://eprint.iacr.org/2022/656

11. Alkim, E., Ducas, L., Pöppelmann, T., Schwabe, P.: Post-quantum key exchange: a new hope. In: Proceedings of the 25th USENIX Conference on Security Symposium, SEC 2016, pp. 327–343. USENIX Association, USA (2016)

12. Banaszczyk, W.: New bounds in some transference theorems in the geometry of numbers. Math. Ann. **296**, 625–635 (1993)

13. Becker, A., Ducas, L., Gama, N., Laarhoven, T.: New directions in nearest neighbor searching with applications to lattice sieving. In: Krauthgamer, R. (ed.) Proceedings of the Twenty-Seventh Annual ACM-SIAM Symposium on Discrete Algorithms, SODA 2016, Arlington, VA, USA, 10–12 January 2016, pp. 10–24. SIAM (2016). https://doi.org/10.1137/1.9781611974331.ch2

14. Brakerski, Z., Langlois, A., Peikert, C., Regev, O., Stehlé, D.: Classical hardness of learning with errors. In: Proceedings of the Forty-Fifth Annual ACM Symposium on Theory of Computing, STOC 2013, pp. 575–584. Association for Computing Machinery, New York (2013). https://doi.org/10.1145/2488608.2488680

15. Brakerski, Z., Vaikuntanathan, V.: Fully homomorphic encryption from ring-LWE and security for key dependent messages. In: Rogaway, P. (ed.) CRYPTO 2011. LNCS, vol. 6841, pp. 505–524. Springer, Heidelberg (2011). https://doi.org/10.1007/978-3-642-22792-9_29

16. Carrier, K., Shen, Y., Tillich, J.P.: Faster dual lattice attacks by using coding theory (2022). https://eprint.iacr.org/2022/1750

17. Dadush, D., Regev, O., Stephens-Davidowitz, N.: On the closest vector problem with a distance guarantee. In: 2014 IEEE 29th Conference on Computational Complexity (CCC), pp. 98–109 (2014). https://doi.org/10.1109/CCC.2014.18

18. Debris, T., Ducas, L., Resch, N., Tillich, J.P.: Smoothing codes and lattices: systematic study and new bounds. Cryptology ePrint Archive, Paper 2022/615 (2022). https://eprint.iacr.org/2022/615
19. Debris-Alazard, T., Remaud, M., Tillich, J.P.: Quantum reduction of finding short code vectors to the decoding problem. Cryptology ePrint Archive, Paper 2021/752 (2021). https://eprint.iacr.org/2021/752
20. Ducas, L., Pulles, L.N.: Does the dual-sieve attack on learning with errors even work? IACR Cryptol. ePrint Arch., p. 302 (2023). https://eprint.iacr.org/2023/302
21. Dürr, C., Høyer, P.: A quantum algorithm for finding the minimum. CoRR **quant-ph/9607014** (1996). http://arxiv.org/abs/quant-ph/9607014
22. Erez, U., Litsyn, S., Zamir, R.: Lattices which are good for (almost) everything. IEEE Trans. Inf. Theory **51**(10), 3401–3416 (2005). https://doi.org/10.1109/TIT.2005.855591
23. Espitau, T., Joux, A., Kharchenko, N.: On a dual/hybrid approach to small secret LWE. In: Bhargavan, K., Oswald, E., Prabhakaran, M. (eds.) INDOCRYPT 2020. LNCS, vol. 12578, pp. 440–462. Springer, Cham (2020). https://doi.org/10.1007/978-3-030-65277-7_20
24. Gentry, C., Peikert, C., Vaikuntanathan, V.: Trapdoors for hard lattices and new cryptographic constructions. In: Proceedings of the Fortieth Annual ACM Symposium on Theory of Computing, pp. 197–206. STOC 2008. Association for Computing Machinery, New York (2008). https://doi.org/10.1145/1374376.1374407
25. Guo, Q., Johansson, T.: Faster dual lattice attacks for solving LWE with applications to CRYSTALS. In: Tibouchi, M., Wang, H. (eds.) ASIACRYPT 2021. LNCS, vol. 13093, pp. 33–62. Springer, Cham (2021). https://doi.org/10.1007/978-3-030-92068-5_2
26. Høyer, P., Mosca, M., de Wolf, R.: Quantum search on bounded-error inputs. In: Baeten, J.C.M., Lenstra, J.K., Parrow, J., Woeginger, G.J. (eds.) ICALP 2003. LNCS, vol. 2719, pp. 291–299. Springer, Heidelberg (2003). https://doi.org/10.1007/3-540-45061-0_25
27. Jaques, S., Rattew, A.G.: QRAM: a survey and critique (2023)
28. Klein, P.: Finding the closest lattice vector when it's unusually close. In: Proceedings of the Eleventh Annual ACM-SIAM Symposium on Discrete Algorithms, SODA 2000, pp. 937–941. Society for Industrial and Applied Mathematics, USA (2000)
29. Kuperberg, G.: A subexponential-time quantum algorithm for the dihedral hidden subgroup problem. SIAM J. Comput. **35**(1), 170–188 (2005). https://doi.org/10.1137/S0097539703436345
30. Loeliger, H.A.: Averaging bounds for lattices and linear codes. IEEE Trans. Inf. Theory **43**(6), 1767–1773 (1997). https://doi.org/10.1109/18.641543
31. Macbeath, A.M., Rogers, C.A.: Siegel's mean value theorem in the geometry of numbers. Math. Proc. Cambridge Philos. Soc. **54**(2), 139–151 (1958). https://doi.org/10.1017/S0305004100033302
32. MATZOV: Report on the Security of LWE: Improved Dual Lattice Attack, April 2022. https://doi.org/10.5281/zenodo.6412487
33. Meyer-Hilfiger, C., Tillich, J.P.: Rigorous foundations for dual attacks in coding theory. Cryptology ePrint Archive, Paper 2023/1460, Accepted to TCC (2023). https://eprint.iacr.org/2023/1460
34. Micciancio, D., Regev, O.: Worst-case to average-case reductions based on gaussian measures. In: 45th Annual IEEE Symposium on Foundations of Computer Science, pp. 372–381 (2004). https://doi.org/10.1109/FOCS.2004.72

35. Micciancio, D., Regev, O.: Lattice-Based Cryptography, pp. 147–191. Springer, Heidelberg (2009). https://doi.org/10.1007/978-3-540-88702-7_5
36. Micciancio, D., Voulgaris, P.: Faster exponential time algorithms for the shortest vector problem. In: Proceedings of the Twenty-First Annual ACM-SIAM Symposium on Discrete Algorithms, SODA 2010, pp. 1468–1480. Society for Industrial and Applied Mathematics, USA (2010)
37. Montanaro, A.: Quantum speedup of Monte Carlo methods. Proc. Royal Soc. Math. Phys. Eng. Sci. **471**(2181), 20150301 (2015). https://doi.org/10.1098/rspa.2015.0301
38. Nguyen, P.Q., Vidick, T.: Sieve algorithms for the shortest vector problem are practical. J. Math. Cryptol. **2**(2), 181–207 (2008). https://doi.org/10.1515/JMC.2008.009
39. Pouly, A., Shen, Y.: Provable dual attacks on learning with errors. Cryptology ePrint Archive, Paper 2023/1508 (2023). https://eprint.iacr.org/2023/1508
40. Regev, O.: On lattices, learning with errors, random linear codes, and cryptography. In: Proceedings of the Thirty-Seventh Annual ACM Symposium on Theory of Computing, STOC 2005, pp. 84–93. Association for Computing Machinery, New York (2005). https://doi.org/10.1145/1060590.1060603
41. Rogers, C.A.: Mean values over the space of lattices. Acta Math. **94**, 249–287 (1955). https://doi.org/10.1007/BF02392493
42. Schnorr, C.P.: Lattice reduction by random sampling and birthday methods. In: Alt, H., Habib, M. (eds.) STACS 2003. LNCS, vol. 2607, pp. 145–156. Springer, Heidelberg (2003). https://doi.org/10.1007/3-540-36494-3_14
43. Schnorr, C.: A hierarchy of polynomial time lattice basis reduction algorithms. Theor. Comput. Sci. **53**(2), 201–224 (1987)
44. Siegel, C.L.: A mean value theorem in geometry of numbers. Ann. Math. **46**(2), 340 (1945). https://doi.org/10.2307/1969027. https://www.jstor.org/stable/1969027?origin=crossref
45. Stephens-Davidowitz, N.: On the Gaussian measure over lattices. Ph.d. thesis, New York University (2017)
46. Wang, Z., Ling, C.: Lattice gaussian sampling by Markov chain Monte Carlo: bounded distance decoding and trapdoor sampling. IEEE Trans. Inf. Theory **65**(6), 3630–3645 (2019). https://doi.org/10.1109/TIT.2019.2901497
47. Zamir, R., Nazer, B., Kochman, Y., Bistritz, I.: Lattice Coding for Signals and Networks: A Structured Coding Approach to Quantization, Modulation and Multiuser Information Theory. Cambridge University Press (2014). https://doi.org/10.1017/CBO9781139045520

Reduction from Sparse LPN to LPN, Dual Attack 3.0

Kévin Carrier[1]($\boxtimes$), Thomas Debris-Alazard[2], Charles Meyer-Hilfiger[3], and Jean-Pierre Tillich[3]

[1] ETIS UMR 8051, CY Cergy-Paris Université, ENSEA, CNRS, Cergy, France
kevin.carrier@ensea.fr
[2] Project GRACE, Inria Saclay-Ile de France, Palaiseau, France
thomas.debris@inria.fr
[3] Project COSMIQ, Inria de Paris, Paris, France
{charles.meyer-hilfiger,jean-pierre.tillich}@inria.fr

Abstract. The security of code-based cryptography relies primarily on the hardness of decoding generic linear codes. Until very recently, all the best algorithms for solving the decoding problem were information set decoders (ISD). However, recently a new algorithm called RLPN-decoding which relies on a completely different approach was introduced and it has been shown that RLPN outperforms significantly ISD decoders for a rather large range of rates. This RLPN decoder relies on two ingredients, first reducing decoding to some underlying LPN problem, and then computing efficiently many parity-checks of small weight when restricted to some positions. We revisit RLPN-decoding by noticing that, in this algorithm, decoding is in fact reduced to a sparse-LPN problem, namely with a secret whose Hamming weight is small. Our new approach consists this time in making an additional reduction from sparse-LPN to plain-LPN with a coding approach inspired by coded-BKW. It outperforms significantly the ISD's and RLPN for code rates smaller than 0.42. This algorithm can be viewed as the code-based cryptography cousin of recent dual attacks in lattice-based cryptography. We depart completely from the traditional analysis of this kind of algorithm which uses a certain number of independence assumptions that have been strongly questioned recently in the latter domain. We give instead a formula for the LPN noise relying on duality which allows to analyze the behavior of the algorithm by relying only on the analysis of a certain weight distribution. By using only a minimal assumption whose validity has been verified experimentally we are able to justify the correctness of our algorithm. This key tool, namely the duality formula, can be readily adapted to the lattice setting and is shown to give a simple explanation for some phenomena observed on dual attacks in lattices in [19].

The work of KC, TDA and JPT was funded by the French Agence Nationale de la Recherche through ANR JCJC DECODE (ANR-22-CE39-0004-01) for KC, ANR JCJC COLA (ANR-21-CE39-0011) for TDA and ANR-22-PETQ-0008 PQ-TLS for JPT. The work of CMH was funded by the French Agence de l'innovation de défense and by Inria.

M. Joye and G. Leander (Eds.): EUROCRYPT 2024, LNCS 14657, pp. 286–315, 2024.
https://doi.org/10.1007/978-3-031-58754-2_11

1 Introduction

1.1 Background

Code-Based Cryptography: Decoding and LPN Problems. Code-based cryptography relies on the hardness of decoding generic linear codes or sometimes also on a closely related problem, namely the LPN problem. The first one corresponds in the binary case to

Problem 1 (decoding a fixed error weight in a linear code). *Let $\mathcal{C}$ be a binary linear code over $\mathbb{F}_2$ of dimension k and length n, i.e., a subspace of $\mathbb{F}_2^n$ of dimension k. We are given $\mathbf{y} \in \mathbb{F}_2^n$, an integer t and we want to find a codeword $\mathbf{c} \in \mathcal{C}$ and an error vector $\mathbf{e} \in \mathbb{F}_2^n$ of Hamming weight $|\mathbf{e}| = t$ for which $\mathbf{y} = \mathbf{c} + \mathbf{e}$.*

Generally the linear code is specified by a *generator matrix*, namely a $k \times n$ binary matrix $\mathbf{G}$ whose rows span the vector space $\mathcal{C}$, in other words $\mathcal{C} = \{\mathbf{u}\mathbf{G} : \mathbf{u} \in \mathbb{F}_2^k\}$. The second one is a version of this problem where the length n is basically unbounded; the code is randomly chosen and the error model is slightly modified to take into account that the length is not fixed.

Problem 2 (LPN problem). *Let $\mathbf{s}$ be chosen uniformly at random in $\mathbb{F}_2^k$. We have unbounded access to an oracle providing at each query a pair $(\mathbf{a}, b)$ where $\mathbf{a}$ is chosen uniformly at random in $\mathbb{F}_2^k$ and b is a bit obtained as $b = \langle \mathbf{s}, \mathbf{a} \rangle + e$ where $e \in \mathbb{F}_2$ is chosen at random and is equal to 1 with probability p. $\langle \mathbf{s}, \mathbf{a} \rangle$ stands for the inner product $\sum_{i=1}^k s_i a_i$ between $\mathbf{s} = (s_i)_{1 \leqslant i \leqslant k}$ and $\mathbf{a} = (a_i)_{1 \leqslant i \leqslant k}$. The aim is to output $\mathbf{s}$ after querying a certain number of times the oracle.*

Sometimes a variation of the LPN problem is considered, namely the *sparse* LPN problem where the only difference is the way $\mathbf{s}$ is chosen, say uniformly at random among the words of length k and Hamming weight t' small, or the entries like i.i.d. Bernoulli random variables of parameter p' small.

The Complexity of the Best Generic Decoding Algorithms and LPN-Solvers. It is of fundamental importance to study the complexity of these problems, the best state of the art algorithms being those that are used to determine secure parameters of code-based cryptosystems. The regime of parameters which is relevant for code-based cryptography depends on the type of primitive, but a large range of parameters is relevant here. For some code-based cryptosystems, t is sublinear in n, [2,3,7,39], for some Stern like signatures schemes [1,13,26,28,47,49] it is precisely decoding at the Gilbert-Varshamov distance that is relevant. It is at this distance that the decoding problem is expected to be the hardest. Recall that the Gilbert-Varshamov distance $d_{\mathrm{GV}}(n, k)$ is given by $d_{\mathrm{GV}}(n, k) \stackrel{\text{def}}{=} n\, h^{-1}(1 - R)$, where $R \stackrel{\text{def}}{=} \frac{k}{n}$ is the code rate, h is the binary entropy function $h(x) \stackrel{\text{def}}{=} -x \log_2 x - (1 - x) \log_2(1 - x)$ and $h^{-1}(x)$ its inverse ranging over $\left(0, \frac{1}{2}\right)$. Above this bound, the number of solutions becomes exponential and this helps to devise more efficient decoders.

Concerning now the LPN problem, it has long been recognized that having an unbounded number of queries or codelength while having a fixed error probability

p per bit as in LPN makes the problem really simpler. The best algorithms for solving this problem, are BKW type algorithms [8, 25] and are of subexponential complexity $2^{\mathcal{O}(k/\log k)}$. However, this is not true anymore if the number of queries is fixed and the error rate p is chosen such that the problem is the hardest, namely when $h(p) = 1 - k/n$. In this case, the best algorithms behave exponentially in $\min(k, n - k)$ despite many efforts on this issue [6, 9, 10, 22, 37, 38, 44, 46].

Reduction from Decoding to an LPN Problem. Note that until very recently, all the best algorithms for solving the decoding problem or the LPN problem when it is the hardest have been ISD algorithms. They all rely crucially on the Prange bet, namely that we have finally found after many trials a subset of positions of size $\approx n - k$ which contains almost all the errors. This was the situation since 1962 [44]. There was at some point, just one exception [20] which relied instead on a collision technique and gave only a slight improvement in a very tiny rate range $R \in (0.98, 1)$, but it was soon found out how to incorporate this technique in ISD algorithms [21, 46] to improve them. However in 2022, a new algorithm called RLPN-decoding was introduced in [10]. It relies on a completely different approach following an old idea called "statistical decoding" due to Al Jabri [31]. The new approach consists in reducing decoding to LPN. For the first time in sixty years a strong competitor for ISD techniques was found: it outperforms ISD techniques in the low rate regime, say $R \in (0, 0.3)$ and the improvement is quite significant in the range $R \in (0, 0.2)$ say. To explain the idea, assume we are given an instance of the decoding problem $\mathbf{y} = \mathbf{c} + \mathbf{e}$, where $\mathbf{c} \in \mathcal{C}$ and $|\mathbf{e}| = t$. As in statistical decoding, decoding relies on low weight parity-check equations, namely vectors $\mathbf{h}$ such that $\langle \mathbf{h}, \mathbf{c} \rangle = 0$ for any $\mathbf{c} \in \mathcal{C}$ (in other words, such $\mathbf{h}$'s belong to the dual code $\mathcal{C}^\perp$). However, in the new approach these parity-check equations are required to be of low weight only on a subset $\mathcal{N}$ of positions. The rest of the positions $\mathcal{P}$ correspond to the entries of $\mathbf{e}$ we aim to recover and is the secret in the LPN problem. The point of the whole approach is that

$$\langle \mathbf{y}, \mathbf{h} \rangle = \langle \mathbf{e}, \mathbf{h} \rangle = \sum_{j \in \mathcal{P}} h_j e_j + \sum_{j \in \mathcal{N}} h_j e_j = \underbrace{\langle \mathbf{e}_\mathcal{P}, \mathbf{h}_\mathcal{P} \rangle}_{\text{lin. comb.}} + \underbrace{\langle \mathbf{e}_\mathcal{N}, \mathbf{h}_\mathcal{N} \rangle}_{\text{LPN noise}}.$$

Here the notation $\mathbf{e}_\mathcal{P}$ means the restriction of $\mathbf{e}$ to the positions in $\mathcal{P}$: $\mathbf{e}_\mathcal{P} = (e_i)_{i \in \mathcal{P}}$. Vector $\mathbf{e}_\mathcal{P}$ is interpreted as the LPN secret $\mathbf{s}$, i.e., $\mathbf{s} \overset{\text{def}}{=} \mathbf{e}_\mathcal{P}$ and $\mathbf{h}_\mathcal{P}$ as the linear combination vector $\mathbf{a}$ while $\langle \mathbf{e}_\mathcal{N}, \mathbf{h}_\mathcal{N} \rangle$ is the LPN noise. Therefore, by computing $(\mathbf{h}_\mathcal{P}, \langle \mathbf{y}, \mathbf{h} \rangle)$ we really have access to the LPN sample

$$\underbrace{\mathbf{a}}_{\mathbf{h}_\mathcal{P}}, \overbrace{\underbrace{\langle \mathbf{s}, \mathbf{a} \rangle}_{\langle \mathbf{e}_\mathcal{P}, \mathbf{h}_\mathcal{P} \rangle} + \underbrace{e}_{\langle \mathbf{e}_\mathcal{N}, \mathbf{h}_\mathcal{N} \rangle}}^{= \langle \mathbf{y}, \mathbf{h} \rangle}.$$

The point of choosing low weight vectors $\mathbf{h}$ on $\mathcal{N}$, is that it is readily verified that this translates into the fact that the binary random variable $\langle \mathbf{e}_\mathcal{N}, \mathbf{h}_\mathcal{N} \rangle$ is biased, say $\mathbb{P}(\langle \mathbf{e}_\mathcal{N}, \mathbf{h}_\mathcal{N} \rangle = 1) = \frac{1 - \varepsilon}{2}$ with a bias ε which gets bigger when the Hamming weight $|\mathbf{h}_\mathcal{N}|$ of $\mathbf{h}$ on $\mathcal{N}$ gets smaller.

Recovering $\mathbf{e}_{\mathscr{P}}$ is then performed by producing enough parity-check equations to have enough information on $\mathbf{e}_{\mathscr{P}}$ (we need about $N \approx 1/\varepsilon^2$ parity-check equations) and amounts to solve the LPN problem. This is done by the Fast Fourier Transform (FFT) and costs about $s2^s$ where $s \overset{\text{def}}{=} |\mathscr{P}|$. We cannot afford more sophisticated techniques like the BKW algorithm which would give a sub-exponential algorithm, because we are very far away from the constant error probability regime. Here the bias ε is exponentially small in the codelength, so we are really in the extreme noise regime, where on top of that we have hardly more LPN samples than the number we need to recover the secret. In other words, we are in a situation where we can only use very basic algorithms, and the FFT which saves a factor N when compared to plain exhaustive search over all possible LPN secrets comes in handy here. The low weight parity-check equations are found by using collision techniques which are borrowed from advanced ISD techniques [6, 21].

The improvement upon statistical decoding given by RLPN is really due to this splitting in two parts. Recall that plain statistical decoding uses parity-checks which are low weight on the *whole support*. In both cases, $\frac{1}{\varepsilon^2}$ of such parity-checks are needed, however in RLPN decoding the bias ε is way bigger because the weight we have on $\mathscr{N}$ is way smaller for our parity-checks.

Dual Attacks, Some Negative Results and a New Analysis. Statistical decoding [31] or its variant, namely RLPN decoding, both fall into the category of *dual attacks* meaning a decoding algorithm that computes in a first step low weight codewords in the dual code and then computes the inner products of the received word $\mathbf{y}$ with those parity-checks to infer some information about the error $\mathbf{e}$. These methods can be viewed as the coding theoretic analogue of the dual attacks in lattice-based cryptography [41]. Similarly to what happened in code-based cryptography, they were shown after a sequence of improvements [4, 12, 23, 29, 36] to be able of being competitive with primal attacks, and the crucial improvement came from similar techniques, namely by a splitting strategy. Like in RLPN decoding, the point is that this splitting in two parts really allows to find dual vectors that are of smaller weight/norm on the restricted subset. Note that this idea was already put forward for statistical decoding (but not exploited there) in [15, §8, p. 33] or [16, p. 21].

However, the analysis in both settings relies on various independence assumptions, see for instance [36, Ass. 4.4, Ass. 5.8] for dual attacks in lattices or [10, Ass. 3.7] for dual attacks for codes. In lattice-based cryptography, the dual attacks were strongly questioned recently in [19] by showing that these independence assumptions made for analyzing dual attacks were in contradiction with some theorems in certain regimes or with well-tested heuristics in some other regimes. Note that it was already noticed in [10, §3.4] that the i.i.d. Bernoulli model implied by the LPN model for the $\langle \mathbf{e}_{\mathscr{N}}, \mathbf{h}_{\mathscr{N}} \rangle$'s is not always accurate, but it was conjectured there that the discrepancy between this ideal model and experiments does not impact the asymptotic analysis of the decoding based on this model. This was proved to be wrong in [40] where it was shown that the number of candidates passing the validity test of the RLPN decoder given in [10] is actually exponentially large for the parameters considered there, whereas there should be only one candidate passing the test if the algorithm was correct. However, this paper gave at the same time an approach for analyzing rigorously dual attacks in coding theory by bringing in a duality equation [40, Prop. 1.3] which relates the fundamental quantity manipulated by the decoder and the weight distribution of translates of a shortened version of the code to be decoded. By studying this weight distribution together with an assumption whose validity has been verified experimentally, a slightly modified RLPN decoder was introduced there and shown to attain the complexity exponent claimed in [10].

1.2   Our Contribution

(i) improving RLPN-decoding by a reduction from sparse LPN to plain LPN,
(ii) a rigorous analysis of the decoding algorithm based on a simple assumption verified experimentally.

Reduction from Sparse LPN to Plain LPN. Notice that the LPN problem we have to solve is actually a *sparse* LPN problem: $\mathbf{e}_{\mathscr{P}}$ is not uniformly distributed among $\mathbb{F}_2^s$ since it is of low weight. Indeed, it is the restriction to $\mathscr{P}$ of a vector which is itself of low weight. Unfortunately, the FFT algorithm used for recovering $\mathbf{e}_{\mathscr{P}}$ is unable to exploit this fact. In a sense, what we need here to improve RLPN decoding is an algorithm for solving sparse secret LPN in the very noisy regime (but with an exponential number of samples). This can be done by using a coded-BKW technique that was introduced in [30]. There it was not used as a technique for solving sparse LPN but as a technique to improve the reduction steps of the BKW algorithm [8] that put together pairs of vectors $\mathbf{a}$ and $\mathbf{a}'$ which are equal on a block of positions and add the corresponding LPN samples to get an LPN sample $(\mathbf{a} + \mathbf{a}', \langle \mathbf{a} + \mathbf{a}', \mathbf{s} \rangle + e + e')$ which is more noisy but with vectors $\mathbf{a}$ which become sparser and sparser as the number of blocks increases. Asking exact collisions on the block needs a lot of LPN samples and this can be relaxed by the coded-BKW technique. It basically uses a code of the same length as the block of positions we are considering during the BKW step and asks only an approximate collision on the block meaning that the closest codewords $\mathbf{c}$ and $\mathbf{c}'$ to $\mathbf{a}$ and $\mathbf{a}'$ restricted to this block should be the same.

To explain what we have in mind here, consider an LPN sample which is of the following form $(\mathbf{h}_{\mathscr{P}}, \langle \mathbf{e}_{\mathscr{P}}, \mathbf{h}_{\mathscr{P}} \rangle + e)$. Choose now a linear code $\mathcal{C}_{\mathrm{aux}}$ of length s and dimension k_{aux} (*i.e.*, a subspace of $\mathbb{F}_2^s$) which we know how to decode for any possible entry, meaning here that we can produce for any entry $\mathbf{y} \in \mathbb{F}_2^s$ a codeword $\mathbf{c}_{\mathrm{aux}} \in \mathcal{C}_{\mathrm{aux}}$ which is close *enough* to $\mathbf{y}$. Codes with this property are known under the name of *lossy source codes* in information theory. In [30] it was proposed to use for instance a product of small codes. There are almost optimal codes (producing for a given dimension k_{aux} almost optimal near codewords) using a low complexity decoder. Basically, the best that can be done is to produce codewords at distance $d_{\mathrm{GV}}(s, k_{\mathrm{aux}})$. For instance polar codes are asymptotically optimal [33], they attain asymptotically this Gilbert-Varshamov distance by using only a decoding algorithm of quasi-linear complexity $\mathcal{O}(s \log s)$.

Consider now a parity-check $\mathbf{h}$ of small weight w on $\mathcal{N}$ that we use for RLPN-decoding and decode $\mathbf{h}_{\mathscr{P}}$ with the lossy source code $\mathcal{C}_{\text{aux}}$: $\mathbf{h}_{\mathscr{P}} = \mathbf{c}_{\text{aux}} + \mathbf{e}_{\text{aux}}$ where $\mathbf{c}_{\text{aux}} \in \mathcal{C}_{\text{aux}}$ and $|\mathbf{e}_{\text{aux}}|$ is small. Consider a generator matrix $\mathbf{G}_{\text{aux}}$ of $\mathcal{C}_{\text{aux}}$, namely a $k_{\text{aux}} \times s$ matrix such that $\mathcal{C}_{\text{aux}} = \{\mathbf{u}\mathbf{G}_{\text{aux}} : \mathbf{u} \in \mathbb{F}_2^{k_{\text{aux}}}\}$ (*i.e.*, the rows of $\mathbf{G}_{\text{aux}}$ generate $\mathcal{C}_{\text{aux}}$). Notice now that

$$\langle \mathbf{e}_{\mathscr{P}}, \mathbf{h}_{\mathscr{P}} \rangle = \langle \mathbf{e}_{\mathscr{P}}, \mathbf{c}_{\text{aux}} + \mathbf{e}_{\text{aux}} \rangle = \langle \mathbf{e}_{\mathscr{P}}, \mathbf{c}_{\text{aux}} \rangle + \langle \mathbf{e}_{\mathscr{P}}, \mathbf{e}_{\text{aux}} \rangle$$
$$= \langle \mathbf{e}_{\mathscr{P}}, \mathbf{u}\mathbf{G}_{\text{aux}} \rangle + \langle \mathbf{e}_{\mathscr{P}}, \mathbf{e}_{\text{aux}} \rangle \quad (\text{where } \mathbf{u} \in \mathbb{F}_2^{k_{\text{aux}}})$$
$$= \langle \mathbf{e}_{\mathscr{P}}\mathbf{G}_{\text{aux}}^{\mathsf{T}}, \mathbf{u} \rangle + \underbrace{\langle \mathbf{e}_{\mathscr{P}}, \mathbf{e}_{\text{aux}} \rangle}_{\text{biased}}.$$

If we plug this expression in the original LPN sample $(\mathbf{h}_{\mathscr{P}}, \langle \mathbf{h}, \mathbf{y} \rangle = \langle \mathbf{e}_{\mathscr{P}}, \mathbf{h}_{\mathscr{P}} \rangle + \langle \mathbf{e}_{\mathcal{N}}, \mathbf{h}_{\mathcal{N}} \rangle)$ we obtain

$$\langle \mathbf{h}, \mathbf{y} \rangle = \langle \mathbf{e}_{\mathscr{P}}\mathbf{G}_{\text{aux}}^{\mathsf{T}}, \mathbf{u} \rangle + \underbrace{\langle \mathbf{e}_{\mathscr{P}}, \mathbf{e}_{\text{aux}} \rangle}_{\text{noise 1}} + \underbrace{\langle \mathbf{e}_{\mathcal{N}}, \mathbf{h}_{\mathcal{N}} \rangle}_{\text{noise 2}}.$$

In other words, we have a new LPN problem where

$$\underbrace{\mathbf{a}}_{\mathbf{u}}, \overbrace{\underbrace{\langle \mathbf{s}, \mathbf{a} \rangle}_{\langle \mathbf{e}_{\mathscr{P}}\mathbf{G}_{\text{aux}}^{\mathsf{T}}, \mathbf{u} \rangle} + \underbrace{e}_{\langle \mathbf{e}_{\mathscr{P}}, \mathbf{e}_{\text{aux}} \rangle + \langle \mathbf{e}_{\mathcal{N}}, \mathbf{h}_{\mathcal{N}} \rangle}}^{\langle \mathbf{y}, \mathbf{h} \rangle}. \tag{1}$$

The new secret is not anymore a part $\mathbf{e}_{\mathscr{P}}$ of the error but a linear combination $\mathbf{e}_{\mathscr{P}}\mathbf{G}_{\text{aux}}^{\mathsf{T}}$ of it and the LPN noise has increased somehow. However, now the secret is way smaller, it belongs to $\mathbb{F}_2^{k_{\text{aux}}}$. The situation is changed significantly by this. Before, basically the optimal parameters for RLPN-decoding were such that the cost of FFT decoding the LPN secret, namely $\mathcal{O}(s2^s)$ is of the same order as $1/\varepsilon^2$ the number of parity-check equations we need. Here ε is defined by $\mathbb{P}(e = 1) = \frac{1-\varepsilon}{2}$. Recall that ε is basically a decreasing function of the weight w of the parity-check equations we are able to produce. Here since we do not pay anymore $\mathcal{O}(s2^s)$ for FFT decoding the new LPN secret but $\mathcal{O}(k_{\text{aux}}2^{k_{\text{aux}}})$ we can take larger values for s which themselves give a smaller support $\mathcal{N}$ resulting in much smaller weight w on $\mathcal{N}$ and thus the bias term coming from $\langle \mathbf{e}_{\mathcal{N}}, \mathbf{h}_{\mathcal{N}} \rangle$ is much smaller. Of course there is an additional noise term now which is $\langle \mathbf{e}_{\mathscr{P}}, \mathbf{e}_{\text{aux}} \rangle$. However, all in all, the gain we have by being able to use a much larger s outweighs the additional noise term. It can also be observed that we do not recover $\mathbf{e}_{\mathscr{P}}$ but k_{aux} linear combinations of bits of $\mathbf{e}_{\mathscr{P}}$. This is easy to fix by running a few times more this algorithm with other lossy source codes $\mathcal{C}_{\text{aux}}$ until getting enough linear combinations to be able to recover $\mathbf{e}_{\mathscr{P}}$.

We call this new algorithm double-RLPN-decoding, since it is based on two successive reductions: first we reduce the problem to sparse-LPN, then we reduce the sparse-LPN to a plain-LPN problem as explained above.

double-RLPN-**Decoding and its Analysis.** It turns out that the LPN problem given in Eq. (1) is more structured than a standard LPN problem and like what happened in the RLPN algorithm [10], producing the most likely candidate for the LPN problem does not necessarily produce the right candidate $\mathbf{e}_{\mathscr{P}}\mathbf{G}_{\text{aux}}^{\mathsf{T}}$ even if we have enough samples for ensuring that in the ideal i.i.d model of the LPN problem the most likely candidate would indeed be the right solution. Again, the i.i.d. model is not accurate. We have to use the whole information given by the FFT and output for L big enough the L most likely solutions to have a chance to have $\mathbf{e}_{\mathscr{P}}\mathbf{G}_{\text{aux}}^{\mathsf{T}}$ in the list. However, verifying whether a candidate $\mathbf{s}$ for $\mathbf{e}_{\mathscr{P}}\mathbf{G}_{\text{aux}}^{\mathsf{T}}$ is indeed valid is relatively straightforward:

(a) we can as in the RLPN algorithm make a bet on the weight $|\mathbf{e}_{\mathscr{P}}|$, say $|\mathbf{e}_{\mathscr{P}}| = t'$ (and run enough double-RLPN decoding steps until finding a partition $\mathscr{P}\cup\mathcal{N}$ for which this bet is valid),

(b) recover $\mathbf{e}_{\mathscr{P}}$ by solving the decoding problem (in its syndrome form) $\mathbf{s} = \mathbf{e}_{\mathscr{P}}\mathbf{G}_{\text{aux}}^{\mathsf{T}}$ and $|\mathbf{e}_{\mathscr{P}}| = t'$,

(c) check whether the putative candidate $\mathbf{v}$ for $\mathbf{e}_{\mathscr{P}}$ we get can be extended to a complete solution by solving the decoding problem $\mathbf{y} = \mathbf{c}+\mathbf{e}$, $\mathbf{e}_{\mathscr{P}} = \mathbf{v}$, $\mathbf{c} \in \mathcal{C}$, $|\mathbf{e}| = t$ which is much easier to solve than the original decoding problem due to the partial knowledge about $\mathbf{e}$ ($\mathbf{e}_{\mathscr{P}} = \mathbf{v}$).

The whole problem we face here for analyzing the problem is the same as the one that was faced to analyze the RLPN algorithm, the i.i.d. LPN model is not valid and we really have to get rid of the independence assumptions. Part of this work is achieved by adapting one of the fundamental tools used for analyzing RLPN decoding, namely [10, Proposition 3.1] which gives a formula of the bias ε in terms of Krawtchouk polynomials. We will obtain a generalization of this proposition adapted to the double-RLPN decoder, namely Proposition 2 in Sect. 3. Note that Proposition 2 does not rely on unproven assumptions contrarily to what is done in dual attacks in lattice-based cryptography where the corresponding result is achieved through independence assumptions.

Estimating the number L of candidates for the LPN problem given in Eq. (1) we have to keep for being sure to have $\mathbf{e}_{\mathscr{P}}\mathbf{G}_{\text{aux}}^{\mathsf{T}}$ is even more delicate. It requires a careful adaptation to our setting of [40] that analyzed the RLPN decoder. Here, we will not be able to completely avoid assumptions for performing the analysis (but this was also the case in [40]). However, again we will not resort to independence assumptions which seem in our context not only to be wrong strictly speaking, but also to be unable to be good enough for capturing the size of L. We will namely develop some tools analogous to what has been achieved in [40]:

(i) a duality result, namely Proposition 4 of Sect. 5.3, which expresses the FFT value of a candidate as a weighted sum of the product of evaluations of Krawtchouk polynomials where the weights come from a certain weight distributions of codes related to $\mathcal{C}$ and $\mathcal{C}_{\text{aux}}$. This is an adaptation of [40, Prop. 3.2] to our setting and is the key for estimating L as explained in Sect. 5.2,

(ii) an estimation of this sum with probabilistic considerations. These probabilistic considerations are rigorous for the part of the sum which is most certainly the dominating term. However for the part of the sum which is very likely to be negligible, we lack accurate tail bounds for the number of codewords of a given weight in a random linear code and we just conjecture that the part of the sum is indeed negligible. This conjecture has been verified experimentally and we even used a very crude approximation of this weighted sum with the help of independent Poisson variables which captures the size of L obtained in our experiments and which implies our conjecture.

All in all with the help of a conjecture that we verified experimentally, we are able to capture the size of L and to obtain a formula for the complexity of double-RLPN decoding. The key tool for performing this analysis, namely the duality result, can be readily adapted to lattices (see Sect. 8). It turns out that even a crude use of this duality result gives a good explanation of the part of the experimental curve departing from the theoretical curve based on the standard independence assumption found in [19, Fig. 3]. This substantiates the claim made in [40, §6] that the code duality result of [40] carries over to the lattice setting and can be used to predict dual attacks without using the independence assumption.

The Results Obtained by this New Approach. This new approach results in a very significant gain compared to RLPN decoding. Our most advanced version of double-RLPN-decoding algorithm performs better than the best ISD algorithm for all rates $R \leqslant 0.42$ as shown in Fig. 1. In the long version of the paper [11, Appendix I] we also give a lower bound for double-RLPNby assuming that we can compute the parity-checks of any weight we need in amortized time one. Additional results can be found on the paper's github page[1]: it includes the memory complexity of double-RLPN, a program to verify our complexity claims and the program used to experimentally verify the Poisson model.

Concurrent/Related Work. Very recently, we became aware that the prediction we have made on the score function for lattices by using our duality result and crude estimates of the relevant sum (see Sect. 8) has also been obtained by using as we do here Bessel functions and related tools in [19]. This paper provides a much more in depth study as we do here.

2   Notation and Coding Theory Background

Basic Notation. Vectors and matrices are respectively denoted in bold letters and bold capital letters such as $\mathbf{a}$ and $\mathbf{A}$. The entry at index i of the vector $\mathbf{x}$ is denoted by x_i or $x(i)$. The canonical inner product $\sum_{i=1}^n x_i y_i$ between two vectors $\mathbf{x}$ and $\mathbf{y}$ of $\mathbb{F}_2^n$ is denoted by $\langle \mathbf{x}, \mathbf{y} \rangle$ where $\mathbb{F}_2$ denotes the binary field. Let $\mathscr{I}$ be a list of indexes. We denote by $\mathbf{x}_{\mathscr{I}}$ the vector $(x_i)_{i \in \mathscr{I}}$. In the same way, we denote by $\mathbf{A}_{\mathscr{I}}$ the sub-matrix made of the columns of $\mathbf{A}$ which are indexed by $\mathscr{I}$. We denote by $\mathbf{0}_n \in \mathbb{F}_2^{n \times n}$ and $\mathbf{Id}_n \in \mathbb{F}_2^{n \times n}$ the null matrix and the identity matrix of size n respectively. The concatenation of two vectors $\mathbf{x}$ and $\mathbf{y}$ is denoted by $\mathbf{x}\|\mathbf{y}$. The Hamming weight of a vector $\mathbf{x}$ and the cardinality of a finite set

---

[1] https://github.com/meyer-hilfiger/Dual-Attack-3.0.

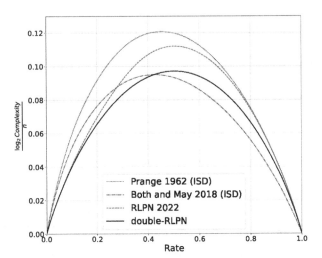

Fig. 1. Asymptotic complexity exponent of some decoding algorithms: our new double-RLPN decoder, the RLPN decoder, Both and May algorithm [9] (with the correction of [10,24]) which is the state-of-the-art of ISD decoders and the Prange decoder [44].

$\mathscr{A}$ are denoted in the same way by $|\mathbf{x}|$ and $|\mathscr{A}|$ respectively. There will be no confusion since they apply to different objects. $[\![a,b]\!]$ stands for the set of the integers between a and b, both included. Furthermore, let $\mathcal{S}_w^n$ be the Hamming sphere of $\mathbb{F}_2^n$ with radius w and centered at $\mathbf{0}$, namely $\mathcal{S}_w^n \overset{\text{def}}{=} \{\mathbf{x} \in \mathbb{F}_2^n : |\mathbf{x}| = w\}$.

Probabilistic Notation. For a finite set $\mathscr{S}$, we write $X \overset{\$}{\leftarrow} \mathscr{S}$ for X drawn uniformly at random in $\mathscr{S}$. For a Bernoulli random variable X, denote by $\text{bias}(X)$ the quantity $\text{bias}(X) \overset{\text{def}}{=} \mathbb{P}(X = 0) - \mathbb{P}(X = 1)$. For a Bernoulli random variable X of parameter $p = \frac{1-\varepsilon}{2}$, i.e., $\mathbb{P}(X = 1) = \frac{1-\varepsilon}{2}$, we have $\text{bias}(X) = \varepsilon$.

Fourier Transform. Let $f : \mathbb{F}_2^n \to \mathbb{R}$ be a function. We define its Fourier transform $\widehat{f} : \mathbb{F}_2^n \to \mathbb{R}$ as $\widehat{f}(\mathbf{x}) = \sum_{\mathbf{u} \in \mathbb{F}_2^n} f(\mathbf{u})(-1)^{\langle \mathbf{x},\mathbf{u} \rangle}$.

Soft-O Notation. For real valued functions defined over $\mathbb{R}$ or $\mathbb{N}$ we define $o()$, $\mathcal{O}()$, $\Omega()$, $\Theta()$, in the usual way and also use the less common notation $\widetilde{\mathcal{O}}()$ and $\widetilde{\Omega}()$, where $f = \widetilde{\mathcal{O}}(g)$ means that $f(x) = \mathcal{O}\left(g(x)\log^k g(x)\right)$ and $f = \widetilde{\Omega}(g)$ means that $f(x) = \Omega\left(g(x)\log^k g(x)\right)$ for some k. We will use this for functions which have an exponential behavior, say $g(x) = e^{\alpha x}$, in which case $f(x) = \widetilde{\mathcal{O}}(g(x))$ means that $f(x) = \mathcal{O}(P(x)g(x))$ where P is a polynomial in x. We also use $f = \omega(g)$ when f dominates g asymptotically; that is when $\lim_{x\to\infty} \frac{|f(x)|}{g(x)} = \infty$.

Coding Theory. A binary linear code $\mathcal{C}$ of length n and dimension k is a subspace of $\mathbb{F}_2^n$ of dimension k. We say that it has parameters $[n,k]$ or that it is an $[n,k]$-code. Its *rate* R given by $R \overset{\text{def}}{=} \frac{k}{n}$. A generator matrix $\mathbf{G}$ for $\mathcal{C}$ is a full rank $k \times n$ matrix over $\mathbb{F}_2$ such that $\mathcal{C} = \{\mathbf{uG} : \mathbf{u} \in \mathbb{F}_2^k\}$. A parity-check matrix $\mathbf{H}$ for $\mathcal{C}$ is a full-rank $(n-k) \times n$ matrix over $\mathbb{F}_2$ such that $\mathcal{C}$ is the null space of $\mathbf{H}$: $\mathcal{C} = \{\mathbf{c} \in \mathbb{F}_2^n : \mathbf{Hc^\mathsf{T}} = \mathbf{0}\}$. The code whose generator matrix is the parity-check matrix of $\mathcal{C}$ is called the dual code of $\mathcal{C}$. It might be seen as the subspace of parity-checks of $\mathcal{C}$ and is defined equivalently as

Definition 1 (Dual Code). *The* dual code $\mathcal{C}^\perp$ *of an* $[n, k]$*-code* $\mathcal{C}$ *is an* $[n, n - k]$*-code which is defined by* $\mathcal{C}^\perp \overset{def}{=} \{\mathbf{h} \in \mathbb{F}_2^n : \forall \mathbf{c} \in \mathcal{C}, \langle \mathbf{c}, \mathbf{h} \rangle = 0\}$.

Sometimes it is considered in the literature the following equivalent version of the decoding problem (see Problem 3 as defined in the introduction) by using instead the parity-check matrix and syndrome point of view

Problem 3 (Decoding a fixed error weight via syndromes). *Let* $\mathcal{C}$ *be an* $[n, k]$*-code with parity-check matrix* $\mathbf{H} \in \mathbb{F}_2^{(n-k) \times n}$. *We are given* $\mathbf{s} \in \mathbb{F}_2^{n-k}$, *an integer* t *and we want to find* $\mathbf{e} \in \mathbb{F}_2^n$ *such that* $|\mathbf{e}| = t$ *and* $\mathbf{He^\mathsf{T}} = \mathbf{s^\mathsf{T}}$.

It is readily seen that both Problems 1 and 3 are equivalent: given $\mathcal{C}$ with parity-check matrix $\mathbf{H}$, then decoding $\mathbf{c} + \mathbf{e}$ with a codeword $\mathbf{c} \in \mathcal{C}$ and $\mathbf{e} \in \mathcal{S}_t^n$ amounts to recover $\mathbf{e}$ from $\mathbf{Hy^\mathsf{T}} = \mathbf{He^\mathsf{T}}$ as by definition $\mathbf{Hc^\mathsf{T}} = \mathbf{0}$.

When $\mathcal{C}$ is an $[n, k]$-code and $\mathbf{x} \in \mathbb{F}_2^n$ we let $\mathcal{C} + \mathbf{x} \overset{def}{=} \{\mathbf{c} + \mathbf{x}, \mathbf{c} \in \mathcal{C}\}$ denote a coset of $\mathcal{C}$ and we denote by $N_i (\mathcal{C} + \mathbf{x})$ the number of words of hamming weight i in the coset $\mathcal{C} + \mathbf{x}$, namely $N_i (\mathcal{C} + \mathbf{x}) \overset{def}{=} |\mathcal{C} + \mathbf{x} \cap \mathcal{S}_i^n|$. An important quantity is the *Gilbert-Varshamov* distance which is defined as

Definition 2 (Gilbert-Varshamov distance). *The Gilbert-Varshamov distance* $d_{GV}(n, k)$ *associated to a length* n *and dimension* k *is defined as the largest integer* d *such that* $2^k |\mathcal{B}_d| < 2^n$ *where* $\mathcal{B}_d$ *is the Hamming ball centered at* $\mathbf{0}$ *in* $\mathbb{F}_2^n$ *and radius* d, *that is* $\mathcal{B}_d \overset{def}{=} \{\mathbf{x} \in \mathbb{F}_2^n : |\mathbf{x}| \leqslant d\}$.

This quantity has two different interpretations. On one hand, it corresponds up to a constant term to the *typical minimum distance* of a linear code of length n and dimension k, but it is also related to the expected number of solutions of the decoding problem for a random linear $[n, k]$-code which is defined as follows.

Problem 4 $((n, k, t)$ Decoding Problem - $\mathsf{DP}(n, k, t))$.

- Given: $(\mathbf{G}, \mathbf{y} \overset{def}{=} \mathbf{mG} + \mathbf{x})$ *where* $\mathbf{m}, \mathbf{G}$ *and* $\mathbf{x}$ *are respectively picked uniformly at random over* $\mathbb{F}_2^k$, $\mathbb{F}_2^{k \times n}$ *and* $\mathcal{S}_t^n$.
- Aim: *find* $\mathbf{e} \in \mathbb{F}_2^n$ *such that* $|\mathbf{e}| = t$ *and* $\mathbf{y} = \mathbf{zG} + \mathbf{e}$ *for some* $\mathbf{z} \in \mathbb{F}_2^k$.

This problem really corresponds to decoding at distance t the $[n, k]$-code admitting $\mathbf{G}$ as generator matrix. The largest weight t for which we might hope for having a single solution (strictly speaking when we look for solutions of weight $\leqslant t$ and not exactly t, but the difference between these two notions is generally irrelevant) is given by the Gilbert-Varshamov distance $d_{GV}(n, k)$. At this distance, the expected number of solutions is readily seen to be $\Theta(1)$

whether we look at codewords at distance exactly t from the received word $\mathbf{y}$ or at distance $\leqslant t$.

It will also be very convenient to consider the operation of puncturing a code, *i.e.*, keeping only a subset of entries in a codeword.

Definition 3 (Punctured Code). *For a code $\mathcal{C}$ and a subset $\mathcal{I}$ of code positions, we denote by $\mathcal{C}_{\mathcal{I}}$ the punctured code obtained from $\mathcal{C}$ by keeping only the positions in $\mathcal{I}$, i.e., $\mathcal{C}_{\mathcal{I}} = \{\mathbf{c}_{\mathcal{I}} : \mathbf{c} \in \mathcal{C}\}$.*

Definition 4 (Shortened Code). *For a code $\mathcal{C}$ and a subset $\mathcal{I}$ of code positions, we denote by $\mathcal{C}^{\mathcal{I}}$ the shortened code defined by $\mathcal{C}^{\mathcal{I}} = \{\mathbf{c}_{\mathcal{I}} : \mathbf{c} \in \mathcal{C} \text{ and } \mathbf{c}_{[\![1,n]\!]\setminus\mathcal{I}} = \mathbf{0}\}$.*

It is readily seen that we have

$$\left(\mathcal{C}^{\mathcal{I}}\right)^{\perp} = \left(\mathcal{C}^{\perp}\right)_{\mathcal{I}} \quad \text{and} \quad \left(\mathcal{C}_{\mathcal{I}}\right)^{\perp} = \left(\mathcal{C}^{\perp}\right)^{\mathcal{I}}. \tag{2}$$

Krawtchouk Polynomial. We recall here some properties about Krawtchouk polynomial that will be useful here. Many properties can be found in [32, §2.2].

Definition 5 (Krawtchouk polynomial). *We define the Krawtchouk polynomial $K_w^{(n)}$ of degree w and of order n as $K_w^{(n)}(X) \overset{def}{=} \sum_{j=0}^{w} (-1)^j \binom{X}{j}\binom{n-X}{w-j}$.*

The following fact is well known: it gives an alternate expression of the Krawtchouk polynomial (see for instance [35, Lemma 5.3.1]).

Fact 1. *For any $\mathbf{x} \in \mathbb{F}_2^n$,*

$$K_w^{(n)}(|\mathbf{x}|) = \widehat{\mathbb{1}_w}(\mathbf{x}) = \sum_{\mathbf{y}\in\mathbb{F}_2^n:|\mathbf{y}|=w} (-1)^{\langle\mathbf{x},\mathbf{y}\rangle}. \tag{3}$$

where $\mathbb{1}_w$ is the characteristic function of the Hamming sphere $\mathcal{S}_w^n$ of radius w.

Recall some known results about Krawtchouk polynomials:

Proposition 1. *[10, Prop. 3.5, Prop. 3.6]*

1. **Value at 0.** *For all $0 \leqslant w \leqslant n$, $K_w^{(n)}(0) = \binom{n}{w}$.*
2. **Reciprocity.** *For all $0 \leqslant t, w \leqslant n$, $\binom{n}{t}K_w^{(n)}(t) = \binom{n}{w}K_t^{(n)}(w)$.*
3. **Roots.** *The polynomials $K_w^{(n)}$'s have w distinct roots which lie in the interval $[\![n/2 - \sqrt{w(n-w)}, n/2 + \sqrt{w(n-w)}]\!]$. The distance between roots is at least 2 and at most $o(n)$.*
4. **Magnitude in and out the root region.** *Let τ and ω be two reals in $[0, 1]$. Let $\omega^{\perp} \overset{def}{=} \frac{1}{2} - \sqrt{\omega(1-\omega)}$, and let $z \overset{def}{=} \frac{1-2\tau-\sqrt{D}}{2(1-\omega)}$ where $D \overset{def}{=} (1-2\tau)^2 - 4\omega(1-\omega)$.*
   Define
   $$\widetilde{\kappa}(\tau,\omega) \overset{def}{=} \begin{cases} \tau\log_2(1-z) + (1-\tau)\log_2(1+z) - \omega\log_2 z & \text{if } \tau \in [0, \omega^{\perp}], \\ \frac{1-h(\tau)+h(\omega)}{2} & \text{otherwise.} \end{cases}$$

– 4.1. If $\tau \leqslant \frac{1}{2} - \sqrt{\omega(1-\omega)}$, then for all $t(n)$ and $w(n)$ such that $\lim\limits_{n\to\infty} \frac{t}{n} = \tau$
and $\lim\limits_{n\to\infty} \frac{w}{n} = \omega$ we have $K_w^{(n)}(t) = 2^{n(\tilde{\kappa}(\tau,\omega)+o(1))}$.

– 4.2. If $\tau > \frac{1}{2} - \sqrt{\omega(1-\omega)}$, then there exists $t(n)$ and $w(n)$ such that
$\lim\limits_{n\to\infty} \frac{t}{n} = \tau$, $\lim\limits_{n\to\infty} \frac{w}{n} = \omega$ and $\left| K_w^{(n)}(t) \right| = 2^{n(\tilde{\kappa}(\tau,\omega)+o(1))}$.

3 Reduction from Sparse to Plain LPN

The purpose of this section is to explain in detail the reduction from sparse to plain LPN and to give an important result about the bias of the resulting RLPN samples. We assume from now on that we are given an $[n,k]$-code $\mathcal{C}$ and a $\mathbf{y} \in \mathbb{F}_2^n$ such that $\mathbf{y} \stackrel{\text{def}}{=} \mathbf{c} + \mathbf{e}$, $\mathbf{c} \in \mathcal{C}$, $|\mathbf{e}| = t$, and we want to find $\mathbf{c}$ and $\mathbf{e}$.

3.1 The Approach

First, we randomly select a subset $\mathscr{P} \subseteq [\![1,n]\!]$ of s positions, where s is a parameter that will be chosen later. Let $\mathscr{N} \stackrel{\text{def}}{=} [\![1,n]\!] \setminus \mathscr{P}$ be the complementary set of $\mathscr{P}$. Here $\mathscr{P}$ corresponds to the entries of $\mathbf{e}$ we aim to recover. As explained in the introduction, the basic step of the decoding algorithm is to compute a large set $\mathscr{W}$ of parity-check equations of low weight w on $\mathscr{N}$ and to compute all the $\langle \mathbf{y}, \mathbf{h} \rangle$ with $\mathbf{h}$ ranging over $\mathscr{W}$. In RLPN decoding, the approach is to exploit directly that we have a number $|\mathscr{W}|$ of LPN samples $(\mathbf{h}_{\mathscr{P}}, \langle \mathbf{h}, \mathbf{y} \rangle)$ which can be viewed as an LPN sample $(\mathbf{a}, \langle \mathbf{a}, \mathbf{s} \rangle + e)$ by letting $\mathbf{a} \stackrel{\text{def}}{=} \mathbf{h}_{\mathscr{P}}$, $\mathbf{s} \stackrel{\text{def}}{=} \mathbf{e}_{\mathscr{P}}$, $e \stackrel{\text{def}}{=} \langle \mathbf{h}_{\mathscr{N}}, \mathbf{e}_{\mathscr{N}} \rangle$. Indeed,

$$\langle \mathbf{h}, \mathbf{y} \rangle = \langle \mathbf{h}, \mathbf{c} + \mathbf{e} \rangle = \underbrace{\langle \mathbf{h}, \mathbf{c} \rangle}_{=0} + \langle \mathbf{h}, \mathbf{e} \rangle = \underbrace{\langle \mathbf{h}_{\mathscr{P}}, \mathbf{e}_{\mathscr{P}} \rangle}_{=\langle \mathbf{a}, \mathbf{s} \rangle} + \underbrace{\langle \mathbf{h}_{\mathscr{N}}, \mathbf{e}_{\mathscr{N}} \rangle}_{\text{LPN noise } e}.$$

Notice that we really have a sparse LPN problem because of the sparseness of the secret $\mathbf{e}_{\mathscr{P}}$ which is not exploited in [10] and only exploited to verify the solution in the corrected RLPN algorithm of [40]. The point of this article is to exploit the sparseness of $\mathbf{e}_{\mathscr{P}} \in \mathbb{F}_2^s$ right away in order to reduce the dimension s of the secret. This is obtained by introducing an auxiliary code $\mathcal{C}_{\text{aux}}$ of length s and dimension k_{aux} which will be instrumental for reducing the dimension s of the secret down to k_{aux}. This is obtained as follows. We will assume that $\mathcal{C}_{\text{aux}}$ is chosen as a code with an *efficient list-decoding procedure* at distance t_{aux}.

Definition 6 (Efficiently list decodable code). *A code $\mathcal{C}$ of length n is said to be efficiently decodable code at distance t if it outputs for any $\mathbf{y} \in \mathbb{F}_2^n$ a non empty list of codewords of $\mathcal{C}$ at distance t in time $2^{o(n)}$.*

Moreover from now on, we assume that

Notation 1. *$\mathcal{C}_{\text{aux}}$ is an $[s, k_{\text{aux}}]$ efficiently list decodable for some distance t_{aux}. We denote by $\mathcal{D}ec(\mathbf{z})$ the set of all codewords of $\mathcal{C}_{\text{aux}}$ at distance t_{aux} from $\mathbf{z} \in \mathbb{F}_2^s$, namely $\mathcal{D}ec(\mathbf{z}) = \{ \mathbf{c}_{\text{aux}} \in \mathcal{C}_{\text{aux}} : |\mathbf{c}_{\text{aux}} + \mathbf{z}| = t_{\text{aux}} \}$.*

Remark 1. In our instantiation, t_{aux} is chosen such that $t_{\mathrm{aux}} \approx d_{\mathrm{GV}}(s, k_{\mathrm{aux}})$, thus we typically have $|\mathcal{D}ec(\mathbf{h}_{\mathscr{P}})| = \Theta(1)$.

Now, let us consider $\mathbf{c}_{\mathrm{aux}} \in \mathcal{D}ec(\mathbf{h}_{\mathscr{P}})$, a codeword of $\mathcal{C}_{\mathrm{aux}}$ at distance t_{aux} of $\mathbf{h}_{\mathscr{P}}$. It is readily seen that $\langle \mathbf{y}, \mathbf{h} \rangle$ decomposes as:

$$\langle \mathbf{y}, \mathbf{h} \rangle = \underbrace{\langle \mathbf{e}_{\mathscr{P}}, \mathbf{c}_{\mathrm{aux}} \rangle}_{\text{linear comb.}} + \underbrace{\langle \mathbf{e}_{\mathscr{P}}, \mathbf{h}_{\mathscr{P}} + \mathbf{c}_{\mathrm{aux}} \rangle + \langle \mathbf{e}_{\mathscr{N}}, \mathbf{h}_{\mathscr{N}} \rangle}_{\text{``new'' LPN noise}}.$$

Let us start by defining $\mathcal{C}_{\mathrm{aux}}$ with a generator matrix $\mathbf{G}_{\mathrm{aux}} \in \mathbb{F}_2^{s \times k_{\mathrm{aux}}}$. Then, knowing $\mathbf{c}_{\mathrm{aux}} \in \mathcal{C}_{\mathrm{aux}}$ is equivalent to know $\mathbf{m}_{\mathrm{aux}} \in \mathbb{F}_2^{k_{\mathrm{aux}}}$ such that $\mathbf{c}_{\mathrm{aux}} = \mathbf{m}_{\mathrm{aux}} \mathbf{G}_{\mathrm{aux}}$.

We can therefore rewrite $\langle \mathbf{e}_{\mathscr{P}}, \mathbf{c}_{\mathrm{aux}} \rangle$ as

$$\langle \mathbf{e}_{\mathscr{P}}, \mathbf{c}_{\mathrm{aux}} \rangle = \langle \mathbf{e}_{\mathscr{P}}, \mathbf{m}_{\mathrm{aux}} \mathbf{G}_{\mathrm{aux}} \rangle = \langle \mathbf{e}_{\mathscr{P}} \mathbf{G}_{\mathrm{aux}}^{\mathsf{T}}, \mathbf{m}_{\mathrm{aux}} \rangle.$$

We have therefore for each parity-check equation $\mathbf{h}$ of weight w on $\mathscr{N}$ that we have computed (*i.e.*, for all $\mathbf{h} \in \mathscr{W}$) and each codeword $\mathbf{m}_{\mathrm{aux}} \mathbf{G}_{\mathrm{aux}}$ of $\mathcal{C}_{\mathrm{aux}}$ at distance t_{aux} from $\mathbf{h}_{\mathscr{P}}$, an LPN sample $(\mathbf{m}_{\mathrm{aux}}, \langle \mathbf{y}, \mathbf{h} \rangle)$ which can be viewed as such by noticing that it is indeed equal to

$$(\mathbf{a}, \langle \mathbf{a}, \mathbf{s} \rangle + e) \quad \text{with} \quad \begin{cases} \mathbf{a} \overset{\text{def}}{=} \mathbf{m}_{\mathrm{aux}} \\ \mathbf{s} \overset{\text{def}}{=} \mathbf{e}_{\mathscr{P}} \mathbf{G}_{\mathrm{aux}}^{\mathsf{T}} \\ e \overset{\text{def}}{=} \langle \mathbf{e}_{\mathscr{P}}, \mathbf{h}_{\mathscr{P}} + \mathbf{c}_{\mathrm{aux}} \rangle + \langle \mathbf{e}_{\mathscr{N}}, \mathbf{h}_{\mathscr{N}} \rangle \end{cases} \tag{4}$$

Notice here that, if $\mathcal{D}ec(\mathbf{h}_{\mathscr{P}})$ contains more than one element, we can compute such LPN samples for each different $\mathbf{c}_{\mathrm{aux}} \in \mathcal{D}ec(\mathbf{h}_{\mathscr{P}})$. The secret in the above LPN sample is no longer given by $\mathbf{e}_{\mathscr{P}}$ that we want to recover (contrarily to RLPN-decoding [10]), but is given by $\mathbf{e}_{\mathscr{P}} \mathbf{G}_{\mathrm{aux}}^{\mathsf{T}} \in \mathbb{F}_2^{k_{\mathrm{aux}}}$ which are $k_{\mathrm{aux}} < s$ linear equations involving the $s = |\mathscr{P}|$ bits of the vector $\mathbf{e}$ we are looking for.

The main advantage of our technique is that we end up with an LPN problem whose dimension of the secret has decreased from s to k_{aux}. However, the noise has increased; let us describe how it behaves in the following paragraph.

3.2   Estimating the New Noise

The error e in Eq. (4) is biased toward zero and its bias is a function of n, s, t and u, w, t_{aux} which are respectively

$$u \overset{\text{def}}{=} |\mathbf{e}_{\mathscr{N}}|, \quad w \overset{\text{def}}{=} |\mathbf{h}_{\mathscr{N}}| \quad \text{and} \quad t_{\mathrm{aux}} \overset{\text{def}}{=} |\mathbf{h}_{\mathscr{P}} + \mathbf{c}_{\mathrm{aux}}|.$$

In the following statement we compute the bias of e over all the possible LPN samples, that is we compute

$$\underset{(\mathbf{h}, \mathbf{c}_{\mathrm{aux}}) \overset{\$}{\leftarrow} \widetilde{\mathscr{H}}}{\mathrm{bias}} (\langle \mathbf{e}_{\mathscr{P}}, \mathbf{h}_{\mathrm{aux}} + \mathbf{c}_{\mathrm{aux}} \rangle + \langle \mathbf{e}_{\mathscr{N}}, \mathbf{h}_{\mathscr{N}} \rangle) = \frac{1}{|\widetilde{\mathscr{H}}|} \sum_{(\mathbf{h}, \mathbf{c}_{\mathrm{aux}}) \in \widetilde{\mathscr{H}}} (-1)^{\langle \mathbf{e}_{\mathscr{P}}, \mathbf{h}_{\mathscr{P}} + \mathbf{c}_{\mathrm{aux}} \rangle + \langle \mathbf{e}_{\mathscr{N}}, \mathbf{h}_{\mathscr{N}} \rangle}$$

where $\widetilde{\mathscr{H}}$ is defined by

Definition 7.

$$\widetilde{\mathscr{H}} \overset{def}{=} \{(\mathbf{h}, \mathbf{c}_{\mathrm{aux}}) \in \mathcal{C}^{\perp} \times \mathcal{C}_{\mathrm{aux}} : |\mathbf{h}_{\mathscr{N}}| = w \text{ and } |\mathbf{h}_{\mathscr{P}} + \mathbf{c}_{\mathrm{aux}}| = t_{\mathrm{aux}}\}. \quad (5)$$

It is tempting to conjecture that this bias is well approximated by the bias of a Bernoulli variable $X \overset{def}{=} \langle \mathbf{e}_{\mathscr{P}}, \mathbf{e}_{\mathrm{aux}} \rangle + \langle \mathbf{e}_{\mathscr{N}}, \mathbf{w} \rangle$ where $\mathbf{e}_{\mathrm{aux}}$ and $\mathbf{w}$ are respectively drawn uniformly at random in the Hamming spheres $\mathcal{S}^{s}_{t_{\mathrm{aux}}}$ and $\mathcal{S}^{n-s}_{w}$. The sum $\langle \mathbf{e}_{\mathscr{P}}, \mathbf{e}_{\mathrm{aux}} \rangle + \langle \mathbf{e}_{\mathscr{N}}, \mathbf{w} \rangle$ is performed over $\mathbb{F}_2$ and all the vectors are independent random variables. Because of the independence of the random variables, from the straightforward fact that $\mathrm{bias}(X_1 + X_2) = \mathrm{bias}(X_1)\,\mathrm{bias}(X_2)$ when X_1 and X_2 are independent Bernoulli variables (and the addition is performed modulo 2). Therefore,

$$\mathrm{bias}(X) = \mathrm{bias}\left(\langle \mathbf{e}_{\mathscr{P}}, \mathbf{e}_{\mathrm{aux}} \rangle\right) \mathrm{bias}\left(\langle \mathbf{e}_{\mathscr{N}}, \mathbf{w} \rangle\right)$$

$$= \frac{K^{(s)}_{t_{\mathrm{aux}}}(t - u)}{\binom{s}{t_{\mathrm{aux}}}} \frac{K^{(n-s)}_{w}(u)}{\binom{n-s}{w}} \quad \text{(by Fact 1).}$$

This kind of approximation was done in the early days of statistical decoding [17,31,42], until [10, Prop. 3.1] which has shown that under certain conditions, *i.e.*, when there are enough available parity-check equations of weight w (essentially when the number is of order $\omega(1/\delta^2)$ where δ is the bias), then this approximation can indeed be shown to hold with overwhelming probability. [10, Prop. 3.1] can be adapted to our setting with some additional technicalities and conditions. It can be shown that with overwhelming probability we indeed have

$$\underset{(\mathbf{h},\mathbf{c}_{\mathrm{aux}}) \overset{\$}{\leftarrow} \widetilde{\mathscr{H}}}{\mathrm{bias}} \left(\langle \mathbf{e}_{\mathscr{P}}, \mathbf{h}_{\mathscr{P}} + \mathbf{c}_{\mathrm{aux}} \rangle + \langle \mathbf{e}_{\mathscr{N}}, \mathbf{h}_{\mathscr{N}} \rangle\right) = (1 + o(1))\,\mathrm{bias}(X).$$

This is in essence what the following proposition shows.

Proposition 2. *Suppose that the parameters are such that for some constant $\alpha > 0$*

$$\frac{\binom{n-s}{w}\binom{s}{t_{\mathrm{aux}}}}{2^{k-k_{\mathrm{aux}}}} = \omega\left(\frac{n^{\alpha}}{\delta^2}\right) \quad \text{where} \quad \delta \overset{def}{=} \frac{K^{(n-s)}_{w}(u)\,K^{(s)}_{t_{\mathrm{aux}}}(t - u)}{\binom{n-s}{w}\binom{s}{t_{\mathrm{aux}}}}. \quad (6)$$

Moreover suppose that

$$\frac{\binom{n-s}{w}\binom{s}{t_{\mathrm{aux}}}}{2^k} = \mathcal{O}(n^{\alpha}) \quad \text{and} \quad \frac{\binom{s}{t_{\mathrm{aux}}}}{2^{s-k_{\mathrm{aux}}}} = \mathcal{O}(n^{\alpha}). \quad (7)$$

Let $\mathscr{N}$ be a set of $n - s$ positions in $[\![1, n]\!]$ and $\mathscr{P} \overset{def}{=} [\![1, n]\!] \backslash \mathscr{N}$. Let $\mathbf{e}$ be a vector of weight u on $\mathscr{N}$ and $t - u$ on $\mathscr{P}$. Let $\mathcal{C}$ and $\mathcal{C}_{\mathrm{aux}}$ be $[n, k]$ and $[s, k_{\mathrm{aux}}]$ linear codes respectively. Let us choose $(\mathbf{c}_{\mathrm{aux}}, \mathbf{h})$ uniformly at random in

$$\widetilde{\mathscr{H}} = \{(\mathbf{h}, \mathbf{c}_{\mathrm{aux}}) \in \mathcal{C}^{\perp} \times \mathcal{C}_{\mathrm{aux}} : |\mathbf{h}_{\mathscr{N}}| = w \text{ and } |\mathbf{h}_{\mathscr{P}} + \mathbf{c}_{\mathrm{aux}}| = t_{\mathrm{aux}}\}.$$

Then for a proportion $1 - o(1)$ of codes $\mathcal{C}_{\mathrm{aux}}$ and $\mathcal{C}$ we have that

$$\underset{(\mathbf{h},\mathbf{c}_{\mathrm{aux}}) \overset{\$}{\leftarrow} \widetilde{\mathscr{H}}}{\mathrm{bias}} \left(\langle \mathbf{c}_{\mathrm{aux}} + \mathbf{h}_{\mathscr{P}}, \mathbf{e}_{\mathscr{P}} \rangle + \langle \mathbf{e}_{\mathscr{N}}, \mathbf{h}_{\mathscr{N}} \rangle\right) = \delta(1 + o(1)).$$

Proof. Available in the long version of the paper [11, Appendix A].

4   The **double-RLPN** Algorithm

We first going to explain the four main ingredients of the double-RLPN algorithm:
(i) computing suitable LPN samples, (ii) FFT decoding, (iii) recovering $\mathbf{e}_{\mathscr{P}}$, (iv)
the bet ensuring that there are u errors on $\mathscr{N}$ at some point. Let us detail each
of these ingredients (or steps of the algorithm).

Computing the LPN Samples. First, our algorithm computes a certain num-
ber of LPN samples by computing a set $\mathscr{W}$ of elements of $\mathcal{C}^{\perp}$ of weight w on $\mathscr{N}$
by using a procedure PARITYCHECKEQUATIONS$(w, \mathscr{N}, \mathcal{C})$ that uses low-weight
codewords search techniques to produce a bunch of parity-check equations of
$\mathcal{C}$ of weight w on $\mathscr{N}$. Then a random code $\mathcal{C}_{\mathrm{aux}}$ is chosen in a family of codes
over $\mathbb{F}_2^{|\mathscr{P}|}$ and dimension k_{aux} that we know how to decode efficiently at distance
t_{aux}. For an element $\mathbf{h}$ in $\mathscr{W}$, each $\mathbf{h}_{\mathscr{P}}$ is decoded at distance t_{aux} to finally
compute the set $\mathscr{H}$ containing pairs $(\mathbf{h}, \mathbf{c}_{\mathrm{aux}})$ in $\mathscr{W} \times \mathcal{C}_{\mathrm{aux}}$ satisfying $|\mathbf{h}_{\mathscr{N}}| = w$
and $|\mathbf{h}_{\mathscr{P}} + \mathbf{c}_{\mathrm{aux}}| = t_{\mathrm{aux}}$. Algorithm 1 gives the pseudo-code of the procedure.

Algorithm 1. The function computing the LPN samples associated to $\mathscr{N}$

1: **function** LPN-SAMPLES$(\mathcal{C}, \mathscr{N})$
2:      $\mathscr{P} \leftarrow [\![1, n]\!] \setminus \mathscr{N}$
3:      $\mathscr{W} \leftarrow$ PARITYCHECKEQUATIONS$(w, \mathscr{N}, \mathcal{C})$ ▷ returns a set of parity-check
   equations of $\mathcal{C}$ of weight w on $\mathscr{N}$
4:      $\mathcal{C}_{\mathrm{aux}} \xleftarrow{\$} \mathscr{F}(\mathscr{P}, k_{\mathrm{aux}}, t_{\mathrm{aux}})$ ▷ returns a code $\mathcal{C}_{\mathrm{aux}}$ in a family of codes $\mathscr{F}$ over $\mathbb{F}_2^{|\mathscr{P}|}$
   and dimension k_{aux} that we know how to decode efficiently at distance t_{aux}
5:      $\mathscr{H} \leftarrow \emptyset$
6:      **for all** $\mathbf{h} \in \mathscr{W}$ **do**
7:          $\mathscr{H} \leftarrow \mathscr{H} \cup \{\mathbf{h}\} \times$ DECODE$(\mathbf{h}_{\mathscr{P}}, \mathcal{C}_{\mathrm{aux}}, t_{\mathrm{aux}})$ ▷ DECODE$(\mathbf{h}_{\mathscr{P}}, \mathcal{C}_{\mathrm{aux}}, t_{\mathrm{aux}})$
   outputs a set of codewords of $\mathcal{C}_{\mathrm{aux}}$ at distance t_{aux} of $\mathbf{h}_{\mathscr{P}}$
8:      **end for**
9:      $\mathbf{G}_{\mathrm{aux}} \leftarrow$ generating matrix of $\mathcal{C}_{\mathrm{aux}}$
10: **return** $(\mathscr{H}, \mathbf{G}_{\mathrm{aux}})$
11: **end function**

FFT Decoding. Computing $\mathscr{H}$ gives a number $|\mathscr{H}|$ of LPN samples, which
from the interpretation given in Eq. (4), leads us to think that the right
choice $\mathbf{x} \in \mathbb{F}_2^{k_{\mathrm{aux}}}$ for $\mathbf{e}_{\mathscr{P}} \mathbf{G}_{\mathrm{aux}}^{\intercal}$ is the one for which bias$_{(\mathbf{h}, \mathbf{m}_{\mathrm{aux}} \mathbf{G}_{\mathrm{aux}}) \xleftarrow{\$} \mathscr{H}}$
$(\langle \mathbf{y}, \mathbf{h} \rangle + \langle \mathbf{x}, \mathbf{m}_{\mathrm{aux}} \rangle)$ would be given by Proposition 2. It should namely be of
order δ which is defined in this proposition. Natural candidates for being equal
to $\mathbf{e}_{\mathscr{P}} \mathbf{G}_{\mathrm{aux}}^{\intercal}$ are those for which this bias is say $\geqslant \delta/2$. This leads to compute
all those biases. This can be done rather efficiently by factoring the common
computations made for computing all those biases for $\mathbf{x} \in \mathbb{F}_2^{k_{\mathrm{aux}}}$ by an FFT trick
which is standard in the LPN context[2]. The link between the bias of the random

---

[2] It dates back in this context to [34], but it can be traced back to decoding the first-
   order Reed-Muller code (which is another way to view the decoding task in case of
   the LPN problem) which was already suggested in [27].

variables we are interested in and the Fourier transform is based on the following simple observation that follows right away from the very definition of the Fourier transform. Before we give this observation, let us bring in a notation that will be helpful for describing it and which will be used throughout the paper from now on.

Notation 2. *For any* $\mathbf{y} \in \mathbb{F}_2^n$, $\mathscr{H} \subseteq \mathcal{C}^\perp \times \mathcal{C}_{\mathrm{aux}}$ *and a generator matrix* $\mathbf{G}_{\mathrm{aux}}$ *of* $\mathcal{C}_{\mathrm{aux}}$ *we define the function* $f_{\mathbf{y}, \mathscr{H}, \mathbf{G}_{\mathrm{aux}}}$ *on* $\mathbb{F}_2^{k_{\mathrm{aux}}}$ *by*

$$f_{\mathbf{y}, \mathscr{H}, \mathbf{G}_{\mathrm{aux}}} : \mathbb{F}_2^{k_{\mathrm{aux}}} \to \mathbb{R}$$

$$\mathbf{x} \mapsto \sum_{\mathbf{h} : (\mathbf{h}, \mathbf{x}\mathbf{G}_{\mathrm{aux}}) \in \mathscr{H}} (-1)^{\langle \mathbf{y}, \mathbf{h} \rangle} \tag{8}$$

With this notation at hand, the link between the biases and the Fourier transform of this function is given by the following lemma.

Lemma 1. *We have for any* $\mathbf{u} \in \mathbb{F}_2^{k_{\mathrm{aux}}}$ *and any* $\mathbf{x} \in \mathbb{F}_2^s$ *such that* $\mathbf{x}\mathbf{G}_{\mathrm{aux}}^{\mathsf{T}} = \mathbf{u}$

$$\widehat{f_{\mathbf{y}, \mathscr{H}, \mathbf{G}_{\mathrm{aux}}}}(\mathbf{u}) = |\mathscr{H}| \operatorname*{bias}_{(\mathbf{h}, \mathbf{m}_{\mathrm{aux}}\mathbf{G}_{\mathrm{aux}}) \xleftarrow{\$} \mathscr{H}} (\langle \mathbf{y}, \mathbf{h} \rangle + \langle \mathbf{u}, \mathbf{m}_{\mathrm{aux}} \rangle)$$

$$= |\mathscr{H}| \operatorname*{bias}_{(\mathbf{h}, \mathbf{c}_{\mathrm{aux}}) \xleftarrow{\$} \mathscr{H}} (\langle \mathbf{y}, \mathbf{h} \rangle + \langle \mathbf{x}, \mathbf{c}_{\mathrm{aux}} \rangle).$$

Proof. Available in the long version of the article [11].

Remark 2. The probabilistic notation hides the fact that computing all these Fourier coefficients and taking the maximum of them allows to decode in a certain code. Indeed let, $\mathcal{D} \stackrel{\text{def}}{=} \left\{ (\langle \mathbf{u}, \mathbf{m}_{\mathrm{aux}} \rangle)_{(\mathbf{h}, \mathbf{m}_{\mathrm{aux}}\mathbf{G}_{\mathrm{aux}}) \in \mathscr{H}} : \mathbf{u} \in \mathbb{F}_2^{k_{\mathrm{aux}}} \right\}$ which is under very mild assumptions a linear code of dimension k_{aux} and length $|\mathscr{H}|$. If we let $c(\mathbf{u}) \stackrel{\text{def}}{=} (\langle \mathbf{u}, \mathbf{m}_{\mathrm{aux}} \rangle)_{(\mathbf{h}, \mathbf{m}_{\mathrm{aux}}\mathbf{G}_{\mathrm{aux}}) \in \mathscr{H}}$ be the codeword associated to $\mathbf{u}$ and $\mathbf{v} = (\langle \mathbf{y}, \mathbf{h} \rangle)_{(\mathbf{h}, \mathbf{m}_{\mathrm{aux}}\mathbf{G}_{\mathrm{aux}}) \in \mathscr{H}}$ then since

$$|\mathscr{H}| \operatorname*{bias}_{(\mathbf{h}, \mathbf{m}_{\mathrm{aux}}\mathbf{G}_{\mathrm{aux}}) \xleftarrow{\$} \mathscr{H}} (\langle \mathbf{y}, \mathbf{h} \rangle + \langle \mathbf{u}, \mathbf{m}_{\mathrm{aux}} \rangle) = |\mathscr{H}| - 2|\mathbf{v} + c(\mathbf{u})|,$$

it follows from Lemma 1 that $c(\mathbf{u}_0)$ is the codeword of $\mathcal{D}$ which is the closest to $\mathbf{v}$, where $\mathbf{u}_0 = \arg\max \widehat{f_{\mathbf{y}, \mathscr{H}, \mathbf{G}_{\mathrm{aux}}}}(\mathbf{u})$. Therefore, vector $\mathbf{u}_0$ is here a likely candidate for being equal to $\mathbf{e}_{\mathscr{P}} \mathbf{G}_{\mathrm{aux}}^{\mathsf{T}}$ when $\mathscr{H}$ is big enough.

We give the pseudo-code of the FFT decoding algorithm producing a list $\mathscr{S}$ of putative candidates for being equal to $\mathbf{e}_{\mathscr{P}} \mathbf{G}_{\mathrm{aux}}^{\mathsf{T}}$ in Algorithm 2.

The point of using the FFT for computing all these biases is that its complexity is of order $\mathcal{O}(k_{\mathrm{aux}} 2^{k_{\mathrm{aux}}} F)$ where F is the complexity of computing $f_{\mathbf{y}, \mathscr{H}, \mathbf{G}_{\mathrm{aux}}}$ which can be bounded by $\mathcal{O}\left(\max\left(1, \frac{|\mathscr{H}|}{2^{k_{\mathrm{aux}}}}\right)\right)$. On the other hand, if we had computed directly all those biases we would have a much bigger complexity of $\mathcal{O}(|\mathscr{H}| 2^{k_{\mathrm{aux}}})$ because $\mathscr{H}$ is of exponential size for the problem at hand.

Algorithm 2. FFT algorithm producing a list of candidates for $\mathbf{e}_{\mathscr{P}}\mathbf{G}_{\mathrm{aux}}^{\mathsf{T}}$

Input: $\mathscr{H}, \mathbf{G}_{\mathrm{aux}}$
Output: $\mathscr{S}$ a list of candidates for $\mathbf{e}_{\mathscr{P}}\mathbf{G}_{\mathrm{aux}}^{\mathsf{T}}$

1: **function** FFT-DECODE($\mathscr{H}, \mathbf{G}_{\mathrm{aux}}$)
2:     $\widehat{f_{\mathbf{y},\mathscr{H},\mathbf{G}_{\mathrm{aux}}}} \leftarrow \mathrm{FFT}(f_{\mathbf{y},\mathscr{H},\mathbf{G}_{\mathrm{aux}}})$
3:     $\mathscr{S} \leftarrow \left\{ \mathbf{u} \in \mathbb{F}_2^{k_{\mathrm{aux}}} : \widehat{f_{\mathbf{y},\mathscr{H},\mathbf{G}_{\mathrm{aux}}}}(\mathbf{u}) > \frac{\delta}{2}|\mathscr{H}| \right\}$ $\triangleright \delta \stackrel{\mathrm{def}}{=} \dfrac{K_w^{(n-s)}(u)K_{t_{\mathrm{aux}}}^{(s)}(t-u)}{\binom{n-s}{w}\binom{s}{t_{\mathrm{aux}}}}$
4:     **return** $\mathscr{S}$
5: **end function**

Recovering $\mathbf{e}_{\mathscr{P}}$ and then e. If we have a candidate **s** for $\mathbf{e}_{\mathscr{P}}\mathbf{G}_{\mathrm{aux}}^{\mathsf{T}}$, then since we expect $|\mathbf{e}_{\mathscr{P}}| = t - u$, recovering $\mathbf{e}_{\mathscr{P}}$ from the equality $\mathbf{s} = \mathbf{e}_{\mathscr{P}}\mathbf{G}_{\mathrm{aux}}^{\mathsf{T}}$ is nothing but solving a decoding problem, namely to decode $t - u$ errors in the code of parity-check matrix $\mathbf{G}_{\mathrm{aux}}$, *i.e.*, $\mathcal{C}_{\mathrm{aux}}^{\perp}$. In other words, we have to solve DP($s, s - k_{\mathrm{aux}}, t-u$). This approach can be generalized by taking N_{aux} different sets of LPN samples associated respectively to the codes $\mathcal{C}_{\mathrm{aux}}^{(1)}, \cdots, \mathcal{C}_{\mathrm{aux}}^{(N_{\mathrm{aux}})}$. For i in $[\![1, N_{\mathrm{aux}}]\!]$, let $\mathbf{G}_{\mathrm{aux}}^{(i)}$ be the generating matrix which is chosen for $\mathcal{C}_{\mathrm{aux}}^{(i)}$. Then each of these sets of LPN samples brings candidates for $\mathbf{e}_{\mathscr{P}}\mathbf{G}_{\mathrm{aux}}^{\mathsf{T}}$. By choosing an N_{aux}-tuple of candidates $(\mathbf{s}^{(1)}, \cdots, \mathbf{s}^{(N_{\mathrm{aux}})})$, where $\mathbf{s}^{(i)}$ is a candidate for $\mathbf{G}_{\mathrm{aux}}^{(i)}\mathbf{e}_{\mathscr{P}}^{\mathsf{T}}$ (we have taken the transpose to have a more readable form) given by the i-th LPN samples set, we get to solve the set of simultaneous equations

$$(\mathbf{s}^{(1)})^{\mathsf{T}} = \mathbf{G}_{\mathrm{aux}}^{(1)}\mathbf{e}_{\mathscr{P}}^{\mathsf{T}}, \cdots, (\mathbf{s}^{(N_{\mathrm{aux}})})^{\mathsf{T}} = \mathbf{G}_{\mathrm{aux}}^{(N_{\mathrm{aux}})}\mathbf{e}_{\mathscr{P}}^{\mathsf{T}}$$

with the constraint $|\mathbf{e}_{\mathscr{P}}| = t - u$. In other words if we set $\mathbf{H}^{\mathsf{T}} \stackrel{\mathrm{def}}{=} \left(\mathbf{G}_{\mathrm{aux}}^{(1)\mathsf{T}} \cdots \mathbf{G}_{\mathrm{aux}}^{(N_{\mathrm{aux}})\mathsf{T}}\right)$ and $\mathbf{s} \stackrel{\mathrm{def}}{=} \left(\mathbf{s}^{(1)} \cdots \mathbf{s}^{(N_{\mathrm{aux}})}\right)$ then we have to solve the decoding problem $\mathbf{H}\mathbf{e}_{\mathscr{P}}^{\mathsf{T}} = \mathbf{s}^{\mathsf{T}}$ with $|\mathbf{e}_{\mathscr{P}}| = t - u$, that is DP$(s, s - N_{\mathrm{aux}}k_{\mathrm{aux}}, t - u)$. We are going to choose a simple ISD algorithm to solve this problem, namely Dumer's algorithm [21] which is a good compromise between efficiency and simple formula for its complexity. We denote by DECODE-DUMER($\mathbf{H}, \mathbf{s}, t$) the call to Dumer's algorithm to decode the syndrome **s** of an error of weight t associated to the parity-check matrix **H**. We assume here that this call produces *all* solutions to this decoding problem.

Once we have recovered $\mathbf{e}_{\mathscr{P}}$, say we know that it is equal to some **v** of weight $t - u$ in $\mathbb{F}_2^s$, we face a much simpler problem. We namely have to solve the problem $\mathbf{y} = \mathbf{c} + \mathbf{e}$ where $\mathbf{c} \in \mathcal{C}$ with $\mathbf{e}_{\mathscr{P}} = \mathbf{v}$ and $|\mathbf{e}_{\mathscr{N}}| = u$. This is nothing but DP($n-s, k-s, u$) which is much simpler. Here we might just use DECODE-DUMER on it. Let us call SOLVE-SUBPROBLEM($\mathcal{C}, \mathscr{N}, \mathbf{y}, \mathbf{v}, u$) the routine which performs this task and which returns a candidate for $\mathbf{e}_{\mathscr{N}}$ and returns $\perp$ otherwise. If this problem has no solution we have of course a false candidate for $\mathbf{e}_{\mathscr{P}}$ and if we have a solution, then we have solved our decoding problem. To verify that we have indeed such a decoding problem, suppose without loss of generality that $\mathscr{P} = [\![1, s]\!]$, $\mathscr{N} = [\![s+1, n]\!]$. We can also assume that $\mathcal{C}_{\mathscr{P}}$ is of full rank dimension s (this holds with overwhelming probability). We can compute $\mathbf{G}$ a generator matrix of $\mathcal{C}$ of the form $\mathbf{G} = \begin{pmatrix} \mathbf{Id}_s & \mathbf{R} \\ \mathbf{0}_{k-s} & \mathbf{R}' \end{pmatrix}$ by applying partial Gaussian elimination on a generator matrix of $\mathcal{C}$. Then SOLVE-SUBPROBLEM$(\mathcal{C}, \mathscr{N}, \mathbf{y}, \mathbf{v}, u)$ decodes at distance u the word $\mathbf{y}' \overset{\text{def}}{=} \mathbf{y}_{\mathscr{N}} - (\mathbf{y}_{\mathscr{P}} - \mathbf{v})\mathbf{R}$ onto the code $\mathcal{C}^{\mathscr{N}}$ of generator matrix $\mathbf{R}'$.

The pseudo-code describing the algorithm for recovering $\mathbf{e}_{\mathscr{P}}$ and then returning $\mathbf{e}$ if a suitable solution is found, is given in Algorithm 3.

Algorithm 3. Algorithm recovering $\mathbf{e}_{\mathscr{P}}$ and then $\mathbf{e}$

Input: $\mathscr{S}^{(1)}, \cdots, \mathscr{S}^{(N_{\text{aux}})} \subset \mathbb{F}_2^{k_{\text{aux}}}$, $\mathbf{G}_{\text{aux}}^{(1)}, \cdots, \mathbf{G}_{\text{aux}}^{(N_{\text{aux}})} \in \mathbb{F}_2^{k_{\text{aux}} \times s}$

1: **function** RECOVER-e$(\mathscr{S}^{(1)}, \cdots, \mathscr{S}^{(N_{\text{aux}})}, \mathbf{G}_{\text{aux}}^{(1)}, \cdots, \mathbf{G}_{\text{aux}}^{(N_{\text{aux}})})$
2:     $\mathbf{H}^{\mathsf{T}} \leftarrow \left(\mathbf{G}_{\text{aux}}^{(1)\,\mathsf{T}} \cdots \mathbf{G}_{\text{aux}}^{(N_{\text{aux}})\mathsf{T}} \right)$
3:     **for** $\left(\mathbf{s}^{(1)}, ..., \mathbf{s}^{(N_{\text{aux}})} \right) \in \prod_{j=1}^{N_{\text{aux}}} \mathcal{S}^{(j)}$ **do**
4:         $\mathbf{s} \leftarrow \left(\mathbf{s}^{(1)} \cdots \mathbf{s}^{(N_{\text{aux}})} \right)$
5:         **for all** $\mathbf{v} \in$ DECODE-DUMER$(\mathbf{H}, \mathbf{s}, t)$ **do**
6:             $\mathbf{e}' \leftarrow$ SOLVE-SUBPROBLEM$(\mathcal{C}, \mathscr{N}, \mathbf{y}, \mathbf{v}, u)$
7:             **if** $\mathbf{e}' \neq \perp$ **then**
8:                 **return** e such that $\mathbf{e}_{\mathscr{P}} = \mathbf{v}$ and $\mathbf{e}_{\mathscr{N}} = \mathbf{e}'$
9:             **end if**
10:         **end for**
11:     **end for**
12: **end function**

Testing Enough Candidates $\mathscr{N}$. It may also happen that when choosing $\mathscr{N}$, we might not have that $|\mathbf{e}_{\mathscr{N}}| = u$. For this, we have to check enough candidates. The probability that a set $\mathscr{N}$ of size $n - s$ satisfies this property is given by $P_{\text{succ}} \overset{\text{def}}{=} \frac{\binom{t}{u}\binom{n-t}{n-u-s}}{\binom{n}{n-s}}$. Performing a number N_{iter} of trials for $\mathscr{N}$ which is of order $\Theta\left(1/P_{\text{succ}}\right)$ will succeed with constant probability. Putting all these ingredients together leads to the whole double-RLPN algorithm given in Algorithm 4.

Complexity of the Algorithm. It is sufficient to take $N_{\text{aux}} = \mathcal{O}(1)$ for the parameters we are interested in which will correspond to a choice of k_{aux} of the form $k_{\text{aux}} = \Omega(s)$. With this choice we immediately get the following complexity for the double-RLPN algorithm

---

Algorithm 4. double-RLPN decoder

Input: $\mathbf{y}$, t, $\mathcal{C}$ an $[n,k]$-code
Parameters: $s, u, k_{\text{aux}}, t_{\text{aux}}, N, \left(\mathcal{C}_{\text{aux}}^{(j)}\right)_{j \in \mathcal{F}}$
Output: $\mathbf{e}$ such that $|\mathbf{e}| = t$ and $\mathbf{y} - \mathbf{e} \in \mathcal{C}$.

1: **function** double-RLPN($\mathbf{y}$, $\mathcal{C}$, t)
2:   **for** i from 1 to N_{iter} **do**   ▷ N_{iter} such that w.o.p one iteration is s.t $|\mathbf{e}_{\mathcal{N}}| = u$
3:     $\mathcal{N} \xleftarrow{\$} \{\mathcal{I} \subseteq [\![1,n]\!] : |\mathcal{I}| = n - s\}$ ▷ Hope that $|\mathbf{e}_{\mathcal{N}}| = u$
4:     **for** $j = 1, \ldots, N_{\text{aux}}$ **do**
5:       $(\mathcal{H}^{(j)}, \mathbf{G}_{\text{aux}}^{(j)}) \leftarrow \text{LPN-SAMPLES}(\mathcal{C}, \mathcal{N})$
6:       $\mathcal{S}^{(j)} \leftarrow \text{FFT-DECODE}(\mathcal{H}^{(j)}, \mathbf{G}_{\text{aux}}^{(j)})$
7:     **end for**
8:     $\text{RECOVER-e}(\mathcal{S}^{(1)}, \cdots, \mathcal{S}^{(N_{\text{aux}})}, \mathbf{G}_{\text{aux}}^{(1)}, \cdots, \mathbf{G}_{\text{aux}}^{(N_{\text{aux}})})$
9:   **end for**
10: **end function**

Proposition 3. *The complexity C of the* double-RLPN *algorithm is given by*

$$C = \tilde{\mathcal{O}}\left(\frac{1}{P_{\text{succ}}} \left(T_{\text{eq}} + N T_{\text{dec}} + k_{\text{aux}} \max\left(2^{k_{\text{aux}}}, |\mathcal{H}|\right) + S^{N_{\text{aux}}} T_{\text{ISD}} \right) \right) \quad (9)$$

where $P_{\text{succ}} = \dfrac{\binom{t}{u}\binom{n-t}{n-u-s}}{\binom{n}{n-s}}$,

$$T_{\text{ISD}} = T_{\text{Dumer}}(s, s - N_{\text{aux}}k_{\text{aux}}, t - u) + N_{\text{ISD}} T_{\text{Dumer}}(n - s, k - s, u)$$

and T_{eq} is the time complexity of PARITYCHECKEQUATIONS, *N is the number of parity-check equations produced by this procedure, T_{dec} is the complexity of decoding $\mathcal{C}_{\text{aux}}$, i.e., it is the complexity of a call to* DECODE, *S is the size of a list output by* FFT-DECODE, *N_{ISD} is the number of solutions to the $(s, s - N_{\text{aux}}k_{\text{aux}}, t - u)$ decoding problem and $T_{\text{Dumer}}(n, k, t)$ stands for the complexity of solving the (n, k, t) decoding problem with Dumer's algorithm when we want to find all solutions to the problem, and, where we supposed that $N_{\text{aux}} = \mathcal{O}(1)$.*

The asymptotic complexity formula for the double-RLPN algorithm, including also the constraints required on our parameters, is given in the long version of the paper [11, App. B, Prop. 9] which was used to generate Fig. 1.

5   Estimating the Number of False Candidates

The goal of this section is to introduce the main tool necessary to make a rigorous analysis of Algorithm 4 and to give a formula for the number of false candidates which is proved by making a certain conjecture whose validity has then been verified experimentally.

5.1 Main Duality Tool

The fundamental quantity when analyzing dual attacks is the bias of $\langle \mathbf{y}, \mathbf{h} \rangle + \langle \mathbf{x}, \mathbf{c}_{\mathrm{aux}} \rangle$ which tells us whether $\mathbf{x}\mathbf{G}_{\mathrm{aux}}^{\intercal}$ has to be put in the list $\mathscr{S}$ of candidates outputted by Algorithm 2. While initially standard independence assumptions were made to analyze its distribution [10, Ass. 3.7] (which are very similar to analyze dual attacks in lattice based cryptography), recently [40] showed that these assumptions were erroneous and, gave for the first time a dual expression [40, Prop 1.] for this quantity which is a key step to understand its behavior and gave with an added assumption a rigorous analysis of the RLPN dual attack. The proposition given there to estimate the number of false candidates turns out to match accurately the experiments. The following proposition is a generalization of [40, Prop 1.] and gives a dual expression for the aforementioned bias.

Proposition 4. *Let $\mathscr{P}$ and $\mathscr{N}$ be two complementary subsets of $[\![1, n]\!]$ of size s and $n - s$ respectively. Let $\mathcal{C}$ be an $[n, k]$-code such that $\mathcal{C}_{\mathscr{P}}$ is of dimension s and let $\mathcal{C}_{\mathrm{aux}}$ be an $[s, k_{\mathrm{aux}}]$-code. We have for any $\mathbf{x} \in \mathbb{F}_2^s$*

$$\operatorname*{bias}_{(\mathbf{h}, \mathbf{c}_{\mathrm{aux}}) \xleftarrow{\$} \widetilde{\mathscr{H}}} (\langle \mathbf{y}, \mathbf{h} \rangle + \langle \mathbf{x}, \mathbf{c}_{\mathrm{aux}} \rangle) = \frac{1}{2^{k - k_{\mathrm{aux}}}} \frac{1}{|\widetilde{\mathscr{H}}|} \sum_{i=0}^{n-s} \sum_{j=0}^{s} N_{i,j} K_w^{(n-s)}(i) K_{t_{\mathrm{aux}}}^{(s)}(j)$$

(10)

where

$$N_{i,j} \overset{def}{=} \left| \left\{ (\mathbf{r}, \mathbf{c}^{\mathscr{N}}) \in (\mathbf{x} + \mathcal{C}_{\mathrm{aux}}^{\perp}) \times \mathcal{C}^{\mathscr{N}} : |\mathbf{r}| = j \text{ and } |(\mathbf{r} + \mathbf{e}_{\mathscr{P}})\mathbf{R} + \mathbf{e}_{\mathscr{N}} + \mathbf{c}^{\mathscr{N}}| = i \right\} \right|,$$

$$\widetilde{\mathscr{H}} = \{ (\mathbf{h}, \mathbf{c}_{\mathrm{aux}}) \in \mathcal{C}^{\perp} \times \mathcal{C}_{\mathrm{aux}} : |\mathbf{h}_{\mathscr{N}}| = w \text{ and } |\mathbf{h}_{\mathscr{P}} + \mathbf{c}_{\mathrm{aux}}| = t_{\mathrm{aux}} \}$$

and where $\mathbf{R} \in \mathbb{F}_2^{s \times (n-s)}$ is such that for any $\mathbf{h} \in \mathcal{C}^{\perp}$ we have $\mathbf{h}_{\mathscr{P}} = \mathbf{h}_{\mathscr{N}} \mathbf{R}^{\intercal}$.

Proof. Available in the long version of the paper [11, Appendix C].

5.2 Intuition on How This Formula Allows to Estimate $|\mathscr{S}|$

As a preliminary remark, notice that $\operatorname*{bias}_{(\mathbf{h}, \mathbf{c}_{\mathrm{aux}}) \xleftarrow{\$} \widetilde{\mathscr{H}}} (\langle \mathbf{y}, \mathbf{h} \rangle + \langle \mathbf{x}, \mathbf{c}_{\mathrm{aux}} \rangle)$ is the same for all $\mathbf{x}$ belonging to a same coset of $\mathcal{C}_{\mathrm{aux}}^{\perp}$ and therefore only possibly allows to distinguish the values $\mathbf{x}\mathbf{G}_{\mathrm{aux}}^{\intercal}$. Second, observe that the expected value of $|\widetilde{\mathscr{H}}|$ is $\frac{\binom{n-s}{w}}{2^{k-s}} \frac{\binom{s}{t_{\mathrm{aux}}}}{2^{s-k_{\mathrm{aux}}}}$ so that we expect $\frac{1}{2^{k-k_{\mathrm{aux}}}} \frac{1}{|\widetilde{\mathscr{H}}|} \approx \frac{1}{\binom{n-s}{w}\binom{s}{t_{\mathrm{aux}}}}$. Third, observe that Proposition 2 means in essence that the bias corresponding to $\mathbf{e}_{\mathscr{P}}$, namely $\operatorname*{bias}_{(\mathbf{h}, \mathbf{c}_{\mathrm{aux}}) \xleftarrow{\$} \widetilde{\mathscr{H}}} (\langle \mathbf{y}, \mathbf{h} \rangle + \langle \mathbf{e}_{\mathscr{P}}, \mathbf{c}_{\mathrm{aux}} \rangle)$ should be $\approx \frac{K_w^{(n-s)}(u) K_{t_{\mathrm{aux}}}^{(s)}(t-u)}{\binom{n-s}{w}\binom{s}{t_{\mathrm{aux}}}}$, *i.e.*, it corresponds roughly to the "first" pair (i, j) (where we range the values according to the product $K_w^{(n-s)}(i) K_{t_{\mathrm{aux}}}^{(s)}(j)$) for which $N_{i,j} \neq 0$, namely $(i, j) = (u, t - u)$ where the pair $(\mathbf{e}_{\mathscr{P}}, \mathbf{0})$ is likely to be the only pair $(\mathbf{r}, \mathbf{c}^{\mathscr{N}})$ in $(\mathbf{e}_{\mathscr{P}} + \mathcal{C}_{\mathrm{aux}}^{\perp}) \times \mathcal{C}^{\mathscr{N}}$ such that $|\mathbf{r}| = t - u$ and $|(\mathbf{r} + \mathbf{e}_{\mathscr{P}})\mathbf{R} + \mathbf{e}_{\mathscr{N}} + \mathbf{c}^{\mathscr{N}}| = u$ (and therefore we likely have $N_{u,t-u} = 1$). Therefore the behavior of the sum appearing in (10) is dominated by this first term $N_{i,j}$ which is non zero, namely $(i, j) = (u, t - u)$ since we really have in this case that the corresponding term in the sum is nothing but $\frac{K_w^{(n-s)}(u)K_{t_{\mathrm{aux}}}^{(s)}(t-u)}{\binom{n-s}{w}\binom{s}{t_{\mathrm{aux}}}}$.

This kind of phenomenon appears to be much more general than this: the $\mathbf{x} \in \mathbb{F}_2^s$ which give a high bias (and are therefore the ones we put in $\mathscr{S}$) are those for which there is an $N_{i,j}$ which is unexpectedly non zero (and therefore most likely equal to 1) in the low values of (i,j) for which the term $K_w^{n-s}(i)K_{t_{\mathrm{aux}}}^{(s)}(j)$ can compete or even supersede the term dominating in the expression (10) of the bias of $\mathbf{e}_{\mathscr{P}}$, namely $K_w^{(n-s)}(u)K_{t_{\mathrm{aux}}}^{(s)}(t-u)$ (we have ignored the common denominator $2^{k-k_{\mathrm{aux}}}\left|\widetilde{\mathscr{H}}\right|$ appearing in both sums). Similarly we expect that the bias of those $\mathbf{x}$ is of order in this case $\frac{K_w^{(n-s)}(i)K_{t_{\mathrm{aux}}}^{(s)}(j)}{\binom{n-s}{w}\binom{s}{t_{\mathrm{aux}}}}$. This intuition is formalized by Conjecture 1 what we make later on.

5.3   Main Proposition

The key step of the analysis is to estimate the number of candidates, namely the size of $\mathscr{S}$ (Instruction 3 of Algorithm 2). Provided that the bet ($|\mathbf{e}_{\mathscr{N}}| = u$) on the error is valid we expect that the secret vector $\mathbf{e}_{\mathscr{P}}\mathbf{G}_{\mathrm{aux}}^{\mathsf{T}}$ belongs to $\mathscr{S}$. But, as we will show in this section this set also contains some false positives, namely any element of $\mathscr{S} \setminus \{\mathbf{e}_{\mathscr{P}}\mathbf{G}_{\mathrm{aux}}^{\mathsf{T}}\}$. Testing if an element of $\mathscr{S}$ is a false positive (Algorithm 3) will be of exponential cost. Estimating their number is therefore crucial to predict the complexity of our algorithm. The following proposition bounds the expected number of candidates in a typical iteration of Algorithm 4.

Proposition 5. *Using Distribution 1 for $\mathcal{C}, \mathcal{C}_{\mathrm{aux}}, \mathbf{e}$ and $\mathbf{y}$ and given that our parameters verify Parameter Constraint 1, that the number of computed* LPN *samples is the total number of available* LPN *samples, i.e., $\mathscr{H} = \widetilde{\mathscr{H}}$ and under Conjecture 1 we have that the expected number of candidates per iteration is bounded by*

$$\mathbb{E}_{\mathcal{C},\mathcal{C}_{\mathrm{aux}}}(|\mathscr{S}|) = \widetilde{\mathcal{O}}\left(\max_{(i,j)\in\mathcal{A}}\frac{\binom{s}{j}\binom{n-s}{i}}{2^{n-k}}\right) + 1 \tag{11}$$

where

$$\mathcal{A} \overset{def}{=} \left\{(i,j) \in [\![0, n-s]\!] \times [\![0, s]\!], \left|\frac{K_w^{(n-s)}(u)K_{t_{\mathrm{aux}}}^{(s)}(t-u)}{K_w^{(n-s)}(i)K_{t_{\mathrm{aux}}}^{(s)}(j)}\right| \leqslant n^{3.2}\right\}. \tag{12}$$

The set $\mathscr{S}$ of candidates is defined by

$$\mathscr{S} \overset{def}{=} \left\{\mathbf{s} \in \mathbb{F}_2^{k_{\mathrm{aux}}} : f_{\mathbf{y},\widetilde{\mathscr{H}},\mathbf{G}_{\mathrm{aux}}}(\mathbf{s}) \geqslant \frac{\delta}{2}\widetilde{H}\right\}, \tag{13}$$

where

$$\widetilde{H} \overset{def}{=} \frac{\binom{n-s}{w}\binom{s}{t_{\mathrm{aux}}}}{2^{k-k_{\mathrm{aux}}}} \quad and \quad \delta \overset{def}{=} \frac{K_w^{(n-s)}(u)K_{t_{\mathrm{aux}}}^{(s)}(t-u)}{\binom{n-s}{w}\binom{s}{t_{\mathrm{aux}}}}. \tag{14}$$

Proof. Available in the long version of the paper [11, Appendix D].

Remark 3. The additional constraint that $\mathcal{H} = \widetilde{\mathcal{H}}$ is only here to simplify the proof. One could make a similar proposition without this constraint. In our instantiation of Algorithm 4 and with our optimal parameters this constraint is de-facto verified. Note also that $\widetilde{H}$ appearing in the expression of the threshold is the expected number of available LPN samples, namely $\mathbb{E}_{\mathcal{C},\mathcal{C}_{\mathrm{aux}}}\left(\left|\widetilde{\mathcal{H}}\right|\right)$.

Distribution 1. *$\mathscr{P}$ and $\mathscr{N}$ are two fixed complementary subsets of $[\![1,n]\!]$ of size s and $n-s$ respectively. The code $\mathcal{C}$ of generator matrix $\mathbf{G}$ is chosen uniformly at random among $[n,k]$ linear codes which are such that $\mathcal{C}_{\mathscr{P}}$ is of dimension s. The code $\mathcal{C}_{\mathrm{aux}}$ of generator matrix $\mathbf{G}_{\mathrm{aux}} \in \mathbb{F}_2^{k_{\mathrm{aux}} \times s}$ is chosen uniformly at random among the $[s, k_{\mathrm{aux}}]$-codes. $\mathbf{e} \in \mathbb{F}_2^n$ is a fixed vector of $\mathcal{S}_t^n$, $\mathbf{c} \in \mathcal{C}$ is a random codeword of $\mathcal{C}$ and we define $\mathbf{y} \stackrel{def}{=} \mathbf{c} + \mathbf{e}$.*

Correctness of our algorithm is ensured by the following constraints.

Constraint 1. *We suppose that the parameters $n, k, t, s, k_{\mathrm{aux}}, t_{\mathrm{aux}}, w, u$ are such that there exists a constant $\alpha > 0$ that is such that*

$$(i)\ \frac{\binom{n-s}{w}\binom{s}{t_{\mathrm{aux}}}}{2^{k-k_{\mathrm{aux}}}} = \omega\left(\frac{n^{\alpha+8}}{\delta^2}\right),\ (ii)\ \frac{\binom{n-s}{w}\binom{s}{t_{\mathrm{aux}}}}{2^k} = \mathcal{O}(n^\alpha),\ (iii)\ \frac{\binom{s}{t_{\mathrm{aux}}}}{2^{s-k_{\mathrm{aux}}}} = \mathcal{O}(n^\alpha).$$
$$(15)$$

where δ is defined in Eq. (6).

Remark 4. Note that these constraints are in fact, up to a polynomial factor, the minimal constraints required for our algorithm to work. Indeed, there are precisely the constraints required in Proposition 2 which estimates the bias of the error of the LPN samples (4).

The difficulty of proving Proposition 5 is similar to the difficulties encountered in analyzing the RLPN algorithm in [40], we know too little about the tails of the distribution of $N_{i,j}$. As such, we will make the following conjecture which formalizes the discussion in Sect. 5.2.

Conjecture 1. Using Distribution 1, under Parameter Constraint 1,

$$\mathbb{P}\left(\sum_{j=0}^{s}\sum_{i=0}^{n-s} K_{t_{\mathrm{aux}}}^{(s)}(j)\, K_w^{(n-s)}(i)\, N_{i,j} \geqslant \frac{1}{2} K_w^{(n-s)}(u)\, K_{t_{\mathrm{aux}}}^{(s)}(t-u)\right) = \tilde{\mathcal{O}}\left(\max_{(i,j)\in\mathcal{A}} \mathbb{P}\left(N_{i,j} \neq 0\right) + 2^{-n}\right)$$

where $\mathcal{A}$ is given in Eq. (12) and $\mathbf{x}$ is taken uniformly at random in $\mathbb{F}_2^s \setminus \{\mathcal{C}_{\mathrm{aux}}^{\perp} + \mathbf{e}_{\mathscr{P}}\}$.

Conjecture 1 is discussed in Sect. 6 where we give experimental evidences that our analysis holds. In the long version of the paper [11, Appendix F] we show that this conjecture is in fact a consequence of a more minimalistic conjecture.

6   Experimental Evidence for Our Analysis

The goal of this section is to provide experimental evidence supporting Proposition 5. We will propose a convenient probabilistic model for the $N_{i,j}$'s and show that this model does not change the output distribution of our algorithm. We will essentially use the same model as in [40, Appendix D] and model the weight distribution of the coset of a random linear code as a Poisson distribution of the right expected value. Recall that $N_{i,j}$ can be written as $N_{i,j} = \sum_{u=1}^{N_j(\mathcal{C}_{\mathrm{aux}}^{\perp} + \mathbf{x})} N_i \left(\left(\mathbf{r}^{(u)} + \mathbf{e}_{\mathscr{P}} \right) \mathbf{R} + \mathbf{e}_{\mathscr{N}} + \mathcal{C}^{\mathscr{N}} \right)$ where $\mathbf{R} \in \mathbb{F}_2^{s \times (n-s)}$ is such that for any $\mathbf{h} \in \mathcal{C}^{\perp}$ we have $\mathbf{h}_{\mathscr{P}} = \mathbf{h}_{\mathscr{N}} \mathbf{R}^{\mathsf{T}}$, $\mathbf{r}^{(u)}$ is the u'th codeword of weight j of $\mathcal{C}_{\mathrm{aux}}^{\perp} + \mathbf{x}$ and $N_j(\mathcal{C}_{\mathrm{aux}}^{\perp} + \mathbf{x})$ is the number of elements in $\mathcal{C}_{\mathrm{aux}}^{\perp} + \mathbf{x}$ of weight j. With our model, we first draw $N_j\left(\mathcal{C}_{\mathrm{aux}}^{\perp} + \mathbf{x}\right)$ according to a Poisson distribution of expected value $\frac{\binom{s}{j}}{2^{k_{\mathrm{aux}}}}$, then we draw each $N_i \left(\left(\mathbf{r}^{(u)} + \mathbf{e}_{\mathscr{P}} \right) \mathbf{R} + \mathbf{e}_{\mathscr{N}} + \mathcal{C}^{\mathscr{N}} \right)$ according to independent Poisson distributions of expected values $\frac{\binom{n-s}{i}}{2^{n-k}}$ (see the long version of the paper [11, App. E, Lem. 9] where we compute $\mathbb{E}\left(N_j\left(\mathcal{C}_{\mathrm{aux}}^{\perp} + \mathbf{x} \right) \right)$ and $\mathbb{E}\left(N_i \left(\left(\mathbf{r}^{(u)} + \mathbf{e}_{\mathscr{P}} \right) \mathbf{R} + \mathbf{e}_{\mathscr{N}} + \mathcal{C}^{\mathscr{N}} \right) \right)$ under Distribution 1). Finally, we get the following model for $N_{i,j}$ by using the fact that the sum of independent Poisson random variables is a Poisson variable:

Model 1 (Poisson Model).   *Under Distribution 1 and when $\mathbf{x}$ is taken uniformly at random in $\mathbb{F}_2^s \setminus \{\mathcal{C}_{\mathrm{aux}}^{\perp} + \mathbf{e}_{\mathscr{P}}\}$ we make the model that $N_{i,j} \sim$ Poisson $\left(N_j \frac{\binom{n-s}{i}}{2^{n-k}} \right)$, where $N_j \sim$ Poisson $\left(\frac{\binom{s}{j}}{2^{k_{\mathrm{aux}}}} \right)$.*

Under Poisson Model 1, the following proposition proves Conjecture 1 and thus it shows that Proposition 5 holds.

Proposition 6. *Under the Poisson Model 1, Conjecture 1 holds.*

Proof. Available in the long version of the paper [11, Appendix F].

In Fig. 2 we computed the expected number of $\mathbf{x}$'s whose bias multiplied by $|\mathscr{H}|$ is bigger than some prescribed quantity T according to: (i) the standard independence model in dual attacks where the $\langle \mathbf{e}, \mathbf{h} \rangle$'s are supposed to be independent, (ii) some experiments, (iii) the case were we replace the right-hand term of $N_{i,j}$ (given in Eq. (10)) by their Poisson model.

As it is shown by Fig. 2, the Poisson model matches remarkably well with the experiments. This shows, as was the case in the analysis [40] of the RLPN algorithm, that the Poisson model allows to predict accurately the size of $\mathscr{S}$.

7   Instantiating the Auxiliary Code $\mathcal{C}_{\mathrm{aux}}$ with an Efficient Decoder

In double-RLPN we need to choose an auxiliary code $\mathcal{C}_{\mathrm{aux}}$ which is efficiently listdecodable (Definition 6) at the smallest as possible distance $t_{\mathrm{aux}} = d_{\mathrm{GV}}(s, k_{\mathrm{aux}})$.

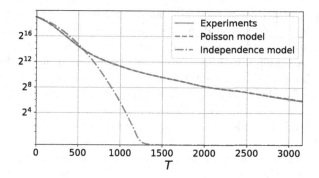

Fig. 2. Expected size of the set $\{\mathbf{x} \in \mathbb{F}_2^{k_{\text{aux}}} \setminus \{\mathbf{e}_{\mathscr{P}}\,\mathbf{G}_{\text{aux}}\} : \widehat{f_{\mathbf{y},\mathscr{H}}}(\mathbf{x}) \geqslant T\}$ as a function of T when $[w, t_{\text{aux}}, k_{\text{aux}}, s, k, n, t] = [5, 2, 20, 28, 30, 60, 8]$, number of LPN samples $N = 65536$. Here the curve "Independence model" has been replaced when modelling the $\langle \mathbf{y}, \mathbf{h} \rangle$'s by i.i.d Bernouilli random variables of parameter $\frac{1}{2}$ (standard independence model in dual attacks).

We propose to use the following product of small random codes (other choices may be more suitable but they are harder to analyze, like polar codes [5,33, 45,48]), $\mathcal{C}_{\text{aux}} \overset{\text{def}}{=} \mathcal{C}_1 \times \cdots \times \mathcal{C}_b$ where the $\mathcal{C}_i$'s are random $\left[\frac{s}{b}, \frac{k_{\text{aux}}}{b}\right]$-codes. Notice that $\mathcal{D}\text{ec}(\mathbf{z}) \overset{\text{def}}{=} \{\mathbf{c}_{\text{aux}} \in \mathcal{C}_{\text{aux}} : |\mathbf{c}_{\text{aux}} + \mathbf{z}| = t_{\text{aux}}\}$ does not look exactly like how it should with a random code for which our analysis given in Propositions 2 and 5 hold. Furthermore, we will compute

$$\mathscr{H} \subseteq \left\{ (\mathbf{h}, \mathbf{c}_{\text{aux}}) \in \mathcal{C}^{\perp} \times \mathcal{C}_{\text{aux}} : \forall i \in [\![1, b]\!], \; |\mathbf{h}_{\mathscr{N}}(i)| = \frac{w}{b} \text{ and } |\mathbf{h}_{\mathscr{P}}(i) + \mathbf{c}_i| = \frac{t_{\text{aux}}}{b} \right\}$$

in Instruction 7 of Algorithm 1. To this aim we will perform exhausting search on the random codes. By choosing the number b of blocks as,

$$b = \Theta(\log n) \tag{16}$$

the above decoding algorithm costs for any parity-check equation $O\left(2^{n/\log n}\right)$ (recall that $t_{\text{aux}} \approx d_{\text{GV}}(n, k)$). As Algorithm 1 running time is exponential (in n) for our considered parameters, it won't affect it. Furthermore, there are false candidates when computing $\mathscr{H}$ and it is crucial to estimate their numbers.

Our analysis of Sects. 3 and 5 has been made in the idealized-model where $\mathcal{C}_{\text{aux}}$ is a random code equipped with genie aided decoders. But, by choosing b as in Eq. (16), analysis of Propositions 2 and 5 is still verified with our particular choice of $\mathcal{C}_{\text{aux}}$ (up to negligible factors) as justified in the long version of the paper [11, Appendix G].

8   Links with Dual Attacks in Lattice Based Cryptography

The purpose of this section is to give more details about the close connection between dual attacks in coding theory (*a.k.a* "statistical decoding" after the pioneering work of [31]) and dual attacks in lattice based cryptography. Basically, with some slight differences highlighted in [43, App. A], the lattice based analogue of the dual attack presented here is the slight improvement [12] of the Matzov attack [36]. The improvement in [12] is based on the fact that the modulus switching technique used in [36] can be viewed as a suboptimal source distortion code for the Euclidean metric which can be replaced by an almost optimal polar code. The approach followed here should carry over to this lattice setting as well and in particular, the fundamental duality Proposition 4. Let us just observe now that a simple duality equality (together with a gross approximation based on the considerations of Sect. 5.2) can be used to explain the results observed in [19, Fig. 3]. It was shown there that predictions of the score function based on standard independence assumptions made for dual attacks in lattice based cryptography seem to be off in some parameter region (what can be called the "error-floor" region due to its similarity with the Low-Density-Parity-Check codes literature). To explain this point, we will use the same notation as in [19] and will not redefine the quantities appearing here.

Let us first observe that an immediate corollary of Proposition 4 is

Corollary 1. *Consider an $[n, k]$ linear code $\mathcal{C}$ and consider some word $\mathbf{y} = \mathbf{c} + \mathbf{e} \in \mathbb{F}_2^n$ where $\mathbf{c}$ is in $\mathcal{C}$. Let $\mathscr{W}$ be the set of codewords of weight w in $\mathcal{C}^\perp$ and let $f_{\mathscr{W}}(\mathbf{y}) \stackrel{def}{=} \sum_{\mathbf{w} \in \mathscr{W}} (-1)^{\langle \mathbf{y}, \mathbf{w} \rangle}$. We have $f_{\mathscr{W}}(\mathbf{y}) = \frac{1}{2^k} \sum_{i=0}^n N_i K_w^n(i)$ where N_i is the number of words of weight i in $\mathcal{C} + \mathbf{e}$.*

It is insightful to view these Krawtchouk polynomials as the Fourier transform of the indicator function of a Hamming sphere, see Fact 1. Similarly, the lattice based analogue of Corollary 1 involving the lattice based analogue of $f_{\mathscr{W}}$, which is called the score function in [19] will involve the Bessel function of the first kind (see for instance [14, Fact 4.9]). We namely obtain

Proposition 7. *Consider a lattice $\Lambda \subseteq \mathbb{R}^n$ and consider some word $\mathbf{y} = \mathbf{x} + \mathbf{e} \in \mathbb{R}^n$ where $\mathbf{x}$ is in Λ. Let $\widetilde{\mathscr{W}}$ be the set of dual lattice vectors of Euclidean weights in $(w - \varepsilon, w + \varepsilon)$ in $\Lambda^\vee$ and let $f_{\widetilde{\mathscr{W}}}(\mathbf{y}) \stackrel{def}{=} \sum_{\mathbf{w} \in \widetilde{\mathscr{W}}} \cos(2\pi \langle \mathbf{x}, \mathbf{y} \rangle)$. We have*

$$f_{\widetilde{\mathscr{W}}}(\mathbf{y}) = \frac{1}{|\Lambda^\vee|} \sum_{j \geqslant 0} \frac{N_j}{j^n (2\pi)^{n/2}} \left((2\pi(w + \varepsilon)j)^{n/2} J_{n/2}(2\pi(w + \varepsilon)j) \right. \tag{17}$$

$$\left. - (2\pi(w - \varepsilon)j)^{n/2} J_{n/2}(2\pi(w - \varepsilon)j) \right)$$

where N_j is the number of words of Euclidean norm j in $\Lambda + \mathbf{e}$ and J_ν is the Bessel function of the first kind of order[3] ν.

Proof. Available in the long version of the paper [11, Appendix H].

Let us take some subset $\mathscr{W}$ of $\widetilde{\mathscr{W}}$ of size N say. We make the approximation $f_{\mathscr{W}}(\mathbf{y}) \approx \frac{N}{|\widetilde{\mathscr{W}}|} f_{\widetilde{\mathscr{W}}}(\mathbf{y})$ and by using the Gaussian heuristic and some computations that are detailed in [11, Appendix H]:

---

[3] Here the j's belong to the discrete set of all possible norms in the lattice and should not be viewed as an integer value.

$$f_{\mathscr{W}}(\mathbf{y}) \approx N \frac{\sqrt{n\pi}}{e} \sum_{j \geqslant 0} N_j \left(\frac{n}{2\pi e w j} \right)^{n/2-1} J_{n/2-1}(2\pi w j). \tag{18}$$

We can use now a similar heuristic as the one described in Sect. 5.2 and predict that the abnormal large values of the score function $f_{\mathscr{W}}(\mathbf{y})$ appear when $\mathbf{y}$ is abnormally close to Λ, say $N_{\leqslant x} \neq 0$, where $N_{\leqslant x} = |\{\mathbf{c} \in \Lambda : |\mathbf{y} - \mathbf{c}| \leqslant x\}|$ when $\mathbb{P}(N_{\leqslant x} \neq 0) \ll 1$. In this case, we make the crude approximation that the sum (18) is dominated by the term j_0 which is the smallest in it:

$$f_{\mathscr{W}}(\mathbf{y}) \approx N \frac{\sqrt{n\pi}}{e} N_{j_0} \left(\frac{n}{2\pi e w j_0} \right)^{n/2-1} J_{n/2-1}(2\pi w j_0). \tag{19}$$

The survival function $\mathbb{P}(f_{\mathscr{W}}(\mathbf{y}) \geqslant X)$ is then crudely approximated as the probability that such an event happens

$$\mathbb{P}\left(f_{\mathscr{W}}(\mathbf{y}) \geqslant N \frac{\sqrt{n\pi}}{e} N_x \left(\frac{n}{2\pi e w x} \right)^{n/2-1} J_{n/2-1}(2\pi w x) \right) \approx \mathbb{P}(N_{\leqslant x} \geqslant 1)$$

$$\approx \mathbb{E}(N_{\leqslant x})$$

$$\approx \left(\frac{x}{\sqrt{\frac{n}{2\pi e}} \cdot (\pi n)^{1/n} \cdot |\Lambda|^{1/n}} \right)^n$$

where the last approximation is the Gaussian heuristic. In the context of the experiments described in [19, §5], $\Lambda \overset{\text{def}}{=} \mathcal{L}(\mathbf{B})$ is given by[4] $\mathbf{B} \overset{\text{def}}{=} \begin{bmatrix} \mathbf{I}_{n/2} & \mathbf{A} \\ \mathbf{0} & q \cdot \mathbf{I}_{n/2} \end{bmatrix}$. $\begin{bmatrix} 2 \cdot \mathbf{I}_{k_{\text{fft}}} & \mathbf{0} \\ \mathbf{0} & \mathbf{I}_{n-k_{\text{fft}}} \end{bmatrix}$. Then we use the same *full sieve* algorithm as in [19] to produce short vectors $\mathscr{W} \subset \Lambda^{\vee}$. In what follows, we use the practical values of N and w that we obtained by experiments. We have reused the implementation for the experiments in [19, §5][5]. This very crude estimation seems to capture the error-floor behavior of the survival function as shown in Fig. 3. The point is that it is precisely this part of the curve which is not predicted by the standard independence assumption and which had no explanation so far. It can also be observed that the duality result is nothing but a straighforward use of the Poisson formula which has also be used very recently in [50] to predict the abnormal variance of the BDD score distribution observed in [19, Table 1]. In the long version of the paper [11, §8] we give a much more precise prediction which matches the observed behavior of the score function on the whole support and not just its tail.

Concurrent Work. Note that very recently we have been made aware of the concurrent work [18] which similarly to what we do here, uses Bessel functions to predict the score with a related approach and similar predictions (see [18, §4.3]).

---

[4] In [19], Λ and $\mathbf{B}$ are actually respectively Λ' and $\mathbf{B}'$.
[5] https://github.com/ludopulles/DoesDualSieveWork.

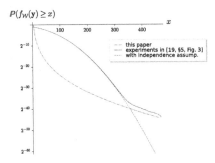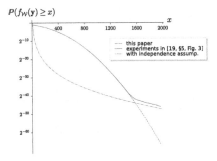

Fig. 3. Crude estimation of the survival function (red, dash-dot line) compared to the experiments in [19, §5] (green, full line) and the prediction with the standard independence assumption (blue, dashed line). (left) $q = 3329$, $n = 60$, $T = 2^{45}$, $N = 5040$ and $w = 0.0320$; (right) $q = 3329$, $n = 80$, $T = 2^{48}$, $N = 89494$ and $w = 0.0376$. (Color figure online)

References

1. Aguilar, C., Gaborit, P., Schrek, J.: A new zero-knowledge code based identification scheme with reduced communication. In: Proceedings of the IEEE Information Theory Workshop - ITW 2011, pp. 648–652. IEEE (2011)
2. Aguilar Melchor, C., et al.: BIKE. Round 3 submission to the NIST post-quantum cryptography call, v. 4.2 (2021). https://bikesuite.org
3. Aguilar Melchor, C., et al.: HQC. Round 3 submission to the NIST post-quantum cryptography call (2021). https://pqc-hqc.org/doc/hqc-specification_2021-06-06. pdf
4. Albrecht, M.R.: On dual lattice attacks against small-secret LWE and parameter choices in HElib and SEAL. In: Coron, J.-S., Nielsen, J.B. (eds.) EUROCRYPT 2017, Part II. LNCS, vol. 10211, pp. 103–129. Springer, Cham (2017). https://doi.org/10.1007/978-3-319-56614-6_4
5. Arıkan, E.: Channel polarization: a method for constructing capacity-achieving codes for symmetric binary-input memoryless channels. IEEE Trans. Inform. Theory **55**(7), 3051–3073 (2009). https://doi.org/10.1109/TIT.2009.2021379, http://dx.doi.org/10.1109/TIT.2009.2021379
6. Becker, A., Joux, A., May, A., Meurer, A.: Decoding random binary linear codes in $2^{n/20}$: how $1 + 1 = 0$ improves information set decoding. In: Pointcheval, D., Johansson, T. (eds.) EUROCRYPT 2012. LNCS, vol. 7237, pp. 520–536. Springer, Heidelberg (2012). https://doi.org/10.1007/978-3-642-29011-4_31
7. Bernstein, D.J., et al.: Classic McEliece: conservative code-based cryptography (2019). https://classic.mceliece.org. Second round submission to the NIST post-quantum cryptography call
8. Blum, A., Kalai, A., Wasserman, H.: Noise-tolerant learning, the parity problem, and the statistical query model. J. ACM (JACM) **50**(4), 506–519 (2003)
9. Both, L., May, A.: Decoding linear codes with high error rate and its impact for LPN security. In: Lange, T., Steinwandt, R. (eds.) PQCrypto 2018. LNCS, vol. 10786, pp. 25–46. Springer, Cham (2018). https://doi.org/10.1007/978-3-319-79063-3_2

10. Carrier, K., Debris-Alazard, T., Meyer-Hilfiger, C., Tillich, J.: Statistical decoding 2.0: reducing decoding to LPN. In: Agrawal, S., Lin, D. (eds.) ASIACRYPT 2022. LNCS, vol 13794, pp. 477–507. Springer, Cham (2022). https://doi.org/10.1007/978-3-031-22972-5_17, https://eprint.iacr.org/2022/1000
11. Carrier, K., Debris-Alazard, T., Meyer-Hilfiger, C., Tillich, J.: Reduction from sparse LPN to LPN, dual attack 3.0. Cryptology ePrint Archive, Report 2023/1852 (2023). https://eprint.iacr.org/2023/1852
12. Carrier, K., Shen, Y., Tillich, J.P.: Faster dual lattice attacks by using coding theory. Cryptology ePrint Archive, Paper 2022/1750 (2022). https://eprint.iacr.org/2022/1750
13. Cayrel, P.-L., Véron, P., El Yousfi Alaoui, S.M.: A zero-knowledge identification scheme based on the q-ary syndrome decoding problem. In: Biryukov, A., Gong, G., Stinson, D.R. (eds.) SAC 2010. LNCS, vol. 6544, pp. 171–186. Springer, Heidelberg (2011). https://doi.org/10.1007/978-3-642-19574-7_12
14. Debris-Alazard, T., Ducas, L., Resch, N., Tillich, J.: Smoothing codes and lattices: systematic study and new bounds. IEEE Trans. Inform. Theory **69**(9), 6006–6027 (2023). https://doi.org/10.1109/TIT.2023.3276921, https://arxiv.org/abs/2205.10552
15. Debris-Alazard, T., Tillich, J.P.: Statistical decoding. Preprint arXiv:1701.07416 (2017)
16. Debris-Alazard, T., Tillich, J.P.: Statistical decoding. Slides of the ISIT talk (2017). https://tdalazard.io/slidesDecoStat.pdf
17. Debris-Alazard, T., Tillich, J.P.: Statistical decoding. In: Proceedings of the IEEE International Symposium Information Theory - ISIT 2017, Aachen, Germany, pp. 1798–1802 (2017)
18. Ducas, L., Pulles, L.N.: Accurate score prediction for dual attacks. Preprint (2023)
19. Ducas, L., Pulles, L.N.: Does the dual-sieve attack on learning with errors even work? In: Handschuh, H., Lysyanskaya, A. (eds.) CRYPTO 2023. LNCS, vol. 14083, pp. 37–69. Springer, Cham (2023). https://doi.org/10.1007/978-3-031-38548-3_2
20. Dumer, I.: On syndrome decoding of linear codes. In: Proceedings of the 9th All-Union Symposium on Redundancy in Information Systems, abstracts of papers (in Russian), Part 2, Leningrad, pp. 157–159 (1986)
21. Dumer, I.: Two decoding algorithms for linear codes. Probl. Inf. Transm. **25**(1), 17–23 (1989)
22. Dumer, I.: On minimum distance decoding of linear codes. In: Proceedings of the 5th Joint Soviet-Swedish International Workshop Information Theory, Moscow, pp. 50–52 (1991)
23. Espitau, T., Joux, A., Kharchenko, N.: On a dual/hybrid approach to small secret LWE. In: Bhargavan, K., Oswald, E., Prabhakaran, M. (eds.) INDOCRYPT 2020. LNCS, vol. 12578, pp. 440–462. Springer, Cham (2020). https://doi.org/10.1007/978-3-030-65277-7_20
24. Esser, A.: Revisiting nearest-neighbor-based information set decoding. Cryptology ePrint Archive, Paper 2022/1328 (2022). https://eprint.iacr.org/2022/1328
25. Esser, A., Kübler, R., May, A.: LPN decoded. In: Katz, J., Shacham, H. (eds.) CRYPTO 2017. LNCS, vol. 10402, pp. 486–514. Springer, Cham (2017). https://doi.org/10.1007/978-3-319-63715-0_17
26. Feneuil, T., Joux, A., Rivain, M.: Syndrome decoding in the head: shorter signatures from zero-knowledge proofs. IACR Cryptol. ePrint Arch. 188 (2022). https://eprint.iacr.org/2022/188
27. Green, R.R.: A serial orthogonal decoder. JPL Space Program. Summary **37-39-IV**, 247–253 (1966)

28. Gueron, S., Persichetti, E., Santini, P.: Designing a practical code-based signature scheme from zero-knowledge proofs with trusted setup. Cryptography **6**(1), 5 (2022). https://doi.org/10.3390/cryptography6010005
29. Guo, Q., Johansson, T.: Faster dual lattice attacks for solving LWE with applications to CRYSTALS. In: Tibouchi, M., Wang, H. (eds.) ASIACRYPT 2021. LNCS, vol. 13093, pp. 33–62. Springer, Cham (2021). https://doi.org/10.1007/978-3-030-92068-5_2
30. Guo, Q., Johansson, T., Löndahl, C.: Solving LPN using covering codes. In: Sarkar, P., Iwata, T. (eds.) ASIACRYPT 2014. LNCS, vol. 8873, pp. 1–20. Springer, Heidelberg (2014). https://doi.org/10.1007/978-3-662-45611-8_1
31. Jabri, A.A.: A statistical decoding algorithm for general linear block codes. In: Honary, B. (ed.) Cryptography and Coding 2001. LNCS, vol. 2260, pp. 1–8. Springer, Heidelberg (2001). https://doi.org/10.1007/3-540-45325-3_1
32. Kirshner, N., Samorodnitsky, A.: A moment ratio bound for polynomials and some extremal properties of krawchouk polynomials and hamming spheres. IEEE Trans. Inform. Theory **67**(6), 3509–3541 (2021)
33. Korada, S.B., Urbanke, R.: Polar codes are optimal for lossy source coding. IEEE Trans. Inform. Theory **56**(4), 1751–1768 (2010)
34. Levieil, É., Fouque, P.-A.: An improved LPN algorithm. In: De Prisco, R., Yung, M. (eds.) SCN 2006. LNCS, vol. 4116, pp. 348–359. Springer, Heidelberg (2006). https://doi.org/10.1007/11832072_24
35. van Lint, J.H.: Introduction to Coding Theory. Graduate Texts in Mathematics, 3rd edn. Springer, Heidelberg (1999). https://doi.org/10.1007/978-3-642-58575-3
36. MATZOV: Report on the Security of LWE: Improved Dual Lattice Attack (2022). https://doi.org/10.5281/zenodo.6412487
37. May, A., Meurer, A., Thomae, E.: Decoding random linear codes in $\tilde{\mathcal{O}}(2^{0.054n})$. In: Lee, D.H., Wang, X. (eds.) ASIACRYPT 2011. LNCS, vol. 7073, pp. 107–124. Springer, Heidelberg (2011). https://doi.org/10.1007/978-3-642-25385-0_6
38. May, A., Ozerov, I.: On computing nearest neighbors with applications to decoding of binary linear codes. In: Oswald, E., Fischlin, M. (eds.) EUROCRYPT 2015. LNCS, vol. 9056, pp. 203–228. Springer, Heidelberg (2015). https://doi.org/10.1007/978-3-662-46800-5_9
39. McEliece, R.J.: A public-key system based on algebraic coding theory, pp. 114–116. Jet Propulsion Lab (1978). dSN Progress Report 44
40. Meyer-Hilfiger, C., Tillich, J.P.: Rigorous foundations for dual attacks in coding theory. In: Rothblum, G., Wee, H. (eds) TCC 2023. LNCS, vol. 14372, pp. 3–32. Springer, Cham (2023). https://doi.org/10.1007/978-3-031-48624-1_1, https://eprint.iacr.org/2023/1460
41. Micciancio, D., Regev, O.: Lattice-based cryptography. In: Bernstein, D.J., Buchmann, J., Dahmen, E. (eds.) Post-Quantum Cryptography, pp. 147–191. Springer, Heidelberg (2009). https://doi.org/10.1007/978-3-540-88702-7_5
42. Overbeck, R.: Statistical decoding revisited. In: Batten, L.M., Safavi-Naini, R. (eds.) ACISP 2006. LNCS, vol. 4058, pp. 283–294. Springer, Heidelberg (2006). https://doi.org/10.1007/11780656_24
43. Pouly, A., Shen, Y.: Provable dual attacks on learning with errors. Cryptology ePrint Archive, Paper 2023/1508 (2023). https://eprint.iacr.org/2023/1508
44. Prange, E.: The use of information sets in decoding cyclic codes. IRE Trans. Inf. Theory **8**(5), 5–9 (1962) https://doi.org/10.1109/TIT.1962.1057777, http://dx.doi.org/10.1109/TIT.1962.1057777

45. Şaşoğlu, E.: Polarization and polar codes. Found. Trends Commun. Inf. Theory **8**(4), 259–381 (2011) https://doi.org/10.1561/0100000041, http://dx.doi.org/10.1561/0100000041

46. Stern, J.: A method for finding codewords of small weight. In: Cohen, G., Wolfmann, J. (eds.) Coding Theory 1988. LNCS, vol. 388, pp. 106–113. Springer, Heidelberg (1989). https://doi.org/10.1007/BFb0019850

47. Stern, J.: A new identification scheme based on syndrome decoding. In: Stinson, D.R. (ed.) CRYPTO 1993. LNCS, vol. 773, pp. 13–21. Springer, Heidelberg (1994). https://doi.org/10.1007/3-540-48329-2_2

48. Tal, I., Vardy, A.: List decoding of polar codes. CoRR abs/1206.0050 (2012). http://arxiv.org/abs/1206.0050

49. Véron, P.: Improved identification schemes based on error-correcting codes. Appl. Algebra Eng. Commun. Comput. **8**(1), 57–69 (1996) https://doi.org/10.1007/s002000050053, http://dx.doi.org/10.1007/s002000050053

50. Wiemers, A., Ehlen, S.: A remark on the independence heuristic in the dual attack. IACR Cryptology ePrint Archive, Report 2023/1238 (2023). http://eprint.iacr.org/2023/1238

Plover: Masking-Friendly Hash-and-Sign Lattice Signatures

Muhammed F. Esgin[1], Thomas Espitau[2(✉)], Guilhem Niot[2], Thomas Prest[2], Amin Sakzad[1], and Ron Steinfeld[1]

[1] Monash University, Melbourne, Australia
{muhammed.esgin,amin.sakzad,ron.steinfeld}@monash.edu
[2] PQShield SAS, Paris, France
thomas@espitau.com, guilhem@gniot.fr, thomas.prest@pqshield.com

Abstract. We introduce a toolkit for transforming lattice-based hash-and-sign signature schemes into masking-friendly signatures secure in the t-probing model. Until now, efficiently masking lattice-based hash-and-sign schemes has been an open problem, with unsuccessful attempts such as Mitaka. A first breakthrough was made in 2023 with the NIST PQC submission Raccoon, although it was not formally proven.

Our main conceptual contribution is to realize that the same principles underlying Raccoon are very generic, and to find a systematic way to apply them within the hash-and-sign paradigm. Our main technical contribution is to formalize, prove, instantiate and implement a hash-and-sign scheme based on these techniques. Our toolkit includes noise flooding to mitigate statistical leaks, and an extended Strong Non-Interfering probing security (SNIu) property to handle masked gadgets with unshared inputs.

We showcase the efficiency of our techniques in a signature scheme, Plover-RLWE, based on (hint) Ring-LWE. It is the *first* lattice-based masked hash-and-sign scheme with quasi-linear complexity $O(d \log d)$ in the number of shares d. Our performances are competitive with the state-of-the-art masking-friendly signature, the Fiat-Shamir scheme Raccoon.

1 Introduction

Post-quantum cryptography is currently one of the most dynamic fields of cryptography, with numerous standardization processes launched in the last decade. The most publicized is arguably the NIST PQC standardization process, which recently selected [1] four schemes for standardization: Kyber, Dilithium, Falcon and SPHINCS+.

Despite their strong mathematical foundations at an algorithmic level, recent years have witnessed the introduction of various side-channel attacks against the soon-to-be-standardized schemes: see this non-exhaustive list of power-analysis attacks against ML-DSA (Dilithium) [7,23], FN-DSA (Falcon) [19,35]

Part of this project was conducted while Guilhem Niot was a student at EPFL and ENS Lyon, interning at PQShield.

M. Joye and G. Leander (Eds.): EUROCRYPT 2024, LNCS 14657, pp. 316–345, 2024.
https://doi.org/10.1007/978-3-031-58754-2_12

or SLH-DSA (SPHINCS+) [22]. This motivates us to consider exploring sound countermeasures allowing secure real-life implementations of mathematically well-founded cryptographic approaches.

Masking Post-quantum Schemes. In general, the most robust countermeasure against side-channel attacks is masking [20]. It consists of splitting sensitive information in d shares (concretely: $x = x_0 + \cdots + x_{d-1}$), and performing secure computation using MPC-based techniques. Masking offers a *trade-off*: while it increases computational efficiency by causing the running time to increase polynomially in d, it also exponentially escalates the cost of a side-channel attack with the number of shares d, see [13,21,26].

Unfortunately, masking incurs a significant computational overhead on the future NIST standards. For example, the lattice-based signature Dilithium relies on sampling elements in a small subset $S \subsetneq \mathbb{Z}_q$ of the native ring $\mathbb{Z}_q$, and testing membership to a second subset $S' \subsetneq \mathbb{Z}_q$. The best-known approaches for performing these operations in a masked setting rely on *mask conversions* [18]. These operations are extremely expensive, and despite several improvements in the last few years [8,10,11], still constitute the efficiency bottlenecks of existing masked implementations of Dilithium, see Coron et al. [12] and Azouaoui et al. [3], and of many other lattice-based schemes, see the works of Coron et al. on Kyber [10], and of Coron et al. on NTRU [11].

Falcon, based on the hash-and-sign paradigm, is even more challenging to mask. The main reason is the widespread use of floating-point arithmetic; even simple operations such as masked addition or multiplication are highly non-trivial to mask. Another reason is a reliance on discrete Gaussian distributions with secret centers and standard deviations, which also need to be masked. Even without considering masking, these traits make Falcon difficult to implement and to deploy on constrained devices.

More recent Hash-and-Sign schemes, such as Mitaka [14], Robin and Eagle [34], also share both of these undesirable traits. Mitaka proposed novel techniques in an attempt to make it efficiently maskable; however, Prest [32] showed that these techniques were insecure and exhibited a practical key-recovery attack in the t-probing model against Mitaka. As of today, it remains an open problem to build hash-and-sign lattice signatures that can be masked efficiently.

1.1 Our Solution

In this work, we describe a general toolkit for converting hash-and-sign schemes into their masking-friendly variants. The main idea is deceptively simple: instead of using trapdoor sampling to generate a signature that leaks no information about the secret key, using noise that is sufficiently large to hide the secret on its own. While similar ideas were described in the Fiat-Shamir setting by Raccoon [29], we show here that the underlying principles and techniques are much more generic. In our case, we replace the canonical choice of Gaussian distribution—which only depends on the (public) lattice and not on the short secret key—with sums of uniform distributions. This allows us to remove all the complications inherent to the sampler, as we now do not need a sampler more complicated than a uniform one. Then since all the remaining operations are linear in the underlying field, we can simply mask all the values in arithmetic form and follow the usual flow of the algorithm.

The security of the scheme in this approach now relies on the hint variant of the underlying problem (namely, Ring-LWE) as the correlation between the signature and the secret can be exploited when collecting sufficiently many signatures. To showcase the versatility of our toolkit, we propose two possible instantiations of our transform: starting from the recent Eagle proposal of [34], we construct a masking-friendly hash-and-sign signature, Plover, based on the hardness of Hint-RLWE. To provide a high-level view, we describe the transformation in Fig. 1a and Fig. 1b. Differences between the two blueprints are highlighted . Operations that need to be masked in the context of side channels are indicated with comments: Easy when standard fast techniques apply to mask, or Hard otherwise. We replace the two Gaussian samples (Eagle L. 3 and 6) by the noise flooding (Plover L. 7, the mask being generated by the gadget AddRepNoise at L.3) in masked form. The final signature $\mathbf{z}$ is eventually unmasked.

Eagle.Sign(sk, msg) $\rightarrow$ sig	Plover.Sign(sk, msg) $\rightarrow$ sig
In: A signing key sk, a message msg.	**In:** A signing key sk, a message msg.
Out: A signature sig of msg under sk.	**Out:** A signature sig of msg under sk.
1: salt $\leftarrow \{0,1\}^{320}$	1: salt $\leftarrow \{0,1\}^{2\kappa}$
2: $\mathbf{u} := H(\mathsf{msg}, \mathsf{salt})$	2: $\mathbf{u} := H(\mathsf{msg}, \mathsf{salt}, \mathsf{vk})$
3: $\mathbf{p} \leftarrow D_{\mathcal{R}^\ell, \sqrt{s^2\mathbf{I}-r^2\mathbf{TT}^*}}$ $\triangleright$ Hard	3: $[\![\mathbf{p}]\!] \leftarrow \mathsf{AddRepNoise}(\mathcal{R}_q^\ell, d, \mathcal{D}, \mathsf{rep})$
4: $\mathbf{c} := \mathbf{u} - \mathbf{A} \cdot \mathbf{p}$ $\triangleright$ Easy	4: $\mathbf{c} := \mathbf{u} - \mathsf{Unmask}(\mathbf{A} \cdot [\![\mathbf{p}]\!])$
5: Decompose $\mathbf{c}$ as $\mathbf{c} = \beta \cdot \mathbf{c}_1 + \mathbf{c}_2$	5: Decompose $\mathbf{c}$ as $\mathbf{c} = \beta \cdot \mathbf{c}_1 + \mathbf{c}_2$
6: $\mathbf{y} \leftarrow D_{\lfloor q/\beta \rceil \cdot \mathcal{R}^\ell + \mathbf{c}_1, r}$ $\triangleright$ Hard	6: [This step is removed]
7: $\mathbf{z} := \mathbf{p} + \mathbf{T} \cdot \mathbf{y}$ $\triangleright$ Easy	7: $\mathbf{z} := \mathsf{Unmask}([\![\mathbf{p}]\!] + [\![\mathbf{T}]\!] \cdot \mathbf{c}_1)$
8: sig $:= (\mathsf{salt}, \mathbf{z})$	8: sig $:= (\mathsf{salt}, \mathbf{z})$
9: **return** sig	9: **return** sig
(a) Blueprint for Eagle [34].	(b) Blueprint for Plover.

Fig. 1. High-level comparison between Eagle [34] and our scheme Plover. In both schemes, the signing key is a pair of matrices $\mathsf{sk} = (\mathbf{T}, \mathbf{A})$, the verification key is $\mathsf{vk} = \mathbf{T}$, and we have $\mathbf{A} \cdot \mathbf{T} = \beta \cdot \mathbf{I}_k$. The verification procedure is also identical: in each case, we check that $\mathbf{z}$ and $\mathbf{c}_2 := \mathbf{A} \cdot \mathbf{z} - \mathbf{u}$ are sufficiently short.

We also provide a similar approach using an NTRU-based signature in the full version of this paper. Our analyses reveal that the NTRU-based approach, at the cost of introducing a stronger assumption, sees its keygen becoming slower but signature and verification get faster. However, as the signature size is slightly bigger and the techniques are similar, we choose to present only the RLWE variant here and describe the NTRU one in the full version.

1.2   Technical Overview

The main ingredients we introduce in this toolkit are the following:

1. *Noise flooding.* The main tool is the so-called *noise flooding* introduced by Goldwasser et al. [17]: we "flood" the sensitive values with enough noise so that the statistical leak becomes marginal. In contrast, other hash-then-sign lattice signatures use trapdoor sampling make the output distribution statistically independent of the signing key. However, marginal does not mean nonexistent and we need to quantify this leakage.

   To achieve this in a *tight* manner, we leverage the recent reduction of Kim et al. [24], which transitions Hint-MLWE to MLWE, providing a solid understanding of the leakage. Noise flooding has recently proved useful in the NIST submission Raccoon [29] to analyze its leakage and optimize parameters. Here also, the tightness of this reduction allows to reduce the relative size of the noise while preserving security, compared to, e.g., using standard Rényi arguments.

2. *SNI with unmasked inputs.* To get a scheme which is *provably* secure in the t-probing model, we need to extend the usual definition of t Strong Non-Interfering (SNI) Gadgets to allow the attacker to know "for free" up to t *unshared inputs* of the gadgets (we call this extended property t-SNIu). This is somehow the "dual" of the (S)NI with public outputs notion (NIo) introduced by Barthe et al. [5].

   In particular, we formally show that the AddRepNoise gadget, introduced by Raccoon [29] to sample small secrets as a sum of small unshared inputs, satisfies our t-SNIu definition and hence enjoys t probing security. This fills a provable security gap left in [29], where the t-probing security of AddRepNoise was only argued informally. Our new model is also sufficient to handle the unmasking present in our signature proposal. We prove the security for the t-probing EUF-CMA notion borrowed from [5].

3. *Masked inversion.* As a natural byproduct of the NTRU-based instantiation, we propose a novel way to perform inversion in masked form. Our proposal combines the NTT representation with Montgomery's trick [28] to speed up masked inversion. It is to the best of our knowledge the first time Montgomery's trick has been used in the context of masking. Our technique offers an improved asymptotic complexity over previous proposals from [11, Section 4.3 and 5]. Due to page limitation, this technique is described in the full version only.

Advantages and Limitations. The first and main design principle of our toolkit is of course its amenability to masking. In effect, we can mask at order $d - 1$ with an overhead of only $O(d \log d)$. This allows masking of Plover at high orders with a small impact on efficiency. High masking orders introduce a new efficiency bottleneck in memory consumption, due to the storage requirements for highly masked polynomials. Second, our proposal Plover relies on (variants of) lattice assumptions that are well-understood (NTRU, LWE), or at least are classically reducible from standard assumptions (Hint-LWE). We emphasize that the simplicity allowed in the design leads to implementation portability. In particular, our scheme enjoys good versatility in its parameter choices—allowing numerous tradeoffs between module sizes, noise, and modulus–enabling target development on various device types. For example, our error distributions can be based on sums of uniform distributions; this makes implementation straightforward across a wide range of platforms. Ultimately, since Plover is a hash-and-sign signature, it does not require masked implementations of symmetric cryptographic components, such as SHA-3/SHAKE. The number of distinct masking gadgets is relatively small, which results in simpler and easier-to-verify firmware and hardware.

As expected, our efficient masking approach comes at the cost of larger parameter sizes (mainly because of the large modulus required) compared to the regular design of hash-and-sign schemes using Gaussian distributions and very small modulus. Additionally, the security is now *query dependant*: as it is the case for Raccoon or most threshold schemes, we can only tolerate a certain number (NIST recommendation being 2^{64}) of queries to the signing oracle with the same private key.

2   Preliminaries

2.1   Notations

Sets, Functions and Distributions. For an integer $N > 0$, we note $[N] = \{0, \ldots, N - 1\}$. To denote the assign operation, we use $y := f(x)$ when f is a deterministic and $y \leftarrow f(x)$ when randomized. When S is a finite set, we note $\mathcal{U}(S)$ the uniform distribution over S, and shorthand $x \xleftarrow{\$} S$ for $x \leftarrow \mathcal{U}(S)$.

Given a distribution $\mathcal{D}$ of support included in an additive group $\mathbb{G}$, we note $[T] \cdot \mathcal{D}$ the convolution of T identical copies of $\mathcal{D}$. For $c \in \mathbb{G}$, we may also note $\mathcal{D} + c$ the translation of the support of $\mathcal{D}$ by c. Finally, the notation $\mathcal{P} \overset{s}{\approx} \mathcal{Q}$ indicates that the two distributions are statistically indistinguishable.

Linear Algebra. Throughout the work, for a fixed power-of-two n, we note $\mathcal{K} = \mathbb{Q}[x]/(x^n + 1)$ and $\mathcal{R} = \mathbb{Z}[x]/(x^n + 1)$ the associated cyclotomic field and cyclotomic ring. We also note $\mathcal{R}_q = \mathcal{R}/(q\mathcal{R})$. Given $\mathbf{x} \in \mathcal{K}^\ell$, we abusively note $\|\mathbf{x}\|$ the Euclidean norm of the $(n\,\ell)$-dimensional vector of the coefficients of $\mathbf{x}$. By default, vectors are treated as *column* vectors unless specified otherwise.

Rounding. Let $\beta \in \mathbb{N}, \beta \geqslant 2$ be a power-of-two. Any integer $x \in \mathbb{Z}$ can be decomposed uniquely as $x = \beta \cdot x_1 + x_2$, where $x_2 \in \{-\beta/2, \ldots, \beta/2 - 1\}$. In this case, $|x_1| \leqslant \left\lceil \frac{x}{\beta} \right\rceil$, where $\lceil \cdot \rceil$ denote rounding up to the nearest integer. For odd q, we note $\mathsf{Decompose}_\beta : \mathbb{Z}_q \to \mathbb{Z} \times \mathbb{Z}$ the function which takes as input $x \in \mathbb{Z}_q$, takes its unique representative in $\bar{x} \in \{-(q-1)/2, \ldots, (q-1)/2\}$, and decomposes $\bar{x} = \beta \cdot x_1 + x_2$ as described above and outputs (x_1, x_2). We extend $\mathsf{Decompose}_\beta$ to polynomials in $\mathbb{Z}_q[x]$, by applying the function to each of its coefficients. For

$c \xleftarrow{\$} \mathbb{Z}_q$ and $(c_1, c_2) := \mathsf{Decompose}_\beta(c)$, we have $|c_1| \leqslant \left\lceil \frac{q-1}{2\beta} \right\rceil$, $\mathbb{E}[c_1] = 0$ and $\mathbb{E}[c_1^2] \leqslant \frac{M^2-1}{12}$ for $M = 2 \left\lceil \frac{q-1}{2\beta} \right\rceil + 1$.

2.2 Distributions

Definition 1 (Discrete Gaussians). *Given a positive definite $\Sigma \in \mathbb{R}^{m \times m}$, we note $\rho_{\sqrt{\Sigma}}$ the Gaussian function defined over $\mathbb{R}^m$ as*

$$\rho_{\sqrt{\Sigma}}(\mathbf{x}) = \exp\left(-\frac{\mathbf{x}^t \cdot \Sigma^{-1} \cdot \mathbf{x}}{2}\right).$$

We may note $\rho_{\sqrt{\Sigma},\mathbf{c}}(\mathbf{x}) = \rho_{\sqrt{\Sigma}}(\mathbf{x} - \mathbf{c})$. When Σ is of the form $\sigma \cdot \mathbf{I}_m$, where $\sigma \in \mathcal{K}^{++}$ and $\mathbf{I}_m$ is the identity matrix, we note $\rho_{\sigma,\mathbf{c}}$ as shorthand for $\rho_{\sqrt{\Sigma},\mathbf{c}}$.

For any countable set $S \subset \mathcal{K}^m$, we note $\rho_{\sqrt{\Sigma},\mathbf{c}}(S) = \sum_{\mathbf{x} \in \mathcal{K}^m} \rho_{\sqrt{\Sigma},\mathbf{c}}(\mathbf{x})$ whenever this sum converges. Finally, when $\rho_{\sqrt{\Sigma},\mathbf{c}}(S)$ converges, the discrete Gaussian distribution $D_{S,\mathbf{c},\sqrt{\Sigma}}$ is defined over S by its probability distribution function:

$$D_{S,\sqrt{\Sigma},\mathbf{c}}(\mathbf{x}) = \frac{\rho_{\sqrt{\Sigma},\mathbf{c}}(\mathbf{x})}{\rho_{\sqrt{\Sigma},\mathbf{c}}(S)}. \tag{1}$$

Definition 2 (Sum of uniforms). *We note $\mathrm{SU}(u, T) := [T] \cdot \mathcal{U}(\{-2^{u-1}, \ldots, 2^{u-1} - 1\})$. In other words, $\mathrm{SU}(u, T)$ is the distribution of the sum $X = \sum_{i \in [T]} X_i$, where each X_i is sampled uniformly in the set $\{-2^{u-1}, \ldots, 2^{u-1} - 1\}$.*

2.3 Hardness Assumptions

In a will of unification and clarification, we choose to present the lattice problems used in this work in their Hint-variants, that is to say with some additional statistical information on the secret values. Of course, not adding any hint recovers the plain problems—here being RLWE, and NTRU in the full version. The Hint-RLWE problem was introduced recently in [24] and reduces (in an almost dimension-preserving way) from RLWE.

Definition 3 (Hint-RLWE). *Let q, Q be integers, $\mathcal{D}_{\mathsf{sk}}, \mathcal{D}_{\mathsf{pert}}$ be probability distributions over $\mathcal{R}_q^2$, and $\mathcal{C}$ be a distribution over $\mathcal{R}_q$. The advantage $\mathsf{Adv}_{\mathcal{A}}^{\mathsf{Hint\text{-}RLWE}}(\kappa)$ of an adversary $\mathcal{A}$ against the Hint Ring Learning with Errors problem $\mathsf{Hint\text{-}RLWE}_{q,Q,\mathcal{D}_{\mathsf{sk}},\mathcal{D}_{\mathsf{pert}},\mathcal{C}}$ is defined as:*

$$\left| \Pr\left[1 \leftarrow \mathcal{A}\left(a, [a\ 1] \cdot \mathbf{s}, (c_i, \mathbf{z}_i)_{i \in [Q]}\right)\right] - \Pr\left[1 \leftarrow \mathcal{A}\left(a, u, (c_i, \mathbf{z}_i)_{i \in [Q]}\right)\right] \right|,$$

where $(a, u) \xleftarrow{\$} \mathcal{R}_q^2$, $\mathbf{s} \leftarrow \mathcal{D}_{\mathsf{sk}}$ and for $i \in [Q]$: $c_i \leftarrow \mathcal{C}$, $\mathbf{r}_i \leftarrow \mathcal{D}_{\mathsf{pert}}$, and $\mathbf{z}_i = c_i \cdot \mathbf{s} + \mathbf{r}_i$. The $\mathsf{Hint\text{-}RLWE}_{q,Q,\mathcal{D}_{\mathsf{sk}},\mathcal{D}_{\mathsf{pert}},\mathcal{C}}$ assumption states that any efficient adversary $\mathcal{A}$ has a negligible advantage. We may write $\mathsf{Hint\text{-}RLWE}_{q,Q,\sigma_s,\sigma_r,\mathcal{C}}$ as a shorthand when $\mathcal{D}_{\mathsf{sk}} = D_{\sigma_s}$ and $\mathcal{D}_{\mathsf{pert}} = D_{\sigma_r}$ are the Gaussian distributions of parameters σ_s and σ_r, respectively. When $Q = 0$, we recover the classical RLWE problem: $\mathsf{RLWE}_{q,\mathcal{D}_{\mathsf{sk}}} = \mathsf{Hint\text{-}RLWE}_{q,Q=0,\mathcal{D}_{\mathsf{sk}},\mathcal{D}_{\mathsf{pert}},\mathcal{C}}$.

The spectral norm $s_1(\mathbf{M})$ of a matrix $\mathbf{M}$ is defined as the value $\max_{\mathbf{x} \neq \mathbf{0}} \frac{\|\mathbf{M}\mathbf{x}\|}{\|\mathbf{x}\|}$. We recall that if a matrix is symmetric, then its spectral norm is also its largest eigenvalue. Given a polynomial $c \in \mathcal{R}$, we may abusively use the term "spectral norm $s_1(c)$ of c" when referring to the spectral norm of the anti-circulant matrix $\mathcal{M}(c)$ associated to c. Finally, if $c(x) = \sum_{0 \leq i < n} c_i x^i$, then the Hermitian adjoint of c, which we denote by c^*, is defined as $c^*(x) = c_0 - \sum_{0 < i < n} c_{n-i} x^i$. Note that $\mathcal{M}(c)^t = \mathcal{M}(c^*)$.

Theorem 1 (Hardness of Hint-RLWE, adapted from [24]). *Let $\mathcal{C}$ be a distribution over $\mathcal{R}$, and let B_{HRLWE} be a real number such that $s_1(D) \leq B_{\mathsf{HRLWE}}$ with overwhelming probability, where $D = \sum_Q c_i c_i^*$. Let $\sigma, \sigma_{\mathsf{sk}}, \sigma_{\mathsf{pert}} > 0$ such that $\frac{1}{\sigma^2} = 2\left(\frac{1}{\sigma_{\mathsf{sk}}^2} + \frac{B_{\mathsf{HRLWE}}}{\sigma_{\mathsf{pert}}^2}\right)$. If $\sigma \geq \sqrt{2}\eta_\varepsilon(\mathbb{Z}^n)$ for $0 < \varepsilon \leq 1/2$, where $\eta_\varepsilon(\mathbb{Z}^n)$ is the smoothing parameter of $\mathbb{Z}^n$, then there exists an efficient reduction from $\mathsf{RLWE}_{q,\sigma}$ to $\mathsf{Hint\text{-}RLWE}_{q,Q,\sigma_{\mathsf{sk}},\sigma_{\mathsf{pert}},\mathcal{C}}$ that reduces the advantage by at most 4ε.*

For our scheme, concrete bounds for B_{HRLWE} will be given in Lemma 2. Finally, we recall the Ring-SIS (RSIS) assumption.

Definition 4 (RSIS). *Let ℓ, q be integers and $\beta > 0$ be a real number. The advantage $\mathsf{Adv}_{\mathcal{A}}^{\mathsf{RSIS}}(\kappa)$ of an adversary $\mathcal{A}$ against the Ring Short Integer Solutions problem $\mathsf{RSIS}_{q,\ell,\beta}$ is defined as:*

$$\mathsf{Adv}_{\mathcal{A}}^{\mathsf{RSIS}}(\kappa) = \Pr\left[\mathbf{a} \xleftarrow{\$} \mathcal{R}_q^\ell, \mathbf{z} \leftarrow \mathcal{A}(\mathbf{a}) : 0 < \|\mathbf{z}\| \leq \beta \wedge \left[1 \; \mathbf{a}^\top\right] \mathbf{z} = \mathbf{0} \bmod q\right].$$

The $\mathsf{RSIS}_{q,\ell,\beta}$ assumption states that any efficient adversary $\mathcal{A}$ has a negligible advantage.

2.4 Masking

Definition 5. *Let R be a finite commutative ring and $d \geq 1$ be an integer. Given $x \in R$, a d-sharing of x is a d-tuple $(x_i)_{i \in [d]}$ such that $\sum_{i \in [d]} x_i = x$. We denote by $[\![x]\!]_d$ any valid d-sharing of x; when d is clear from context, we may omit it and simply write $[\![x]\!]$. A probabilistic encoding of x is a distribution over encodings of x.*

- A d-shared circuit C is a randomized circuit working on d-shared variables. More specifically, a d-shared circuit takes a set of n input sharings $(x_{1,i})_{i \in [d]}, \ldots, (x_{n,i})_{i \in [d]}$ and computes a set of m output sharings $(y_{1,i})_{i \in [d]}, \ldots, (y_{m,i})_{i \in [d]}$ such that $(y_1, \ldots, y_m) = f(x_1, \ldots, x_n)$ for some deterministic function f. The quantity $(d - 1)$ is then referred to as the *masking order*.
- A probe on C or an intermediate variable of C refers to a wire index (for some given indexing of C's wires).
- An evaluation of C on input $(x_{1,i})_{i \in [d]}, \ldots, (x_{n,i})_{i \in [d]}$ under a set of probes P refers to the distribution of the tuple of wires pointed by the probes in P when the circuit is evaluated on $(x_{1,i})_{i \in [d]}, \ldots, (x_{n,i})_{i \in [d]}$, which is denoted by $C((x_{1,i})_{i \in [d]}, \ldots, (x_{n,i})_{i \in [d]})_P$.

In the following, we focus on a special kind of shared circuits which are composed of gadgets. A (u, v)-gadget is a randomized shared circuit as a building block of a shared circuit that performs a given operation on its u input sharings and produces v output sharings.

2.5   Probing Model

The most commonly used leakage model is the probing model, introduced by Ishai, Sahai and Wagner in 2003 [20]. Informally, it states that during the evaluation of a circuit C, at most t wires (chosen by the adversary) leak the value they carry. The circuit C is said to be t-probing secure if the exact values of any set of t probes do not reveal any information about its inputs.

Definition 6 (t-probing security). *A randomized shared arithmetic circuit C equipped with an encoding $\mathcal{E}$ is t-probing secure if there exists a probabilistic simulator $\mathcal{S}$ which, for any input $x \in \mathbb{K}^\ell$ and every set of probes P such that $|P| \leqslant t$, satisfies $\mathcal{S}(C, P) = C(\mathcal{E}(x))_P$.*

Since the computation of distributions is expensive, the security proof relies on stronger simulation-based properties, introduced by Barthe et al. [4], to demonstrate the independence of the leaking wires from the input secrets. Informally, the idea is to perfectly simulate each possible set of probes with the smallest set of shares for each input. We recall the formal definitions of t-non-interference and t-strong non-interference hereafter. These provide a framework for the composition of building blocks, which makes the security analysis easier when masking entire schemes, as is the case here.

Definition 7 (t-non-interference). *A randomized shared arithmetic circuit C equipped with an encoding $\mathcal{E}$ is t-non-interferent (or t-NI) if there exists a deterministic simulator $\mathcal{S}_1$ and a probabilistic simulator $\mathcal{S}_2$, such that, for any input $x \in \mathbb{K}^\ell$, for every set of probes P of size t,*

$$(\mathcal{I}_1, \mathcal{I}_2, \ldots, \mathcal{I}_\ell) \leftarrow \mathcal{S}_1(C, P) \quad with \ |\mathcal{I}_1|, |\mathcal{I}_2|, \ldots, |\mathcal{I}_\ell| \leqslant t$$
$$and \quad \mathcal{S}_2((x_{1,i})_{i \in \mathcal{I}_1}, (x_{2,i})_{i \in \mathcal{I}_2}, \ldots, (x_{\ell,i})_{i \in \mathcal{I}_\ell}) = C(\mathcal{E}(x))_P.$$

If the input sharing is uniform, a t-non-interferent randomized arithmetic circuit C is also t-probing secure. One step further, the strong non-interference benefits from stopping the propagation of the probes between the outputs and the input shares and additionally trivially implies t-NI.

We now introduce the notion of t-strong non-interference with unshared input values (t-SNIu). The new notion is very much similar to that of t-SNI of Barthe et al. [5] with a special additional *unshared* input values x' along with the usual shared input values x. In addition, there will be no unshared outputs in t-SNIu, hence the interface with other gadgets is with the shared inputs only as with the original definition.

Definition 8 (*t*-strong non-interference with unshared input values).
A randomized shared arithmetic circuit C equipped with an encoding $\mathcal{E}$ is t-strong non-interferent with unshared input values (or t-SNIu) if there exists a deterministic simulator $\mathcal{S}_1$ and a probabilistic simulator $\mathcal{S}_2$, such that, for any shared inputs $x \in \mathbb{K}^\ell$ and unshared input values $x' \in \mathbb{K}^{\ell'}$, for every set of probes P of size t whose P_1 target internal variables and $P_2 = P \backslash P_1$ target the output shares,

$$(\mathcal{I}_1, \mathcal{I}_2, \ldots, \mathcal{I}_\ell, \mathcal{I}') \leftarrow \mathcal{S}_1(C, P) \quad with \; |\mathcal{I}_1|, |\mathcal{I}_2|, \ldots, |\mathcal{I}_\ell|, |\mathcal{I}'| \leqslant |P_1|$$
$$and \quad \mathcal{S}_2((x_{1,i})_{i \in \mathcal{I}_1}, (x_{2,i})_{i \in \mathcal{I}_2}, \ldots, (x_{\ell,i})_{i \in \mathcal{I}_\ell}, (x'_i)_{i \in \mathcal{I}'}) = C(\mathcal{E}(x, x'))_P.$$

We remark that for usual gadgets with no unshared inputs, our above definition of t-SNIu reduces to the usual t-SNI notion. Looking ahead, we will model our AddRepNoise gadget's internal small random values as unshared inputs to the AddRepNoise gadget.

Common Operations. Arithmetic masking, which we use in this paper, is compatible with simpler arithmetic performed in time $O(d^2)$ and is shown to be t-SNI by Barthe et al. [4, Proposition 2].

A t-SNI refresh gadget (Refresh), given in Algorithm 1, with complexity $O(d \log d)$ has been proposed by Battistello et al. [6]. Its complexity has been improved by a factor 2 by Mathieu-Mahias [27], which also proves that it is t-SNI in [27, Section 2.2]. We use this improved variant as a building block of our schemes. For completeness, it is reproduced in Algorithms 1 and 3.

Finally, a secure decoding algorithm Unmask is described in Algorithm 2. It is shown by Barthe et al. [5] to be t-NIo [5, Definition 7] .

Refresh and Unmask take as a (subscript) parameter a finite abelian group $\mathbb{G}$. When $\mathbb{G}$ is clear from context, we may drop the subscript for concision.

Algorithm 1. $\mathsf{Refresh}_{\mathbb{G}}(\llbracket x \rrbracket) \to \llbracket x \rrbracket'$

Require: A d-sharing $\llbracket x \rrbracket$ of $x \in \mathbb{G}$
Ensure: A fresh d-sharing $\llbracket x \rrbracket$ of x

1: $\llbracket z \rrbracket \xleftarrow{\$} \mathsf{ZeroEncoding}(\mathbb{G}, d)$
2: **return** $\llbracket x \rrbracket' := \llbracket x \rrbracket + \llbracket z \rrbracket$

Algorithm 2. $\mathsf{Unmask}_{\mathbb{G}}(\llbracket x \rrbracket) \to x$

Require: A d-sharing $\llbracket x \rrbracket = (x_i)_{i \in [d]}$
of $x \in \mathbb{G}$
Ensure: The clear value $x \in \mathbb{G}$
1: $\llbracket x \rrbracket \leftarrow \mathsf{Refresh}(\llbracket x \rrbracket)$
2: **return** $x := \sum_{i \in [d]} x_i$

Algorithm 3. $\mathsf{ZeroEncoding}(\mathbb{G}, d) \to \llbracket z \rrbracket_d$

Require: A power-of-two integer d, a finite
abelian group $\mathbb{G}$
Ensure: Uniform d-sharing $\llbracket z \rrbracket \in \mathbb{G}^d$ of $0 \in \mathbb{G}$
1: **if** $d = 1$ **then**
2:   **return** $\llbracket z \rrbracket_1 := (0)$
3: $\llbracket z_1 \rrbracket_{d/2} \leftarrow \mathsf{ZeroEncoding}(\mathbb{G}, d/2)$
4: $\llbracket z_2 \rrbracket_{d/2} \leftarrow \mathsf{ZeroEncoding}(\mathbb{G}, d/2)$
5: $\llbracket r \rrbracket_{d/2} \xleftarrow{\$} \mathbb{G}^{d/2}$
6: $\llbracket z_1 \rrbracket_{d/2} := \llbracket z_1 \rrbracket_{d/2} + \llbracket r \rrbracket_{d/2}$
7: $\llbracket z_2 \rrbracket_{d/2} := \llbracket z_2 \rrbracket_{d/2} - \llbracket r \rrbracket_{d/2}$
8: **return** $\llbracket z \rrbracket_d := (\llbracket z_1 \rrbracket_{d/2} \; \| \; \llbracket z_2 \rrbracket_{d/2})$
   ▷ ($u \| v$) denote shares concatenation.

AddRepNoise The AddRepNoise procedure (Algorithm 4) is one of the key building blocks of our scheme. It is an adaptation of the eponymous procedure from the Raccoon signature scheme [29].

Algorithm 4. AddRepNoise($\mathbb{G}, d, \mathcal{D}^{\text{ind}}, \text{rep}) \to \llbracket v \rrbracket$

Require: A finite Abelian group $\mathbb{G}$, the number of shares d, a noise distribution $\mathcal{D}^{\text{ind}}$, a repetition count parameter rep

Ensure: A masked element $\llbracket v \rrbracket \in \mathbb{G}^d$ such that $v \sim [d \cdot \text{rep}] \cdot \mathcal{D}^{\text{ind}}$

1: $\llbracket v \rrbracket = (v_j)_{j \in [d]} := (0_{\mathbb{G}})^d$ $\triangleright \llbracket v \rrbracket \in \mathbb{G}^d$
2: **for** $i \in [\text{rep}]$ **do**
3:     **for** $j \in [d]$ **do**
4:        $r_{i,j} \leftarrow \mathcal{D}^{\text{ind}}$
5:        $v_j := v_j + r_{i,j}$
6:     $\llbracket v \rrbracket \leftarrow \text{Refresh}(\llbracket v \rrbracket)$ $\triangleright$ Refresh $\llbracket v \rrbracket$ on each repeat
7: **return** $\llbracket v \rrbracket$

We prove that the AddRepNoise gadget satisfies the SNI with both shared and *unshared* inputs notion (t-SNIu), as defined in Sect. 2.1. In particular, there exists a simulator that can simulate $\leqslant t$ probed variables using $\leqslant t$ unshared input values and $\leqslant t$ shared input values. The underlying intuition (see Sect. 4.2 in [29] for an informal discussion) is that the t-SNI property of the Refresh gadget inserted between the rep MaskedAdd gadgets effectively isolates the MaskedAdd gadgets and prevents the adversary from combining two probes in different MaskedAdd gadgets to learn information about more than two unshared inputs, i.e. t probes only reveal $\leqslant t$ unshared inputs. The formal statement is given in Lemma 1.

Lemma 1 (AddRepNoise probing security). *Gadget AddRepNoise is t-SNIu, considering that AddRepNoise has no shared inputs, and that it takes as* unshared *input the values* $(r_{i,j})_{i,j}$.

Proof. The AddRepNoise consists of rep repeats (over $i \in [\text{rep}]$) of the following Add-Refresh subgadget: a MaskedAdd gadget (line 5) that adds sharewise the d unshared inputs $(r_{i,j})_{j \in [d]}$ to the internal sharing $\llbracket v \rrbracket$, followed by a Refresh($\llbracket v \rrbracket$) gadget (line 6). For $i \in [\text{rep}]$, we note:

1. $t_{1,R}^{(i)}$ the number of probed internal variables (not including outputs);
2. $t_{2,R}^{(i)}$ the number of simulated or probed output variables in i'th Refresh;
3. $t_A^{(i)}$ the total number of probed variables in the i'th MaskedAdd gadget (i.e. including probed inputs and probed outputs that are not probed as inputs of Refresh).

We construct a simulator for the t probed observation in AddRepNoise by composing the outputs of the [rep] simulators for probed observations in the Add-Refresh subgadgets, proceeding from output to input. For $i = \text{rep} - 1$ down to 0, the simulator for the i'th Add-Refresh subgadget works as follows.

The Refresh gadget is t-SNI according to [4]. Therefore, there exists a simulator $\mathcal{S}_R^{(i)}$ that can simulate $t_{1,R}^{(i)} + t_{2,R}^{(i)} \leqslant t$ variables using $t_{in,R}^{(i)} \leqslant t_{1,R}^{(i)}$ input shared values $[\![v]\!]$ of the i'th Refresh gadget. The latter is also equal to the number of outputs of MaskedAdd gadget that need to be simulated to input to $\mathcal{S}_R^{(i)}$.

Since the ith MaskedAdd gadget performs addition sharewise, we can now construct a simulator $\mathcal{S}_A^{(i)}$ that simulates the required $\leqslant t_A^{(i)} + t_{in,R}^{(i)} \leqslant t_A^{(i)} + t_{1,R}^{(i)}$ variables in the i'th MaskedAdd gadget using $t_{in,A}^{(i)} \leqslant t_A^{(i)} + t_{1,R}^{(i)}$ additions and the corresponding summands: $t_{in,A}^{(i)}$ input shares of the first MaskedAdd gadget in $[\![v]\!]$ and $t_{in,A}^{(i)}$ unshared inputs $r_{i,j}$.

Over all $i \in [\mathsf{rep}]$, the composed simulator $\mathcal{S}$ for AddRepNoise can simulate all t probed observations in AddRepNoise using a total of $t_{in,ARN,u} \leqslant \sum_{i \in [\mathsf{rep}]} t_{in,A}^{(i)} \leqslant \sum_{i \in [\mathsf{rep}]} t_A^{(i)} + t_{1,R}^{(i)} \leqslant t$ unshared input values $r_{i,j}$ of AddRepNoise, where $t_{in,ARN,u} \leqslant t$ since the above $\sum_{i \in [\mathsf{rep}]} t_A^{(i)} + t_{1,R}^{(i)}$ variables are distinct probed variables in AddRepNoise. $\qquad\square$

3 Plover-RLWE: Our RLWE-Based Maskable Signature

This section presents a maskable hash-and-sign signature scheme based on RLWE. It leverages the compact lattice gadget from Yu et al. [34], and its mostly linear operations to construct a maskable scheme relying on noise flooding, i.e. Gaussian sampling is replaced by a large noise provably hiding a secret value. We describe the unmasked scheme in Sect. 3.1, and the masked scheme in Sect. 3.3. We introduce additional notations.

- ExpandA: $\{0,1\}^\kappa \to \mathcal{R}_q$ deterministically maps a uniform seed seed to a uniformly pseudo-random element $a \in \mathcal{R}_q$.
- $H : \{0,1\}^* \times \{0,1\}^{2\kappa} \times \mathcal{V} \to \mathcal{R}_q$ is a collision-resistant hash function mapping a tuple $(\mathsf{msg}, \mathsf{salt}, \mathsf{vk})$ to an element $u \in \mathcal{R}_q$. We note that H is parameterized by a salt salt for the security proof of Gentry et al. [16] to go through, and by the verification key vk.

3.1 Description of Unmasked Plover-RLWE

Parameters. We sample RLWE trapdoors from a distribution $\mathcal{D}_{\mathsf{sk}}$, and noise in the signature from a distribution $\mathcal{D}_{\mathsf{pert}}$. Additionally, we introduce an integer parameter β; it is used as a divider in the signature generation to decompose challenges in low/high order bits via $\mathsf{Decompose}_\beta$. Despite its name, we do not require that β divides q; that was only required by the Gaussian sampler of [34].

Key Generation. The key generation samples a public polynomial a, derived from a seed. The second part of the public key is essentially an RLWE sample shifted by β. A description of the key generation is given in Algorithm 5.

Algorithm 5. Plover-RLWE.Keygen(1^κ) $\rightarrow$ (vk, sk)

Require: The ring $\mathcal{R}_q$, a divider β, a distribution $\mathcal{D}_{\mathsf{sk}}$ over $\mathcal{R}^2$

Ensure: A verification key vk $= (\mathsf{seed}, b) \in \{0,1\}^\kappa \times \mathcal{R}_q$, a signing key sk $= (s, e) \in \mathcal{R}^2$

1: seed $\xleftarrow{\$} \{0,1\}^\kappa$
2: $a := \mathsf{ExpandA}(\mathsf{seed})$ ▷ ExpandA maps a seed to an element in $\mathcal{R}$
3: $(s, e) \leftarrow \mathcal{D}_{\mathsf{sk}}$
4: $b := \beta - (as + e) \bmod q$
5: **return** vk $:= (\mathsf{seed}, b), := (\mathsf{vk}, s, e)$

Signing Procedure. The signature generation is described in Algorithm 6. It first hashes the given message msg to a target polynomial u. It then uses its trapdoor to find a short pre-image $\mathbf{z} = (z_1, z_2, z_3)$ such that $\mathbf{A} \cdot \mathbf{z} := z_1 + a z_2 + b z_3 = u - c_2 \bmod q$ for a small c_2 and $\mathbf{A} := \begin{bmatrix} 1 \ a \ b \end{bmatrix}$. In order to prevent leaking the trapdoor, a noise vector $\mathbf{p}$ is sampled and added to the pre-image $\mathbf{z}$. As in [34], the actual signature is (z_2, z_3), since $z_1 + c_2 = u - a z_2 - b z_3$ can be recovered in the verification procedure. Additionally, c_1 is public and does not require to be hidden by noise. Signature size is then dominated by sending z_2.

Ahead of Sect. 3.3, we note that, except for Line 5, all operations in Algorithm 6 either (i) are linear functions of sensitive data ($\mathbf{T}$ and $\mathbf{p}$), and can therefore be masked with overhead $\tilde{O}(d)$, or (ii) can be performed unmasked.

Algorithm 6. Plover-RLWE.Sign(msg, sk) $\rightarrow$ sig

Require: A message msg, the secret key sk $= ((\mathsf{seed}, b), s, e)$, a bound $B_2 > 0$

Ensure: A signature $(\mathsf{salt}, z_2, z_3)$

1: $a := \mathsf{ExpandA}(\mathsf{seed})$
2: salt $\xleftarrow{\$} \{0,1\}^{2\kappa}$
3: $u := H(\mathsf{msg}, \mathsf{salt}, \mathsf{vk})$
4: $\mathbf{A} := \begin{bmatrix} 1 \ a \ b \end{bmatrix}, \mathbf{T} := \begin{bmatrix} e \\ s \\ 1 \end{bmatrix}$
5: $\mathbf{p} \leftarrow \mathcal{D}_{\mathsf{pert}} \times \{0\}$ ▷ Recall $\mathcal{D}_{\mathsf{pert}}$ is over $\mathcal{R}_q^2$
6: $c := u - \mathbf{A} \cdot \mathbf{p}$
7: $(c_1, c_2) := \mathsf{Decompose}_\beta(c)$ ▷ $c = \beta \cdot c_1 + c_2$
8: $\mathbf{z} \leftarrow \mathbf{p} + \mathbf{T} \cdot c_1$ ▷ $\mathbf{z} = (z_1, z_2, z_3)$ and $z_3 = c_1$
9: **return** sig $:= (\mathsf{salt}, z_2, z_3)$, $\mathsf{aux}_{\mathsf{sig}} = c_2$ ▷ $\mathsf{aux}_{\mathsf{sig}}$ used in security proof, but not in verification.

Verification. The verification first recovers $z_1' := u - a z_2 - b z_3$ (equal to $z_1 + c_2$), followed by checking the shortness of (z_1', z_2, z_3). A formal description is given in Algorithm 7. Using notations from Algorithm 6, correctness follows from:

$$\mathbf{A}\mathbf{z} = \mathbf{A}\mathbf{p} + \mathbf{A}\mathbf{T}c_1 = (u - c) + \beta \cdot c_1 = u - c_2$$

To provide a more modular exposition to our algorithms and security proofs, we next prove the EUF-CMA security of our unmasked signature proposal. Later

---

Algorithm 7. Plover-RLWE.Verify(vk, msg, sig) → **accept** or **reject**

Require: sig = (salt, z_2, z_3), msg, vk = (seed, b), and a bound $B_2 > 0$
Ensure: Accept or reject.
1: $a := \mathsf{ExpandA}(\mathsf{seed})$,
2: $u := H(\mathsf{msg}, \mathsf{salt}, \mathsf{vk})$
3: $z'_1 := (u - a\, z_2 - b\, z_3) \bmod q$ $\triangleright\ z'_1 = z_1 + c_2$
4: **accept if** $\{\ \|(z'_1, z_2, z_3)\| \leqslant B_2 \text{ and } \|z_3\|_\infty \leqslant q/(2\beta) + 1/2\ \}$, **else reject**

---

in Sect. 3.4, we will reduce the t-probing security of our *masked* construction from the EUF-CMA security of the *unmasked* construction. To facilitate the latter reduction, we show the EUF-CMA security of the unmasked construction even when the signing oracle outputs the auxiliary signature information $\mathsf{aux}_{\mathsf{sig}} = c_2$ (see Algorithm 6) along with the signature sig.

3.2 EUF-CMA Security of Unmasked Plover-RLWE

For the Hint-RLWE reduction in Theorem 2, we introduce Definition 9. Note that in the definition, if β divides q, then c_1 and c_2 are independent and uniformly random in their supports but this is not necessary for our reduction.

Definition 9 (Distributions for Hint-RLWE). *Let (c_1, c_2) be sampled from the joint distribution induced by sampling c uniformly at random from R_q and setting $(c_1, c_2) := \mathsf{Decompose}_\beta(c)$. Then:*

- *We let $\mathcal{C}_1$ denote the marginal distribution of c_1.*
- *For a fixed c'_1, we let $\mathcal{C}_2^{|c'_1}$ denote the conditional distribution of c_2 conditioned on the event $c_1 = c'_1$.*

Before we move into the formal security statement, we emphasize that the security of unmasked Plover reduces to the standard RLWE and RSIS problems when the distributions $\mathcal{D}_{\mathsf{sk}}, \mathcal{D}_{\mathsf{pert}}$ are chosen to be discrete Gaussians (with appropriate parameter). This is due to the fact that Hint-RLWE reduces to RLWE as proven in [25], see also Theorem 1.

Theorem 2. *The* Plover-RLWE *scheme is* EUF-CMA *secure in the random oracle model if* $\mathsf{RLWE}_{q, \mathcal{U}([-B_2/\sqrt{2n}, B_2/\sqrt{2n}]^n)^2}$, $\mathsf{Hint\text{-}RLWE}_{q, Q_{\mathsf{Sign}}, \mathcal{D}_{\mathsf{sk}}, \mathcal{D}_{\mathsf{pert}}, \mathcal{C}_1}$ *and* $\mathsf{RSIS}_{q, 2, 2B_2}$ *assumptions hold. Formally, let $\mathcal{A}$ be an adversary against the* EUF-CMA *security game making at most Q_{Sign} signing queries and at most Q_H random oracle queries. Denote an adversary $\mathcal{H}$'s advantage against* $\mathsf{Hint\text{-}RLWE}_{q, Q_{\mathsf{Sign}}, \mathcal{D}_{\mathsf{sk}}, \mathcal{D}_{\mathsf{pert}}, \mathcal{C}_1}$ *by $\mathsf{Adv}_{\mathcal{H}}^{\mathsf{Hint\text{-}RLWE}}(\kappa)$, and an adversary $\mathcal{D}$'s advantage against* $\mathsf{RLWE}_{q, \mathcal{U}([-B_2/\sqrt{2n}, B_2/\sqrt{2n}]^n)^2}$ *by $\mathsf{Adv}_{\mathcal{D}}^{\mathsf{RLWE}}(\kappa)$. Then, there exists an adversary $\mathcal{B}$ running in time $T_{\mathcal{B}} \approx T_{\mathcal{H}} \approx T_{\mathcal{D}} \approx T_{\mathcal{A}}$ against* $\mathsf{RSIS}_{q, 2, 2B_2}$ *with advantage $\mathsf{Adv}_{\mathcal{B}}^{\mathsf{RSIS}}(\kappa)$ such that*

$$\mathsf{Adv}_{\mathcal{A}}^{\mathsf{EUF\text{-}CMA}} \leqslant p_c + Q_{\mathsf{Sign}} Q_H / 2^{2\kappa} + \mathsf{Adv}_{\mathcal{H}}^{\mathsf{Hint\text{-}RLWE}}(\kappa) + Q_H \cdot \mathsf{Adv}_{\mathcal{D}}^{\mathsf{RLWE}}(\kappa) + \mathsf{Adv}_{\mathcal{B}}^{\mathsf{RSIS}}$$

for some $p_c \leqslant 2^{-n \cdot \left(2\log_2(2B_2/\sqrt{2n}) - \log_2(q)\right)}$.

Proof. We prove the security of the above scheme with intermediary hybrid games, starting from the EUF-CMA game against our signature scheme in the ROM and then finally arriving at a game where we can build an adversary $\mathcal{B}$ against $\mathsf{RSIS}_{q,2,2B_2}$. Let $\mathcal{A}$ be an adversary against the EUF-CMA security game.

Game_0. This is the original EUF-CMA security game. A key pair $(\mathsf{vk}, \mathsf{sk}) \leftarrow$ Plover-RLWE.Keygen(1^κ) is generated and $\mathcal{A}$ is given vk. $\mathcal{A}$ gets access to a signing oracle $\mathsf{OSign}(\mathsf{msg})$ that on input a message msg (chosen by $\mathcal{A}$) outputs a signature, along with the auxiliary signature information $(\mathsf{sig}, \mathsf{aux}_{\mathsf{sig}}) \leftarrow$ Plover-RLWE.Sign($\mathsf{msg}, \mathsf{sk}$) and adds $(\mathsf{msg}, \mathsf{sig}, \mathsf{aux}_{\mathsf{sig}})$ to a table $\mathcal{T}_s$. The calls to the random oracle H are stored in a table $\mathcal{T}_H$ and those to OSign are stored in a table $\mathcal{T}_s$.

Game_1. Given a message msg, we replace the signing oracle OSign as follows:

1. Sample $\mathsf{salt} \xleftarrow{\$} \{0,1\}^{2\kappa}$. Abort if an entry matching the $(\mathsf{msg}, \mathsf{salt}, \mathsf{vk})$ tuple exists in $\mathcal{T}_H$ (Abort I).
2. Sample $u' \xleftarrow{\$} \mathcal{R}_q$ and decompose it as $(c_1, c_2) := \mathsf{Decompose}_\beta(u')$ (i.e., $u' = \beta \cdot c_1 + c_2$).
3. Sample $\mathbf{p} \leftarrow \mathcal{D}_{\mathsf{pert}} \times \{0\}$.
4. Compute $\mathbf{z}' := \mathbf{p} + \mathbf{T} \cdot c_1 + \begin{bmatrix} c_2 & 0 & 0 \end{bmatrix}$. Program the random oracle H such that $H(\mathsf{msg}, \mathsf{salt}, \mathsf{vk}) := \mathbf{A}\mathbf{z}'$. Store in $\mathcal{T}_H$ the entry $((\mathsf{msg}, \mathsf{salt}), \mathbf{z}')$.
5. Return $\mathsf{sig} := (\mathsf{salt}, z_2', z_3')$ and $\mathsf{aux}_{\mathsf{sig}} := c_2$, where $\mathbf{z}' = (z_1', z_2', z_3')$, and store $(\mathsf{msg}, \mathsf{sig}, \mathsf{aux}_{\mathsf{sig}})$ in $\mathcal{T}_s$.

Observe that Abort I happens with probability at most $Q_{\mathsf{Sign}} Q_H / 2^{2\kappa}$. If it does not, then the view of $\mathcal{A}$ in Game_1 is distributed identically to their view in Game_0. Indeed, in Game_1, the value u output by H for signed values is still uniform in $\mathcal{R}_q$ and independent of $\mathbf{p}$. This is due to the fact that $u := \mathbf{A}\mathbf{z}' = \mathbf{A}\mathbf{p} + \mathbf{A}\mathbf{T} \cdot c_1 + c_2 = \mathbf{A}\mathbf{p} + \beta c_1 + c_2 = \mathbf{A}\mathbf{p} + u'$ and u' is uniform in $\mathcal{R}_q$ and independent of $\mathbf{p}$. Hence, there is an advantage loss only if Abort I occurs; that is,

$$\left| \mathsf{Adv}_{\mathcal{A}}^{\mathsf{Game}_0} - \mathsf{Adv}_{\mathcal{A}}^{\mathsf{Game}_1} \right| \leqslant Q_{\mathsf{Sign}} Q_H / 2^{2\kappa}.$$

Game_2. In this game, we make a single change over Game_1 and replace $b = \beta - (as + e)$ by $b = \beta - b'$ where b' is a uniformly random polynomial in $\mathcal{R}_q$. This means that b also follows uniform distribution over $\mathcal{R}_q$.

We can observe that this reduces to Hint-RLWE problem with Q_{Sign} hints. In particular, given Hint-RLWE instance $(a, b', \{c_{1,i}, (h_{1,i}, h_{2,i})\}_{i \in [Q_{\mathsf{Sign}}]})$ with $c_{1,i} \leftarrow \mathcal{C}_1$, and $h_{1,i} := p_{1,i} + e \cdot c_{1,i}$ and $h_{2,i} := p_{2,i} + s \cdot c_{1,i}$, adversary $\mathcal{H}$ runs $\mathcal{A}$ with verification key (a, b') and simulates the view of $\mathcal{A}$ as in Game_1, computing the values of $z_{1,i}', z_{2,i}'$ in step 4 of the i'th query to OSign in Game_1 using the hints $h_{1,i}, h_{2,i}$ as follows: $z_{1,i}' = h_{1,i} + c_{2,i}$, $z_{2,i}' = h_{2,i}$, with $c_{2,i}$ sampled from the conditional distribution $\mathcal{C}_2^{|c_{1,i}}$. At the end of the game, $\mathcal{H}$ returns 1 if $\mathcal{A}$ wins the game, and 0 otherwise. Observe that if b' in the Hint-RLWE instance is from the real RLWE (resp. uniform in R_q) distribution, then $\mathcal{H}$ simulates to $\mathcal{A}$ its view in Game$_1$ (resp. Game$_2$), so $\mathcal{H}$'s advantage is lower bounded as

$$\left| \mathsf{Adv}_{\mathcal{A}}^{\mathsf{Game}_1} - \mathsf{Adv}_{\mathcal{A}}^{\mathsf{Game}_2} \right| \leqslant \mathsf{Adv}_{\mathcal{H}}^{\mathsf{Hint\text{-}RLWE}}(\kappa).$$

Game$_3$. In this game, we replace the random oracle H as follows. If an entry has not been queried before, H returns $\mathbf{Az}$ where $\mathbf{z} \xleftarrow{\$} \{0\} \times \left([-B_2/\sqrt{2n}, B_2/\sqrt{2n}]^n\right)^2$ (observe that $\|\mathbf{z}\| \leqslant B_2$). We store in $\mathcal{T}_H$ the entry $((\mathsf{msg}, \mathsf{salt}), \mathbf{z})$ for an input query $(\mathsf{msg}, \mathsf{salt}, \mathsf{vk})$. Note that the result of $\mathbf{Az}$ is indistinguishable from a uniformly random value in R_q by the $\mathsf{RLWE}_{q, \mathcal{U}([-B_2/\sqrt{2n}, B_2/\sqrt{2n}]^n)^2}$ assumption. Hence, we have

$$\left| \mathsf{Adv}_{\mathcal{A}}^{\mathsf{Game}_2} - \mathsf{Adv}_{\mathcal{A}}^{\mathsf{Game}_3} \right| \leqslant Q_H \cdot \mathsf{Adv}_{\mathcal{D}}^{\mathsf{RLWE}}(\kappa).$$

Game$_4$. Let $\mathsf{sig}^* := (\mathsf{salt}^*, z_2^*, z_3^*) \notin \mathcal{T}_s$ be the forged signature output by $\mathcal{A}$ for a message msg^*. Define $z_1^* := u - a z_2^* - b c_1^*$ and $\mathbf{z}^* := (z_1^*, z_2^*, z_3^*)$. Without loss of generality, we assume that the pair $(\mathsf{msg}^*, \mathsf{salt}^*)$ has been queried to the random oracle H. From $\mathcal{T}_H$, we retrieve $\widehat{\mathbf{z}} = (\widehat{z}_1, \widehat{z}_2, \widehat{z}_3)$ corresponding to $(\mathsf{msg}^*, \mathsf{salt}^*)$. If $\widehat{\mathbf{z}} = \mathbf{z}^*$, then we abort (Abort II).

- **Case 1:** Suppose $H(\mathsf{msg}^*, \mathsf{salt}^*, \mathsf{vk})$ was called by the signing oracle OSign. Then, since $\mathsf{sig}^* := (\mathsf{salt}^*, z_2^*, z_3^*) \notin \mathcal{T}_s$, we must have $(\mathsf{salt}^*, z_2^*, z_3^*) \neq (\mathsf{salt}^*, \widehat{z}_2, \widehat{z}_3)$, which implies $\widehat{\mathbf{z}} \neq \mathbf{z}^*$. Hence, Abort II never happens in this case.
- **Case 2:** Suppose $H(\mathsf{msg}^*, \mathsf{salt}^*, \mathsf{vk})$ was queried directly to H. Then, since the first entry of $\widehat{\mathbf{z}}$ (resp. $\mathbf{z}^*$) is uniquely determined by the remaining entries of $\widehat{\mathbf{z}}$ (resp. $\mathbf{z}^*$), Abort II happens with a probability

$$p_c := \max_u \Pr[(z_2^*, z_3^*) = (\widehat{z}_2, \widehat{z}_3) \mid H(\mathsf{msg}^*, \mathsf{salt}^*, \mathsf{vk}) = u = \mathbf{A}\widehat{z}] \leqslant 2^{-H_\infty((\widehat{z}_2, \widehat{z}_3)|u)}$$

Since $H_\infty((\widehat{z}_2, \widehat{z}_3)) \geqslant 2n \log_2(2B_2/\sqrt{2n})$ and $H_\infty(u) \leqslant n \log_2(q)$, we have:

$$\begin{aligned} H_\infty((\widehat{z}_2, \widehat{z}_3)|u) &\geqslant H_\infty((\widehat{z}_2, \widehat{z}_3, u)) - H_\infty(u) \\ &\geqslant H_\infty((\widehat{z}_2, \widehat{z}_3)) - H_\infty(u) \\ &\geqslant n \cdot (2 \log_2(2B_2/\sqrt{2n}) - \log_2(q)) \end{aligned}$$

Hence, we get

$$\left| \mathsf{Adv}_{\mathcal{A}}^{\mathsf{Game}_3} - \mathsf{Adv}_{\mathcal{A}}^{\mathsf{Game}_4} \right| \leqslant p_c \quad \text{for} \quad p_c \leqslant 2^{-n \cdot (2 \log_2(2B_2/\sqrt{2n}) - \log_2(q))}.$$

Observe from the verification algorithm (Algorithm 7) that $\mathbf{Az}^* = u = H(\mathsf{msg}, \mathsf{salt}, \mathsf{vk})$ and $\|\mathbf{z}^*\| \leqslant B_2$. Also, by the construction of H, $u = \mathbf{A}\widehat{z}$ with $\|\widehat{\mathbf{z}}\| \leqslant B_2$ (see Game$_3$). Consequently, if Abort II does not happen, we can construct an adversary $\mathcal{B}$ that solves the $\mathsf{RSIS}_{q,2,2B_2}$ problem for $\mathbf{A}$ since $\mathbf{A}(\hat{\mathbf{z}} - \mathbf{z}^*) = 0 \bmod q$ for $\hat{\mathbf{z}} - \mathbf{z}^* \neq \mathbf{0}$ where $\mathbf{A} = \begin{bmatrix} 1 & a & b \end{bmatrix}$ for a random a (modelling ExpandA as a random oracle) and random b (as discussed in Game_2). More concretely, let $\mathbf{A} = \begin{bmatrix} 1 & a & b \end{bmatrix}$ be the challenge RSIS vector given to $\mathcal{B}$ where $a, b \xleftarrow{\$} \mathcal{R}_q$. The adversary $\mathcal{B}$ samples $\mathsf{seed} \xleftarrow{\$} \{0,1\}^\kappa$ and provides $\mathsf{vk} = (\mathsf{seed}, b)$ to $\mathcal{A}$ against Game_4 and programs $\mathsf{ExpandA}(\mathsf{seed}) = a$ (modelling $\mathsf{ExpandA}$ as a random oracle). Note that the distribution of (seed, b) matches perfectly the distribution of vk produced in Game_4 due to the change of b in Game_2. Since OSign is run using only with publicly computable values in Game_4, $\mathcal{B}$ simulates OSign queries as in Game_4. $\mathcal{B}$ also simulates the queries to H as in Game_4 and stores the corresponding tables $\mathcal{T}_H$ and $\mathcal{T}_s$. As discussed above, provided that Abort II does not happen, $\mathcal{B}$ can use $\mathcal{A}$'s output forgery to create an $\mathsf{RSIS}_{q,2,2B_2}$ solution. Hence, $\left| \mathsf{Adv}_{\mathcal{B}}^{\mathsf{RSIS}} - \mathsf{Adv}_{\mathcal{A}}^{\mathsf{Game}_4} \right| \leqslant p_c$ and $T_\mathcal{B} \approx T_\mathcal{A}$. As a result, we get

$$\left| \mathsf{Adv}_{\mathcal{B}}^{\mathsf{RSIS}} - \mathsf{Adv}_{\mathcal{A}}^{\mathsf{EUF\text{-}CMA}} \right| = \left| \mathsf{Adv}_{\mathcal{B}}^{\mathsf{RSIS}} - \mathsf{Adv}_{\mathcal{A}}^{\mathsf{Game}_4} + \mathsf{Adv}_{\mathcal{A}}^{\mathsf{Game}_4} - \mathsf{Adv}_{\mathcal{A}}^{\mathsf{EUF\text{-}CMA}} \right|$$

$$\leqslant p_c + Q_{\mathsf{Sign}} Q_H / 2^{2\kappa} + \mathsf{Adv}_{\mathcal{H}}^{\mathsf{Hint\text{-}RLWE}}(\kappa) + Q_H \cdot \mathsf{Adv}_{\mathcal{D}}^{\mathsf{RLWE}}(\kappa).$$

This concludes the proof. $\qquad\qquad\qquad\qquad\qquad\qquad\qquad\qquad\qquad\qquad\square$

3.3   Description of Masked Plover-RLWE

This section describes our main construction, the masked Plover-RLWE. $\mathcal{D}_{\mathsf{sk}}$ and $\mathcal{D}_{\mathsf{pert}}$ are respectively replaced by sums of distributions $[d\,\mathsf{rep}_{\mathsf{sk}}] \cdot \mathcal{D}_{\mathsf{sk}}^{\mathsf{ind}}$ and $[d\,\mathsf{rep}_{\mathsf{pert}}] \cdot \mathcal{D}_{\mathsf{pert}}^{\mathsf{ind}}$ to enable the masking, where $\mathsf{rep}_{\mathsf{sk}}$ and $\mathsf{rep}_{\mathsf{pert}}$ are newly introduced parameters.

Key Generation. The key generation generates d-sharings small secrets $(\llbracket s \rrbracket, \llbracket e \rrbracket)$ and the corresponding RLWE sample $b = a \cdot s + e$. As in Raccoon [29], a key technique is the use of AddRepNoise for the generation of the small errors which ensures that a t-probing adversary learns limited information about (s, e).

Algorithm 8. Plover-RLWE.MaskKeygen(1^κ) $\rightarrow$ (vk, sk)

Require: The ring $\mathcal{R}$, a modulus q
Ensure: A public key $(\mathsf{seed}, b) \in \{0,1\}^\kappa \times \mathcal{R}$, a private key $(s, e) \in \mathcal{R}^2$
1: $\mathsf{seed} \xleftarrow{\$} \{0,1\}^\kappa$
2: $a := \mathsf{ExpandA}(\mathsf{seed})$ $\triangleright$ Map a seed to an element in $\mathcal{R}$
3: $\llbracket (s, e) \rrbracket \leftarrow \mathsf{AddRepNoise}\left(\mathcal{R}_q^2, d, \mathcal{D}_{\mathsf{sk}}^{\mathsf{ind}}, \mathsf{rep}_{\mathsf{sk}}\right)$ $\triangleright$ Samples s, e from $\mathcal{D}_{\mathsf{sk}}$
4: $\llbracket b \rrbracket := \beta - (a \cdot \llbracket s \rrbracket + \llbracket e \rrbracket)$
5: $b := \mathsf{Unmask}(\llbracket b \rrbracket)$
6: **return** $(\mathsf{vk} := (\mathsf{seed}, b), \mathsf{sk} := (\mathsf{vk}, \llbracket s \rrbracket))$

Signature Procedure. The signature procedure is adapted to remove the computation of z_1 and save on masking. It recovers $z_1' = z_1 + c_2$ from unmasked values as done in the verification Algorithm 7 from unmasked values. This also allows to drop e from the private key and significantly reduces its size. A formal description is given in Algorithm 9.

Algorithm 9. Plover-RLWE.MaskSign(msg, sk) $\rightarrow$ sig

Require: A message msg, the secret key sk $= ((\text{seed}, b), [\![s]\!])$
Ensure: A signature (salt, $z_2, z_3,$ msg)

1: salt $\overset{\$}{\leftarrow} \{0,1\}^{2\kappa}$
2: $u := H(\text{msg}, \text{salt}, \text{vk})$
3: $a := \text{ExpandA}(\text{seed})$
4: $[\![\mathbf{p}]\!] \leftarrow \text{AddRepNoise}(\mathcal{R}_q^2, d, \mathcal{D}_{\text{pert}}^{\text{ind}}, \text{rep}_{\text{pert}})$ $\quad\quad\quad\quad\quad \triangleright \mathbf{p} = (p_1, p_2) \in \mathcal{D}_{\text{pert}}^2$
5: $[\![\mathbf{w}]\!] \leftarrow [\![p_1]\!] + a \cdot [\![p_2]\!]$
6: $w := \text{Unmask}([\![w]\!])$
7: $c := u - w$
8: $(c_1, c_2) := \text{Decompose}_\beta(c)$ $\quad\quad\quad\quad\quad\quad\quad\quad\quad\quad \triangleright c = \beta \cdot c_1 + c_2$
9: $[\![s]\!] \leftarrow \text{Refresh}([\![s]\!])$ $\quad\quad\quad\quad\quad\quad\quad\quad\quad \triangleright \text{Refresh } [\![s]\!] \text{ before re-use}$
10: $[\![z_2]\!] := [\![p_2]\!] + c_1 \cdot [\![s]\!]$
11: $z_2 := \text{Unmask}([\![z_2]\!])$
12: $z_3 := c_1$
13: **return** sig $:= (\text{salt}, z_2, z_3), \text{aux}_{\text{sig}} = c_2$ $\quad \triangleright \text{aux}_{\text{sig}} \text{ is used in security proof, but not in verification.}$

Verification. The verification first recovers $z_1' := u - az_2 - bz_3 = z_1 + c_2$. It then checks the shortness of (z_1', z_2, z_3). A formal description is given in Algorithm 7.

3.4 Security of Masked **Plover-RLWE**

We now turn to the security of the masked version of Plover, in the t-probing model. Contrary to proofs for less efficient masking techniques, which have no security loss even in the presence of the probes, we propose a fine-grained result where we quantify precisely the loss induced by the probes and show how the security of this leaky scheme corresponds to the security of the leak-free unmasked Plover, but with slightly smaller secret key parameters and slightly larger verification norm bound.

Theorem 3. *The masked* Plover-RLWE *scheme with parameters* $(d, \mathcal{D}_{\text{sk}}^{\text{ind}}, \text{rep}_{\text{sk}},$ $\mathcal{D}_{\text{pert}}^{\text{ind}}, \text{rep}_{\text{pert}}, B_2)$ *is t-probing EUF-CMA secure in the random oracle model if the unmasked* Plover-RLWE *scheme with parameters* $(\mathcal{D}_{\text{sk}}, \mathcal{D}_{\text{pert}}, B_2')$ *is EUF-CMA secure in the random oracle model, with*

$$\begin{cases} \mathcal{D}_{\text{sk}} & := [d \, \text{rep}_{\text{sk}} - t] \cdot \mathcal{D}_{\text{sk}}^{\text{ind}}, \\ \mathcal{D}_{\text{pert}} & := [d \, \text{rep}_{\text{pert}} - t] \cdot \mathcal{D}_{\text{pert}}^{\text{ind}} \\ B_2' & := B_2 + t \cdot (B_{\text{pert}} + n(q/(2\beta) + 1/2) B_{\text{sk}}), \end{cases} \quad (2)$$

where B_{pert} and B_{sk} denote upper bounds on the ℓ_2 norm of samples from $\mathcal{D}_{\text{pert}}^{\text{ind}}$ and $\mathcal{D}_{\text{sk}}^{\text{ind}}$, respectively. B_2' is the norm bound used by the unmasked Plover-RLWE.

Formally, let $\mathcal{A}$ denote an adversary against the t-probing EUF-CMA security game against masked Plover-RLWE making at most Q_{Sign} signing queries and at most Q_H random oracle queries and advantage $\mathsf{Adv}_{\mathcal{A}}^{\mathsf{pr\text{-}EUF\text{-}CMA}}$. Then, there exists an adversary $\mathcal{A}'$ against EUF-CMA security of unmasked Plover-RLWE, running in time $T_{\mathcal{A}'} \approx T_{\mathcal{A}}$ and making $Q'_{\mathsf{Sign}} = Q_{\mathsf{Sign}}$ sign queries and $Q_{H'} = Q_H$ random oracle queries with advantage $\mathsf{Adv}_{\mathcal{A}'}^{\mathsf{EUF\text{-}CMA}}$ such that:

$$\mathsf{Adv}_{\mathcal{A}}^{\mathsf{pr\text{-}EUF\text{-}CMA}} \leqslant \mathsf{Adv}_{\mathcal{A}'}^{\mathsf{EUF\text{-}CMA}} + Q_{\mathsf{Sign}}Q_H/2^{2\kappa}.$$

Proof. We describe the reduction with several hybrid games starting from the t-probing EUF-CMA game played with adversary $\mathcal{A}$ against the masked signature with random oracle H and ending with a game where we can build an adversary $\mathcal{A}'$ against the EUF-CMA security for the unmasked signature with a random oracle H'. In this and the following games we let S_i denote the event that $\mathcal{A}$ wins the t-probing EUF-CMA game.

Game_0. This corresponds to the t-probing EUF-CMA unforgeability game [5] played with adversary $\mathcal{A}$. At the beginning of the game, $\mathcal{A}$ outputs a key gen. probing set P_{KG} of size $\leqslant t$, then a masked key generation oracle OKG runs $\mathsf{MaskKeygen}(1^\kappa)$ to output $(\mathsf{vk} := (\mathsf{seed}, b), \mathsf{sk} := (\mathsf{vk}, [\![s]\!]))$ and $\mathcal{A}$ is given $(\mathsf{vk}, \mathcal{L}_{\mathsf{KG}})$, where $\mathcal{L}_{\mathsf{KG}} = \mathsf{MaskKeygen}_{P_{\mathsf{KG}}}$ denotes the observed values of the t probed variables during the execution of Plover-RLWE.MaskKeygen with oracle access to Algorithms 8 and 9 with adversary $\mathcal{A}$. In addition, the adversary is allowed to probe and learn the values of t variables during each execution of Algorithms 8 and 9.

The adversary gets access to a (masked) signing oracle $\mathsf{OSign}(m, P_S)$, where m is a message and P_S is a signing probing set of size at most t. The oracle returns $(\mathsf{sig}, \mathcal{L}_S)$ where $\mathsf{sig} \leftarrow \mathsf{Plover\text{-}RLWE.MaskSign}(m, \mathsf{sk})$ and $\mathcal{L}_S$ is the observed values of the t probed variables during the execution of Plover-RLWE.MaskSign. Before each such OSign query, the $\mathsf{Refresh}([\![s]\!])$ gadget is called by the challenger to refresh the secret key shares (this challenger-run gadget is not probed by $\mathcal{A}$). The adversary can also query the random oracle H for the masked scheme. In this game, queries to the masked random oracle H are answered using an internal random oracle H' (not accessible directly to $\mathcal{A}$). The oracles in this game are similar to those in Fig. 2 but *without* the highlighted lines that are introduced in the following game. The adversary wins the game if it outputs a valid forgery message/signature pair $(\mathsf{msg}^*, \mathsf{sig}^*)$, where msg^* has not been queried to OSign.

Game_1 *(Fig. 2)*. In this game, we change the computation of the probed observations $(\mathcal{L}_{\mathsf{KG}}, \mathcal{L}_S)$ given to $\mathcal{A}$, from the actual values to the values simulated by probabilistic polynomial time algorithms $\mathsf{SimKG}(P_{\mathsf{KG}}, \mathsf{aux}_{\mathsf{KG}})$ and $\mathsf{SimSig}(P_S, \mathsf{aux}_{\mathsf{MS}})$, respectively. The simulation algorithms simulate the probed values using auxiliary information $\mathsf{aux}_{\mathsf{KG}}$ (resp. $\mathsf{aux}_{\mathsf{MS}}$) consisting of public values and certain leaked internal values as indicated in the highlighted lines of Fig. 2. The main idea (see Sect. 4.2 of [29] for a similar proof) is that the internal t-probed observations in all the gadgets except $\mathsf{AddRepNoise}$ can be simulated without the secret shared inputs, whereas by SNI with unshared inputs property of AddRepNoise in Lemma 1, only $\leqslant t$ *unshared* inputs (captured by the auxiliary values $(\breve{s}_i, \breve{e}_i)_{i\in[t]}$ and $(\breve{\mathbf{p}}_i)_{i\in[t]}$ in the masked key generation and signing algorithms, respectively) suffice to simulate its t-probed observations. Note that Game_1 writes z_1' as $z_1' = p_1 + c_1\, e + c_2$ instead of $z_1' = u - a\, z_2 - b\, z_3$; this is a purely syntactic change, as the two expressions are equal and we assume that the secret key includes the error e.

We construct the simulators SimKG and SimSig by composing the outputs of the simulators for each gadget, going from the last gadget to the first gadget, similar to the analysis in [5]. In the following description, we use the following notations: For the i'th gadget in SimKG (resp.SimSig), we let t_i denote the number of probed variables in this i'th gadget and by aux_i the auxiliary (leaked) information needed to simulate the internal view of the i'th gadget. Simulator SimKG for the probed observations $\mathcal{L}_{\mathrm{KG}}$ works as follows:

1. The Unmask($[\![b]\!]$) gadget (gadget 3) in Plover-RLWE.MaskKeygen is t-NIo (by Lemma 8 in [5]) with public output b. Hence, the probed observations in Unmask can be simulated by SimKG using $\leqslant t_3$ input shares in $[\![b]\!]$ and the auxiliary information $\mathsf{aux}_3 := b$.
2. The multiplication gadget $a \cdot [\![s]\!] + [\![e]\!]$ (gadget 2) in Plover-RLWE.MaskKeygen is computed share-wise and therefore is t-NI. Hence, the probed observations in this gadget can be simulated by SimKG using $\leqslant t_2 + t_3$ input shares in $[\![s]\!], [\![e]\!]$.
3. The AddRepNoise gadget in Plover-RLWE.MaskKeygen is t-SNIu with $d \cdot$ rep unshared inputs $(r_{i,j})_{i\in[\mathrm{rep}],j\in[d]} := ((\widehat{s}_k, \widehat{e}_k)_{k\in[d\cdot\mathrm{rep}-t]}, (\breve{s}_k, \breve{e}_k)_{k\in[t]})$ by Lemma 1.
   Hence, the probed observations in AddRepNoise can be simulated by SimKG using $\leqslant t_1 + t_2 + t_3 \leqslant t$ leaked unshared inputs $(\breve{s}_k, \breve{e}_k)_{k\in[t]}$ (i.e. the set of safe (unleaked) unshared inputs of AddRepNoise are denoted by $(\widehat{s}_k, \widehat{e}_k)_{k\in[d\cdot\mathrm{rep}-t]}$).

Overall, SimKG can simulate the probed observations in P_{KG} using auxiliary information $\mathsf{aux}_{\mathrm{KG}} := (\mathsf{vk}, (\breve{s}_i, \breve{e}_i)_{i\in[t]})$, as shown in Fig. 2.

Similarly, simulator SimSig for the probed observations $\mathcal{L}_S$ works as follows:

1. The Unmask($[\![z_2]\!]$) gadget (gadget 6) in Plover-RLWE.MaskSign is t-NIo (by Lemma 8 in [5]) with public output z_2. Hence, the probed observations in Unmask can be simulated by SimSig using $\leqslant t_6$ input shares in $[\![z_2]\!]$ and the auxiliary information $\mathsf{aux}_6 := z_2$.
2. The multiplication gadget $[\![p_2]\!] + c_1 \cdot [\![s]\!]$ (gadget 5) in Plover-RLWE.MaskSign is t-NI. Hence, the probed observations in this gadget can be simulated by SimSig using $\leqslant t_5 + t_6 \leqslant t$ input shares in $[\![p_2]\!], [\![s]\!]$.
3. The Refresh($[\![s]\!]$) gadget (gadget 4) in Plover-RLWE.MaskSign is t-SNI (by [27]). Hence, the probed observations in this gadget can be simulated by SimSig using $\leqslant t_4 \leqslant t$ input shares in $[\![s]\!]$ (note that those t_4 input shares in $[\![s]\!]$ can be simulated by SimSig as independent uniformly random shares due to the Refresh($[\![s]\!]$) called by the challenger before each OSign call).

4. The $\mathsf{Unmask}(\llbracket w \rrbracket)$ gadget (gadget 3) in Plover-RLWE.MaskSign is t-NIo (by Lemma 8 in [5]) with public output w. Hence, the probed observations in Unmask can be simulated by SimSig using $\leqslant t_3$ input shares in $\llbracket w \rrbracket$ and the auxiliary information $\mathsf{aux}_3 := w$.

5. The multiplication gadget $\llbracket p_1 \rrbracket + a \cdot \llbracket p_2 \rrbracket$ (gadget 5) in Plover-RLWE.MaskSign is t-NI. Hence, the probed observations in this gadget can be simulated by SimSig using $\leqslant t_2 + t_3 \leqslant t$ input shares in $\llbracket p_1 \rrbracket, \llbracket p_2 \rrbracket$.

6. The AddRepNoise gadget (gadget 1) in Plover-RLWE.MaskSign is t-SNI with $d \cdot \mathsf{rep}$ unshared inputs $(\hat{\mathbf{p}}_k)_{k \in [d \cdot \mathsf{rep} - t]}, (\check{\mathbf{p}}_k)_{k \in [t]})$ by Lemma 4. Hence, the probed observations in AddRepNoise can be simulated by SimSig using $\leqslant t_1 \leqslant t$ leaked unshared inputs $(\check{\mathbf{p}}_k)_{k \in [t]})$ (i.e. the set of safe (unleaked) unshared inputs of AddRepNoise are denoted by $(\hat{\mathbf{p}}_k)_{k \in [d \cdot \mathsf{rep} - t]}$).

Overall, SimSig can simulate the probed observations in P_S using auxiliary information $\mathsf{aux}_{MS} := (\mathsf{msg}, \mathsf{vk}, (\check{\mathbf{p}}_i)_{i \in [t]}, \mathsf{sig}, \mathsf{aux}_{sig})$, as shown in Fig. 2. (note that $\mathsf{aux}_3 = w$ can be computed from aux_{MS} since $w = u - c$, $u = H(\mathsf{msg}, \mathsf{salt}, \mathsf{vk})$ with salt taken from sig, and c computed from c_1 in sig and c_2 in aux_{sig}).

$\mathsf{OKG}(1^\kappa, P_{KG}) \rightarrow (\mathsf{vk}, \mathsf{sk}, \mathcal{L}_{KG})$

1: $\mathsf{seed} \xleftarrow{\$} \{0,1\}^\kappa$
2: $a := \mathsf{ExpandA}(\mathsf{seed})$
3: $(\hat{s}, \hat{e}) \leftarrow [d\,\mathsf{rep}_{sk} - t] \cdot \mathcal{D}_{sk}^{ind}$ ▷ Safe
4: $(\check{s}_i, \check{e}_i)_{i \in [t]} \leftarrow (\mathcal{D}_{sk}^{ind})^t$ ▷ Leaked
5: $(s, e) := (\hat{s} + \sum_{i \in [t]} \check{s}, \hat{e} + \sum_{i \in [t]} \check{e}_i)$
6: $b := \beta - (a\,s + e)$
7: $\mathsf{vk} := (\mathsf{seed}, b)$
8: $\mathsf{sk} := (\mathsf{vk}, s)$
9: $\mathsf{aux}_{KG} := (\mathsf{vk}, (\check{s}_i, \check{e}_i)_{i \in [t]})$
10: $\mathcal{L}_{KG} \leftarrow \mathsf{SimKG}(P_{KG}, \mathsf{aux}_{KG})$
11: **return** $\mathsf{vk}, \mathsf{sk}, \mathcal{L}_{KG}$

$H(\mathsf{msg}, \mathsf{salt}, \mathsf{vk}) \rightarrow u$

1: $u := H'(\mathsf{msg}, \mathsf{salt}, \mathsf{vk})$
2: **return** u

$\mathsf{OSign}(\mathsf{msg}, \mathsf{sk}, P_S) \rightarrow (\mathsf{sig}, \mathcal{L}_S)$

1: $\mathsf{salt} \xleftarrow{\$} \{0,1\}^{2\kappa}$
2: $u := H(\mathsf{msg}, \mathsf{salt}, \mathsf{vk})$
3: $a := \mathsf{ExpandA}(\mathsf{seed})$
4: $\hat{\mathbf{p}} \leftarrow [d\,\mathsf{rep}_{pert} - t] \cdot \mathcal{D}_{pert}^{ind}$ ▷ Safe
5: $(\check{\mathbf{p}}_i)_{i \in [t]} \leftarrow (\mathcal{D}_{pert}^{ind})^t$ ▷ Leaked
6: $\mathbf{p} := \hat{\mathbf{p}} + \sum_{i \in [t]} \check{\mathbf{p}}_i$
7: $w := [1\ a] \cdot \mathbf{p}$
8: $c := u - w$
9: $(c_1, c_2) := \mathsf{Decompose}_\beta(c)$
10: $z_2 := p_2 + c_1\,s$
11: $z_3 := c_1$
12: $z_1' := p_1 + c_1\,e + c_2$
13: $\mathsf{sig} := (\mathsf{salt}, z_2, z_3)$
14: $\mathsf{aux}_{sig} := c_2$
15: $\mathsf{aux}_{MS} := (\mathsf{msg}, \mathsf{vk}, (\check{\mathbf{p}}_i)_{i \in [t]}, \mathsf{sig}, \mathsf{aux}_{sig})$
16: $\mathcal{L}_S \leftarrow \mathsf{SimSig}(P_S, \mathsf{aux}_{MS})$
17: **return** $(\mathsf{sig}, \mathcal{L}_S)$

Fig. 2. Algorithms in Game_1

Since the view of $\mathcal{A}$ is perfectly simulated in this game as in the previous game, we have $\Pr[S_1] = \Pr[S_0]$.

Game$_2$ *(Fig. 3)*. In this game, we re-arrange the computation in OKG to first compute a 'safe' verification key $\hat{b} := \beta - (a\hat{s} + \hat{e})$ using the 'safe' part $(\hat{s}, \hat{e})$ of the secret key, and only later sample the 'leaked' part $(\check{s}, \check{e}) := \sum_{i \in [t]} (\check{s}_i, \check{e}_i)$ of the secret key and use this leaked secret and $\hat{b}$ to compute the full verification key $b := \hat{b} - (a\check{s} + \check{e})$. The above change to OKG is just a re-ordering of the computation and thus does not change the view of $\mathcal{A}$.

In this game, we also similarly re-arrange the computation in OSign to first compute a 'safe' part of the signature $\widehat{\text{sig}}$ with $\hat{z}_2 = \hat{p}_2 + \hat{c}_1 \hat{s}$, using the 'safe' perturbation part $\hat{p}_2$ and 'safe secret key part $\hat{s}$, and later compute the full signature sig from the $\hat{z}_2$ by adding the 'leaked' signature part to get $z_2 = \hat{z}_2 + \sum_{i \in [t]} \check{p}_{i,2} + c_1 \sum_{i \in [t]} \check{s}_i = (\hat{p}_2 + \check{p}_2) + \hat{c}_1 \hat{s} + c_1 \check{s} = (\hat{p}_2 + \check{p}_2) + c_1 (\hat{s} + \check{s})$, where the last equality holds if $\hat{c} = c$. Hence, for this re-arranged computation to preserve the correctness of the final signature (in particular z_2) as in the previous game (and thus preserve $\mathcal{A}$'s view), we need to ensure that $\hat{c} := \hat{u} - \hat{w}$ in the top 'safe' part of the computation, is equal to $c := u - w$ used in the bottom 'leaked' part of the computation. To achieve this, we use the random oracle H' (not directly accessible to $\mathcal{A}$) to compute $\hat{u} := H'(\text{msg}, \text{salt}, \text{vk})$ in the 'safe' part of the computation, and we change the simulation of the random oracle H accessible to $\mathcal{A}$ by programming H so that $u = H(\text{msg}, \text{salt}, \text{vk}) := \hat{u} + [1\ a] \cdot \check{p}$, where $\check{p}$ is sampled by the simulation and stored in the table T_H for H. Defining $\check{w} := [1\ a] \cdot \check{p}$, we have $c = u - w = (\hat{u} + \check{w}) - (\hat{w} + \check{w}) = \hat{u} - \hat{w} = \hat{c}$, as required.

Since $\hat{u} := H'(\text{msg}, \text{salt}, \text{vk})$ is uniformly random in R_q and independent of $[1\ a] \cdot \check{p}$, the simulation of H is identical to the previous game from $\mathcal{A}$'s view, except if an abort happens in OSign line 18 (we say then that the event B_2 occurs). However, since salt is uniformly random in $\{0, 1\}^{2\kappa}$ for each sign query, the event B_2 occurs with negligible probability $\Pr[B_2] \leqslant Q_{\text{Sign}} Q_H / 2^{2\kappa}$. Therefore, overall we have $\Pr[S_2] \geqslant \Pr[S_1] - \Pr[B_2] \geqslant \Pr[S_1] - Q_{\text{Sign}} Q_H / 2^{2\kappa}$.

We now construct an adversary $\mathcal{A}'$ against the EUF-CMA of the unmasked signature scheme Sign with random oracle H', secret key distribution $\mathcal{D}_{\text{sk}} := [d \, \text{rep}_{\text{sk}} - t] \cdot \mathcal{D}_{\text{sk}}^{\text{ind}}$, and perturbation distribution $\mathcal{D}_{\text{pert}} := [d \, \text{rep}_{\text{pert}} - t] \cdot \mathcal{D}_{\text{pert}}^{\text{ind}}$ that simulates view of $\mathcal{A}$ in Game$_2$, such that $\mathcal{A}'$ wins its game with probability $\geqslant \Pr[S_2]$. The challenger for $\mathcal{A}'$ generates a challenge key pair $(\widehat{\text{vk}}, \widehat{\text{sk}})$ by running lines 1–6 of OKG in Game$_2$ (this corresponds exactly to the key gen. algorithm for the unmasked scheme) and runs $\mathcal{A}'$ on input vk'. Then $\mathcal{A}'$ runs as follows.

1. It first runs $\mathcal{A}$ to get P_{KG} and then runs lines 7–12 of OKG in Game$_2$ to get $(\text{vk}, \text{sk}, \mathcal{L}_{\text{KG}})$ and runs $\mathcal{A}$ on input $(\text{vk}, \mathcal{L}_{\text{KG}})$.
2. Similarly, to respond to each OSign query (msg, P_S) of $\mathcal{A}$, $\mathcal{A}'$ calls its Sign algorithm on input msg (this corresponds to running lines 1–11 of OKG in Game$_2$), and using the returned $\widehat{\text{sig}}$ and $\widehat{\text{aux}}_{\text{sig}}$, $\mathcal{A}'$ runs lines 12–26 of OSign in Game$_2$ to compute and return $(\text{sig}, \mathcal{L}_S)$ to $\mathcal{A}$ (note that $\hat{w} = \hat{u} - \hat{c}$ is computed by $\mathcal{A}'$ from $\hat{u} = H'(\text{msg}, \text{salt}, \widehat{\text{vk}})$ and $\hat{c}$ obtained from c_1 in $\widehat{\text{sig}}$ and c_2 in $\widehat{\text{aux}}_{\text{sig}}$).

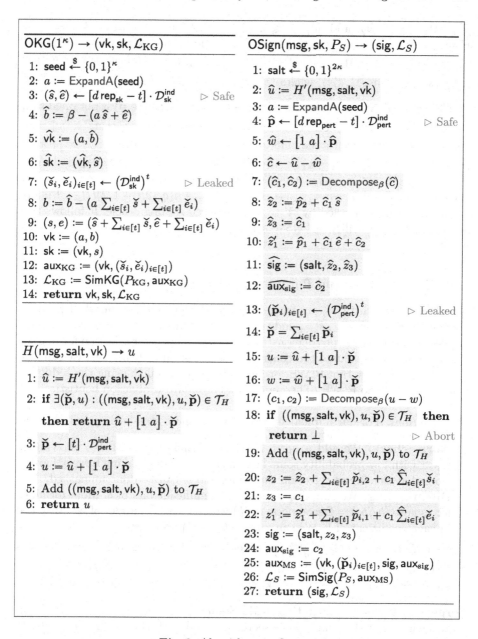

Fig. 3. Algorithms in Game_2

3. $\mathcal{A}'$ also runs the H simulator in Game_2 to respond to $\mathcal{A}$'s H queries, where H' is the random oracle provided to $\mathcal{A}'$ by its challenger.

Consequently, the view of $\mathcal{A}$ is perfectly simulated as in Game_2, so with probability $\Pr[S_2]$, $\mathcal{A}$ outputs a valid forgery $(\mathsf{msg}^*, \mathsf{sig}^* = (\mathsf{salt}^*, z_2^*, c_1^*))$ such that

$\|(z_1'^*, z_2^*, z_3^*)\| \leqslant B_2$, and $\|c_1^*\|_\infty \leqslant q/(2\beta) + 1/2$ and $z_1'^* + az_2^* + bc_1^* = u^* = H(\mathsf{msg}^*, \mathsf{salt}^*, \mathsf{vk})$ where msg^* has not been queried by $\mathcal{A}$ to OSign. Then, $\mathcal{A}'$ computes $(\breve{z}_1'^*, \breve{z}_2^*) = \breve{\mathbf{p}} + c_1^*(\breve{e}, \breve{s})$ with $(\breve{s}, \breve{e}) = (\sum_{i \in [t]} \breve{s}_i)$ and returns its forgery $(\mathsf{msg}^*, \widehat{\mathsf{sig}}^* = (\mathsf{salt}^*, \widehat{z}_2^*, c_1^*))$, where $(\widehat{z}_1'^*, \widehat{z}_2^*) := (z_1'^*, z_2^*) - (\breve{z}_1'^*, \breve{z}_2^*)$.

Note that, defining $\breve{w}^* := [1 \ a] \cdot \breve{\mathbf{p}}^*$ and $\breve{b} := a\breve{s} + \breve{e}$ (where $\breve{\mathbf{p}}^*$ is obtained from $\mathcal{T}_H$ entry for the forgery H-query $(\mathsf{msg}^*, \mathsf{salt}^*, \mathsf{vk})$), we have $\breve{z}_1'^* + a\breve{z}_2^* - \breve{b}c_1^* = \breve{w}^*$ and so forgery $\widehat{\mathsf{sig}}^*$ satisfies the unmasked scheme validity relation $\widehat{z}_1'^* + a\widehat{z}_2^* + \widehat{b}c_1^* = (z_1'^* + az_2^* + bc_1^*) - (\breve{z}_1'^* + a\breve{z}_2^* - \breve{b}c_1^*) = u^* - \breve{w}^* = H'(\mathsf{msg}^*, \mathsf{salt}^*, \widehat{\mathsf{vk}})$, as required. Also, $\|(\widehat{z}_1'^*, \widehat{z}_2^*, c_1^*)\| \leqslant \|(z_1'^*, z_2^*, c_1^*)\| + \|(\breve{z}_1'^*, \breve{z}_2^*, 0)\| \leqslant B_2 + t \cdot (B_{\mathsf{pert}} + n\frac{q}{2\eta}B_{\mathsf{sk}}) := B_2'$, since $\|(\breve{z}_1'^*, \breve{z}_2^*)\| \leqslant \|\breve{\mathbf{p}}\| + n\|c_1^*\|_\infty\|(\breve{e}, \breve{s})\| \leqslant (tB_{\mathsf{pert}} + n(q/(2\beta)+1/2)tB_{\mathsf{sk}})$. Finally, msg^* has not been queried by $\mathcal{A}$ to its unmasked signing oracle. It follows that $\mathcal{A}'$ wins with probability $\geqslant \Pr[S_2] \geqslant \Pr[S_0] - Q_{\mathsf{Sign}}Q_H/2^{2\kappa}$. This concludes the proof. □

3.5 Cryptanalysis and Parameter Selection

Now that the security of our scheme is formally proven in unmasked form for general distributions $\mathcal{D}_{\mathsf{sk}}, \mathcal{D}_{\mathsf{pert}}$ and the security of the masked form reduces to its unmasked form, we wish to demonstrate concrete parameter selection for masked Plover-RLWE. We evaluate the concrete security of our scheme against RSIS for forgery, and against Hint-RLWE for key-indistinguishability using the reduction from Hint-RLWE to RLWE (Theorem 1) and standard evaluation heuristics.

Optimizations. For our implementation, we use these standard optimizations:

- **Norm check.** We add a norm check in MaskSign against B_2, allowing to reject with low probability some large signatures, and making forgery harder. Note that this is *not* rejection sampling, and it can be done unmasked.
- **Bit-dropping.** We can drop the ν least significant bits of b. More formally, let us note $(b_1, b_2) = \mathsf{Decompose}_{\{2^\nu\}}(b)$ where ν is the number of bits dropped in each coefficient of b. We can set $2^\nu \cdot b_1$ as a public key. As long as $\nu = O\left(\log\left(\frac{\sigma_{\mathsf{pert}}}{q\sqrt{n}}\right)\right)$, we can show that breaking inhomogeneous RSIS for $[1 \ a \ 2^\nu \cdot b_1]$ implies breaking it for $[1 \ a \ b]$ with comparable parameters. This reduces the size of vk, while preserving the security reduction.

Forgery Attacks and Practical RSIS Security. Let $\sigma_{\mathsf{sk}}, \sigma_{\mathsf{pert}}$ denote the standard deviation of the (unmasked) secret key and perturbation, respectively. In a legitimate signature:

$$\mathbb{E}\left[\|\mathbf{z}'\|^2\right] = \mathbb{E}\left[\|p_1 + e \cdot c_1 + c_2 + b_2 \cdot c_1\|^2\right] + \mathbb{E}\left[\|p_2 + s \cdot c_1\|^2\right] + \mathbb{E}\left[\|c_1\|^2\right]$$

$$\approx n\left(2\sigma_{\mathsf{pert}}^2 + \frac{\beta^2}{12} + \frac{q^2 n}{6\beta^2}\sigma_{\mathsf{sk}}^2 + n\frac{2^{2\nu}}{12}\frac{q^2}{12\beta^2}\right)$$

Based on this analysis, we set $B_2 = 1.2 \sqrt{n \left(2\,\sigma_{\mathsf{pert}}^2 + \frac{\beta^2}{12} + \frac{q^2\,n}{6\,\beta^2}\,\sigma_{\mathsf{sk}}^2 + n\frac{2^{2\nu}}{12}\frac{q^2}{12\beta^2} \right)}$.
The "slack" factor 1.2 allows an extremely large number of generated signatures to satisfy $\|\mathbf{z}'\| \leqslant B_2$, which means that the restart rate will be very low.

Solving Inhomogeneous RSIS. To forge a message, an adversary must either break the collision resistance of H or solve the equation:

$$\left(\begin{bmatrix} 1 \ a \ \beta \cdot b_1 \end{bmatrix} \cdot \mathbf{z}' = u \right) \wedge \left(\|\mathbf{z}'\| \leqslant B_2 \right) \tag{3}$$

Note that $\begin{bmatrix} 1 \ a \ \beta \cdot b_1 \end{bmatrix} \cdot \mathbf{z}' = \begin{bmatrix} 1 \ a \ b \end{bmatrix} \cdot \mathbf{z}''$, where $\mathbf{z}'' = \mathbf{z}' - (z_3 \cdot b_2, 0, 0)$, and that $\|z_3 \cdot b_2\| \leqslant \|c_1\|_1 \cdot \|b_2\| \leqslant n^{3/2} \cdot \frac{q\,2^{\nu-2}}{\beta}$. Then Eq. (3) is an instance of the inhomogeneous RSIS problem, with a bound $B_{\mathsf{RSIS}} = B_2 + n^{3/2} \cdot \frac{q\,2^{\nu-2}}{\beta}$.

We estimate its hardness based on Chuengsatiansup et al. [9] and Espitau and Kirchner [15]. Under the geometric series assumption, [15, Theorem 3.3] states that Eq. (3) can be solved in $\mathsf{poly}(n)$ calls to a CVP oracle in dimension B_{BKZ}, as long as:

$$B_{\mathsf{RSIS}} \leqslant \left(\delta_{B_{\mathsf{RSIS}}}^{3n}\, q^{1/3} \right), \quad \text{where} \quad \delta_{B_{\mathsf{RSIS}}} = \left(\frac{(\pi \cdot B_{\mathsf{BKZ}})^{1/B_{\mathsf{BKZ}}} \cdot B_{\mathsf{BKZ}}}{2\pi e} \right)^{1/(2(B_{\mathsf{BKZ}}-1))}. \tag{4}$$

This attack has been optimized in [9] by omitting $x \leqslant n$ of the first columns of $\mathbf{A}$ (when considered as a $n \times 3n$ matrix). The dimension is reduced by x, however, the co-volume of the lattice is increased to $q^{\frac{n}{3n-x}}$. This strengthens Eq. (4) to the more stringent condition $B_{\mathsf{RSIS}} \leqslant \min_{x \leqslant n} \left(\delta_{B_{\mathsf{RSIS}}}^{3n-x}\, q^{\frac{n}{3n-x}} \right)$.

Key-Indistinguishability and Hint-RLWE. In order to apply Theorem 1, we need quantitative bounds on B_{HRLWE}. These are given in Lemma 2, which is a minor adaptation of [30, Lemma B.2]. A proof is provided in the full version for completeness.

Lemma 2. *For $j \in [Q_{\mathsf{Sign}}]$, let $c^{[j]} \leftarrow \mathcal{C}_1$, where $\mathcal{C}_1$ is defined as in Definition 9. Let $D = \sum_{j \in [Q_{\mathsf{Sign}}]} c^{[j]} (c^{[j]})^*$. Let $M = 2\left\lceil \frac{q-1}{2\beta} \right\rceil + 1$. We then have* $\Pr\left[s_1(D) \geqslant B_{\mathsf{HRLWE}} \right] \leq 2^{-\kappa}$, *where* $B_{\mathsf{HRLWE}} = \frac{Q_{\mathsf{Sign}}\,n\,M^2}{12} \left(1 + \frac{O(\kappa\,n \log n)}{\sqrt{Q_{\mathsf{Sign}}}} \right)$. *Specifically, when $Q_{\mathsf{Sign}} = \omega(\kappa\,n \log n)^2$, then $s_1(D)$ is equivalent to $\frac{Q_{\mathsf{Sign}}\,n\,M^2}{12}$.*

Advantage Against Hint-RLWE. An adversary breaking the key-indistinguishability of vk is also able to break Hint-RLWE$_{q, Q_{\mathsf{Sign}}, \widehat{\mathcal{D}}_{\mathsf{sk}}, \widehat{\mathcal{D}}_{\mathsf{pert}}, \mathcal{C}}$. In the Gaussian case, $\mathcal{D}_{\mathsf{sk}} \overset{s}{\sim} D_{\hat{\sigma}_{\mathsf{sk}}}$ and $\mathcal{D}_{\mathsf{pert}} \overset{s}{\sim} D_{\hat{\sigma}_{\mathsf{pert}}}$, where $\frac{\hat{\sigma}_{\mathsf{sk}}}{\sigma_{\mathsf{sk,ind}}} = \frac{\hat{\sigma}_{\mathsf{pert}}}{\sigma_{\mathsf{pert,ind}}} = \sqrt{d\,\mathsf{rep} - t}$.

Theorem 1 and Lemma 2 state that such an adversary is also able to break RLWE$_{q, D_{\sigma_{\mathsf{red}}}}$, where $\frac{1}{\sigma_{\mathsf{red}}^2} = 2 \left(\frac{1}{\sigma_{\mathsf{sk}}^2} + \frac{B_{\mathsf{HRLWE}}}{\hat{\sigma}_{\mathsf{pert}}^2} \right)$ and B_{HRLWE} is as in Lemma 2. For the parameters we choose in practice, this entails: $\frac{\sigma_{\mathsf{red}}}{\sigma_{\mathsf{pert}}} \approx \frac{\beta}{q} \sqrt{\frac{6}{n\,Q_{\mathsf{Sign}}}}$ Estimating the concrete hardness of RLWE is well-documented. We rely on the lattice estimator [2], an open-source tool available at https://github.com/malb/lattice-estimator.

Parameter Selection. Despite the many variables involved, parameter selection is fairly straightforward. We set $\beta = \Theta(\sigma_{\mathsf{pert}})$, $\nu = \Theta\left(\log\left(\frac{\sigma_{\mathsf{pert}}^2}{q\sqrt{n}}\right)\right)$ and $\sigma_{\mathsf{sk}} = o\left(\frac{\beta\,\sigma_{\mathsf{pert}}}{q\sqrt{n}}\right)$. This guarantees efficiency while ensuring that $B_{\mathsf{RSIS}} = O(\sigma_{\mathsf{pert}}\sqrt{n})$.

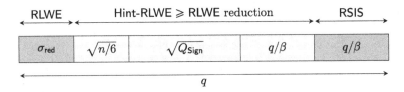

Fig. 4. Illustration of the constraints on q (in log scale): RSIS and RLWE must be hard, and the Hint-RLWE $\geqslant$ RLWE reduction must be non-vacuous.

These parameters also guarantee an efficient reduction in Theorem 1. We estimate the number of queries, Q_{Sign}, by increasing it for as long as the RLWE instance entailed by the reduction of Theorem 1 and Lemma 2 remains secure according to the state-of-the-art. Q'_{Sign} corresponds to the number of queries allowed when the condition $\sigma \geqslant \sqrt{2}\eta_\varepsilon(\mathbb{Z}^n)$ is dropped in Theorem 1.

We illustrate constraints over the modulo q in Fig. 4. Selected parameters are provided in Table 1, and the evolution of allowed number of queries as a function of $\log q$ is illustrated in Fig. 5.

Table 1. Parameter sets for $\kappa = 128$. All parameter sets feature $n = 2048$.

$\lceil\log q\rceil$	35	36	37	38	39	40	41	42	43	44	45	46	47	48	49	50
$\log\beta$	31	32	33	34	35	36	37	37	38	38	39	39	40	40	41	41
$\log\sigma_{\mathsf{pert}}$	30	31	32	33	34	35	36	36	37	37	38	38	39	39	40	40
$\log\sigma_{\mathsf{sk}}$	21	22	23	24	25	26	27	26	27	26	27	26	27	26	27	26
ν	15	16	17	18	19	20	21	20	21	20	21	20	21	20	21	20
Q_{Sign}	2^{40}	2^{42}	2^{44}	2^{46}	2^{48}	2^{50}	2^{52}	2^{51}	2^{52}	2^{49}	2^{50}	2^{47}	2^{48}	2^{45}	2^{46}	2^{43}
Q'_{Sign}	2^{46}	2^{48}	2^{48}	2^{50}	2^{52}	2^{53}	2^{54}	2^{50}	2^{52}	2^{49}	2^{50}	2^{47}	2^{48}	2^{45}	2^{46}	2^{43}
$\lvert\mathsf{vk}\rvert$	5136	5136	5136	5136	5136	5136	5136	5648	5648	6160	6160	6672	6672	7184	7184	7696
$\lvert\mathsf{sig}\rvert$	11488	11843	12198	12533	12908	13263	13617	13617	13972	13972	14327	14327	14682	14682	15037	15037

3.6 Implementation

We provide both a Python and a C reference implementation for Plover-RLWE, available at https://github.com/GuilhemN/masksign-plover. They are designed to match the high-level pseudo-code from Subsect. 3.3 and allows one to read a concrete implementation of each of the functions we introduced. The Python implementation aims for simplicity and is not constant-time, while the C implementation is constant-time and uses optimization techniques. We include scripts for parameters selection under the folder *params* based on the lattice estimator [2].

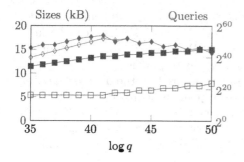

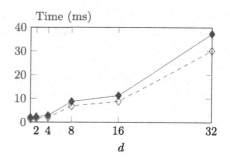

Fig. 5. Number of signing queries (conservative:—◇—, standard: —◆—) and bytesizes (|vk|:—□—, |sig|:—■—) as functions of q. Parameter sets as in Sect. 3.5.

Fig. 6. Timings of Plover-RLWE (Keygen:- ◇- , Sign:—◆—) as functions of d. Parameter set from Sect. 3.5 with $\lceil \log q \rceil = 41$, and concrete parameters from Table 2.

These reference implementations re-use several components of Raccoon reference implementations [29] for the NTT, Montgomery modular reduction, and randomness generators. They are portable and can target various masking orders $d - 1$. Note however that they suffer from the same issues as Raccoon reference implementations. Specifically, a deterministic portable code written in a high-level language cannot realistically be considered to be fully resistant to side-channel attacks, and notably due to the use of the *randombytes* function defined by NIST, which represents an abstract RBG (Random Bit Generator), but is only suitable to ease reproducibility and generation of test vectors. Additionally, our reference implementations are severely limited in their key management as the NIST API does not allow for a refresh of the secret key, which is required for t-probing security. We argue that these implementations still provide evidence that Plover-RLWE is easy to mask at high masking orders.

General Implementation Characteristics. Plover-RLWE has building blocks resembling those of Raccoon [29], as well as a modulus q of same magnitude and format (product of two Solinas primes). In particular we reuse part of their codebase and of their implementation tricks.

Signature Encoding. We encode low-order bits using binary encoding, and high-order bits using Huffman/unary-type encoding. This encoding is similar to the ones in Falcon and Raccoon. We chose this technique over ANS encoding – although ANS could compress signatures further – as the latter proved hard to implement securely in NIST Call for Additional Digital Signature Schemes, with vulnerabilities discovered in the HuFu and HAETAE proposals[1].

Mask Compression Technique. Our implementation uses the mask compression technique introduced in [29,33] in order to reduce the size of the stored secret

---

[1] See https://groups.google.com/a/list.nist.gov/g/pqc-forum/c/Hq-wRFDbIaU.

key, which contains the masked polynomial $[\![s]\!]$. A masked polynomial at order d can be compressed into one polynomial and $d - 1$ seeds which can be later expanded into full polynomial masking shares. We refer to [29, Algorithms 14 and 15] and [33] for a detailed specification of this technique.

This technique could also be used to drastically reduce the memory requirements of Plover-RLWE. Our masking gadgets can be adapted to do runtime computations on compressed masked polynomials to limit the impact of a larger d on memory requirements. For reference, Raccoon [29, section 3.3.2] reduced memory usage for a masking order $d = 32$ by a factor of 15 using this technique.

Hardware. Plover-RLWE could be implemented on hardware in a similar manner to Raccoon. Several versions of Raccoon were implemented on FPGA architecture, one is reported in [31]. These implementations contain a RISC-V controller, a Keccak accelerator, and a lattice unit with direct memory access via a 64-bit interface, using hard-coded support for Raccoon's arithmetic modulus q. Plover-RLWE can share a large part of these implementations.

As for Raccoon [29, section 3.3.1] the usage of SHAKE as hash function in the implementation of ExpandA and AddRepNoise can be highly optimized in hardware, and the hardware XOF (eXtendable-Output Functions) sampler can implement a full Keccak round and produce output at a very high rate.

Table 2. Performance of the Plover-RLWE reference implementation for different masking orders on our reference platform. Across all parameter sets, we have $(\kappa, n, \lceil \log q \rceil, \log \beta, \nu) = (128, 2048, 41, 37, 21)$, and we set $\mathsf{rep}_{\mathsf{sk}} = \mathsf{rep}_{\mathsf{pert}} = \mathsf{rep}$.

Variant	Parameters			Keygen			Sign			Verify		
$\kappa - d$	rep	u_{sk}	u_{pert}	ms	Mclk	stack	ms	Mclk	stack	ms	Mclk	stack
128-1	8	27	36	1.341	2.546	49312	1.989	3.788	164128	0.432	0.820	32864
128-2	4	27	36	1.595	3.030	114848	2.272	4.316	246048	=	=	=
128-4	2	27	36	2.045	3.885	213184	2.835	5.386	410016	=	=	=
128-8	4	26	35	6.887	13.083	409856	8.732	16.588	737760	=	=	=
128-16	2	26	35	8.832	16.782	803200	11.288	21.460	1393248	=	=	=
128-32	4	25	34	30.213	57.404	1589888	37.350	70.959	2704224	=	=	=

Performance. We evaluated the performance of Plover-RLWE on a Ryzen Pro 7 5850U (16CPU threads at 3 GHz), boost disabled, and running Manjaro 22.1. The results are provided in Table 2 and Fig. 6. The reference implementation instantiates the parameter set from Table 1 such that $\lceil \log q \rceil = 41$, as it is optimal for the number of possible queries for $n = 2048$ and $\kappa = 128$. Other parameter sets perform very similarly since – performance-wise – only the encoding differs between them. The implementation packages parameters for d shares, $d \in \{1, 2, 4, 8, 16, 32\}$, and the distributions $\mathcal{D}_{\mathsf{sk}}$ and $\mathcal{D}_{\mathsf{pert}}$ are sums of uniforms $\mathrm{SU}(u_{\mathsf{sk}}, d \cdot \mathsf{rep}_{\mathsf{sk}})$ and $\mathrm{SU}(u_{\mathsf{pert}}, d \cdot \mathsf{rep}_{\mathsf{pert}})$ with $\mathsf{rep} := \mathsf{rep}_{\mathsf{sk}} = \mathsf{rep}_{\mathsf{pert}} \in \{2, 4, 8\}$ a function of d. u_{sk} and u_{pert} are chosen as to achieve a standard deviation close to σ_{sk} and σ_{pert}. Plover-RLWE has performance very similar to Raccoon; in particular, we observe a (quasi-)linear increase in the execution times and stack usage of our functions with d, which makes the use of a high masking order practical. For instance, Plover-RLWE masked with a number of shares $d = 8$ still performs better than Dilithium masked with $d = 2$ [29, Table 6].

References

1. Alagic, G., Apon, D., Cooper, D., Dang, Q., Dang, T., Kelsey, J., Lichtinger, J., Miller, C., Moody, D., Peralta, R., Perlner, R., Robinson, A., Smith-Tone, D., Liu, Y.K.: NISTIR 8413 – Status Report on the Third Round of the NIST Post-Quantum Cryptography Standardization Process (2022), https://doi.org/10.6028/NIST.IR.8413
2. Albrecht, M.R., Player, R., Scott, S.: On the concrete hardness of learning with errors. J. Math. Cryptol. **9**(3), 169–203 (2015), http://www.degruyter.com/view/j/jmc.2015.9.issue-3/jmc-2015-0016/jmc-2015-0016.xml
3. Azouaoui, M., Bronchain, O., Cassiers, G., Hoffmann, C., Kuzovkova, Y., Renes, J., Schneider, T., Schönauer, M., Standaert, F., van Vredendaal, C.: Protecting dilithium against leakage revisited sensitivity analysis and improved implementations. IACR Trans. Cryptogr. Hardw. Embed. Syst. **2023**(4), 58–79 (2023). https://doi.org/10.46586/tches.v2023.i4.58-79
4. Barthe, G., Belaïd, S., Dupressoir, F., Fouque, P.A., Grégoire, B., Strub, P.Y., Zucchini, R.: Strong non-interference and type-directed higher-order masking. In: Weippl, E.R., Katzenbeisser, S., Kruegel, C., Myers, A.C., Halevi, S. (eds.) ACM CCS 2016. pp. 116–129. ACM Press (Oct 2016). https://doi.org/10.1145/2976749.2978427
5. Barthe, G., Belaïd, S., Espitau, T., Fouque, P.A., Grégoire, B., Rossi, M., Tibouchi, M.: Masking the GLP lattice-based signature scheme at any order. In: Nielsen, J.B., Rijmen, V. (eds.) EUROCRYPT 2018, Part II. LNCS, vol. 10821, pp. 354–384. Springer, Heidelberg (Apr / May 2018). https://doi.org/10.1007/978-3-319-78375-8_12
6. Battistello, A., Coron, J.S., Prouff, E., Zeitoun, R.: Horizontal side-channel attacks and countermeasures on the ISW masking scheme. In: Gierlichs, B., Poschmann, A.Y. (eds.) CHES 2016. LNCS, vol. 9813, pp. 23–39. Springer, Heidelberg (Aug 2016). https://doi.org/10.1007/978-3-662-53140-2_2
7. Berzati, A., Viera, A.C., Chartouny, M., Madec, S., Vergnaud, D., Vigilant, D.: Exploiting intermediate value leakage in dilithium: A template-based approach. IACR Trans. Cryptogr. Hardw. Embed. Syst. **2023**(4), 188–210 (2023). https://doi.org/10.46586/tches.v2023.i4.188-210
8. Bronchain, O., Cassiers, G.: Bitslicing arithmetic/boolean masking conversions for fun and profit with application to lattice-based KEMs. IACR TCHES **2022**(4), 553–588 (2022). https://doi.org/10.46586/tches.v2022.i4.553-588
9. Chuengsatiansup, C., Prest, T., Stehlé, D., Wallet, A., Xagawa, K.: ModFalcon: Compact signatures based on module-NTRU lattices. In: Sun, H.M., Shieh, S.P., Gu, G., Ateniese, G. (eds.) ASIACCS 20. pp. 853–866. ACM Press (Oct 2020). https://doi.org/10.1145/3320269.3384758

10. Coron, J., Gérard, F., Montoya, S., Zeitoun, R.: High-order polynomial comparison and masking lattice-based encryption. IACR Trans. Cryptogr. Hardw. Embed. Syst. **2023**(1), 153–192 (2023). https://doi.org/10.46586/tches.v2023.i1.153-192

11. Coron, J., Gérard, F., Trannoy, M., Zeitoun, R.: High-order masking of NTRU. IACR Trans. Cryptogr. Hardw. Embed. Syst. **2023**(2), 180–211 (2023). https://doi.org/10.46586/tches.v2023.i2.180-211

12. Coron, J., Gérard, F., Trannoy, M., Zeitoun, R.: Improved gadgets for the high-order masking of dilithium. IACR Trans. Cryptogr. Hardw. Embed. Syst. **2023**(4), 110–145 (2023). https://doi.org/10.46586/tches.v2023.i4.110-145

13. Duc, A., Faust, S., Standaert, F.X.: Making masking security proofs concrete (or how to evaluate the security of any leaking device), extended version. J. Cryptol. **32**(4), 1263–1297 (2019). https://doi.org/10.1007/s00145-018-9277-0

14. Espitau, T., Fouque, P.A., Gérard, F., Rossi, M., Takahashi, A., Tibouchi, M., Wallet, A., Yu, Y.: Mitaka: A simpler, parallelizable, maskable variant of falcon. In: Dunkelman, O., Dziembowski, S. (eds.) EUROCRYPT 2022, Part III. LNCS, vol. 13277, pp. 222–253. Springer, Heidelberg (May / Jun 2022). https://doi.org/10.1007/978-3-031-07082-2_9

15. Espitau, T., Kirchner, P.: The nearest-colattice algorithm. Cryptology ePrint Archive, Report 2020/694 (2020), https://eprint.iacr.org/2020/694

16. Gentry, C., Peikert, C., Vaikuntanathan, V.: Trapdoors for hard lattices and new cryptographic constructions. In: Ladner, R.E., Dwork, C. (eds.) 40th ACM STOC. pp. 197–206. ACM Press (May 2008). https://doi.org/10.1145/1374376.1374407

17. Goldwasser, S., Kalai, Y.T., Peikert, C., Vaikuntanathan, V.: Robustness of the learning with errors assumption. In: Yao, A.C. (ed.) Innovations in Computer Science - ICS 2010, Tsinghua University, Beijing, China, January 5-7, 2010. Proceedings. pp. 230–240. Tsinghua University Press (2010), http://conference.iiis.tsinghua.edu.cn/ICS2010/content/papers/19.html

18. Goubin, L.: A sound method for switching between Boolean and arithmetic masking. In: Koç, Çetin Kaya., Naccache, D., Paar, C. (eds.) CHES 2001. LNCS, vol. 2162, pp. 3–15. Springer, Heidelberg (May 2001). https://doi.org/10.1007/3-540-44709-1_2

19. Guerreau, M., Martinelli, A., Ricosset, T., Rossi, M.: The hidden parallelepiped is back again: Power analysis attacks on falcon. IACR TCHES **2022**(3), 141–164 (2022). https://doi.org/10.46586/tches.v2022.i3.141-164

20. Ishai, Y., Sahai, A., Wagner, D.: Private circuits: Securing hardware against probing attacks. In: Boneh, D. (ed.) CRYPTO 2003. LNCS, vol. 2729, pp. 463–481. Springer, Heidelberg (Aug 2003). https://doi.org/10.1007/978-3-540-45146-4_27

21. Ito, A., Ueno, R., Homma, N.: On the success rate of side-channel attacks on masked implementations: Information-theoretical bounds and their practical usage. In: Yin, H., Stavrou, A., Cremers, C., Shi, E. (eds.) ACM CCS 2022. pp. 1521–1535. ACM Press (Nov 2022). https://doi.org/10.1145/3548606.3560579

22. Kannwischer, M.J., Genêt, A., Butin, D., Krämer, J., Buchmann, J.: Differential power analysis of XMSS and SPHINCS. In: Fan, J., Gierlichs, B. (eds.) COSADE 2018. LNCS, vol. 10815, pp. 168–188. Springer, Heidelberg (Apr 2018). https://doi.org/10.1007/978-3-319-89641-0_10

23. Karabulut, E., Alkim, E., Aysu, A.: Single-Trace Side-Channel Attacks on ω-Small Polynomial Sampling: With Applications to NTRU, NTRU Prime, and CRYSTALS-DILITHIUM. In: IEEE International Symposium on Hardware Oriented Security and Trust, HOST 2021, Tysons Corner, VA, USA, December 12-15, 2021. pp. 35–45. IEEE (2021). https://doi.org/10.1109/HOST49136.2021.9702284

24. Kim, D., Lee, D., Seo, J., Song, Y.: Toward practical lattice-based proof of knowledge from hint-MLWE. In: Handschuh, H., Lysyanskaya, A. (eds.) CRYPTO 2023, Part V. LNCS, vol. 14085, pp. 549–580. Springer, Heidelberg (Aug 2023). https://doi.org/10.1007/978-3-031-38554-4_18

25. Kim, M., Lee, D., Seo, J., Song, Y.: Accelerating HE operations from key decomposition technique. In: Handschuh, H., Lysyanskaya, A. (eds.) CRYPTO 2023, Part IV. LNCS, vol. 14084, pp. 70–92. Springer, Heidelberg (Aug 2023). https://doi.org/10.1007/978-3-031-38551-3_3

26. Masure, L., Rioul, O., Standaert, F.: A nearly tight proof of duc et al.'s conjectured security bound for masked implementations. In: Buhan, I., Schneider, T. (eds.) Smart Card Research and Advanced Applications - 21st International Conference, CARDIS 2022, Birmingham, UK, November 7-9, 2022, Revised Selected Papers. Lecture Notes in Computer Science, vol. 13820, pp. 69–81. Springer (2022). https://doi.org/10.1007/978-3-031-25319-5_4

27. Mathieu-Mahias, A.: Securisation of implementations of cryptographic algorithms in the context of embedded systems. Theses, Université Paris-Saclay (Dec 2021), https://theses.hal.science/tel-03537322

28. Montgomery, P.L.: Speeding the pollard and elliptic curve methods of factorization. Math. Comput. **48**(177), 243–264 (1987). https://doi.org/10.1090/s0025-5718-1987-0866113-7

29. del Pino, R., Espitau, T., Katsumata, S., Maller, M., Mouhartem, F., Prest, T., Rossi, M., Saarinen, M.J.: Raccoon, A Side-Channel Secure Signature Scheme. Tech. rep., National Institute of Standards and Technology (2023), available at https://csrc.nist.gov/Projects/pqc-dig-sig/round-1-additional-signatures

30. del Pino, R., Katsumata, S., Maller, M., Mouhartem, F., Prest, T., Saarinen, M.J.: Threshold raccoon: Practical threshold signatures from standard lattice assumptions. Cryptology ePrint Archive, Paper 2024/184 (2024), https://eprint.iacr.org/2024/184, https://eprint.iacr.org/2024/184

31. del Pino, R., Prest, T., Rossi, M., Saarinen, M.O.: High-order masking of lattice signatures in quasilinear time. In: 44th IEEE Symposium on Security and Privacy, SP 2023, San Francisco, CA, USA, May 21-25, 2023. pp. 1168–1185. IEEE (2023). https://doi.org/10.1109/SP46215.2023.10179342

32. Prest, T.: A key-recovery attack against mitaka in the t-probing model. In: Boldyreva, A., Kolesnikov, V. (eds.) PKC 2023, Part I. LNCS, vol. 13940, pp. 205–220. Springer, Heidelberg (May 2023). https://doi.org/10.1007/978-3-031-31368-4_8

33. Saarinen, M.J.O., Rossi, M.: Mask compression: High-order masking on memory-constrained devices. Cryptology ePrint Archive, Paper 2023/1117 (2023), https://eprint.iacr.org/2023/1117

34. Yu, Y., Jia, H., Wang, X.: Compact lattice gadget and its applications to hash-and-sign signatures. In: Handschuh, H., Lysyanskaya, A. (eds.) CRYPTO 2023, Part V. LNCS, vol. 14085, pp. 390–420. Springer, Heidelberg (Aug 2023). https://doi.org/10.1007/978-3-031-38554-4_13

35. Zhang, S., Lin, X., Yu, Y., Wang, W.: Improved power analysis attacks on falcon. In: Hazay, C., Stam, M. (eds.) EUROCRYPT 2023, Part IV. LNCS, vol. 14007, pp. 565–595. Springer, Heidelberg (Apr 2023). https://doi.org/10.1007/978-3-031-30634-1_19

Updatable Public-Key Encryption, Revisited

Joël Alwen[1]($^{(\boxtimes)}$), Georg Fuchsbauer[2], and Marta Mularczyk[1]

[1] AWS Wickr, New York, USA
{alwenjo,mulmarta}@amazon.com
[2] TU Wien, Vienna, Austria
Georg.Fuchsbauer@tuwien.ac.at

Abstract. We revisit Updatable Public-Key Encryption (UPKE), which was introduced as a practical mechanism for building forward-secure cryptographic protocols. We begin by observing that all UPKE notions to date are neither syntactically flexible nor secure enough for the most important multi-party protocols motivating UPKE. We provide an intuitive taxonomy of UPKE properties – some partially or completely overlooked in the past – along with an overview of known (explicit and implicit) UPKE constructions. We then introduce a formal UPKE definition capturing all intuitive properties needed for multi-party protocols.

Next, we provide a practical pairing-based construction for which we provide concrete bounds under a standard assumption in the random oracle and the algebraic group model. The efficiency profile of the scheme compares very favorably with existing UPKE constructions (despite the added flexibility and stronger security). For example, when used to improve the forward security of the Messaging Layer Security protocol [RFC9420], our new UPKE construction requires less than 1.5% of the bandwidth of the next-most efficient UPKE construction satisfying the strongest UPKE notion considered so far.

1 Introduction

Spurred on by the seemingly never-ending procession of data breaches, 0-day exploits and system compromises, it is becoming ever more important in to design protocols with the ability to automatically limit the blast radii of key and state compromises. Among other techniques, this has lead to interest in primitives designed to provide cheap but effective *forward security*, namely the property that security holds despite possible future compromises.

A naïve (though not ineffective) approach to providing forward security for, say, public-key encryption (PKE) is for the owner of a key pair (pk, sk) to periodically sample a fresh and independent key pair (pk', sk') that replaces its old keys. While this does provide forward security – old ciphertexts encrypted to pk remain secure even if the adversary learns sk' – it comes with a serious drawback from the protocol perspective. After each key rotation the receiver must first inform prospective senders of the new public key before new messages can be

© International Association for Cryptologic Research 2024
M. Joye and G. Leander (Eds.): EUROCRYPT 2024, LNCS 14657, pp. 346–376, 2024.
https://doi.org/10.1007/978-3-031-58754-2_13

sent privately to the receiver again.[1] Besides increasing communication complexity, the biggest issue with this is that it forces potentially onerous coordination requirements on protocol participants.

Avoiding this cost motivated the study of *Puncturable Public-Key Encryption* [GM15] (PPKE) as a stand-alone primitive. PPKE provides essentially the same security as the naïve approach but without further coordination between parties beyond the initial public key distribution. After that, any number of senders may independently send any number of ciphertexts to the receiver which can be delivered in any order (or not at all). Despite the lack of coordination between parties, PPKE guarantees that at any point, leaking the receiver's secret key reveals nothing about messages in ciphertexts it had already received and decrypted.

Clearly a powerful tool for building forward-secure protocols, PPKE lies at the heart of recent forward-secure 0-round trip key agreement protocols [GHJL17]. But minimizing round and communication complexity for forward-secure key agreement underpins other classes of cryptographic protocols. Notably, these include 2-party ratcheting [JS18, PR18, JMM19, DV19, CCD+20], the multi-party analogue: continuous group key agreement (CGKA) [ACDT20, AAN+22, ACJM20] and secure group and 2-party messaging [ACDT21]. In this work, we are especially interested in CGKA and secure group messaging (SGM) applications of forward-secure encryption primitives as these demand new, and hitherto seemingly overlooked, properties of the underlying primitive.

Updatable Public Key Encryption. Unfortunately, despite its wide-ranging practical applications, to date, PPKE constructions are not practically efficient for many real-world use cases, in particular in the ratcheting and messaging settings. This has given rise to a new class of "off-brand" forward-secure encryption schemes in the messaging literature called *Updatable Public-Key Encryption* (UPKE). They aim for a happy middle ground between forward secrecy with minimal interaction and truly practical efficiency.

Intuitively, UPKE is public-key encryption where senders can also generate *update tokens*. Applying a token up to a public key pk produces an updated public key $pk \rightarrow_{up} pk'$. Similarly, applying up to the secret key sk of pk yields the secret key $sk \rightarrow_{up} sk'$ corresponding to pk'. The essential promise of UPKE is that ciphertexts encrypted to pk remain secure even when an adversary learns pk, the token up and the updated *secret* key sk'. Thus, a protocol in which parties update receivers' key pairs whenever encrypting to them can achieve relatively strong forward secrecy properties. Indeed, no secret key is ever used more than once by a party and is immediately deleted (and replaced) upon first use.

However, there is a caveat to this. While using UPKE this way doesn't require as much coordination between parties as the naïve approach, it does require more than PPKE. To ensure a receiver has the correct secret key available, a sender must encrypt to the *most recent version* of the receiver's public key. In other words, senders must see each others' *up* tokens (or at least the most recently updated public key) before they can send. Otherwise, two senders may

---

[1] Note that new keys cannot prepared and distributed too far in advance since this only extends the window of time during which forward secrecy is *not* provided.

concurrently produce update tokens up_0 and up_1 for one public key pk giving rise to two sibling key pairs (pk_0, sk_0) and (pk_1, sk_1). We refer to this as a "fork". When a fork occurs, a receiver will typically only derive one of the forked secret keys sk_b since it must then immediately delete sk to ensure forward security. Thus, when it later receives up_{1-b}, it can no longer produce sk_{1-b} meaning it can't decrypt anything sent to pk_{1-b} (or any of its descendent keys). A similar restriction is that the receiver must decrypt ciphertexts in the same order they were sent (even when sent by different senders).

Still, compared to the naïve technique this represents a qualitative reduction in coordination since the receiver can essentially stay silent after initial public key distribution. Crucially, this makes asynchronous communication (as understood in asynchronous (group) messaging) possible, because senders need not wait for a receiver to announce new public keys before they can encrypt new messages to them. Thus, UPKE provides to secure messaging protocol designers the benefits of strong forward secrecy without forcing them to compromise on the ability of parties to privately message each other despite receivers potentially being off-line for extended periods of time.

Unfortunately, no UPKE scheme to date is sufficiently flexible, nor has all of the requisite security properties for natural use in CGKA and SGM applications which UPKE was partly designed for. Indeed, the initial academic work [ACDT20] in this area introduced rTreeKEM, a CGKA protocol which provides strong forward security by using UPKE in place of the PKE. The goal was to provide a more secure CGKA upon which to re-base the IETF's Messaging Layer Security (MLS) protocol, an open SGM standard specified in RFC9420 [BBR+23]. However, rTreeKEM (and the resulting SGM based on rTreeKEM [ACDT21]) were only analyzed in a restricted model, which lead to relatively lightweight demands being placed on the underlying UPKE (both in terms of functionality and security).

Since then, however, the much more realistic "insider security" paradigm [AJM22] has established itself as a standard in the CGKA and SGM literature [HKP+21, AHKM22, AMT23]. Unlike the security models of [ACDT20, ACDT21], which assume authenticated channels, insider security only uses an insecure network. More challengingly maybe, insider security also provides meaningful security guarantees to parties joining "fake" groups; that is, sessions created arbitrarily by the adversary. These additions mean that insider security better captures the practical security concerns for SGM and CGKA. However, they also mean that to date, all UPKE schemes lack either the flexibility or security necessary for a CGKA (or SGM) application like rTreeKEM to be insider-secure.

Fake-Group Security. One such missing security property of existing UPKE notions is the (intuitive) property we call "joiner" security. When UPKE is used in higher-level CGKA/SGM protocols as a forward-secure replacement for PKE (as in rTreeKEM, for example), the joiner security of the UPKE scheme plays a central role in ensuring that the resulting CGKA/SGM protocol provides the "fake group" security aspect of insider security.

In more detail, CGKA and SGM protocols allow for dynamic groups (i.e. groups with evolving membership). Thus, a party P might receive an invitation to join an existing group mid-session. To join the group, P also receives the group state including the signature verification keys for each group member (authenticated by some trusted PKI). Fake-group security (for SGM) considers the case when the invitation (and accompanying group state) were produced maliciously by the adversary (who may also corrupt parties). It mandates that if P validates the invitation and state (as specified by the protocol) and subsequently proceeds with the execution to a point where no corrupt signing keys are left in the group's state, then the session should return to a secure state. For example, P's messages to the group should remain hidden from the adversary. Notably, this should be the case even though the group state could still includes (U)PKE keys obtained by P from the adversary.

Fake-Group Security in MLS. To date, the only protocol we are aware of that achieves fake-group security is MLS. It does so by including signatures in the public group state, which give P a way to identify which PKE keys in the state were (supposedly) generated by which party and to whom the party sent the decryption keys as part of the protocol execution. Whenever a party is removed from the group, so too are any keys they either (supposedly) generated or were sent. In the insider corruption model, leaking a party's signing key also leaks all other secret keys it knows. Thus, if at some point only secure verification keys remain in the group state, we can conclude that all remaining public keys were generated by and sent to uncorrupted parties. As a result, under those conditions, MLS can provide P with meaningful security guarantees for the session.

UPKE Breaks MLS's Fake-Group Security Mechanism. When [ACDT20] proposed replacing PKE with UPKE to improve MLS's forward security, the authors left as an open problem how to adapt MLS's mechanism for fake-group security accordingly (at least without growing the group state in the number of updates to UPKE keys). This was one of the primary barriers to adopting UPKE in MLS.

Indeed, in general, the state of a group mid-session would include UPKE keys pk that are (nominally) the result of updates to some prior original key pk_0. So, to guarantee that pk is still secure, a new member must validate that (i) pk_0 was generated by an honest party, and (ii) that pk is the result of honestly using the update algorithm starting from pk_0.

One approach to providing (ii) could be to include in the group state all update tokens up leading from pk_0 to pk along with proofs that they were generated by the update algorithm. But this results in a state size and computational cost of joining that grow linearly in the number of updates between pk_0 and pk, which is prohibitive in practice. (MLS sessions can be expected to last for years and have, say, $n = 50,000$ group members; so some of the $2n$ public keys in an MLS state could have been updated $n/2$ times by the time a new member joins.) It is also not an adequate solution to have receivers (i.e., members who can compute the updated sk, which could be as few as a single party) sign the updated pk to attest to its correctness, as it conflicts with the asynchronous nature of MLS.[2]

This motivates the *joiner security* property of UPKE identified in this work. It provides a joiner P with a concise tag for validating that some UPKE public key pk is the result of an (unknown) sequence of honest updates to a given "origin" UPKE public key pk_0. Thus, if an uncorrupted honest party attests to having generated pk_0 via a signature (just as with the PKE keys in MLS) then we can again conclude, in the insider security model, that pk must be secure.

Our Proposal: UPKE Allowing for Fake-Group Security. These issues show that there seems to be no easy way to efficiently adapt MLS's fake-group security mechanism to UPKE. So instead, we ask the UPKE scheme to directly provide a comparable public key validation mechanism for new members (and a matching security guarantee). A *joiner-secure* UPKE scheme thus includes an algorithm Verify_{jt} with 3 inputs: (i) a UPKE public key pk to be validated, (ii) an original public key pk_0 and (iii) a "joiner tag" jt. The tag must be constant-size, in particular, independent of how many updates might have lead to from pk_0 to pk.

The UPKE security game chooses the initial pk_0 honestly at the start of the game (reflecting that in the application we only expect security from pk if an honest party attested to having generated pk_0, e.g. via a signature). Then, the UPKE adversary may update pk_0 with honest (i.e., generated by the challenger) or potentially malicious tokens up. The adversary wins if it can come up with pk^* and jt^* which pass Verify_{jt} and for which it can break privacy (IND-CCA) of a ciphertext c^* encrypted to pk^*. However, the adversary loses if it corrupts a secret key created before requesting c^*.

This restriction excludes trivial attacks in which pk^* is an updated version of a corrupted key. On the other hand, the restriction is not tight in the sense that it also excludes corruptions that do not lead to trivial attacks. We believe that our joiner security is a good compromise for the following reasons. First, defining UPKE security that only excludes trivial attacks would require UPKE schemes with additional functionality, which seems to require inefficient constructions.[3] Second, our joiner security is sufficient to prove that MLS with UPKE achieves the same fake-group security as today's MLS with PKE. In fact, the above can be proven even using UPKE joiner security with *no corruptions at all*. This means that our joiner security notion with corruption could enable an even stronger flavor of fake-group security for MLS with UPKE. Indeed, in the full version we give an example of an MLS execution where MLS with UPKE satisfying our stronger joiner security is secure, but would not be so if its UPKE only satisfied

---

[2] Indeed, after an update by one group member, new members could only join the group after a different (receiving) group member comes online to validate and sign the updated key. This would mean that at least 2 existing group members are needed to invite a new member to the group.

[3] Essentially, the challenger needs some way to identify which pk's are old versions of pk^* provided by the adversary. This seems to require storing the whole update history in pk^* or jt^*.

a notion disallowing corruptions. Such a stronger notion for MLS has not been defined yet, and we leave this as an interesting open problem.

UPKE Taxonomy. Hiding beneath the term "UPKE" and the high-level intuition above, we actually find a series of concrete schemes in the literature (e.g. [JMM19, ACJM20, EJKM22, HLP22, DKW21, AMT23, AW23, HPS23]) that differ in their syntax, security properties and even the purposes they serve in the applications they were conceived for. To better interpret the results in our work, it is instructive to categorize these differences.

Long vs. Short Syntax: The most obvious differences between UPKE schemes are their various syntaxes. UPKE was first introduced in [JMM19] using an *(asymmetric) long* syntax also used in [AAN+22, EJKM22]. Here, "long syntax" means that key updates are generated and applied using stand-alone algorithms. In contrast, in this work (as in [ACDT20, ACJM20, ACDT21]) we use a *short syntax*, where keys are updated as a side-effect of encryption and decryption, thereby obviating the need for explicit update algorithms. We opted for the simpler syntax as it suffices for the dynamic group protocol applications we focus on and converting to long syntax is trivial.

Further, [EJKM22] defines two variants of a long syntax. "Asymmetric" long syntax means an update $up = (pu, su)$ includes a public component pu for updating public keys and a private component su for updating corresponding secret keys. "Symmetric" long syntax uses a single value to update both public and private keys. The notions in [DKW21, HLP22, AW23, HPS23] can be viewed as having a symmetric long syntax where the random coins used by the public key update algorithm are also the update token used for the private key.

CPA vs. CCA: The first UPKE applications needed only CPA-style UPKE as they either included additional mechanisms reducing the role of UPKE in their protocol [JMM19, AAN+22] or their application was analyzed in a model that disables all attacks that might leverage honest parties as decryption oracles. (For example, the use of ideal authenticated channels in [ACDT20] trivially prevents the adversary from injecting ciphertexts to honest parties.) However, subsequently, the stronger and more realistic "insider security" model [AJM22] has become the standard in the field [HKP+21, AHKM22, AMT23]. This motivated the need for CCA-style UPKE. Indeed, all subsequent UPKE constructions (including in this work) are now regularly proven secure with CCA-style security games.

Forking Security: Almost all UPKE applications in the group setting involve multiple parties using the same UPKE secret key. An adversary that, say, controls the network can easily cause such parties to have diverging views of a protocol session's transcript. This can result in forked UPKE keys (i.e., the initial key is updated using different sequences of updates). Thus, for such settings UPKE schemes must provide security in the face of forks. To date, we know of no (explicitly defined) UPKE scheme with this property, including those in

Table 1. Comparison of security properties of different UPKE schemes. The last two columns indicates whether they are practically efficient and in which model they are proven secure. AGM stands for the algebraic group model [FKL18].

Scheme	Syntax	Privacy	Forking	Agnos-tic	Update validation	Joinersec.	PQ	Practical	Model
[JS18]	long	CCA		✓			✓		ROM
[PR18]	long	CCA		✓			✓		ROM
[JMM19]	long	CPA		✓				✓	ROM
[ACDT20]	short	CPA		✓				✓	ROM
[EJKM22]	long	CPA		✓			✓		standard
[DKW21]	long	CCA		✓	✓		✓		standard
[HLP22]	long	CCA		✓	✓			✓	ROM
[AW23]	long	CCA					✓		ROM
[HPS23]	long	CCA			✓		✓	✓	ROM
[ACJM20]	long	CCA	✓	✓	✓		✓		standard
[AMT23]	long	CCA	✓	✓	✓		✓		standard
This work	short	CCA	✓		✓	✓		✓	ROM+AGM

[JMM19, EJKM22, HLP22, AW23, DKW21, HPS23] making them, a priori, insufficient for such applications.[4]

Notable exceptions are the schemes of [ACJM20, AMT23] that are (implicitly) based on hierarchical identity-based encryption (HIBE). Unfortunately, owing to their use of unbounded-depth HIBE, these are decidedly impractical for real-world applications leaving the state of UPKE for the group setting unsatisfactory.

Decryption Oracles for Old Keys: Even assuming there are no forks, in a setting with multiple parties using the same UPKE secret key, one has to account for parties not seeing some of the updates (yet) and hence holding old versions of the secret key. Accordingly, UPKE security notions should account for the attacker trying to inject ciphertexts to such parties. More precisely, assume we want to prove that an SGM scheme using UPKE is secure against adversaries who can inject ciphertexts but can *not* create forks. Even this weaker notion requires a UPKE security notion where, even after receiving the challenge ciphertext, the adversary can use the decryption oracle for any old secret key. However, this is not covered by any CCA-style UPKE definition we know of, in particular, not for [AW23, DKW21, HLP22, HPS23] (Table 1).

Agnostic Updates: The applications of UPKE considered in [JS18, PR18, JMM19, AAN+22] require update tokens to be generated without knowing the public key to which they will ultimately be applied which we refer to as "agnostic" updates.

---

[4] This seems to have happened because initial applications of UPKE are either in the 2-party setting, where forking is inherently not possible [JMM19] or they used very restricted models that artificially avoided forking by definition. Later UPKE constructions relied on UPKE security notions inspired by these early works but were not analyzed in their motivating applications using newer models. We provide a concrete scheme in the full version satisfying the definition [DKW21] but which leads to simple attacks when plugged into rTreeKEM.

Consequently, the UPKE schemes in those works are agnostic (as is the one in [EJKM22] and the implicit ones in [ACJM20, AMT23], although this is not necessary for the applications in those works). Conversely, the constructions of [AW23, DKW21, HLP22, HPS23] create updates for a target key.

Protocol Usage: While UPKE is usually used as a tool for achieving forward security in an application, the work of [AAN+22] applies updates to a possibly leaked secret key to refresh it to a new *secure* secret key. In other words, their protocol also relies on UPKE updates to ensure *post-compromise security* (PCS).[5] Thus, unlike any other use for UPKE we are aware of, [AAN+22] needs the additional intuitive property that secret keys of updated public keys have high (computational) entropy given the old secret key and updated public key. Fortunately, to the best of our knowledge, most UPKE schemes already have this property with the exception of the HIBE-based implicit schemes in [JS18, PR18, ACJM20, AMT23]. For the purpose of this work we focus on using UPKE for forward secrecy, so we leave such an entropy requirement for future work.

Publicly Verifiable Updates: In multi-party protocols like MLS and rTreeKEM, a common feature is that more than one user might encrypt messages to a particular public key. Suppose we use UPKE in this setting and a party P_1 updates a public key pk to pk'. It is important that everyone in the group is convinced that pk' was generated via an honest update. Otherwise, a corrupt group member P_1 (called an *insider*) might generate a key pair (pk^*, sk^*) using KeyGen and then convince someone that pk^* is the updated key. Clearly this would make all future ciphertext sent to the "updated key" pk^* insecure.

For group members that know sk, avoiding this is usually not too difficult. For example, P_1 could encrypt to pk the coins used to produce the update [ACDT20]. However, revealing those coins to members who do *not* know sk would be problematic since UPKE security notions only ensure forward secrecy for updated keys if the coins used to update sk to sk' are kept secret.

So, to prevent an insider from tricking parties that don't know sk into accepting arbitrary new public keys, the UPKE scheme should provide a method to publicly verify that pk' was produced from pk via the update algorithm. To achieve this, the verification procedure can also take as input a *validation tag* provided by P_1 as part of the message it sends to the group to announce the update. Intuitively, UPKE security should guarantee that if pk is secure and the pair (pk, pk') passes validation (with some tag), then pk' is also secure. Accordingly, the UPKE constructions [HLP22, DKW21, HPS23] include a special VerifyUpdate algorithm. For the implicit HIBE-based schemes of [ACJM20, AMT23], update verification is quite trivial and the step is left implicit.

To summarize, no UPKE scheme to date is known to satisfy the (CCA and) forking security properties needed to use UPKE in a CGKA protocol

---

[5] PCS is the mirror image of forward security where *future* keys should be secure despite *past* compromises.

like rTreeKEM [ACDT20] and meet the standard insider security for CGKA. (See the full version for a toy scheme that satisfies the UPKE security notion of [DKW21,HLP22,HPS23], yet leads to a trivial insider security attack when used in place of PKE in MLS as proposed in [ACDT20]. The attack leverages the lack of forking security in those UPKE notions.)

Our Contributions

New Model. In this work, we study CCA-secure Updatable Key Encapsulation Mechanisms (UKEM); the KEM analogue of UPKE. Note that building UPKE from a UKEM is straightforward (for both the long and short syntax) e.g. using a standard KEM/DEM construction of CCA-secure PKE from a CCA-secure KEM and a CCA-secure authenticated encryption scheme, as done for example in Hybrid Public Key Encryption (HPKE) [BBLW22].

We present a new UKEM syntax and security definition designed to meet the needs of dynamic group protocols such as MLS and rTreeKEM of [ACDT20]. In particular, it captures CCA-type confidentiality with forks and joiner security. Our notion for UKEM can be easily extended to model UPKE security.

The new syntax does not require agnostic updates as this is not needed for these applications. It is based on the short UPKE syntax augmented with two public key validation algorithms. The first, Verify_{jt}, lets new members joining a group validate the public keys they download as part of the group's state. It takes as input a public key pk_0, a public key pk_i being validated and a *joiner tag* jt_i. The joiner tag is generated along with pk_i. In particular, the tag jt_0 is generated alongside pk_0 by KeyGen and for $i > 0$, the tag jt_i is generated by Encaps when encrypting to and updating pk_{i-1}, given only pk_{i-1} and jt_{i-1}.

Joiner tags can be used to provide new-member security in protocols like MLS and rTreeKEM as follows. In addition to each UPKE public key pk_i, the group state contains the associated tag jt_i, as well as the original key pk_0 signed by the group member who generated it.[6] Whenever a group member encrypts to pk_{i-1}, they replace pk_{i-1} and jt_{i-1} by pk_i and jt_i. Note that this can be done by all members, including new ones who did not see $pk_1, \ldots, pk_{i-2}$. Further, new members can verify the signature on pk_0 and verify jt_i, which convinces them, respectively, that pk_0 was honestly generated and then updated to get pk_i.

The second algorithm, Verify_{mt} plays the same role as VerifyUpdate in the syntax of [HLP22,DKW21,HPS23]. It allows existing group members that do not know the secret keys to validate an updated public key. It takes as input the previous public key pk_{i-1}, the updated public key pk_i and a member tag mt_i, also produced as part of the output when encapsulating to pk_{i-1}.

One may wonder why Verify_{mt} is needed and why members cannot verify Verify_{jt} instead. Indeed, there may exist schemes for which this is the case. However, constructing Verify_{mt} is much easier. Intuitively, this is because the creator of mt_i can use the actual "witness" (i.e., secret randomness) for updating pk_{i-1}

---

[6] The number of signatures can be reduced by half using the same "hashing down the path" optimization as in the parent hash mechanism of MLS.

to pk_i. On the other hand, jt_i must be generated without knowledge of the witnesses of the updates from pk_0 up to pk_{i-1}. As a result, our efficient construction achieves better security for Verify_{mt}. On the other hand, joiners cannot profit from this additional security.

Our Construction. We provide a practically efficient construction of UKEM satisfying our model based on pairing-friendly elliptic curves. We prove it secure in the combination of the random oracle model (ROM) and the algebraic group model (AGM) [FKL18] (see below) under the co-discrete-log assumption, which in the AGM directly implies the co-CDH assumption [BLS01].[7]

Our starting point is the ElGamal-based KEM of DHIES [ABR98]. Public keys are of the form $u = g^x \in \mathbb{G}$ in a group $\mathbb{G}$ of prime order p with secret key $x \in \mathbb{Z}_p$. To encapsulate a symmetric key K, one chooses $r \leftarrow_\$ \mathbb{Z}_p$, computes the ciphertext $v := g^r$ and sets $K := H(u, u^r)$, where H is treated as a random oracle.

To update a public key u in our scheme, we choose a random $d \leftarrow_\$ \mathbb{Z}_p$, which defines a new key $u' := u \cdot g^d$. The associated member tag mt is a *proof of knowledge* of d. Intuitively, this proof guarantees that if u was "secure" then so is u'. Indeed, suppose an adversary could update a random key $u = g^x$ to $u' = g^y$ for which it knows the secret key y while also proving knowledge of d such that $u' = u \cdot g^d$. Then by extracting d from the PoK we can use the adversary to compute the discrete log $x = y - d$ for a random u. For our scheme, this intuition about the one-wayness of u and u' also extends to CCA-security. To allow receivers to update their secret keys accordingly, d is encrypted under u. Decrypters can thus recover d and update secret key x to $x' := x + d$ for u'.

In fact, in our construction, d is actually derived via a random oracle (like the encapsulated key K). This achieves three goals. First, it allows us to deal with adaptive corruptions, a problem resulting from forks (see below). Second, unlike in [JMM19, ACDT20] we can use the KEM ciphertext directly to transmit d, which saves on encrypting d explicitly. Third, using encryption would require key-dependent message security.

Our UKEM *member security* notion requires CCA-security for any public key whose member tag is valid. The notion is strong in that it allows the adversary to adaptively corrupt any secret key sk as long as sk does not let the adversary learn the challenge secret key in a trivial way. We achieve this leveraging the random oracle and by devising a careful guessing strategy: the security reduction guesses the first key u^* on the path of key updates leading from an initial honestly generated public key u_0 to the challenge public key for which (i) the adversary breaks an encryption (which, as in DHIES, corresponds to solving CDH) or (ii) it breaks an encryption of any key the adversary derived from pk^*. Note that the reduction does not know this path and so it simply guesses a key.

---

[7] The co-DL assumption in groups $\mathbb{G}$ and $\hat{\mathbb{G}}$, both of prime order p and generated by g and h, respectively, states that given $g^x \in \mathbb{G}$ and $h^x \in \hat{\mathbb{G}}$ for $x \leftarrow_\$ \mathbb{Z}_p$, it is hard to compute x. The co-CDH assumption states that given (g^x, g^r, h^x) for $x, r \leftarrow_\$ \mathbb{Z}_p$, it is hard to compute g^{xr}.

Despite allowing adaptive corruption, our reduction achieves a security loss of only the number of ciphertexts (and thus new keys) the adversaries asks for. For this to work, we need to assume that the proofs of knowledge of d (i.e., mt) are *simulation-sound*, that is, even after the adversary has seen simulated proofs (which the reduction creates when embedding its CDH challenge as a key), we can extract from an adversarial proof mt. This lets us "translate" a CDH solution for a key the adversary derived from the embedded key u^* to a solution for u^*.

Aiming for efficiency, we instantiate these proofs of knowledge of logarithms with Schnorr proofs, which consist of one element from $\mathbb{G}$ and one from $\mathbb{Z}_p$. These proofs were shown simulation-sound in the ROM and the algebraic group model [FPS20,FO22], which provides "straight-line extractability". That is, extraction of the witness does not require rewinding the adversary (as in the security proof in the ROM), which means we can extract from several proofs without risking an explosion of the running time due to interleaved rewinds for several proofs.

Joiner Security. A trivial construction of a joiner tag jt would be to include all mt proofs and intermediary public keys on the path from u_0 to u', which guarantee knowledge of $d_1, \ldots, d_k$ s.t. $u' = u_0 \cdot g^d$ for $d = d_1 + \cdots + d_k$. However, this is inefficient and our goal is constant-size joiner tags. Since the updater does not know the value d, we need a way to "aggregate" the proofs mt_i guaranteeing honest hops from u_{i-1} to u_i into a single short proof jt guaranteeing honest hops from u_0 all the way to u'. An inherent problem with aggregatable proofs is that aggregation introduces malleability, which conflicts with our requirement that mt should be simulation-sound. Thus, we cannot hope that an instantiation of jt can also play the role of mt.

A very simple proof of knowledge of a logarithm is to assume that there exists a second generator h of $\mathbb{G}$ of which no one knows the discrete log. To prove knowledge of the logarithm of $v = g^d$, one sets $\pi := h^d$. The knowledge-of-exponent assumption [Dam92] states that π can only be computed if one knows d; formally, for any algorithm outputting (g^d, h^d), there exists an extractor that outputs d. These proofs can be aggregated: given a proof $\pi = h^d$ for $u = g^x$ w.r.t. $u_0 = g^{x_0}$, that is $d = x - x_0$, a proof for $u' := u \cdot g^d$ is computed as $\pi' := \pi \cdot h^d$.

The problem is how to verify whether π was correctly computed. This is why we embed our scheme in a *bilinear group*. That is, we assume a second group $\hat{\mathbb{G}}$ and a bilinear map e: $\mathbb{G} \times \hat{\mathbb{G}} \to \mathbb{G}_T$ for some target group $\mathbb{G}_T$.[8] We can now set the basis h for the proofs as a generator of $\hat{\mathbb{G}}$ and use the pairing to verify a proof $\pi \in \hat{\mathbb{G}}$ for $v \in \mathbb{G}$ by checking whether e$(v, h) = $ e(g, π).

We prove joiner security directly in the algebraic group model. This model implies states that after having received elements $h, \pi_1, \ldots, \pi_k \in \hat{\mathbb{G}}$, whenever the adversary returns some $\pi \in \hat{\mathbb{G}}$, it must have computed π as a linear

---

[8] In particular, we use an *asymmetric* pairing. That is, there are no efficiently computable homomorphisms between $\mathbb{G}$ and $\hat{\mathbb{G}}$. In practice, this type of pairing yields the most efficient constructions. Note also that assuming a pairing lets one prove the security of DHIES from co-CDH instead of the interactive assumption *gap-CDH* [OP01,ABR01] which is also the case for our UKEM (see below).

Table 2. Comparison of object sizes in {kilo, mega}-bytes of recent UPKE schemes. By ϕ we denote the bit-length of a NIZK that the update was generated correctly. A similar NIZK is needed to make the CPA scheme [DKW21] CCA-secure, while the CRS for the NIZK is included in public keys. In all UPKE applications considered in this work (e.g. rTreeKEM and MLS) ciphertexts are always sent together with a public key, an update up, joiner tag jt and member tag mt.

Scheme	Security	PQ	ROM	$|sk|$	$|pk|$	$|ctxt|$	$|up|$	$|jt|$	$|mt|$
[DKW21]	CPA	✓		166 B	41 KB	41 KB	52.375 MB		
[HPS23]	CCA	✓				1.8 KB	10.8 KB + ϕ		
[HLP22]	CCA		✓	589 B	1.15 KB	11.375 KB	13.125 KB		
[AW23]	CCA		✓	32 B	80 B	96 B	128 B		
This work	CCA		✓	48 B	48 B	96 B		96 B	96 B

combination ("algebraically") of all the $\hat{\mathbb{G}}$ elements it has received. In particular, the AGM assumes that the adversary outputs $\alpha_0, \dots, \alpha_k \in \mathbb{Z}_p$ such that $\pi = h^{\alpha_0} \cdot \pi_1^{\alpha_1} \cdots \pi_k^{\alpha_k}$. In our security proof, h and the proofs $\pi_1, \dots, \pi_k$ computed by the reduction will be all $\hat{\mathbb{G}}$ elements given to the adversary. As the reduction knows the discrete logarithms of the π_i's, it can compute the logarithm of π from $\alpha_0, \dots, \alpha_k$.

Weaker Assumption for Member Security. It turns out that the proofs π for joiner security also allow us to prove member security of our construction under weaker assumptions. In particular, we only require a notion of simulation-soundness for mt where extraction is done *after* all simulations. Recall that a co-CDH instance consists of $u = g^x$, $v = g^r \in \mathbb{G}$ and $\hat{u} = h^x \in \hat{\mathbb{G}}$ and the goal is to compute $w = g^{xr}$. In the security proof of DHIES, the reduction embeds u as the public key and v as the ciphertext and searches for w among the random oracle queries made by the adversary. Using co-CDH (rather than CDH) the reduction can efficiently find $w = g^{xr}$ the pairing e, by checking if $e(v, \hat{u}) \stackrel{?}{=} e(w, h)$.

Our reduction for UKEM embeds u as some (honestly updated) public key and v as some ciphertext it hopes the adversary breaks. However, v may not be created for u but for some $u' = u \cdot g^{d'}$ derived from u by the adversary, who needs to provide proofs mt and jt for u'. The reduction thus searches the random oracle queries for a value $w' = g^{(x+d')r}$. It could do so by extracting d' from the proof of knowledge mt. However, using $\pi = h^{d'}$, it can directly check $e(v, \hat{u} \cdot \pi) \stackrel{?}{=} e(w', h)$ without extracting anything at all. Extraction of the value d' is then only needed when a CDH solution is found (and the reduction stops): computing $w := w'/v^{d'} = g^{(x+d')r}/g^{rd'}$ yields the co-CDH solution g^{xr}.

Efficiency of Our Scheme. We describe the efficiency profile of our scheme when instantiated with the BLS12-381 curve [SKSW22,Bow], which is a concrete 128-bit-secure instance of a BLS curve [BLS04]. It is equipped with an asymmetric pairing from source groups $\mathbb{G} \times \hat{\mathbb{G}}$ to target group $\mathbb{G}_T$. Elements of $\mathbb{G}$ and $\hat{\mathbb{G}}$ are of size 48 B and 96 B respectively. As a NIZK we use a Schnorr proof of knowledge of the discrete log of elements in $\mathbb{G}$, which results in proofs of length 96 B. Based on this, in our scheme, public keys are 48 B, ciphertexts are 48 B and both joiner and member tags are 96 B. As seen in Table 2 this represents a *very* significant improvement over all CCA-secure UPKE (and UKEM) schemes to date (despite the new scheme satisfying a considerably stronger security notion).

For example, using UPKE in rTreeKEM to achieve insider security involves sending multiple tuples of the form $(pk, ctxt, t)$ where t is either an update token up or a joiner and member tag pair (jt, mt), depending on which UPKE syntax is used and $ctxt$ is a ciphertext under the previous key. The tuples of the new UPKE construction in this work are $< 1.5\%$ the size of those of [HLP22]. For other CCA-secure schemes with publicly verifiable updates, the tuples are orders of magnitude larger still (despite none of these schemes providing forking or joiner security like the new construction).

We note that in our scheme, neither key generation, encapsulation nor decapsulation use pairing operations. One pairing is computed during each of the public key validation algorithms (which is run by parties holding the secret key before decapsulation as well).

Further Results. In the full version, we discuss extensions of our security model and efficiency improvements of the construction. We also dive into details of the impact of using variants of UPKE, including ours and less secure ones from the literature, on the security of MLS.

2   Preliminaries

Bilinear Groups. Our scheme will be defined over a bilinear group with an asymmetric pairing, that is, a tuple $(p, \mathbb{G}, \hat{\mathbb{G}}, \mathbb{G}_T, g, h, e)$, where $\mathbb{G}$ and $\hat{\mathbb{G}}$ are groups of prime order p generated by g and h, respectively, and e: $\mathbb{G} \times \hat{\mathbb{G}} \to \mathbb{G}_T$ is a non-degenerate (i.e., $e(g, h)$ generates $\mathbb{G}_T$) bilinear map (i.e., for all $a, b \in \mathbb{Z}_p$: $e(g^a, h^b) = e(g, h)^{ab}$).

The security of our scheme relies on the hardness of the co-discrete-logarithm problem in bilinear groups, defined as follows. We also state co-CDH [BLS01].

Definition 1 (co-DL). *Let* $\mathcal{G} = (p, \mathbb{G}, \hat{\mathbb{G}}, \mathbb{G}_T, g, h, e)$ *be a bilinear group. The advantage of an adversary $\mathcal{A}$ in solving the co-DL problem over $\mathcal{G}$ is defined as*

$$\mathsf{Adv}_{\mathcal{G}}^{\mathsf{co-DL}}(\mathcal{A}) := \Pr\left[y = x \,\middle|\, x \leftarrow_{\$} \mathbb{Z}_p, u \leftarrow g^x, \hat{u} \leftarrow h^x, y \leftarrow \mathcal{A}(u, \hat{u})\right].$$

Definition 2 (co-CDH). *Let* $\mathcal{G} = (p, \mathbb{G}, \hat{\mathbb{G}}, \mathbb{G}_T, g, h, e)$ *be a bilinear group. The advantage of an adversary $\mathcal{A}$ in solving the co-CDH problem over $\mathcal{G}$ is defined as*

$$\mathsf{Adv}_{\mathcal{G}}^{\mathsf{co-CDH}}(\mathcal{A}) := \Pr\left[w = g^{xr} \,\middle|\, \begin{array}{c} x, r \leftarrow_{\$} \mathbb{Z}_p, u \leftarrow g^x, \hat{u} \leftarrow h^x, v \leftarrow g^r \\ w \leftarrow \mathcal{A}(u, \hat{u}, v) \end{array}\right].$$

For any $u = g^x$, $v = g^r$, we denote a CDH solution $w = g^{xr}$ by $w = \mathrm{DH}(u, v)$.

The Algebraic Group Model. We analyze our scheme in the algebraic group model (AGM) [FKL18], which assumes that an adversary is *algebraic*, meaning that it computes any group element it outputs as a linear combination of the group elements it was given. More precisely, if the adversary, given input $g :=$ $u_0, u_1, \ldots, u_k \in \mathbb{G}$, outputs a group element $v \in \mathbb{G}$, then it must have computed v as $v = u_0^{\alpha_0} \cdots u_k^{\alpha_k}$ for some $\alpha_0, \ldots, \alpha_k$. Formally, the AGM assumes that such coefficients α_i, i.e., the "representation" of v are output by the adversary. The following is implicit in [FKL18]; we include a proof in the full version.

Lemma 1. *In the algebraic group model, co-DL tightly implies co-CDH. In particular, for any algebraic adversary $\mathcal{A}$ against co-CDH in $\mathbb{G}$, there exists $\mathcal{B}$ against co-DL in $\mathcal{G}$ with approximately the same running time as $\mathcal{A}$ s.t.* $\mathsf{Adv}_{\mathcal{G}}^{\mathsf{co-DL}}(\mathcal{B}) \geq \mathsf{Adv}_{\mathcal{G}}^{\mathsf{co-CDH}}(\mathcal{A})$.

Simulation-Extractable Zero-Knowledge Proofs. Our UKEM scheme uses a proof system PoL ("proof of logarithm") for statements of the form $\theta := (u, u')$ proving knowledge of a witness d s.t. $u'/u = g^d$. Formally, PoL may use a random oracle H and comprises the following algorithms: $\tau \leftarrow \mathsf{PoL.Prove}_H((u, u'), d)$ outputs a proof τ and $0/1 \leftarrow \mathsf{PoL.Verify}_H((u, u'), \tau)$ verifies τ.

We require two security notions: *Zero-knowledge* (in the random oracle model) means that the reduction, which can program the random oracle H, can create proofs τ_i for statements θ_i without knowing a witness, using an algorithm $\mathsf{PoL.Simulate}_H$. The programmed random oracle and simulated proofs are, together, indistinguishable from a fresh random oracle and proofs computed honestly via $\mathsf{PoL.Prove}_H$ using a witness. We denote by $\epsilon_{\mathsf{PoL},n}^{\mathsf{sim}}$ the simulation error of PoL when simulating at most n proofs.

Strong Simulation Extractability (sSE) is an adaptation of *strong simulation soundness* [Sah99] to proofs of knowledge [DP92]. It is defined via the following game: an adversary $\mathcal{A}$ has access to random oracle H and an oracle that, on input a statement θ_i of $\mathcal{A}$'s choice, returns a simulated proof τ_i (and programs H as needed). Eventually, $\mathcal{A}$ returns a statement/proof pair $(\theta^*, \tau^*) \notin \{(\theta_i, \tau_i)\}_i$. If τ^* is a valid proof for θ^* (using the final programmed version of H) then a witness for θ^* can be extracted from $\mathcal{A}$. (The notion is *strong* since after querying a simulated proof for a statement, a different proof for the same statement must be extractable.) We require a *multi-extraction* version of sSE, in which, after having queried simulated proofs, the adversary returns *several* valid pairs (θ_i^*, τ_i^*) with $\{(\theta_i^*, \tau_i^*)\}_i \cap \{(\theta_i, \tau_i)\}_i = \emptyset$ and one can extract witnesses for all statements θ_i^*. We denote by $\epsilon_{\mathsf{PoL},n}^{\mathsf{ext}}(\mathcal{A})$ the advantage of the adversary $\mathcal{A}$ in breaking simulation extractability of PoL when returning at most n proofs.

Schnorr Signatures. (Key-prefixed) Schnorr signatures are defined over a group $\mathbb{G}$ of order p and a hash function $H \colon \{0,1\}^* \to \mathbb{Z}_p$, modeled as a random oracle. Using signing key $x \in \mathbb{Z}_p$, a signature on a message $m \in \{0,1\}^*$ is computed by sampling $r \leftarrow_\$ \mathbb{Z}_p$ and returning

$$(v := g^r, s := (r + cx) \bmod p) \quad \text{with} \quad c := H(v, g^x, m).$$

A signature (v, s) is valid for message m under public key $u = g^x$ iff $g^s = v \cdot u^c$ with $c = H(v, u, m)$.

In the combination of the random oracle model and the algebraic group model, [FO22] show that Schnorr signatures are sSE zero-knowledge proofs of knowledge of the logarithm of the public key. That is, they are proofs of knowledge (of the witness) for the NP-relation $\{((u, m), x) \mid u = g^x, m \in \{0, 1\}^*\}$.

Proofs for statements (u_i, m_i) can be simulated by programming the random oracle (as done in the original security proof for Schnorr [PS00]). Suppose an algebraic adversary $\mathcal{A}$ receives simulated proofs (v_i, s_i) for statements (u_i, m_i) of its choosing and then outputs a valid statement/proof pair $((u^*, m^*), (v^*, s^*)) \notin \{((u_i, m_i), (v_i, s_i))\}$. Then, [FO22] showed that from the representations for the group elements $u_1, u_2, \ldots, u^*$ and v^*, which $\mathcal{A}$ outputted during the game, one can efficiently compute a witness for the statement (u^*, m^*) with overwhelming probability.[9] In particular, extraction is straight-line and we can extract witnesses for *multiple* proofs produced during a single execution of an adversary. Thus, Schnorr signatures are *multi-extraction* sSE proofs in the ROM and AGM, which we formally prove in the full version.

The proof system PoL for member tags is defined as taking input a statement (u, u') and a witness $d = \log(u'/u)$ and returning a Schnorr signature under key u'/u on the message (u, u'). Then, sSE guarantees that after receiving simulated proofs for pairs (u_i, u_i'), if the adversary returns a new valid statement/proof pair $((u_*, u_*'), (v_*, s_*))$, we can extract d such that $u_*'/u_* = g^d$.

3 Updatable Key Encapsulation (UKEM)

3.1 Functionality

Intuitively, a UKEM scheme is a key encapsulation mechanism with the following modifications. First, on input a public key pk_i, the Encaps algorithm outputs – in addition to the key K and the ciphertext c – the updated public key pk_{i+1}. Accordingly, on input sk_i, the Decaps algorithm outputs – in addition to K – the

---

[9] One might wonder why extraction is not trivial in the AGM anyway: an algebraic adversary that has only seen the generator g and returns u^* must know a representation α s.t. $u^* = g^\alpha$. In the context of security proofs, this is not the case: Consider e.g., an *algebraic* reduction $\mathcal{R}$ to the DL problem. This means that $\mathcal{R}$ receives a DL instance g^* and simulates the game to an adversary $\mathcal{A}$, providing it with group elements it computes *as linear combinations* of g and g^*. When $\mathcal{A}$ outputs a group element z, it accompanies it by a representation in basis all group elements received from $\mathcal{R}$. From this, $\mathcal{R}$ can compute a representation (α_0, α_1) in basis (g, g^*), that is, $z = g^{\alpha_0} \cdot (g^*)^{\alpha_1}$. To argue that $\mathcal{R}$ can extract from proofs of knowledge made by $\mathcal{A}$, we need to turn $\mathcal{R}$ together with $\mathcal{A}$ into an adversary against simulation-extractability. This adversary is algebraic, but only in the sense that it can give representations in basis (g, g^*) where g^* is a group element of which the extractor will not know the discrete logarithm. Therefore, [FO22] (and our proof in the full version) actually show that even in the presence of an "auxiliary-input" g^*, one can extract the witness from a Schnorr proof.

updated secret key sk_{i+1}. This is analogous to any UKEM/UPKE with short syntax from the literature.

Second, Encaps also outputs a "member tag" mt_{i+1} which can be used by entities holding pk_i to validate pk_{i+1}. In particular, running $\mathsf{Verify_{mt}}(pk_i, pk_{i+1}, mt_{i+1})$, such entities can verify that if pk_i is "honest" then pk_{i+1} is so, too. In MLS (more precisely, rTreeKEM [ACDT20]), $\mathsf{Verify_{mt}}$ is run by members (not joiners) who do not know sk_i but know and have validated pk_i.

Third, Encaps also generates a "joiner tag" jt_{i+1} which can be used by entities holding pk_0 to validate pk_{i+1}: running $\mathsf{Verify_{jt}}(pk_0, pk_{i+1}, jt_{i+1})$, such entities can verify that if pk_0 is "honest" then pk_{i+1} is so, too. In MLS, $\mathsf{Verify_{jt}}$ is run by joiners after checking that pk_0 was signed by the member who generated it using KeyGen. Moreover, Encaps takes the last joiner tag jt_i as input.

Decaps takes additional input pk_{i+1} and should output $\bot$ if it does not "match" sk_{i+1}. In MLS, members who *do* know sk_i can thus reject "incorrect" (e.g. adversarially chosen) pk_{i+1}.

Formally, a UKEM scheme consists of the following algorithms:

Key Generation. $\mathsf{KeyGen}(\kappa) \to (pk_0, sk_0, jt_0)$, on input the security parameter, outputs a key pair (pk_0, sk_0) and the first joiner tag jt_0.

Encapsulation. $\mathsf{Encaps}(pk_i, jt_i) \to (K, c, pk_{i+1}, mt_{i+1}, jt_{i+1})$ takes as input the current public key and joiner tag and returns an encapsulated key K, a ciphertext c, an updated public key pk_{i+1}, a new member tag mt_{i+1} and an updated joiner tag jt_{i+1}.

Verification of member tags. $\mathsf{Verify_{mt}}(pk_i, pk_{i+1}, mt_{i+1}) \to 0/1$ verifies the update from pk_i to pk_{i+1} using the tag mt_{i+1}.

Verification of joiner tags. $\mathsf{Verify_{jt}}(pk_0, pk_{i+1}, jt_{i+1}) \to 0/1$ verifies the update from pk_0 to pk_{i+1} using the tag jt_{i+1}.

Decapsulation. $\mathsf{Decaps}(sk_i, c, pk_{i+1}) \to (K, sk_{i+1})/\bot$ outputs the decapsulated key K and the updated secret key sk_{i+1}, but only if pk_{i+1} matches sk_{i+1}.

Using UKEM Schemes. Importantly, Decaps *does not validate any tags*. Therefore, applications using a UKEM scheme *should always run* $\mathsf{Verify_{mt}}$ *and* $\mathsf{Verify_{jt}}$ *before* Decaps. This is reflected in our security notion.

3.2 Security

The IND-CCA security of UKEM schemes is formalized by the experiment in Fig. 1.

Intuitively, during the experiment, a tree is created where each node is identified by an integer i and has a public key pk_i and a joiner tag jt_i. The root is identified by $i = 0$. Each non-root node has a parent par_i and a member tag mt_i. Further, some nodes have a secret key sk_i. If a node has a secret key, we call it *full*, and otherwise we call it a *half node*.

The root node $i = 0$ is created by the challenger at the beginning of the experiment. Its public key pk_0, secret key sk_0 and joiner tag jt_0 are generated using KeyGen (the root is thus a full node). All other nodes j are created by updating existing nodes in one of three ways:

Game UKEM IND-CCA Security

$\text{Exp}^{\text{IND-CCA}}(\mathcal{A})$

$(pk_0, sk_0, jt_0) \leftarrow \text{KeyGen}(\kappa)$
$(mt_0, par_0, rev_0, j) \leftarrow (\epsilon, \epsilon, 0, 0)$
$b \leftarrow_{\$} \{0,1\}$
$b' \leftarrow \mathcal{A}^{\text{Enc,Dec,Rev,MChal,JChal}}(pk_0, jt_0)$
$S \leftarrow \textbf{chall-set}(chall)$
return $b = b' \wedge \forall j \in S : \neg rev_j$

Oracle Enc(i)

$(K, c) \leftarrow \textbf{create-honest-node}(i)$
return (K, c, pk_j, mt_j, jt_j)

Oracle MChal(i)

---

req $chall = \bot$
$K^{(0)} \leftarrow_{\$} \{0,1\}^{\kappa}$
$(K^{(1)}, c^*) \leftarrow \textbf{create-honest-node}(i)$
$chall \leftarrow (\text{"member"}, i, c^*, pk_i)$
return $(K^{(b)}, c^*, pk_j, mt_j, jt_j)$

Oracle Rev(i)

---

req $sk_i \neq \bot$
$rev_i \leftarrow 1$
return sk_i

Oracle JChal(pk', jt')

---

req $chall = \bot$
req $\text{Verify}_{jt}(pk_0, pk', jt')$
$K^{(0)} \leftarrow_{\$} \{0,1\}^{\kappa}$
$(K^{(1)}, c^*, pk, mt, jt) \leftarrow \text{Encaps}(pk', jt')$
$chall \leftarrow (\text{"joiner"}, j, c^*, pk')$
return $(K^{(b)}, c^*, pk, mt, jt)$

Oracle Dec(i', c', pk', mt', jt')

---

req $pk_{i'} \neq \bot$ // i-th node exists
if $chall = (*, *, c^*, pk^*)$ **then**
  req $c^* \neq c' \vee pk^* \neq pk_{i'}$
req $\text{Verify}_{mt}(pk_{i'}, pk', mt')$
req $\text{Verify}_{jt}(pk_0, pk', jt')$
j++
$(pk_j, mt_j, jt_j, sk_j, par_j, rev_j)$
$\qquad\qquad \leftarrow (pk', mt', jt', \bot, i', 0)$
if $sk_{i'} \neq \bot$ **then**
  $out \leftarrow \text{Decaps}(sk_{i'}, c', pk')$
  if $out \neq \bot$ **then**
    $(K, sk_j) \leftarrow out$
    return K
return $\bot$

Helper create-honest-node(i)

---

req $pk_i \neq \bot$ // i-th node exists
j++
(K, c, pk_j, mt_j, jt_j)
$\qquad\qquad \leftarrow \text{Encaps}(pk_i, jt_i)$
if $sk_i \neq \bot$ **then**
  // i-th node is *full*
  $(*, sk_j) \leftarrow \text{Decaps}(sk_i, c, pk_j)$
else $sk_j \leftarrow \bot$
$(par_j, rev_j) \leftarrow (i, 0)$
return (K, c)

Helper chall-set($chall$)

---

if $chall = (\text{"member"}, i^*, *, *)$ **then**
  $base \leftarrow \{i_0, \ldots, i_\ell\}$ where $i_0, \ldots, i_\ell$ is
  the path from $i_0 = 0$ to $i_\ell = i^*$
else if $chall = (\text{"joiner"}, i^*, *, *)$ **then**
  $base \leftarrow \{0, \ldots, i^*\}$
else return $\emptyset$
$extd\text{-}base \leftarrow \{i' \mid \exists i \in base :$
  $\qquad\qquad (pk_{i'}, mt_{i'}, jt_{i'}) = (pk_i, mt_i, jt_i)\}$
  // include duplicates
return dec-closure($extd\text{-}base$)

Helper dec-closure(S)

Return the set of all j reachable from
some $i \in S$ via only edges created by
Dec queries.

Fig. 1. The experiment formalizing UKEM IND-CCA security. By default, all variables are initialized to $\bot$. We use **req** *condition* to denote that if *condition* is false, then the current function, and any function calling it, stops and returns $\bot$.

1. When the adversary $\mathcal{A}$ calls the oracle $\mathsf{Enc}(i)$, the challenger creates a child j of i by running Encaps. If i is a full node, j is also a full node with secret key generated by running Decaps.
2. A child of i with a possibly "adversarial" public key may be created when $\mathcal{A}$ calls the oracle $\mathsf{Dec}(i, c, pk', mt', jt')$. In such case, the challenger verifies mt' and jt' and, if the check passes, creates the node j using these values. If i is a full node and $\mathsf{Decaps}(sk_i, c, pk')$ outputs (K, sk_j) (and not $\bot$), then j is also a full node with secret key sk_j; in that case, $\mathcal{A}$ also receives K, which reflects CCA-security. Otherwise, j is a half node. Observe that j is a half node if $\mathcal{A}$ provides correct (publicly verifiable) tags but c inconsistent with pk' (which is not publicly verifiable).
3. A node can be created during a challenge call. We address such calls next. There are two challenge oracles: member challenge MChal and joiner challenge JChal. Without loss of generality, $\mathcal{A}$ can only call one of them, and only once.

Member Security. Consider the case that $\mathcal{A}$ calls MChal, which means that the notion implies security for group members when used in a secure messaging application. On query $\mathsf{MChal}(i^*)$, the challenger creates a child j^* of i^* just like during an Enc query creating a "real" key $K^{(1)}$. $\mathcal{A}$ gets either $K^{(1)}$ or a random and independent key $K^{(0)}$ and has to decide which is the case. It also receives the resulting tags, public key and the ciphertext c^*. To disable trivial wins, on inputs i and c the Dec oracle returns $\bot$ if $pk_i = pk_{i^*}$ and $c = c^*$.

Furthermore, our notion implies forward secrecy by giving $\mathcal{A}$ access to an oracle Rev, which reveals secret keys (of full nodes). In particular, $\mathcal{A}$ can ask for the secret key of any node outside the *challenge set of* i^*, which consists of three parts. First, the *base* of the challenge set, which is the path from the root 0 to i^*. Clearly, revealing the secret key for any such node would allow $\mathcal{A}$ to trivially win by computing the secret key of i^* by running Decaps sequentially on the ciphertexts between the corrupted and the challenged node, and then decapsulating c^*. This *base* is extended to *extd-base*, which also includes *duplicates*, i.e., any nodes that have the same public key and tags as a node in *base*.[10]

Finally, the challenge set contains *branches*, which are nodes reachable from *extd-base* via nodes created by Dec queries. This is where our notion does not formalize optimal security: there exist UKEM schemes, notably the ones based on HIBE that achieve security even when $\mathcal{A}$ can corrupt keys on branches. However, we are not aware of any *efficient* schemes that achieve this. Observe that the secret keys of nodes on branches are generated by updating a secret key on the challenge path (or a duplicate node) with updates generated by $\mathcal{A}$. Therefore, for optimal security we would need a mechanism that does not allow $\mathcal{A}$ to undo its updates, which resembles PPKE.

---

[10] This restriction prevents trivial attacks, as in the following example: $\mathcal{A}$ queries $\mathsf{Enc}(0)$, which creates node 1 with (pk_1, mt_1, jt_1) and ciphertext c_1. It next queries $\mathsf{Rev}(1)$, to obtain the corresponding sk_1. It then queries $\mathsf{Dec}(0, c_1, pk_1, mt_1, jt_1)$, which creates node 2 with $sk_2 = sk_1$, and finally $\mathsf{MChal}(2)$, to receive $(c^*, K^*, pk_3, mt_3, jt_3)$ and checks whether for $(K', sk_3) \leftarrow \mathsf{Decaps}(sk_1, c^*, pk_3)$ it holds that $K' = K^*$.

We note that $\mathcal{A}$ is allowed to ask for the secret key for j^* created by MChal, which corresponds to the fact that in typical UPKE security notions [DKW21, HPS23, HLP22, AW23] the challenge oracle returns the updated secret key. However, $\mathcal{A}$ can also obtain many other keys, e.g., any node created by Enc and not on the challenge path (and all their children).

Joiner Security. Next, consider the case that $\mathcal{A}$ calls JChal, formalizing a notion that implies security for joiners when used in a secure messaging application. On query $\text{JChal}(pk', jt')$, the challenger verifies jt' for pk' w.r.t. the (honest) pk_0 and, if the check passes, runs Encaps on pk' to generate the "real" key $K^{(1)}$. As for member security, $\mathcal{A}$ is also given the resulting ciphertext, public key and tags. $\mathcal{A}$'s goal is to distinguish $K^{(1)}$ from a random and independent $K^{(0)}$. To disable trivial wins, on inputs i and c the Dec oracle returns $\perp$ if $pk_i = pk'$ and $c = c^*$.

Reveal queries are more restricted for joiner security than for member security. In particular, the challenge set $base$ now contains all nodes generated before the call to JChal was made (which is thus a superset of the set $base$ in the MChal setting). Analogously to member security, $\mathcal{A}$ is not allowed to corrupt keys for nodes in the set $base$, any duplicates of such nodes and $branches$ (i.e., nodes derived from these via Dec queries).

The above restriction cannot be relaxed without enabling "trivial" attacks against any correct scheme (with our syntax). To illustrate this, consider the following adversary $\mathcal{A}$. By calling Enc(0) twice, $\mathcal{A}$ generates two children of node 0 with keys pk_1, pk_2 and tags jt_1, jt_2. Then by running $\text{Encaps}(pk_1, jt_1)$ (possibly repeating this to create a longer path), $\mathcal{A}$ computes a new pair (pk', jt') on its own and submits it to its JChal oracle. If $\mathcal{A}$ was allowed to query Rev(1), it could then, by running Decaps (possibly consecutively), compute the secret key for pk'.

In general, pk' may have been derived via Encaps from any pk_i that $\mathcal{A}$ saw before generating pk'. Our restriction thus disallows Rev(i) for all such pk_i, including pk_0, pk_1 and pk_2 in the above example, even though corrupting pk_2 would not lead to an attack. However, the challenger cannot identify keys that can be revealed, as the UKEM syntax does not allow to decide, given the challenger's information, whether pk' could not have been derived from them.

Remark 1. One could consider relaxing the above restriction on reveal queries for a UPKE with modified syntax, e.g. with an additional algorithm that decides, given pk', jt', pk_i and sk_i (and any other information the challenger has), whether pk_i is an ancestor of pk'. However, implementing such an algorithm seems to require inefficient techniques, such as storing all ancestor public keys in jt'.

Remark 2. One could imagine achieving stronger joiner security by having $\text{JChal}(pk', jt')$ create an (incomplete) node i' with $pk_{i'} = pk'$ and $jt_{i'} = jt'$ and allowing the adversary $\mathcal{A}$ to create a (detached) tree rooted at i'. (Note that, by the arguments in Remark 1, we cannot define a parent of i'.) However, the resulting notion would be equivalent to our notion. Since i' has no parent, its sub-tree contains only half-nodes without secret keys. So no oracle call related to such nodes uses any secrets unknown to $\mathcal{A}$ (which are the secret keys of full nodes and the bit b.) Thus, $\mathcal{A}$ could emulate such oracle calls itself.

Definition 3 (UKEM Security). *Let* $\mathrm{Exp}^{\mathsf{IND\text{-}CCA}}(\mathcal{A})$ *be as defined in Fig. 1. The advantage of an adversary $\mathcal{A}$ against the* IND-CCA *security of a* UKEM *scheme is defined as*

$$\mathsf{Adv}^{\mathsf{IND-CCA}}(\mathcal{A}) := 2\Pr\left[\mathrm{Exp}^{\mathsf{IND\text{-}CCA}}(\mathcal{A}) = 1\right] - 1.$$

4 Construction

The basis of our construction is the KEM part of DHIES [ABR98], which is basically "hashed ElGamal" for a hash function (modeled as a random oracle) $H\colon \{0,1\}^* \to \mathcal{K}$, the symmetric key space. We use groups $\mathbb{G}$ and $\hat{\mathbb{G}}$ of order p with a pairing e from $\mathbb{G} \times \hat{\mathbb{G}}$ and define the KEM in $\mathbb{G}$: Public keys are of the form $u = g^x \in \mathbb{G}$ and symmetric keys K are encapsulated by choosing $r \leftarrow_\$ \mathbb{Z}_p$, defining the ciphertext as $v := g^r$ and deriving $K := H(u, u^r)$. Using the secret key x, keys are decapsulated from v as $K := H(g^x, v^x)$.

We extend this to derive updated public keys as follows: using a second random oracle H_1, we define $d := H_1(u, u^r)$ and set the new public key as $u' := u \cdot g^d$. Decapsulation now takes as additional argument the updated key u', derives $d := H_1(g^x, v^x)$, updates the secret key to $x' := x + d$ and checks if $u' = g^{x'}$. To guarantee that u' was derived correctly (and not chosen freshly with a known secret key), we add a proof of knowledge (PoK) τ of d, that is, a PoK of the discrete log of u'/u. (For our security notion allowing adaptive corruption, τ needs to be simulation-sound.) This τ corresponds to mt in the UKEM model.

The tag jt given to joiners will be a PoK of $D' := x' - x_0$, with x_0 the secret key of the root key u_0 and x' the secret key of the updated key u'. This guarantees that u' is linked to the root key u_0. A straightforward solution would be to define $jt_j := (u_1, mt_1, \ldots, u_{j-1}, mt_{j-1}, mt_j)$To avoid a growth in size depending on the number of updates, we would require a direct proof of knowledge of $D' = x' - x_0$, but the updater will not know D'. Our solution is to use "aggregatable" proofs, that is, given a PoK of $D = x - x_0$ corresponding to key u, and deriving u' from u using d, one should be able to derive a PoK of $D' := D + d$.

We use the second pairing source group $\hat{\mathbb{G}}$, generated by h, to instantiate these aggregatable proofs. A proof π proving knowledge of the logarithm of an element $u = g^x \in \mathbb{G}$ is defined as $\pi := h^x \in \hat{\mathbb{G}}$. Using the pairing, a proof can be verified by checking $\mathrm{e}(u, h) = \mathrm{e}(g, \pi)$. Making "knowledge-of-exponent"-type assumptions (in our security proof we will directly rely on the algebraic group model), we get that from any algorithm that returns u and π satisfying the above equation, one can extract $x = \log_g u = \log_h \pi$, meaning π is a proof of knowledge.

Using these proofs for jt allows the updater to transform a proof π for u into a proof $\pi' := \pi \cdot h^d$ for $u' = u \cdot g^d$. A proof π' for u' w.r.t. u_0 is verified by checking $\mathrm{e}(u'/u_0, h) = \mathrm{e}(g, \pi')$. Our UKEM scheme is formally defined in Fig. 2.

5   Security of the Construction

Security of our construction is expressed by the following theorem.

Theorem 1. *If PoL is a strongly simulation-extractable proof system and co-CDH holds for $\mathcal{G}$, and assuming adversary $\mathcal{A}$ is algebraic, then the UKEM construction from Fig. 2 is* IND-CCA *secure in the ROM. More precisely, for any adversary $\mathcal{A}$, there exist reductions $\mathcal{B}$ and $\mathcal{B}'$ such that*

$$\mathsf{Adv}^{\mathsf{IND-CCA}}(\mathcal{A}) \leq (n_e + 2)\left(\epsilon^{\mathrm{sim}}_{PoL,n_e+1} + \epsilon^{\mathrm{ext}}_{PoL,n_d}(\mathcal{B}') + \mathsf{Adv}^{\mathsf{co-CDH}}_{\mathcal{G}}(\mathcal{B})\right),$$

where n_e (n_d, resp.) are upper bounds on the number of Enc (Dec, resp.) queries made by $\mathcal{A}$, and $\epsilon^{\mathrm{sim}}_{PoL,n}$ ($\epsilon^{\mathrm{ext}}_{PoL,n_d}(\cdot)$, resp.) are the probabilities that simulation of n proofs (extraction from n_d proofs, resp.) fails for PoL.

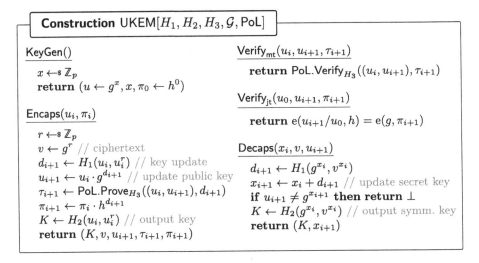

Fig. 2. The UKEM construction. Here H_1, H_2 and H_3 are hash functions modeled as random oracles, $\mathcal{G} = (p, \mathbb{G}, \hat{\mathbb{G}}, \mathbb{G}_T, g, h, \mathrm{e})$ is a bilinear group, and PoL is a proof of knowledge system for discrete logarithm statements in $\mathbb{G}$, which might use H_3.

Together with Lemma 1, Theorem 1 implies that the security of our construction can be reduced to co-DL. Moreover, using the fact that Schnorr proofs, against algebraic adversaries, are strongly simulation-(multi-)extractable (as we show in the full version) with simulation error $\epsilon^{\mathrm{sim}}_n := n/(p - n_h - n)$ and (multi-)extraction error $\epsilon^{\mathrm{ext}}_n = n/p$, yields the following:

Corollary 1. *Let $\mathcal{G}$ be an asymmetric bilinear group. If PoL is instantiated using Schnorr (cf. Sect. 2) and co-DL holds for $\mathcal{G}$, then the UKEM construction from Fig. 2 is* IND-CCA *secure in the ROM and the AGM. More precisely, for any algebraic adversary $\mathcal{A}$, there exist a reduction $\mathcal{B}$ such that*

$$\mathsf{Adv}^{\mathsf{IND-CCA}}(\mathcal{A}) \leq (n_e + 2)\left(\frac{n_e + 1}{p - n_h - n_e - 1} + \frac{n_d}{p} + \mathsf{Adv}^{\mathsf{co-DL}}_{\mathcal{G}}(\mathcal{B})\right),$$

where n_e, n_d and n_h are upper bounds on the number of, respectively, Enc, Dec and RO queries made by $\mathcal{A}$.

Proof of Theorem 1. We split the security notion IND-CCA into two: CCA-M, in which the JChal oracle is disabled, and CCA-J, in which the MChal oracle is disabled. The advantages $\mathsf{Adv}^{\mathsf{CCA-M}}$ and $\mathsf{Adv}^{\mathsf{CCA-J}}$ are defined accordingly. In Lemmas 2 and 3 we then bound these advantages. Theorem 1 then follows by summing them and letting $\mathcal{B}$ and $\mathcal{B}'$ be those adversaries from Lemma 2 or Lemma 3 that have the greater advantage.

5.1   Member Security

We start with the following lemma, which formalizing member security, CCA-M, of our UKEM scheme. For space reasons, we defer the full proof to the full version.

Lemma 2. *If PoL is a strongly simulation-extractable proof system and co-CDH holds for $\mathcal{G}$, then the UKEM construction from Fig. 2 is CCA-M-secure in the ROM. More precisely, for any adversary $\mathcal{A}$, there exist reductions $\mathcal{B}$ and $\mathcal{B}'$ such that*

$$\mathsf{Adv}^{\mathsf{CCA-M}}(\mathcal{A}) \leq (n_e + 1)\left(\epsilon^{\mathsf{sim}}_{\mathsf{PoL},n_e+1} + \epsilon^{\mathsf{ext}}_{\mathsf{PoL},n_d}(\mathcal{B}') + \mathsf{Adv}^{\mathsf{co-CDH}}_{\mathcal{G}}(\mathcal{B})\right),$$

where n_e and n_d are upper bounds on the number of $\mathcal{A}$'s Enc and Dec queries, resp.

Proof Intuition. Let $\mathcal{A}$ be any adversary against the CCA-M security of our UKEM scheme. We will construct a reduction $\mathcal{B}$ against the co-CDH problem, i.e., given u^*, $\hat{u}^*$ and v^*, $\mathcal{B}$ must compute $w^* = \mathrm{DH}(u^*, v^*)$.

We start by adapting the proof idea for the security of the KEM of DHIES in the ROM. $\mathcal{B}$ embeds u^* as some u_j generated by the challenger, that is, either as u_0 or some u_j returned by an Enc(i) query, hoping that $\mathcal{A}$ calls MChal(j). If this happens, $\mathcal{B}$ embeds v^* as the ciphertext returned by the oracle. Now as long as $\mathcal{A}$ never queries (u^*, w^*) to the RO H_2 with $w^* = \mathrm{DH}(u^*, v^*)$, the challenge key $K^{(b)}$ is independently random in both the real and the ideal game, and so no information on b is revealed. On the other hand, querying (u^*, w^*) means $\mathcal{A}$ solved CDH; moreover, $\mathcal{B}$ can test this by checking if $\mathrm{e}(w^*, h) = \mathrm{e}(v^*, \hat{u}^*)$.

Embedding u^*. Consider embedding $u^* = g^x$ as u_{i^*} during a query Enc(p^*) (with p^* the parent of i^*), which returns ciphertext v_{i^*}. Recall that Encaps would compute $d_{i^*} = H_1(u_{p^*}, w_{i^*})$ with $w_{i^*} := \mathrm{DH}(u_{p^*}, v_{i^*})$ and define $u_{i^*} := u_{p^*} \cdot g^{d_{i^*}}$ and $\pi_{i^*} := \pi_{p^*} \cdot h^{d_{i^*}} = h^{x_{i^*} - x_0}$. So when setting $u_{i^*} := u^*$, the reduction $\mathcal{B}$ does not know $d_{i^*} = \log(u^*/u_{p^*})$. It thus generates the proof τ_{i^*} using the simulator guaranteed by zero knowledge of PoL. To compute π_{i^*}, it uses $\hat{u}^* = h^x$ from its co-CDH challenge and sets $\pi_{i^*} := \hat{u}^*/h^{x_0}$ (and $\pi_{i^*} := h^0$ if $j = 0$).

While $\mathcal{B}$ can simulate the proofs, not knowing d_{i^*}, it cannot consistently answer if $\mathcal{A}$ queries H_1 on (u_{p^*}, w_{i^*}). On the other hand, as long as this query has not been made, the simulation is consistent. Now, to make this query, $\mathcal{A}$ would have to solve CDH w.r.t. u_{p^*} and v_{i^*}. But if $\mathcal{A}$ ever does so, then $\mathcal{B}$ should have guessed differently and embedded u^* as u_{p^*} and v^* as v_{i^*} (assuming for the moment there are no Dec queries). $\mathcal{B}$'s guessing strategy will therefore be to guess the index i^* of the *first* key u_{i^*} generated during a query $Enc(p^*)$ on the path to the challenge for which $\mathcal{A}$ will solve CDH via an RO query. (Note that $\mathcal{B}$ does not know the path; it simply guesses the index of an Enc query.)

For now we only considered the case that $\mathcal{A}$ makes the query $MChal(j^*)$ or $Enc(j^*)$ assuming u_{j^*} was itself created during an Enc query; but u_{j^*} might have been created during a Dec query. That is, the attacked key (i.e., the one for which $\mathcal{A}$ solves CDH) has been generated by the adversary. Security now relies on the fact that ultimately the attacked key was derived (possibly via many Dec queries) from an honest key, say u_{i^*} (which might be u_0).

Since $\mathcal{A}$ must provide proofs τ_i for the hops from u_{i^*} to u_{j^*} (where τ_i proves knowledge of $d_i = x_i - x_{par_i}$), $\mathcal{B}$ can extract the values d_i and sum them to $d_{i^* \to j^*} := x_{j^*} - x_{i^*}$, which it can use to "translate" CDH solutions for u_{j^*} to u_{i^*}. Thus, it can embed u^* as u_{i^*} and embed v^* as the ciphertext the adversary breaks. A solution $w = DH(u_{j^*}, v^*)$ then yields a solution $w/(v^*)^{d_{i^* \to j^*}} = g^{x_{j^*} r}/g^{r(x_{j^*} - x_{i^*})} = DH(u^*, v^*)$.

Our strategy is thus to guess the following index i^*: if the first attacked key is u_{j^*}, then i^* is the closest ancestor of j^* with a public key generated by the challenger. That is, at the latest $i^* = j^*$ (if j^* is generated during an Enc query), and at the earliest $i^* = 0$.

Answering Rev Queries. Say $\mathcal{B}$ embeds u^* as u_{i^*} and consider a query $Enc(i^*)$, which creates a new key u_j. If node j turns out not to lie on the challenge path, then $\mathcal{A}$ is allowed to query $Rev(j)$. However, if $\mathcal{B}$ ran Encaps to answer the query, setting $u_j := u^* \cdot g^{d_j}$ with $d_j := H_1(u_{i^*}, DH(u_{i^*}, v_j))$, then it would not know $x_j = \log u_j$ to answer the Rev query.

But recall that $\mathcal{B}$ hopes that $\mathcal{A}$ attacks key u_{i^*}! Every time Enc or MChal is queried on i^*, the reduction thus embeds v^* from its co-CDH challenge into the ciphertext. In particular, using random self-reducibility, $\mathcal{B}$ chooses a uniform s_j and defines the new ciphertext as $v_j := v^* \cdot g^{s_j}$. If $\mathcal{A}$ ever queries $H_1(u_{i^*}, w_j)$ for $w_j := DH(u_{i^*}, v_j)$, the game stops and $\mathcal{B}$ returns $w^* := w_j/(u^*)^{s_j} = g^{x^*(r+s_j)}/g^{x^* s_j} = DH(u^*, v^*)$. On the other hand, as long as no such query is made, d_j is not defined, and thus $\mathcal{B}$ can simply sample x_j, set $u_j := g^{x_j}$ (which implicitly defines d_j) and simulate the proofs τ_j and π_j. This way, $\mathcal{B}$ can then answer the query $Rev(j)$.

The case $Enc(i)$ for an index i whose path from i^* consists of only Dec queries is dealt with similarly: $\mathcal{B}$ embeds $v^* \cdot g^{s_j}$ as v_j and samples x_j freshly. As long as $\mathcal{A}$ does not query $H_1(u_i, w_j)$ with $w_j = DH(u_i, v_j)$, the simulation is perfect. If the adversary makes that query, it can be translated back to a solution $DH(u^*, v_j)$, and thus to $DH(u^*, v^*)$, by extracting $d_{i^* \to i} = x_i - x^*$ from the τ-proofs provided

by the adversary when making the Dec queries linking u_{i^*} to u_i: we have $w^* :=$
$$w_j \cdot (u^*)^{-s_j} \cdot v_j^{-d_{i^*\to i}} = g^{(x^*+d_{i^*\to i})(r+s_j)} g^{-x^*s_j} g^{-(r+s_j)d_{i^*\to i}} = \mathrm{DH}(u^*, v^*).$$

Extracting from Adversarial Proofs. Simulation-extractability of τ-proofs only lets us extract from proofs computed by the adversary (and not ones created by the simulator). So what happens if the adversary "copies" proofs simulated by the challenger?

In particular, consider the situation where we embedded our challenge key u^* as u_{i^*} and the adversary attacked one of its Dec-descendants u_{j^*}. If none of the key/proof pairs (u_i, τ_i) on the path from i^* to j^* appear elsewhere in the tree, then the statement/proof pairs are different from those of the simulated proofs, and we can extract their witnesses. On the other hand, assume that on this path, there is a pair (u_{k^*}, τ_{k^*}) which appears elsewhere as $(u_{k'}, \tau_{k'})$ in the tree. If (and only if) k' was created in a query $\mathrm{Enc}(i')$ and i' is a Dec-descendant of i^*, then $\tau_{k'}$ was simulated, and thus we cannot extract from $\tau_{k'} = \tau_{k^*}$. (Note that since for every u_k there is a unique valid π_k, we have $(u_{k^*}, \tau_{k^*}, \pi_{k^*}) = (u_{k'}, \tau_{k'}, \pi_{k'})$.)

However, this just means that we should have guessed differently: assume k^* is the last "copied" node on the path from i^* to j^*. If we had embedded our challenge key u^* as u_{k^*} (when we created it as $u_{k'}$ when answering an Enc query) then we could now solve CDH: since, by assumption, no nodes between u_{k^*} and u_{j^*} are copied, we can extract from their τ-proofs and thus compute $d_{k^*\to j^*} = x_{j^*} - x_{k^*}$, which lets us shift a CDH solution for u_{j^*} to one for u_{k^*}. Note that we would not be able to answer Rev for k' and its Dec-descendants, but such queries are disallowed (as they are part of *chall-set*, cf. Fig. 1).

Our actual guess strategy is therefore: let u_{j^*} be the first key the adversary attacks during the game; then what is the index of the Enc query that creates the node (u_{k^*}, τ_{k^*}) so that when starting from u_{j^*} and moving up Dec-edges, (u_{k^*}, τ_{k^*}) is the first key/proof pair created by the challenger during an Enc query (at latest, this is u_0).

Answering Dec Queries. We address answering decryption queries $\mathrm{Dec}(i)$ for nodes whose secret key is not known to the reduction. These are all nodes whose public key u^* is the embedded co-CDH instance, or any Dec-descendant of such nodes. Here, we again follow the ideas for proving CCA-security of DHIES, namely to inspect the random-oracle table. We moreover use the fact that CDH solutions can be checked via the pairing using the associated proof π_i: given a ciphertext v_j for key $u_i = g^{x_i}$, we have $K_j = H_2(u_i, w_j)$ with $w_j := \mathrm{DH}(u_i, v_j)$ and the latter can be efficiently checked: setting $\hat{u}_i := \pi_i \cdot h^{x_0} = h^{x_i}$ (where $h^{x_0} := \hat{u}^*$ if $i^* = 0$), check if $e(w_j, h) \overset{?}{=} e(v_j, \hat{u}_i)$.

So to decrypt ciphertext v_j for key u_i we do the following: if there has been a query $(u_i, \mathrm{DH}(u_i, v_j))$ to H_2, then we return the same key again; if there has not been such a query, we sample a fresh key K_j and (implicitly) program the random oracle: store an entry $(u_i, v_j, \bot, K_j)$, meaning that $(u_i, \mathrm{DH}(u_i, v_j))$ gets mapped to K_j. To detail how the Dec queries are answered, we first address programming of the random oracles.

Programming the Random Oracles. Answering Enc, Dec and MChal queries results in defining the entries of the random oracle tables for H_1 and H_2. The inputs are of the form (u, w), on which H_1 outputs d and H_2 which outputs K. For certain queries, these entries are partial, since the reduction does not know all inputs/outputs, i.e., the RO is programmed implicitly. The reduction thus stores RO entries of the form $(u, \hat{u}, v, w, u', d, K)$, some of whose components can be $\perp$. For $u = g^x$, the (non-$\perp$) values are: $\hat{u} = h^x$, $w = v^x = \mathrm{DH}(u, v)$, $u' = u \cdot g^d$ and d and K are the outputs of, respectively, H_1 and H_2, on input (u, w). Note that $\hat{u}$, w and u' are determined by the other values. During Enc and MChal queries, implicit programming happens at the following positions:

1. When embedding the key u^* as u_{i^*} for $i^* \neq 0$, letting $p^* := par_{i^*}$, the reduction implicitly defines the oracles at $(u_{p^*}, v_{i^*}^{x_{p^*}})$ (where x_{p^*} was chosen by the reduction); H_1 is set to $d_{i^*} := \log(u_{i^*}/u_{p^*})$ (unknown to the reduction) and H_2 is set to K_{i^*} (chosen by the reduction). When answering this query, the reduction thus stores the following entry (where $\hat{u}_{p^*} := h^{x_{p^*}}$):

$$(u_{p^*}, \hat{u}_{p^*}, v_{i^*}, \perp, u_{i^*}, \perp, K_{i^*})$$

2. For any call of Enc or MChal at position i with $u_i = u^*$ or i being a Dec-descendant of a node with public key u^*, the reduction creates v_j (embedding v^* from its co-CDH instance) and u_j ($:= g^{x_j}$ for fresh j) and defines H_1 and H_2 at position $(u_i, \mathrm{DH}(u_i, v_j))$, which is unknown to the reduction. While the reduction chooses the value K_j at this position for H_2 (for the MChal query, K_j corresponds to "$K^{(1)}$"), it will not know the value $d_j = \log(u_j/u_i)$ for H_1. The reduction thus stores $(u_i, \hat{u}_i, v_j, \perp, u_j, \perp, K_j)$, where, as above, $\hat{u}_i = \hat{u}^*$ if $i^* = 0$ and $\hat{u}_i := \pi_i \cdot h^{x_0} = h^{x_i}$ otherwise.

For every random-oracle query (u, w) the adversary makes, the reduction checks if $(u, w) = (u_i, \mathrm{DH}(u_i, v_j))$ holds when $i = i^*$, or $i = par_{i^*}$ or i is a Dec-descendant of i^*. It does this by checking $u \stackrel{?}{=} u_i$ and $e(w, h) \stackrel{?}{=} e(v_j, \hat{u}_i)$. (Note that such queries to H_1 cannot be answered, since the reduction does not know $d_j = \log(u_j/u_i)$.)

If this is the case for $i = par_{i^*}$, the reduction stops, since the guess i^* was wrong, as par_{i^*} would have been the right guess. If it happens for i^* or any of its Dec-descendants, the reduction stops and returns the co-CDH solution (computed as described above). Otherwise, fresh values d and K are sampled and a new entry $(u, \perp, \perp, w, u \cdot g^d, d, K)$ is created. We say that in this case the RO was *explicitly* programmed.

Details of Answering Dec Queries. Let us consider a query $\mathrm{Dec}(i', v', u', \tau', \pi')$. If τ' and π' are valid, a new (for now: half-)node is created. If i' is a full node, the oracle would do the following: run Decaps on $sk_{i'}$, that is, compute $d' := H_1(u_{i'}, \mathrm{DH}(u_{i'}, v'))$; check if $u' = u_{i'} \cdot g^{d'}$; if so, return $K := H_2(u_{i'}, \mathrm{DH}(u_{i'}, v'))$ and declare the new node a full node; else return $\perp$.

If i' is a half-node, then the reduction can simulate the Dec oracle perfectly, as the latter uses only public values. Moreover, if $i' \notin$ *chall-set*, then the reduction knows $sk_{i'}$ and can thus simulate the oracle perfectly as well. For $i' \in$ *chall-set* and i' being a full node, the reduction uses its extended RO table as follows:

(i) If there is an entry $(u_{i'}, *, v', \bot, u'', d, K)$ for some u'', d (where possibly $d = \bot$) and K, then the RO was already implicitly programmed at $(u_{i'}, \mathrm{DH}(u_{i'}, v'))$ (either during and Enc or MChal query as described above, or during a Dec query as described below). The reduction checks if $u' = u''$ (as Decaps does) and if so, it declares the new node a full node and returns K; else, it declares the new node a half node and returns $\bot$.

(ii) Else if there is an entry $(u_{i'}, \bot, \bot, w, u'', d, K)$ for some u'' and $w = \mathrm{DH}(u_{i'}, v')$, which can be checked using $\hat{u}_{i'} = \pi_{i'} \cdot h^{x_0}$, then the RO was already explicitly programmed at $(u_{i'}, \mathrm{DH}(u_{i'}, v'))$. As above, the reduction checks if $u' = u''$ (as Decaps does); if so, it declares the new node a full node and returns K; else, it declares the new node a half node and returns $\bot$.

(iii) If none of the above apply, then sample d and K, create new entry $(u_{i'}, \hat{u}_{i'}, v', \bot, u_{i'} \cdot g^d, d, K)$ and proceed as in Decaps. (Note that, with overwhelming probability, this will return $\bot$, since d will be inconsistent with $u_{i'}$ and u'.)

Finally, note that the only RO query that would reveal the challenge bit b is querying H_2 on $(u_{i_c}, \mathrm{DH}(u_{i_c}, v_{j_c}))$, where i_c is the value queried to MChal and j_c the current value of j at that point. "Explicit" queries are dealt with by our guessing strategy: if the guess i^* was correct then such a query is used to solve co-CDH. On the other hand, "implicit" queries via the Dec oracle cannot occur, since this would correspond to $\mathrm{Dec}(i', v', u', \tau', \pi')$ with $u' = u_{i_c}$ and $v' = v_{i_c}$, which is forbidden (as trivial wins).

5.2 Joiner Security

We next state the following lemma, which formalizes the joiner security, CCA-J, of our UKEM scheme. The full proof is deferred to the full version.

Lemma 3. *Let $\mathcal{G}$ be an asymmetric bilinear group. If PoL is a simulation-extractable proof system, co-CDH holds for $\mathcal{G}$ and adversary $\mathcal{A}$ is algebraic in $\hat{\mathbb{G}}$, the UKEM construction from Fig. 2 is CCA-J secure in ROM. More precisely, for any algebraic adversary $\mathcal{A}$, there exist reductions $\mathcal{B}$ and $\mathcal{B}'$ such that*

$$\mathsf{Adv}^{\mathsf{CCA-J}}(\mathcal{A}) \leq \epsilon_{\mathsf{PoL}, n_e}^{\mathsf{sim}} + \epsilon_{\mathsf{PoL}, n_d}^{\mathsf{ext}}(\mathcal{B}') + \mathsf{Adv}_{\mathcal{G}}^{\mathsf{co-CDH}}(\mathcal{B}),$$

where n_e and n_d are upper bounds on the number of $\mathcal{A}$'s Enc and Dec queries, resp.

Proof Intuition. We build upon the proof of Lemma 2 (member security). The only difference is that instead of MChal, the adversary $\mathcal{A}$ now calls $\mathrm{JChal}(u', \pi')$. Accordingly, instead of embedding v^* in the ciphertext returned by the MChal oracle, the reduction $\mathcal{B}$ against co-CDH now embeds v^* in the ciphertext v' returned by JChal; specifically, using random self-reducibility, it sets $v' := v^* \cdot g^{s'}$ for a random s'. The security of v' encrypted to u' hinges on the link between u'

and the honest u_0 via the associated proof π'. More precisely, unless $\mathcal{A}$ queries H_2 on $w' := \mathrm{DH}(u', v')$, both the "random" key $K^{(0)}$ and the "real" key $K^{(1)} = H_2(u', w')$ are random and independent, so $\mathcal{A}$'s advantage is 0. On the other hand, if $\mathcal{A}$ makes such an RO query, $\mathcal{B}$ can compute the co-CDH solution by extracting from the proof π' as follows.

Extracting from the π' Proof. Since $\mathcal{A}$ is algebraic, when it calls $\mathrm{JChal}(u', \pi')$, $\mathcal{B}$ can extract the representation of π' as a linear combination of all $\hat{\mathbb{G}}$ elements given to $\mathcal{A}$ so far, which are (precisely) the π_j proofs returned by the Enc oracle. $\mathcal{B}$ knows the logarithm of each such π_j because it emulates the Enc oracle by running Encaps honestly. Thus, $\mathcal{B}$ can use the representation of π' and the known logarithms to compute the logarithm d' of π'. Since π' is valid, d' is equal to the logarithm of $u'/u_0 = u'/u^*$. Thus $\mathcal{B}$ can use d' and s' chosen when embedding v' as $v' = v^* \cdot g^{s'}$ to translate $w' = \mathrm{DH}(u', v') = \mathrm{DH}(u^* \cdot g^{d'}, v^* \cdot g^{s'})$ from $\mathcal{A}$'s RO query to the solution $w^* = \mathrm{DH}(u^*, v^*)$ analogously to the reduction for member security: $w^* = w' \cdot (u^*)^{-s'} \cdot (v')^{-d'}$.

Answering Rev Queries. If, after the JChal call, $\mathcal{A}$ makes a query $\mathrm{Enc}(i)$ creating a node j, then it is allowed to query $\mathrm{Rev}(j)$. $\mathcal{B}$ deals with such queries the same way as the reduction for member security: It samples the secret key x_j itself. This implies that $\mathcal{B}$ cannot answer a query $(u_i, \mathrm{DH}(u_i, v_j))$ to H_1, which should return $d_j = \log(g^{x_j}/u_i)$. But again, such a query would allow $\mathcal{B}$ to solve its co-CDH instance, had it embedded v^* in v_j.

In more detail, recall that Rev queries are allowed for nodes outside of *chall-set* which is the *dec-closure* of all nodes (and their duplicates) created before the JChal call. If after the JChal query $\mathcal{A}$ queries $\mathrm{Enc}(i)$ for some $i \in$ *chall-set*, $\mathcal{B}$ samples x_j itself and returns $v_j = v^* \cdot g^{s_j}$ for a random s_j together with simulated proofs π_j and τ_j. If $\mathcal{A}$ later "breaks" v_j by making an RO query (u_i, w_j) with $w_j = \mathrm{DH}(u_i, v_j)$ then $\mathcal{B}$ translates w_j to the co-CDH solution $\mathrm{DH}(u^*, v^*)$: it does so by collecting and summing all d values on the path from node 0 to node i: for any Dec edge, $\mathcal{B}$ extracts d from the τ proof provided by $\mathcal{A}$; for any Enc edge, $\mathcal{B}$ generated d itself, as all Enc edges in *chall-set* were created before JChal and hence by running Encaps. Knowing $d_{0 \to i}$ s.t. $u_i = u_0 \cdot g^{d_{0 \to i}} = u^* \cdot g^{d_{0 \to i}}$ and s_j s.t. $v_j = v^* \cdot g^{s_j}$, the reduction can compute $\mathrm{DH}(u^*, v^*) = \mathrm{DH}(u_i, v_j) \cdot (u^*)^{-s_j} \cdot v_j^{-d_{0 \to i}}$.

Observe that for the above "simulated" edges, $\mathcal{B}$ does not know the logarithm of the simulated π_j. This does not affect extraction from the proof π' above, since extraction is done when JChal is called, thus before any proofs are simulated.

Extracting from Adversarial τ Proofs. Say $\mathcal{A}$ breaks some v_j embedded in the response to $\mathrm{Enc}(i)$ as described above. Simulation-extractability allows $\mathcal{B}$ to extract from τ-proofs for Dec edges as long as these were not simulated. However, $\mathcal{A}$ could copy a node with a simulated proof via a Dec query. Therefore, we need to modify $\mathcal{B}$'s strategy, similarly to the proof of member security.

Consider the following example : $\mathcal{A}$ starts by calling JChal and then queries $\mathrm{Enc}(0)$ creating node 1, at which point $\mathcal{B}$ picks x_1 and sets $u_1 = g^{x_1}$ as described above. Now $\mathcal{A}$ forwards the outputs of the above Enc query to $\mathrm{Dec}(0)$, creating node 2 with $(u_2, \tau_2) = (u_1, \tau_1)$. Finally, $\mathcal{A}$ queries $\mathrm{Enc}(2)$, which creates node

3. Since node 2 is in *chall-set*, $\mathcal{B}$, following the above strategy, would choose a fresh key x_3 for $u_3 := g^{x_3}$. However, if $\mathcal{A}$ queries $(u_2, \mathrm{DH}(u_2, v_3))$ to H_1, then $\mathcal{B}$ would not be able to answer, since it does not know $d_3 := x_3 - x_2$; moreover, the value $\mathrm{DH}(u_2, v_3)$ is of no use, as $\mathcal{B}$ can compute it itself as $v_3^{x_2} = v_3^{x_1}$. $\mathcal{B}$ should thus just have computed u_3 honestly as $u_3 = u_2 \cdot g^{d_3}$. It could then still answer Rev(3), as required, since it knows $x_3 = x_1 + d_3$.

$\mathcal{B}$'s strategy is thus the following: u^* is embedded as u_0, and before the JChal query, every Enc query is answered by running Encaps (and thus $\mathcal{B}$ does not know the resulting secret key). After the JChal query, every query $\mathrm{Enc}(i)$ creating node j must be answered in a way so $\mathcal{B}$ knows the resulting secret key x_j. We distinguish two cases: (1) $\mathcal{B}$ knows x_i, or x_k for any Dec-"ancestor" k of i: then $\mathcal{B}$, knowing x_i, runs Encaps, and will thus know x_j. (2) Else $\mathcal{B}$ sets the resulting key as $u_j := g^{x_j}$ and $v_j := v^* \cdot g^{s_j}$ for fresh x_j, s_j, and simulates the proofs.

Note that for every $i \notin$ *chall-set*, $\mathcal{B}$ either knows x_i, or it can compute it by running Decaps between the node k for which it knows x_k and i in order to derive x_i. Therefore, $\mathcal{B}$ can answer all Rev queries for such i.

Moreover, when $\mathcal{A}$ makes an unanswerable RO query, $\mathcal{B}$ can use it to break co-CDH. Any such query is of the form $(u_i, w_j = \mathrm{DH}(u_i, v_j))$ where j is a node created in mode (2) above (for which $\mathcal{B}$ does not know d_j). $\mathcal{B}$ extracts all d values from the proofs τ on the path from the root to node i. This must succeed as long as none of the proofs was simulated, which we show next.

Towards a contradiction, assume that for some k on that path, τ_k for the statement (u_{par_k}, u_k) was simulated. $\mathcal{B}$ must have simulated the proof when, after the JChal call, $\mathcal{A}$ called $\mathrm{Enc}(par_{k'})$, creating node k' with $u_{k'} = u_k$. However, this means that $\mathcal{B}$ chose $x_{k'}$ itself, and thus i has a Dec-ancestor with a known secret key, meaning that node j was not created in mode (2), which is a contradiction.

Since $\mathcal{B}$ can extract all values d and thus compute $d_{0\to i}$ with $u_i = u^* \cdot g^{d_{0\to i}}$, and since $v_j = v^* \cdot g^{s_j}$, it can translate $\mathrm{DH}(u_i, v_j)$ to $\mathrm{DH}(u^*, v^*)$, as done above.

Acknowledgments. This work was funded by the Vienna Science and Technology Fund (WWTF) [10.47379/VRG18002] and by the Austrian Science Fund (FWF) [10.55776/F8515-N]. The authors would like to thank the anonymous reviewers for their valuable comments and suggestions.

References

[AAN+22] Alwen, J., et al.: CoCoA: concurrent continuous group key agreement. In: Dunkelman, O., Dziembowski, S. (eds.) EUROCRYPT 2022. LNCS, vol. 13276, pp. 815–844. Springer, Cham (2022). https://doi.org/10.1007/978-3-031-07085-3_28

[ABR98] Abdalla, M., Bellare, M., Rogaway, P.: DHIES: an encryption scheme based on the Diffie-Hellman problem. In: Contributions to IEEE P1363a, September 1998

[ABR01]   Abdalla, M., Bellare, M., Rogaway, P.: The oracle Diffie-Hellman assumptions and an analysis of DHIES. In: Naccache, D. (ed.) CT-RSA 2001. LNCS, vol. 2020, pp. 143–158. Springer, Heidelberg (2001). https://doi.org/10.1007/3-540-45353-9_12

[ACDT20]   Alwen, J., Coretti, S., Dodis, Y., Tselekounis, Y.: Security analysis and improvements for the IETF MLS standard for group messaging. In: Micciancio, D., Ristenpart, T. (eds.) CRYPTO 2020. LNCS, vol. 12170, pp. 248–277. Springer, Cham (2020). https://doi.org/10.1007/978-3-030-56784-2_9

[ACDT21]   Alwen, J., Coretti, S., Dodis, Y., Tselekounis, Y.: Modular design of secure group messaging protocols and the security of MLS. In: Vigna, G., Shi, E. (eds.) ACM CCS 2021, pp. 1463–1483. ACM Press, November 2021

[ACJM20]   Alwen, J., Coretti, S., Jost, D., Mularczyk, M.: Continuous group key agreement with active security. In: Pass, R., Pietrzak, K. (eds.) TCC 2020. LNCS, vol. 12551, pp. 261–290. Springer, Cham (2020). https://doi.org/10.1007/978-3-030-64378-2_10

[AHKM22]   Alwen, J., Hartmann, D., Kiltz, E., Mularczyk, M.: Server-aided continuous group key agreement. In: Yin, H., Stavrou, A., Cremers, C., Shi, E. (eds.) ACM CCS 2022, pp. 69–82. ACM Press (2022)

[AJM22]   Alwen, J., Jost, D., Mularczyk, M.: On the insider security of MLS. In: Dodis, Y., Shrimpton, T. (eds.) CRYPTO 2022. LNCS, vol. 13508, pp. 34–68. Springer, Cham (2022). https://doi.org/10.1007/978-3-031-15979-4_2

[AMT23]   Alwen, J., Mularczyk, M., Tselekounis, Y.: Fork-resilient continuous group key agreement. In: Handschuh, H., Lysyanskaya, A. (eds.) CRYPTO 2023. LNCS, vol. 14084, pp. 396–429. Springer, Cham (2023). https://doi.org/10.1007/978-3-031-38551-3_13

[AW23]   Asano, K., Watanabe, Y.: Updatable public key encryption with strong CCA security: security analysis and efficient generic construction. IACR Cryptology ePrint Archive, p. 976 (2023)

[BBLW22]   Barnes, R., Bhargavan, K., Lipp, B., Wood, C.A.: Hybrid public key encryption. RFC 9180, February 2022

[BBR+23]   Barnes, R., Beurdouche, B., Robert, R., Millican, J., Omara, E., Cohn-Gordon, K.: The messaging layer security (MLS) protocol. RFC 9420, July 2023

[BLS01]   Boneh, D., Lynn, B., Shacham, H.: Short signatures from the weil pairing. In: Boyd, C. (ed.) ASIACRYPT 2001. LNCS, vol. 2248, pp. 514–532. Springer, Heidelberg (2001). https://doi.org/10.1007/3-540-45682-1_30

[BLS04]   Barreto, P.S.L.M., Lynn, B., Scott, M.: On the selection of pairing-friendly groups. In: Matsui, M., Zuccherato, R.J. (eds.) SAC 2003. LNCS, vol. 3006, pp. 17–25. Springer, Heidelberg (2004). https://doi.org/10.1007/978-3-540-24654-1_2

[Bow]   Bowe, S.: Bls12-381: New zk-snark elliptic curve construction

[CCD+20]   Cohn-Gordon, K., Cremers, C., Dowling, B., Garratt, L., Stebila, D.: A formal security analysis of the signal messaging protocol. J. Cryptol. 33(4), 1914–1983 (2020)

[Dam92]   Damgård, I.: Towards practical public key systems secure against chosen ciphertext attacks. In: Feigenbaum, J. (ed.) CRYPTO 1991. LNCS, vol. 576, pp. 445–456. Springer, Heidelberg (1992). https://doi.org/10.1007/3-540-46766-1_36

[DKW21] Dodis, Y., Karthikeyan, H., Wichs, D.: Updatable public key encryption in the standard model. In: Nissim, K., Waters, B. (eds.) TCC 2021, Part III. LNCS, vol. 13044, pp. 254–285. Springer, Cham (2021). https://doi.org/10.1007/978-3-030-90456-2_9

[DP92] De Santis, A., Persiano, G.: Zero-knowledge proofs of knowledge without interaction (extended abstract). In: 33rd FOCS, pp. 427–436. IEEE Computer Society Press, October 1992

[DV19] Durak, F.B., Vaudenay, S.: Bidirectional asynchronous ratcheted key agreement with linear complexity. In: Attrapadung, N., Yagi, T. (eds.) IWSEC 2019. LNCS, vol. 11689, pp. 343–362. Springer, Cham (2019). https://doi.org/10.1007/978-3-030-26834-3_20

[EJKM22] Eaton, E., Jao, D., Komlo, C., Mokrani, Y.: Towards post-quantum key-updatable public-key encryption via supersingular isogenies. In: AlTawy, R., Hülsing, A. (eds.) SAC 2021. LNCS, vol. 13203, pp. 461–482. Springer, Cham (2022). https://doi.org/10.1007/978-3-030-99277-4_22

[FKL18] Fuchsbauer, G., Kiltz, E., Loss, J.: The algebraic group model and its applications. In: Shacham, H., Boldyreva, A. (eds.) CRYPTO 2018. LNCS, vol. 10992, pp. 33–62. Springer, Cham (2018). https://doi.org/10.1007/978-3-319-96881-0_2

[FO22] Fuchsbauer, G., Orrù, M.: Non-interactive mimblewimble transactions, revisited. In: Agrawal, S., Lin, D. (eds.) ASIACRYPT 2022, Part I. LNCS, vol. 13791, pp. 713–744. Springer, Cham (2022). https://doi.org/10.1007/978-3-031-22963-3_24

[FPS20] Fuchsbauer, G., Plouviez, A., Seurin, Y.: Blind Schnorr signatures and signed ElGamal encryption in the algebraic group model. In: Canteaut, A., Ishai, Y. (eds.) EUROCRYPT 2020, Part II. LNCS, vol. 12106, pp. 63–95. Springer, Cham (2020). https://doi.org/10.1007/978-3-030-45724-2_3

[GHJL17] Günther, F., Hale, B., Jager, T., Lauer, S.: 0-RTT key exchange with full forward secrecy. In: Coron, J.-S., Nielsen, J.B. (eds.) EUROCRYPT 2017, Part III. LNCS, vol. 10212, pp. 519–548. Springer, Cham (2017). https://doi.org/10.1007/978-3-319-56617-7_18

[GM15] Green, M.D., Miers, I.: Forward secure asynchronous messaging from puncturable encryption. In: 2015 IEEE Symposium on Security and Privacy, pp. 305–320. IEEE Computer Society Press, May 2015

[HKP+21] Hashimoto, K., Katsumata, S., Postlethwaite, E., Prest, T., Westerbaan, B.: A concrete treatment of efficient continuous group key agreement via multi-recipient PKEs. In: Vigna, G., Shi, E. (eds.) ACM CCS 2021, pp. 1441–1462. ACM Press, November 2021

[HLP22] Haidar, C.A., Libert, B., Passelègue, A.: Updatable public key encryption from DCR: efficient constructions with stronger security. : Yin, H., Stavrou, A., Cremers, C., Shi, E. (eds.) ACM CCS 2022, pp. 11–22. ACM Press, November 2022

[HPS23] Haidar, C.A., Passelégue, A., Stehlé, D.: Efficient updatable public-key encryption from lattices. Cryptology ePrint Archive, Paper 2023/1400 (2023). https://eprint.iacr.org/2023/1400

[JMM19] Jost, D., Maurer, U., Mularczyk, M.: Efficient ratcheting: almost-optimal guarantees for secure messaging. In: Ishai, Y., Rijmen, V. (eds.) EUROCRYPT 2019. LNCS, vol. 11476, pp. 159–188. Springer, Cham (2019). https://doi.org/10.1007/978-3-030-17653-2_6

[JS18]   Jaeger, J., Stepanovs, I.: Optimal channel security against fine-grained state compromise: the safety of messaging. In: Shacham, H., Boldyreva, A. (eds.) CRYPTO 2018. LNCS, vol. 10991, pp. 33–62. Springer, Cham (2018). https://doi.org/10.1007/978-3-319-96884-1_2

[OP01]   Okamoto, T., Pointcheval, D.: The gap-problems: a new class of problems for the security of cryptographic schemes. In: Kim, K. (ed.) PKC 2001. LNCS, vol. 1992, pp. 104–118. Springer, Heidelberg (2001). https://doi.org/10.1007/3-540-44586-2_8

[PR18]   Poettering, B., Rösler, P.: Towards bidirectional ratcheted key exchange. In: Shacham, H., Boldyreva, A. (eds.) CRYPTO 2018, Part I. LNCS, vol. 10991, pp. 3–32. Springer, Cham (2018). https://doi.org/10.1007/978-3-319-96884-1_1

[PS00]   Pointcheval, D., Stern, J.: Security arguments for digital signatures and blind signatures. J. Cryptol. **13**(3), 361–396 (2000)

[Sah99]   Sahai, A.: Non-malleable non-interactive zero knowledge and adaptive chosen-ciphertext security. In: 40th FOCS, pp. 543–553. IEEE Computer Society Press, October 1999

[SKSW22]   Sakemi, Y., Kobayashi, T., Saito, T., Wahby, R.S.: Pairing-friendly curves. internet-draft draft-IRTF-CFRG-pairing-friendly-curves-11, Internet Engineering Task Force, November 2022. Work in Progress

Author Index

A
Albrecht, Martin R.   90
Alwen, Joël   346

B
Briaud, Pierre   3
Bros, Maxime   3

C
Carrier, Kévin   286

D
Das, Dipayan   205
De Feo, Luca   181
Debris-Alazard, Thomas   286
Ducas, Léo   151

E
Esgin, Muhammed F.   316
Espitau, Thomas   316
Esser, Andre   151
Etinski, Simona   151

F
Fenzi, Giacomo   90
Fouotsa, Tako Boris   181
Fuchsbauer, Georg   346

H
Han, Shuai   120

J
Joux, Antoine   205

K
Kirshanova, Elena   151

L
Lapiha, Oleksandra   90
Liu, Shengli   120

Lyu, You   120

M
Meyer-Hilfiger, Charles   286
Mularczyk, Marta   346
Mureau, Guilhem   226

N
Nguyen, Ngoc Khanh   90
Niot, Guilhem   316

P
Pan, Jiaxin   59
Panny, Lorenz   181
Pellet-Mary, Alice   226
Perlner, Ray   3
Pliatsok, Georgii   226
Pouly, Amaury   256
Prest, Thomas   316

R
Riepel, Doreen   59

S
Sakzad, Amin   316
Shen, Yixin   256
Smith-Tone, Daniel   3
Steinfeld, Ron   316

T
Tillich, Jean-Pierre   286

W
Wallet, Alexandre   226

X
Xagawa, Keita   30

Z
Zeng, Runzhi   59

M. Joye and G. Leander (Eds.): EUROCRYPT 2024, LNCS 14657, p. 377, 2024.
https://doi.org/10.1007/978-3-031-58754-2